MARXISM IN RUSSIA
Key Documents 1879-1906

MARXISM IN RUSSIA

Key Documents 1879-1906

Edited, with an introduction by

NEIL HARDING
Senior Lecturer in Politics and Russian Studies,
University College of Swansea

With translations by

RICHARD TAYLOR
Lecturer in Politics and Russian Studies,
University College of Swansea

CAMBRIDGE UNIVERSITY PRESS
Cambridge
London   New York   New Rochelle
Melbourne   Sydney

Published by the Press Syndicate of the University of Cambridge
The Pitt Building, Trumpington Street, Cambridge CB2 1RP
32 East 57th Street, New York, NY 10022, USA
296 Beaconsfield Parade, Middle Park, Melbourne 3206, Australia

© Cambridge University Press 1983

First published 1983

Printed in Great Britain at the University Press, Cambridge

Library of Congress catalogue card number: 82–19754

British Library Cataloguing in Publication Data

Marxism in Russia.
1. Communism — Soviet Union — Sources
I. Harding, Neil
320.5'315   HX724
ISBN 0 521 25123 0

WD

To the memory of J.C.R.

Contents

Acknowledgements   *page* xi
Preface   xiii
Introduction   1

DOCUMENTS

Section 1. 1879–1893: theoretical foundations and worker projects   39

1   Programme, NORTHERN UNION OF RUSSIAN WORKERS (1879)   41

2   Socialism and the Political Struggle, G.V. PLEKHANOV (1883):
    extracts   44

3   Programme of the Social Democratic Emancipation of Labour Group,
    G.V. PLEKHANOV (1884)   55

4   'Propaganda Among the Workers', from *Our Differences*,
    G.V. PLEKHANOV (1884)   59

5   From the Publishers of the 'Workers' Library', G.V. PLEKHANOV
    AND P. AKSELROD (1884)   68

6   The Demands of the Morozov Workers (1885)   72

7   A Draft Programme for Russian Social Democrats, and Statutes of
    the Fund, BLAGOEV GROUP (1885)   74

8   Second Draft Programme of the Russian Social Democrats,
    G.V. PLEKHANOV (1885)   81

9   Four Speeches by Petersburg Workers (1891)   84

10 Report [to the International] by the Editorial Board of the Journal
    Sotsial-Demokrat, G.V. PLEKHANOV AND V. ZASULICH (1891)   92

11 The Tasks of the Social Democrats in the Struggle against the
    Famine in Russia, G.V. PLEKHANOV (1891): extracts   100

12 Manuscript Programme for Studies with the Workers, M.I. BRUSNEV
    (1892)   108

13   A Programme of Action for the Workers, N.E. FEDOSEEV
      (1892)   *page* 109

14   The Tasks of the Worker Intelligentsia in Russia, P. AKSELROD
      (1893): extracts   113

Section 2. 1894–1897: bridges to the workers – economic agitation   121

15   The Working Day, ANON. (1894)   123

16   Questionnaire on the Situation of Workers in Enterprises, V.I. LENIN
      (1894/5)   138

17   To the Workers of the Semyannikov Factory, V.I. LENIN (1895)   140

18   What Should the Port Workers Strive for?, ANON. (1895)   143

19   Appeal to the Workers to Unite into a Workers' Union, MOSCOW
      'WORKERS' UNION' (1895)   145

20   Appeal to the Workers to Unite and Demand the Shortening of the
      Working Day, MOSCOW 'WORKERS' UNION' (1895)   146

21   To the Working Men and Women of the Thornton Mill, V.I. LENIN
      (1895)   146

22   What Are the Demands of the Women Workers at the Laferme
      Factory?, ST PETERSBURG UNION OF STRUGGLE (1895)   149

23   From the Union of Struggle for the Emancipation of the Working
      Class, ST PETERSBURG UNION OF STRUGGLE (1895)   150

24   What Is a Socialist and a Political Offender?, I.V. BABUSHKIN
      (1895)   151

25   To the Weavers of the Lebedev Mill, ST PETERSBURG UNION
      OF STRUGGLE (1896)   152

26   The Demands of the Weavers at the Lebedev Mill, ST PETERSBURG
      UNION OF STRUGGLE (1896)   153

27   Draft and Explanation of a Programme for the Social Democratic
      Party, V.I. LENIN (1895/6)   153

28   The Workers' Holiday of 1 May (19 April by our Calendar),
      ST PETERSBURG UNION OF STRUGGLE (1896)   171

29   To the Workers in All the Petersburg Cotton Mills, ST PETERSBURG
      UNION OF STRUGGLE (1896)   174

30   To All Petersburg Workers, ST PETERSBURG UNION OF
      STRUGGLE (1896)   175

31   Report Presented by the Russian Social Democrats to the (London)
      International Congress of Socialist Workers and Trade Unions,
      G.V. PLEKHANOV (1896)   176

ix   *Contents*

32   To All St Petersburg Workers, ST PETERSBURG UNION OF
      STRUGGLE (1896)   *page* 187
33   To the Tsarist Government, V.I. LENIN (1896)   188
34   On Agitation, A. KREMER AND YU. MARTOV (1896)   192
35   To the Workers in the Petersburg Cotton Spinning and Weaving
      Mills, ST PETERSBURG UNION OF STRUGGLE (1897)   206
36   To All Petersburg Workers, ST PETERSBURG UNION OF
      STRUGGLE (1897)   209
37   The World-Wide Workers' Holiday of 1 May, ST PETERSBURG
      UNION OF STRUGGLE (1897)   210
38   The First of May, ST PETERSBURG UNION OF STRUGGLE
      (1897): extracts   212
39   To All Moscow Workers, MOSCOW WORKERS' UNION (1897)   215
40   Letter to All Kiev Workers, KIEV UNION OF STRUGGLE
      (1897): extracts   216

Section 3. 1898–1902: political agitation and the critics of orthodoxy   221

41   Manifesto of the Russian Social Democratic Labour Party,
      P. STRUVE (1898)   223
42   Decisions of the First Congress of the RSDLP, RUSSIAN SOCIAL
      DEMOCRATIC LABOUR PARTY (1898)   225
43   On the Question of the Present Tasks and Tactics of the Russian
      Social Democrats (Draft Programme), P.B. AKSELROD (1898)   227
44   Our Reality, K.M. TAKHTAREV (1899): extracts   242
45   Credo, E.D. KUSKOVA (1899)   250
46   A Protest by Russian Social Democrats, V.I. LENIN (1899)   253
47   The Urgent Tasks of Our Movement, V.I. LENIN (1900)   259
48   Where to Begin?, V.I. LENIN (1901)   263
49   Our New Programme, RABOCHEE DELO (1902)   268

**Section 4. The Bolshevik/Menshevik dispute – organisational questions
and appraisals of the 1905 revolution**   277

50   Second Party Congress: The Debate on Clause 1 of the Party Rules,
      RUSSIAN SOCIAL DEMOCRATIC LABOUR PARTY (1903)   279
51   The Programme of the Russian Social Democratic Labour Party,
      RUSSIAN SOCIAL DEMOCRATIC LABOUR PARTY (1903)   288

52   The Organisational Statutes of the RSDLP, RUSSIAN SOCIAL
       DEMOCRATIC LABOUR PARTY (1903)   *page* 293

53   Organisational Questions of Russian Social Democracy,
       R. LUXEMBURG (1904)   295

54   Petition of the Workers and Inhabitants of St Petersburg to
       Nicholas II, G. GAPON AND I. VASIMOV (1905)   309

55   On an Armed Uprising, MENSHEVIK CONFERENCE
       RESOLUTION (1905)   313

56   On the Seizure of Power and Participation in a Provisional
       Government, MENSHEVIK CONFERENCE RESOLUTION (1905)   314

57   Two Tactics of Social Democracy in the Democratic Revolution,
       V.I. LENIN (1905): extracts   315

58   The People's Duma and the Workers' Congress, P.B. AKSELROD
       (1905): extracts   331

59   Our Revolution, L. TROTSKY (1906): extracts   337

60   The Driving Forces of the Russian Revolution and Its Prospects,
       with Preface by V.I. Lenin, K. KAUTSKY (1906)   352

Notes   373
List of sources   404
Guide to further reading   406
Glossary   408
Index   410

Acknowledgements

Thanks to: Caryl Johnston and Pat Rees for their fortitude in preparing so lengthy and unmanageable a manuscript; Mary Ghullam for help in the initial collecting of documents; Alan Bodger and Bruce Waller for their expert counsel on knotty problems of Russian and German respectively; the staff of the International Institute of Social History in Amsterdam for their legendary courtesy and expertise; finally, to the Centre for Russian and East European Studies, University College of Swansea, for financial support.

Preface

There has long been a lack of balance in the literature on the development of Marxism in Russia. On the one hand there has been an abundance of scholarly commentary and biography, and on the other a virtual absence (Lenin and Plekhanov excepted) of translated texts and source materials. It is obvious that, in seeking to redress the balance, no single volume could be comprehensive – the Russian Marxists were too numerous and too prolix for that. And yet there are certain texts whose centrality is undoubted. No one would, for instance, dispute that Plekhanov's *The Tasks of the Russian Social Democrats in the Struggle against the Famine*, Kremer's and Martov's *On Agitation*, the anonymous brochure *The Working Day*, Akselrod's *The Present Tasks and Tactics of the Russian Social Democrats*, Takhtarev's *Our Reality* or Kautsky's *The Driving Forces of the Russian Revolution* were, in their differing ways, of cardinal importance. Commentators and biographers repeatedly return to them offering their rival interpretations and all the non-Russian reader can do is to select that interpretation that seems most cogent, for not one of the above texts has previously been translated into English. Nor is there anything by Blagoev, Brusnev or Fedoseev, none of the agitational leaflets of the 1890s, nor the May Day proclamations, available in translation. Of the sixty documents presented here only sixteen have previously been translated and even readers of Russian would struggle to obtain them. No single library in Europe has them all. Wherever possible documents have been presented in their entirety. Where extracts have been resorted to this is indicated in the document's heading.

Previously translated documents which have been included are, for the most part, either programmatic statements of the Russian Social Democratic Labour Party (RSDLP) or writings of Plekhanov and Lenin. There is an obvious merit in bringing the party statements together in one book and it would have been odd to have included none of the influential writings of Plekhanov and Lenin. *All* the translations in the volume are new translations done from the earliest available copies of the originals and, where necessary, as for instance in the case of Luxemburg's *Organisational Questions of Russian Social Democracy* and Kautsky's *The Driving Forces of the Russian Revolution*, checked against the contemporaneous German publication. In the case of Luxemburg's piece this has revealed some serious shortcomings in currently available translations.

xiii

Difficulty of access was, then, one of the criteria for inclusion and it reinforced the other main objective of the volume which was to reveal the levels of articulation within the Russian Marxist tradition. Works of 'high theory' elaborating and extending the full complexity of Marxist thought, such as Plekhanov's *Our Differences* or his *The Development of the Monist View of History* or Lenin's *The Development of Capitalism in Russia*, are readily available in decent translations and have not therefore been included.

Apart from the works of high theory, addressed to intellectuals, there exists a formidable volume of source materials in which the Russian Marxists simplified and popularised their propositions in the attempt to win a mass following. By the second half of the 1890s Russian Marxists were quite consciously engaged in the task of disseminating their message through carefully graduated levels of articulation which corresponded, in their minds, to the differing levels of consciousness and organisation of their followers.

At the most primitive level were the flysheets, at first hand-written, but later run off on hectograph machines, issued by local social democratic groups which set out to formulate the immediate grievances of particular groups of workers in specific plants. They were addressed to the uninitiated, unpoliticised mass of workers and were therefore couched in popular idiomatic language. Generally, indeed, it was made to appear that the flysheets had been composed by the workers themselves. If they did contain any overt general message it was almost invariably the simplest and most basic call to the workers to unite and steadfastly defend their interests.

At the next level were the May Day leaflets, brochures like *The Working Day*, and the flysheets addressed to the workers of an entire industrial area. These set out to generalise the grievances of all working people, to present them systematically and to show them to be not local or adventitious but endemic in the structure of Russian and international capitalism. They were written in a language that would be accessible to the average worker and therefore avoided abstraction. General propositions were, rather, seen to follow from carefully cited examples. Their message was nonetheless more elevated than those in our first group and often leaned on the experience of the labour movement in other countries to support the contention that without a nation-wide organisation of the workers, without political freedoms of association and propaganda for their cause, the movement to improve working conditions would be doomed to impotence.

For the advanced worker and social democratic activist, brochures on the general line of the movement, like Kremer's and Martov's *On Agitation*, Lenin's *Draft and Explanation of a Programme*, Akselrod's *Present Tasks and Tactics*, or even Kuskova's *Credo* and Takhtarev's *Our Reality*, set out to relate Marxist theoretical constructs to generalised statements about political and economic goals and to outline broad strategies for achieving them. These were of the nature of programmatic statements more sophisticated in reasoning and abstract in formulation.

In selecting the documents I have also had in mind their interdependence. Russian Marxism was very much a self-conscious tradition of thought. Each of its principal contributors was well aware of the work of his predecessors and contemporaries and made repeated references to them, either to demonstrate their error or to appropriate their authority. The numerous cross-references in the notes to this volume are evidence enough of this. They are evidence too of the rather obvious point that the thought of none of the principal Russian Marxists can be understood unless an effort is made to reconstruct the stock of shared ideas and memories which constituted the tradition to which he contributed. The major disputes which divided the movement were, precisely, disputes about the continued relevance of those ideas and those evaluations of the past.

NEIL HARDING
Oxford, May 1982

Introduction

It was in the period from the 1880s to 1905 that Russian Marxism emerged and developed its particular character and reputation. Its reputation in the international socialist movement for undiluted propriety in matters of Marxist theory and uncompromising militance in matters of practice was a product of its struggles and pronouncements of these years — its heroism in the battle with the Russian autocracy for political freedom and a better deal for the workers, its emphatic rejection of revisionism of all hues and its militant role in leading the revolution of 1905. It had also acquired a reputation that was the obverse side of its devotion to Marxist principle — it was thought to be hopelessly schismatic. By 1905–6 deep internal divisions had rent Russian Marxism and the broad lines of affiliation and opposition which were to characterise the movement in 1917 had already emerged. A large part of the explanation for the uniquely uncompromising character of Russian Marxism lies in the relationship of the Russian Marxists to their native labour movement. Almost everywhere else in Europe Marxism had to be grafted on to existing, and often powerful, labour movements. These movements had developed their own traditions of thought and organisation long before Marxism began to have an appreciable impact upon the European labour movement in the 1880s.

The most spectacular instance of this general phenomenon was of course the British labour movement where the Marxist proselytes of the eighties and nineties found powerful and self-confident associations of unionists and cooperators suspicious of their intentions and anxious to preserve their own organisations and the structure of beliefs bound up both with these organisations and with their shared memories of past battles.

In France the Proudhonists had long propagandised and organised quite a large proportion of the artisans and urban workers in pursuit of the mutualist dream of re-establishing their economic independence. In Spain and Italy Bakuninist propaganda had struck strong roots and established a heroic tradition of struggle which continued to be more potent than Marxism throughout this period. Even in Germany, though Marxism was notionally triumphant by the early 1890s, the resilience of the older Lassallean traditions was clearly apparent by the end of that decade. Certainly in its attitude towards the revisionist followers of Bernstein none could accuse the German Marxists of want of compromise on basic issues.

1

Only in Russia was there an emergent working class that was quite devoid of strong traditions of thought and organisation, which had, moreover, no corporate memory to bind its identity. It was kept in its atomised state by the autocratic government which saw every attempt at working class organisation as a threat to its own prerogatives that had to be ruthlessly stamped upon. The attempts, therefore, of such groups as the North Russian Workers' Union[1] and the projects of groups associated with individuals like Blagoev,[2] Brusnev[3] and Fedoseev[4] attained momentary and generally very localised success but certainly did not beget a continuous or broadly shared tradition. There was another factor, apart from ruthless government suppression, which, no doubt, partly accounts for these failures. This was the obvious fact that it was not until the early 1890s that a settled urban proletariat began to emerge in Russia to any significant degree. In almost all the other countries of Europe Marxism had, as we have seen, only begun to make a significant impact in the 1880s, i.e. after the urban proletariat had established itself. In Russia, however, the Marxist intelligentsia, if it did not actually pre-date the class emergence of the proletariat, at least emerged contemporaneously with it. Consequently the Russian Marxist intelligentsia (and it is crucially important to remember that, at least until 1905, the Marxist movement was almost *exclusively* recruited from the intelligentsia) began their activities with far more of a *tabula rasa* than had been the case elsewhere. They had before them an almost clean sheet of infinite possibility and they were determined that what they wrote upon it would be word-perfect according to the textbooks of Marxism.

The effective absence of prior organisation and systems of thought was at once advantage and drawback: advantage in the sense alluded to above, that the Russian intelligentsia Marxists would not have to temporise or conciliate in adapting their Marxism to native traditions, and drawback in that there were no ready-made organisations which might be utilised to propagate the message, to use as a lever to convert the class.

The selection of documents presented here demonstrates quite clearly the twin preoccupations of Russian Marxists which derived from their rather unique situation as an intelligentsia movement dealing with a disorganised, emergent working class. Throughout the documents there is an almost obsessive and very self-conscious discussion of how to characterise the proletariat. What were its defining attributes, its immediate and ultimate objectives? To answer these problems the Russian acolytes looked to the Master and they were more faithful to Marx's specification than most other Marxists. It was precisely the earnestness with which Plekhanov, Akselrod, Lenin and Martov clung to Marx's account of the essential role of the proletariat that accounts for the vehemence with which they rounded on all varieties of Economism and revisionism; for what were these but attempts to renege upon the obligations Marx had laid upon the proletariat and its party?

Inextricably bound to their characterisation of the proletariat and its mission in history was the enormous practical problem of how to make the Russian proletariat conscious of its class objectives and organised and enthused to fulfil them. This organisational 'practical' problem could not, in the view of the Russian Marxists, be separated from the 'theoretical' specification of the proletariat's mission. The examples of other countries provided object lessons enough of how attachment to inappropriate organisational forms had perverted the proletariat's awareness of its objectives. The organisation had to be consonant with the objective in hand and, therefore, as the objectives changed from lower to higher ones, as the proletariat increasingly approximated its *essential* role, so its organisational forms would have to change. That at least was what the practical experience of the 1890s taught the Russian Marxists.

The 'practical' activity of the Russian Marxists in building bridges to the workers and attempting to develop the class consciousness of the proletariat cannot, according to this analysis, be separated from their 'theoretical' views on the process of history and the role of the proletariat within it. Those views were, of course, explicitly derived from Marx.

Marx: the class characteristics of the proletariat

Marx's specification of what constituted the proper class activity of the proletariat is crucial for any understanding of what Russian Social Democrats were attempting to do in this period. It was, after all, this specification that *defined* the proletariat for the Social Democrats. The workers only began to emerge as a class properly so-called when they began to exhibit the characteristics Marx had long previously set out. The task of the Social Democrats, as the Russians were very self-consciously aware, was not simply to act as the passive instrument of the working class but to raise the class to accept and prosecute the role allotted to it. Theory, Marx maintained, must not only strive towards reality but reality must strive towards thought. The working class must strive to realise those universal elements which philosophy had allotted to it. Thus, in Marx's early conception, the proletariat was characteristically viewed as the vehicle to resolve the problems of German philosophy that, in Hegel's system, had finally arrived at an impasse. Marx and some other radical Young Hegelians came to the conclusion that speculative philosophy could go no further: it had exposed the rottenness of German reality and revealed religion as an aspect of man's self-alienation. The critical problem which now emerged was how could German political and social life, which had fallen so lamentably behind that of Europe generally, be raised to the level of European history? How could the huge discrepancy between what German *thinkers* had attained and German *reality* displayed be overcome? How could man re-appropriate all those parts of himself he had so prodigally alienated to the state, to religion and to the pursuit of Mammon? Where was the force that would regenerate a decrepit civilisation?

Where, then, is the *positive* possibility of a German emancipation? *Answer*: In the formation of a class with *radical chains*, a class of civil society which is not a class of civil society, an estate which is the dissolution of all estates, a sphere which has a universal character by its suffering and claims no *particular right* because no *particular wrong* but *wrong generally* is perpetrated against it; which can no longer invoke a *historical* but only a *human* title; which does not stand in any one-sided antithesis to the consequences but in an all-round antithesis to the promises of the German state; a sphere, finally, which cannot emancipate itself without emancipating itself from all other spheres of society and thereby emancipating all other spheres of society, which in a word, is the *complete loss* of man and hence can win itself only through the *complete rewinning of man*. This dissolution of society as a particular estate is the *proletariat*.[5]

Like Moses Hess, Marx came to the conclusion that speculation had run its course and ended eventually in a blind alley. The philosophical questions had been solved, the outstanding problems were practical ones. Reality had to be changed to make it conform to the goals of philosophy. Man had now not so much to think as to act upon reality to change his world, and, from the French, Hess groped towards a philosophy of practice.[6] He came to the very French conclusion that the main vehicle in the *practical* transformation of existing society could only be the proletariat. The essential germs of the way out of the impasse had been discovered and were seized on and developed by Marx.

The proletariat is a force at once inside civil society yet not of civil society. All its features are drawn by Marx long before he had any practical involvement with the proletariat quite explicitly in order to complete the philosophical picture he was creating. To be the agent of *universal* regeneration it was essential that the proletariat be shown to be the victim not of any particular or partial wrong but of universal and complete maltreatment. To be not simply the agency for resolving peculiarly German problems the proletariat must, moreover, be shown to be the vehicle of a world-historical rebirth, a global regeneration of mankind to properly human existence. 'The proletariat', Marx insisted, 'can thus only exist world-historically, just as communism, its activity, can only have a "world-historical" existence'.[7] Its object in history was not merely to end exploitation but to overcome alienation in all its aspects for all classes of the population. Its revolution was to secure the triumph of humanism not merely for the oppressed, exploited and debased, but also for the exploiters who had been wont to see in their wealth and power a semblance of their self-realisation and affirmation.[8]

The proletariat, for Marx, existed as such only insofar as it fulfilled the universal characteristics theory allotted to it. Its mission in history was to realise (or negate) philosophy and in so doing realise itself as human.

The imperative to achieve this realisation proceeded, according to Marx, from a two-pronged spur. In the first place the development of the division of labour which modern industry inexorably produced resulted in a progressive whittling down of the skills of the worker, and his aggregation into a vast anonymous mass made it impossible to take any personal satisfaction in the article produced.

Owing to the extensive use of machinery and to division of labour, the work of the proletarians has lost all individual character, and, consequently, all charm for the workman. He becomes an appendage to the machine, and it is only the most simple, most monotonous and most easily acquired knack, that is required of him.[9]

The worker was not only alienated from his skills and his product, which should have encapsulated his innate drive to act on nature to produce things in accordance with the norms of beauty, he was also alienated from his fellow man. Each worker set in competition with every other made flagrant mockery of the natural instinct to produce cooperatively. Man the worker was in this way, according to Marx's *1844 Manuscripts* and the first part of the *German Ideology*, robbed of his humanity yet still preserved a presentiment of what he might be if his self-activity were allowed to flourish.

Apart from the urge to recover a lost humanity there was, of course, the ever-present imperative to escape from physical, material need. The experience of the workers would, however, reveal to them that the capitalist structure was inherently unable to provide even the bare necessities of a tolerable existence. Marx's later economic studies confirmed that:

Along with the constantly diminishing number of the magnates of capital, who usurp and monopolise all advantages of this process of transformation, grows the mass of misery, oppression, slavery, degradation, exploitation; but with this grows the revolt of the working-class, a class always increasing in numbers, and disci-plined, united, organised by the very mechanism of the process of capitalist pro-duction itself.[10]

The capitalist system therefore stands condemned not only because it consigns the majority of the population to pauperism, not only because 'it is incompetent to assure an existence to its slave within his slavery',[11] but also because it is endemi-cally anti-human. Together these provide a sufficient and compelling rationale, or rather imperative, to overthrow it.

Since in the full-formed proletariat the abstraction of all humanity, even of the *semblance* of humanity, is practically complete; since the conditions of life of the proletariat sum up all the conditions of life of society today in their most inhuman form; since man has lost himself in the proletariat, yet at the same time has not only gained theoretical consciousness of that loss, but through urgent, no longer removable, no longer disguisable, absolutely imperative *need* – the practical expression of *necessity* – is driven directly to revolt against this inhumanity, it follows that the proletariat can and must emancipate itself. But it cannot emanci-pate itself without abolishing the conditions of its own life. It cannot abolish the conditions of its own life without abolishing *all* the inhuman conditions of life of society today which are summed up in its own situation.[12]

The tasks of the proletariat are truly of epic proportions, they are to recast the world in its entire economic, social, political and general cultural relations. These essential goals of the proletariat are given by the role it must play in Marx's philos-ophical schema and it is hardly accidental that Marx, having specified them in the passage given above, immediately proceeds to make this clear. The workers them-selves, Marx argues, may well be lamentably unaware of their great goal but that does not invalidate it. One does not, Marx seems to be arguing, discover the goal of the proletarian movement by opinion sampling of the proletariat, for the proletariat itself is only gradually forged and made conscious (i.e. aware of its mission) in a long progress of historical struggles. Only those blessed with a prescient awareness of its *future* development can properly define its aim, the proletariat itself is for a long while fated to have only a very inadequate grasp of it.

It is not a question of what this or that proletarian, or even the whole proletariat, at the moment *regards* as its aim. It is a question of *what the proletariat is*, and what, in accordance with this *being*, it will historically be compelled to do. Its aim and historical action is visibly and irrevocably foreshadowed in its own life situation as well as in the whole organisation of bourgeois society today.[13]

Marx's whole analysis is clearly dependent upon the presence of at least some individuals who have the inclination, education and leisure to stand back and appraise the historical evolution of the proletariat, what it is and what it must become. The *essential* being of the proletariat must be known to some of its observers if not to itself. These people clearly have a prescient awareness of what the ultimate goals of the proletariat amount to. They are those who 'have over the great mass of the proletariat the advantage of clearly understanding the line of march, the conditions, and the ultimate general results of the proletarian movement'.[14] The crucial role of the intellectuals in the movement begins to emerge but is little developed by Marx — his Russian disciples were to be more forthright and in many ways more cogent and honest in their accounts. All that Marx will say (as clearly, from the above account, he *has* to say, since the whole system is predicated upon some individuals with prescient awareness providing the initial impetus and steering the movement in its nascent phase of ill-developed consciousness) is that 'a portion of the bourgeoisie goes over to the proletariat, and, in particular, a portion of the bourgeois ideologists, who have raised themselves to the level of comprehending theoretically the historical movement as a whole'.[15]

The actual way in which the proletariat itself is brought to consciousness and acquires the organisation necessary to implement its grand objectives is rarely directly dealt with by Marx. Perhaps the closest Marx comes to an account of these processes is in his historical essays on the experience of the French working class in the period 1848–51. *The Class Struggles in France* and *The Eighteenth Brumaire of Louis Bonaparte* both contain the same essential message. The proletariat *began* its revolutionary activity with all sorts of illusions, under the direction of all sorts of charlatans, crackpots and naive idealists. It imagined variously that its goals were quite compatible with those of the bourgeois democrats and could be accommodated within the bourgeois democratic republic; it convinced itself that the guarantee of the right to work, or the promotion of cooperatives or *phalanstères*, would be the social revolution accomplished. Only the experience of the revolution itself, only the polarities which emerged in the actual historical struggle when the bourgeoisie moved to counter-revolution and bloody suppression of the workers' most modest demands, only when the schemes of utopian crackpots for partial amelioration were shown in practice to be utterly useless, only then did the proletariat purge itself of illusions in the hard school of historical experience.

In a word: the revolution made progress, forged ahead, not by its immediate tragicomic achievements, but on the contrary by the creation of a powerful, united counter-revolution, by the creation of an opponent in combat with whom alone the party of overthrow ripened into a really revolutionary party.[16]

The process of political polarisation was, according to Marx's account, the process wherein all who aspired to *any* change in the existing structure of society were obliged to assume a position of unqualified antagonism to its bourgeois defenders and obliged also to acknowledge the dominance of the proletariat in the opposition camp.

Little by little we have seen peasants, petty bourgeois, the middle classes in general, stepping alongside the proletariat, driven into open antagonism to the official republic and treated by it as antagonists. *Revolt against bourgeois dictatorship, need of a change of society, adherence to democratic-republican institutions as organs of their movement, grouping round the proletariat as the decisive revolutionary power* — these are the common characteristics of the *so-called party of social democracy, the party of the Red republic.* This *party of Anarchy*, as its opponents christened it, is no less a coalition of different interests than the *party of Order*. From the smallest reform of the old social disorder to the overthrow of the old social order, from bourgeois liberalism to revolutionary terrorism — as far apart as this lie the extremes that form the starting-point and the finishing-point of the party of 'Anarchy'.[17]

All the strata which are marginal to modern society (i.e. all those apart from the proletariat and the bourgeoisie) are forced to choose and align themselves whenever great political issues are fought out. Having no possibility of an autonomous political, and therefore class, existence of their own, they must side with one or the other of the great social and political powers. Revolutions act in this way as *'the locomotives of history'* by enormously accelerating the process of class development: 'in this vortex of movement, in this torment of historical unrest, in this dramatic ebb and flow of revolutionary passions, hopes and disappointments, the different classes of French society had to count their epochs of development in weeks where they had previously counted them in half centuries'.[18]

The process of political polarisation did not, however, end here; it was not just a matter of obliging peripheral or marginal groups to choose sides, it also entailed, in Marx's account, a process of ideological and organisational consolidation *within* the proletariat and the bourgeoisie. The bourgeoisie became ever more monolithically committed to the maintenance of *all* its privileges quite intact, and to the defence of its economic prerogatives. To guarantee their defence it had little compunction in transferring its political power into the hands of the military and revealing itself as an overtly anti-democratic force. For its part the proletariat, chastened by its recent experiences and rid of its utopianism:

increasingly organises itself around *revolutionary Socialism*, around *Communism*, for which the bourgeoisie has itself invented the name of *Blanqui*. This socialism is the *declaration of the permanence of the revolution*, the *class dictatorship* of the proletariat as the necessary transit point to the *abolition of class distinctions generally*, to the abolition of all the relations of production on which they rest, to the abolition of all the social relations that correspond to these relations of production, to the revolutionising of all the ideas that result from these social relations.[19]

Marx has in this way resolved the difficulty which was inherent in his earlier account of consciousness. The essential being of the proletariat or the proper location of its aim was, as we have seen, for some time unattainable by the proletariat itself. It could only be *theoretically* apprehended by some few renegade bourgeois ideologists who undertook the initial leadership of the Communist movement. The proletariat was not, then, nor arguably is it ever, in a position to apprehend its situation and its goal *theoretically*. Its mode of learning, Marx appears to argue in *The Class Struggles in France* and *The Eighteenth Brumaire of Louis Bonaparte*, is practical and sensuous. Its practical experience of struggle *is* the process of its class development and the maturation of its consciousness. The process of realisation of proletarian consciousness is shown to be an historical and practical process which vindicates the theoretical prescience of the intellectual pioneers.

An essential part of the process of class formation of the proletariat is its organisational cohesion and especially its ability to organise to articulate its interests on a nation-wide basis. Until it is able to achieve this it cannot lay claim to a properly class existence. It was of course on these grounds that Marx, in his famous passage in *The Eighteenth Brumaire*, found the peasants incapable of constituting a class:

Insofar as millions of families live under economic conditions of existence that separate their mode of life, their interests and their culture from those of the other classes, and put them in hostile opposition to the latter, they form a class. Insofar as there is merely a local interconnection among these small-holding peasants, and the identity of their interests begets no community, no national bond and no political organisation among them, they do not form a class . . . They cannot represent themselves, they must be represented.[20]

Clearly the sharing of a common relationship to the ownership of the means of production is a *necessary* but by no means a *sufficient* definition of class in Marx's account. Earlier, in *The Poverty of Philosophy*, in a tantalisingly brief comment, Marx had distinguished between the 'economic' and 'political' attributes and had implied that these were ascending phases of class existence. A recognition of a community of interest on the purely economic plane would seem, in this account, to be no more than rudimentary class consciousness:

Economic conditions had first transformed the mass of the people of the country into workers. The domination of capital has created for this mass a common situation, common interests. This mass is thus already a class as against capital, but not yet for itself. In the struggle, of which we have pointed out only a few phases, this mass becomes united, and constitutes itself as a class for itself. The interests it defends become class interests. But the struggle of class against class is a political struggle.[21]

The conclusion that Marx arrives at here was elevated by his Russian disciples into the single most important and influential precept of Marxism. The text from which it was taken was directed against the apoliticism of Proudhon's scheme of social regeneration and it long served the Russian Marxists as a valuable quarry of materials to use against their native apolitical Populists. Given the dominance of the Russian anarchist tradition on social thought in the 1870s it was hardly surprising that Plekhanov, when making his first translation of Marxism to Russian conditions, should take as his prefatory text Marx's epigram 'Every class struggle is a political struggle',[22] and that he should entitle his first work as a thorough-going Marxist *Socialism and the Political Struggle*.

For Marx the form of organisation best able to articulate the ultimate aims of the proletariat on a national scale was the political party. Given that the conquest of the state machine and the establishment of a transitional political regime, to be known as the dictatorship of the proletariat, were held to be necessary in pursuit of these aims, it followed that the proletariat had to be organised into a political party. The 'immediate aim of the Communists', as announced in *The Manifesto of the Communist Party*, was the 'formation of the proletariat into a class, overthrow of the bourgeois supremacy, conquest of political power by the proletariat'.[23] A little earlier in the same text the connection is even more precisely made, 'This organisation of the proletarians into a class, and consequently into a political party'.[24] It was hardly surprising that Marx's Russian followers regarded the degree to which the proletariat was politically organised as the acid test of its class development. Only in proportion as it was organised in a political party and conscious of its great political tasks could the proletariat emerge as a class.

It will be convenient at this point to summarise Marx's account of the necessary and sufficient conditions for proletarian class existence.

    i. The aggregation of large numbers of non-owners of the means of production in one place consequent upon the extensive use of machinery.

    ii. The adhesion to the proletarian cause of some renegade bourgeois intellectuals able to generalise about the workers' conditions of life and, from their theoretical understanding of the historical line of march, able to formulate the ultimate aims of the movement.

    iii. The pursuit of economic objectives in the course of which the workers became aware that they share certain interests.

    iv. The struggle for political rights led by a revolutionary political party, in the course of which many of the illusions of the proletariat are purged and adequate consciousness and organisation begin to emerge.

We shall not begin to understand the controversies that consumed the social democratic and labour movements in Russia in this period unless we bear these criteria for defining the proletariat as firmly in mind as the Russian Marxists did.

Plekhanov's translation of the problem to Russian conditions

There is a striking and important similarity between Marx's and Plekhanov's motives for discovering the proletariat and attributing to it the goals they did. Both were expressly and self-consciously searching for a force which would lift their country out of an intolerably backward and anachronistic social and political reality and raise it to the advanced European level.

In Russia of course this search had, ever since Chaadaev, constituted a sort of full-time occupation for the intelligentsia who followed the trail of every West European innovation remorselessly to its terminus in the hope that it might afford a solution to Russia's appalling social and political plight. With all the seriousness and commitment which ever characterised this preoccupation the Russian intelligentsia wholeheartedly embraced liberalism, Utilitarianism, Fourierism, Owenism and every latest product of the West European forcing-house – only to see each in turn wilt and die in the inhospitable Russian environment. Then, after the failure of the 1848 revolutions and the renegacy of the 'liberal' middle classes of the West, a reaction set in. Herzen, taking over some of the Slavophiles' ideas, backing them with Haxthausen's sociological findings on the continued vitality of the peasant commune, and blending both with French socialist ideas, began to distil a native brand of Russian socialism which in various guises was to dominate the social and political thought of Russia for the next forty odd years. In this distillation the peasant was to be the agent of Russia's regeneration. The *muzhik* – the authentic man of the Russian *narod* (people) – preserved within himself a dislike of state or any other kind of centralisation and disparaged all politics which had to do with the domination of one group of men by another. Politics was not the vocation of the Russian people. Their destiny was to show the world the way to a humane, decentralised, non-political society of equals where the governance, and therefore dominance, of men by men would no longer hold sway. 'The Slavic peoples', Herzen declared, 'like neither the state nor centralisation. They prefer to live in scattered communes, as far as possible from all interference on the part of the government. They hate military organisation, they hate the police. A federation would be the most authentically national form of organisation for the Slavic peoples'.[25]

In achieving her destiny Russia was uniquely aided by the continued strength of the ancient communal landholding system where the peasant communes continued to hold land and to distribute it according to need. The federation of free communes, the libertarian socialist ideal, was shown to be, in the Russian environment, no idle utopia but a project rooted in the consciousness and institutions of the Russian people.

Plekhanov himself had been a prominent Russian Socialist in his younger days and had enthusiastically endorsed the militantly libertarian version of Populism inspired by Bakunin's writings and example. Plekhanov's faith survived until the end of the seventies and the beginning of the eighties but by that time three factors intruded themselves which were, cumulatively, to cause him to reject the Populist resolution of Russia's problems. In the first place there was the inescapable evidence of the failure of Populist strategy. The great hopes of Zemlya i Volya (Land and Freedom) to inaugurate the social revolution by sending its socialist missionaries among the naturally revolutionary Russian peasants, had issued in lamentable failure. The idealistic 'Going to the People' exposed the naive hopes and extravagant expectations of the young revolutionaries: nowhere did they succeed in rousing the peasants to revolutionary activity.[26] On the contrary they were met with incomprehension, suspicion and, frequently, animosity which did not stop short at turning the youthful revolutionaries over to the authorities. The gap between the revolutionary intelligentsia and the 'people' had been shown to be as wide as ever and the pretensions of the youngsters to articulate the 'real' interests of the peasants had been rudely shattered.

The second factor which disrupted Plekhanov's Bakuninist faith was the split in the Land and Freedom organisation that resulted from the failure of the 'Going to the People'. The majority of the surviving activists decided to abandon the policy of inciting mass rebellions and went over to the tactic of terrorising the government and plotting the assassination of the tsar. In March 1881 the Executive Committee of the Narodnaya Volya Party (People's Will) did succeed in assassinating the tsar but this act, far from unleashing the popular instinct of rebellion, led instead to ruthless government suppression of all revolutionary and political activity. For the rest of the 1880s the revolutionary movement was effectively emasculated.

Plekhanov had, even in 1879, objected to the new tactic of terrorism: it appeared to him to offer no positive answers to the crucial problems facing Russia – how to put an end to the hated autocracy and introduce a humane socialist regime, with its ancillary problem of how to realise these objectives in view of the seemingly unbridgeable gulf between the people and the intelligentsia. Without the active support of the people, without their conscious participation, no serious movement towards socialism in Russia was, in his view, possible.

The final causal factor in Plekhanov's conversion to Marxism and his adoption of the proletariat as the regenerator of Russia was the doubt which he began to have about the economic viability of Bakuninist socialism in Russia. He had assumed (as had all Populist theorists since Herzen) that the peasant commune was alive and flourishing in Russia and protecting her peasants against poverty, proletarianisation and all the baneful consequences of commodity economy. Now Plekhanov discovered that recently collected data on the state of the communes in the Moscow district ran directly counter to these suppositions. The commune, according to Orlov's thorough research, was already divided into hostile groups of wealthy and poor peasants with the latter often suffering the crudest exploitation at the hands of the former. Differentiation of the peasantry, Orlov found, was already far advanced and was proceeding at an accelerated tempo due to the tendency (which was both cause and effect of the ongoing process of differentiation) for the periods between redistribution of the land to become longer and longer. Plekhanov's faith in the solidarity of the peasants and his belief in the commune as the stepping-stone to socialism in Russia took a heavy blow. Within a few years he emerged as a convinced Marxist.

Perhaps the most remarkable feature of the early reception of Marxism by the Russians was the extraordinary similarity between the positions of the radical Young Hegelians in Germany in the 1840s and the small group of ex-Populists grouped around Plekhanov in the 1880s. Both groups were painfully aware of how far their respective countries had lagged behind the social and political norm of Western Europe. Both groups were self-consciously searching for a force which would revivify the national life and overcome the unbearable divide between what philosophers and social theorists aspired to, and the uncouth, restrictive and barbarised social relations that actually prevailed. Both groups were self-conscious seekers for that bridge via which the ideals of philosophy could reach the mass of the people and thus become an irresistible force acting upon an anachronistic reality and raising it to the level of thought. In this sense the legacy of the great French Revolution weighed heavily on both: 'It is not enough for thought to strive for realisation,' Marx at his most Promethean had written, 'reality must itself strive towards thought.'[27] The watchword of this radical philosophy of practice Marx had already given out in a slogan which might, in a way, serve as an epitaph for the efforts of Russian Marxists in the nineteenth century: 'Theory also becomes a material force as soon as it has gripped the masses.'[28]

The problem of the ineffectual nature of speculative philosophy had no doubt been solved by adopting a philosophy of practice in which the proletariat was to be the major protagonist. 'As philosophy finds its *material* weapons in the proletariat, so the proletariat finds its *spiritual* weapons in philosophy.'[29] The success of Marx's historical venture was predicated upon the fusion of these two elements. Each, without the strength of the other, would end in banality: 'Philosophy cannot be made a reality without the abolition of the proletariat, the proletariat cannot be abolished without philosophy being made a reality.'[30] This did not, however, in any way solve the practical problem which obviously emerged — how to make the proletariat aware of the role allotted to it and organised to fulfil it? The problem of how to unite 'philosophy' and the 'proletariat' is, clearly, not only central to the logical structure of Marxism but had also to be the paramount concern of social democratic practice.

As far as the Russian neophytes of Marxism in the early 1880s were concerned, there was hardly need to press the logical and practical importance of accomplishing this fusion. Their own immediate past experience had made them poignantly aware of the utter helplessness of a small group of intellectuals attempting to rouse an unorganised mass of peasants to revolutionary action. The great idealistic 'Going to the People' of the 1870s had foundered precisely because the huge gap in culture, dress, speech and education which separated the 'students' from the peasants had made communication almost impossible. The mass they had come to save turned them over to the authorities.

In a certain sense their own experience prepared the Russian revolutionaries for Marxism. The belief that the peasant mass was spontaneously revolutionary had been shown to be illusory. One of the theorists of Russian socialism who had long questioned this myth and the *buntarist* tactic derived from it was Peter Lavrov. Lavrov had, since the beginning of the seventies, bitterly criticised what he took to be the naive nihilistic anti-intellectualism of Bakunin and the *buntarists*. Then his sober voice had been out of tune with the frenzied times; the young intelligentsia could not, or would not, wait to prepare themselves and the mass before attempting a revolutionary onslaught. Plekhanov, in his youth, had indeed been prominent in polemic against Lavrov's words of caution and his pleas for clarity and self-preparation on the part of the intelligentsia and patient propaganda among the people.[31] Only in this way, Lavrov argued, would any real and lasting socialist society be produced, only in this way could the real danger of a revolutionary bloodbath which threatened all culture and progress in Russia be avoided. The crucial thing for Lavrov, as for Marx, was not the engineering of a revolution as an anarchic all-consuming outburst. The aim was not retribution but progress towards a humane society, the force of the people must be so channelled as to realise philosophy, or, as Lavrov would have it, to implement 'critical thought'. The intelligentsia had been able to acquire this most precious human gift of being able to think critically only because they were privileged with leisure. But leisure for the few in contemporary society, and especially in Russia, Lavrov argued, rested upon the exploitation, suffering and gross ignorance of the great majority. The obligation to implement the conclusions of critical thought therefore derived not solely from the general moral principle that man should act in accordance with his conception of the good but also from the fact that his very ability to perceive the good was established upon the degradation of the mass. The critically thinking individual, as the repository of knowledge and civilisation, had a huge debt to repay to the barbarised mass around him. The socialist revolution, in Lavrov's view, depended for its success upon two factors: the theoretical clarity and ideological preparedness of the 'critically thinking' leaders and their patient and persistent work in propagandising the mass, explaining to it the full magnitude of the socialist objective. The lesson of 1789–93, of 1848–51 and of 1871 was always the same – these tasks had not been carried out. 'Knowledge', Lavrov insisted 'is the fundamental power of the revolution which is under way and the force essential to carry it out.'[32]

It was hardly surprising that by the end of the seventies Lavrov was himself inclining more and more towards Marxism. It was hardly surprising either that when Plekhanov came to Geneva to begin his long exile, he too fell under the joint sway of Marx and Lavrov.

Lavrov's prestige as a major ideologist of the revolutionary movement was magnified in Plekhanov's eyes by the fact that he personally knew Marx and Engels. Besides, certain traits of character drew the two together. Lavrov shared with Plekhanov a great respect for learning, which both translated into an emphasis on the importance of theory for the revolutionary movement.[33]

For the three years that Plekhanov was undergoing his apprenticeship in Marxism and beginning his career as a Marxist publicist he was working in close collaboration with Lavrov and this circumstance undoubtedly left its impress upon his interpretation of the doctrine.

With Lavrov, Plekhanov insisted on the all-importance of knowledge and adequate theoretical preparation for the revolutionary cause 'for without knowledge there is no strength'.[34]

The application of proper theory, study of the laws of history and of Russia's level of economic development would, according to Plekhanov, enable the Marxists to avoid the errors of the past. The revolutionary movement could at last pitch its demands and set its objectives according to the precise stage of social and economic development. Marxism served, therefore, not to debase, but to augment the role of the intelligentsia for their knowledge of historical laws, and their awareness of the limitations to action were to be crucial to the movement. 'Once I know the laws of social and historical progress I can influence the latter according to my aims . . . in broad outline I shall know the direction of the forces of society, and it will remain for me only to rely on their resultant to achieve my ends.'[35] There is much in Plekhanov that smacks of the young Marx. There is in particular the same Promethean insistence that reason must strive to transform the world and remake it in its own image.

Dialectical materialism says that human reason could not be the demiurge of history, because it is itself the *product of history*. But once that product has appeared, it *must* not — and in its nature it *cannot* — be obedient to the reality handed down as a heritage by previous history; of necessity it strives to transform that reality after its likeness and image, *to make it reasonable*.

Dialectical materialism says, like Goethe's Faust:

>   *Im Anfang war die Tat!*

Action (the activity of men in conformity to law in the social process of production) explains to the dialectical materialist the historical development of the reason of social man. It is to action also that all his *practical philosophy* is reduced. *Dialectical materialism is the philosophy of action.*[36]

To have been really precise Plekhanov should have added that dialectical materialism was a philosophy of action precisely tailored to the needs of the Russian intelligentsia. By pointing to the proletariat as the force of the future, the intelligentsia singled out the most compactly organised and least conservative work force in the country. Here was a comparatively manageable group of men upon whom the puny forces of the intelligentsia would not be spread too thin, a force which was, moreover, concentrated in the towns — the natural habitat of the intelligentsia and its only place of asylum from the attentions of the police.[37] The industrial workers were, for all these reasons, *the* group through which the Russian intelligentsia could at last overcome its prolonged isolation from the mass of the people, 'We point out to them the industrial workers as the intermediary force able to promote the intelligentsia's merger with the "people".'[38] 'Having secured the powerful support of this section, the socialist intelligentsia will have far greater hope of success in extending their activity to the peasantry as well.'[39] As it had been for Marx, the proletariat was seen as the bridge connecting radical philosophy with the mass. It was, Plekhanov claimed, 'only through the intermediary of this class that the people can take part in the progressive strivings of civilised humanity.'[40]

If anything Plekhanov credits the intellectuals with a far more forward role than does Marx. Plekhanov is quite unequivocal that it is they who initiate the struggle, they 'bring *consciousness* into the working class'[41] and play the leading role in the creation of a separate working class political party. Once again, however, one gets the impression that all of this activity is directed not so much at alleviating the felt grievances of the working class but rather at overcoming the problems of the revolutionary intelligentsia. The creation of a separate workers' political party, according to Plekhanov, 'alone is capable of solving all the contradictions which now condemn our intelligentsia to theoretical and practical impotence. We have already seen that the most obvious of those contradictions is at present the necessity to overthrow absolutism and the impossibility of doing so without the support of the people.'[42] It is hard to escape the conclusion that there is about this sort of formulation more than a whiff of a patrician stance in which the proletariat is viewed as but the instrument of intelligentsia designs. It was indeed the 'most obvious' of the contradictions besetting the *intelligentsia* — the overthrow of autocracy — which Plekhanov stipulates as *the* task which the nascent workers' movement is duty-bound to carry out. Some of the contemporary detractors of this sort of Marxism, Mikhailovsky in the late 1880s and early 1890s, the *praktiki*, Economists and revisionists in the late 1890s and early years of the twentieth century, repeatedly alleged that in this, as in other perhaps even more unworthy respects, the intelligentsia was simply using the labour movement, foisting on to it political goals which might have been appropriate to them but which were alien to the proletariat.

There was no doubt an element of *hauteur* in the way in which Plekhanov conceived of the proletariat, but his insistence upon the centrality of the political struggle for the workers' movement, his insistence that the proletariat only existed as such to the degree that it was organised and acted politically, all of this is, as we have seen, Marxism of the most pure.

Plekhanov's need to insist upon the primacy of the political struggle as an index of the class development of the proletariat stemmed not only from axioms derived from Marx, that the Social Democrats should 'give political expression to the economic antagonism', it was also intended to combat the prevalent apoliticism of the Russian revolutionary movement. In this respect Marxism demanded a total break with the old traditions of political abstentionism and anarchism. It stipulated the urgent need for constitutional rights so that the labour movement and social democracy, its political arm, could develop. Only on the basis of legal guarantees of freedom of assembly, freedom from censorship, protection of the funds and personnel of voluntary political and trade associations would it be possible to begin an extensive propaganda campaign for socialism. Without the growth of proletarian consciousness which presupposed legitimation of the agencies through which it could be propagated, there would be no serious hope for socialism. In any case the prospects for socialism were still in the somewhat distant future. Plekhanov conceded in 1883 that 'we by no means believe in the early possibility of a socialist government in Russia'.[43] The reason why is obvious enough; the development of the productive forces in Russia was nowhere near the requisite level. 'In other words, socialist organisation, like any other, requires the appropriate basis. But that basis does not exist in Russia.'[44] Plekhanov's rejection of socialism as an immediate goal of social democracy in Russia was not to be challenged until 1905 and then only fleetingly in the euphoria of the first revolution.

The immediate political objective of the proletariat in Russia was, therefore, the securing of the democratic revolution. In the battle for democratic liberties and an end to all feudal prerogatives, however, the proletariat had to recognise from the outset that it was unlikely to receive any steadfast support from the bourgeoisie. There was no evidence to suggest, Plekhanov maintained, that the Russian bourgeoisie would prove any more committed to the realisation of democracy and freedom than had its peers in Europe. Paraphrasing Marx, Plekhanov reminded his audience 'that whenever the "red spectre" took at all threatening forms the "liberals" were ready to seek protection in the embraces of the most unceremonious military dictatorship'.[45]

There was no doubt whatsoever in Plekhanov's mind that the proletariat would have to assume the leading role in the political battle for democracy. This is no accidental or peripheral point of his teaching, it is central and is one that is repeatedly made: 'In conclusion I repeat — and I insist upon this important point: the revolutionary movement in Russia will triumph only as a *working class movement* or else it will never triumph!'[46] The proletariat's obligation to assume the leading role in the struggle against autocracy, for the realisation of the democratic revolution, is without doubt the most important precept of orthodox Russian Marxism up to 1905 at least. It is an idea which recurs, in one guise or another, in the majority of the documents cited in this collection. In the *Programme of the Social Democratic Emancipation of Labour Group* (1884), whose principles served to define a Social Democrat until the adoption of a new party programme in 1903 it presented as follows:

One of the most harmful consequences of this backward state of production was, and still is, the underdeveloped state of the middle class which in our country is incapable of taking the initiative in the struggle against absolutism.
   That is why the socialist intelligentsia has been obliged to head the contemporary emancipation movement whose immediate task must be the creation of free political institutions in our country.[47]

In *On Agitation* the same point is made — the bourgeoisie merely uses the proletariat in pursuit of its own partial interests and allows few of the crumbs of any victory to fall to the proletariat.[48] Even more emphatic was the manifesto adopted by the First Congress of the RSDLP, the only unassailably authoritative document of the period up to 1903. The attainment of democratic freedoms is stipulated as fundamental to the development of the proletariat, then comes the clear warning:

But only the Russian proletariat *itself* can win the political liberty that it needs.
   The further east one goes in Europe, the meaner, more cowardly and politically weak the bourgeoisie becomes, and the greater are the cultural and political tasks that fall to the proletariat. On its own sturdy shoulders the Russian working class must, and will, carry the cause of the achievement of political liberty.[49]

Finally, Akselrod in his very important programmatic statement of 1898 — *The Present Tasks and Tactics of the Russian Social Democrats* — is emphatic: 'if there is no possibility of giving the Russian proletariat an independent pre-eminent role in the fight against tsarist police autocracy and arbitrary rule, then Russian social democracy has no historical right to exist'.[50] It was hardly fortuitous that it was to be Akselrod who first coined the phrase 'the hegemony of the proletariat in the democratic revolution', first used in the spring of 1901 and meaning, according to the gloss he put on it, 'our party will become the liberator *par excellence*, a centre to which all democratic sympathies will gravitate and where all the greatest revolutionary protests will originate'.[51]

This idea of the hegemony of the proletariat in the democratic revolution was the bedrock of the whole political strategy of the orthodox Russian Marxists and, when it was threatened in the last years of the nineteenth and at the beginning of the twentieth centuries, the orthodox responded by closing ranks in a monolithic and impassioned defence of the key element of their strategy.

One of the first to dispute the role of leader of the democratic revolution against autocracy was E.D. Kuskova who penned a private declaration of faith which clearly owed a good deal to Bernstein's ideas. Her *Credo*[52] directly contested not merely the hegemonic role of the proletariat but even the mere possibility or desirability of creating an independent working class party. '[In Russia] the line of least resistance will never lead to political activity. The intolerable political oppression will prompt much talk about it and will concentrate attention precisely on this question, but it will never prompt political action.'[53] The economic struggle, Kuskova maintained, was hard enough, particularly in Russia where conditions were so difficult. Her conclusion therefore was that 'Talk of an independent workers' political party is nothing but the result of transplanting alien aims and alien achievements on to our soil.'[54]

Kuskova's was not, as some maintain, a lone and isolated voice. There was at the turn of the century a genuine crisis in the Russian Marxist movement which paradoxically followed and stemmed from the significant successes it had attained in winning over the labour movement during the latter half of the 1890s. The ramifications of this crisis may perhaps become clearer if, for the moment, we explore the tactics employed by the Social Democrats in winning support from the labour movement in the 1890s.

Bridges to the workers: propaganda and economic agitation

The initial problem the youthful student Marxists faced was quite simply that of establishing contact with their clients and this was by no means as easy as might be supposed. In the early 1890s the Marxists of St Petersburg and Moscow, as well as those in provincial centres (with the exception of the Jewish Pale of Settlement), were almost exclusively drawn from the ranks of the professional middle classes or the gentry and nobility. The gap in manners, life-style, even in dress and language, between them and the workers of the capitals was not much less than that which had separated the activists of Zemlya i Volya from the peasants. Throughout the period covered by these documents there was in Russia, as there was elsewhere, a significant section of the workers who resented the 'students' and intellectuals and who were quite prepared to believe government and clerical propaganda that all Socialists were enemies of the people and criminals. One of the first 'agitational' leaflets brought out by the Petersburg Social Democrats was indeed concerned to quash these illusions.[55] Many of the student Marxist memoirs of this period recall the lengths which the youngsters went to just to meet genuine working men to gain an entrée into the class they had set out to cultivate. Perhaps the most successful in this connection were the women Marxists who took an active and increasingly prominent part in the adult education classes in St Petersburg. These legal and open classes, funded from benevolent bequests, proved to be by far the most effective means of recruiting intelligent and ambitious workmen to the movement.[56]

Gradually, through these individual contacts which the intellectuals secured, they built up small circles of workmen generally working in the same factory or living in the same district of the city. By the mid-1890s there had emerged a fairly well-defined division of labour with particular groups of intellectuals being responsible for circle work in particular quarters of the city, the whole work being supervised by a leading circle of intellectuals.

The rationale behind the patient educational work of the circles was simple enough and quite logical given the forces then available to the Marxists. Given that they could not, without extensive contacts, make any impact on the mass of the workers in the capitals, given that they themselves were not at this time very strong in numbers (their forces were counted in hundreds rather than thousands at this time), they had little option but to work with the small groups of 'advanced' workers grouped in the circles or *kruzhki*. This period of the *kruzhovshchina*, as it was later called, signified above all the attempt by the intelligentsia to mould the advanced workers in their own image. They were to be inducted into the toils of philosophy, economics, dialectics of history and sociology, so that they might gain a comprehensive and scientific awareness of the proletarian life situation. As the future leaders of the working class, the advanced workers had to develop a fully rounded, integrated knowledge of *all* the problems of politics, economics and culture which confronted the working class. This was the phase of 'propaganda' where, following Plekhanov's specification,[57] the Marxists concentrated exclusively on the in-depth, theoretical preparation of a comparatively small number of workers. The task of 'propaganda' was to impart many and complex ideas to the few. It was hoped that this small élite corps would then go out into the working class and each would train new worker-leaders and they, in their turn, would go and do likewise in geometrical progression until, with accelerating rapidity the whole class became conscious. This was what I refer to elsewhere[58] as the chain letter theory of the generation of socialist consciousness. It was soon abandoned. It was found to be a tactic which was not simply unproductive but actually counter-productive.

Far from producing zealous missionaries impatient to carry the message to their untutored comrades, the Marxist leaders of the circles discovered that they were raising men who aspired to the learning of the Renaissance polymaths. The intellectuals found themselves hoist on their own petard. The advanced workers, once embarked upon scholarship, seemed to fall prey to a kind of Socratic awareness of ignorance. As might have been predicted, this, far from inspiring them with the urgency of action, made them more and more aware of their own limitations and the need for more and more study. They could not yet, they maintained, begin to win over their worker comrades when their own world views were so lamentably deficient by comparison with the genuine intellectuals. Not for the first nor the last time was the concept of unripe time invoked as the pretext for avoiding any practical attempt to extend the revolutionary movement.

Throughout the early 1890s the advanced workers, organised in their rather incestuous circles, kept themselves studiously aloof from the working class 'disturbances' which began to break out with increasing regularity. Indeed they were often positively hostile to intelligentsia attempts to get them actively involved, fearing that the new 'mass' tactic would mean the end to the self-education sessions they had come to value so dearly. It was, they felt, no part of their lofty business to have any truck with Luddite wreckers and anarchic arsonists.

This attitude came out very clearly in the disturbances which broke out in the Semyannikov factory just before Christmas in 1894. Some of the worker members of one of Lenin's circles were employed at the Semyannikov factory but they gave him no inkling of the fact that grievances were developing to breaking point. Takhtarev, who has left one of the best accounts of the Russian labour movement in the 1890s,[59] noticed how the 'advanced' members of the workers' circles almost ostentatiously held themselves aloof even from disturbances in the factories in which they themselves worked. On this occasion they did not even inform Lenin of the build-up of tensions and, indeed, stoutly justified their refusal to participate with a 'rabble' that stooped to breaking windows and fire-raising.

Lenin's evaluation of the abortive rising of the Semyannikov workers in one sense sided with that of the advanced workers; he agreed that spontaneous violence simply played into the hands of the factory managers and their agents — the police and soldiery. He also came, however, to a conclusion which was far from flattering, which implied indeed a comprehensive critique of their earlier exclusively theoretical concerns. The key sentence in the flysheet Lenin wrote out by hand for distribution in the Semyannikov works was 'The capacity for struggle may only be evoked by struggle.'[60] This was the first 'agitational' leaflet put out by the Petersburg Marxists. Others followed as the year 1895 brought a crop of disturbances and strikes, at Laferme's tobacco factory and at the Admiralty shipyards at the New Port.[61] Each was made the occasion for a leaflet outlining the workers' grievances, calling upon them to act peaceably and in unison and ending with a simplified formulation of the common interests of all workers in the struggle for better conditions of work.

The strategy of utilising the immediate grievances of particular groups of workers in particular plants as a lever for spreading social democratic ideas and influences among the workers had already been adopted in a somewhat haphazard way by some of the St Petersburg Marxists before the arrival of *On Agitation* in the spring of 1895. It was this programmatic statement, however, which first coherently developed its implications. The adoption of the programme of *On Agitation* signalled a very self-conscious reorientation of the practical activities of the Social Democrats especially in their relations with the labour movement.[62] It was written by Arkadi Kremer and edited by Julius Martov, two prominent activists of the Jewish workers' movement centred on Vilna. The Jewish movement, itself strongly influenced by the Polish labour movement, was, at least until the second half of the nineties, considerably more advanced than the Russian. It had for a time gone over to the tactic of extensive mass agitation and Kremer did no more than justify this transition and summarise the defects that had become so evident during the phase of small circle intensive propaganda. It was a résumé of the recent past of the Jewish movement that struck the many Russians as a convincing diagnosis of their own present ills.

The new programme (for such, in effect, *On Agitation* became) pulled no punches: its first paragraph bluntly declared that 'the first steps taken by the Russian Social Democrats were the wrong ones and that, in the interests of the cause, their tactics must be changed'.[63] According to *On Agitation*, propaganda conducted through the circles had done more harm than good. It had created a rather precious stratum of educated workers more knowledgeable about Western European than Russian labour conditions and contemptuous of the practical struggle. It had, in effect, succeeded in emasculating precisely those most intelligent and militant workers who ought to have emerged as the natural leaders of their class. 'By creating a worker socialist intelligentsia, alienated from the mass, we harm the cause of the development of the proletariat, we harm our own cause.'[64]

On Agitation argued two closely related propositions in accounting for this lamentable state of affairs within the movement, both had to do with the manner in which consciousness was produced in the class as a whole. The first had it that proletarian consciousness arose not out of theoretical work and the proselytising work of intellectuals and worker-intellectuals but had its origins and was refined and developed only in the course of the struggle for existence of the working mass. Secondly, the brochure argued that it was utopian and unhistorical to expect the mass, even if blessed with great cohorts of worker-intellectuals, to emerge at one stroke into full social democratic consciousness. It argued that, on the contrary, the process of self-education through its own activity must take the working class through a series of transitional stages before this could be realised.

The first step in this progression, according to Kremer and Martov (the authors of *On Agitation*), was to develop the workers' awareness of common economic objectives — to produce what they termed 'a strongly developed class egoism'. Only experience would teach them that conditions everywhere were essentially the same, that exploitation was neither accidental nor localised but systemic. Only the struggle for particular improvements in particular plants would teach them the importance of statutory guarantees to protect their conditions of work, and therefore of the need to win the support of all workers in their particular trade and eventually in all trades.

The struggle to obtain partial improvements in particular factories would quickly reveal to the workers where the government and its armed forces stood. It would hardly be difficult for the social democratic propagandists to point up the conjunction of economic and political power when every strike, no matter how peaceably conducted, met with immediate police repression, arrests of leaders, impounding of strike funds and beatings for the strikers. It would not be difficult to point out that until legal guarantees were granted which allowed the workers to organise themselves to withdraw their labour and protect their funds and their officials, there could be little hope of attaining any serious improvement in their lot. Politics was to come via economics. Out of the growing awareness of a community of *economic* interests there would quickly emerge the realisation of the need for *political* and legal changes, and this would signal the second phase of the struggle when new objectives and new modes of organisation would become appropriate.

The first phase of the struggle for petty demands, towards which the worker is propelled by a calculation that is easily grasped — exploitation by the owner being easy to explain — demands from the workers a certain degree of energy and unanimity. In the second phase, when it is necessary to make common cause against the entire bourgeois class, which the government will immediately rush to help, a much greater degree of endurance, solidarity and courage will be required. Moreover, a certain level of consciousness will also be demanded, the ability to link one's own interests with the interests of other workers in the same branch of production, sometimes even of another, but such consciousness can be developed only when the worker comes, through his own experience, to the conclusion that success in a particular struggle for the interests of workers in separate factories is not feasible. This very struggle with separate owners will develop in the working class a degree of stability and endurance, of unity, a sense of independence and class self-confidence, which it will need when it comes face to face with the inevitability of the class struggle in the proper meaning of the word. As it enters this stage, the workers' movement will begin little by little to take on a political tinge.[65]

The quotation ends with the impeccably orthodox proposition that insofar as the proletariat begins to lay claim to objectives which have to do not with this or that section of the wage labourers but with the general conditions in which all are employed (claims like the right to strike, or for the reduction of the working day, or for a minimum wage or proper system of factory inspection), insofar as it articulates these demands the proletariat becomes political. Its representatives must transcend the particularity of specific trade demands and must press these objectives not with particular employers nor employers' federations but with the most generalised and potent representative of the bourgeois interest — the state. The political party exists, therefore, to articulate the generalised interests of the working class as a whole, to represent its goal in history not vis-à-vis the employers as such but vis-à-vis those who command the state. The great virtue of the *On Agitation* programme was that it offered a plausible line of ascent from the particular to the most generalised grievances of the working class. It did so, moreover, within the framework of an epistemology far closer to Marx's (and Plekhanov's) philosophy of action than the over-abstract and theoretical mode of approach they had started with.

Lenin's *Draft and Explanation of a Programme for the Social Democratic Party*[66] was written in the heyday of social democratic obsession with *On Agitation* as the means at last discovered for the Social Democrats to make a substantial impact upon the working class and to develop its consciousness through a series of demarcated and ascending phases. 'This transition of the workers to an unflinching struggle for their vital needs, a struggle for concessions, for better living conditions, wages and hours means that the Russian workers have taken an enormous step forward.[67] In the very process of this struggle for their immediate needs, the workers, according to Lenin:

learn to understand the social order that is based upon the exploitation of labour by capital. Secondly, in the course of this struggle the workers test their strength, learn to act together and learn to appreciate the necessity for and significance of their unity. The extension of this struggle and the increasing frequency of conflict lead inevitably to an extension of the struggle, to the development of a sense of unity, a sense of their own solidarity, at first among the workers of a particular locality and then among the workers of the country as a whole, among the whole working class. Thirdly, this struggle develops the political consciousness of the workers. The living conditions of the mass of working people put them in a position where they (can) have neither the leisure nor the opportunity to reflect on any matters of state. But the workers' struggle with the factory owners for their every-day needs in itself inevitably leads the workers [to reflect on] state, political questions, the questions of how the Russian state is governed, how laws and regulations are promulgated and whose interests they serve. Every confrontation in the factory inevitably leads the workers into a confrontation with the laws and representatives of state authority.[68]

The demarcation of distinct stages in the development of consciousness — from the primitive awareness on the part of workers of one plant that they shared interests in common, through to a similar awareness of a national community of economic interest shared by all workers, to a political consciousness 'that in order to achieve their aims, the workers must gain influence on affairs of state'[69] — was to play an important role, not only in Lenin's account of the revolutionary process, but in the whole strategy of the Russian Marxists up to 1905 at least. Here at last the Russian Marxists had discovered a manageable progression, a sort of timetable in terms of which their goal of raising the Russian working class to the level of political consciousness attained by its German or French comrades did not appear quite as remote as it had at the beginning of the 1890s.

By 1897, indeed, it appeared that gigantic steps had already been taken by both the Social Democrats and the labour movement. In May of 1896 they had achieved a most impressive demonstration of their joint power when virtually the whole force of St Petersburg cotton spinners came out on strike demanding payment for the holiday in honour of Nicholas II's coronation and the shortening of the working day.[70] This strike of some 30,000 operatives in one city was certainly by far the largest witnessed in Russia and there could have been few European strikes at that time to match it. The actual influence of Social Democrats in instituting and subsequently leading the strike is, however, disputed. Professor Pipes has it that the later claims of the Social Democrats were grossly exaggerated and concludes that their influence was simply advisory: 'the Union performed the function of an editorial and printing centre. There is no evidence whatsoever for the assertion frequently made in Soviet histories that the Union directed the 1896 textile strike.'[71] 'Directed' may perhaps be too strong a word, neither then nor subsequently did the Social Democrats pretend that they could initiate strikes at will or 'direct' them once started. Lenin's own *Draft Programme* of this time is more modest and probably sums up the Social Democrats' general objectives at this time quite well: 'the task of the party is not to dream up fashionable ways of helping the workers, but to join up with the workers' movement, to bring light into it, to assist the workers in the struggle that they have already begun to wage.'[72]

Partly no doubt this assistance would take the form of acting as 'an editorial and printing centre' and the leaflets translated in the collection make it clear that it was the Union of Struggle that did formulate, print and circulate the demands of a whole succession of strikes in the 1895—6 period culminating in the great textile strike.[73] The impact of these seemingly modest endeavours should not, however, be underestimated. There can be no doubt that the simple appearance of a printed leaflet was often sufficient to fire the workers with a previously absent confidence to assert themselves and claim redress of their grievances. At last they had been noticed by 'The Committee' which would help them against their employers. Takhtarev recounts how quickly the spirits of the newly leafleted workers were raised, how they enthused about 'our boys who notice everything and write it all down. Tell it to the Union, they say, we've got to let them know about this.'[74] Nor was the naivety confined exclusively to the workers; police reports also greatly exaggerated the potency and working class support enjoyed by 'The Labour Union' to whose evil influence they attributed almost all the strikes of this period.[75] No doubt too, many employers confronted with sudden and unwonted militancy from workers whose demands were well-presented and distributed in printed copies complied with at least some of the demands with uncustomary rapidity. Each capitulation of this sort adding, of course, to the notoriety and legendary power of the Labour Union.

It can hardly have been accidental that the textile workers — considered the *least* developed and organised of industrial workers — who had in their whole previous history displayed little initiative to redress their grievances, had for the first time received social democratic agitational leaflets in 1895 and early 1896. Lenin's leaflet *To the Working Men and Women of the Thornton Mill*[76] had been addressed to striking weavers, and so had Martov's directed at the workers in the Koenig plant. Many other textile plants had been leafleted specifically with regard to the grievances of striking weavers.[77] Furthermore the 1896 May Day leaflet put out by the Union of Struggle attained a broad circulation and is known to have been distributed in at least seven textile plants.[78]

There is, finally, the fact that the St Petersburg strikers held out quite insistently for a reduction of the working day to ten and a half hours[79] which indicates rather clearly the impact that the May Day campaign was beginning to have on the Russian workers. It was, of course, a decision of the Second International that the main objective of an international labour day should be that of reducing the hours of labour, and this had naturally been taken up in the social democratic leaflets put out for 1 May. It was a theme which was also presented in one of the most popular and influential agitational brochures which the Russian Social Democrats had appropriated from their Polish comrades — the pamphlet *The Working Day*.[80] Making use of comparative material collected by the International the pamphlet stressed the vital significance of reducing the hours of work for the entire economic, social and intellectual well-being of the working class. It was not, of course, very difficult to demonstrate how lamentable were Russian conditions in this respect. What is surprising is that the comparatively 'advanced' demand made an enormous impact upon the Russian workers in this period. According to one history of the Russian labour movement: 'This new type of strike was started by the St Petersburg workers in 1895, and the movement spread all over the country. The strikers everywhere insisted on the introduction of a ten-and-a-half hours working day (from 7 a.m. to 7 p.m. with an interval of one and a half hours for lunch) and a shorter working day on Saturday.'[81] According to this account there were 'according to the official data, 303 strikes of this nature, involving 90,162 workers',[82] though unofficial data which perhaps came nearer the truth put the figure considerably higher.

According to Wildman's account of the St Petersburg textile strikes, social democratic propaganda, in particular the campaign for the reduction of the hours of work and the wide distribution of the pamphlet *The Working Day*, had a very considerable impact not merely in rousing the weavers to strike in the first place, but also in providing them with a simple common programme which strengthened their resolve in the two week long strike. 'It is quite probable that the circulation of this pamphlet contributed more than any other single factor to the transformation of a disorderly protest over non-payment for the Coronation days into a remarkably coordinated general strike seeking government regulation of the hours of work.'[83]

The great crop of strikes which continued unabated into 1897, all insistently calling for a reduction of the working day, eventually forced the Russian government to do something it had never before been so obviously obliged to do – it yielded to the public, or rather to the workers', pressure. In 1896 at the time of the textile strikes it promised to examine the possibility of a general reduction of hours but it was not until June 1897, after many more strikes had insisted upon the same point, that an Act was finally published limiting the working day to eleven and a half hours, or ten hours where the work was done in two shifts.

The new law was no doubt a triumph for the Russian working class and for the Social Democrats. The latter greeted it, however, with cautionary words. The workers had won these minor concessions, they argued, only through intensive struggle. Only continued struggle on their part would ensure that the provisions of the new law were not ignored wholesale or attenuated via ministerial 'interpretations'. The workers' vigilant protection of their own interests, it was repeatedly pointed out, was so enormously difficult in a country where they enjoyed none of the elementary rights enjoyed by their comrades in other lands:

The employers have thousands of ways of exerting pressure on the government: they have their societies and associations; employers are members of numerous government commissions and boards (for example, the Factory Boards), they have personal access to ministers; they may write as much as they like in the press about their wishes and demands, and the press has tremendous influence in our times. As to the workers, they have *no* legal means of exerting pressure on the government. There is only one thing the workers can do, and that is to join forces, to spread the consciousness of their interests as members of one class among all the workers, and to put up united resistance to the government and the employers. Every worker can now see that the enforcement of the new law will depend entirely on who exerts strongest pressure on the government, the employers or the workers. It was only by struggle, by a conscious and staunch struggle, that the workers secured the *passage* of the law. Only by struggle will they be able to secure the actual enforcement of the law, and its enforcement in the interests of the workers. Without a stubborn struggle, without the staunch resistance of the united workers to every claim the employers make, the new law will remain a scrap of paper.[84]

In the opinion of many social democratic leaders in Russia the successful struggle of these years, the mass strikes which had, for the first time, roused sections of the 'backward' workers with such dramatic results spelt the start of a new phase of development. The workers, they argued, had begun to emerge as a class. Not only had the strikes forged a sense of shared interests opposed to the interests of other classes but they had also been conducted under the emphatically national and all-class slogan of a reduction of the working day. The realisation of that slogan in its turn clearly demanded legislation. The Russian working class had, in other words, in the space of two years begun to make political demands. In this short period it had demonstrated the correctness of the watchword of Marx and Plekhanov that every class struggle is a political struggle.

Political agitation, proletarian hegemony and Economism

The task which now appeared on the agenda was that which Plekhanov had specified and which all the documents of orthodoxy insisted upon – the proletariat's next step was to assume the leadership of the democratic revolution against feudalism.

We have already seen that this was the main strategic directive of the manifesto of the First Congress of the Russian Social Democratic Labour Party (RSDLP) convened in the aftermath of the strike wave in 1898. It was a strategy which expressed, according to the orthodox Russian Marxists, the very *raison d'être* of the party. In the same year as the First Congress was convened Akselrod had insisted that:

if there is no possibility of giving the Russian proletariat an independent, pre-eminent role in the fight against tsarist police autocracy and arbitrary rule, then Russian social democracy has no historical right to exist. It becomes, in this event, no longer viable, and its very existence, far from assisting the revolutionary movement, retards it.[85]

It was, paradoxically, the very success of the strike movement of the years 1895–7 which directly led to this social democratic shibboleth being questioned.

Perhaps the single most important factor to notice is that the successes of social democracy and the labour movement led directly to more intensive police suppression. In December 1895 the leaders of the St Petersburg *stariki*, unquestionably the most important Marxist leaders in Russia proper (here, again, we exclude the

Jewish Pale), had been arrested. Their places were filled by the 'candidate members' but these too were soon swept away. Arrests both of Social Democrats (500 of the most prominent remaining leaders were rounded up after the First Congress of the party) and of the veteran labour leaders proceeded apace and, by the end of 1898, there were very few social democratic or labour leaders of any prominence or experience still at large.

The places of the veterans were, necessarily, filled with young inexperienced men. Lenin, and some of the other veterans, had encountered some of the youngsters who were to replace them at a meeting in St Petersburg arranged in the few days of freedom allowed to political prisoners to make family and private arrangements before travelling to their places of exile. The meeting had not been very cordial. The veterans suspected the youngsters of insufficient theoretical preparation with the consequent inclination to follow the workers rather than lead them.

How far these recollections were blessed with hindsight is, as ever in examining reminiscences of the Russian revolutionary movement, impossible to tell. What is beyond doubt is that within a year or so of taking effective control of the social democratic movement in Russia (if we date this from the arrests of the remaining veterans in spring of 1898) the young *praktiki* had precipitated a severe crisis by renouncing the specification of social democratic politics hitherto agreed upon by all the orthodox Russian Marxists.

The first, rather surreptitious document in this attempt to revise the orthodoxy was a statement outlining the proper strategy of the Russian Social Democrats and the Russian labour movement in an emphatically Bernsteinian way written by E.D. Kuskova. Its conclusions we have already alluded to before embarking upon this historical diversion. Kuskova's statement, Lenin declared, 'was such an excellent weapon against Economism that, had there been no *Credo*, it would have been necessary to invent one'.[86] Kuskova's views were openly espoused by her husband S.N. Prokopovich and he in turn was for a time the main spokesman for the young opposition to Plekhanov which, from the turn of the century, constituted a majority in the Union of Social Democrats Abroad. It was, moreover, no secret that the Prokopoviches were close, in both personal and political terms, to the editors of the newspaper *Rabochaya Mysl* (*Workers' Thought*), which the 'orthodox' viewed as the main vehicle of Economism and revisionism in the Russian labour and socialist movement. Before going on to examine the substantive arguments between the 'orthodox' and the 'revisionists' during this period, we ought first to establish who were the parties to the dispute and what political and personal issues were at stake.

There was, in the first place, the 'young' opposition to Plekhanov in the émigré movement. The Union of Russian Social Democrats Abroad had been founded in 1894 as an organisational focus for socialist émigrés but within it the veteran Emancipation of Labour Group retained its exclusive structure and insisted on supervising the larger organisation and editing its publications. Understandably frictions arose which were quickly exacerbated by Plekhanov's well-known prickliness and intellectual arrogance. He was not a man who took kindly to criticism of himself but felt quite free to deal out the most biting censure of other people's literary and ideological shortcomings. The youngsters, stung by Plekhanov's tactless critiques of their literary ventures and dismayed that he and the other veterans of the Emancipation of Labour Group steadfastly refused to sully *their* pens with popular agitational literature, carried out what amounted to a coup d'état. Plekhanov and Akselrod were defeated on a whole number of issues within the Union and, consequently, the Emancipation of Labour Group decided, in 1898, to refuse to undertake the editing of any more of the Union's publications. This self-denying ordinance was to have quite a dramatic effect because the youngster-controlled Union immediately proceeded to lay plans for a regular newspaper to be distributed in Russia under the title *Rabochee Delo* (*The Workers' Cause*). When this journal began publication in March 1899 Plekhanov and the other 'orthodox' veterans, who had for so long striven for exactly such a rostrum through which to address the Russian workers, found themselves out in the cold.

Lenin's *Protest*[87] written in the last months of his Siberian exile and signed by seventeen of his comrades-in-exile was the first blow struck by the orthodox in their counter-campaign. Emboldened by Lenin's support for the tenets of 'the old current' and his explicit support for Plekhanov and Akselrod against the youngsters who presumed to 'improve' upon the old orthodoxy, Plekhanov took to his pen and dipped it liberally in the gall which he had stored up in the past few years. His *Preface to the 'Vademecum' for the Editorial Board of Rabochee Delo*[88] might have had a cumbersome title but was full of the most biting invective and cruelly polished phrases. Plekhanov rounded on these 'narrow-minded pedants' and 'political castrates'[89] barely out of nappies, with scant literary attainment and the most rudimentary theoretical training, who nonetheless presumed to tell the Emancipation of Labour Group what the workers *really* wanted. In actual fact, Plekhanov argued, what the young *praktiki* were doing was merely satisfying the *existing* level of working class consciousness, taking *existing* demands as the only proper or feasible ones to pursue.[90] According to their logic the Social Democrats ought to restrict themselves to those interests and objectives of which the workers were already conscious. Such 'leaders', Plekhanov maintained, were renegades to the ideals and final goals of socialism just as surely as Bernstein was. They had renounced the central obligation of Social Democrats to *develop* the consciousness of the working class into a comprehensive and revolutionary critique of capitalist society in its entirety. There was, Plekhanov concluded, precious little either of socialism or of democracy in the social democracy of the 'youngsters' who dominated the Union.[91]

The fundamental error of both *Rabochee Delo* and *Rabochaya Mysl*, in the opinion of Akselrod, Plekhanov and Lenin, was their belief that the labour movement would spontaneously, automatically, tend towards socialism. *Rabochaya Mysl* was, without doubt, the most important socialist publication in Russia until the appearance of *Iskra* (*The Spark*) in December 1900. It was in many ways a most remarkable journal. Most remarkable of all was the fact that it had been started and the first two issues produced exclusively by a group of St Petersburg workers. Throughout its career the paper retained what has been termed its 'worker patriot' disposition, not rejecting the intelligentsia but certainly making it plain that its function was simply to help formulate and publish proletarian views rather than to foist intelligentsia designs on to the proletariat. Even after arrests had destroyed the initiating workers' group and the project was taken over by sympathetic émigré intellectuals, the paper retained its 'workerphile' stamp.

Throughout the period up to 1901 *Rabochaya Mysl* held to a consistently Economist list. It proclaimed the object of the workers' movement to be the satisfaction of their immediate economic and professional demands. It saw little place for the struggle for political rights and none at all for the formation of an illegal revolutionary political party of the working class. This position was forcibly put in its seventh issue (parts of the *Separate Supp,ement* to which appear as Document 44): 'the organisation by intellectuals of small circles of leading workers for the overthrow of autocracy – seems to us a theory which has long outlived its life, a theory abandoned by all in whom there is the least sensitivity to and understanding of reality'.[92] This did not mean to say that *Rabochaya Mysl* wholly ignored politics, nor was it part of the orthodox case to argue that it did so. What it *did* deny, as the above quotation makes clear, was the specification of properly social democratic politics which the orthodox had always held sacrosanct – the insistence upon the proletariat and its party assuming hegemony over the democratic revolution. For *these* politics *Rabochaya Mysl* had nothing but disdain, echoing Kuskova's sentiments that these were but alien *intelligentsia* designs. The demands which must determine the direction of the movement must, however, be authentically proletarian. These demands were according to *Rabochaya Mysl*:

increases in wages, the shortening of the working day, the ending of fines . . . of the crude and oppressive behaviour of the administration, the right to have elected representatives, workers' deputies, in all cases of conflict with the bosses, with their administration and the police . . . and other local demands that depend on the local, particular conditions of the life and work of particular workers. The immediate general political demands of the workers still remain the legal shortening of the working day (to ten hours) and the restoration of the holidays abolished by the law of 2 June 1897. But we shall be accused of heresy by those who criticise the narrowness of our attitude, the revolutionaries who call us the lowest strata of the proletariat.[93]

In short, the political role of the working class should for the time being be restricted to 'the legislative defence of labour'. The bourgeoisie could be left to pull its own chestnuts from the fire and the advent of socialism could not be hastened or foreshortened; as the orthodox seemed to imagine, it would arrive in its own good and properly determined time. Socialism was but the inevitable outcome of the growing extensiveness and maturity of the working class, it would arise as an efflux of the movement itself. 'In conclusion, a few words on our conception of workers' socialism. We see it in the workers' movement itself, in the present and future development of the independent social and political activity of the workers, in the development of workers' organisations.' Socialism would arise quite naturally out of 'workers participation in independent social management and finally in the country's general representative institution.'[94]

Rabochaya Mysl, or at least the author of the editorial statement *Our Reality*, stood for a kind of gradualist socialist pluralism. The vision of Takhtarev was for the bourgeoisie gradually to make encroachments on the prerogatives of autocracy through its expanding organs of self-government and its example would, in due course, be followed by the working class which, in proportion to its level of maturity, consciousness, and organisation, would gradually assume self-governing functions in a democratic state.

In the meantime the readers of *Rabochaya Mysl* were exhorted not to lose heart, not to be concerned about problems their grandchildren would have to solve, rather they should fight the great fight for their immediate physical needs since that was the only part the present generation of workers could play in the gradually unfolding drama. They were unequivocally advised not to be seduced by nebulous vistas but to get on with the job they understood and had already begun. In a formulation which Lenin was to put to his own polemical purposes several times in the next few years, Takhtarev summed up his position: 'What kind of struggle should the workers wage? Is it not the only one they can wage in present circumstances? But is not the struggle that is possible in present circumstances the one that they are in actual fact presently waging?'[95]

It was this historical optimism which ended in a fatalistic acceptance of what *is* that so offended the orthodox. It offended against the heroic activism which they took to lie at the centre of Marxism. In particular they all rejected the idea that the labour movement would spontaneously strive towards socialism, as a mechanistic, false and dangerous interpretation of Marx, which lay at the heart of all opportunism. Akselrod, who was acknowledged as the Russian Marxist pundit on the Western labour movement, in his *Present Tasks and Tactics* makes it perfectly clear that there is no question of any such ineluctable progress to socialism. In fact the burden of his remarks suggests the exactly opposite process at work. The English labour movement, he pointedly reminds his Russian readers, began as a 'pure' and authentically proletarian movement. It had developed the largest, best organised labour movement in the world, yet it had displayed barely a glimmer of socialist striving in its entire history. It was *the* object lesson of the fatal disjunction between socialism and the labour movement. Akselrod's conclusion was that, however extensive the labour movement, however consolidated its organisational base, it did not necessarily produce even political consciousness let alone a striving for socialism. If political strivings did emerge among the workers they almost invariably fell under the sway of the bourgeoisie.[96]

In exactly similar vein Plekhanov, in almost all of his major writings since the early 1880s, had insisted, as we have seen, on the cardinal importance of the intelligentsia in introducing socialism, knowledge and organisation into the working class. In his polemical sallies against *Rabochee Delo* he was, if anything, even more emphatic on this point. His *Preface to the 'Vademecum'* insisted that the workers do not and cannot for some considerable time know the full nature of their position and their aims within society. There was, according to Plekhanov, a lag of working class consciousness behind the 'objective development' of society. Only the determined intervention of the 'revolutionary bacilli', conscious Social Democrats from the working class or the intelligentsia, could overcome the lag.[97] It was precisely the job of the social democratic agitator to open the eyes of the workers to those ways and means of improving their situation which had not yet occurred to them. In particular it was his job to demonstrate from the struggle itself how economic improvement was inextricably bound to political change and political action.[98] His argument was the same as the one Lenin employed so centrally in *What Is To Be Done?* Unless economic agitation was used as a means to produce *political* consciousness it had no social democratic content, it was but Economism, a species of revisionist opportunism. In Plekhanov's considered opinion (which most commentators might locate as a mark of specifically Leninist pessimism), unless political agitation was immediately taken up as the main preoccupation of the movement, *unless* the workers were welded into an independent political party, they would shortly become but the political tool of the bourgeoisie.[99]

It was left to Lenin to prepare the authoritative rebuttal of the revisionism of *Rabochaya Mysl* and the Economism of *Rabochee Delo* and this he eventually spelt out in *What Is To Be Done?* Almost all the ideas of that lengthy pamphlet were developed earlier in a series of leading articles for *Iskra*, the journal which united Plekhanov and Akselrod with their Russian disciples Lenin and Martov, the journal which was to be the mouthpiece of revived Marxist orthodoxy in Russia. In the leading article for the very first number of *Iskra*[100] Lenin immediately located the central issue in question – whether the Party, which all sections of the movement demanded should be reconstituted, should define its most immediate task as the economic struggle for improvements, or that of leading the political confrontation with the autocracy. Lenin's piece of course comes down decisively in favour of the latter objective but warns that the actual realisation of the role of vanguard in the democratic revolution will demand very considerable changes in the organisational structure of the movement. There must be an end to the 'isolation of small workers' circles', whose parochial horizons inevitably encouraged the preponderance of the economic struggle and hence the jettisoning of the *political* and *class* objectives of the proletariat.

Social democracy is the fusion of the workers' movement with socialism. Its task is not to serve the workers' movement passively at each of its separate stages but to represent the interests of the movement as a whole, to direct this movement towards its ultimate goal, its political tasks, and to safeguard its political and ideological independence. Divorced from social democracy, the workers' movement degenerates and inevitably becomes bourgeois: in carrying on the purely economic struggle, the working class loses its political independence, becomes an appendage of the other parties and betrays the great principle that 'the emancipation of the workers should be a matter for the workers themselves'.[101]

The specification of party *objectives* was, therefore, in the view of Lenin and the orthodox, tantamount to the specification of party *organisation*. If the objectives were primarily *economic* then the party should retain its prevailing localism and the lack of a central directing organ: if leadership of the political struggle against autocracy then, as Lenin went on to make clear, proper organisational methods, rigorous training of professionals to combat the gendarmes and the building up of 'an organisation that is large enough to allow a strict division of labour between the different aspects of our work' became necessary.[102] 'Without such organisation the proletariat is not capable of rising to the conscious class struggle, without such organisation the workers' movement is condemned to impotence.'[103] By the time that the Second Party Congress convened in 1903, it was clear that the orthodox had triumphed. They set about the task of dominating the local committees of the party in Russia with a single-minded professionalism which their rivals could not match. The contacts which Lenin built up in the frenzied months of travelling up and down Russia before once again going into exile in July 1900 were preserved and extended by the agents he left behind, especially Martov. *Iskra*, the journal of the orthodox, took advantage of the network Lenin had built up and was itself meant to provide an organisational framework for the spread of their influence. There can be no doubt either that the publication and wide circulation of Lenin's *What Is To Be Done?* provided the *Iskra* agents in Russia with a compendium of powerful arguments against all those groups which had strayed from the narrow path of orthodoxy. Lenin's pamphlet, as I have argued elsewhere,[104] was explicitly intended as a re-statement of the old current, the orthodoxy of Russian Marxism, and it was received precisely as such both by his fellow editors of *Iskra* (the only people after all with a claim to have created and defended that orthodoxy) as well as by his opponents.

The Bolshevik/Menshevik dispute, organisational questions and appraisal of 1905 revolution

The solidarity of the orthodox in the *Iskra* camp did not last long. It hardly survived their first significant victories over the Economists at the Second Party Congress. No sooner was the Bund defeated on its claim for autonomous status within a federal party and the Economists put down on a number of issues, than the *Iskra* camp itself split on the question of how to define a party member. The famous dispute over clause 1 of the party rules was, as every novitiate to the study of Russian Marxism knows, resolved in favour of Martov's formulation.[105]

According to most commentators the subsequent history of the Bolshevik/Menshevik dispute is the story of how this allegedly profound difference on organisational matters, which was itself a reflection of quite distinct attitudes towards the labour movement, was refined and developed. The Mensheviks, it is commonly argued, turned their backs on the old Russian Marxist infatuation with the underground party with its implied tutelage of intellectuals over the workers. It became, according to the legend, much more closely modelled on the West European social democratic parties, loose in structure, easy of access and as nearly democratic in structure as conditions would allow. The dramatic complement to this scenario is the picture of the Bolsheviks as that section of the party most attached to the conspiratorial hierarchical structure of organisation inherited from earlier revolutionary trends, dedicated, disciplined, confident in the ability of professional revolutionaries, and especially of Lenin their leader, to dispense with the role of the working class in history. The Mensheviks thereafter are blessed with the reputation of being the orthodox, i.e. Western style, Social Democrats whereas the Bolsheviks are seen as revisionists par excellence of Marx's historical determinism.

The difficulty for the historian is that this alluring pastiche is almost nowhere supported by the evidence. It is, for instance, impossible to explain in this light Akselrod's assurances to Kautsky in 1904 that no issue of principle divided Bolsheviks and Mensheviks but only the 'application or execution of organisational principles . . . we have all accepted'.[106] How, indeed, are we to explain the fact that at the Menshevik-dominated Fourth (or Unity) Congress of the RSDLP, convened in 1906, Lenin's formulation of rule 1 was adopted in preference to Martov's *nem. con?*[107] As Lenin ironically remarked, none of the Mensheviks in 1905 or early 1906, when conditions of political life were freer than they had ever been, recommended dispensing with the underground or relaxing the centralised structure of the Party. It was, paradoxically, Lenin who was calling for a looser, more decentralised 'democratic centralism' at this time[108] and there is indeed evidence to suggest that of the two factions the Bolsheviks had a more open structure than their opponents.[109]

It was not until the revolution of 1905–6 and its immediate aftermath that clear differences of political strategy emerged to distinguish the rival factions in Russian social democracy. These differences were, as we shall see, rooted in fundamentally differing estimations of the political capacity of the Russian working class. The essence of this divide was that the Mensheviks now no longer believed that the working class and its party could or should exercise hegemony over the democratic revolution whereas the Bolsheviks continued to hold fast to this central tenet of the old orthodoxy.

The whole course of the revolution, in Lenin's eyes, provided an amazing confirmation of Marx's analysis of the rapid process of class formation and growth of political consciousness which revolutionary situations produced. Just like the French workers of 1848, the Russian working class in 1905 had initially followed all sorts of utopian crackpots. At first they had, in their thousands, followed the priest/police agent Gapon to the Winter Palace in the ancient belief that once the 'Little Father' was made aware of their sufferings and grievances he would put things to right. Their modest and very generalised demands met with nothing but the salvoes of the imperial troops.[110] The massacre of the innocents before the Winter Palace was the first harsh political lesson the working class was obliged to undergo in the revolutionary process. The revolution progressed, Lenin maintained in paraphrase of Marx, by building the reaction. Each stage in the process involved the progressive polarisation of society – either for the radical democratic republic, or for the preservation of the autocracy and the existing landowning structure and the preservation therewith of the old organs of coercion. All the bewildering varieties of political strategies and political formations would eventually refine themselves down to that dialectical choice. The leading force urging a radical democratic solution of the agrarian problem and a genuinely free republic could only be the proletariat, its only ally with a vested interest in this programme – the poor peasants. The leading force urging the preservation of the existing landholding structure and the retention of the monarchy, even if in some constitutional garb, was the big bourgeoisie, backed by the landowners and nobility and eventually joined, in the course of the revolution, by the liberal bourgeoisie. Only in the course of the struggle itself, only from witnessing the treachery of the bourgeoisie in the revolution, would the proletariat come to realise that it alone could win democracy for Russia.[111]

The argument that it was heretical for Socialists to assume the leadership of the democratic revolution was, in Lenin's view, no more than a caricature of Marxism. It was a caricature, he contended because for Marx the democratic revolution referred above all to the economic and social content of the changes which the objective development of the productive forces made imperative. The economic and social structure of landlordism with its innumerable remnants of feudal servitude in the countryside would *have* to be destroyed. The fundamental objective of the democratic revolution was then, in Lenin's view, not so much a revision of constitutional procedures, not simply the installation of the bourgeoisie in place of the gentry and nobility in the seats of power, but rather the demolition of feudalism and landlordism. Without that, no constitutional paper guarantees, or checks and balances of the most cunning construction, would be of any avail in the face of inevitable reaction in the future. Only the poor peasants had a common interest with the proletariat in seeing the anti-feudal revolution through to its radical completion – *all* the other groups and classes would, as the revolution progressed, throw in their lot with the bourgeoisie.

But can the socialist proletariat accomplish the bourgeois revolution independently and as the guiding force? Does not the very concept bourgeois revolution imply that it can be accomplished only by the bourgeoisie?

The Mensheviks often fall into this error, although, as a viewpoint, it is a caricature of Marxism. A liberation movement that is bourgeois in social and economic content is not such because of its motive forces. The motive force may be, not the bourgeoisie, but the proletariat and the peasantry. Why is this possible? Because the proletariat and the peasantry suffer even more than the bourgeoisie from the survivals of serfdom, because they are in greater need of freedom and the abolition of landlord oppression. For the bourgeoisie, on the contrary, complete victory constitutes a danger, since the proletariat will make use of full freedom against the bourgeoisie, and the fuller that freedom and the more completely the power of the landlords has been destroyed, the easier will it be for the proletariat to do so.[112]

Lenin's conclusion (which guided his strategy from the outset and was, in this sense, more a *prediction* based on propositions derived from Marx) was that the revolution would have to be made *against* the bourgeoisie. Its leading force would be the proletariat with the poor peasantry (which had no class existence of its own. Together they would form a 'revolutionary-democratic dictatorship'. There could, however, Lenin forcibly argued, be no talk of a *socialist* revolution as many of the unstable Mensheviks under Trotsky's influence originally believed. The objective level of development of the productive forces, and therewith of social relations in Russia, would emphatically not allow such a transformation. He rebuked those who dreamed of:

the absurd and semi-anarchist idea of giving effect to the maximum programme and the conquest of power for a socialist revolution. The degree of Russia's economic development (an objective condition), and the degree of class consciousness and organisation of the broad masses of the proletariat (a subjective condition inseparably bound up with the objective condition) make the immediate and complete emancipation of the working class impossible.[113]

Lenin's economic analysis firmly set the parameters of the politically possible and it was on this sure ground that throughout 1905 and 1906 he rejected the idea of a workers' government, dictatorship of the proletariat, immediate advance to socialism dispensing with the democratic phase, or any similar notion. 'Whoever wants to reach socialism by any path other than that of political democracy, will inevitably arrive at conclusions that are absurd and reactionary both in the economic and political sense.'[114]

The response of Trotsky to Lenin's reasoning was that at a certain rather abstracted level Lenin might well be correct but what his rather rigid self-denying ordinance failed to take into account was the actual class dynamics of the revolution. It was not so much that he and Parvus were theoretically convinced of the propriety of an advance to socialism in Russia but that they could see no way of stopping the revolution at the minimum programme (i.e. the implementation of radical democracy) given the fact that the proletariat, and it alone, would be its leading force. For Trotsky, indeed, the proletariat was the *only* revolutionary force. He had nothing but the deepest suspicion for the revolutionary initiative and stability of the peasantry. It followed, therefore, that in any coalition government the peasant representatives would inevitably play second fiddle to those of the proletariat. It further followed, in Trotsky's view, that the party of the proletariat having assumed hegemony over the revolution through its position of dominance within the revolutionary government would find it impossible to set clear and restrictive limits to the self-activity of the proletarian and peasant masses. They would justifiably demand some of the fruits of victory, they would necessarily propel the revolution in a collectivist direction and it would be idle pedantry to attempt to stop this movement. On the contrary the revolutionary government would have to promote it in order to sap the power of the possessing classes to stage a counter-revolution, and in order to fire the workers in Western Europe with sufficient enthusiasm to conduct their own unequivocally socialist revolutions which would, in turn, serve to strengthen and preserve the turn to socialism in Russia.

All this quite clearly shows that social democracy cannot enter a revolutionary government, having given the workers an advance undertaking that it will not *give way* on the minimum programme, and having at the same time promised the bourgeoisie that it will not *go beyond* the limits of the minimum programme. This kind of bilateral undertaking would be quite impossible to realise. The very fact that the proletariat's representatives enter the government, not as impotent hostages, but as the leading force, destroys the dividing line between the minimum and maximum programmes: i.e. *it makes collectivism the order of the day*. The point at which the proletariat will be held up in its advance in this direction depends upon the relation of forces but in no way upon the original intentions of the proletarian party.[115]

The differences between Lenin and Trotsky at this time were important but hardly crucial; they certainly did not prevent adherents of the two different lines from cooperating closely on the immediate tasks of organising a genuinely militant party – a party of fighters, for both recognised that the issue would have to be resolved by force of arms. Their dispute was over *how* the proletariat should exercise its hegemony over the democratic revolution, and the form and objectives of the revolutionary government in which it would be the leading force. The controversy between Lenin and the Menshevik supporters of Plekhanov, Akselrod and Martynov was, however, quite different in nature. The question here was *whether* the proletariat should lay claim to hegemony over the democratic revolution in the changed political environment of 1905.

Almost from the outset, and certainly from October 1905 onwards, both Plekhanov and Martynov felt that it would, in the new circumstances, be inopportune and even dangerous to the cause of democracy to insist on the old claim to proletarian leadership. The essential factor which had now changed the situation was, they argued, the emergence of a strong and self-confident bourgeois liberal party – the Constitutional Democrats, or Cadets as they were popularly known. At last the heroic action of the proletariat had shamed the bourgeoisie into organising itself into a cohesive party which was very radical by the standards of bourgeois parties and appeared uncompromising in its stand for genuine democracy in Russia. The great danger existed, they believed, that precipitate action by the proletariat or extravagant claims by the Social Democrats, would frighten the well-meaning bourgeois liberals into the camp of the reaction. Besides, as they repeatedly argued, this was only the first stage of the revolution, the democratic revolution in which Marxism allotted the leadership role to the bourgeoisie who, after all, stood to gain most from it. In the opinion of Plekhanov, Akselrod and the moderate Mensheviks, the Social Democrats should drop all talk of a 'workers' government' or a 'revolutionary democratic dictatorship of the proletariat and the poor peasantry' and accept the role of an extreme opposition to a bourgeois government. In this way social democracy could preserve the purity of its socialist objectives and avoid the danger of compromising itself in the hopeless task of trying to supervise the democratic revolution. Only in this way, furthermore, was there any prospect of obtaining any real and lasting results from the Russian revolution. Like Trotsky, Plekhanov was no believer in the revolutionary potential of the peasantry, and the Mensheviks generally were in agreement with him. The only other force available as an ally to the comparatively small and weak proletariat was, therefore, the radical and liberal bourgeoisie. Without winning the support and confidence of this group the proletariat could not hope to secure for itself the democratic rights so essential for its future development. It must, therefore, Plekhanov argued, be guided by prudence and restraint 'lest the bourgeoisie recoil'. The respective attitudes of Plekhanov and Lenin to the Moscow Rising of December 1905 graphically illustrate the huge divide which now separated them.

For Lenin the Moscow Rising was a vital stage in the class evolution of the proletariat. It had progressed from its *economic* or industrial phase of the mid-1890s, with its appropriate organisational form in the strike fund, through to *political* activity in the early years of the century under the direction of *Iskra* as a proto-party. The political preparation of the proletariat had been completed with the re-establishment of the Party in 1903. Now the proletariat had moved on to the ultimate, most heightened form of practice, to active service in the revolutionary war against autocracy. As with all the earlier phases of its practice, the proletariat could only learn from its own experience. The proletariat as a whole developed as a class only by following its most advanced representatives who, at each stage of the historical progress, undertook resolute action to expose as clearly as possible the polarities into which society was riven. The final and most heightened form of such activity was the prosecution of civil war against the autocracy and its class supporters. Only in this war would the proletariat as a whole become conscious of the true nature of social polarity, only in the struggle would it forge the organisation, leadership, courage and military technique requisite to overthrow the *ancien régime*. In Lenin's activist epistemology, which is remarkably similar to the one Marx outlined in his analysis of 1848–51, the Moscow Rising signified the most extensive coming to consciousness and militant organising of the proletariat compatible with the Russian economic 'base'. The progress in these respects which Marx had described the European proletariat undergoing had been mirrored almost exactly in the Russian experience. From being but the glint in the eye of an isolated faction of the intelligentsia, which saw in the proletariat the weapon to realise philosophy, the Russian proletariat had, through the process of its own history, realised itself as a conscious class. It had been disciplined and organised by the struggles its own life situation obliged it to take up. The immanent reality of the proletariat, which Marx set out in the *Holy Family* and which revealed itself in the progress of the 1848–51 revolution, was also realised, according to Lenin's writings, in the marvellous decade of Russian Marxism from 1895 to 1905.

For Plekhanov, by contrast, the Moscow Rising was an unmitigated disaster. Not only did it serve to alienate the sympathy of the liberals, its failure also contributed to sapping the morale of the proletariat and encouraging the reaction. It ought never to have been undertaken, and the losses it caused to the democratic movement in general, and the proletariat in particular, were directly attributable to the *putschist* leadership of the RSDLP in Russia – especially to the Bolsheviks.

In many accounts Plekhanov was in 1905 the sounding board of orthodox 'Western' Marxism, stressing the modest limits which the development of productive forces in Russia dictated to the movement. He was the 'determinist' moderate against the 'voluntarist' extremism of Lenin's and Trotsky's differing designs for some kind of proletarian dictatorship. The documents presented here tend to invert this case. It was not Plekhanov but Lenin and Trotsky who could lay claim to the orthodoxy of Russian Marxism whose principal political tenet had ever been that the proletariat alone could exercise hegemony over the democratic revolution in Russia.

Plekhanov was not only in breach of the canons of Russian Marxist orthodoxy, he was also running directly counter to all the advice which the pope of European socialism, Karl Kautsky himself, bestowed upon the Russian movement. His authoritative judgement on the Russian Revolution was set out in a series of articles for *Neue Zeit* subsequently translated into Russian and translated with a Preface by Lenin. Kautsky, as one might imagine from the haste with which Lenin published his pamphlet, supported the Bolsheviks on every one of the major points at issue with Plekhanov and the 'revisionist' Mensheviks. Kautsky rejected outright the fundamental idea of Plekhanov that the revolution, being a democratic revolution, had to be led by the bourgeoisie. The bourgeoisie, Kautsky firstly declared, could not in Russia be trusted with the leadership role. That role could only be played by the proletariat and its only ally was the peasantry which still had very considerable revolutionary potential in the Russian environment. In a withering assault on Plekhanov's position, Kautsky argued that it was impossible to fight whilst renouncing beforehand the possibility of success. It was futile to expect the proletariat to fight for the democratic revolution if the party of the proletariat ostentatiously refused even to consider a share in a revolutionary government.[116]

Akselrod, whilst not so openly 'revisionist' as Plekhanov, was, nonetheless, from early 1906 onwards, urging a similar policy of caution and restraint. Akselrod's message became increasingly attractive as the year progressed since its 'realistic' recognition that the revolutionary wave was now over, and that therefore a more or less prolonged phase of quiet preparation of the proletariat was likely to ensue, struck a responsive chord in a large part of the party which had been dispirited by the way in which the autocracy had recovered from the onslaught and was now actually taking the initiative. Akselrod's plan for a Labour Congress, patiently organised on the basis of democratic and authentically proletarian local organisations, was intended to serve many purposes. It was, at last, to emancipate the party from the incestuous pseudo-revolutionism of the 'underground'. It would revivify and cleanse the party, it would indeed effect a 'revolution' within it. More positively the Labour Congress would gradually emerge as a focal point for the articulation of general national grievances. It would enjoy such enormous moral support from the population at large that the autocracy would have to listen and make concessions to it. In its gradually expanding sphere of activity it would assume new functions and would become transformed into a People's Duma and in this way the objectives of the 1905 revolution could be achieved piecemeal and the party would become genuinely democratic and fused with the masses.[117]

By the end of 1906, as we can see from the documents, a broad range of political strategies had emerged. The differences between them reflected differences in estimation of the political capabilities of the Russian working class and, more basically, differences in accounting for the way in which the class became conscious of its mission in history and organised to fulfil it. To an extent these differences reflected the duality in the structure of Marxism with which we started. Some of Marx's Russian disciples tended to view the development of consciousness and organisation proceeding step by step with the evolution of the productive forces and therewith of social relations. Others, leaning upon just as impeccable a stock of texts, contended that the essence of the Marxist teaching on the class function of the proletariat was its self-creation through struggle. The determined leadership of the intelligentsia Socialists and the advanced workers was itself a prime condition for drawing the mass into activity through which alone it would emerge with adequate consciousness and appropriate organisation. This duality inherent in Marxism was nowhere more self-consciously and repeatedly teased out than in the disputes which wracked the Russian Marxists and which directly or indirectly runs through all the documents collected here.

1879-1893: theoretical foundations and worker projects

1. PROGRAMME (1879)[1]

Northern Union of Russian Workers

To the Russian workers

Recognising the extremely harmful aspect of the political and economic oppression which descends on our heads with all the force of its implacable arbitrariness; recognising the whole intolerable burden of our social condition which deprives us of every opportunity and hope for some kind of tolerable existence; recognising finally that it is becoming more and more impossible to endure this order of things, which threatens us with complete material deprivation and the paralysis of our spiritual strength, we, the workers of Petersburg, at a general assembly from 23 to 30 December 1878[2] have conceived the idea of organising an all-Russian union of workers which, uniting the uncoordinated forces of the urban and rural working population and explaining to it its own interests, aims and aspirations, will serve it as a sufficient bulwark in the struggle with social injustice and will give it the organic internal bond that it needs for the successful conduct of the struggle.

The organisation of the Northern Union of Russian Workers should have a strictly defined character and should pursue precisely those aims which are laid down in its programme.

Workers will only be elected to membership of this Union by at least two people who are more or less well known.

Every worker who wishes to become a member of the Union must acquaint himself beforehand with the programme which follows and with the essence of its social teaching.

All members of the Union must maintain complete solidarity amongst themselves and whoever breaches this will be immediately excluded. A member who attracts the suspicion that he has betrayed the Union will submit to a special elected court.

Every member is obliged to contribute to the general fund of the Union a fixed sum determined at the general assembly of members.

The affairs of the Union will be conducted by an elected committee consisting of ten members, in whose charge will also lie the responsibility for the fund and the library. General assemblies of the membership are held once a month, at which the activity of the committee is reviewed and the affairs of the Union are discussed.

The assembly authorises the committee to undertake only those activities which are directly in the interests of the entire Union.

The duties of the committee also comprise the right to establish relations with the representatives of provincial circles and sections of the workers of Russia who have accepted the programme of the Northern Union.

The provincial sections of the Union retain for themselves autonomous competence in that sphere of activity defined by the general programme and are subject only to the decisions of general representative assemblies.

The central fund is to be exclusively directed towards expenditure which is necessary to fulfil the plans of the Union and to support workers during strikes.

The library is intended to supply free of charge the needs of the workers of the capital, even of those who do not belong to the Union.

The cost of stocking it and of issuing books is to come from the Union fund and from sums donated by the workers.

The Northern Union of Russian Workers, closely allied in its objectives with the Social Democratic Party of the West,[3] lays down as its programme:

1. The overthrow of the existing political and economic order of the state as one which is extremely unjust.
2. The establishment of a free popular federation of communes [*obshchiny*], founded on complete political equality and with full internal self-government on the principles of Russian common law.
3. The abolition of private land ownership and its replacement by communal land ownership.
4. The just associative organisation of labour, placing in the hands of the worker-producers the products and tools of production.

As political freedom assures for each person independence of beliefs and actions and as it above all assures the resolution of the social question, the following should be the immediate demands of the Union:

1. Freedom of speech and of the press, the right of assembly and meeting.
2. The abolition of the criminal investigation department and trial for political crimes.
3. The abolition of class rights and privileges.
4. Compulsory and free education in all schools and educational institutions.
5. A reduction in the size of the standing army or its complete replacement by the arming of the people.
6. The right of the rural commune to decide matters that concern it, such as: the rate of tax, allotment of land and internal self-government.
7. Freedom of movement and the abolition of the passport system.
8. The abolition of indirect taxes and the institution of direct taxation corresponding to income and inheritance.
9. The limitation of working hours and the prohibition of child labour.
10. The institution of production associations, loan funds and free credit for the workers' associations and the peasant communes.

That, in its main features, is the programme that the general assembly of Petersburg workers resolved to be guided by on 23–30 December.

By tireless and active propaganda among its brothers the Northern Union hopes to achieve results that will advance the workers' estate and compel it to start talking about itself and its rights; and hence it is the sacred duty of every member of this Union to do what lies in his power to carry out agitation among the working mass, oppressed and sympathetic to demands for justice. His services will not be forgotten by posterity and his name will be revered as an apostle of the evangelical truth and will be written in the chronicle of history.

Workers! We summon you now; we appeal to your voice, your conscience and your consciousness!

The great social struggle has already commenced – and we must not wait: our brothers in the West have already raised the banner of the emancipation of the millions – and we have only to join them. Arm in arm with them we shall move forward and in brotherly unity merge into a single fearful fighting force.

Workers, a great task has fallen to us – the task of our emancipation and the emancipation of our brothers; it is our duty to renew the world, which is wallowing in luxury and draining our strength – and we must carry it out.

Remember who was the first to respond to the great words of Christ, who was the first bearer of his teaching that love and brotherhood would overturn the whole of the old world? – the simple settlers . . . We are also called upon to preach, we are also summoned to be the apostles of a new, but in essence only a misunderstood and forgotten, teaching of Christ. We shall be persecuted as the first Christians were persecuted; we shall be beaten and taunted, but we shall be undaunted and we shall not be ashamed of their desecrations, because this animosity towards us itself demonstrates its weakness in the struggle with the moral greatness of the ideas, in the struggle with the force that we represent.

'You corrupt the world', they say to us, 'you destroy the family, you scorn property and profane religion.'

Now, we shall reply to them, we are not the ones who are corrupting the world, it is you; we are not the cause of evil – you are. On the contrary, we are going to renew the world, revive the family, establish property as it should be and resurrect the great teaching of Christ on brotherhood and equality . . .

Workers! Stand bravely beneath our banner of social revolution, join a harmonious, fraternal family and, arming yourselves with the spiritual sword of truth, go and preach your gospel in the towns and villages!

Your future lies in this propaganda of salvation, and your success depends on your moral strength; with it you are mighty, with it you will subdue the world. Know that in you is contained the entire strength and significance of the country, you are the flesh and blood of the state and without you the other classes, which now suck your blood, would not exist. You realise this dimly but you have no organisation, no idea to lead you, in the final analysis no moral support, which is so essential to deliver a joint rebuff to the enemy. But we, the worker-organisers of the Northern Union, give you this leading idea, give you the moral support in the unity of your interests and, finally, give you the organisation that you lack.

And so, workers, the last word is yours, and on you depend the fate of the great Union and the success of the social revolution in Russia!

Printed at the request of the workers, *Petersburg Free Press*, 12 January 1879.

2. SOCIALISM AND THE POLITICAL STRUGGLE (1883): EXTRACTS[4]

G.V. Plekhanov

Having made this reservation, let us now try to determine in what sense the causal connection between economic relations and the political structure of a particular society should be understood.

What does history teach us in this respect? It shows us that whenever and wherever the process of economic development has given rise to a fragmentation of society into classes, the contradictions between the interests of those classes have inevitably led them to struggle for political domination. This struggle has arisen not only between the various strata of the ruling classes but also between these classes on the one hand and the people on the other, provided that the latter were accorded conditions that were even remotely favourable for their intellectual development. In the states of the ancient Orient we see the struggle between the warriors and the priests; the whole drama of the history of the ancient world is contained in the struggle between the aristocracy and the *demos*, the patricians and the plebeians; the Middle Ages bring forth the burghers who try to achieve political hegemony within the confines of their own communes; finally, the contemporary working class is waging a political struggle against the bourgeoisie which has achieved complete domination in the modern state. Whenever and wherever [this has occurred], political power has at all times and in all places been the lever by which a class that has achieved a dominant position has completed the social revolution that is essential for its well-being and future development. So that we do not stray too far afield, let us recall the history of the 'third estate', a class that can look with pride upon a past full of brilliant achievements in all branches of life and thought. It will hardly occur to anyone to reproach the bourgeoisie with a lack of tact or ability in achieving its ends by the most appropriate means. Nor will anyone deny that its efforts have always had a quite definite economic character. That has not, however, prevented it from embarking on the path of political struggle and political gains. Sometimes through arms, sometimes through peace treaties, sometimes in the name of the republican independence of its cities, sometimes in the name of consolidating royal power, the nascent bourgeoisie has for centuries waged a ceaseless and tenacious struggle against feudalism and, long before the French Revolution, it could proudly draw its enemies' attention to its successes. 'The opportunities varied and success was uneven in the burghers' great struggle against the feudal lords,' the historian says, 'and not only did the sum total of the liberties achieved by force or obtained by peaceful agreement differ from place to place but, even under exactly the same political forms, the cities frequently enjoyed differing degrees of liberty and independence.'[5] Nevertheless, the sense of the movement was everywhere identical and it marked the beginning of the social emancipation of the third estate and the decline of the aristocracy, both secular and spiritual. Generally speaking, this movement brought the burghers 'municipal independence, the right to elect all the local authorities and a precise definition of their duties', guaranteed the rights of the individual within the urban communes, gave the bourgeoisie a more elevated position in the estate-based states of the *ancien régime* and brought it finally, by a series of permanent gains, to complete domination in contemporary society. Setting itself socio-economic aims which, although they changed with time, were perfectly defined, and deriving the means of continuing the struggle from the advantages of the material position that it had already attained, the bourgeoisie has not missed a single opportunity of giving legal expression to the stages of economic progress that it has attained; on the contrary, it has demonstrated the same skill in utilising each political gain for new achievements in the economic sphere. As recently as the mid-forties of this century the English Anti-Corn-Law League, following Richard Cobden's ingenious plan,[6] strove to increase its *political* influence in the shires in order to secure the abolition of the 'monopoly' it despised and which was, apparently, exclusively *economic* in character.

History is the greatest of dialecticians: if, in the course of its progress, reason is, in the words of Mephistopheles, transformed into unreason and blessings become a plague, just as often in the historical process an effect becomes a cause and a cause proves to be an effect. Deriving from the economic relations of its own time, the political might of the bourgeoisie in its turn served, and serves, as an indispensable factor in the further development of those relations.

Now that the bourgeoisie is nearing the end of its historical role and the proletariat is becoming the sole representative of progressive aspirations in society, we may observe a phenomenon similar to that mentioned above but taking place in changed conditions. In all the advanced states of the civilised world, in Europe as well as in America, the working class is entering the arena of political struggle and, the more conscious it becomes of its economic tasks, the more furiously it resolves to form a separate political party of its own . . .

. . . But, just as the bourgeoisie did not merely fight the autocracy on the basis of pre-existing political relations, but also sought to rearrange these relations in its own interests, so the proletariat does not confine its political programme to the seizure of the contemporary state machine. The conviction becomes more and more widespread among its members that 'any order of things that determines the relations between citizens and governs their property and labour relations, corresponds to a particular form of government that serves at the same time as the means of realising and preserving that order'.[7] While the representative (monarchical or republican) system was the brainchild of the bourgeoisie, the proletariat *demands direct popular legislation as the sole political form* under which its social aspirations can be realised. This demand by the working class occupies one of the foremost places in the socialist democratic programme in every country and is very closely linked with all the other points in its programme.[8] In spite of Proudhon, the proletariat continues to regard 'political revolution' as the most powerful means of achieving an economic revolution.

This testimony of history should in itself be enough to predispose us towards thinking that the political tendencies of the various social classes are based not on an erroneous theory, but on a correct practical instinct. If, regardless of the complete dissimilarity in other respects, all the classes that are waging a conscious struggle against their opponents begin at a particular stage in their development to strive to secure political influence and later domination for themselves, then it is clear that the political structure of society is a far from indifferent condition for their development. If, moreover, we see that no single class that has achieved political domination has had cause to regret its interest in 'politics' but, on the contrary, each one of them attained the highest, the culminating point of its development only after it had achieved political domination, then we must admit that the political struggle is an instrument of social reconstruction whose effectiveness has been proven by history. Every teaching that runs counter to this historical induction loses a considerable part of its credibility and, if contemporary socialism were really to condemn the political efforts of the working class as inadvisable, then by that token alone it could not be called scientific.

Let us now test our induction by the deductive method, taking Marx's philosophical and historical views as the premisses for our conclusions.

Let us imagine a society in which a particular class enjoys complete domination. It achieved this domination through the advantages of its economic position which, according to our premisses, open before it the path to all other forms of success in public life. In its capacity as the *ruling* class it naturally adapts the organisation of society to provide the most favourable conditions for its own existence and it carefully removes from it everything that could in any way weaken its influence. 'The ruling class at any particular period', Schäffle correctly remarks,

is also the one that creates law and morality. Its members are only obeying their instinct for self-preservation when they try to consolidate their domination and preserve it for as long as they can for their descendants as a necessary condition of their privileged position and as a means of exploiting the oppressed . . . Almost no other section of positive law commands such respect among the ruling estates at a particular period; no other section is used to such an extent to justify the character of 'external' institutions or even the 'sacred' foundations of society as that which consolidates the law of their estate and safeguards the domination of their class.[9]

And, as long as the ruling class remains the vehicle for the most progressive social ideals, the system it has established will satisfy all the demands of social development. But, as soon as the economic history of a particular society promotes new elements of a progressive movement, as soon as its 'productive forces come into conflict with the existing relations of production or – what is but a legal expression for the same thing – with the property relations within which they have been at work',[10] the progressive role of a particular ruling class will have come to an end. It will change from a representative of progress to its sworn enemy and it will, of course, make use of the state machine to defend itself. In its hands political power will become the most powerful weapon of reaction. To open the way for the development of the productive forces in society it is necessary to remove the property relations that impede that development, i.e., as Marx says, to carry out a social revolution. But this is impossible as long as legislative power remains in the hands of the representatives of the old order, i.e., in other words, as long as it safeguards the interests of the ruling class. It is therefore not surprising that the innovators, i.e. the representatives of the oppressed class or classes, will strive to wrest this terrible weapon from the hands of their opponents and turn it against them. The very logic of things will force them on to the path of political struggle and the seizure of state power, even though they define their aim as economic revolution. Lassalle uttered a profound truth when he noted in the preface to his *System of Acquired Rights* that, 'where juridical attitudes, moving into the sphere of private right, lost any apparent connection with politics, *they are far more political than politics itself*, because they then represent a social element'.[11]

As far as one can judge *a priori*, things move far more slowly in practice. The oppressed class only gradually distinguishes the link between its *economic* situation and its *political* role in the state. For a long time it does not even fully understand its economic task. Its individual members wage a hard struggle for their daily subsistence without even considering which aspects of social organisation they owe their wretched condition to. They try and avoid the blows aimed at them without asking where or whom they come from in the final analysis. As yet they have no class consciousness and there is no guiding idea in their struggle against individual oppressors. The oppressed class does not yet perceive *its own existence*; in time it *will* become the advanced class in society, but it is not yet *becoming* that. The consciously organised power of the ruling class is confronted only by the separated individual efforts of isolated individuals or isolated groups of individuals. Even now, for instance, it is not unusual to meet a worker who detests a particularly energetic exploiter but does not yet suspect that he must fight the whole class of exploiters and remove the very possibility of the exploitation of man by man.

Little by little, however, the process of generalisation does its job and the oppressed begin to be conscious of themselves as a class. But their understanding of the peculiarities of their class position remains too one-sided: the springs and motive forces of the social mechanism as a whole are still hideen from their mind's eye. The exploiting class appears to them as the simple sum of individual employers, not connected by the threads of political *organisation*. At this stage of development the connection between 'society' and 'state' is not yet clear in the minds of the oppressed, or in the mind of Professor Lorenz von Stein.[12] They suppose that state power stands above class antagonism; its representatives appear as the natural judges and conciliators of the opposing sides. The oppressed class has complete faith in them and is very surprised when its requests for help from them remain unanswered. Without dwelling on particular examples, we shall note only that a similar conceptual confusion was recently displayed by the English workers who have waged a highly energetic struggle on the economic front and yet thought it possible to figure in the ranks of one or another of the bourgeois political parties.

It is only in the next and final stage of development that the oppressed class comes to a thorough recognition of its position. *It now understands the connection between society and state and it does not appeal for restrictions on its exploiters to those who constitute the political organ of that same exploitation.* The oppressed class knows that the state is a fortress that serves as the bulwark and defence of its oppressors, a fortress that it can and must capture and rebuild in the interests of its own defence, but that it cannot bypass by relying on its neutrality. Relying only on themselves, the oppressed begin to understand that '*political* self-help is', as Lange[13] says, 'the most important form of *social* self-help'. They then strive for political domination in order to help themselves by changing existing social relations and adapting the social order to the conditions of their own development and welfare. They do not, of course, achieve domination immediately; it is only gradually that they become a terrible force, driving any thought of resistance from the minds of their opponents. For a long time they ask only for the concessions, demand only the reforms that will give them not domination but the opportunity to grow and mature towards future domination; the reforms that would satisfy the most urgent and immediate of their demands and extend only slightly their sphere of influence on the public life of the country. It is only by going through the tough school of the struggle for separate little patches of enemy territory that the oppressed class acquires the persistence, daring and maturity that is necessary for the decisive struggle. But, once it has acquired these qualities, it may look upon its opponents as a class that has been finally condemned by history; it need have no doubts about its victory. The so-called revolution is only the last act in the long drama of revolutionary class struggle which becomes conscious only insofar as it becomes a *political* struggle.

The question is now: would it be expedient for the Socialists to restrain the workers from 'politics' on the grounds that the political structure of society is determined by its economic relations? Of course not. They would be depriving the workers of the focal point of their struggle, of the opportunity to concentrate their efforts and direct their blows at the social organisation established by their exploiters. Instead, the workers would have to wage partisan warfare against individual exploiters or, at most, against separate groups of these exploiters, who would always have the organised power of the state on their side. It was precisely this kind of mistake that the Russian Socialists from among the so-called intelligentsia made when they censured the Northern Russian Workers' Union in no. 4 of *Zemlya i Volya* because it had put forward certain political demands in its programme . . . [14]

All this is very well, some readers may say, but your arguments are not to the point. We do not deny that it would be *useful* for the working class to gain political influence and take state power into its own hands; we only maintain that at present that is *impossible* for many reasons. Your reference to the history of the bourgeoisie proves nothing because the position of the proletariat in bourgeois society is in no way comparable to the position of the third estate in the states of the *ancien régime*. Marx himself recognises this difference and formulates it in *The Manifesto of the Communist Party* in the following manner:

The serf, in the period of serfdom, raised himself to membership in the commune, just as the petty bourgeois, under the yoke of feudal absolutism, managed to develop into a bourgeois. The modern labourer, on the contrary, instead of rising with the progress of industry, sinks deeper and deeper below the conditions of existence of his own class. He becomes a pauper, and pauperism develops more rapidly than population and wealth in bourgeois countries.[15]

There is nothing surprising in the fact that every progressive step taken by the bourgeoisie in the field of production and exchange has been accompanied by 'corresponding political gains':[16] everyone knows that an improvement in the material well-being of a particular class is accompanied by a growth in its political influence. But the very fact that the political gains of the bourgeoisie presupposed an increase in its wealth compels us to view the political movements of the working class as hopeless. Becoming more and more 'pauperised', the workers must apparently forfeit even the share of influence that they had won in the struggle for the interests of the bourgeoisie, 'fighting the enemies – the remnants of absolute monarchy, the landowners, the non-industrial bourgeois' and so on. The political struggle of the working class is pointless because it is doomed to failure by its economic position.

For all its internal inconsistency, this objection seems at first sight so final that it cannot be passed over in silence. It is the last plank of the argument put forward by those supporters of the theory of political non-interference who count themselves followers of Marx. If, therefore, it is disposed of, the theory of non-interference falls completely and the political tasks of contemporary socialism emerge in their true light.

The working class's share of the national product is constantly diminishing: there is not the slightest doubt about that. It is being impoverished not just in relative terms but in absolute terms too; its income is not only not increasing in the same progression as the income of other classes, but is falling; the real wage of the contemporary proletarian (the quantity of consumer goods that he receives) is less than a worker's pay was 500 years ago. This has been shown by the researches of Rogers, Du Châtelet and others.[17] But it by no means follows from this that economic conditions now are less favourable to the political movement of the working class than they were in the fourteenth century. We have already said that, in appraising the economic conditions of a particular country in this manner, we must take account not only of the distribution of national income, but above all of the organisation of production and mode of exchange of the products. The strength of the emerging bourgeoisie consists not so much in its wealth as in the socio-economic progress for which it was once the vehicle. It was not the increase in its income that drove it on to the path of revolutionary struggle and secured the growth of its political influence, but the contradiction between the productive forces that it summoned into existence and the conditions under which the production and exchange of goods took place in feudal society. Once it had become the representative of the progressive demands in that society, it rallied all the discontented elements under its banner and led them into battle against a regime that the great majority of the people hated. It was not money but the immaturity of the working class that gave [the bourgeoisie] the leading role in that movement for emancipation. Its wealth and its already relatively fairly elevated social position were naturally necessary for it to fulfil this role. But what determined that necessity? Above all the fact that the bourgeoisie could not destroy the old order without the help of the lower strata of the population. Here it was assisted by its wealth. It brought it influence over that same mass that was to fight for its domination. If it had not been rich, the bourgeoisie would have had no influence and, without influence over the people, it would not have defeated the aristocracy, because it was strong, not of its own accord but through the power that it had already mastered and that it commanded by virtue of its capital. The question now arises as to whether it is *possible* for the proletariat to exert this kind of influence over another class of the population and whether it is *necessary* to ensure victory. It is enough to ask the question and we hear a decisive 'No!' from everyone who understands the present position of the working class. It is *impossible* for the proletariat to influence lower classes in the same way that the bourgeoisie once influenced it for the simple reason that there are no classes below it. It is itself the very lowest economic group in contemporary society. *Nor does it need* to strive for such influence as it is at the same time the *most numerous* stratum in this society because it has always been the proletariat, with the other strata of the working population, whose intervention has resolved political issues. We say the most numerous class because all

the other classes decay and finally disappear in the face of modern industry; the proletariat is its special and essential product. The lower middle class, the small manufacturer, the shopkeeper, the artisan, the peasant, all these fight against the bourgeoisie, to save from extinction their existence as fractions of the middle class. They are therefore . . . conservative. Nay more, they are reactionary, for they try to roll back the wheel of history. If by chance they are revolutionary, they are so only in view of their impending transfer into the proletariat, they thus defend not their present, but their future interests, they desert their own standpoint to place themselves at that of the proletariat.[18]

Previously the working class was victorious under the command of the bourgeoisie and only naively wondered at the strange fact that nearly all the burdens of the struggle fell to it while nearly all the spoils and honours of victory went to its ally. Now it is not satisfied with this servile role and it is directing against the bourgeoisie that very strength that won the latter its victory. But now this strength has significantly increased. It has grown and continues to grow in proportion to the concentration of capital and the spread of large-scale production. In addition, it has grown in the same proportion as the political experience of the working class, which the bourgeoisie itself brought into the arena of social activity. Can there be any doubt that the proletariat, which, under the leadership of the bourgeoisie, was once strong enough to smash feudal absolutism, will in time be strong enough to destroy the political domination of the bourgeoisie on its own initiative? The bourgeoisie was able to defeat feudalism only through its wealth; the proletariat will defeat the bourgeoisie precisely because its lot — 'pauperism' — is becoming the lot of an increasing part of contemporary society.

But in the history of its development the bourgeoisie's wealth has rendered it another and indeed an extremely *'productive* service', as its economists would put it. It gave it knowledge and made it the most advanced and educated stratum of society at that time. Can the proletariat acquire that knowledge, can it be at one and the same time both the poorest and the most advanced of all classes in society? Political domination is impossible for [the proletariat] without this condition, for without knowledge there is no strength!

We have already said that it was the bourgeoisie itself that initiated the political education of the proletariat. It took care of its education in as far as it needed it for the struggle against its own enemies. It shattered its religious faith whenever this was required to undermine the political significance of the clergy; it broadened its legal outlook wherever it needed to oppose 'natural' law to the written law of a state based on estates. Now the economic question has come to the fore and political economy now plays, as a very clever German[19] observed, just as important a role as natural law played in the eighteenth century. Will the bourgeoisie consent to give the lead to the working class in investigating the relationship between labour and capital, this question of questions for the whole of social economy? It is reluctant to take upon itself even that role, advantageous as it would be for it, because simply to raise the question is to threaten the domination of the bourgeoisie. But *can* it perform that role, if only in the way it once did with regard to religion and to law? No! Blinded by the interests of its own class, its representatives in the world of scholarship long ago lost their capacity for the objective scientific investigation of social questions. Therein lies the whole secret of the present decline in bourgeois economics. Ricardo was the last economist who, while remaining a bourgeois through and through, had sufficient wit to understand the diametrical opposition of interests between labour and capital. Sismondi was the last bourgeois economist with sufficient sensitivity to bewail this antagonism without hypocrisy. Since then the *general* theoretical researches of the bourgeois economists have on the whole lost all scientific significance. To convince oneself of this it is enough to recall the history of political economy since Ricardo and to consult the works of Bastiat, Carey, Leroy-Beaulieu or even the contemporary *Kathedersozialisten.*[20] Bourgeois economists have changed from being peaceful and objective thinkers into militant guardians and watchdogs of capital, devoting all their efforts to reconstruct the very edifice of science for the purposes of war. But, despite these warlike exertions, they continually retreat and leave in the enemies' hands the scientific territory over which they once ruled absolutely. Nowadays people to whom any 'demagogic' aspirations would be completely foreign assure us that the workers are 'better able than any Smith or Faucher to master the most abstract concepts' in economic science. This was the opinion, for instance, of a man who is regarded by German economists as the great authority but who, for his part, viewed them with utter scorn. 'We look upon the workers as children', this man added, 'whereas they are already head and shoulders above us.'[21]

But is he not exaggerating? Can the working class comprehend 'abstract' questions of social economics and socialism at least as well as, if not better than, people who have spent whole decades on their education?

What are the principles of contemporary scientific socialism based on? Are they the concoctions of some leisured benefactor of the human race or are they a generalisation of the very phenomena that we all, in one way or another, come up against in our daily lives, an explanation of the very laws that determine our part in the production, the exchange, or simply the distribution of goods? Whoever answers this question in the latter sense will agree that the working class has many opportunities for a correct understanding of the 'most abstract' laws of social economics, for grasping the most abstract principles of scientific socialism. Difficulty in understanding the laws of a particular science arises from an incomplete knowledge of the data underlying those laws. Wherever it is merely a matter of everyday phenomena, where the scientific law only generalises facts of which everyone is aware, people in the practical field not only understand the theoretical principles perfectly, they can sometimes even teach the theoreticians themselves. Ask a farmer about the effect that distance from the market has on the price of his produce or the effect the fertility of the soil has on the size of the land rent. Ask the factory owner about the effect the expansion of the market has in making production cheaper. Ask the worker where his employer gets his profits from . . . You will see that all these people know their Ricardo, although they have never even seen the cover of his works. Yet these questions are supposed to be very complex and 'abstract'; oceans of ink have been used up on them and such an enormous number of tomes have been written on them that they are enough to terrify anyone beginning to study economics. It is the same in each and every area of social economics! Take the theory of exchange value. You can explain to the worker how and why it is determined in a couple of words, but many bourgeois economists are still unwilling or unable to comprehend this perfectly simple theory and, in their arguments about it, they succumb to gross errors of logic that no teacher of arithmetic would hesitate to give an elementary pupil a bad mark for. That is why we think that the writer we quoted was right: the only audience today that will understand burning social issues is an audience of proletarians or people who hold the proletarian point of view. Once the basic principles of social economics have been mastered, there is no difficulty in understanding scientific socialism: here too the worker will only follow the dictates of his practical experience. This aspect of the question was explained very well by Marx himself: 'By proclaiming the dissolution of the *hitherto existing world order*', we read in his *Critique of Hegel's Philosophy of Law*,

the proletariat merely states the secret of *its own existence*, for it is *in fact* the *dissolution* of that order. By demanding the *negation of private property*, the proletariat merely raises to the rank of a *principle of society* what society has made the principle of the *proletariat*, what, without its own cooperation, is already incorporated in *it* as the negative result of society.[22]

So we see that the proletariat does not need material wealth to achieve an understanding of the conditions for its emancipation. Its pauperism (which is determined *not by the poverty or barbarism of society but by defects in the organisation of society*), far from hindering an understanding of these conditions, actually makes it easier.

The laws governing the distribution of products in capitalist society are extremely unfavourable to the working class. But the organisation of production and form of exchange that are characteristic of capitalism create for the first time both the objective and the subjective opportunity for the emancipation of the workers. Capitalism broadens the worker's outlook and destroys all the prejudices that he inherited from the old society; it drives him into the struggle and at the same time guarantees his victory by increasing his numbers and putting at his disposal the economic opportunity to organise the kingdom of labour. Technical progress increases man's power over nature and raises the productivity of labour to such a degree that the obligation to work cannot be an obstacle but, on the contrary, will become an indispensable condition for the all-round development of all members of socialist society. At the same time the socialisation of *production* that is characteristic of capitalism paves the way for the conversion of its *instruments and products* into common property. The joint-stock company, this highest form of organisation for industrial enterprises at the present time, excludes the capitalists from any active role in the economic life of society and turns them into drones whose disappearance is incapable of causing the slightest disruption in the course of that life. 'If the energetic race of major-domos once managed without any difficulty to depose a royal dynasty that had grown indolent', the Conservative Rodbertus says,

why should a living and energetic organisation of workers (the white-collared personnel of companies are *qualified workers*), why should this kind of organisation not in time remove the owners who have become mere *rentiers*? . . . And yet capital is no longer able to take another road! Having outlived its period of prosperity, capital is becoming its own grave-digger!

Why, we in turn ask, should not the very same organisation of workers that will be in a position to 'remove the owners who have become mere *rentiers*', why should not such an organisation be in a position to take state power into its own hands and thus achieve political domination? For the former presupposes the latter: the only organisation that can 'remove' the owners is one that is in a position to overcome their *political resistance*.

But that is not all: there are other social phenomena that also enhance the probability of a *political* victory for the proletariat:

entire sections of the ruling classes are, by the advance of industry, precipitated into the proletariat, or are at least threatened in their conditions of existence. These also supply the proletariat with fresh elements of enlightenment and progress.

Finally, in times when the class struggle nears the decisive hour, the process of dissolution going on within the ruling class, in fact within the whole range of old society, assumes such a violent, glaring character, that a small section of the ruling class cuts itself adrift, and joins the revolutionary class, the class that holds the future in its hands. Just as, therefore, at an earlier period, a section of the nobility went over to the bourgeoisie, so now a portion of the bourgeoisie goes over to the proletariat, and, in particular, a portion of the bourgeois ideologists, who have raised themselves to the level of comprehending theoretically the historical movement as a whole.[23]

There is a really remarkable legend among the negroes of North Guinea. In the words of this legend:

One day God summoned the two sons of the first human couple. One of them was white, the other dark-skinned. Placing before them a pile of gold and a book, God ordered the dark-skinned brother, being the elder, to choose one of the two. He chose the gold and so the younger brother received the book. An unknown power immediately transported him and his book to a cold and distant country. But, thanks to his book, he became learned, terrifying and strong. But the elder brother remained at home and lived long enough to see how superior science is to wealth.

The bourgeoisie once possessed both knowledge and wealth. Unlike the dark-skinned brother in the negro legend, it owned both the gold and the book because history, the god of human societies, does not recognise the right of classes that are under age and makes them the wards of their elder brothers. But the time came when the working class, deprived by history, outgrew its childhood and the bourgeoisie was forced to share with it. The bourgeoisie kept the gold, while the younger brother received the 'book', thanks to which, despite the darkness and the cold of his cellars, he has now become strong and terrifying. Little by little scientific socialism is edging bourgeois theories off the pages of this book of magic and soon the proletariat will read in the book how it can achieve material satisfaction. Then it will throw off the shameful yoke of capitalism and show the bourgeoisie 'how superior science is to wealth'.

3. PROGRAMME OF THE SOCIAL DEMOCRATIC EMANCIPATION OF LABOUR GROUP (1884)[24]

G.V. Plekhanov

The Emancipation of Labour Group sets itself the aim of spreading socialist ideas in Russia and working out the elements for organising a Russian workers' *socialist party*.

The essence of its outlook can be expressed in the following few propositions:[25]

I. The economic emancipation of the working class will be achieved only by the transfer to collective ownership by the working people of all means and fruits of production and the organisation of all the functions of social and economic life in accordance with the requirements of society.

II. The modern development of technology in civilised societies not only furnishes the *material opportunity* for such organisation but makes it *necessary and inevitably* for solving the contradictions which hinder the peaceful and all-round development of those societies.

III. This radical economic revolution will entail the most fundamental changes in the entire constitution of social and international relationships.

Abolishing the class struggle by destroying the classes themselves, making the economic struggle of individuals impossible and unnecessary by abolishing commodity production and the competition resulting from it, briefly, putting an end to the struggle for existence between individuals, classes and whole societies, it renders unnecessary all the social organs that have developed as the weapons of the struggle during the many centuries it has been proceeding.

Without falling into utopian fantasies about the social and international organisation of the future, we can now already foretell the abolition of the most important of the organs of chronic struggle inside society, namely, *the state, as a political organisation opposed to society* and safeguarding mainly the interests of the ruling section. In exactly the same way we can now already foresee the international character of the impending economic revolution. The contemporary development of the international exchange of products necessitates the participation of all civilised societies in this revolution.

That is why socialist parties in all countries acknowledge the international character of the present-day working class movement and proclaim the principle of the international solidarity of producers.

The Emancipation of Labour Group also acknowledges the great principles of the former *International Working Men's Association*[26] and the common interests of the working people of the whole civilised world.

IV. Introducing *consciousness* where *blind economic necessity* now dominates, replacing the modern mastery of the *product* over the *producer* by that of the *producer* over the *product*, the socialist revolution simplifies all social relationships and gives them a purpose, at the same time providing each citizen with the real opportunity to participate directly in the discussion and resolution of all social matters.

This direct participation of citizens in the management of all social matters presupposes the abolition of the modern system of political representation and its replacement by *direct popular legislation.*

In their present-day struggle, the Socialists must bear in mind this necessary political reform and aim to realise it by all the means at their disposal.

This is all the more essential as the political self-education and rule of the working class are a necessary preliminary condition for its economic emancipation. Only a completely *democratic* state can carry out the economic revolution that conforms to the interests of the producers and demands their intelligent participation in the organisation and regulation of production.

At present the working class in the advanced countries is becoming increasingly aware of the necessity of the above-mentioned socio-political revolution and is organising itself into a special labour party that is hostile to all the parties of the exploiters.

Basing itself on the principles of the International Working Men's Association, this organisation, however, has as its principal aim the achievement by the workers of political hegemony within each of their respective states. 'The proletariat of each country must, of course, first of all settle accounts with its own bourgeoisie.'

This introduces an element of variety into the programmes of the socialist parties in the different states, compelling each of them to conform to the social conditions in their own country.

It goes without saying that the practical tasks, and consequently also the programmes, of the Socialists are bound to have a more original and complex character in countries where capitalist production has not yet become dominant and where the working masses are under a double yoke – that of developing capitalism and that of decaying patriarchal economy.

In those countries the Socialists must simultaneously organise the working class for the struggle with the bourgeoisie and wage war against the remnants of old pre-bourgeois social relations that are harmful both to the development of the working class and to the welfare of the people as a whole.

The Russian Socialists find themselves in precisely this position. The working population of Russia directly bears the whole burden of the enormous machinery of the despotic police state and at the same time suffers all the miseries that characterise the epoch of capitalist *accumulation* and in places – in our industrial centres – it is already experiencing the yoke of capitalist *production* which is not yet limited by any decisive intervention on the part of the state or by the organised resistance of the workers themselves. Present-day Russia is suffering – as Marx once said of the western part of the European continent – not only from the development of capitalist production, but also from the inadequacy of that development.

One of the most harmful consequences of this backward state of production was, and still is, the underdeveloped state of the middle class which in our country is incapable of taking the initiative in the struggle against absolutism.

That is why the socialist intelligentsia has been obliged to head the contemporary emancipation movement whose immediate task must be the creation of free political institutions in our country, the Socialists being, for their part, obliged to provide the working class with the opportunity to play an active and fruitful part in the future political life of Russia.

The first way of achieving this aim must be agitation for a democratic constitution that guarantees:

1. The right to elect and be elected to the Legislative Assembly as well as to the provincial and communal organs of self-government for every citizen who has not been sentenced by a court to deprivation of political rights for certain *shameful* activities strictly specified by law.[27]
2. A financial emolument determined by law for the representatives of the people that will permit their election from among the poorest classes of the population.
3. Inviolability of the person and the citizen's dwelling-place.
4. Unlimited freedom of conscience, speech, the press, assembly and association.
5. Freedom of movement and employment.
6. Complete equality of all citizens irrespective of religion and racial origin.[28]
7. The replacement of the standing army by general arming of the people.
8. The revision of all our civil and criminal legislation, the abolition of class distinctions and of punishments that are incompatible with human dignity.

But this goal will remain unfulfilled, the political initiative of the workers will be unthinkable, if the fall of absolutism finds them completely unprepared and disorganised.

That is why the socialist intelligentsia has a duty to organise the workers and *prepare* them as far as possible for the struggle against the present system of government as well as against the bourgeois parties in the future.

It must *immediately set to work to organise* the workers in our industrial centres, as the foremost representatives of the whole working population of Russia, into secret circles that are linked with one another and have a definite social and political programme that corresponds to the present-day needs of the entire class of producers in Russia and to the basic tasks of socialism.

Whilst appreciating that the details of such a programme can be worked out only in the future and by the working class itself when it is called upon to participate in political life and is united in its own party, the *Emancipation of Labour* Group presupposes that the main points of the *economic section* of the workers' programme must be the demands:

1. For a radical revision of our agrarian relations, i.e. the conditions for the redemption of the land and its allotment by peasant communes. The granting of the right to renounce their allotments and leave the commune to those peasants who find this arrangement suits them, etc.

2. For the abolition of the present system of dues and the institution of a progressive income tax.
3. For the legislative regulation of relations between the workers (urban and rural) and employers and the organisation of the relevant *inspectorate with worker representation*.
4. For state aid for production *associations* organised in every possible branch of agriculture, mining and manufacturing industry (by peasants, miners, factory and plant workers, craftsmen, etc.).

The *Emancipation of Labour* Group is convinced that not just the success but even the very possibility of such a meaningful movement of the Russian working class depends in large degree upon the above-mentioned work by the intelligentsia in its midst.

But the group mentioned assumes that as a preliminary step the intelligentsia itself must adopt the standpoint of contemporary scientific socialism, adhering to Populist traditions only insofar as they are not inconsistent with its principles.

In view of this, the Emancipation of Labour Group sets itself the aim of propaganda for contemporary socialism in Russia and the preparation of the working class for a conscious social and political movement; it is devoting all its energies to this aim, summoning our revolutionary youth to assistance and cooperation.

Pursuing this aim by all the means at its disposal, the Emancipation of Labour Group does at the same time recognise the need for terrorist struggle against the absolutist government and differs from the Narodnaya Volya Party only on the question of the so-called seizure of power by the revolutionary party and of the *tasks of the immediate activity of the Socialists among the working class.*

The Emancipation of Labour Group in no way disregards the peasantry who constitute the major part of the working population of Russia. But it assumes that the work of the intelligentsia, especially in the present conditions of social and political struggle, must be aimed primarily at the most advanced stratum of the population, the industrial workers. Having secured the strong support of this stratum, the socialist intelligentsia will have a far greater hope of successfully extending its influence to the peasantry as well, particularly if, by that time, it has achieved freedom of agitation and propaganda. Incidentally, it goes without saying that the disposition of the resources of our Socialists *will have to be changed if an independent revolutionary movement emerges among the peasantry* and that, even at the present time, people who are in direct contact with the peasantry could, through their activity amongst them, render an important service to the socialist movement in Russia. The Emancipation of Labour Group, far from rejecting these people, will exert every effort to agree with them on the basic positions of the programme.

4. 'PROPAGANDA AMONG THE WORKERS', FROM *OUR DIFFERENCES* (1884)[29]

G.V. Plekhanov

But is such a merger possible at present? Is propaganda among the workers at all possible in the present political circumstances?

Impossibility is a particular case of difficulty. But there are two forms of difficulty that occasionally become impossibility. One type of difficulty depends on the personal qualities of the agents, on the dominant character of their aspirations, views and inclinations. This type of difficulty is created by social surroundings through the intermediary of individuals, and therefore its shades are as varied as are the qualities of individuals. What was *difficult* for Goldenberg was *easy* for Zhelyabov; what is impossible for a man of one type of character and convictions may appear necessary and therefore possible, though perhaps difficult, for another with different habits and views.[30] The impossible is often not what is in itself impossible, but what, in the opinion of a particular individual, brings rewards that do not compensate for the efforts exerted. But the appraisal of the rewards brought by a particular political matter depends entirely on the agent's view of that matter. Mr V.V.,[31] being convinced that the government itself will undertake the organisation of national production that he thinks desirable, will naturally consider superfluous the sacrifices and efforts that propaganda among the workers will require at present. Similarly, the conspirator who relies mainly on some 'committee' or other will declare without great inner conflict that propaganda is impossible among the workers, who, in his opinion, are *important* only 'for the revolution' but are far from being the only representatives of the revolution. This is by no means the way the Social Democrat speaks; he is convinced not that the workers are necessary *for the revolution*, but that the revolution is necessary *for the workers*. For him propaganda among the workers will be the main aim of his efforts, and he will not give it up until he has tried all the means at his disposal and exerted all the efforts he is capable of. And the more our revolutionary intelligentsia becomes imbued with socialist views, the easier and more feasible work among the workers will seem to them, for the simple reason that their desire for such work will be all the greater.

We do not wish to deceive anybody and we would not be able to do so. Everybody knows how many difficulties and persecutions await the propagandist and popular agitator in our country today. But those difficulties must not be exaggerated. Every kind of revolutionary work without exception is made very difficult in our country today by police persecution, but that does not mean that the white terror has achieved its aim, i.e. that it has 'rooted out sedition'. Action calls for counteraction, persecution gives rise to self-sacrifice, and no matter how energetic the reactionary steps taken by the government, the revolutionary will always be able to evade them if only he devotes the necessary amount of energy to that purpose. There was a time when blowing up the Winter Palace and tunnelling under Malaya Sadovaya Street would have seemed impracticable and unrealistic to the revolutionaries themselves. But people were found who did the impossible, carried out the unrealistic. Can such persistence be unthinkable in other spheres of revolutionary work? Are the spies that track down the 'terrorists' less skilful and numerous than those who guard our working class against the 'pseudo-science of socialism and communism'? The only person who can affirm that is someone who has made up his mind to avoid any kind of work that he finds unpleasant.

As far as the qualities of the working class itself are concerned, they do not by any means justify the gloomy prophecies of our pessimists. Properly speaking, hardly anybody has ever undertaken propaganda among the workers in our country with any consistency or system. And yet experience has shown that even the scattered efforts of a few dozen men were sufficient to give a powerful impulse to the revolutionary initiative of our working class. Let the reader remember the Northern Union of Russian Workers, its social democratic programme and its organisation, which was very widespread for a secret society. This Union has disintegrated but, before accusing the workers of responsibility, our intelligentsia should recall whether they did much to support it. Yet it would have been quite possible and not even all that difficult to support it. In their 'Letter to the Editors of *Zemlya i Volya*'[32] representatives of the Union even defined the type of help that they wanted and needed. They asked for cooperation in setting up a secret print-shop for the publication of their working class paper. The 'intellectual' society Zemlya i Volya considered it untimely to fulfil that request. The main efforts of our 'intellectual' Socialists were then aimed in a completely different direction. The result of those efforts was not support for the workers but intensification of the police persecutions whose victims, among others, were the workers' organisations. Is it surprising that, left to their own resources in a conspiracy to which they were by no means accustomed, the Workers' Union broke up into small sections not linked together by any unity of plan or of action? But those small circles and groups of socialist workers have still not ceased to exist in our industrial centres; all that is needed to unite them again in one impressive whole is a little conviction, energy and perseverance.

Needless to say the workers' secret societies do not constitute a workers' party. In this sense, those who say that our programme is meant far more for the future than for the present are quite right. But what follows from that? Does it mean we need not set to work immediately on its implementation? The exceptionalists who argue in that way are again being caught in a vicious circle of conclusions. A widespread working class movement presupposes at least a temporary triumph of free institutions in the country concerned, even if those institutions are only partly free. But to secure such institutions will in turn be impossible without political support from the most progressive sections of the people. Where is the way out? West European history broke this vicious circle by slow political education of the working class. But there is no limit to our revolutionaries' fear of that punctilious old woman history's slowness. They want the revolution as soon as possible, at whatever cost. In view of this, one can only wonder at them not remembering the proverb: if you want to ride the sledge, pull it up the hill – a proverb whose political meaning amounts to the irrefutable proposition that anyone who wishes to win freedom quickly must try to interest the working class in the fight against absolutism. The development of the political consciousness of the working class is one of the chief forms of the struggle against the 'principal enemy which prevents any at all rational approach' to the question of creating in our country a workers' party on the West European pattern. What, indeed, is the meaning of the assurances given by historians that in such and such a historical period the bourgeoisie – or, which comes to almost the same, society – was fighting against absolutism in such and such a country? It was none other than the bourgeoisie that was inciting and leading the working class to fight, or at least was counting on its support. Until the bourgeois was guaranteed that support it was cowardly, because it was powerless. What did the republican bourgeoisie – deservedly deprived of that support – do against Napoleon III? All that it could do was to choose between hopeless heroism and hypocritical approval of the accomplished fact. When did the revolutionary bourgeoisie show courage in 1830 and 1848? When the working class was already getting the upper hand at the barricades. Our 'society' cannot count on such support from the workers; it does not even know at whom the insurgent workers will aim their blows – the defenders of absolute monarchy or the supporters of political freedom. Hence its timidity and irresolution, hence the leaden, hopeless gloom that has come over them now. But, if the state of affairs changes, if our 'society' is guaranteed the support from at least the city suburbs, you will see that it knows what it wants and will be able to speak to the authorities in the language worthy of a citizen. Remember the Petersburg strikes in 1878–9.[33] The Socialists were far from being the only people to show an interest in them. They became the event of the day and nearly all the intelligentsia and thinking people in Petersburg showed an interest in them. Now imagine that those strikes had expressed, besides the antagonism of interests between the employers and the workers of a given factory, the political discord which was appearing between the Petersburg working *class* and the absolute monarchy. The way the police treated the strikers gave occasion enough for such political discord to be manifested. Imagine that the workers at the New Cotton Mill had demanded, besides a wage rise for themselves, definite political rights for all Russian citizens. The bourgeoisie would then have seen that it had to consider the workers' demands more seriously than before. Besides this, all the liberal sections of the bourgeoisie, whose interests would not have been immediately and directly threatened had the strikes been successful, would have felt that its political demands were at least being provided with some solid foundation and that support from the working class made the success of their struggle against absolutism far more probable. The workers' political movement would have inspired new hope in the hearts of all supporters of political freedom. The Narodniks themselves might have directed their attention to the new fighters from among the workers and have ceased their barren and hopeless whimpering over the destruction of the 'foundations' they cherished so much.

The question is who, if not the revolutionary intelligentsia, could promote the political development of the working class? During the 1878–9 strikes even the self-reliant intelligentsia could not boast of clear political consciousness. That was why the strikers could not hear anything at all instructive from them about the connection between the economic interests of the working class and its political rights. Now, too, there is much confusion in the heads of our 'revolutionary youth'. But we are willing to entertain the hope that confusion will at last give way to the theories of scientific socialism and will cease to paralyse the success of our revolutionary movement. Once that fortunate time comes, the workers' groups will also not delay in adopting the correct political standpoint. Then the struggle against absolutism will enter a new phase, the last; supported by the working masses, the political demands of the progressive section of our 'society' will at last receive the satisfaction they have been awaiting for so long.

Had the death of Alexander II been accompanied by vigorous action from the workers in the principal cities of Russia, its results would probably have been more decisive. But widespread agitation among the workers is unthinkable without the help of secret societies previously set up in as large numbers as possible, which would prepare the workers' minds and direct their movement. It must therefore be said that, without serious work among the workers and, consequently, without conscious support from the secret workers' organisations, the terrorists' most daring feats will never be anything more than brilliant sorties. The 'principal enemy' will only be hit, not destroyed, by them; that means that the *terrorist* struggle will not achieve its aim, for its only aim must be the complete and merciless destruction of absolutism.

Thus, far from the political situation in Russia today compelling us to renounce activity among the workers, *it is only by means of such activity that we can free ourselves from the intolerable yoke of absolutism.*

Let us now consider another aspect of the matter. The preceding exposition has once more confirmed for us the truth that the working class is very important 'for the revolution'. But the Socialist must think first and foremost of making the revolution useful for the working population of the country. Leaving the peasantry aside for the time being, we shall note that the more clearly the working class sees the connection between its economic needs and its political rights, the more profit it will derive from its political struggle. In the 'West European' countries the proletariat often fought absolutism under the banner and the supreme leadership of the bourgeoisie. Hence its intellectual and moral dependence on the leaders of liberalism, its faith in the exceptional holiness of liberal mottoes and its belief in the inviolability of the bourgeois system. In Germany it took all Lassalle's energy and eloquence merely to *undermine* the moral link of the workers with the progressives. Our 'society' has no such influence on the working class and there is no need or use for the Socialists to create it from scratch. They must show the workers their own working class banner, give them leaders from their own working class ranks; briefly, they must make sure that not bourgeois 'society', but the workers' secret organisations gain a dominant influence over the workers' minds. This will considerably hasten the formation and growth of the Russian workers' socialist party, which will be able to win itself a place of honour among the other parties after having, in its infancy, promoted the fall of absolutism and the triumph of political freedom.

In order thus to contribute to the intellectual and political independence of the Russian working class, our revolutionaries need not resort to any artificial measures nor place themselves in any false or ambiguous position. All they need is to become imbued with the principles of modern social democracy and, not confining themselves to political propaganda, constantly to impress upon their listeners that 'the economical emancipation of the working classes is . . . the great end to which every political movement ought to be subordinate as a means'.[34] Once it has assimilated this thought, our working class will itself be capable of steering between Scylla and Charybdis, between the political reaction of state socialism and the economic quackery of the liberal bourgeoisie.

In promoting the formation of the workers' party, our revolutionaries will be doing the most fruitful, the most important thing that is open to a 'progressive man' in present-day Russia. The workers' party alone is capable of solving all the contradictions that now condemn our intelligentsia to theoretical and practical impotence. We have already seen that the most obvious of those contradictions is at present the need to overthrow absolutism and the impossibility of doing so without the support of the people. Secret workers' organisations will solve this contradiction by drawing into the political struggle the most progressive sections of the people. But that is not enough. Growing and strengthening under the protection of free institutions, the Russian workers' socialist party will solve another, no less important, contradiction, this time of an economic character. We all know that the village commune of today must give place to communism or ultimately disintegrate. At the same time, the economic organisation of the commune has no springs to start it off on the road to communist development. While easing our peasants' transition to communism, the commune cannot impart to it the initiative necessary for that transition. On the contrary, the development of commodity production is more and more undermining the traditional foundations of the commune principle. And our Narodnik intelligentsia cannot remove this basic contradiction in one fell swoop. Some of the village communes are declining, disintegrating before their eyes and becoming a 'scourge and a brake' for the poorest of the commune members. Unfortunate as this phenomenon may seem to the intelligentsia, they can do nothing to help the commune at present. There is absolutely no link whatever between the 'lovers of the people' and the 'people'. The disintegrating commune is still alone on its side, and the grieving intelligentsia are alone on theirs, neither being able to put an end to this state of affairs. How can a way out of this contradiction be found? Will our intelligentsia indeed have to dismiss all practical work with a wave of the hand and console themselves with 'utopias' of the kind Mr G. Uspensky likes?[35] Nothing of the sort! Our Narodniks can at least save a certain number of village communes if only they will consent to appeal to the dialectics of our social development. But such an appeal is also possible only through the intermediary of a workers' socialist party.

The disintegration of our village commune is an indisputable fact. But the speed and intensity of the process differs according to localities in Russia. To halt it completely in places where the commune is still fresher and more stable, our Narodniks must use the forces now being freed by the breaking up of communes in provinces where industry is more developed. These forces are none other than the forces of the rising proletariat. They, and they alone, can be the link between the peasantry and the socialist intelligentsia; they, and they alone, can bridge the historical abyss between the 'people' and the 'educated' section of the population. Through them and with their help socialist propaganda will at last penetrate every corner of the Russian countryside. Moreover, if they are united and organised at the right time into a single workers' party, they can be the main bulwark of socialist agitation in favour of economic reforms that will protect the village commune against general disintegration. And when the hour of the decisive victory of the workers' party over the upper sections of society strikes, it will once more be that party, and only that party, that will take the initiative in the socialist organisation of national production. Under the influence of (and, if the case presents itself, under pressure from) that party, the village communes still in existence will in fact begin the transition to a higher, communist form. Then the advantages offered by communal land tenure will become not only possible, but actual, and the Narodnik dreams of our peasantry's exceptionalist development will come true, at least as far as a certain portion of the peasantry is concerned.

Thus the forces that are being freed by the disintegration of the village commune in some places in Russia can safeguard it against total disintegration in other places. All that is necessary is the ability to make correct and timely use of those forces and to direct them, i.e. to organise them as soon as possible into a social democratic party.

But, the champions of exceptionalism may object, the small landowners will offer vigorous resistance to the socialist tendencies of the workers' party. Most probably they will, but, on the other hand, there will be somebody to fight that resistance. The appearance of a class of small landowners is accompanied by the growth in numbers and strength of the revolutionary proletariat, which will at last impart life and movement to our clumsy state apparatus. Resistance need not be feared where there is a historical force capable of overcoming it; this is just as true as, on the other hand, a presumed absence of resistance is by no means a cause for celebration when the people are not capable of beginning the socialist movement, when the heroic exertions of separate individuals are shattered by the inertia of the obscure and ignorant masses.

It must be borne in mind, moreover, that this workers' party will also be for us a vehicle of influence from the West. The working man will not turn a deaf ear to the movement of the European proletariat, as could easily be the case with the peasant. And the united forces of the home and international movement will be more than enough to defeat the reactionary efforts of the small landowners.

So once more: *the earliest possible organisation of a workers' party is the only means of solving all the economic and political contradictions of present-day Russia.* On that road success and victory lie ahead; all other roads can lead only to defeat and impotence.

And what about terror?, the Narodovoltsy will exclaim. And the peasants?, the Narodniks, on the other hand, will shout. You are prepared to be reconciled with the existing reaction for the sake of your plans for a distant future, some will argue. You are sacrificing concrete interests for the victory of your doctrines, others will say, horrified. But we ask our opponents to be patient for a while and we shall try to answer at least some of the questions showered on us.

First of all, we by no means deny the important role of the terrorist struggle in the present emancipation movement. It has grown naturally from the social and political conditions under which we are placed, and it must just as naturally promote a change for the better. But in itself so-called terror only destroys the forces of government and does little to further the conscious organisation of its opponents. The terrorist struggle does not widen our revolutionary movement's sphere of influence; on the contrary, it reduces it to heroic actions by small partisan groups. After a few brilliant successes our revolutionary party has apparently weakened as a result of the great tension and cannot recover without an influx of fresh forces from new sections of the population. We recommend it to turn to the working class as to the most revolutionary of all classes in present-day society. Does that mean that we advise it to suspend its active struggle against the government? Far from it. On the contrary, we are pointing out a way of making the struggle broader, more varied, and therefore more successful. But it goes without saying that we cannot consider the cause of the working class movement from the standpoint of how important the workers are 'for the revolution'. We wish to make the very victory of the revolution profitable to the working population of our country, and that is why we consider it necessary to further the intellectual development, the unity and organisation of the working population. By no means do we want the workers' secret organisations to be transformed into secret nurseries rearing terrorists from among the workers. But we understand perfectly that the political emancipation of Russia coincides completely with the interest of the working class, and that is why we think that the revolutionary groups existing in that class must cooperate in the political struggle of our intelligentsia by propaganda, agitation and, occasionally, open action on the street. It would be unjust to leave all the hardships of the emancipation movement to be borne by the working class, but it is perfectly just and expedient to bring the workers, as well as others, into it.

There are other sections of the population for whom it would be far more convenient to undertake the terrorist struggle against the government. But, apart from the workers there is no section that could at the decisive moment knock down and kill off the political monster already wounded by the terrorists. Propaganda among the workers will not remove the necessity for terrorist struggle, but it will provide it with opportunities which have so far never existed.

So much for the terrorists. Let us now speak to the Narodniks.

They are grieved at all programmes in which revolutionary work among the peasants is not given first place. But, although such work is all that their own programme contains, the result is that

> The people's gains are still but small,
> Their life's not easier yet at all!

Since the late seventies, i.e. since the splitting of the Zemlya i Volya society,[36] revolutionary work among the peasants, far from being extended, has become increasingly narrow. At present it would not be a great error to rate it at nil. And yet all this time there has been no lack of people who assumed that the main stress of our entire revolutionary movement should be immediately transferred to the peasantry. Whence this contradiction? It would be unjust to suspect the Narodniks of inactivity, cowardice or lack of resolution. So one must think that they have set themselves a task which they cannot carry out in present circumstances, that it is not with the peasantry that our intelligentsia must begin its merger with the people. That is in fact what we think. But that is far from meaning that we *attribute no importance* to revolutionary work among the peasants. We note the fact and try to understand what it really means, convinced that, once they have understood the true reasons for their failure, the Narodniks will manage to avoid repeating it. It seems to us that the formation of a workers' party is what would free us from the contradiction as a result of which the Narodniks in Russia have been able to exist for the last seven years in a state of complete alienation from the people.

How the workers' party will do this can be seen from what has been set forth above. But it will do no harm to say a few words more on this subject.

To have influence on the numerous obscure masses one must have a certain minimum of forces without which all the efforts of separate individuals will never achieve any more than absolutely negligible results. Our revolutionary intelligentsia do not have that minimum, and this is why their work among the peasants has left practically no trace. We point out to them the industrial workers as the intermediary force able to promote the intelligentsia's merger with the 'people'. Does that mean that we ignore the peasants? Not at all. On the contrary, it means that we are looking for more effective means of influencing the peasantry.

Let us continue. Besides the definite minimum of forces necessary to influence the sections in question, there must be a certain community of character between the sections themselves and the people who appeal to them. But our revolutionary intelligentsia has no community with the peasantry either in its habits of thought or in its ability for physical labour. In this respect, too, the industrial worker is an intermediary between the peasant and the 'student'. He must, therefore, be the link between them.

Finally, one must not lose sight of still another, far from negligible, circumstance. No matter what is said about the alleged exclusively agrarian character of present-day Russia, there is no doubt that the countryside cannot exert an attraction on the whole force of our revolutionary intelligentsia. That is unthinkable if only because it is in the town, not in the countryside, that the intelligentsia is recruited, that the revolutionary seeks asylum when he is persecuted by the police, even if it is for propaganda among the peasants. Our principal cities are, therefore, the centres in which there is always a more or less considerable contingent of the intelligentsia's revolutionary forces. It goes without saying that the intelligentsia cannot avoid being influenced by the town or living its life. For some time this life has assumed a political character. And we know that, despite the most extreme 'Narodnik' plans, our intelligentsia have not been able to hold out against the current and have found themselves forced to take up the political struggle. As long as we have no workers' party, the revolutionaries 'of the town' are compelled to appeal to 'society', and therefore they are, in fact, its revolutionary representatives. The 'people' are relegated to the background and thus not only is the establishment of a link between them and the intelligentsia delayed, but even the link which formerly existed between the intellectual revolutionaries 'of the town' and those 'of the countryside' is severed. Hence the lack of mutual understanding, the disagreements and differences. This would not be the case if the political struggle in the town were mainly of a working class character. Then the only difference between the revolutionaries would be representatives of the *popular* movement in its various forms, and the Socialists would not need to sacrifice their lives in the interests of a '*society*' which is alien to their views.

Such harmony is not an impracticable utopia. It is not difficult to realise in practice. If at present it is impossible to find ten Narodniks who have settled in the countryside because of their programme, because of their duty to the *revolution*; on the other hand, there are quite a number of educated and sincere democrats who live in the countryside because of duty in the service of the *state*, because of their profession. Many of these people do not sympathise with our political struggle *in its present form* and at the same time do not undertake systematic revolutionary work among the peasantry for the simple reason that they see no party with which they could combine their efforts and we know that a single man on a battlefield is not a soldier. Begin a social and political movement among the workers, and you will see that these rural democrats will little by little come over to the standpoint of social democracy and in their turn will serve as a link between the town and the countryside.

Then our revolutionary forces will be distributed in the following very simple manner: those who are obliged by professional duties to be in the countryside will go there. It goes without saying that there will be a fair number of them. At the same time, those who have the opportunity to settle in towns or industrial centres will direct their efforts at work among the working class and endeavour to make it the vanguard of the Russian social democratic army.

Such is our programme. It does not sacrifice the countryside to the interests of the town, does not ignore the peasants for the sake of the industrial workers. *It sets itself the task of organising the social-revolutionary forces of the town to draw the countryside into the channel of the world-wide historical movement.*

5.   FROM THE PUBLISHERS OF THE 'WORKERS' LIBRARY' (1884)[37]

G.V. Plekhanov and P. Akselrod

The publication of pamphlets and booklets for the workers that the Emancipation of Labour Group has undertaken will be directed mainly at the more advanced strata among them, in other words, at the worker intelligentsia. Notwithstanding our desire to work for the creation of a literature that can be understood by the entire *mass* of peasants and workers, we are nevertheless compelled to restrict our popular literary activity *for the time being* to a tight circle of more or less intelligent readers from amongst the working class. We are driven to this by our position far from our homeland and by the extremely small number of people upon whom we can at present rely to support such an undertaking. We hope that the true friends of the working classes among the Russian revolutionaries will not be slow to take serious steps to fulfil one of their most important obligations – the creation of a peasants' and workers' literature that can be understood by readers at various levels of intellectual development. In the meantime, may our effort serve as the first step along this path.

Directing its publications mainly at the worker intelligentsia, the Emancipation of Labour Group considers it necessary to offer it a few clarifications of the immediate tasks of the Workers' Library.

These tasks depend above all on the aims that the working class in Russia must and can pursue. The duty of literature – books and newspapers – consists in helping to clarify in people's minds the aims and means that will most surely lead to their well-being.

Russia is now living on the eve of great changes. Its population is suffering beneath the yoke of tsarist autocracy and the tyranny of officials, gendarmes and police – right down to the arbitrary behaviour of the local constable. Lawlessness and tyranny reign throughout the country and stifle everyone, from the peasant and the worker to the scholars, publishers and authors of books and newspapers, the student youth etc. This monstrous order or, more accurately, disorder must inevitably soon collapse under the pressure of the struggle against it by the revolutionaries and because of its own savagery. In these circumstances would the working strata of Russia gain anything and, if so, what? Every advanced thinking worker and every true friend of the people must ask himself this question, whichever class of the population he belongs to.

The gains made by the peasant and worker population of Russia from the impending changes in its government will depend above all on the degree of consciousness and energy with which they fight against the tsarist police autocracy and participate in the establishment of any new order on its ruins. Everywhere the labouring classes have, with their blood, facilitated the overthrow of tsarist despotism in favour of the establishment of constitutional norms, i.e. the government of the country by means of laws promulgated by delegates elected by the population. But it has been rare for these changes to be accompanied by any appreciable improvement in the material life of the peasants and workers – an increase in the allotment of land, an alleviation of redemption payments, an increase in pay etc. Moreover, in the vast majority of cases, the upper classes and their educated representatives – the intelligentsia – knew how to discourage the peasant smallholders and the workers from making use even of political rights such as the election of legislators and representatives to the *Zemskii sobor*[38] and the Duma, or their rights to assemble and form unions to defend their own interests etc. Meanwhile, in constitutional states these rights offer one of the most important means of struggle of the various classes for their own emancipation. The backwardness of the lower classes, their lack of understanding of the events occurring around them or of their own interests, were the reasons why they served for such a long time in all countries as mere cannon-fodder in the hands of the rich and educated minority of the population.

Can we be certain that this will not happen in our country if the present system of governing the country collapses? We cannot answer this question with complete certainty. In any case every advanced and honest man is obliged to use every effort to preserve our labouring classes from the degrading role of a blind tool in the hands of their exploiters.

Anyone who is more or less acquainted with the present living conditions of the peasant population will agree with us that they are extremely unfavourable for the development among them of the consciousness of their own resources and interests that is essential for an independent *rational* struggle against unjust practices. This is not the place to throw doubt on this idea. Let us merely observe that the very fragmentation of the peasant population in the villages, their isolation from any contact with the highly populated centres of trade, industry and education and, lastly, the extraordinary difficulty in getting any correct information to them about what is happening outside the tight circle of the village, are big enough obstacles to the emergence in their midst of a fully conscious movement for the overthrow of tsarist tyranny and the establishment of better conditions in Russia.

But, if our peasantry cannot of its own accord produce from within its own ranks a coherent force of conscious fighters for its own interests, it might nonetheless become a significant revolutionary force under the energetic influence of the section of the exploiting strata that has found itself in circumstances more favourably disposed to the development within it of the capacity and ability for struggle with existing ways. We are talking of the working class in the industrial and commercial centres.

This class is, it is true, still too small in this country in comparison with the whole mass of the population for it to be able by itself in the near future to gain the strength enjoyed, for example, by the workers in England or even Germany and France. But, to make up for it, life in the heavily populated towns of Russia provides it with the opportunity to develop within itself those qualities that are necessary for it to become the conscious leader of the toiling masses of Russia in their struggle for their liberty and well-being. The concentration of workers from all four corners of Russia in great masses in a few places, in factories and plants, gives them the opportunity to inform one another about the life of the population throughout the Empire and eases their path towards a common agreement on the great needs of all working people and the methods of struggle to satisfy these needs. Close contact (by comparison with those who live in the country) with the highest authorities and their educated people and, lastly, easy access to newspapers and booklets – all this gives the urban workers the opportunity to find out the truth about the character of our government, about the customs prevailing in various countries and the paths that lead to general equality and true liberty for all mankind.

Only ten or twelve years have elapsed since the best part of our student youth went 'to the people' to propagate socialist doctrines.[39] In spite of every imaginable kind of government persecution, even in spite of the fact that the propagandists themselves thought that their activity among the urban workers was of very little importance when compared with revolutionary activity among the peasantry, and for this reason treated it far less seriously than it deserved, in spite of all this, our working class has already managed to demonstrate in this short time both its receptivity to the ideas of socialism and its ability to fight for them.

At the beginning of the 1870s there was only one stratum in this country – the 'intelligentsia' – that was composed of more or less educated people from among the propertied classes. The 'people', the 'workers', opposed it then as an undifferentiated mass of ignorant and backward people. Who would begin to deny that we have a *worker intelligentsia* in our country, consisting of several thousand people who consciously sympathise with the aspirations of the Russian revolutionaries and react to the most important social questions with the same interest as the mass of educated representatives of the upper and middle classes? Hundreds of worker Socialists languishing in exile, prison or hard labour, dozens of brave fighters from the working class appearing at various trials and many other phenomena from the life of that class over the last ten years demonstrate that it is capable of conducting serious propaganda in its midst. Let us recall, lastly, the remarkable fact that in the shape of the North Russian Workers' Union the working class was the *first* in this country to take up, even in *defiance* of the so-called revolutionary intelligentsia, the demands of political liberty. It came completely independently to the realisation that any improvement in the life of the lower classes was impossible without their acquiring political rights for themselves.[40]

These brief remarks on the achievements of socialist propaganda among the workers offer sufficiently convincing support for the view that the Russian working class is greatly disposed towards emerging as the conscious representative of the interests of the whole labouring mass of Russia. But, to ensure that it might in good time achieve this degree of significance in Russian life, the revolutionaries must undertake far more seriously and consistently the business of propaganda for socialism in their midst and of their merger into secret unions with clearly thought-out aims and methods of struggle.

This obligation lies above all and in the main with the *worker* intelligentsia and in particular with its most advanced and daring representatives. But, in order to fulfil this obligation adequately, [the worker intelligentsia] must itself be profoundly immersed in a consciousness of the *intimate link* between the well-being of the peasants and industrial workers and an understanding of the tasks of the working class as the leader of all the labouring strata in Russia. It must itself be imbued with the idea that the serious and tireless preparation of the working class for its great historical role constitutes one of the necessary conditions for protecting the labouring masses of Russia from making fatal mistakes and from the deceit and coercion of the exploiting classes.

Obviously, the first step in preparing the workers of the industrial centres for their emergence on the field of struggle with the enemies of the people's well-being must be for our worker intelligentsia to organise itself into an *independent* force. Instead of following in the tail of so-called intelligentsia circles, it must direct all its efforts, all its energy, to the formation of a single *independent workers'* union or *workers' party* in the full sense of this word. The sincere friends of the people's independent activity from the upper and middle classes will no doubt not stint their support for the efforts of the worker intelligentsia in this direction.

The more energetically it pursues this aim and the more boldly and tirelessly it strives to achieve it, the larger will be the number of revolutionaries from what we call the intelligentsia who will do it the honour of joining the workers' circles and acting on their behalf and in their name. An undoubted consequence of the activity of the worker intelligentsia will in the final analysis be that all sincere and conscious Socialists, whatever their name or origin, will enter a general workers' union; instead of the present revolutionary circles, each of which acts on behalf of the people and in the name of the people, a *single socialist workers'* party will be formed and, as in Germany at present, all true friends of the labouring classes of the population will join it.

The task of the 'Workers' Library' follows naturally from everything that has been mentioned above. It amounts principally to explaining to the worker intelligentsia its tasks and the conditions through which they can best be accomplished. With this aim it will acquaint the Russian workers:

1. With the concepts of human well-being, liberty and justice with which advanced workers and their scholarly representatives in the civilised countries are acquainted. These concepts are the fruit of many centuries of extremely difficult experience on the part of the most advanced nations and their acquaintance with them might save the working class of Russia from many extremely important errors.

2. As a necessary addition to this the 'Workers' Library' will publish booklets on the history of the formation of workers unions and parties in Europe and acquaint [its readers] with the present position and methods of activity of these unions.

3. Finally, it will explain, on the one hand, the position of the various strata of the working class and the indissoluble reciprocal link between their

interests, and, on the other hand, the ways and means that, in the view of the members of the Emancipation of Labour Group, might lead to the working class gaining enough strength for a successful struggle for its liberty and well-being.

The Editors: P. AKSELROD, G. PLEKHANOV.
Geneva, 15 September 1884.

6.   THE DEMANDS OF THE MOROZOV WORKERS[41]

By the common consent of us workers at the factory of Savva Morozov Co. and Son. Also, concerning our demand that the employer should pay back the fine levied on the workers (the weavers and spinners) since Easter 1884 and that he should take no more than 5% of every rouble of our earnings. Concerning the employer's desire to dismiss workers, he is obliged to keep to the agreement according to our record of it, i.e. no deductions before Easter, 23 March 1885.

Also by general consent we, the workers, have for several years wanted to raise the matter of our earnings during the years 1880, 1881 and 1882, when all of us workers were content with our earnings and had no claims at all on our employer; also, none of us workers in 1884 and 1885 had secure jobs so that we cannot support ourselves or our families and are unable to meet our obligations to our communes.

The workers demand:

1. According to the published state law the employer must not levy excessive fines which would be a burden on their workers. We, the workers, request and demand that the fines should not exceed 5% of our wages and that the worker should be warned about his bad work and should not be reported more than twice a month.

2. Deductions for absence from work should not exceed one rouble and the employer should also be obliged to pay the worker for absences that were the employer's responsibility, e.g. for time wasted because of warps, mechanical breakdowns and re-tooling for other work, etc., etc., so that every rest hour should be noted down in either the pay or wages book, and would be counted for earnings at not less than forty kopeks a day (40) or twenty kopeks a shift (20).

3. A complete transformation in the conditions of hire between the employer and the workers in accordance with the published state law, so that every worker may receive his full wages without any deductions or delays if the worker gives fifteen days' notice that he does not wish to continue working. Similarly, the

employer should have to give the worker fifteen days' notice of dismissal and all this would be recorded in the accounts book. If these conditions are not fulfilled by either side, two weeks' wages must be surrendered by either the worker or the employer.

4. [We demand that] high quality material, corresponding to the requirements of the work, should be certified by the men working nearby and recorded in the goods receipt book.

The record in the book of surplus measure in *arshins* is not to exceed the weight of the goods, increase the frequency of the reeds [in the loom] or the strength of the material. Until now no demand of this kind has been accepted from us. Newly designated work, not specified in the rates, would be done at the daily rate of pay until the workers eventually master the work and can state how much the material can be worked for. In the absence of a general agreement on rates, set by the office, state control must be instituted and this would even out the wages.

Complete reimbursement of the workers for absences from work since our strikes that were the employer's fault. A day off work is, at the worker's request, to be calculated at not less than 40 kopeks a day. Free distribution of food until the workers' demands have been met, without any account kept, because deductions for it have already been taken from us and a stamp has been put on every account to show (that the monies have been received in full).

Also, in future nothing must be held back, because our employer has kept our wages for the month of December. Wages should not be kept back after the 15th of the month or the first Saturday after the 15th. Free election of the elders in artels, and the elders must not be able to serve longer than three months and they should produce a monthly account so that they cannot misappropriate anything. Those employers and foremen whom the workers deem it necessary to sack should be sacked: they will be listed separately.

7. A DRAFT PROGRAMME FOR RUSSIAN SOCIAL DEMOCRATS, AND STATUTES OF THE FUND (1885)[42]

Blagoev Group

a. A draft programme for Russian Social Democrats

The unification of people into social forms has as its aim an increase in, and a development of, the material and moral forces of mankind.

The most complex and powerful social form is the *state*, i.e. a society having a political and economic organisation.

The state order in one or another form is always the embodiment of a certain moral principle but until now the state, thanks to the narrowness of these principles, has always served the interests of separate classes to the detriment of the people.

Contemporary government serves as an expression of the principle of individualism which requires, in politics, the freedom of the individual and, in the economic sphere, free competition.

Influenced by competition, the distribution of products under all political forms takes the wrong path: the mass of the working population is left with the minimum degree of satisfaction of its essential demands and the whole surplus is concentrated in the hands of the capitalist class.

But competition inevitably brings individualism to a renunciation of its very self: under its influence the working class is organised, through the socialisation of labour, into large units of production, as they are the most profitable, and through long suffering it comes to the idea of socialism — equality and brotherhood.

Socialism appears as the logical conclusion to the historical course of events. It demands the socialisation of labour and the equal distribution of products amongst everyone; this is attainable in full measure only through the expropriation of land and the tools of production (factories and plants) into state ownership, and through the organisation of labour on the foundations of collectivism. Only with these forms is it possible to achieve the full development of the forces of mankind, both material and moral.

But the process of the socialisation of labour under the power of capital is taking a slow and tortuous path and we must not wait idly until such time as the iron laws of competition organise the working class and set it against a small group of the capitalists of the time, when a complete and radical revolution in social relationships is possible.

We must direct our efforts towards accelerating and facilitating this process and prepare the way for the future accession of socialism, which is possible only through state intervention in economic relationships.

There is no chance of stopping the development of large-scale production and there would be no point in it. The aim of the government should consist in replacing individual capitalism by production associations of workers, both agricultural and industrial, retaining for itself the supreme right of ownership of land and the tools of production.

But for state power really to serve the people it must become the expression of the popular will and this can only be achieved by the granting of universal franchise without distinction of sex, nationality or confession.

With the abolition of serfdom the Russian state embarked on the same path of economic competition as Western Europe. Capitalism has already arisen here and is growing.

But, as Russia embarked on this path significantly later than Western states, it is difficult for her to compete with them in the struggle for the foreign market, while the home market is extremely limited due to the poverty of the population. The development of capitalism has met more obstacles here than anywhere else: the process of socialisation of labour under the banner of competition is moving along an even slower and more tortuous path than in the West.[43] Class relationships have been less clearly defined here, [class] interests have not been cast in sufficiently clear moulds, the peasant population is scattered across an enormous area and it is difficult to reach and organise, so that here state intervention seems even more necessary to facilitate the process of the formation of the new social order.

There is no reason whatsoever to count on a single revolution which would suddenly lead to the transfer of land and the tools of labour to the hands of the people.

The only possible path lies in gradual democratisation and the transfer of economic and political influence from the hands of the privileged classes to the hands of the people, which is only possible with its active collaboration through a whole series of popular movements that will fundamentally alter the power of the state and turn it to the people's advantage rather than to the advantage of a handful of privileged classes. Our programme is developed in accordance with this. We should indicate those demands that mark a logical approach to our ideal and, on the other hand, indicate the significance of all the elements of Russian life in the struggle for this ideal, and define our attitude towards them.

The fundamental requirements for the transition to the realisation of the socialist order are:

1. The abolition of private land ownership and the transfer of all land to state ownership; the transfer of factories and plants to workers' associations.
2. A fundamental reform in taxation — the replacement of all direct taxes by a progressive income tax.
3. The organisation of the political forms of the state on a federal basis.

4. Free elementary education. To realise these demands fully we must organise state power on democratic foundations and this can only be achieved in the following conditions:
5. Freedom of conscience, speech, the press, education and assembly.
6. The transfer of state power to a representative assembly whose members are elected through direct and universal franchise and the organisation along similar lines of local self-government.
7. The transformation of the standing army into a militia (home guard).

These are the tasks that we have set ourselves for the time when our popular revolutionary forces are mature. But even in the preparatory period, during the period of maturation, these forces cannot remain silent. They will inevitably announce themselves in one or another form of active protest; they will exert pressure on the government before they are in a position to overthrow it altogether. As a result of this pressure there will be various concessions from the government along the lines of the demands stated, but these will have to be supplemented by yet more demands that will have essential meaning for this preparatory period and will serve as the best subject for agitation, as the most easily attainable and obvious demands. To these belong:

1. A guarantee of individual inviolability from the arbitrary rule of government and the jurisdiction of the general court of jurors over political offences.
2. The calling of an assembly [*Zemskii sobor*] [44] with real representation of the peasants and workers.
3. The broadening of local self-government and the abolition of the property qualification.
4. The equalisation of the rights of subject nationalities with those of the predominating people.
5. The wider use of state credit for peasants' societies and workers' associations for use in the purchase of land, factories and plants.
6. The arrangement of cheap government credit to satisfy the current demands and needs of the national economy.
7. State control of the railways and waterways.
8. State regulation of the market, i.e. the arrangement of stores for grain and for the products of cottage industry.
9. State organisation of resettlement and seasonal employment.
10. The lowering of the payments levied on the people's labour and their transfer to land and industrial capital.
11. The shortening of the period of military service.

At the present time revolutionary elements already exist amid the Russian people — the landless proletariat. Thanks to the progressive development of the *kulak* class and of capitalism the proletariat will inevitably grow and multiply; on the other hand the obstacles to the development of Russian industry, limiting [the proletariat's] sphere of activity, will provoke constant unrest in its midst. It is impossible to predict the forms that this popular movement will adopt but our task is to regulate as far as is possible the path of the revolution, to direct its material strength through the combination of a peasants' revolution with the political movement of the workers and the intelligentsia in the centres.

The large mass of the population in this country consists of the peasantry. In its midst there exists a view of land as the property of the state (divine and royal land) [*zemlya bozhya da tsarskaya*] and there is an agrarian movement which fights private land ownership. The general aim of our work in this context should consist in bringing light and understanding to the social movement of the people, in showing them the most reasonable and practicable formulations of the demands that they should present to the government and the paths that the struggle should follow.

Rejecting the possibility of a broad fighting organisation in the peasant sphere, we see as our immediate task the consolidation of the link between the intelligentsia of socialism and the people. This is only possible through the organisation of local groups from the intelligentsia and workers who have been prepared for this in the cities with the aim of attracting to them the most suitable elements of the peasantry and of putting autonomous popular propaganda on its feet. In individual cases of peasant disturbances or agrarian terror the initiative should rest with the population itself; our task is merely to point to the best methods and to the possible consequences, to cooperate in the realisation of an already existing desire, when it is just and for this reason has some educational significance.

Among urban workers, communicating the same ideas as among the peasantry, we should pay particular attention to their political education, because they represent the most suitable element [of the population] for this [education]. That section of the workers which returns to the countryside, adequately prepared and supplied with suitable literature, will serve as the best purveyor of revolutionary ideas and political progress to the peasant sphere. But those workers who remain in the centres should serve as the nucleus for the political strength of the people. The atmosphere of political interest created in their midst will serve them as a necessary school of political education. But their active participation in the field of the political struggle is not desirable before similar workers' groups have been prepared in all the large centres, before they constitute a significant force; otherwise all their separate attempts will easily be suppressed and will lead to demoralisation and to the unproductive waste of resources. So, in the case of separate disturbances among the working population, and also in the case of strikes, displays of terror in the factories, etc., we shall behave as in similar occurrences in the peasant sphere.

Propaganda among the soldiers in the army is possible only to a limited extent by infiltrating into their midst prepared workers and by the influence of officers on individual soldiers. But we should pay great attention to the officers themselves because, by their moral influence and power, even without preparatory propaganda, they will exert pressure in the desired direction at the moment of action.

Among the privileged classes and the intelligentsia our attention should be directed towards the propagation of our ideas and the attraction of new forces. We cannot concentrate our forces together in one place but we shall try to organise them into local provincial and urban central groups. These groups should make arrangements between themselves on such matters as mutual support, the exchange of information and publication. To make such relationships easier – the regularisation of free financial resources, the direction of people into the desired and accessible places, the editing of the leading organ – there must be a known centre with representatives from the local groups. But it should not have compulsory power; its function is only distributive, local groups preserving complete autonomy.

There remains our relationship towards existing tendencies and programmes.

Recognising the desirability and utility of the demands of the liberals with regard to the limitation of all forms of governmental tyranny, we reject the other side of the liberal constitution, the protection of the owning classes at the expense of the people. Central seizure of power, from our point of view, can only have real significance if it marks the culmination of the revolution of the whole people of the peasants and workers, but not if it ends in a preliminary conspiracy with the military or some other [force].

As far as political terror as a system of forcing concessions from the government is concerned, we must say that, in present circumstances – in the absence of a strong workers' organisation powerful enough to give immediate support to the effects of a terrorist act – we do not recognise the utility of terror in that sense and will practise it only in the following cases:

1. When the population itself selects victims from the administration.
2. When the victims are selected by the party from the ranks of the highest administration and when their death cannot stir up public opinion and popular discontent against us.
3. In cases of self-defence against spies.

b. The statutes of the fund

Having set as our immediate task the unification of the largest possible number of workers into a single 'workers' party', which would be able to transform the existing order of things in favour of the working class, we think that the success of the cause will only be assured when the workers are strong both materially and through the knowledge and consciousness of [their] moral unity. Without these three conditions the struggle for a better future would be, if not completely impossible, in any event extremely difficult. Everyone who strives for a better future for the whole people, and not just for himself personally, may surrender himself to the cause of popular liberation in the full consciousness of its justice and with unlimited devotion to it only when he knows in full the falsehood upon which the contemporary order rests and those prejudices that illuminate this falsehood: when at last he can clearly perceive, albeit only in its principal features, how the contemporary conditions of the life of the people should be altered, how [those conditions] influence [that life] and how much easier life would [then] be for the people. Yes, he should perceive this clearly, should have faith in the possibility of the realisation of this great task and devote his whole life to the struggle for it. Belief in the justice of this task and labour on its behalf on the part of every honest man should join everyone together, compelling them to support one another in the difficult struggle. It should be easier for each one of you to sacrifice yourself when you know that you are not alone, that your comrades will always support you, when you know that your family will not be left without food and shelter, that among your comrades it will always find kindness, comfort and support. Only when someone understands that will he stand so far morally and intellectually above those who surround him that he will be in a position to influence them, to attract the best of them into the ranks of those fighting for the truth, and to facilitate their unification into a single popular party. Of course moral influence alone counts for little: much has to be done before our aim is achieved. We must devote a great deal of effort to detailed preparatory work. [We must] find those few conscientious people who wander about in isolation and unite them[we must] arrange study circles with the workers, in which they could be moulded into active members of the people's party; we must organise libraries and procure material assistance for the cause. These are the tasks to which we should devote the major part of our time and energy before we can create from all this a powerful popular party which will be capable of openly shaking the foundations of the contemporary order and of founding a new one.

Let every one of us do everything in his power for the cause of the people; let every one of us try to work himself and not leave the work to others.

The funds are one of the means with which the realisation of the task of the unification of the workers should begin. Let us set out a programme for them.

The funds which are now being established should have a circle character and only through their great development and through the close connection between the different circles should all these funds be merged into a single general fund — the 'fund of the workers' party'.

The principal aims of the fund:

1.[45] Aid to people who have suffered for the cause and to their families.
2.[45] An allowance for people who have commended themselves by their useful activity for the cause in the event that they be put out of work.
3.   An allowance for people who rent flats in which [party] activities or other meetings have to be held.
4.   The organisation of stores of leaflets.
5.   The provision of funds for travel, and recompense for people who do not go out to work if the cause requires this.

The resources of the fund are received:

1. From a once-for-all levy of 1 rouble made on each member when he joins.

2. From the monthly membership fees which should be not less than 30 kopeks.
3. From irregular income, donations, lotteries, etc.

The resources of the fund are distributed in the following manner:

first, to meet running expenses,

second, part is set aside for reserve capital which is given to the savings fund and,

third, to support the 'Basic Fund'.

If expenses cannot be met from the resources of the fund that discrepancy is made up from the 'Basic Fund'. As the fund is not a charitable institution, whose programme involves the paying out of funds to its members at a certain rate of interest but should serve as one of the means of uniting the workers for the struggle for a better future, only those who are striving for the alteration of the contemporary order may be members of the circle; for this reason entry into the fund requires the recommendation of at least three people. On leaving the fund, for whatever reason, nobody may ask for a refund of their contributions because they are intended to support the cause of the emancipation of the people. The monies entering the fund are given to the treasurer. As everything here is based on trust the treasurer must be someone who is elected unanimously. As the fund develops, when there are many members and the sum of contributions increases, two treasurers must be elected. The treasurers are elected for a set period (for a half-year) and are changed at the wish of the membership. The members of the fund, in turn and two at a time, audit the accounts every week. There should be meetings of the [members of the] fund every month to receive a report from the treasurer. At these meetings the estimates of expenses for the following month and the residue from the previous month are divided into two parts as described above. Matters are resolved by majority vote. With larger numbers the membership is divided into circles which are related [to the centre] through their representatives; in every such circle fund there should be approximately ten people.

8.   SECOND DRAFT PROGRAMME OF THE RUSSIAN SOCIAL DEMOCRATS (1885)[46]

G.V. Plekhanov

The Russian Social Democrats, like the Social Democrats in other countries, aim at the complete emancipation of labour from the yoke of capital. This emancipation can be achieved by the transfer to social ownership of all the means and objects of production, a transfer which will entail:

a. the abolition of the present commodity production (i.e. the purchase and sale of products on the market) and

b. its replacement by a new system of social production according to a previously drawn-up plan with a view to satisfying both all the requirements of society as a whole and of each one of its members within the limits permitted by the condition of the productive forces at the given time.

This communist revolution will give rise to the most radical changes in the whole constitution of social and international relationships.

Replacing the present mastery of the product over the producer by that of the producer over the product, it will introduce consciousness where there now reigns blind economic necessity; by simplifying and giving purpose to all social relationships it will at the same time provide each citizen with the real economic opportunity for participating directly in the discussion and resolution of all social matters.

This direct participation of each citizen in the management of social affairs presupposes the abolition of the present system of political representation and its replacement by direct popular legislation.

Moreover, the international character of the impending economic revolution may now already be foreseen. Given the present development of international exchange, it is possible to consolidate this revolution only by the participation in it of all or at least several civilised societies. Hence follows the solidarity of interests between producers of all countries, already recognised and proclaimed by the International Working Men's Association.[47]

But as the emancipation of the workers must be a matter for the workers themselves, as the interests of labour in general are diametrically opposed to the interests of the exploiters, and as, therefore, the higher classes will always hinder the above described reorganisation of social relationships, the necessary preliminary condition for this reorganisation is the seizure of political power by the working class in each of the countries concerned. Only this temporary domination of the working class can paralyse the efforts of counter-revolution and put an end to the existence of classes and their struggle.

This political task introduces an element of variety into the programmes of the Social Democrats in the different states, in accordance with the social conditions in each of them individually.

The practical tasks and, consequently, the programmes of the Social Democrats are bound, of course, to be more complex in countries where modern capitalist production is still only striving for dominance and where the working masses are oppressed by a double yoke — that of rising capitalism and that of obsolescent patriarchal economy. In these countries the Social Democrats must, as a transitional stage, strive for the forms of social organisation that already exist in the advanced countries and that are necessary for the further development of the workers' party. Russia is in precisely such a position. Capitalism has achieved enormous success there since the abolition of serfdom. The old system of natural economy is giving way to commodity production and thereby opening up an enormous home market for large-scale industry. The patriarchal communal forms of peasant land tenure are rapidly disintegrating, the village commune is being transformed into a simple medium for the enslavement of the peasant population to the state and in many localities it serves also as an instrument for the exploitation of the poor by the rich. At the same time, in binding the interests of an enormous section of the producers to the land, it hinders their intellectual and political development by limiting their outlook to the narrow bounds of village traditions. The Russian revolutionary movement, whose victory would first and foremost serve the interests of the peasants, receives almost no support, sympathy or understanding from them. The main bulwark of absolutism is precisely the political indifference and intellectual backwardness of the peasantry. An inevitable consequence of this is the powerlessness and timidity of those educated strata of the upper classes whose material, intellectual and moral interests are incompatible with the present political system. Raising their voice in the name of the people, they are astonished to see the people indifferent to their appeals; hence the instability of our intelligentsia's political outlook and their occasional despondency and complete disillusionment.

This state of affairs would be absolutely hopeless if the above-mentioned movement of Russian economic relations had not created new chances of success for those defending the interests of the working people. The disintegration of the village commune is creating in our country a new class of industrial proletariat. Being more receptive, mobile and advanced, this class responds to the appeal of the revolutionaries more readily than the backward peasant population. Whereas the ideal of the village commune member lies in the past, under conditions of patriarchal economy, the complement of which was tsarist autocracy, the lot of the industrial worker can be improved only thanks to the development of the more modern and free forms of communal life. With this class our people achieve for the first time the economic conditions that are common to all civilised peoples and hence it is only through the agency of this class that the people can take part in the progressive efforts of civilised mankind. On these grounds the Russian Social Democrats consider their primary and principal duty to be the formation of a revolutionary workers' party. The growth and development of such a party, however, will find a very powerful obstacle in modern Russian absolutism.

That is why the struggle against absolutism is obligatory even for those working class groups that are now the embryo of the future Russian workers' party. The overthrow of absolutism must be the first of their political tasks.

The principal means for the political struggle of the workers' groups against absolutism, in the opinion of the Russian Social Democrats, is agitation among the working class and the further spread of socialist ideas and revolutionary organisations among that class. Closely bound together in a single harmonic whole, these organisations, not content with frequent clashes with the government, will not delay in passing, at the appropriate time, to general and resolute attacks upon it and in this they will not stop even at so-called acts of terrorism if that proves to be necessary in the interests of the struggle.

The aim of the struggle of the workers' party against absolutism is to win a democratic constitution which will guarantee:

1. The right to vote and be elected to the Legislative Assembly as well as to the provincial and village self-government bodies, for every citizen who has not been sentenced by court to deprivation of his political rights for certain shameful activities strictly specified by law.
2. A money payment fixed by law for the representatives of the people, which will allow them to be elected from the poorest classes of the population.
3. Universal, civil, free and compulsory education, the state being obliged to provide poor children with food, clothing and school requisites.
4. Inviolability of the person and the home of citizens.
5. Unlimited freedom of conscience, speech, press, assembly and association.
6. Freedom of movement and of employment.
7. Complete equality for all citizens, irrespective of religion and racial origin.
8. The replacement of the standing army by the general arming of the people.
9. A revision of all our civil and criminal legislation, the abolition of division according to estates and of punishments incompatible with human dignity.

Basing itself on these fundamental political demands, the workers' party puts forward a number of immediate economic demands, such as:

1. Radical revision of our agrarian relations, i.e. the conditions for the redemption of land and its distribution to peasant communes. The right to renounce allotments and to leave the village communes for those peasants who find this convenient for themselves, etc.
2. The abolition of the present system of dues and the institution of a progressive taxation system.
3. Legislative regulation of relations between workers (in town and country) and employers, and the organisation of the appropriate inspection with representation of the workers.
4. State assistance for production associations organised in all possible branches of agriculture, the mining and manufacturing industries (by peasants, miners, factory and plant workers, craftsmen, etc.).

These demands are as favourable to the interests of the peasants as they are to those of the industrial workers; for this reason, by achieving their implementation, the workers' party will open up the broad path of reconciliation with the agrarian population. Thrown out of the village as an impoverished member of the commune, the proletarian will return to it as a social democratic agitator. His appearance in this role will transform the present hopeless lot of the commune. The disintegration of the latter is inevitable only until such time as this very disintegration gives rise to a new popular force that is powerful enough to put an end to the reign of capitalism. The working class and the poorest part of the peasantry, drawn along in its wake, constitute a force of this kind.

Note. As is seen from above, the Russian Social Democrats presume that the work of the intelligentsia, particularly under present-day conditions of social and political struggle, must be aimed first at the most developed part of the working population, which consists of the industrial workers. Having secured the powerful support of this section, the Social Democrats may have far greater hope of success in extending their action to the peasantry, especially when they have won freedom of agitation and propaganda. Incidentally, it goes without saying that, even at present, people who are in direct touch with the peasantry could, by their work among them, render an important service to the socialist movement in Russia. The Social Democrats, far from rejecting such people, will exert all their efforts to agree with them on the basic principles and methods of their work.

9.   FOUR SPEECHES BY PETERSBURG WORKERS (1 MAY 1891)[48]

a. First speech

Comrades!

This day should remain indelibly printed on all our minds. It is only today that we have been able to assemble for the first time from all corners of Petersburg for this modest gathering and to hear for the first time from our comrade workers an impassioned speech calling us to the struggle with our powerful political and economic enemies. Yes, comrades, seeing an enemy like that and now knowing where his strength lies, seeing our own small handful of people who take this struggle upon themselves, a few of our number cannot trust in the achievement of our victory: they leave our ranks in despair and cowardice. No, comrades, we should trust firmly in our victory. We need only arm ourselves with a powerful weapon — and this weapon is the knowledge of the historical laws of the development of mankind — we have only to arm ourselves with this and we shall defeat the enemy everywhere. None of his acts of oppression – sending us back to our birthplaces, imprisoning us or even exiling us to Siberia – will take this weapon away from us. We shall find the field of victory everywhere, we shall transmit our knowledge in all directions: in our birthplaces to our peasants, in prison to the men detained there we shall explain that they too are human beings and are entitled to all human rights, so that they will recognise these rights, transmit their knowledge to others and organise them into groups.

This is the guarantee of our success!

Yes, comrades, we often have occasion to read, or even hear, about workers' demonstrations in the West which move in enormous, orderly columns through the cities and fill their exploiters with fear; but we should look at the history of the development of this orderly mass and then it will become clear to us that this mass originated with a small group of people like ourselves. Let us look, albeit fleetingly, at the historical development of the Social Democratic Party in Germany,[49] the strongest and most orderly organisation in the West. It also originated with a small handful of people grouped in a single centre of production, like our Petersburg. These workers first recognised their human rights and began to communicate their beliefs to other workers; for this the government started to persecute them and send them into the countryside. But even this dispersal acted to the workers' advantage. These workers found comrades and, by organising them together, formed a single, indivisible union. What of us, Russian workers, who despair and flee from these fighting comrades who are involved in a cause as great as the cause of the liberation of the people? Having regard to all the historical facts, which compel us to trust boldly in victory, we should think of our Russian people in the same light. They will bear the burdens piled upon them until they recognise that they have human rights and that he, the worker, above all should have the right to enjoy all the wealth produced by his labour. Our worker should also know that labour *is the motor of all human progress, that it is the creator of all science, art and inventions.* It is only when the people are conscious of all this that no army will be able to restrain them from their self-liberation, and to bring such consciousness to the people is the immediate, inalienable right of all advanced workers. This was demonstrated to us by the struggle of our intelligentsia in the 70s and 80s. Look, comrades, at this struggle from a historical point of view, at how these friends of and warriors for the people brought all their knowledge to the people, often even sacrificing their lives, and justified themselves before history and did not just remain indebted to the people. Everywhere they responded to the people's complaints and gave a helping hand but the people did not recognise them as friends and regarded them with distrust. Now we, comrades, must carry our modest knowledge to the people: can we not transmit it to the people and won't they understand us now because we, as an intelligentsia, stand closer to them? There's only one pity, comrades, and that is that we, *unlike the workers in the past, will get no help from anywhere,* except from a small handful of people to whom we shall always be profoundly grateful. Present-day youth does not hear the complaints of the people and does not see their grief — it does not even think about the people. This youth is nothing more than a parasitic element in society: they are capable only of destroying the products of common labour and they do not think of paying the people for their labours.

b. Second speech

It is a great pity, comrades, that for the foreseeable future we must come to terms with the impossibility of gathering and spending the First of May together, as the workers in Western countries do, and must be satisfied with the chance to assemble on a Sunday. Every one of us knows, of course, that now we can have no demonstrations at all, and not just ones like those held by the workers in the West. I think that now every one of us automatically compares our strength with that of the Western workers; but I dare to hope that none of us, bearing in mind our small numbers, will fall into despair as a result of this comparison, because we all still have sufficient strength and energy for our spirits not to sink and our hands not to droop merely because the work is only just beginning.

Western workers suffer, as we do, under the yoke of the capitalist system, i.e. the system by which all the products of the workers' labour are sold by the factory owner for his own profit and he pays the workers for their labour only enough to prevent them from starving to death. Dissatisfied with such a shocking system, which deprives them of the benefits of their labour, they have often pondered over the situation in which they find themselves and they have come to the conclusion that the only possible way out is through the intellectual development of the people, because everything depends upon their development.

Having reached this conclusion they have not rested solely on their words but are attempting to develop and organise themselves and others into a tightly knit organisation and within this they have a fund [*kassa*] ; with its monies they distribute books and publish journals and newspapers through which they transmit their ideas: they try to support strikes, although they do not consider them to be the principal method of destroying evil because, even assuming a favourable outcome, they can only marginally improve the position of the workers and cannot emancipate them from the yoke of capital. Gradually growing in strength, thanks to their energetic activity, they have from time to time made both society and government feel their strength by various means; they have proclaimed their demands and the government has been forced to meet some of them. For instance, it has granted a constitution, freedom of the press, freedom of assembly and organisation and similar rights which have made it much easier for them to begin the struggle against the existing economic order.

One of the means by which they wished to make their strength felt, and at the same time make known one of their important demands, was the vast demonstration on 1st May. At this demonstration they demanded the establishment by law of the eight-hour day. A comparison of the demonstration last year with that this year makes it clear that their strength has grown and this gives rise to the hope that in the not too distant future we shall see the better and just order for which they are striving.

If we turn our attention to the plight of our own workers we see that they too suffer severely from the arbitrary exploitation of the kulaks, which is almost unrestrained because our workers, due to the efforts of the government and the factory owners, find themselves in a down-trodden condition and in complete ignorance and cannot offer any resistance to this arbitrary extortion: and this causes even more brazen behaviour on the part of the pitiless vultures.

This situation does not, of course, please any of the workers; but they remain silent and suffer because they can see no way out, and so the responsibility falls to us, as the more advanced workers, of explaining to the workers the causes of their wretched condition and of pointing to a way out of them.

It is to our credit, I may say, that we have really recognised our responsibilities and, regardless of all the obstacles and threats from our vile government, we are trying, in accordance with our strength and our capabilities, to advance the workers around us . . . Hence recently, with a sincere feeling of gratitude towards Shelgunov as the man 'who had pointed the way to freedom and brotherhood', we attempted, by presenting an address to him and by attending his funeral with a wreath, to draw the attention of society to the workers' question and, as you know, we succeeded in this.[50] But it is clear that our attempt and its success did not please the government and it gave orders for the punishment of the workers who had dared to contemplate an improvement in their living conditions, sending three of them to little country towns.

As you know, at the slightest appearance of dissatisfaction with the current outrages it always exiles and imprisons workers and the intellectuals who are genuinely striving (and for this we are eternally grateful to them) with all their strength and knowledge to help the workers in their struggle with the existing plunderous order. But I trust, comrades, that these measures on the government's part will not frighten any of us, but will only evoke a greater hatred both for it and for the existing order that it protects and a stronger desire to achieve as quickly as possible a situation in which there are neither rich nor poor but where everyone enjoys happiness and satisfaction in equal measure.

In this way, comrades, by advancing and supporting one another, we shall continue the struggle that has begun against the existing evil and for the realisation of *Freedom, Truth and Brotherhood*!

2. Third speech

Comrades!

If we look at our situation we see that all our sufferings stem from the existing economic order.

Consequently, to improve our situation we must strive for the replacement of the existing economic order, which gives full rein to arbitrary exploitation by the kulaks, by a better and more just socialist order.

But in order to realise such an economic order in practice we must obtain the political rights that we do not have at the moment. We shall only be in a position to gain these political rights when there is an organised force on our side whose demands the government would be unable to reject and which would insistently demand the following concessions from it: first, the promulgation of a constitution, based on general and direct franchise, i.e. where all the laws of the country are approved and amended, not by the savage tyranny of the tsar, but by discussion in a supreme legislative assembly in which deputies elected by the people would sit.

Elections to the legislative assembly should be carried out by the people and every citizen of the country, apart from those sentenced for dishonest behaviour, should be able to elect, and be elected as, a deputy to the legislative assembly. The expenses for these deputies should come from the state and should be paid to them in the form of a salary. This is necessary so that deputies do not have to be rich men but men who are devoted to the cause of the people and who are fully equipped for it.

Second, it is necessary that the number of men in the army should be determined by the assembly of deputies and that the army may at any time be disbanded on its orders. So that the soldiers should not forget that they are also of the people and that their interests are identical with those of the people, the period of military service should be made as short as possible and arranged so that citizens spend it in their birthplace and, while they are there, have a chance to establish close contacts with their family. Then the soldier, conscious of his solidarity with the people, will never resolve to move against them. This is essential if the government is not to have the means of compelling citizens by force of arms to obey laws which have not been approved, or which have been amended by the assembly of deputies.

Third, the freedom of electoral campaigning, freedom of the spoken word and freedom of the press, i.e. the complete absence of any form of censorship so that everyone may express his convictions by spoken or by written word and also there should be no deposits for the publication of books and journals; this is necessary so that the workers too should have the opportunity of publishing them.

Fourth, freedom of assembly and organisation.

Fifth, freedom of religion.

Sixth, free elementary education for the people.

Seventh, all forms of crime should be tried by jury.

Comrades, do not forget these demands because they are the first and most important that we should present to the government at the earliest opportunity and because only then shall we be able to have everything that is set out in these demands!

Once we possess such rights we can then elect deputies to the legislative assembly who will draft and approve only those laws which will be to the benefit of the majority of the people and reject laws which exist to their detriment. In this way we shall have an opportunity to transform the whole of the existing economic order into a better and more just one.

I shall not unravel before you a picture of this better and more just order because, however good it is, nobody can guarantee that with the passage of time someone will not think up a better one and also because you can acquaint yourselves with it fully by reading Schäffle's *The Quintessence of Socialism* or Bellamy's novel *Looking Backward*.

A transitional stage towards the future economic order could comprise: the nationalisation of land, i.e. the state should buy up all land in public ownership and let it to people who wish to engage in agricultural activity in lots that they could work with their own labour. To acquire the farms necessary for agriculture and to build the factories and plants for the workers who want to work on an *artel* basis a bank must be established which will give funds to the workers who need them.

In this manner, by improving their position gradually, the workers will have an opportunity to reach a state of well-being that at the moment only the most advanced of them can contemplate.

From all that I have said we see that, in order to have the opportunity of achieving a full and bright future, we must first of all form an organised force from the workers, consciously striving for the improvement of their lot, that could compel the government to concede it political rights; it is only when we have these that we shall have the opportunity of undertaking a transformation of the existing economic order.

Consequently at the present time there only remains to us the possibility of busying ourselves with the advancement and organisation of the workers, a possibility that I hope we shall use regardless of any obstacles and threats made by our government. So that our activity should bear as much fruit as possible we should try as best we can to improve ourselves and others both mentally and morally and to act more energetically so that the people around us look upon us as intelligent, honourable and brave people and therefore regard us with greater trust and set us up as an example to themselves and others.

Consequently, the success of the advancement and organisation of the workers depends exclusively on our knowledge and our energy, and therefore, comrades, it is our duty, as honourable and intelligent people, to prepare ourselves and [other] suitable people as experienced propagandists and organisers for the social democratic cause and as energetic fighters for the rights of man and for a bright future.

d. Fourth speech

Comrades!

I should like to say a few words on this, for us triumphal, day, organised, after the example of our brothers, the Western workers.

Brothers, we shall enjoy this first bright moment of our spiritual delight to have appeared on the horizon of our Russian life. Our Western brothers have long enjoyed the holidays which we are just beginning to use to express our spiritual sympathy, and even now not on a legal basis; but this, too, is good, comrades. It is good that we too are beginning to awaken from our centuries of slumber under the yoke of lordly, priestly and tsarist slavery; we are beginning, I say, to awaken and this is the contribution of the Russian workers to general progress. Certainly, comrades, nothing is done straight away in the world but everything happens in accordance with the definite laws of nature. And human genius cannot embrace everything at once, cannot foresee everything, but it gradually becomes conscious of the sacred truth. It falls to it to share the most difficult task in the whole history of human life – to awaken consciousness in humanity itself and move it along the path of true progress and happiness. Of course, comrades, this happiness is never achieved easily but costs humanity itself a great deal. We see the same thing in the case of our brothers, the Western workers. They already have strength and freedom: this is already a particle of happiness. But this particle was obtained by them at the high cost of their own human blood. They fought a long time for the particle of happiness that they now enjoy. They fought for many decades with weapons in their hands for freedom, truth, equality and brotherhood. Now, comrades, we see that their demands have already been accepted by law, such as strikes, funds, cooperatives, unions, libraries and other social institutions. But here there is nothing, because we have not exerted ourselves for these things. Here, as you yourselves know, every declaration on the people's rights is counted as rebellion! There are only cries, the bayonet, the birch, Siberia, prison, hard labour and, of course, the Cossack whips! But there in the West our brother workers are already enjoying full political rights. We are serfs, slaves. We have to doff our caps to the meanest policeman. But there they are all free and equal citizens, in England, France, Germany, Belgium and in all other European states. We can judge their strength by last year's elections to the German parliament: the workers gave their leaders around one and a half million votes in an electorate of seven millions – i.e. one fifth of the whole people, the state, are on the workers' side, under their direction. As a result they have 104 newspapers of their own with six hundred thousand (600,000) subscribers, and their general fund in 1880 had 37,000 marks, in 1883, 95,000, in 1887 it already had 188,000, and last year it had even risen to 390,000 marks! You see, comrades, how quickly they have grown and how strong they have become. They have made themselves into an organised party, a force which neither their exploiters nor the government itself with its army can fight. That, comrades, is how their strength has grown since 1848, since the day when the cry was heard: 'Workers of all countries, unite!' Yes, comrades, these great words belong to the cause of human intelligence. Human intelligence, the sower of this sacred truth, planted its seed around almost the entire globe and in our forgotten Russia in the 60s and 70s, at first mainly in the ranks of young students, our best friends, and through them it filters through, then as now, to us.

Gentlemen, as we see, this little transplanted seedling is growing, ripening and spreading its shoots through the whole Russian land. It is growing but it has terrible enemies in the shape of kulaks, priests, nobles and the tsar with his army and police. It is hard to carry on the struggle. Tens of thousands of young men have already perished for us in the snows of Siberia and the casemates of St Peter and St Paul and Schlüsselburg.[51] Let us start to fight for ourselves: we shall not find it easy to begin with. Our every step, our every act threatens us with imprisonment or exile, but what can we do, comrades? We have no alternative if it is a matter of life and death. We must think of our present position in which we are condemned to vegetate by our exploiters and rulers.

Comrades, you yourselves see that here in all corners of Russia there reigns fearful economic deprivation amongst both industrial and agricultural workers. The only thing that can be heard is a single wailing groan.

'Here this groan is called a song!' says Nekrasov. Indeed, everywhere there is deprivation, hunger, arbitrary police rule (and this is not the worst of it: they are now making nobles into land captains to make things even worse), destitution, illness, premature death, amongst us, our wives and children. They suck our blood like leeches, they turn us into a different kind of person, pale, greenish, sickly, but what is all this done for? It is done so that a handful of factory owners, landowners, bureaucrats and even the tsar can live in luxury, drunkenness and depravity! So in the name of these bestial lusts they have fettered the whole people, a hundred million, in shameful, servile, slavish chains that don't give us a chance to stand, to speak or to breathe.

Comrades, brothers! Are we really not human, have they reduced us utterly to a state of slavery, with a complete degradation of our human dignity? And they tell us that that is how it has to be. All our lives they tyrannise us and do not give us a chance to see beyond our unjust social life; for how many centuries have they been feeding us with the idea of patience and hope for the Kingdom of God so that they could live in peace and drink our blood! No, it is bad to believe in these fairy tales. Our consciousness tells us that we are also human. But we are still slaves of the Russian tsar with no rights and bearing the mark of shame. So, comrades, let us wash off this servile mark of shame! Then we shall gain for ourselves rights that we should enjoy in the name of our human dignity so that we can live like people, think, speak, assemble and discuss our public affairs without any obstacles being placed in our way, such as spies of the vile police.

Comrades, it will be difficult for us in the first stages to take up the struggle with our enemies for our economic and political rights, but let us remember that even now at this very moment thousands of intellectuals are languishing on our behalf in Siberia, sentenced to prison or hard labour. Let us remember that our brothers, the Western workers, did not find it easy to improve their position, just as it will not be easy for us to improve ours in the face of despotic reaction, which will pursue us at every step. Comrades, it will be difficult for us, but science has liberated the Western workers, it will help us to enlighten ourselves and to fill our souls with the sacred truth of love for one another. Let us, comrades, fight for truth, not retreating until our death agony, for truth, equality, brotherhood and freedom! Let us study, join together, ourselves and our comrades, let us organise ourselves into a strong party! Let us, brothers, sow this great seed from sunrise till sunset in all four corners of the Russian land.

10. REPORT [TO THE INTERNATIONAL] BY THE EDITORIAL BOARD OF THE JOURNAL *SOTSIAL-DEMOKRAT* (AUGUST 1891)[52]

G. V. Plekhanov and V. Zasulich

Citizens!

The Russian Social Democrats are not represented at the International Congress of Social Democracy this year.

Their absence will not cause you any practical difficulties: our voice can have no great significance in your decisions or, rather, it would have had *no weight at all*. Nevertheless we think it would be useful to put before you the reasons for our abstention.

Citizens, those of you who have the time and the will to read these pages will have the opportunity of receiving a report on the actual position of the Russian revolutionary movement that a decade ago caused such an uproar throughout the whole civilised world.[53]

We shall speak openly, without undue mercy, without resonant phrases. To conceal anything would be harmful to our movement and unworthy of you, the representatives of world social democracy.

Our *duty* to tell you the truth is a duty that we can carry out all the more easily as our present position is far from grievous. On the contrary, it is only now that we can perceive in the economic life of Russia the phenomena that may serve as a serious basis for the hopes of all those who oppose the existing order.

Our political situation is, as you know, distinguished by a terrible governmental despotism, which is almost unparalleled in history – a despotism that combines the worst aspects of the sad memory of Western absolutism with all the horrors of Oriental despotism. Russian tsarism depends at one and the same time on the discoveries of European science and on the Asiatic ignorance of the peasants. It exploits science to organise its resources more effectively, it exploits the ignorance of the peasants, regarding itself as the government that most closely corresponds to the *national spirit* of the Russian people.

We can easily see that this notorious national spirit is only an absurd piece of sophistry thought up by a government that can find nothing better to justify its existence. There is no point in arguing that no people could have an organic predisposition towards the sort of shameful and wretched existence that is the lot of all the subjects of His Imperial Majesty. The Russian people have never had this predisposition. What the government calls the national *spirit* of the people was only this spirit's *failure to develop*, caused by the economic backwardness of Russia.

This economic backwardness is seen as a very sympathetic manifestation of our national spirit. Both our Slavophile reactionaries and our Bakuninist revolutionaries praised it with one voice. With equal diligence they both contrasted it to the 'bour-geois' development of the West. Russia had been delivered from the bourgeoisie, from the proletariat, from class antagonism and class struggle, so they both main-tained. Consequently, the social revolution that threatens Europe is impossible in Russia, said the reactionaries. Consequently, socialism cannot triumph here today or tomorrow, asserted the Bakuninists. This was the only point of difference in the theory of the two parties.

I do not have to prove to you, the representatives of the revolutionary prolet-ariat, the revolutionary role that has fallen to the lot of the contemporary prolet-ariat in history. In just the same way I also do not have to prove to you that where there is no proletariat there can be no socialist movement worthy of the name. You all know very well that contemporary socialism is only the 'theoretical expression of the proletarian movement', as F. Engels says.[54] Where there is no proletariat, there is no basis for socialism.

If we do have to prove our assertions, it will be for a completely different reason. It may surprise you that a similar doctrine, that of *socialism without a proletariat*, could nowadays find adherents among the revolutionaries of any country.

But this fact will not seem improbable if you recall that these strange theories are closely connected with the propaganda of Bakunin. You are probably familiar with the contradictory, obscure and metaphysical doctrines of this man, whom people once regarded as a remarkable dialectician but who was only a low-grade sophist.

A decade ago Russia was the citadel of Bakuninism. Thanks to the propaganda of Bakunin's supporters, the very name 'Social Democrat' seemed shameful to Russian revolutionaries and when at the end of 1883 we began our propaganda for scientific socialism our opponents thought they were making a terrible accusation when they maintained that we were encouraging sympathy for both the ideas and the activity of German social democracy.

This accusation was in fact justified: we really were encouraging this sympathy. We told our fellow citizens that German social democracy had performed many services for the proletariat and that an acquaintance with its theories and its activity was all the more necessary for the Russians because hitherto even in Western Europe they had studied only the doctrines and practice of the Bakuninists.

Driven out of the revolutionary party, reviled by everybody, persecuted by the government, we had for many years to fight various aspects of Bakuninist doctrines. This was tiresome. But it is almost over.[55] We can now congratulate ourselves on having cleared the ground for scientific socialism and, although Bakuninist preju-dices have left many traces in the ideas of a large number of Russian Socialists, none of those who confess to any kind of revolutionary ideas would dare to con-sider our sympathies for social democracy to be a crime. On the contrary, these sympathies are increasing among Russian revolutionaries . . . You will note that in using the name 'Bakuninists' we are not referring only to a small number of anarch-ists. The late Tkachev considered himself a follower of Blanqui. He fought the anarchists and engaged in polemics with Bakunin himself. Nonetheless all his ideas on social conditions in Russia were permeated with the purest Bakuninism.

Like Bakunin, he saw in the backward condition of our economic life the guarantee of our rapid future progress. Like Bakunin, in his theories he contrasted the Western European proletarian with the Russian peasant whom he imagined to be imbued with *communist ideals.* [56]

In just the same way for the Narodnaya Volya Party, led by its famous 'Executive Committee', the development of a proletariat in Russia was only a historical misfortune. This party attempted to search out proofs of Russia's backwardness and, the more it found these proofs, the more it was convinced of its triumph. The contrast between Russia and Western Europe was one of the favourite themes of these writers.

This party was composed of representatives from the social stratum that we call the intelligentsia, i.e. of students, members of all the liberal professions and officers from different sections of the armed forces. It did not hold the workers at bay, but it did not attach great significance to their membership. To it, a single officer was of much greater significance than a hundred workers.

The Narodnaya Volya Party rendered great services to Russia. Thanks to it the struggle with the government began to be waged with hitherto unheard-of energy. But, in recruiting its members almost exclusively from the 'intelligentsia', the Narodnaya Volya Party could not be very numerous. It had sufficient resources for brilliant skirmishes but not for the decisive battle.

In our country the name of this party is closely linked with what we call the terrorist struggle, i.e. attempts on the lives of the official representatives of tsarism, including the tsar himself.

This method of struggle was not invented by Narodnaya Volya but it was practised by this party with the greatest energy and the greatest success.

We Social Democrats were considered opponents of 'terrorism'. But we have never been opposed to the 'terrorist' struggle on principle.

We were only opposed to it in as far as it bore witness to the weakness of the revolutionary party. By 'terrorising' our government momentarily, this struggle in the final analysis proved dangerous only to *individuals.* Terrorism did not undermine the *system.*

Several people perished. Their places were immediately taken by others and tsarism, far from wavering, went from strength to strength because it had the support of the upper classes who were simultaneously afraid of reaction from above and the audacity of the terrorists.

The revolutionary party expended greater resources than it attracted. It is easy to understand what happened. After the death of Alexander II in March 1881 our movement visibly began to die.

A few more successful attempts did not, and could not, improve the situation. In the three or four years following the death of Alexander II there existed several more or less revolutionary groups of young people in Russia but there was no party, not a single secret revolutionary society that presented any kind of danger to tsarism.

But that is not all. At almost the same time one could discern a decline in revolutionary enthusiasm in the social stratum that had hitherto taken the initiative in the movement.

It was clear that, if the revolutionaries could not manage to attract new social strata to their cause, it would perish once and for all. All the revolutionaries were agreed on this point; their differences arose only when a decision had to be made as to which class, which social stratum they should approach.

Some maintained that the revolutionaries should merge with 'society', i.e. the upper classes; others advised an approach to the proletariat in the industrial centres.

The former inevitably inclined towards liberalism, the latter towards social democracy.

Our liberals are far from power: a man with liberal views is suspect in the eyes of our government.

In their capacity as a party opposed to our present regime the liberals obviously constitute a progressive force in our country.

Unfortunately they have never engaged in active struggle with the government. They have never dared to transgress the narrow limits of *'peaceful'* and *'legal'* opposition.

The revolutionaries could merge with the liberals only by renouncing all forms of revolutionary activity.

In addition we should note that the weakness of our liberals also depends to a certain degree on their theories.

Our industrial bourgeoisie has so far adopted liberal ideas only in a very small way.

For the most part our liberals, like the revolutionaries of the old Bakuninist stamp, have belonged to the so-called 'intelligentsia'. For many people from this social stratum liberalism is frequently only one of the phases in their evolution.

The same man who was a *'socialist'* at university becomes a *'liberal'* when he receives his degree, when he has managed to settle down and find himself a job.

For this reason it is not surprising that our liberals still bear traces of the prejudices of 'Russian socialism'. Like the Socialists, they like to hold forth, arguing that the class struggle, the antagonism between labour and capital, has no meaning in our country.

These theories would be very handy for our liberals if they had not reduced them to absurdity. If the struggle of labour against capital has no meaning in Russia, why do the liberals not turn to the working people of Russia? Why do they not unite them beneath their banner? It is precisely on this point that an enormous difference emerges between the ideas of our Russian liberals and the ideas of Western liberals.

The Western liberals say that the worker can gain a great deal by living in peace with capital.

Russian liberals say nothing of this because they deny the very existence of a proletariat in Russia.

When they talk of the people our liberals have only the *peasant* in mind.

But liberal ideas have no influence on the peasants; the liberals know this very well and they make no attempt to attract the peasants over to their side.

What is the consequence of this? Because the peasant is indifferent and the proletariat does not exist, hope can only be placed in the liberals themselves. But these gentlemen know better than anyone the price of this deceptive hope.

You know, citizens, that, wherever liberal parties have exerted influence on the political life of their country, they have owed this influence to the support of the people, and, in particular, the proletariat. Without this valuable support they lose all their strength because a liberal party that is divorced from the people is like a general staff without an army, and general staffs cannot frighten anyone on their own.

Thus, by closing its eyes to the revolutionary strength of the proletariat and even denying the existence of this proletariat, and by rejecting as useless any attempt to approach the working masses of our big cities, Russian liberalism condemns itself to complete impotence.

Thus, tsarism has nothing to fear from an opponent like this and in fact it does not fear him at all.

Our reactionaries, who are more numerous than the revolutionary party, treat the liberals with suspicion. As a gibe they call our liberals *pseudo-liberals*. And they will be right as long as the liberals ignore the ABC of the political struggle, which consists in the absolute necessity of an approach to the working population of our big cities.

But they cannot understand this ABC unless they first abandon all their old ideas on the social life of Russia.

They know Russia only in its static economic condition; they must study it from the standpoint of economic *movement*, recognise what *is* and what will *grow* steadily, instead of going into ecstasies over what *was* once and what nowadays is turning more and more into patriotic nostalgia.

Studied from this angle, the economic structure of Russia appears completely different from the one that was so dear to our reactionaries, our liberals and our Bakuninists.

At the time of Nicholas the 'Unforgettable' it was still possible to contrast the political economy of 'Holy' Russia with the political economy of the 'rotten' West.

Serfdom, which bound the Russian peasant to the land, was an insurmountable obstacle preventing the growth of an industrial proletariat; communications were in an extremely primitive state; industry and trade were very underdeveloped; exchange did not yet include the agricultural peasant economy.

And it seemed that the heavy hand of police supervision made any progressive movement quite out of the question.

But at this time perceptive people were already realising that our old economic order could not remain unchanged.

By the end of Nicholas' reign, industry and trade had already developed to such an extent that even the Ministry for Internal Affairs had to concede that serfdom did not correspond to the economic interests of Russia.

After Nicholas' death came an era of reforms. The Crimean war 'showed that Russia, even from a purely military point of view, was short of railways and large-scale industry. The government therefore began to concern itself with increasing the capitalist class. But this class could not exist without a proletariat, and, in order to generate a proletariat, the so-called emancipation of the serfs had to be carried out. For their personal freedom the peasants paid the nobility the best part of the land that belonged to them.[57] What was left was too large for them to starve to death but too small for them to live. When the Russian peasant commune was uprooted in this way, the new upper bourgeoisie was force-grown in the hothouse atmosphere of railway preferences, a protective tariff and all sorts of other privileges. In both the towns and the villages all this produced a complete social revolution in which intellectual movement, once started, could not be stopped'.[58]

This social revolution continues to the present day. The number of peasants leaving their land or not having the necessary means to work it is growing with frightening rapidity. Statistics have shown that this number reaches 60% of the total number of Russian peasants.

The rural petty bourgeoisie completely dominates the peasantry while the upper bourgeoisie is buying up the estates of the nobility, which more and more is approaching ruin.

The disappearance of the old economic order leaves the field wide open for the development of capitalism. But already it is not satisfied with the domestic market.

The Russian bourgeoisie attacks foreign capitalists, accusing them of unfair competition. It tries to open up markets for itself in Central Asia, Persia, Mongolia and China, and even in Abyssinia. The Trans-Caspian railway brought great rewards to our industrialists. The Siberian railway will bring even greater rewards. In a word, if the Emperor Nicholas was merely the soldiers' tsar, Alexander II was the tsar of the bourgeoisie, and in this respect his son is faithfully following his father's example.

We may cite as a characteristic sign of our times the ideals of the party that calls itself the *Russian Party or the National Party*. In Paris in 1890 a member of this party published a very instructive and in many respects a very interesting book. This patriotic defender of tsarism and orthodoxy tries to educate his French readers in the finer qualities of the true Russian spirit. A beautiful theme for Slavophile eloquence! But the author achieves eloquence only when he is talking about the future of Russian trade. 'In the new geographical situation', he says,

Russia has been summoned to serve as the natural transit route for the products of Asia and of Western countries. Thus Russia has been called to become in the more or less immediate future the indispensable middle-man in both Western and Eastern trade. On the day that Russia drives the railway that is now being built into the heart of China the rich shipping and transport companies whose ships now plough the Eastern seas will perish, no matter what flag they sail under, and on that day England will lose her naval sceptre.

But to achieve this objective [he continues] it will not be enough for a route from the Eastern provinces of Russia to penetrate Asia; in addition there must be a network of routes, even sea routes, linking up with the great artery. It is precisely this that prompts the idea of Russia's domination of the Black Sea. Constantinople, as everyone knows, can, because of its position, serve as an office and warehouse for the whole of Asia [etc].[59]

These are the ideals of our reactionaries. You see that even a partial realisation of their desires would make Russia dangerous for Western Europe and particularly for the European proletariat, not only because of her guns and bayonets but also because of her industry.

Our government is straining all its resources to realise this patriotic programme.

Thanks to this skilful tactic our industrial and commercial bourgeoisie is not crossing over to the liberal opposition, whose supporters are for the most part recruited from amongst the bourgeois ideologists of the 'liberal professions'.

The European proletariat can no longer continue to regard Russia as a country that figures on the international market only with raw agricultural produce. The time is already not far off when Russian industry will compete fiercely with Western European industry in Eastern markets. *For this reason the vital interests of social democracy throughout the whole world are intimately linked to the progress of the Russian workers' movement.*

The emergence in Russia of a significant industrial proletariat is a social fact of enormous historical importance. Since the beginning of this century many people have spoken of the *Europeanisation of Russia*. More than one Slavophile writer has won his literary laurels by bemoaning the Europeanisation. But for a long time the nobility were the only ones who did not resist European culture. All the other classes, and especially the peasants, led a completely Asiatic way of life. Now Europeanisation embraces the *economic structure* of Russia and consequently the whole *Russian people*. With the emergence of the industrial proletariat we have for the first time in our history a revolutionary force that is capable of overthrowing tsarism and leading our country into the great family of civilised nations. And without any exaggeration we can say that the *entire future evolution of Russia depends on the intellectual development of the Russian proletariat.*

The Russian peasant of the good old days had nothing in common with the culture and liberal ideas of Europe. His ignorance was the best possible basis for tsarist despotism. *The Russian proletarian* is trying to learn, to acquire European culture. Wherever the emperor's inquisition allows public libraries to exist, worker readers appear in large numbers. At every public reading the audience is so great that there is no room for them.

It is obvious that anyone who can serve the cause of popular education has to slip through the filter of the carping censorship. *Legal* propaganda for any kind of progressive political ideas is completely impossible. We have to resort to secret presses to print books and brochures against the present regime, or even print them abroad. It goes without saying that these editions can only be distributed in secret.

This situation clearly and logically dictates to the revolutionary party the programme that it must follow.

What we need is propaganda for socialist ideas among the workers and the organisation of workers' societies with the same aim of propaganda and agitation.

The Russian proletarian is no novice in the revolutionary movement. You know that it was a worker who blew up the imperial palace in February 1880.[60] The very idea for this action was conceived in a workers' group. For twenty years now revolutionary circles have continued to exist despite all the efforts of the political police.

As long as our revolutionaries were imbued with Bakuninist prejudices they were unable to exert a great influence on the proletariat. Their sights were set on the past. They had an inkling of the revolutionary role of the Russian proletariat.

They dismiss the political freedoms as bourgeois sophistry. If by chance they do turn to the workers, it is only to rally them to the banner of *'purely economic'* revolution. Around the beginning of 1879 a secret workers' society, the *Northern Union of Russian Workers*, issued a programme in which the political freedoms were placed at the head of the demands of the Russian proletariat.[61] The well-known revolutionary society Zemlya i Volya, which consists almost exclusively of more or less 'intellectual' Bakuninists, felt it its duty to fight the 'bourgeois' tendencies of the workers' union.

In Russia and throughout the world the workers' movement can flourish only beneath the banner of *scientific socialism*, i.e. beneath the banner of *social democracy*.

In no instance is social democracy indifferent to political freedoms. Russian social democracy is convinced that the *first efforts of the workers' party in Russia should be directed towards the achievement of precisely these freedoms*.

A party that was mainly recruited among the 'intelligentsia' could not have overthrown tsarism. It was not even strong enough to attack it in the decisive battle. Inevitably, the terrorist struggle, this *partisan* war, dictated to it. The entry of the industrial proletariat into the struggle provides the opportunity for going *further*. Henceforward danger will no longer threaten an *individual* sitting on the tsar's throne; the threat will be directed against the existence of the throne itself.

This is our programme, dear citizens. We have set ourselves the duty of covering the whole of Russia with a network of workers' societies. Until this aim has been achieved we shall abstain from participating in your meetings. Until that time any representation of Russian social democracy would be fictitious.

And we do not want fiction.

We are convinced that soon there will no longer be any grounds for our abstention. It is very possible that at the next international congress you will see amongst you true representatives of the Russian workers.

In the meantime we think that all of you, regardless of nationality, will wish us success.

Long live social democracy!

Long live the alliance of proletarians of all countries!

For the editorial board of *Sotsial-Demokrat*

G. PLEKHANOV V. ZASULICH.

11. THE TASKS OF THE SOCIAL DEMOCRATS IN THE STRUGGLE AGAINST THE FAMINE IN RUSSIA (1891): EXTRACTS[62]

G.V. Plekhanov

What is the socialist movement?

If you had put such a question to a Socialist in the 30s, to one of the followers of the famous Fourier, for instance, he would have replied more or less in the following manner: 'Our brilliant teacher discovered and expounded in his works a whole series of truths, whose existence mankind had not previously suspected. On the basis of these discoveries he worked out a detailed plan of the new social order which alone can save man from his countless moral and material misfortunes. The contemporary socialist movement, the true socialist movement and worthy of the name, is resolved to spread the ideas of our teacher and to realise them in practice, i.e. to form the *phalansteries* that he has devised.'[63]

An answer of this sort would have been quite correct in the 30s. At that time the socialist movement was really concerned to spread the ideas of the various schools of socialism and to try to realise them in practice. In these circumstances each school clearly thought that the teaching of its particular founder was the true socialism.

But now things are different. To a contemporary Socialist the socialist movement does not look anything like it did to a Socialist in the 30s. Even shortly before the revolutionary year of 1848 there emerged among the Socialists men who looked at socialism in a completely new perspective. Seen in this new perspective the principal error of previous Socialists was precisely the fact that, 'Future history resolves itself, in their eyes, into propaganda and the practical implementation of their social plans.'[64] The Socialists with the new outlook saw in the future history of the civilised world something else, something incomparably more promising.

What precisely did the Socialists with the new outlook see in it? Above all *class struggle*, the struggle *of the exploited with the exploiters, the proletariat with the bourgeoisie*. In addition they saw in it the inevitability of the impending triumph of the proletariat, the fall of the present bourgeois social order, the socialist organisation of production and the corresponding alteration in the relationships between people, i.e. even the destruction of classes, among other things. Although they knew full well (better than their predecessors) that the socialist revolution involves a complete transformation in all social relationships, the Socialists of the new tendency did not concern themselves at all with working out a plan for the future organisation of society. They thought this a complete waste of time because the details of the future order would be determined in their own time by circumstances that it was impossible to foresee, and its general principles would be sufficiently determined by a *scientific* critique of existing social relationships, i.e. by a critique based not on the sympathies and antipathies of the reformers but on an examination of the historical development of the present social order. The Socialists with the new outlook broke once and for all with *utopias* and took their stand on the basis of *science*. Even their enemies gave them credit for this when they began to call the new socialism *scientific socialism*. The followers of scientific socialism seem nowadays to be the only Socialists worthy of the name.

If for the followers of scientific socialism the whole future history of bourgeois society resolves itself in the struggle of the proletariat with the bourgeoisie, all their practical tasks are prompted by precisely this class struggle. Standing resolutely on the side of the proletariat, the new Socialists do everything in their power to facilitate and hasten its victory. But what exactly can they do in this case? A necessary condition for the victory of the proletariat is its recognition of its own position, its relations with its exploiters, its historic role and its socio-political tasks. For this reason the new Socialists consider it their principal, perhaps even their only, duty to promote the growth of this consciousness among the proletariat, which for short they call its *class consciousness*. The whole success of the socialist movement is measured for them in terms of the growth in the class consciousness of the proletariat. Everything that helps this growth they see as useful to their cause: everything that slows it down as harmful. Anything that has no effect one way or the other is of no consequence for them, it is *politically* uninteresting . . .

There is no doubt that the development of capitalism hastens the social revolution. Consequently, every bourgeois whose activity furthers the development of capitalism hastens the social revolution. But it would be very strange if, because of this, someone were to think of the bourgeois activists as Socialists. Even people whose activity is directly aimed at fighting socialism can hasten the social revolution. Some German Social Democrats think that the famous law of exclusion against the Socialists has to some extent helped their party. If this view is correct then it follows that Bismarck, in introducing the law of exclusion, has by that very fact hastened the social revolution in Germany.[65] But who would describe as a Socialist the man who was trying to deal the death-blow to the Social Democratic Party?

I reiterate that, however much you have discussed the *consequences* of your political activity, you will only be recognised as a Socialist if your activity has *directly* facilitated the growth of the class consciousness of the proletariat. If it does not exert this direct influence then you are not a Socialist at all, even though the more or less remote consequences of your *non*-socialist activity may bring some degree of advantage for the cause of socialism.

Comrades, it is clear that, in identifying the most important and the most direct sign of socialist activity, I do not wish to say that anyone who does not want to betray the Red Flag should unfailingly engage either in writing socialist books or in distributing them and generally in propaganda among the proletariat and its organisations. *Individuals*, belonging to the socialist *party*, may be involved in other matters *without ceasing to be* Socialists for a single moment. Let us suppose that the socialist party of a particular country has decided to arrange secret hiding places for its members who are the objects of government persecution. It entrusts the matter to me and to several other comrades. We willingly and zealously carry out this assignment. Our individual activity is not directly aimed at the development of the class consciousness of the proletariat. But is it conceivable that, in doing this, we cease to be Socialists? No one could say that. But why should they not say that? Because, in engaging in this activity, not only did we remain members of *the party that directly promotes the growth of the class consciousness of the proletariat* but we also undertook this activity on its instructions. Another example. The socialist party of a particular country decides that in the near future it will have to come out into open conflict with the government. The success of its struggle depends to a great extent of course on how the army behaves at the decisive moment. And so the party assigns a certain number of its members to engage in revolutionary propaganda in the army. The soldiers may of course be regarded as proletarians in military uniform. Consequently, as far as the people who explain the ideas of socialism to them are concerned, the question that interests us cannot even arise. But it is entirely appropriate for the people who deal exclusively with the officers. Do these people cease to be Socialists? Not at all. Why not, then? Once again because their activity is determined by the needs of the party that directly promotes the growth of the class consciousness of the proletariat. And if they had not belonged to it? In that case they would have ceased to be Socialists because then their work would immediately have lost any connection with the direct and immediate socialist cause. One could cite very many such examples. But my view, I hope, is sufficiently clear. It is expressed in its entirety in the epigraph to this letter: *without workers who are conscious of their class interests there can be no socialism* . . .

. . . The conflict between the proletariat and the bourgeoisie is not the contrivance of the Socialists of a particular school and is by no means a tactical device dreamed up by a fanatical revolutionary, but is that same fateful historical inevitability as was the conflict between the bourgeoisie and the feudal aristocracy in its own time. Nowadays it would be superfluous even to say that the example of the 'owning class' in Germany proves and exact opposite of what the German Utopian Socialist of the 40s wanted to prove. This class did absolutely nothing to resolve the 'social question', but, if the young men of the time who belonged to it took a fancy to socialism then, from their point of view, this was of course a very good thing, but it can easily be explained by the political condition of Germany at that time. After 1848 the German 'intelligentsia' was really only interested in socialism as a fearful monster, which must be overcome at all costs, even though to do this it might be necessary to waive the 'inalienable' rights of the citizen. In Germany now, as in France, it is *only* the worker, only the 'non-owning' class that marches under the banner of socialism and it is for this reason that the laws of exclusion against them have been devised. Nowadays judgements like those above may be heard only in Russia, where quite often even the revolutionaries carry on about how we are not 'the West' and so on. (In addition we now count Germany as a Western country, whereas the German Utopians used to contrast it with the West.) Since the 1840s Western European life has progressed a great deal, and the further it has progressed, the clearer the fateful and revolutionary significance of the class struggle has become both for the Socialists and even for their enemies, the defenders of the current social order.

Before I proceed, I shall make one more reservation. If I assert that the promotion of the growth of the class consciousness of the proletariat is the sole purpose and the direct and sacred duty of the Socialists, then this does not mean that the contemporary Socialists stand for propaganda, for propaganda alone, and for nothing but propaganda. In the broad sense of the word this is perhaps true, but only in the *very* broad sense. When at the International Congress in Paris in 1889 the Socialists resolved to strive for the eight-hour day they obviously had it in mind that workers' demonstrations in favour of their resolution would be a marvellous method of propagating their ideas. But a demonstration is at the same time a method of *agitation*. In general it is not easy to draw the line between agitation and what is usually called propaganda. Agitation is also propaganda, but propaganda that takes place in particular circumstances, that is in circumstances in which even those who would not normally pay any attention are forced to listen to the propagandist's words. Propaganda is agitation that is conducted in the normal everyday course of the life of a particular country. Agitation is propaganda occasioned by events that are not entirely ordinary and that provoke a certain upsurge in the public mood. Socialists would be very bad politicians if they were not to use such notable events for their own ends.

Let us suppose that the agitation in favour of the eight-hour day has been crowned with success. Frightened by constantly growing pressure from the workers' movement, the bourgeoisie has yielded. In all civilised countries the law has limited the working day to eight hours. This is a great victory for socialism but the question arises: were all the workers whose efforts contributed to the victory Socialists? Probably not. There were of course Socialists among them. There were many Socialists who played a leading role, stepping out in front and sweeping the hesitant and the indecisive along in their wake. But were there really then people who were hesitant and indecisive? Why did they hesitate, why were they indecisive? Was it because they were generally indecisive and inclined to hesitation? It was partly for that reason perhaps but partly, and perhaps even probably, because they had not fully appreciated the benefits of the eight-hour day and because, on a general level, not having assimilated socialist ideas, they were not yet imbued with the thirst for the battle for a better future that is aroused by a consistent and ordered revolutionary outlook. In a word, these people were not yet Socialists. But now look at what has happened. The Socialists have drawn people who were not yet Socialists into the struggle for a cause that will be very useful to socialism. In other words, people who were not yet Socialists have already been working for socialism. And it is agitation that has done this! Because of this Socialists can use for the cause not just the forces that belong to them at the present time, but also those that will belong

to them only subsequently. What has happened is rather like drawing on the socialist account which history will pay for. And this payment will bring the victory of
socialism significantly closer.

Propaganda, in the strict sense of the word, would lose all historical significance
if it were not accompanied by agitation. Propaganda conveys the correct views to
dozens, hundreds, thousands of people. But people holding the correct views only
become historical activists when they exert a direct influence on public life. And
influence on the public life of contemporary civilised countries is unthinkable without influence on the mass, i.e. without agitation. (In barbaric despotisms things are
different: there the mass has no importance. But we are not talking about them.)
Consequently agitation is essential for any party that wishes to have historical
meaning. A sect may be content with propaganda in the narrow sense of the word,
but a political party never.

If I had to clarify further the relationship between agitation and propaganda I
should add that the propagandist conveys *many* ideas to a single person or to a few
people, whereas the agitator conveys *only one or a few* ideas, but he conveys them
to *a whole mass of people*, sometimes to almost the entire population of a particular locality. But history is made by the mass. Consequently agitation is the aim of
propaganda: I conduct propaganda so that I shall have the opportunity to transfer
to agitation.

However, let us return to our example. We supposed that the Socialists had
managed to secure an eight-hour day by law. Such a law brings very great benefit to
the working class. Even the least advanced, least comprehending and most backward workers soon become convinced of this once it has become a reality. And
they all know that the eight-hour day was introduced on the initiative of the Socialists. For this reason all workers, even the most backward, will be thoroughly convinced that the realisation of at least some socialist demands benefits the working
class. And this knowledge will in any case bring them incomparably closer to a
complete sympathy with socialism than a complete indifference to socialist teaching would have done. But let us go further. By increasing the worker's leisure time,
the eight-hour day gives him the opportunity for greater intellectual development
and consequently for the easier assimilation of socialist ideas. That means that in
this way too the eight-hour day brings nearer the inevitable reckoning: it 'hastens
the social revolution'.

If, at the same time as we engaged in socialist propaganda among the workers,
Russia were standing still, then the mutual relationship between the social forces in
our country would also remain unchanged. The autocracy would be just as strong
and durable after ten, twenty or thirty years as it had been when we started our
propaganda: the fact that several thousand 'propagandised' workers hated it would
only diminish its durability to a minute degree, which would have not the slightest
practical significance. But would social relations in Russia remain unchanged? We
have seen that they are changing very rapidly. But the mutual relationship between
the social forces does, clearly, change with them. The autocracy weakens as the

historical soil that has nurtured it crumbles and decomposes. At the same time some forces are growing stronger and stronger, and it is the collision with these forces that drives [autocracy] to its ruin. This means that, while our propaganda is training *revolutionaries*, history creates the *revolutionary milieu* 'essentially for their activity; while we are preparing the leaders of the revolutionary mass, the officers and NCOs of the revolutionary army, this very army is being created by the inevitable course of social development. But in this case can we describe our activity as fruitless or unproductive? On the contrary, is it not absolutely necessary and uniquely productive from the revolutionary point of view?

On the other hand it is clear that, as long as the *individuals* that we have 'propagandised' exert no direct revolutionary influence on the *mass*, they are only its leaders *in theory*. If they are to become its leaders *in reality* they will have to influence them in the revolutionary sense.

That is where *agitation* comes into its own. Thanks to it the necessary link between the 'heroes' and the 'crowd', between the mass and its leaders is established and strengthened. The more strained matters become, the more the old social edifice will rock, and the more rapidly the revolution approaches, the more important agitation will become. To it belongs the principal role in the drama that we call the *social revolution*.

From this it follows that, if the Russian Socialists want to play an active role in the coming Russian revolution, they must know how to become *agitators*.

This is essential. But it is not easy. The task of the agitator involves putting into circulation in each particular case the maximum possible number of revolutionary ideas in a form that is accessible to the mass. For every mistake he makes one way or another a harsh punishment awaits the agitator. If he overestimates the revolutionary mood of the mass he will at best remain unintelligible but he may be ridiculed or even assaulted. If, on the other hand, because of extreme caution he puts to the mass demands that it has already outgrown in its rapid revolutionary development, he will fall into the awkward position of agitator-brake, an agitator who inspires the crowd with 'moderation and tender conscience'. The whole skill of the agitator consists in his ability to avoid such excesses. But if he has this skill he has no need to fear failure. His task will be carried out of its own accord. You may perhaps say that he is giving the mass nothing: he is only giving fully conscious expression to the attitude that it already holds, which it is not itself aware of. But in this lies the secret of his influence and the guarantee of his future successes. Seeing in his words merely the expression of its own demands, the mass willingly follows him. And if only it has not become estranged from the causes of its revolutionary attitude, it may even itself push ahead of the agitator. Realising that only yesterday it was still frightened by its boldness and novelty it rapidly goes further, inclining to more daring demands. In this way, learning from its own experience, carried along by its own movement, encouraged by its own success, it gradually, but on the other hand assuredly, becomes more and more revolutionary, until in the end it deals with a single decisive movement the death-blow to the existing order. But when the edifice of this order, made shaky, weak and decrepit by history, has shattered, new tasks will unfold before it, it will have to build things better in its new home, not falling into the net of the political exploiters, flatterers and tricksters. Then the services and the directions of its devoted agitator-friends will be just as important for it as they were earlier in the heart of the struggle with the old order.

Orators are born, according to the well-known saying. Agitators are also 'born' and no science can replace the inborn agitational gift. Agitation cannot be conducted according to a particular pattern. But this does not prevent us from thinking about its significance and preparing for it with all the means at our disposal at a time when we can foresee that there will soon be a broad scope for agitational activity.

A necessary condition for this activity is a merger of the revolutionary forces that have already been prepared. Through circle propaganda we can involve people who have no connection with one another and do not even suspect one another's existence. Of course the absence of organisation always affects propaganda, but it does not make it impossible. In epochs of great social upheaval, when the political atmosphere is charged with electricity and when here and there for the most varied, most unforeseen reasons there are increasingly frequent explosions that testify to the approach of the revolutionary storm, in short when it is necessary either to agitate or to rally to the flag – in these epochs *only organised* revolutionary forces can exert a serious influence on the course of events. The individual is then powerless, and only units of a higher order are equal to the revolutionary task: *revolutionary organisations*.

Organisation is the first, the essential step. However insignificant the prepared revolutionary forces of contemporary Russia, they will be increased tenfold by organisation. Counting their forces and stationing them where appropriate, the revolutionaries set to work. By means of spoken and printed propaganda they spread the correct view of the causes of the present famine through all strata of the population. Wherever the mass is not yet sufficiently advanced to understand their teaching, they give it, as it were, object lessons. They appear wherever it protests, they protest with it, they explain to it the meaning of its own movement and hence they increase its revolutionary preparedness. In this way the elemental movements of the mass gradually merge with the conscious revolutionary movement, and the idea that the *Zemskii sobor* must be summoned becomes increasingly popular: the Russian people becomes more and more convinced that it must snatch its fate from the hands of tsarist officials.

This is one side of things. On the other side we must ensure that the people, once it has risen against the existing order, should win *political rights for itself* and not *political privileges for its exploiters*. We must ensure that the *Zemskii sobor*[66] is an assembly of the whole people, that the working mass may send *its own* representative, that the electors and the elected are all adult Russian citizens. *Direct universal suffrage* is the first and most important demand of the Russian Socialists. If they do not achieve this, they will still be in a position to achieve their other demands, which are very closely related: freedom of the spoken word, of assembly, of association, freedom to strike, etc., etc.

The agitators must win the mass over to every one of these demands.

But from which stratum will the people's representatives in the assembly be elected? Direct universal suffrage certainly does not guarantee that the workers will not elect their bosses, the poor peasants their kulaks or landowners and generally that the exploited will not elect the exploiters. Direct universal suffrage is a double-edged sword which the government or the bourgeoisie can easily direct against us. How should we fend off their blows?

The worker will only stop voting for his boss when he recognises the irreconcilable contradiction that exists between his own economic interests on the one hand and the interests of the boss on the other. As soon as he does recognise this, he will no longer want to be the political tool of the exploiter, and he will try to give *political* expression to his *economic* needs, he will give his vote to the *Socialist*.

The poor peasant will only stop voting for the kulak, the landowner or the government candidate when the socialist workers' party — in putting forward its well-known economic demands like those outlined above, for instance — demonstrates to him that there is a close connection between his interests and the interests of the revolutionary proletariat.

Consequently we come once more to the familiar conclusion that our political agitation will bear fruit for us only if it *corresponds to the growth in the class consciousness of the proletariat.*

The class consciousness of the proletariat is the protective layer that deflects, like water off a duck's back, all the attacks of the parties opposed to us.

I am coming to the end. I have openly set forth our views on the tasks of the Russian Socialists in the struggle with the causes of the famine in Russia and I hope that now there can be no misunderstandings on that account. I welcome those who agree with them as comrades and I remind those who find them too 'extreme' that we are Socialists and in the eyes of Socialists moderation is by no means something to be proud of.

People will probably tell me that the time is not ripe for an open exposition of our views because this could frighten the liberals. To that I reply: it would be absurd on our part to frighten them deliberately; but if by chance they are frightened of us, against our will, then we can only pity their completely 'inopportune' timidity. In any case for us the most insidious form of intimidation is the intimidation of Socialists by the spectre of the intimidated liberal. The harm done by this intimidation is infinitely greater than the advantage to be gained by convincing the liberal gentlemen of our moderation and our tender conscience.

12. MANUSCRIPTS PROGRAMME FOR STUDIES WITH THE WORKERS (1892)[67]

M.I. Brusnev

I. Reading, writing and thinking.

II. Chemistry, physics, botany, zoology, physiology, anatomy, hygiene: briefly, geology, cosmography and astronomy. The differing theories of the formation of the earth and the origin of the universe.

III. The theory of Darwin, the theory of the origin and development of organisms and the origin of man.

IV. The history of culture. The period of savagery and the period of barbarism. The life of man in each of these periods (his food, pursuits, family, habits, laws, beliefs, property, social life and the full communism of the time) and the evolution of all this, the development and evolution of power, religion, morality, the family and property. The dependence of all aspects of human life on the economic situation.

The period of civilisation. A similar, but more detailed, study of this period with the addition of the political history of ancient and modern peoples – and in this context the whole evolution of all aspects of the life of the Russian people – and especially Russian history. The history of science, philosophy, discoveries and inventions.

V. Political economy. The history of the development of the forms of organising labour (slavery, feudalism, capitalism, the inevitable evolution of the latter in the direction of collectivism). The history of political economy.

VI. The position and history of the peasants in Russia and in the West. The commune, artel, allotments, foodstuffs and taxes. Banks – for the peasantry (and the nobility). Migration, schism and sectarianism.

VII. The position of the working class in Russia and the West. The history of the workers' movement in the light of the theories of various reformers. Palliatives in the workers' question (producers' and consumers' societies, etc.), factory legislation.

VIII. The history of the social movement in Europe and, in the fullest and greatest detail, in Russia (NB). The contemporary position and significance of all the classes in Russia (the nobility, clergy, bourgeoisie, peasantry and the workers; the bureaucracy, army and the government).

IX. Economic policy and its history in the West and in Russia. The essence of socialism.

X. The full, detailed, and precisely and definitely substantiated programme of minimum demands for the present time.[68]

13. A PROGRAMME OF ACTION FOR THE WORKERS (1892)[69]

N.E. Fedoseev

You will not doubt that the situation of the Russian worker is terrible in all respects; this condition is far below the level which can be described as a human existence. The condition of the Russian worker is immeasurably worse that the condition of the working class (proletariat) in Western Europe where, as you know, the struggle with the owners has produced glittering results for the working class and is leading this class to an undoubted, and imminent, complete victory over the owners or, in other words, is leading it to complete economic emancipation. The working class in Western Europe conducts the struggle, preparing for it in large and harmonious unions consisting of workers from all branches of industry. The majority of workers in the West have recognised the common interest of the workers not only of a particular country (e.g. England) but have recognised the common interest of the workers of the whole world; the working class in the West unites beneath a banner on which is written, 'Workers of all countries, unite!' This consciousness of common interest is reflected in the fact that every year an ever greater number of workers joins the workers' party. The workers of the West are in a very favourable position to unify a large number rapidly; they enjoy freedom of the press, of assembly and of association. *They have won all this for themselves.* In addition the worker in the West has now already reached an economic position by comparison with which the position of our worker may be described as a terribly impoverished, wretched and slave-like condition.

This condition of our working class is explained by the fact that it has not united, its separate members have not come to a clear recognition of the common interests of all workers (not even of the workers of a single factory or locality, for a start). The Russian worker has not yet understood that he can only improve his difficult, oppressed and impoverished condition by constant struggle with the owners, that the owners are his enemies and enemies solely because they are in possession of capital (of machines, factories, 'goods', wages, i.e. the workers' means of living); the Russian workers have not yet appreciated that they can only improve their lot by joining with one another in a strong and large *lasting* union to begin the real struggle with the owners for the improvement of their lot. This struggle should end, even for our worker, with the complete victory of the worker, with his complete emancipation from oppression, his emancipation from slavery to capital. Our Russian worker will only rise, unite as one man, 'rebel', as the owners and their most ardent defenders say, when they 'can stand no more'. Rising immediately against the owners, with no preparation, with no *clear goals*, our workers destroy the factories and shops and drive out the police and the directors. But such uprisings almost never give them anything that will alleviate their condition. At the same time in the majority of cases such uprisings end very sadly for them: the government treats the workers' leaders cruelly. Even recently the government has cruelly punished as a state criminal every worker who has dared to raise his voice to explain to his comrades the causes of their miserable condition (that's not bad! The government itself openly admits that it is the defender of the owners' interests if it considers that workers who unite to fight the owners are state criminals), and it was only after huge strikes, in which the majority of the workers participated, that the government was forced to 'reduce the punishment' and now punishes the preparation of strikes with about one year's imprisonment. Apart from the large strikes, our workers have achieved almost no improvement in their situation. This is because Russian workers unite only *temporarily*, to hold a strike when things have already become insufferable and because they have not yet worked out any clear goals for themselves towards which they can strive, and because they have not understood the *principal* causes of their impoverished condition.

For this reason we must strive with all our strength to explain to the workers the correct view of the principal causes of their impoverished condition. We must strive to put their incipient struggle with the owners on a straight path leading ever closer to the principal aim — the complete emancipation of the working class. For this we must strive to unite the workers of every factory in a lasting union, which would have clear views on the means by which the struggle should be conducted, on the final, principal aim of the struggle, and on the immediate *tasks attainable* at the present moment. The resolution of these matters would at least somewhat improve the distressing condition of the workers and at the same time make them more amenable to the struggle.

The present economic subjugation of the working class to the owners who possess the capital is the cause of the enslavement of the workers in all its forms: destitution, intellectual stupefaction and political dependence. For this reason economic emancipation is the most important goal that the working class should strive for. The emancipation of the working class may be achieved only by the working class itself. In fighting for their own emancipation, the workers are fighting for the complete abolition of all inequalities; the workers, in fighting for their own emancipation, are fighting for identical rights and duties for all. The economic emancipation of the working class can only be achieved by way of force, through the seizure of political power (the state), of all the instruments and means of production (capital) from the hands of the owner-capitalists. For this reason the workers, firstly of every separate factory, then of every locality (or province) and, finally, the workers of all branches of production, should join unanimously into a strong, steadfast and lasting workers' union. Union with the workers of the West is absolutely necessary and essential for our workers: our workers should learn a great deal from their Western brothers, who have fought more than they have and are therefore more experienced. But at the present time such a union is completely impossible.

When the Russian workers unite into a great force they will be able to set about the struggle for the improvement of their condition; and the Russian workers will above all demand and urgently obtain *political freedom*: the freedom of their own workers' press (newspapers and books) to discuss and defend the interests of the working class, the freedom of political assembly and the complete immunity from prosecution of workers' unions. To obtain all this for the workers is a very important task. Having obtained political freedom the workers will quickly move to the true, straight path to their complete emancipation from their economic yoke, and at the same time from the political injustice and subjugation that is associated with this yoke.

When the Russian workers unite into a great force they will be able to strive for the improvement of their economic condition, i.e. they will be able to do battle with the owners for a reduction in the working day and for an increase in wages, because a reduction in the working day and an increase in wages are necessary for a more rapid union of the greatest possible number of workers. This improves the conditions of the workers and thus makes them more amenable to their own intellectual development. I am not talking here about the large number of other very important gains for the workers after the realisation of these demands because you know about these from the marvellous book by Mr G.V. Plekhanov.

I consider it a very great fortune for me to inform you, in conclusion, of the programme put forward by the great teacher of the workers of all countries, the German Karl Marx.

'Socialists, "Social Democrats," ' so the editors say in their introduction to *The Manifesto of the Workers' (Communist) Party*,

Social Democrats consider it shameful to hide their opinions and intentions. They openly proclaim that their aims can be achieved by the forcible overthrow of the whole existing system. Let the ruling classes tremble before the revolt and victory of the workers. The workers (when they unite into a great force) have nothing to lose in revolt, *except their chains*, and they will gain the whole world. Workers of all countries, unite![70]

The workers are striving to destroy the contemporary order not merely because they are unfortunate oppressed paupers. No! The workers are striving for hegemony because they are the class that produces all the enormous wealth of society. They are striving to destroy the contemporary order because a large part of the wealth *produced by them* passes into the hands of the owners and the workers receive wages that they can hardly live on.

The workers want to abolish wages and enjoy all the wealth that they produce.

From their enormous share of the wealth the owners pay the workers only their wages because the instruments of production are in their hands. The instruments of production should be transferred to the hands of the workers. Not to the hands of the workers of any particular factory — that would be simply plunder — but to the hands of the workers of the whole state, because individual workers have as little right to the factories and machines they work with as each individual one of them has to the wealth produced by them all. Consequently the workers do not want to abolish property at all but, on the contrary, want everyone to own what he has earned.

At the moment the workers earn all the wealth but receive only their wages, while the owners merely possess the capital and do not work, but receive an enormous share of the wealth created by the workers. The owners cannot eat or squander all this wealth that remains in their hands: an enormous part of the money that they receive for the goods produced by the workers is spent by the owners on the purchase of machines, the employment of new workers, and this increases their wealth even further.

But the worker who produces this wealth and works day after day like a convict to the point of complete exhaustion receives only his wages. The wealth created by the workers grows enormously but they continue to receive the same wretched wage merely because they have to sell themselves to the owners as a work force. The workers want to destroy the order under which they receive their wages because they create all the wealth and not merely that part of it that they receive in the form of wages.

The workers do not want merely to increase wages, but to receive all that they earn.

The workers do not recognise the legitimacy of an order under which they are deprived of the right to own what they have earned. For this reason they wish to overthrow completely the existing order which is founded on injustice.

They can do this only by depriving the owners of their factories, machines, etc. (capital).

This capital belongs to all the workers of the state and for this reason it should pass into the ownership of all the workers of the state.

The leaders of the working class should not, even at the present time, oppose workers' strikes. They should not themselves encourage strikes, because at the present moment strikes are almost useless; but, once the workers have embarked on a strike, the leaders should point out to them the most important demands that they should make, and point out the necessity for a *lasting* union among them so that the struggle with the owners may meet with every possible success. Finally, once the strike has begun, the leaders should explain to the workers that destruction and pillage positively harm the cause and at the same time they should encourage the workers in a broad discussion of their interests.

14. THE TASKS OF THE WORKER INTELLIGENTSIA IN RUSSIA (1893): EXTRACTS[71]

P. Akselrod

Letter to socialist workers
(In lieu of a preface)

Dear comrades!

The booklet before you first appeared in print more than three years ago as a 'Letter to the Russian Workers'. The ideas expressed in it on the whole correspond to those that were expressed by your orators on the occasion of the world-wide workers' festival at the May gatherings of 1891 and 1892.[72] Like you, the social democratic circle of Russian émigré revolutionaries, which raised the banner of the independent political activity of the working class in Russia about ten years ago,[73] recognises that the principal immediate task of the latter is the achievement of political rights for the Russian people. Like you, we also think that, in order to achieve this goal, the advanced workers in Russia must direct all their energy towards the creation among the popular masses of an 'organised force' that would be in a position to force the government to concede its demands. My brochure is, therefore, the literary expression of your own political aspirations; hence, in publishing it again, we mean to help to explain your aims to the workers who have already considered the problem of the removal of the injustice of the present social order but who, unlike you, have not yet come into contact with the teaching of world social democracy.

The period that Russia is now living through is an especially favourable one for you to gain a powerful influence among the lower classes and create the revolutionary force at whose head you could initiate the daring war against the government and the exploiters of the people. They say that 'every cloud has a silver lining'. This adage is exactly suited to the harvest failure that has afflicted our native land last year and this. It has brought great calamities to the Russian people. But these calamities could become the catalyst for its deliverance from the government tyranny that oppresses it if we could find people capable of explaining to it the true causes of its sufferings and of rousing it to battle with them.

The government and the exploiters that it supports have been fleecing the peasants and workers for so long and with such inhumanity that they have driven Russia to ruin and now they themselves do not know how to extricate themselves from the troubles they have created. For you cannot collect from a ruined people the taxes necessary to maintain the splendour of the tsar, his court and authorities. Five or ten years ago it was only the revolutionaries and very educated people who could appreciate what great harm the despotism of the tsar and his gendarmerie and police is doing to Russia. But now the sorrowful predictions of these people have been fully realised. When the despotic government has led the entire country to the edge of ruin and seems completely unable even temporarily to relieve the sufferings of the people, it is not difficult to explain to even the most backward person the need for a radical transformation in our state order. Really it is only the Sysoiki who would now respond unsympathetically to the call to struggle for political liberty and for the summoning of a *Zemskii sobor* with elected representatives of the whole people. And none of us can turn to the labouring masses with this appeal with as much success as you, dear comrades. In so doing you would be rendering an inestimable service to Russia in general and to its working class in particular.

But, in order to utilise the misfortunes that the Russian people are now experiencing in the interests of their emancipation, you must above all else organise yourselves and make yourselves as nearly as possible into the kind of strong revolutionary nucleus that was provided some fifteen years ago by the Zemlya i Volya organisation, and later by Narodnaya Volya.[74] A popular union of this kind would probably have made use of popular discontent, such as the Astrakhan uprising and the cholera disorders that involved 20,000 of the working population in the Ekaterinoslav province. Until such time as the revolutionary representatives of our workers in the principal towns of the Empire have merged into a single all-Russian union of indefatigable propagandists and agitators, until such time, I say, popular resentment against the tyranny of the authorities and the exploiters will inevitably break out in wild forms and serve only the cause of tsarist despotism.

That these kinds of popular 'protests' frighten to no avail only that part of the upper classes that would be happy to get rid of the tsarist autocracy, that they therefore serve precisely to consolidate the tyranny of the government is quite obvious. The government uses the cholera, antisemitic and other disorders to depict the oppressed working masses as infuriated wild beasts to whom it would be dangerous to give their freedom. But the government's enemies among the upper classes are beginning to make their peace with it as a necessary evil. Without it, they say to themselves, there'll be nobody to tame the wild beasts.

I know very well that an efficient organisation cannot be created straight away. For this reason we need time and a series of individual actions in which the revolutionaries get to know one another and learn to act together. It is of course difficult for us to judge from abroad, in the absence of regular dealings with you, to what extent your work on these matters has progressed. But the very absence of any connection between you and us demonstrates that even your preparatory organisational work has not advanced very far. We are your comrades in aims and views, and in the cause. We are trying to promote the triumph of these aims through books and journals, in a word, by literary means. There should, consequently, be the very closest link between us. For socialist literature is for you too what the tools are to the craftsman or, more accurately, what the gunpowder and the rifle are to the soldier. But can this literature really flourish and be supplied regularly to Russia when there is no direct link at all between those who publish the books and those who distribute them.

I have mentioned this among other things because it is precisely the establishment of such a link and the transformation of the publishing and literary activity into the general concern of all the workers' circles of Russia that might serve as the first serious point for their merger into a single whole. The supply of socialist literature to Russia, its distribution to the major towns, the collection of funds for its publication – all this might serve to maintain and consolidate the link between the revolutionary workers who are at present uncoordinated and unaware of one another's existence. From the agreement and the dealings between them on the matter of foreign revolutionary publications a lasting all-Russian workers' organisation would gradually develop and strengthen: it would embrace all aspects of revolutionary activity: propaganda, agitation, the printing and distribution of appeals to the people in the name of the workers' union, etc.

You, comrades, have embarked upon the path of revolutionary activity at a time when the revolutionary movement of the 'intelligentsia' has gone into decline. This circumstance, of course, seriously hinders your first steps. But, on the other hand, it assures you of support on the part of all those upper class people who sympathise with the cause of political liberty. They will support you without fail if only because they see in you a serious revolutionary force. Their desperate position vouchsafes this.

The resources of the so-called 'intelligentsia' in this country are far from adequate for the struggle with the government. This was fully proven by the experience of the revolutionaries in the 1870s. The movement at that time did not achieve its aim and for this reason the intelligentsia began more and more to recognise that, without the assistance of the workers, there was no way in which it could overthrow the long-standing edifice of tsarist autocracy.

If our revolutionaries had until recently paid so little attention to propaganda among the workers, the reason for this was their false view of the inability of this stratum to interest itself in political questions. Generally speaking, it was rare until recently even for one of the representatives of the upper classes who had gone over to the people to admit that even among the Russian workers a stratum of intelligent people had formed who had thought about the unjust position of the Russian people and about the means of emancipating them. Three years ago, in addressing a letter to the 'worker intelligentsia', I came to terms in advance with the fact that it would provoke derisive smiles on the lips of many of the representatives of the privileged intelligentsia. But, dear comrades, you have already managed to uproot completely the prejudices of our intelligentsia about the apparent political inability of the Russian workers. For this it was enough to have two or three facts proving that you – the worker Socialists and worker 'intellectuals' – exist and that you are *preparing* to take into your own hands the political awakening of the oppressed and deprived masses of Russia. The few serious manifestations of your activity and the previously scornful attitude of our educated strata towards the Russian workers will give way to respect for them. Then, all the best representatives of the 'intelligentsia' will realise that it is not the workers who should support them but, on the contrary, they who should support the workers in the struggle for the political emancipation of the Russian people.

In energetically helping the worker Socialists to call forth an independent revolutionary movement among the working classes of Russia, the revolutionaries from so-called society perform a great service, not only to these classes, but also to themselves. But it is precisely your own energy that can propel them to this new activity. The more tirelessly you pursue your aim, the more *the news will spread both inside and outside Russia* of your aspirations and your efforts to realise them, and the more rapidly the ranks of your assistants from the educated strata will grow. And once again all this can only be achieved through the gradual agreement and collaboration on various matters and for various reasons of the uncoordinated units and circles of worker Socialists into a single organised whole.

In conclusion I send you on my own behalf and on that of my comrades fraternal greetings on the publication of social democratic booklets and fervent wishes for success in the path that lies before you, such a difficult path and, at the same time, such an attractive one for people who are really advanced and courageous. Europe considers Russia to be an Asiatic country. You have the great historic task of making the Russian people a worthy member of the family of civilised nations.

Zürich, February 1893

IV

The purpose of my letter was to explain very briefly to our worker intelligentsia their immediate tasks and duties with regard to the labouring classes of Russia. The principal evil from which our fatherland is now suffering is the fact that it is governed by the tyranny of one man and his servants, like the private domain of some despotic landowner. It is, therefore, the obligation, the duty, of every honest and educated person to work for its liberation from the yoke of tsarist autocracy. But the true friends of the people are obliged in this process to concern themselves in addition with ensuring that the new state order (after the fall of absolutism) preserves for it the greatest possible rights for the protection of its interests. Political rights are the most powerful weapon in the struggle for economic welfare. The axe, the saw, the plough, machines and factories can none of them in themselves provide either food or shelter. But they are the tools without which it would be almost impossible for people to produce the articles that are essential for life. And the more these tools are perfected, the more easily and rapidly we can produce with their assistance an abundance not only of the essentials but also of articles for pleasure and even luxury goods. But, because the machines, factories etc. are now the property of private individuals, they serve simultaneously as instruments for the exploitation of those millions of people who do not have the opportunity of indulging in such perfected methods of labour. Political rights have a similar significance. In the hands of the rich classes they serve as an instrument for the still greater augmentation of their wealth and power over the people; in the hands of the latter they are, in contrast, a means for their own emancipation from subjection and for the improvement of their well-being.

But the extent of the political rights that a future Russian constitution grants to our labouring classes is determined above all by the strength and significance of these classes when the constitution is drawn up. What can constitute their strength, if not the energy, solidarity and consciousness with which they, or at least a significant number of them, will uphold their political and economic demands! The awakening among the people of dissatisfaction with the present system of government, the spread among them of the correct conceptions of the importance of political rights for its material welfare, the encouragement among them of the desire to fight for these rights — these must therefore be the principal task of our advanced workers and revolutionary Socialists from among the intelligentsia. As the workers of the commercial and industrial centres constitute the advanced stratum of the people,[75] it is to the awakening and encouragement of their political consciousness that the principal efforts of their own representatives among the intelligentsia and in addition, and with their assistance, the efforts of our revolutionary intelligentsia from the other classes must be directed.

But to ensure successful activity on this new path our advanced workers must first of all be organised into circles and must try, as rapidly as possible, to form a single workers' party or a single all-Russian workers' union from these circles. It is fifteen years since the workers of St Petersburg and Moscow manifested their half-hearted desire to unite into an independent union. They even sent a delegate abroad (a locksmith, later sentenced to eight years' penal servitude) to buy a printing press and to negotiate with an émigré writer for him to edit the newspaper of the workers' union.[76] Unfortunately the revolutionaries from the intelligentsia did not at that time sympathise with the cause that our advanced workers were promoting and the latter did not have enough experience of secret revolutionary activity to carry the matter through to a successful conclusion. For this reason a number of members of the newborn union were soon imprisoned and others, like the joiner Khalturin,[77] who [tried to] blow up the Winter Palace and took part in the murder of Strelnikov, were attracted to terrorist activity and were lost in the general mass of revolutionaries from among the students and the so-called intelligentsia in general. The result was that very few people heard anything of the revolutionary achievements of the minority of our workers, and many did not even recognise their ability to comprehend political questions, considering absurd the very idea of conscious activity on their part on behalf of the political struggle.

Recently our revolutionary youth has begun to realise that their own resources alone are far from adequate to ensure any degree of success for their struggle with the government. Some of their representatives have understood that, in order to ensure the success of the struggle, they must enlist the active sympathy and serious support of the factory workers. May the advanced representatives of the latter hasten to make use of this mood among the revolutionary intelligentsia in order to create, with their assistance and collaboration, an independent workers' movement in Russia. The more energetically and persistently they pursue their goal, the more rapidly the present far from complimentary view that educated people hold of our workers will give way to sympathy and respect for them. Alongside the growth of workers' circles and their unification into a single union there will be an increasing readiness on the part of revolutionaries from other classes not only to promote the cause of these circles but also to enter them as members. The final consequence of the activity of our worker intelligentsia along the path indicated will be the fact that all sincere and conscious *revolutionary Socialists*, whatever their name or provenance, will join a general workers' union: instead of the present workers' circles, every one of which acts on behalf of the people and in the name of the people, a single *Socialist Workers'* party will be formed and its members will be 'all true friends of the labouring classes in the population'.[78]

Embarking on the path of the organisation of our emancipatory movement among Russian workers, their advanced minority will have to be clear in their own minds about the position and the demands of the labouring classes of Russia and will have to work out a detailed programme of their aims and immediate demands, both political and *economic*. Our workers will be greatly assisted in the drafting of this programme and in the choice of path towards its realisation by an acquaintance with the emancipatory efforts of their brothers in the advanced countries. Because they were first on the field of battle for their own emancipation, the workers of these countries had, as it were, to grope to find the way and the means to wage their struggle. It is not surprising that in so doing they made many mistakes. But in the end, through many years of hard experience, they have reached a true conception of the conditions for welfare and liberty that are common to all mankind. Acquaintance with this experience and this conception will help our workers to avoid many mistakes and to set off at once along the appropriate path in their public activity.

As has already been said in the preface, the preceding pages were first printed some four years ago. Unfortunately, the matter of the unification of the Russian workers into a revolutionary party does not appear to have moved forward at all in this time. Only this can explain the extremely sad fact that our worker intelligentsia has hitherto exerted no influence on the mass of the people. At the same time the ground for this influence has been more than prepared by the ruinous rule of the autocratic tsar and his servants. The popular disturbances and 'disorders' of recent years demonstrate that the masses of the people are no longer willing to tolerate the tyranny and plunder imposed upon them by tsarist officials in collaboration with the landowners, kulaks and all sorts of exploiters of the people's labour. But in none of these disturbances has the banner of liberty been held aloft, none of the 'insurgents' has proclaimed the need to summon elected representatives from the whole people to destroy the whole of our antiquated state edifice and erect a new one on foundations of popular self-government. For this reason, the people's blood has flowed in vain, it did no damage to autocracy and helped to an even lesser degree to promote the spread of the ideas and aims of the advanced workers among the people.

The calamities that Russia is now experiencing and the ever increasing and instructive outbursts of popular indignation against its oppressors may be turned into instruments for the emancipation of the people only on one condition: with energetic agitation by advanced Russian workers among the mass of the population against tsarist and police tyranny and for the summoning of *an assembly of all the people* [*vsenarodnyi Zemskii sobor*] . But for such agitation they must first of all themselves merge into a strong organisation with a definite programme of action. The immediate future of the poorest classes in our fatherland will depend on the conduct of our worker intelligentsia. Let them keep this firmly in their minds and act accordingly.

1894-1897: bridges to the workers – economic agitation

15. THE WORKING DAY (1894)[79]

Anon.

We all know very well what it means to be a worker: it means above all else to labour and to labour hard! Hard and long. The tailor, the cobbler, the locksmith, the factory worker — life is not easy for any of them. Working a machine, sitting doubled up over a bench, wielding a heavy hammer, using a plane — and doing this not for an hour, a day, a month, or even a year, but for your whole life. Yes, the worker's lot is a sad one! It is not, therefore, surprising that the workers are constantly complaining about their miserable fate. In doing so, they observe: it is true that life is hard but what can we do? Can anything be done? We have to eat and drink somehow, after all, and we have to earn our bread: nobody gives us anything for nothing — so how could things be different?

Thus, the constant worry about our daily bread deprives us of the opportunity to review our position and discuss it properly. In isolation, the individual worker devotes little time to considering whether his working conditions could be alleviated in any way or whether, if he has to work, only reasonable and acceptable demands should be made of him.

Yes, reasonable! But, of course, if we reduce the scale of our labour, we shall have nothing to live on. So what good is less work to us if we do not have the food and drink that we need? No, this is not the way to alleviate our conditions!

But, enough of this: what are things really like, what do we all think? Let us try and discuss with one another what things are like: would we earn less if, for instance, instead of working a thirteen- to fourteen-hour day, we started to work for only twelve hours?

We all know that we do not always earn the same, that a worker's life goes through different periods: some better and some worse, some very bad, and even more when there is no work at all. When the boss is short of labour the workers get more pay: on the other hand, when he is not short, the workers queue for jobs and the boss, exploiting their need, reduces pay.

But when exactly is the boss short of labour? When he has a lot of work and in addition very few surplus workers. For example, when the boss has to complete a particular job in a single day which should take, let us say, sixty hours, and they work, let us say, a twelve-hour day in his workshop or factory, then five men can do this job for him in a single day. But imagine that these men work a ten-hour day — what happens then? What would the boss do? Obviously in that case his workers

23

will not finish the whole job for him in a single day and he will have only one option left: he will take on a sixth worker. Thus, if he needs six workers instead of five, then he requires more and, because he has to take on more workers, there will be fewer remaining unemployed and for these two reasons he will not be able to reduce their pay: hence, the workers will do less work and get more pay.

Now we can return to our earlier question: if this is so, are the workers right in assuming that they cannot achieve shorter working hours? Clearly, they are wrong.

However, there are probably people in our ranks who will say: 'It's true, of course, that the whole of this discussion has been about people who work by the day, the week or the month. What about the piece-workers? There can be no doubt that it is more profitable for them to work as long as possible because the more they work, the more they get.'

Let us take the same example and see if this is true. Let us suppose that the same boss we have already mentioned pays on a piece-work basis, what would happen then? The workers would try and work for fifteen hours a day and they would, it is true, earn more but this could go on only for a very short time.

How many people could in fact be employed on this work? Four at the most, and the other two of the previous six would stay out of work. Nonetheless, they have to live and so they would come to the boss and tell him that they were prepared to work for less pay provided only that they got work. He would of course take advantage of this and tell his own piece-workers, 'I can find cheaper workers who are willing to work for such-and-such pay. So, if you agree to the same conditions, you can stay. If not, thank you and goodbye!!' So the piece-workers would be forced to work a fifteen-hour day and get as much as they previously got for a twelve-hour day and thus they too would lose something from the lengthening of their working day: they would increase the number of unemployed, who would of necessity push pay down, and the piece-workers would make fools of themselves.

We can see from the following calculation that the workers would not in fact earn less from doing less work. Here in Russia at the present time there are about 1,400,000 factory workers, excluding handicraftsmen and artisans, and they work on average for fourteen hours a day: if they worked for thirteen hours, another 100,000 workers would be employed and fewer people would be out of work, all workers could get better pay and, consequently, while working less, they would be earning more.

But how would this apply to trades and industries where the work can be done only at a certain time of year, i.e. where so-called 'seasonal labour' operates, as, for instance, among stonemasons, plasterers, tailors, milliners etc? How would they all be affected? Could masons and plasterers really reduce their working day when they are dependent on the time of year and have to take advantage of it? Or let us take tailors: could they really work shorter hours when their work only lasts for a certain time, after which they have nothing to do? What would they gain? For them, on the contrary, it is more profitable to do more work, as time is short and they must value every minute. No – it is not like that.

If they were to do less work, more of them would be needed, and they would be able to demand higher pay so that they would earn more at the same time.

That is precisely what would happen in seasonal work that is completely dependent on the time of year; as far as other areas are concerned, e.g. tailoring and millinery, where there is not the same dependence on the time of year, the workers would, by shortening their working day, reach a position in which the season itself was prolonged because, if the work is not done on time, part of it remains to be done another time and, thanks to this, the workers will be out of work for a shorter period. In addition, when customers get used to the fact that tailors find it difficult to complete orders on time before holidays or before the arrival of spring or autumn, they will start to place their orders earlier and the season will thus prolong itself of its own accord.

Now you can clearly see that a reduction in the working day would be useful for these workers as well.

In a word, it is obvious that all workers would benefit from a reduction in the working day, that they would thereby earn, not just as much, but even more than, before, and that they would be out of work for a shorter period. Many facts of working life confirm that this is correct. In Germany, for instance, joiners have not always worked the same hours and received the same pay: when they worked thirteen hours a day, i.e. seventy-eight hours a week, they received 7 roubles 30 kopeks a week; when they started to work a twelve-hour day they began to receive 8 roubles 43 kopeks a week. When they achieved a reduction in their working day to eleven hours their pay rose correspondingly to 8 roubles 60 kopeks and, finally, it reached 10 roubles 80 kopeks a week for a nine- to ten-hour day. So their pay rose from 7 to 10 roubles when they started to work four hours a day less. The joiners were not alone: the bakers also achieved a reduction of two hours in their working day and at the same time their pay rose by 6 roubles a week. The same thing happened in England: in London the gas board workers obtained the introduction of an eight-hour working day, instead of a nine-hour one and, as a result, several thousand unemployed found work and, in addition, earnings increased.

Here in Russia, in the province of Minsk, earnings in the weaving mill have altered in the following manner: when the working day lasted fifteen to sixteen and a half hours, average monthly earnings reached 16 roubles 16 kopeks; when they started to work fourteen to fifteen hours a day, pay rose to 18 roubles 89 kopeks, i.e. it increased by 2 roubles 73 kopeks. When they achieved a further reduction in the working day, i.e. when it began to last thirteen to fourteen and a half hours, pay rose again, by 1 rouble 11 kopeks, to 20 roubles, and it finally reached 21 roubles 66 kopeks a month when they started to work a total of eleven and one third to twelve and three-quarter hours a day. Thus, if we compare earnings for a fifteen- to sixteen-hour day with current earnings for a twelve- to thirteen-hour day, i.e. after the working day has been reduced by three hours, then we see that earnings have risen from 16 roubles 16 kopeks to 21 roubles 66 kopeks – in other words by 5 roubles 50 kopeks.[80]

In the western region, since they began to achieve a shorter working day and since they started demanding that the day's work should last only as long as the law designated for artisans, i.e. twelve hours, an increase has also been discernible in the earnings of cobblers, brush-makers and several other trades. The brush-maker, for instance, used to work fifteen hours a day in winter and thirteen and a half in summer and earn on average 2 roubles 75 kopeks a week, but, when he started working a twelve-hour day the whole time, his earnings increased to 3 roubles 25 kopeks a week. Once more, then, a reduction in the working day by one, two or four hours (currently some workshops work from 7 a.m. till 7 p.m., some from 7 till 8, and others from 7 till 9) has been accompanied by increased earnings of 50 kopeks a week, and the same thing happened to cobblers and type-setters. In a word, the same phenomenon can be observed everywhere: *earnings increase with a shorter working day*.

Many people, however, do not accept these facts and maintain that this cannot be so because the opposite is true: it is more profitable for the boss to pay his workers more if they work longer for him. But this is not true. More examples from the life of the workers will serve as proof of this.

The workers of — began to work twelve hours a day instead of eight and their earnings should, as a result, have risen by half, but they increased by only a quarter. And this increase came only in the initial stages and then the opposite occurred: because they produced more goods, fewer workers were needed to do the same work and so more of them were laid off; these unemployed people, by offering their services, naturally depressed the earnings of those who were employed. Hence, it is obvious that in the end the workers gained nothing from the increase in their working day: all that happened was that they had to work longer for the same pay.

So we have seen many examples to prove that all this is true. But these examples have for the most part been chosen from countries, regions and towns where industry is highly developed, where the machine has to a significant extent replaced the labour of man and where, for that reason, the worker is needed less and they can manage more easily without skilled workers, i.e. those men who have learned a particular trade, because the machine simplifies labour to the point where anyone can learn and, consequently, if the worker demands a pay increase or a shorter working day, he can always be replaced by someone else.

However, despite all this, the workers have nonetheless managed, while shortening their working day, to achieve a simultaneous increase in their pay because in all circumstances a reduction in the working day always leads to a decrease in the overall number of unemployed and, by that very fact, consequently increases the earnings of the employed workers.

In the case of those towns and areas where large-scale mechanised industry is still in the early stages of development, where manual labour dominates the majority of trades, and where, as a result, both the quality and quantity of labour depend, in the main, on the skill of every individual worker there it is even easier for the workers to achieve their demands: if the worker refuses to work in the conditions that the boss offers him, he cannot be replaced so easily by a machine or by other workers.

We saw earlier that all the circumstances that in one way or another influence the earnings of workers who are paid on a daily basis exert the same influence on piece-workers: for this reason everything that has been said about the former is also wholly applicable to the latter. Against all their objections that with a shorter working day they would produce less and therefore also earn less we can show them the same incontrovertible proof: if they work less time more workers will have to be employed, there will be fewer unemployed, competition between workers will be reduced and they will therefore be in a position to increase their piece-work earnings, so that in the final analysis a shorter working day will not mean any reduction in their daily or weekly earnings. And we can confirm that by another example taken from the actual life of the workers. In Berlin in 1862 every bricklayer laid 623 bricks a day but in 1873, after the working day had been shortened, every worker could lay 304 bricks in all; at the same time earnings rose from 1 rouble 5 kopeks to 2 roubles 25 kopeks. This shows that even for piece-workers a reduction in the working day increases earnings. After everything that has been said this should already be quite clear to you.

A short working day has many other advantages which may however not be noticeable at first. For instance, a reduction in working hours creates an opportunity to produce more because labour becomes more strenuous or, as they say, more intensive: this means the worker producing more goods per hour than with a long working day. We are convinced that this is correct by numerous facts and examples, both from the life of the workers and from daily life in general.

Every one of us, for example, knows that, when you have to cover a long distance on foot, you walk much more slowly at the end of the journey than at the beginning when you started off with fresh strength. But in work this is much less noticeable because the workers have already grown so used to their hard lot that, in the view of many, the reduction of the working day by an hour or two would not represent any real improvement but would only reduce the quantity of goods produced. But both the one and the other are completely wrong: even the most minute reduction in working hours makes the worker brighter and stronger and, because of his greater leisure, he always sets to work with renewed strength and therefore produces as many goods as he did before. This fact is already well known to the factory owners and some of them have themselves begun to introduce a shorter working day because under this arrangement the quantity of goods produced does not decrease but their quality improves, for the same reason once again.

In Australia, for instance, the eight-hour day has been introduced almost everywhere and there they now produce no less than in other places where they work a thirteen-, fourteen- or fifteen-hour day. The accounts of one factory show that, with the same instruments of production, they started to work 776–777 pounds of yarn. Further, in France every worker produces goods to the value of 1,337 roubles a year, whereas in America (US), where the working day is three hours shorter than in France, a worker produces goods to the value of 4,073 roubles a year. We can find similar examples here in Russia. In 1893 the Scheibler factory in Łódź introduced a twelve-hour day instead of a thirteen-hour one. Other factory owners followed this example and now they say that nobody regrets it: just as many goods as before are produced in their factories because the worker, less exhausted and enfeebled by excessive labour, can produce more. In the Moscow province people work day and night, in all about fifteen to sixteen hours out of twenty-four; in Petersburg there is no night work but nevertheless the Petersburg factory owners maintain that their factories produce more and that the quality of their goods is superior.

To this you will probably say: but if, in the final analysis, just as many goods are produced in a shorter working day, then the old story will be repeated – fewer workers will be required, more people will be unemployed and earnings will be reduced once more!

That would be the case if only you had not forgotten one important thing: in order to obtain a shorter working day the workers must merge, unite and stand firmly together. For this reason, when, by reducing the working day, they provoke an increase in earnings, it will not be easy to deprive them of what they have achieved: having learned from experience and joined together, they will defend their earnings with the same strength with which they previously achieved a reduction in the working day, for it is much easier to keep something that you already have than to get something new.

Thus, to your first question as to whether you would not be reducing your share of food, drink and general provisions by reducing the working day, there is one and the same answer: *no, not only will you not be reducing it, you will even be increasing it.*

Let us now look at the other advantages, apart from an immediate increase in earnings, that would accrue to the workers from a shorter working day. Above all would it not be beneficial to their health? Without doubt it would, because a long working day is for them the source of all sorts of illnesses and even of premature death.

To understand all this better you should first of all know that generally man must work, but he must work in good measure: both insufficient and excessive work are equally harmful to man – they weaken his organism and cause him both illness and suffering. You will probably respond by saying that the rich do not work but nevertheless they do not suffer much as a result. But this is not so. The idle rich, instead of straightforward work, turn to artificial methods like gymnastics, cycling and so on, or they really fall ill and as a result they are constantly taking cures, going on cruises etc. The excessive toil of the working poor produces significantly greater suffering so that exhaustion or an ailment in one organ tells on their whole body.

But, you ask, what is the relationship between, for instance, the hand and the head and heart?

The fact is that the human body is completely normal and healthy only when all parts of the body, all the organs, are exercised. If only some of the organs are exercised they develop at the expense of the others: thus, the right hand is stronger than the left. Besides, what does working generally mean? It means moving our organs; but they come to move because of the existence within us of a multiplicity of fine fibres which are called *nerves*. They are distributed throughout our whole body and they all lead to one place, our brain, where they are interwoven and joined to one another. Thus, tiredness in a particular organ causes the appropriate nerves to suffer and through them this is transmitted to the whole head. You know from your own experience that strenuous labour with the hands gives you pains in the chest, makes your back ache and your head spin. But this kind of strenuous work lasts, not for an hour or a day, but for years, for your whole life — it is not surprising, therefore, that the workers fall ill so frequently and so quickly grow tired and old, and die. Everyone knows that the death rate among the working class is much higher than among the more comfortably off. In Hamburg, for instance, it has been calculated that the average life expectancy for the upper classes is around thirty-five, whereas for the workers it is only fifteen! Quite a difference! This occurs because the worker labours to a degree and in a manner that does not correspond to the requirements of the nature of his organism, but that far exceed them — and in conditions which are directly fatal to his good health. A man needs fresh air to breathe, but the workers live in close, stifling dwellings, which make them feverish. It is bad for a man to move quickly from the heat to the cold: nonetheless in the spinning mills, for example, there are sections where a very high temperature is maintained to dry the wool and in winter the workers have constantly to leave these sections and go outside into the frost! This kind of temperature change rapidly destroys the worker's health: he starts suffering from rheumatism and minor illnesses, but is that all? In fact, if we think about it carefully, we shall see that the worker, even before he makes his appearance in the world, is already suffering in his mother's womb from all kinds of illnesses that will contribute to his premature death. Excessive toil under these conditions is particularly harmful to women who succumb to female illnesses and give birth prematurely: you can appreciate what kind of generation this will give rise to! If the children eventually survive to the age of six to eight, they will be sent into this industrial hell because the father, who works long hours in the factory, has in so doing severely depressed wages, as you know, and these are now insufficient to feed his family, so that he is forced to send both his wife and his children to the factory. But has anyone not seen workers' children? Not seen these pale, slender, emaciated little faces in the match or matting factories? In these young and prematurely aged faces you can read better than in any table, better than in the doctors' reports, how penal labour in a polluted atmosphere (air) affects the already weak health of children.

These are the unfortunate children, who are born weak, as we saw earlier, who grow up uncared for, who from an early age have to go to these factories that are so bad for them, that cripple them and make their teeth fall out as, for instance, in the match factories where the children's gums rot from the sulphur and their teeth fall out. These are the unfortunate children who, if they do manage to reach adulthood, become weak, exhausted, prematurely aged workers who, I repeat, show us more clearly than anything else the effect of excessive labour. In fact illnesses that are insignificant in children become more serious in adults and every worker suffers from some kind of illness.

Hence compositors always suffer from consumption and, in addition, from the lead that they inhale, and their gums and teeth decay. Because they are always working at a machine dressmakers contract female illnesses. Both male and female workers in the cigarette factories suffer from pains in the head and eyes, their hands tremble and so on. In a word every trade produces its own illnesses and it is therefore understandable that the more people work the more rapidly they will succumb to those illnesses.

These are some of the most obvious facts: workers' children die two years earlier than anybody else's. Why is this? Because their mothers give birth prematurely, because they are themselves weak and ill and, naturally, they produce children who are the same, and because they are unable to nurse them and care for them. What factory labour does to women can be seen from the following figures: in America they once examined and recorded all the women who had entered one factory: 16,360 of them were in full health, 882 in moderate health and 185 in weak health. After eight years' work in this factory 14,557 of them were in full health (i.e. almost 2,000 fewer than before), 2,385 were in moderate health (i.e. almost three times more than before). In the course of eight years the number of healthy workers had fallen by two thousand and the number of those in weak health had tripled.

Factory labour, especially when it is prolonged, also causes curvature of the limbs. One doctor recounts that in 1832 in one part of London it was difficult to find a man with straight knees: all the workers had pale, dull faces and bent backs. But twenty-five years later after the introduction of the shorter working day, in the same place and according to the testimony of the same doctor it was, in contrast, difficult to find factory cripples: nobody's face was anywhere near as pale, their backs were not as bent, and in general the workers had a much more cheerful and healthy look. All this was because they did not have to work as long in an unhealthy environment and because they had more rest. Here again are some figures to prove how harmful a long working day is for the workers: the following table compares the number of deaths per thousand among the workers with the number among the rich.

Why is there such an enormous discrepancy? Principally because the workers labour too hard so that they are treated worse than cattle.[81] At least cattle are allowed to rest. If a horse works by day it rests by night because the owner knows that the horse might perish from excessive labour and so he looks after it as his own property. But the worker does not concern him; if he falls ill or dies the owner can replace him without any difficulty and without making a loss. That is why he tortures his workers with hard work without any pangs of conscience, forcing them to labour day and night.

Deaths per thousand

	Class	
Age	Rich	Worker
5	57	345
10	62	402
20	144	434
30	204	514
40	305	674
50	443	767
60	602	828
70	765	935
80	943	991

But if you try to talk to him about it he will make a most innocent face. What! Is he really forcing his workers to do excessive labour? Surely, they come to him themselves and ask for work and they voluntarily agree to work until late at night! Is it really the boss's job to worry about rest for the workers? It is in his interest to forget about it but the workers should remind him. The factory owner who is concerned only that the machinery should not stop for a moment will divide his work force into two shifts, a day one and a night one, and at lunchtime the night workers, who have been sleeping after a hard working night, are woken to replace the day workers who are having their lunch break. Often the factory owner fails completely to designate a particular time even for food, having resolved that (the workers) can eat and work at the same time. We are well aware of the methods and the tricks used by the factory owner to prolong the working day and, consequently, to torture the worker all the more.

But we should never forget the evil of uninterrupted forced labour, we must always remember that we need rest.

So far we have examined the harm done to the worker's health by a long working day; now let us look at the effect it has on his mental capacities and on the degree of his consciousness. Doctors testify that workers generally suffer from nervous disorder, i.e. from head-aches and breathing difficulties, because, as you know, every organ is joined through the nerves to the brain and a pain in one organ provokes a pain in the brain. In addition, as you already know from the above, every organ can be healthy only if it is properly and constantly exercised; if we never use a particular organ in our body at all then it grows weaker. In fact, because workers, thanks to the division of labour, have to work with fewer and fewer of their organs, their remaining organs grow ever weaker and degenerate: for instance, tailors, who have to lead a sedentary existence, usually have weak and bandy legs.

It will be understood that all this applies to the brain as well. The worker rarely has to use his head so that his brain gradually weakens, becomes stunted, less receptive and less capable of being used. The harder the workers labour, the more they lose their capacities, their intelligence, their consciousness. Because this weakness is passed on to posterity, and sick parents cannot produce healthy children, with each generation the workers grow ever weaker, become ever more stunted and degenerate ever further. Thus the workers must know and be thoroughly aware that a *long working day ruins their health, deprives them of their strength, stunts their mental capacities* and they must remember this themselves, because the boss and the factory owner are not concerned about it: they require a certain number of workers and they are never short of them. The more stunted and backward the workers, so much the better for the boss, because they will be less conscious of their situation, the less they will manifest their discontent, the less they will insist on their rights, organise strikes and generally disturb the boss.

But the workers themselves must realise that they are people, they must remember what harms them and *they must fight against it themselves*. The bosses seek out ways of prolonging the working day, reducing wages, in a word, of depriving the workers of their health and consciousness in order to exploit them freely and stuffing their own pockets. The workers, in turn, must seek out ways of reducing the working day and, by so doing, of facilitating an increase in wages. They must demand a short working day to protect their health, to have more time for rest and, finally, to have the time and means to educate themselves.

Apart from the damage to their health, the factory workers become crippled for various reasons: they are left without arms, legs, fingers or, if they fall between the wheels of a machine, they even perish. What is the cause of these misfortunes? Once again the principal cause is the long working day. If the worker has to stand at a machine for twelve, thirteen, fourteen and fifteen hours without even pausing for breath, if the worker never has the opportunity for a good rest after the penal labour that saps his strength completely, if, in a word, the worker is like the wheel of a machine, which is poorly greased and constantly in motion, then is it really surprising that the wheel breaks, cracks, loses its teeth and generally stops moving? Is it really surprising, you may ask, that it is so difficult for this worker to escape from his unfortunate circumstances,[82] this worker whose whole body is constantly exhausted, as if he has been beaten, whose head scarcely moves on his shoulders and spins with tiredness, and whose eyes are dark, because he never has any rest? But these circumstances occur so frequently that it is quite terrible to think of how many innocent people are being sacrificed to that omnivorous capital!

But, if the working day were shorter, if the worker could have more rest, could preserve consciousness and clarity of intellect, then he would be in a position to be more wary of, and less vulnerable to, the tortures of the factory. We are convinced that this view is correct by the fact that all kinds of accidents occur far less frequently in the mornings, when the worker arrives at the factory after a night's rest, and particularly frequently in the evenings, when the worker is tired, both physically and mentally, and when his limbs are shattered. If we count from the beginning of the working day to the end, the number of accidents increases by the hour; it is only in the middle of the day, i.e. after the lunch break when the workers have rested their weary limbs a little and between 6 and 7 p.m., when the machines are cleaned, that the number of accidents is again reduced. (See table below, compiled on the basis of the accident statistics in Germany for 1887.) Thus we see that when the workers rest more they have fewer accidents, but the more they work, the more tired they become and the more often they have the accidents that have crippled tens of thousands of people.

But, you will say, it is not just the length of the working day that causes accidents. They occur in the mornings too, so what causes them then?

We must look for the cause of these accidents above all in the working conditions themselves: in factories, for instance, for reasons of economy the machines are frequently placed so close together that the workers really do have no room to turn round and it is therefore not surprising if they fall between the wheels which cut off their hand, leg etc. Consequently in this case the cause of the accident lies in the overcrowding. In addition, both in Russia and abroad, hundreds of thousands of workers are employed in coal-mines (in underground shafts and pits) where many noxious gases accumulate which will easily ignite at the slightest provocation, causing explosions and killing or maiming everyone who is working in the shaft at the time. There are, it is true, machines that extract the gases from underground shafts, and many other methods, but all these methods cost money and the managers and owners of the mines and factories, the rich millionaires, begrudge the money and prefer to sacrifice hundreds and thousands of workers, worrying about their profits and thinking them much more valuable than human lives.

It is, of course, with astonishment that you will ask if it is really possible that there are no laws obliging the owners to introduce preventive measures against accidents in their factories. Yes, it is true that there is a law of this kind but it is worded as follows: 'The owner who does not introduce in his factory the preventive measures that have already been introduced in neighbouring factories will be punished.' This is the letter of the law. But what happens if the owners of neighbouring factories do not introduce any measures of this kind, considering them unnecessary? In that case the original factory owner will of course feel that he is freed from any obligation towards his workers and the law will remain a dead letter. Where is justice to be found? And how can the worker find it? By law, in the event of an accident, the worker must prove that it was caused by the owner and not by the worker himself. But for this he needs both the time and the money for litigation in the courts and he has neither the one nor the other, so that he is quite powerless against the factory owner. At the same time the latter has at his disposal lawyers whom he hires and who are ready to prove whatever he wants and who bend the law in his favour and who are generally able, with the encouragement of money, to avoid putting into effect the laws which, as we know, are enacted solely to be circumvented.

Thus the workers cannot find protection in either the court or the law. But surely, you will say, there are inspectors who are obliged to supervise the factories, to defend the workers from the wrongs and harm perpetrated by the entrepreneurs, and to supervise the prevention of accidents. Why do they not intervene? First of all, we have so few factory inspectors that they are simply not in a position to look after everything. Secondly, they are also guilty, no better than the rest and far from averse to taking bribes. Thirdly, in the final analysis, the law itself, as we have already seen, can be interpreted in several ways so that the workers cannot expect any help from the factory inspectors.

We have thus examined all the means by which it appears that some improvement might be achieved: amongst them were the law, and the courts, from which one usually expects help, and we saw how much help they give the workers. Yes, they help a lot! *Ten thousand workers* are crippled in Russia every year.

Ten thousand! Out of a total of two million workers – but, you will say, that is appalling!

It is appalling but it is unfortunately true. They are unwilling to introduce strong measures to protect us from premature death. For us there are neither laws nor justice: so what can we do? To whom can we turn? To ourselves, to our brother workers who carry the same burden and who drink the same bitter cup of suffering!

But, you may ask, when on earth can the workers give any thought to themselves and, in particular, to their brothers and sisters, the working class as a whole? The worker gets home from work between 10 and 11 p.m. or even later; he is tired, completely shattered, hardly able to hold his head up. It is cold and miserable where he lives and his exhausted children sleep like the dead. His wife, who has been slaving away all day just as much as he has, has also gone to sleep. He is left to lie down on his rough bed so that tomorrow he can set out once more to his hard labour. So it goes on day in day out for the whole of his life – from factory to a cold dark dungeon and back again! When boredom drives him from his home on to the street what pleasures can he find there? He sets off for the tavern for a glass of vodka which warms his exhausted body; there he also finds both cards and billiards which drive his boredom away and temporarily cheer him up. Because of these diversions he once again has no time to ponder over his situation because in the tavern there is no food for thought or for feelings which therefore become constantly more dulled, and with every day that passes the worker looks at himself and at his surroundings with increasing indifference. But, if he does have moments of consciousness from time to time and sees and understands his unfortunate position, how can he help himself? If he has no time to think of himself or to care for his wife and children, can he really be expected to think of others and worry about the needs of the working class? Hence the workers become rougher and rougher because their life is spent either at the machine, or in the tavern or in a cold dark corner, with no books and no pleasures which would exert a beneficent influence on the character of a man so that he could be told apart from a wild beast!

However, if the workers worked less, they would not be so tired and weak and they would not feel the need to revive themselves with a glass of vodka: coming home early they would find their wife and children waiting for dinner and, finding relaxation there, enjoying the endearments of their family, they would not be forced to flee from their home to the tavern. In fact, in England, for instance, in the twenty-five years after the introduction of a shorter working day, drunkenness among workers decreased significantly. If a long working day has this kind of effect on the parents, what must its effect be on the children and on the formation of their character? We know, of course, that there are in fact things in the workers' way of life that give their enemies cause to assert that the workers are spoiled, depraved, and so on.

But could it be otherwise? That is the question. Could it be otherwise when their wage, because of a working day that is too long, is extremely small, when the workers have to send their wife and children to the factory to earn enough to live on, and when workers' children are in the constant company of adults and are party to discussions and scenes that they should not be party to? Here in Russia adult workers and their children, men and women, are together the whole time, and not just at work but while they are asleep – in these conditions how can the workers change? How can the children remain innocent if they see themselves surrounded by so many instances of tyranny, plunder and of violence that goes unpunished, and if the boss himself, the rich factory owner, thinks only of how to amass more, how to deprive the worker of his pittance? From whom can the worker learn his morality?

Thus we have seen that the workers do not have the slightest opportunity of growing into honest and moral people, because their life is spent in the factory and when they have finished work they do not have even a moment to consider their situation, to improve their character, to develop their tastes or to study. We have seen that excessive labour deprives the workers of their energy, their health and their intellectual capabilities and that this excessive labour means that their wages are extremely low and deprives them of the opportunity of satisfying their most basic needs. Finally, we have seen that excessive labour cripples the workers and is a contributory factor to their premature death and that it forces them to send their weakling children almost from the age of six to the factory where their health deteriorates and they age prematurely. *For the workers all this is a result of the long working day.*

Hence, in order to increase our wages, to protect our health and to live as other people live, to escape from a position akin to that of beasts of burden, who are not aware of their situation, to have the opportunity to study, to ensure that we can bring up our children too as honest people and save them from crime and debauchery, to have the time to think over the affairs and needs, both of our own and of the whole working class, for all this *we must direct all our efforts to ensuring that we have to work less and thus to securing a shorter working day.*

But how can this be achieved? How can we secure a reduction in working hours?

As far as handicraft workers are concerned this is a very simple matter in its early stages. In Russia we have a law, according to which handicraft workers should not work for more than twelve hours a day, and this time includes half an hour for breakfast and one and a half hours for lunch; this law has existed for over a hundred years. It states: 'The daily hours for handicraft workers are: from 6 a.m. to 6 p.m., excluding half an hour for breakfast and one and a half hours for lunch and rest.'[83]

However, this law is not observed, because it would be unprofitable for the workshop bosses to observe it and because the workers are ignorant benighted men who are unaware of its existence and do not appreciate the good it might do them. It is, therefore, not surprising that in many workshops the working day lasts fourteen, fifteen and sixteen hours.

But how can the workers reach a position where their work lasts for only twelve hours a day? What do they have to do to bring this about?

They must, first of all, explain to one another all the gains that would accrue from a shorter working day. Then they must submit to the Governors petitions signed by all the workers urging that the police should be used to compel the workshop bosses to release their workers after twelve hours' labour.

It is possible that a worker will ask: 'Why should I talk to workers and explain to them the gains from a short working day? I'd be better off sending a petition to the Governor myself and pointing out to him that in certain workshops the law on a twelve-hour day is being broken. Then the police would probably force the bosses to abide by the law and I should thus be rendering a great service without any effort on the past of the workers.'

This kind of attitude has no justification. Until such time as the workers themselves are imbued with an awareness of the advantage of and need for a short working day they will be helping the police in the circumvention of the law: they will tell the police that they only work for twelve hours, they will hide when the police inspect the workshops and will set to work again when they have gone. This has been the usual pattern until now. In other words it is only when the workers really understand the enormous significance for them of a short working day, and when they consciously begin to strive for it, that they will be able to realise their demands.

However, although there is a law, even if the workers want to work shorter hours, it is not enough to ensure that in practice they work for less than twelve hours a day: the bosses know very well that there is a very convenient and simple method of dealing with the police – passing them a few roubles so that the police do not start to interfere, just as if the workers were content to work fourteen and fifteen hours. Hence the bosses very quietly dispose of their apprentices who are unwilling to work for more than twelve hours.

Consequently the principal method available to worker handicraftsmen for shortening the working day appears to be strikes, i.e. a complete work stoppage until the boss has agreed to the demands put forward by the workers.

For the factory workers, who are not affected by the aforementioned law, strikes are almost the only method both of persuading individual factory owners to shorten the working day and of achieving a factory law that limits the number of working hours.

But, in order to ensure that the workers can stop working immediately and that, during their strike, they can hold firm and not be deflected from their demands, they must unite, they must form a union. It is only by joining in unions that the workers will develop mutual trust, will recognise their common interests, and will

Before lunch		After lunch	
Time	No. of accidents	Time	No. of accidents
6–7	436	12–1	587
7–8	794	1–2	745
8–9	815	2–3	1,037
9–10	1,069	3–4	1,243
10–11	1,598	4–5	1,178
11–12	1,590	5–6	1,306
		6–7	979

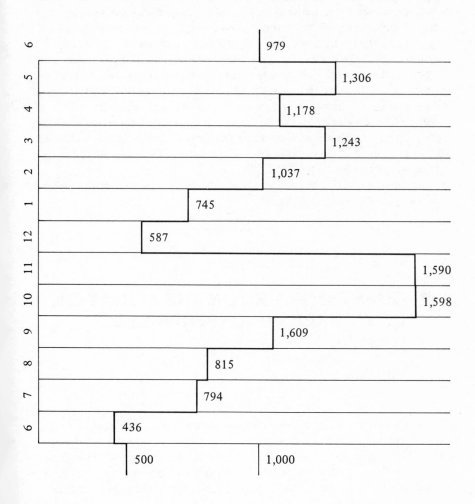

support one another. It is only by joining a workers' union that each [individual worker] can be sure that nobody will start work again until everybody's demands have been met. It is, in the final analysis, only then that the workers will hold firm during a strike.

In addition, to organise a strike you need funds to support the striking workers during the strike so that they do not have to give in through lack of means. With this end in view the workers joining unions should surrender whatever they can afford to a general fund for a rainy day, they must collect money, in short, they must organise general *workers' funds*. By forming unions and organising funds, by standing firmly together so that, if one man gives up his work, the others will not replace him, the workers will achieve everything: they will ensure that they work eleven, ten or even fewer, hours a day. First of all, they will force the bosses to observe the law on the twelve-hour day, then, having a twelve-hour working day, they will have the leisure in which to consider their position and, step by step, they will begin to achieve more and more improvements. In all this you must not forget that all these improvements are to the *advantage and profit of the workers* and are not profitable for the owners and bosses. For this reason the workers must always rely only on *themselves* and must not depend on any benefactors!

Let the workers join forces and do everything together, let them combine their limited separate resources and form a single enormous force so that they can then achieve a reduction in the working day, and, at the same time, alleviate, and bring light into their own difficult working life.

Unity, unions and the struggle for a short day – this is the first, the major way to improve the life of the workers!!!

16.   QUESTIONNAIRE ON THE SITUATION OF WORKERS IN ENTERPRISES (1894/5)[84]

V.I. Lenin

(1) The number of workers in the institution – men, women, adolescents, children, the total number. (2) When and how long the employment is for, or if it is without a definite term. Is there anything special about it? (Employment through a contractor, the district authorities, an artel, etc.) (3) Does the owner break the terms of employment before their term has expired, e.g. by paying less? (4) Do workers leave the employer before their term has expired? In droves or one at a time? How does the owner react? Does he complain to a court or to an inspector, does he

protest to other owners? (5) How many hours a day does the work last? Is there night and holiday work? Always or from time to time? How are the shifts arranged? Is there frequently work outside hours? Can one refuse to work on holidays and outside hours? (6) Information on monthly output. The number of workers. The jobs given to men and women. Working together or apart? The monthly output: of the ordinary worker, the skilled worker, the slow worker. Who provides the food? Who provides the quarters? Is it piece-work, or is it done by day or by month? (7) How much higher is the pay for holiday or out-of-hours work? (8) How many times a month are wages paid out and in what manner: in cash, in goods, in shop tokens? Are there any abuses in the payment (delays, miscalculations, etc.)? (9) Have the wages recently been increased or reduced? If so, what explanation has been given? (10) Deductions from wages in roubles and kopeks: to the artel, the shops, for arrears. (11) A list of fines. In round numbers how much a month does this affect the individual? Are there irregularities in the penalties? (1) How do the masters and owners treat the workers? Give examples. (13) Is there dissatisfaction among the workers with conditions in the factory? How is this dissatisfaction manifested? Revolts. Is it possible to give more details of all the strikes in this institution or in others in which [the workers] have participated, or about which they have known: when, for what reason, how many people took part, how it went – peacefully or violently, were the army called in, how did it end – whether it was a success or a failure and why it ended as it did? (14) Are the factory laws of any use to the workers? What kind of man is the factory inspector? How does he treat the workers? Give some of his actions as an example. (15) Are there factory shops and consumers' cooperatives in the institution? If yes, give the following figures: what are the prices on the open market and in the factory shop for rye-flour, high quality wheat, salt beef, lard, eggs, milk, potatoes, sugar, salt, kerosene etc.? (16) As far as the worker, single and married, is concerned [the cost] per month [of]: accommodation, food (in artels and individually), heating, light, and per year: taxes, debt loan payments, clothing, shoes, tobacco, vodka?

17. TO THE WORKERS OF THE SEMYANNIKOV FACTORY (JANUARY 1895)[85]

V.I. Lenin

... *And so in each of these numerous similar riots the worker who understands first of all disregards the example of all kinds of outrages perpetrated by the factory authorities in their ... * of his brother workers. That is the first thing. Secondly he is convinced once again that, however uneducated are the people who rebel only in this way, the very instance of such an explosion shows that they are discontented and would be willing to sacrifice a great deal to escape from their accursed fate; but they simply don't know how [to go about it]. That is the second thing. Thirdly, whether he wants to or not, he is forced to recognise that neither he nor his comrades who are at a similar stage of development have done much to ease the lot of all workers, when the majority of Russian workers has not yet thought up any other method of struggle. But isn't all this really sad?

Sadness however is sadness, and work is work. We work our whole lives for the capitalists – how about working for ourselves? We recall that our first duty is to know in advance about all these circumstances, to intervene in the event of their appearance in the crowd, which relies on its fists alone, and to explain to it how and why all this occurs and why we should act in a different way. This is not all that difficult, and the main thing is that without it the lot of the workers will never be changed. Let us take our example. In this case it would have been possible to tell in advance that the destruction of the masters' houses would only lead to the rapid involvement of the police, the workers would be silenced and the affair would end as it has ended.

But everybody knows that the factory owners, the police and the whole authority of the state are all one, and that they are all against us. They are glad that we started the fisticuffs; they then sent out the men who had more than their fists to rely on and declared, 'What can we do with these pigs? Let them go, and they start beating one another up.'

Then those very people would turn out to be right who ought to be tried and driven out of St Petersburg for not paying wages on time, for demanding longer working hours than those agreed, for demanding them and mocking. Here our example shows how all these upright gentlemen have collaborated!

You know that there's a toy where you press a spring and up jumps a soldier with a sabre. That's what happened at the Semyannikov factory and that's what will happen all over the place. The factory owners and their toadies are the spring: push it just once and the puppet that it activates will appear – the public procurators, the police and the gendarmes.

*The beginning of the pamphlet has not been preserved.

If you take a steel spring, press it, it will hit you and that will be that. But we all know that if you press the spring constantly and persistently, without releasing it, then it will lose its strength and the whole mechanism will be spoiled, even if it's as cunning a toy as ours. We must impress this fact on every worker's mind.

We press this spring occasionally but it weighs upon us all the time. The first thing that we must do is to imitate its manner and the spring yields to just a single press: let us imagine that the Semyannikov workers had pressed, that they had been paid their wages and that the puppets had been sent in panic; even the city governor had sent an officer with some money. Once the pressure had weakened the spring stretched out once more and the governor, sitting in his cosy office, gave orders as to which of the best workers were to be exiled from St Petersburg and where they were to be sent. That means that we must press, but if we're going to press, then we must press together, all in one direction, and not let go, or we shall only be beaten more severely again.

The Russian worker still has many tasks in front of him and he will have to make many sacrifices but his labour is not without hope and the time has come, the time is long overdue, for him to tackle them. But what choice does life itself offer him? Being transformed completely into a beast of burden that merely stares blankly, as everyone shoves one unbearable burden after another on to him – isn't this really equivalent to the destruction of humanity in him, and not only in him, but in those near to him, all those for whom you live and work? Moving to another place? But where? In his native village there is only destitution, the fists and rods of the estate managers; the people don't flee there, but from there to the town. Leaving for another factory or another town? But won't it be the same there? Leaving for somewhere and having to be thrashed day after day, and expecting to be dismissed, if not today then the day after, for some little trifle, or simply because another, or even cheaper, employee has been found, or an employee with 'protection'. And if you peer deeper into life you will see that it will be like that in the future: starvation and unemployment will grow, the number of people willing to do backbreaking work for a pittance will increase. This will be used by every proprietor and by the police, and the whole power of the state will assist them in this attempt which is 'legal' in our times. (How else could it be? Everyone is looking after his own profit!)

And so it will be until the workers realise that they will never find salvation anywhere but in themselves, and until they act together to exert constant pressure on the detestable group of people who live off the toil of others.

In the struggle the Western worker has, by a united effort, already achieved an infinitely better lot than ours; we too should look for salvation in the same struggle. In England the worker receives three times, in America six times as much as our worker, while their working day is shorter, and in England the cost of living is only a little higher than in cities here like St Petersburg and Moscow, while in America it is even cheaper. This is to say nothing of the other things: workers there assemble freely and talk of their affairs, they have large funds to support their comrades even in case of strikes or unemployment, they publish their own papers and even participate in the administration of the state! But even there all this was not achieved overnight, even there the workers were at first persecuted and victimised for their attempts to unite, and the factory owners also wore them out in their factories, just as ours do. But the workers fought indefatigably and now all the authorities there are forced to tremble before their strength.

The capacity for struggle may only be evoked by struggle.

The greater the number of people who participate in every incident, the greater the rationality and equanimity with which they will be able to judge what they have begun, and the greater will be the success of the whole common cause of the workers.

As soon as conditions become intolerable in a factory, general discontent grows. It is the duty of every knowledgeable worker to intervene in the affair, to unite those who are willing to fight, to show which demands they should put to all their oppressors; with this knowledge things will always improve, because both the position of the workers has improved, if you like, beyond all recognition, and the number of people who understand the value of the struggle has increased.

If in that same Semyannikov factory the workers, who so long ago suffered a delay in the payment of their wages and the deception and mockery of the factory managers, had agreed in advance in as large a number as possible either to stop work altogether or to achieve the fulfilment of even a few minor demands, such as the immediate payment of wages on Saturdays straight after knocking-off time, the payment of all wages before Christmas – then, acting not with their fists but by a general agreement specifically directed at the factory owner, they would probably have gained this concession, and without so many pointless sacrifices. In this case they could have seen which of their comrades could be relied upon, who stood for himself and betrayed the others, who was the worker's friend and who his enemy, who knew more and could help with this knowledge and advice. Lo and behold the next time it would be easier to lead the fight and it would be easier to gain an even greater improvement in their situation. 'Struggle and knowledge!' – that is what Russian life demands from the Russian worker.

18.   WHAT SHOULD THE PORT WORKERS STRIVE FOR? (FEBRUARY 1895)[86]

Anon.

Comrades, we all know how hard life is for the port workers. We all know that it would be difficult to find another place in Petersburg where the wages were as low, where there was as much fault-finding and as many deductions [from the workers' pay], where the workers ate and lived as badly. But very few people know that many of the restrictions even constitute a breach of the agreement reached between the workers and the yard. Very few know what the workers should strive for above all and how they should act in order to improve their position even just a little.

Let us talk a bit about this.

Above all the workers must strive to ensure that the foremen should set the final rate for work, as is done in all other plants, so that the boss cannot lower the rate promised by the foreman. Otherwise the worker agrees on one rate with the foreman and starts work, but the boss sometimes reduces the rate by half.

They must ensure that deductions of 25 kopeks in the rouble are not made in the rate for unfinished work. This is illegal because it is forbidden to make deductions from wages. It is unjust and extremely hard on the workers who have to leave the factory empty-handed and wait for whole months for the 25 kopeks that has been held back.

They must strive for the repeal of the rule by which piece-work cannot be paid at more than 50 kopeks in the rouble above the rate for time-work. They must demand that the worker always has the right to a calculation based on the same rate, i.e. that there is no 'shrinkage', that the works management under no circumstances has the right to reduce wages to below the time-rate, which even so is low enough. At other yards, for instance at the Baltic Yard, the worker always has the right to demand payment at the time-rate.

They must strive for the abolition of overtime, so that work can never under any circumstances last for longer than ten hours a day, so that there is no work on holidays. It seems to the workers that overtime gives them the chance to earn more but in actual fact it only allows the owner to depress the rate further and further and to oppress the worker with outrageous, harmful and exhausting work.

These are the most necessary, the minimum demands, based on the agreement between the worker and the yard; a breach of them is simply illegal and is something against which the workers should stand firmly, together as one man. Otherwise they will not achieve any improvement in their situation. Otherwise the management, seeing that the workers bow to everything, will reduce pay even further, make overtime longer and more frequent, think up new forms of deduction and extortion like the contract stamps introduced at the New Year.[87] Why do other yards function without these stamps? Why should the workers pay for these stamps when they receive next to nothing, and not the authorities?

To achieve these demands the workers must act differently — not in the way they have usually acted until now. If the workers will not clearly recognise just what they should demand, if their dissatisfaction is blind and expresses itself in throwing stones at the management, then the workers will achieve nothing. But if every one of them knows exactly which demands they should defend against the bosses, if they make these demands peacefully and firmly then the bosses will not be able to claim that the workers are simply 'in revolt', then the bosses will appreciate that you do not ignore workers who understand their interests and stand together for them, and they will have to yield. They will not dare to break their agreements with the workers and bring in new pressures when the workers begin to defend firmly and consciously every article of the agreement and when they stand together against new restrictions.

So that it should be easier for the workers to make representations they must demand the right to elect permanent deputies in every workshop (like those elected, for instance, at the Baltic Yard) and they must elect as deputies intelligent and honest workers who will not be afraid to stand up for everyone and put the common demands openly and skilfully. If the workers had permanent representatives it would be impossible to forbid these deputies to enter into negotiations with the bosses; it would be impossible to brand these deputies as troublemakers and simply seize and arrest them, as they do now with deputies elected by the workers in a particular dispute.

Let the workers try to understand properly how they can explain more clearly to one another precisely how the bosses at the yard are breaking the law and the agreement reached with the workers when they oppress the workers. Let them try and explain and clarify this to every worker. Let them insist that everyone should act together and let them punish severely those who act against the common decision of the workers: only then will they be in a position to achieve their demands.

19. APPEAL TO THE WORKERS TO UNITE INTO A WORKERS' UNION (JUNE 1895)[88]

Moscow 'Workers' Union'

Appeal

Comrades, workers!

Our situation gets worse and worse each year. In the hope of earning more, we work for longer hours, working at nights and on holidays. But what will come of this? Will our situation improve? Where 150 men worked previously the owner makes do with 100 working harder. The other 50, unemployed, go from factory to factory and, whether they like it or not, they are forced to agree to work for the very lowest pay and they depress our earnings too. If one of us so much as mentions his low pay, then the owner replies by pointing to the unemployed: if you don't like it, he says, there are ten men at the gates waiting for your job.

Comrades, what are we to do? How are we to fight?

We see that you will do nothing on your own. It is probably still possible to conduct the struggle in whole factories and plants, but even this is extremely difficult and rarely meets with success. Only when the workers of every factory and plant join together, apply themselves jointly to their workers' cause, only then is it possible to be sure of success.

For this reason the workers who have understood the need to fight together have joined in the *Workers' Union* and invite the workers of every factory and plant to join them for the common struggle for the common workers' cause.

Let us unite, comrades, and let us begin to fight together for the right to assemble freely to discuss our own affairs. We shall fight until we have thrown off the yoke of the capitalists, until the whole world, every factory and every plant has been made common property.

20. APPEAL TO THE WORKERS TO UNITE AND DEMAND THE SHORTENING OF THE WORKING DAY (NOVEMBER 1895)[89]

Moscow 'Workers' Union'

Comrades, we sleep and do not see how the capitalists are robbing us. Enough of their drinking our blood: we have done the work and it is time we recognised it. And so, comrades, let us follow the example of our comrades and brothers in toil, the foreign workers. They have laws that they won for themselves and now they prosper but we, as beasts of burden, work fifteen and sixteen hours a day, lining the pockets of the rich with our blood and toil. Comrades, all our working blood belongs to the capitalists. Are they really stronger than us? They are a handful, and we are millions. Comrades, we are brothers amongst ourselves. Let us forget the quarrels and the squabbles, let us unite, found [mutual aid] funds and [face] the enemy together! Let us march arm in arm and ask for a short working day. Comrades, awake, the time has come to begin avenging blood for blood. Workers of all countries, unite!

21. TO THE WORKING MEN AND WOMEN OF THE THORNTON MILL (10 NOVEMBER 1895)[90]

V.I. Lenin

Working men and women of the Thornton mill!

The 6 and 7 November are days that we should all remember ... By their concerted resistance to the bosses' pressure the weavers have proved that at a difficult moment there are still people in our midst who can stand up for our common interests as workers, and that our beneficent bosses have not yet managed to turn us once and for all into the pitiful slaves of their bottomless purse. Comrades, let us then carry on firmly and steadfastly to the end, let us remember that we can improve our lot only by our common and concerted efforts. Above all, comrades, do not fall into the trap that Messrs Thornton have so cunningly laid for us. They reason thus: 'There is a lull now in the demand for our goods, so that, if we keep to the old working conditions in the mill, we shall not make our old profit ... And we are not prepared to take less . . . So we shall have to lean on the working fraternity and let them bear the brunt of the bad market prices . . . But the matter must be handled cleverly and not just any old how so that the worker in his simplicity will not appreciate what kind of treat we have in store for him . . . If we tackle them all at once, they will all rise up at once and we shall be unable to handle them, so we shall first dupe the wretched weavers and then the others will not get away . . . We are not used to restraint in our dealings with these creatures, and why should we be? New brooms sweep cleaner here.' So the bosses, who are so solicitous of the well-being of the worker, want stage by stage to prepare the same future for the workers in all sections of the mill as they have already put into practice for the weavers . . . That is why, if we all remain indifferent to the fate of the weaving sheds, we shall be digging with our own hands a grave in which we too shall soon be buried. Recently the weavers have been earning, in round figures, 3 roubles 50 kopeks a fortnight, and during the same period families of seven have somehow contrived to live on five roubles, and families comprising a husband, wife and child on 2 roubles in all. They have sold the last of their clothes and used up the last pennies that they earned by their hellish labour at the same time as the Thorntons, their benefactors, were adding millions to their existing millions. To crown it all, before their very eyes more and more victims of the bosses' greed have been thrown out on to the street, and the pressure has been regularly increased with the most heartless cruelty. Without any explanation they have started to mix noils[91] and clippings in with the wool, which slows the work down terribly; delays in getting the warp have increased as if by chance; lastly, they have without further ado started to introduce short time and now they are bringing in pieces that are five lengths long, instead of nine, so that the weaver has to fuss about longer and more frequently getting the warps and fixing them, for which, as we know, he is not paid a penny. They want to starve our weavers out, and the fortnightly pay of 1 rouble 62 kopeks that has already started appearing in the pay books of some weavers might soon become the usual rate in the weaving sheds . . . Comrades, do you too want to wait for this sort of kindness from the bosses? If not — if, when it comes to the crunch, your hearts have not turned completely to stone when faced with the suffering of poor people like yourselves, rally together round our weavers: let us put forward our common demands, and on every suitable occasion let us wrest better conditions from our oppressors. Workers of the spinning sheds, do not be deceived by the stability and the slight increase in your pay . . . After all, almost two-thirds of your brother workers have already been sacked from the mill and your better earnings have been bought at the cost of the starvation of your very own spinners who have been sacked. This is another of the bosses' cunning tricks, and it is not difficult to understand it if only you work out how much was earned by the entire spinning section before and how much it earns now. Workers of the new dyeing section . . . For fourteen and a half hours work every day, saturated from head to foot in the poisonous fumes of the dyes, you now earn 12 roubles a month in all. Take note of our demands: we also want to have done with the illegal deductions made from you for your foreman's inefficiency. To casual workers and all unskilled workers in the mill generally: do you really hope to keep your 60–80 kopeks a day when the skilled weaver has to content himself with 20? Comrades, do not be blind, do not fall into the bosses' trap, stand up for one another more resolutely, otherwise we shall all have a bad time this winter. We must keep a very close eye on our bosses' manoeuvres towards reducing rates of pay and we must resist with all our strength this trend, which would be fatal for us . . . turn a deaf ear to all their pleading about business being bad: for them it only means less return on their capital — for us it means the sufferings of starvation for our families, deprived of the last crust of stale bread. Can there really be any comparison between the two? Now they are putting pressure on the weavers above all, and we must ensure:

1. an increase in the weavers' rates of pay to their level last spring, i.e. by about 6 kopeks a length;

2. that the weavers are also brought under the law that says that a worker must be told how much he will earn on a job before he starts it. Let the table of rates of pay, bearing the factory inspector's signature, exist not just on paper but also in reality, as required by law. In the case of weaving, to the existing rates should be added: information about the quality of the wool, the number of noils and clippings in it, and an estimate of the time required for preparatory work;

3. that the working time should be so arranged that we do not stand idle through no fault of our own; now, for instance, things are so arranged that the weaver loses a day on each piece waiting for warp and, since the piece is being reduced to almost half its former size, the weaver will suffer a double loss, regardless of the table of rates of pay. If the boss wants to steal our earnings in this way, let him do so openly, so that we know exactly what he wants to squeeze out of us;

4. that the factory inspector sees to it that there is no subterfuge in the rates of pay, that there are no dual rates. That means, for instance, that he should not permit two different rates of pay in the table for one and the same job under different names. We received 4 roubles 32 kopeks a piece for weaving Bieber, and only 4 roubles 14 kopeks for Ural[92] — but, as far as the work is concerned, is it not one and the same thing? An even more impudent bit of trickery is the dual rate for work on a job of the same name. By this means Messrs Thornton have dodged the laws on fines, which stipulate that a fine may only be imposed for damage that results from the worker's carelessness; in these circumstances the deduction must be recorded in the worker's pay book in the 'fines' column not later than three days after its imposition. A strict record of all the fines must be kept and the sum total is to go, not into the factory owner's pocket, but to meet the needs of the workers of the factory concerned. But here — you have only to look at our books — there are blank spaces, there are no fines, and one might think that our bosses are the kindest of the lot. In actual fact, however, because of our ignorance, they get round the law and easily arrange things to suit themselves . . . We are not fined, you see, but they make deductions from us by paying us at the lower rates: as long as two rates, a higher and a lower rate, exist, there is no way of complaining about them — they counted out the money for themselves and counted it into their own pockets.

5. that, in addition to the introduction of single rates of pay, every deduction should be recorded in the fines column with an indication of why it has been made. Then unjust fines will be obvious, less of our labour will be done for nothing and there will be a decline in the incidence of the disgraceful things that happen now, as, for example, in the dyeing sheds where the workers earn less because of the foreman's inefficiency which, by law, cannot be a reason for the non-payment of labour, since there can be no question in this instance of the worker's carelessness. And we have all had deductions like that for things for which we are in no way to blame.

6. We demand that the payment we make for lodgings should be at the pre-1891 level, i.e. 1 rouble per person per month, because, our earnings being what they are, we have absolutely nothing to pay the 2 roubles with and, in any case, what are we paying for? . . . For this filthy, smelly, crowded fire hazard of a kennel? Do not forget, comrades, that all over St Petersburg 1 rouble a month is considered enough: it is only our considerate bosses who are not satisfied with this and here too we must force them to curb their greed. In defending these demands, comrades, we are by no means rebelling: we are only demanding that we be given what the workers in other factories already enjoy by law. They took it away from us, hoping that we should be unable to uphold our own rights.

This time let us show that our 'benefactors' are mistaken.

22. WHAT ARE THE DEMANDS OF THE WOMEN AT THE LAFERME FACTORY? (NOVEMBER 1895)[93]

St Petersburg Union of Struggle

Demand the release of all those who have been arrested, as they were not the instigators and the disturbances were caused by the insolence of the owners.

Demand an increase in the rate to 40 kopeks a thousand at the machine.

Demand that there should be no oppression in the factory, that they should not dare to reject goods that are going on sale.

Demand the abolition of the illegal dues of 10 kopeks a month (for storing their clothing and providing hot water, etc.).

23. FROM THE UNION OF STRUGGLE FOR THE EMANCIPATION OF THE WORKING CLASS (15 DECEMBER 1895)[94]

St Petersburg Union of Struggle

Comrade workers, the recent strikes have brought about an unusual degree of confusion among our capitalist bosses. They have seen with horror that the workers of Petersburg have begun to fight against their intolerable yoke. Influenced by a fear of this solidarity, Laferme and Thornton have tried to calm the impatient workers by a few concessions; seeing the disturbance caused by the appearance of leaflets at the Putilov works,[95] the factory management rushed to reduce the cut in pay that had been announced. Even the factory inspectorate began to treat its responsibilities more seriously: recently, in a special circular, the factory inspector recognised as illegal the rejection of defective articles that the milliners of the Laferme factory had complained about. But, having yielded where it would have been dangerous not to yield, the capitalists turned to the government for assistance against the workers who had dared to make a move. True to their duty – to protect the interests of the wealthy – the authorities enthusiastically set about sparing the Thorntons from future distasteful concessions to their despised workers. What could they do to ensure that in future there would be no such strikes? In the opinion of the police strikes and disorders are not caused by the destitution and sufferings of those by whose labour the whole of society lives; in their opinion all this is the responsibility of 'fire-brands', disturbed people. Of course. Who, if not fire-brands, would at every new act of oppression distribute the demands, the mere sight of which makes the capitalists' hair stand on end. And so, on the night of 8 to 9 December, in order to uproot this evil at once, the police carried out raids all over the city: dozens of suspects were thrown into prison, the factories were inundated with spies. 'Order has been established. There will be no more strikes. The leaflets will disappear', is what the capitalists think while their police friends lick their lips at the prospect of their forthcoming holiday reward for their cruel diligence. Now, after the arrests and before the holidays, the Thorntons are throwing several dozen weavers who had gone on strike on to the street, blaming them for their own forced compliance. The new city governor kindly offers them their only hope – a free ticket home to the starving countryside . . . The money bag and the police uniform know no pity. Nevertheless the strikes are not coming to an end. There is talk of new disturbances at the Laferme factory, of a strike at the Lebedev mill[96] and at the Sampson mill. And the leaflets go on appearing as before, they are read, and everywhere they meet with agreement, and the Union of Struggle for the Emancipation of the Working Class, which distributes them, remains intact and will continue its activity. The police got hold of the wrong address. The workers' movement will not be defeated by arrests and deportations: the strikes and the struggle will not cease until the complete emancipation of the working class from the yoke of capitalism has been achieved. *Comrades, we shall continue to defend our interests together.*

24. WHAT IS A SOCIALIST AND A POLITICAL OFFENDER? (DECEMBER 1895)[97]

I.V. Babushkin

Brothers, comrades, how hard it is to see that we stand so far behind in our development. Most of us do not even understand what 'Socialist' means. We are ready to betray people who are called 'Socialists' and 'political offenders' by denouncing them, to ridicule and even to destroy them, because we think of them as our enemies. Is it true, comrades, that these people are our enemies? Let us look more closely at them and we shall probably see that on the whole they are not as terrible as they seem. These people, whom we abuse and betray into the hands of our enemies to gain a gratitude that we expect from them but do not get, sacrifice their lives on our behalf. You yourselves, comrades, know that the owner is robbing us – the *factory owner* or *plant owner*, whose side is taken by the *government*. The Socialists are those people who strive for the emancipation of the oppressed working people from the yoke of capitalist owners. They are called political or state offenders because they oppose the aims of our barbaric government, which defends the interests of the factory and plant owners and wants to squeeze the poor peasant and worker in his hands so as to deprive him peacefully of the last drops of his blood to satisfy the splendour and bestial whims of the bureaucrats. Think, comrades, and you will understand clearly how sad it is that people in their ignorance are ready to betray their defenders into the hands of their enemies. We shall not, brothers and comrades, submit to the deceptive talk of those who hold us in the darkness of ignorance, we shall try to find out the truth for ourselves so that we shall move towards emancipation from our present condition of slavery.

Our strength is great, nothing will stand in our way if we all march together arm in arm.

Your comrade worker

Published by the Union of Struggle for the Emancipation of the Working Class

25. TO THE WEAVERS OF THE LEBEDEV MILL (1 JANUARY 1896)⁹⁸

St Petersburg Union of Struggle

Comrades!

On 20 December you showed that the bosses' ruthless oppression had not yet finally beaten you into submission, that Lebedev has not yet succeeded in making you his serfs. You showed that all patience comes to an end: you responded to his inhuman action with a strike. The whole year round you strained yourselves to the limit trying to increase his wealth and, as a reward for your effort, he brought you a present for the holiday: your wages were reduced by almost two and a half times. The grateful boss did not even think it necessary to keep his word and give you 5 kopeks on top of the rouble you had earned. Why? Because the weavers agree without a murmur at his first utterance to tolerate deprivation and starvation. When he saw clearly that the weavers, having refused to work until midnight, were beginning to demand a wage increase, the boss found an effective method of dealing with the troublemakers: he set the police dogs on them. On the night of 21–22 December, without any reason, the police *illegally* detained a large number of weavers as a warning to the others.

Comrades, on the side of your thief – the boss – lay the strength of his capital, at his disposal were the factory inspector, the police, the gendarmes, and on his side he had the Russian laws as well, which forbid the workers to arrange their own affairs and to stop work together when work becomes intolerable. On your side you received no combined help from the workers in other sections: nobody had explained to them that they should support their comrades. Not foreseeing a case like this, you did not create amongst yourselves a *comradely workers' union* to keep the money collected in times of peace for use during strikes.

You had none of this; it is no wonder that, forced by hunger and cold, you have *temporarily* submitted to the boss's tyranny and work as much as he asks and at whatever rate he wants. But *do not forget that by combined actions* at the first available opportunity *you will easily achieve success*. Prepare for the struggle and, when it becomes possible, *you should all as one man stop work and peacefully but firmly announce your wishes*.

Stay together, comrades, and bravely defend your interests.

For the New Year we send you our greetings and our wishes for success and promise you our constant collaboration.

Union of Struggle for the Emancipation of the Working Class
St Petersburg, 1 January 1896

26. THE DEMANDS OF THE WEAVERS AT THE LEBEDEV MILL (1896)[99]

St Petersburg Union of Struggle

We demand:

1. That our comrades who have been arrested should be released immediately and reinstated at the mill.
2. That the old rate of pay that prevailed until 15 December should be restored. To do this the owner should bring back the old piece-time and increase the pay for each piece. We cannot live on 40 kopeks a day.
3. That pay books should be handed to the worker, as is required by law.[100]

Comrades in all sections, support our just demands.

Published by the Union of Struggle for the Emancipation of the Working Class.

27. DRAFT AND EXPLANATION OF A PROGRAMME FOR THE SOCIAL DEMOCRATIC PARTY (DECEMBER 1895-JULY 1896)[101]

V.I. Lenin

Draft programme

A. 1. Large factories and plants are developing in Russia at an increasingly rapid pace, ruining the small craftsmen and the peasants, turning them into propertyless workers and driving an ever-increasing number of people into the towns, the factory and industrial villages and settlements.

2. This growth in capitalism signifies an enormous growth in the wealth and luxury of a handful of factory owners, merchants and landowners and an even more rapid growth in the poverty and oppression of the workers. The improvements in production introduced in the large factories and the machines that facilitate the increased productivity of social labour serve to strengthen the power of the capitalists over the workers, to increase unemployment and, at the same time, to underline the defencelessness of the workers.

3. But, by pushing the oppression of labour by capital to its extreme, the large factories are creating a special class of workers who have the chance to wage the

struggle against capital because the very conditions of their life are destroying all their ties with their own petty production; and, by uniting the workers through their common labour and shifting them from factory to factory, [these factories] are rallying the masses of the working people together. The workers are beginning the struggle against the capitalists and an intensified desire for unity is emerging among them. From the isolated rebellions of the workers there grows the struggle of the Russian working class.

4. This struggle of the working class against the capitalist class is a struggle against all the classes that live off the labour of others; and against all forms of exploitation. It can only end with the transfer of political power to the hands of the working class, the handing-over of all land, tools, factories, machines and mines to society as a whole for the organisation of socialist production under which everything that the workers produce, and all improvements in production, must benefit the workers themselves.

5. The Russian working class movement is, in accordance with its character and aims, a part of the international (social democratic) movement of the working class of all countries.

6. The main obstacle in the struggle of the Russian working class for its emancipation is the unbridled autocratic power of the government and its officials who are not accountable. Relying on the privileges of the landowners and capitalists and on a subservience to their interests, they continue to deprive the lower classes of all their rights and thus restrict the workers' movement and retard the development of the people as a whole. For this reason the struggle of the Russian working class for its emancipation necessarily provokes a struggle against the unbridled power of the autocratic government.

B. 1. The Russian Social Democratic Party declares that its aim is to promote this struggle of the Russian working class by developing the class consciousness of the workers, by promoting their organisation, by indicating the aims and objects of the struggle.

2. The struggle of the Russian working class for its emancipation is a political struggle and its first task is the achievement of political liberty.

3. For this reason the Russian Social Democratic Party will, without divorcing itself from the workers' movement, support any social movement against the unbridled power of the autocratic government, against the privileged landed nobility and against all the remnants of serfdom and the class system that hinder free competition.

4. On the other hand, the Russian Social Democratic Labour Party will wage war on all attempts to patronise the labouring classes with the protection of the absolutist government and its officials, to retard the development of capitalism and thus also the development of the working class.

5. The emancipation of the workers must be a matter for the workers themselves

6. The Russian people need, not the assistance of the absolutist government and its officials, but emancipation from their yoke.

C. Following on from these views, the Russian Social Democratic Party demands above all:

1. The summoning of a *Zemskii sobor* composed of representatives of all citizens to draw up a constitution.

2. Universal direct suffrage for all Russian citizens who have reached the age of twenty-one, irrespective of religion or nationality.

3. Freedom of assembly and association, and the right to strike.

4. Freedom of the press.

5. The abolition of social classes and complete equality for all citizens before the law.

6. Freedom of religion and equality for all nationalities. The transfer of the registration [of births, marriages and deaths] to independent civic officials, i.e. independent from the police.

7. Every citizen should have the right to prosecute any official without having to lodge a complaint with his superiors.

8. The abolition of pass-books and complete freedom of movement and residence.

9. Freedom of trade and occupation, and the abolition of guilds.

D. The Russian Social Democratic Party demands for the workers:

1. The establishment of industrial courts in all branches of industry with judges chosen in equal number from among the capitalists and the workers.

2. Legislation to limit the working day to eight hours in any twenty-four.

3. Legislation to prohibit night work and shifts. The prohibition of child labour under fifteen years of age.

4. Legislation to enact public holidays.

5. Application of factory laws and the factory inspectorate to all branches of industry throughout Russia, including government-owned factories and also handicraftsmen working at home.

6. The factory inspectorate must be independent and not subject to the Ministry of Finance. Members of industrial courts must enjoy equal rights with the factory inspectorate in supervising the observance of the factory laws.

7. Absolute prohibition in all cases of the truck system.

8. Supervision, by workers' elected representatives, of the proper calculation of rates, the rejection of [sub-standard] goods, the expenditure accruing from fines and the workers' quarters owned by the factory.

A law that the total deductions from workers' wages, whatever the reason for their imposition (fines, rejects, etc.), cannot, when taken together, exceed 10 kopeks in the rouble.

9. A law making employers responsible for injuries caused to workers, the employer being required to prove that the worker is to blame.

10. A law making employers responsible for the maintenance of schools and the provision of medical aid for the workers.

The Russian Social Democratic Party demands for the peasants:

1. Abolition of land redemption payments and compensation to the peasants for the redemption payments made. Reimbursement for the peasants of excess payments made to the Treasury.

2. Return to the peasants of their land that was sequestrated in 1861.

3. Complete equality of taxation for the peasants' and the landlords' land.

4. Abolition of collective responsibility and the repeal of all laws that restrict the peasants in disposing of their land.

Explanation of the programme

The programme is divided into three main parts. The first part sets out the views from which the other parts of the programme follow. This part indicates the position that the working class occupies in contemporary society, the meaning and significance of its struggle with the factory owners and the political position of the working class in the Russian state.

The second part sets out the *aim of the party* and indicates its attitude towards other political tendencies in Russia. It deals with what the activity of the party and of all the workers who are conscious of their class interests should be, and what their attitude towards the interests and aspirations of the other classes in Russian society should be.

The third part contains the party's practical demands. This part is divided into three sections. The first section contains demands for general state reforms. The second section contains the demands and programme of the working class, and the third section the demands on behalf of the peasants. Some preliminary explanations of these sections are given below, before we proceed to the practical part of the programme.

A. 1. The programme deals first of all with the rapid growth of large factories and plants because this is the principal phenomenon of contemporary Russia that is completely changing all the old conditions of life, and especially the living conditions of the labouring class. Under the old conditions practically all the wealth was produced by small proprietors, who constituted the vast majority of the population. The population lived in their villages, never moving, producing the greater part of their wares either for their own consumption or for a small market of neighbouring villages with little contact with other adjacent markets. These very same small proprietors worked for the landlords who compelled them to produce mainly for their own consumption. Domestic produce was handed over for processing to artisans who also lived in the villages or travelled in the surrounding areas to find work.

But, since the emancipation of the peasants those living conditions of the mass of the people have undergone a complete transformation: small artisan establishments began to be replaced by large factories, which grew with extraordinary rapidity; they drove the small proprietors out, turning them into wage labourers producing enormous quantities of goods that are sold throughout Russia.

The emancipation of the peasants destroyed the immobility of the population and left the peasants in conditions where they could no longer feed themselves off the plots of land that they were left with. Masses of people went to work in the towns, participated in the construction of factory and commercial premises, in the provision of fuel for the factories and in the preparation of raw materials for them. Finally, many people were employed at home, working for merchants and factory owners who could not expand their establishments [fast enough]. There were similar changes in agriculture: the landlords began to produce grain for sale, large-scale cultivators emerged from among the peasants and merchants and hundreds of millions of poods of grain began to be sold abroad. Production required wage labour and hundreds of thousands and millions of peasants abandoned their tiny plots and went to work as regular or day labourers for the new bosses who were producing the grain for sale. These changes in the old conditions of life are also described in the programme which states that the large factories and plants are ruining the small handicraftsmen and peasants and turning them into wage labourers. Small-scale production is everywhere giving way to large, and in this large-scale production the masses of workers are nothing but hirelings employed for a wage by the capitalist who owns vast amounts of capital, builds vast workshops, buys up vast quantities of raw material and pockets all the profit from this mass-scale production by the combined forces of the workers. Production has become capitalist and it exerts merciless and ruthless pressure on all small proprietors, destroying their life of immobility in the villages, forcing them to travel the length and breadth of the country as ordinary unskilled labourers, selling their labour to capital. An ever-increasing portion of the population is being separated once and for all from the countryside and from agriculture, and is concentrating in the towns, factory and industrial villages and settlements, forming a special class of people who have no property, a class of hired worker-proletarians, living only from the sale of their labour power.

These are what constitute the enormous changes in the life of the country produced by the large factories and plants: small-scale production is replaced by large, small proprietors are turned into wage labourers. What does this change mean for the whole of the working population and what will it lead to? This is dealt with further in the programme.

A. 2. The replacement of small-scale production by large is accompanied by the replacement of small-scale financial resources in the hands of the individual proprietor by enormous sums of capital, and the replacement of small insignificant profits by profits running into millions. For this reason the growth of capitalism leads everywhere to the growth of luxury and wealth. A whole class of big financial magnates, factory owners, railway owners, merchants and bankers has grown up in Russia, a whole class of people who live off income from money capital loaned against interest to industrialists; the great landowners have made their fortunes drawing money from the peasants in the form of land leased, and setting up large sugar refineries and spirit distilleries on their estates. The luxury and extravagance of all these wealthy classes have reached unparalleled dimensions and the main streets of our large cities are lined with their princely palaces and luxurious mansions. But, as capitalism has grown, the position of the worker has steadily deteriorated. If earnings increased here and there after the emancipation of the peasants, they did so very slightly and for a short time, because the mass of hungry people pouring in from the countryside pushed rates down while the price of food and other necessities rose steadily, so that, even with their increased wages, the workers had to make do with less; it became more and more difficult to make a livelihood and, side by side with the palatial mansions of the rich (or on the city outskirts), there grew up the slums where the workers were forced to live in basements, in overcrowded, cold, damp quarters, and even in dug-outs next to the new industrial plants. As capital grew ever more powerful, it increased its pressure on the workers, pauperising them and forcing them to devote all their time to the factory, driving the workers' wives and children to go to work. This, therefore, is the first change to which the growth of capitalism is leading: enormous wealth is accumulated in the hands of a small handful of capitalists, while the mass of people are reduced to paupers.

The second change consists in the fact that the replacement of small-scale production by large-scale has led to many improvements in production. First of all work done individually, separately in each little workshop, each little household, has given way to the joint labour of workers toiling together in a single factory, for a single landowner, a single contractor. Joint labour is considerably more effective (productive) than individual labour and it facilitates the production of goods much more easily and much more quickly. But all these improvements help only the capitalist, who pays the workers their pittance and for next to nothing appropriates all the profit from the joint labour of the workers. The capitalist emerges even stronger, the worker even weaker, because he has got used to a particular kind of work and it is more difficult for him to change to a different job, to alter his occupation.

Another, far more important improvement in production is the introduction of *machines* by the capitalist. The effectiveness of labour is increased many times over by the use of machines. But the capitalist turns the whole of this gain against the worker: he takes advantage of the fact that machines require less physical labour, he assigns women and children to them and pays them less. Taking advantage of the fact that far fewer workers are needed where machines are used, he throws them out of the factory in large numbers and then takes advantage of this unemployment to enslave the worker even further, to increase the working day, to deprive the worker of his night's rest and turn him into a simple adjunct to the machine. The unemployment created by the machine constantly increases and now makes the worker completely defenceless. His skill loses its value, he can easily be replaced by a plain unskilled worker who quickly gets used to the machine and gladly works for a lower wage. Any attempt to resist the increased oppression of capital leads to dismissal. On his own the worker is quite helpless against capital and the machine threatens to crush him.

A. 3. In clarifying the previous point, we showed that on his own the worker is helpless and defenceless against the capitalist who introduces machines. At all costs the worker must find a means of resisting the capitalist in order to protect himself. And he finds this means in *unification*. Helpless on his own, the worker, when united with his comrades, becomes a force and has a chance to fight the capitalist and resist him.

Unification becomes a necessity for the worker in the face of big capital. But is it possible to unite a motley mass of people who are strangers to one another even if they work in the same factory? The programme indicates the conditions that prepare the workers for union and develop in them the capacity and ability to organise. These conditions are as follows: (1) The large factory, with mechanised production that requires regular work the whole year round, completely severs the link between the worker and the land and his own smallholding, making him into an out-and-out proletarian. But individual smallholdings on a small plot of land divided the workers and gave each one a particular interest that was separate from the interests of his fellow worker and in this way served as an obstacle to union. The worker's break with the land removes these obstacles. (2) Further, the combined labour of hundreds and thousands of workers in itself teaches the workers to discuss their ideas with one another, to take joint action, and clearly demonstrates to them that the position and interests of the whole mass of workers are identical. (3) Lastly, the constant transfer of workers from one factory to another teaches them to contrast conditions and practices in different factories and compare them and they become convinced of the identical nature of the exploitation in every factory and acquire the experience of other workers in their confrontations with the capitalist so that the unity and solidarity of the workers is strengthened. It is because of these conditions, taken together, that the emergence of large factories has led to the unification of the workers. Among Russian workers this unification is expressed most frequently and most strongly in strikes (we shall deal later with the reasons why it is beyond the reach of our workers to join in unions or mutual aid funds). The more the large factories and plants develop, the more frequent, powerful and determined the workers' strikes become so that the greater the oppression of capitalism, the greater the need for joint resistance by the workers. As the programme says, strikes and isolated disturbances by the workers constitute at the present time the most widespread phenomenon in Russian factories. But, as capitalism continues to grow and the strikes become more frequent, they prove to be inadequate. The employers take joint measures against them: they conclude agreements among themselves, bring in workers from other areas, turn for assistance to the state, which helps them to put down the workers' resistance. The workers are now opposed, not by the one individual owner of each separate factory but by the *entire capitalist class* with the aid of the government. The entire *capitalist class* enters into battle with the entire *working class*: it devises common measures against strikes, it persuades the government to legislate against the workers, it moves plants and factories to remoter localities, it resorts to employing people who work at home and to a thousand other tricks and ruses against the workers. The unification of the workers in a particular factory, even in a particular branch of industry, is not enough to resist the entire capitalist class: joint action by the *entire working class* becomes absolutely necessary. In this way isolated disturbances among the workers grow into the struggle of the working class as a whole. The struggle between the workers and the factory owners is transformed into a *class struggle*. All the factory owners are united by a single interest: keeping the workers in subjection and paying them as little as they can. And the owners realise that the only way they can safeguard their interests is by joint action on the part of the entire factory-owning class, by gaining influence over the state authorities. The workers are likewise bound by a single common interest: preventing capital from crushing them, defending their right to life and a human existence. And the workers likewise become convinced that they too need unity, joint action by the entire class – the working class – and that to this end they must gain influence over the state authorities.

A. 4. We have explained how and why the struggle between the factory workers and the factory owners becomes class struggle, the struggle of the working class – the proletarians – against the capitalist class – the bourgeoisie. The question arises as to what significance this struggle has for the people as a whole and for all the workers. In present conditions, which we have already mentioned in our explanation of the first point, production by wage labourers increasingly displaces small-scale production. The number of people *who live by wage labour* is rapidly growing: it is not only the number of regular factory workers that is growing, but the number of peasants who have to seek the same wage employment in order to live is increasing even more. At the present time labour for wages, labour for the capitalist, has already become the most widespread form of labour. The role of capital over labour has embraced the mass of the population, not only in industry, but also in agriculture. And it is this exploitation of wage labour, which lies at the basis of contemporary society, that the large factories take to an extreme. All the methods of exploitation utilised by all the capitalists in all branches of industry, from which the whole mass of Russia's working population suffers, are concentrated, intensified, regularised here in the factory and spread to all aspects of the worker's life and labour; they create a whole routine, a whole system, whereby the capitalist squeezes everything out of the worker. Let us illustrate this with an example: at all times and in all places anyone in employment takes a rest, leaves his work at holiday times, if the holiday is celebrated in his area. It is completely different in the factory: having employed a worker, the factory uses him as it sees fit, paying no attention to what the worker is used to, to his customary way of life, his family position, his mental requirements. The factory drives him to work when it needs his labour, forces him to arrange his whole life to suit its requirements, to take his rest period in fragments and, if he is on shift work, it compels him to work at night and on holidays. The factory employs every imaginable abuse of working hours and, at the same time, it introduces its own 'rules', its own 'practices', which are binding on every worker. Factory practice is deliberately designed to extract from the employee all the labour that he can muster, to extract it as quickly as possible, and then to throw him out! Another example: anyone taking a job undertakes, of course, to submit to the employer, to do whatever he commands. But someone employed on a temporary job does not surrender his freedom at all; if he finds his employer's demands unjust or excessive, he leaves. But the factory requires that the worker renounce his freedom completely; it introduces discipline within its own four walls, forces the worker to start and stop work when a bell rings, it takes upon itself the right to punish the worker by a fine or a deduction for every infringement of the rules that it has itself devised. The worker becomes part of an enormous complex of machinery: he must be just as submissive and servile, just as devoid of his own free will, as the machine itself.[102]

A third example as well: anyone taking a job has frequent occasion to be dissatisfied with his employer and complains about him to a court or to a government official. Both the court and the official usually settle the dispute in the boss's favour and give him their support, but this promotion of the employer's interest is based, not on a general rule or law, but on the subservience of individual officials, who offer him a varying degree of protection and decide unjustly in the employer's favour either because of their acquaintance with him or because of their ignorance of working conditions or their inability to understand the worker. Each individual case of this kind of injustice depends upon each individual conflict between the worker and the boss and upon each individual official. But the factory brings together such a mass of workers, it takes oppression to such an extreme, that it becomes impossible to examine each case individually. General rules are drawn up, a law governing the relations between workers and employers is drafted, and it is a law that is binding on everyone. In this law the promotion of the employer's interests is backed up by the authority of the state. The unfairness of individual officials gives way to the unfairness of the law itself. For example, rules like these emerge: a worker who is absent from his work not only loses his wages but also has to pay a fine, whereas the employer pays him nothing if he sends him home; the boss may sack the worker for rudeness but the worker cannot leave if treated in the same way; the boss may at will impose fines, make deductions, or demand that overtime be worked, etc.

All these examples demonstrate the way in which the factory intensifies the exploitation of the workers and makes this exploitation universal, makes a whole '*system*' out of it. Whether he likes it or not, the worker now has to deal not with an individual employer and his willpower and oppression, but with the tyranny and oppression of the whole class of employers. The worker sees that his oppressors are not just a single capitalist, but the whole capitalist class, because the system of exploitation is the same in every enterprise. The individual capitalist cannot even depart from this system: if, for instance, he were to contemplate shortening the working hours, his goods would cost more than those produced by his neighbour, another factory owner, who makes his employees work longer hours for the same wage. To secure an improvement in his position, the worker must now take issue with the whole social order that is designed for the exploitation of labour by capital. The worker is no longer confronted by the individual unfairness of an individual official but by the injustice of state power itself, which takes the whole capitalist class under its wing and promulgates laws favouring that class that are binding on everyone. Thus the struggle of the factory workers against the factory owners inevitably turns into a struggle against the whole capitalist class, against the whole social order based on the exploitation of labour by capital. That is why the workers' struggle acquires social significance and becomes a struggle on behalf of all who labour against all the classes who live off the labour of others.

What then is the basis of the hegemony of the capitalist class over the whole mass of working people? It is the fact that all the factories, mills, mines, machines and instruments of labour are held by the capitalists as their private property; the fact that they own vast tracts of land (of all the land in European Russia more than one third belongs to fewer than half a million landed proprietors). The workers do not own any instruments of labour or raw materials and so they are obliged to sell their labour power to the capitalists, who pay the workers only what is necessary for their keep and pocket all the surplus that labour produces; thus they pay only for part of the working hours that they use and keep the rest for themselves. The whole of the increase in wealth that results from the combined labour of the mass of workers or from improvements in production goes to the capitalist class, and the workers, who toil from generation to generation, remain propertyless proletarians. That is why there is only one way to put an end to the exploitation of labour by capital and that is to abolish the private ownership of the instruments of labour, to hand over all the factories, mills, mines, and likewise all the large estates, etc., to society as a whole and introduce common socialist production that is directed by the workers themselves. The goods produced by common labour will then go to benefit the workers themselves, while the surplus they produce over and above their keep will serve to satisfy the needs of the workers themselves, develop all their capabilities and give them equal access to all the achievements of science and art. That is why the programme says that the struggle between the working class and the capitalists can only end in this way. But, for that to happen, it is necessary for political power, i.e. the power to control the state, to pass from the hands of a government that is under the influence of the capitalists and landowners, or from the hands of a government that is directly made up of the elected representatives of the capitalists, into the hands of the working class.

This is the ultimate aim of the struggle of the working class; this is the condition for its complete emancipation. It is to this ultimate aim that conscious united workers should strive. But here in Russia they still encounter enormous obstacles in their struggle for their own emancipation.

A. 5. The struggle against the hegemony of the capitalist class is already being waged by the workers of every European country, and also by the workers of America and Australia. The unification and solidarity of the working class is not confined to a single country or a single nationality: the workers' parties of different states loudly proclaim the complete identity (solidarity) of the interests and aims of the workers of the whole world. They meet at joint congresses, and put forward common demands to the capitalist class in every country, establish an international holiday for the entire united proletariat striving for its own emancipation (1 May), thus welding the working class of every nationality and every country into one great workers' army. This unity of the workers of every country is necessary because the capitalist class, which rules over the workers, does not confine its rule to a single country. The commercial ties between different states are becoming ever closer and more extensive: capital is constantly being transferred from one country to another. The banks – those enormous repositories of capital, gathering it from all over the place and distributing it in loans to the capitalists – move from the national to the international plane, collecting capital from every country and distributing it to the capitalists of Europe and America. Enormous joint-stock companies are already being organised to set up capitalist enterprises not just in one country but in several countries at the same time; international associations of capitalists make their appearance. The rule of capital is international. That is why the emancipation struggle of the workers of every country will only be successful if the workers wage a combined war against international capital. That is why the Russian worker's comrade-in-arms in the struggle against the capitalist class is the German worker, the Polish worker or the French worker, just as his enemy is the Russian, Polish or French capitalist. Thus, foreign capitalists have recently been particularly eager to transfer their capital to Russia, to build branches of their own factories in Russia, and to found companies for new enterprises in Russia. They fling themselves greedily on this young country, where the government is more favourable and obsequious towards capital than anywhere else and where they find workers who are less united and less capable of resistance than in the West, where the workers' standard of living, and therefore also their wages, are much lower, so that foreign capitalists can make enormous profits on a scale undreamt of in their own countries. International capital has already stretched out its hand to Russia. The Russian workers are stretching out their hands to the international workers' movement.

A. 6. We have already mentioned how large factories and plants carry the oppression of labour by capital to an extreme, how they create a whole system of methods of exploitation; how the workers, in their revolt against capital, inevitably come to appreciate the need to unite all workers, the need for joint struggle by the whole of the working class. In this struggle against the capitalist class the workers come into conflict with the general laws of the state, which protect the capitalists and their interests.

But then, if the workers, when united, are strong enough to wring concessions from the capitalists, to offer them resistance, they might also, through their unity, influence the laws of the state and obtain changes in them. That is what the workers in every other country are doing, but the Russian workers cannot exercise direct influence upon the state. The conditions of the Russian workers are such that they are deprived of the most elementary civil rights. They do not dare to meet, to discuss their affairs together, to organise unions, to publish their manifestos – in other words the laws of the state have not merely been drafted in the interests of the capitalist class, but they openly deprive the workers of any opportunity to influence these laws or obtain changes in them. This follows from the fact that in Russia (and in Russia alone of all European states) the unbridled power of an autocratic government survives to this day, i.e. a system of government exists under which laws that are binding on everyone can be promulgated by the tsar alone, at his own discretion, while only officials appointed by him may put these laws into effect. Citizens are not allowed to participate in the promulgation or discussion of laws, or in proposing new laws or demanding changes in the old ones. They have no right to hold officials to account for their activity, to check their activity or prosecute them. Citizens do not even have the right to discuss affairs of state: they do not dare to organise meetings or associations without the permission of those same officials. The officials are therefore irresponsible in the full sense of the word: they constitute, as it were, a special caste placed above the citizens. The irresponsibility and tyranny of the officials and the fact that the population itself has no say give rise to the kind of scandalous abuse of power by officials and the kind of violation of the rights of the common people that are scarcely possible in any European country.

Thus, in law, the Russian government has unlimited authority and is considered to be, as it were, completely independent of the people, standing above all social estates and classes. But, if this were really so, why, in every conflict between the workers and the capitalists, should the law and the government take the capitalists' side? Why should the capitalists meet with ever-increasing support as their numbers rise and their wealth grows, while the workers meet with ever-greater resistance and restriction?

In reality the government does not stand above classes but protects one class from another, protects the propertied class from the propertyless, the capitalists from the workers. An absolutist government could not control such a vast country if it did not provide the propertied classes with all sorts of privileges and favours.

Although in law the government has unlimited and independent authority, in reality the capitalists have thousands of ways in which they can influence the government and the affairs of state. They have their own associations based on social estate – the noblemen's and merchants' societies, chambers of trade and manufacturing guilds, etc., – and these are recognised by law. Their elected representatives either become officials outright and participate in the running of the state (e.g. the marshals of the nobility) or they are given positions in all sorts of government institutions: e.g. by law factory owners participate in factory courts (the principal authority over the factory inspectorate), to which they elect their own representatives. But they do not confine themselves to this direct participation in the running of the state. In their associations they discuss state laws and draft bills, and the government usually consults them on every issue, submitting draft bills to them and asking for their observations.

The capitalists and landowners organise all-Russian congresses at which they discuss their own affairs, devise various measures to benefit their own class and, on behalf of all the landed gentry or 'the merchants of the whole of Russia', they petition for the promulgation of new laws and the amendment of old ones. They can discuss their affairs in the newspapers for, however great the restrictions placed by the government's censorship on the press, it would never dare dream of depriving the propertied classes of their right to discuss their own affairs. They have all sorts of ways and means of access to the highest representatives of state authority and can more easily discuss the tyrannical conduct of lower officials and they can easily obtain the repeal of particularly irritating laws and regulations. And, while there is not a single country in the world with such a multiplicity of laws and regulations, such unexampled police supervision by the government that extends to every petty detail and depersonalises every aspect of life, there is also not a single country in the world where these bourgeois regulations are so easily disregarded and these police laws are so easily circumvented simply by kind permission of the highest authorities. And this kind permission is never refused.

B. 1. This is the most important, the principal point in the programme, because it indicates the proper activity of the party in defending the interests of the working class and the proper activity of all conscious workers. It indicates the way in which the striving for socialism, the striving to abolish the age-old exploitation of man by man should be linked to the popular movement that is a product of the living conditions created by large-scale factories and plants.

The activity of the party should consist in promoting the workers' class struggle. The task of the party is not to dream up fashionable ways of helping the workers, but to join up with the workers' movement, to bring light to it, to assist the workers in the struggle that they have already begun to wage. The task of the party is to protect the interests of the workers and to represent the interests of the whole workers' movement. What then should this assistance to the workers in their struggle consist in?

The programme states that this assistance should consist, first of all, in developing the workers' class consciousness. We have already described the way in which the struggle between the workers and the factory owners becomes a class struggle between the proletariat and the bourgeoisie.

What we mean by the workers' class consciousness follows from what we have said. The class consciousness of the workers means the workers' realisation that the only way of improving their position and achieving their own emancipation is to wage a struggle against the capitalist and factory-owning class that has been created by the large factories and plants. Further, the class consciousness of the workers means a realisation that the interests of all the workers in a particular country are common and identical, that they all constitute a single class that is distinct from all the other classes in society. Lastly, the class consciousness of the workers means the realisation by the workers that, in order to achieve their aims, the workers must gain influence on affairs of state, just as the landowners and capitalists have done, and continue to do.

How will the workers come to realise all this? The workers come to it by constantly learning from the very same struggle that they are beginning to wage against the factory owners and that is increasingly developing, sharpening and involving larger numbers of workers as the large-scale factories and plants expand. There was a time when the enmity felt by the workers towards capital found its expression only in a vague sense of hatred for their exploiters, in a dim recognition of their oppressed and servile condition, and in the desire to *wreak vengeance* on the capitalists. At that time the struggle found its expression in isolated workers' disturbances, the destruction of buildings and wrecking of machines, and in attacks on the factory management, etc. This was the *first*, the original form of the workers' movement, and it was a necessary one because a hatred of the capitalist has in all places and at all times acted as the initial impulse towards awakening in the workers a desire to defend themselves. But the Russian workers' movement has already outgrown this original form. Instead of a vague hatred for the capitalist the workers have already begun to understand the antagonism between the interests of the workers and the interests of the capitalists. Instead of a dim sense of oppression they have already begun to distinguish *the ways and means* by which capital oppresses them, and they are rebelling against various forms of oppression, defining limits to the oppression of capital, defending themselves against the capitalist's greed. Instead of wreaking vengeance on the capitalists, they are now turning to the struggle for concessions, they are beginning to put one demand after another to the capitalist class and they are demanding improved working conditions, higher wages, and shorter working hours for themselves. Every strike concentrates all the attention and all the efforts of the workers on one or other of the conditions under which the working class lives. Every strike provokes a discussion of these conditions and helps the workers to appraise them, to understand what constitutes the oppression of capital in a particular case and the means by which this oppression can be countered. Every strike enriches the experience of the entire working class. If a strike is successful, it shows them the strength of the workers when they are united and provokes others to make use of their comrades' success. If it is unsuccessful, it provokes a discussion of the causes of its failure and a search for better methods of struggle. All over Russia a transition is now taking place: this transition of the workers to an unflinching struggle for their vital needs, a struggle for concessions, for better living conditions, wages and hours means that the Russian workers have taken an enormous step forward, and that is why the principal attention of the Russian Social Democratic Party and of all conscious workers should be focussed on this struggle and on its promotion. Assistance for the workers should consist in indicating the most vital needs that they should fight to satisfy, in analysing the factors that are particularly responsible for worsening the conditions of various groups of workers and in explaining the factory laws and regulations, violation of which (together with the deceptive tricks of the capitalists) so frequently exposes the worker to twofold robbery. Assistance should consist in giving more precise and definite expression to the workers' demands and in stating them publicly, in choosing the best moment for resistance, in choosing the method of struggle, in discussing the position and strength of the two opposing sides and, in discussing whether an even better method of struggle might be chosen (such methods as, for instance, a letter to the factory owner, an appeal to the inspector or to a doctor, according to the circumstances, where immediate resort to strike action is inadvisable, etc.).

We have said that the Russian workers' transition to this kind of struggle shows what an enormous step forward they have taken. This struggle leads the workers' movement on to the high road and serves as a firm guarantee of its future success. In the course of this struggle the masses of working people learn, firstly, how to diagnose and investigate the methods of capitalist exploitation one by one, to contrast them with the law, with their living conditions and with the interests of the capitalist class. By investigating the different forms and instances of exploitation, the workers learn to understand the significance and essence of exploitation as a whole, learn to understand the social order that is based upon the exploitation of labour by capital. Secondly, in the course of this struggle the workers test their strength, learn to act together and learn to appreciate the necessity for and significance of their unity. The extension of this struggle and the increasing frequency of conflict lead inevitably to an extension of the struggle, to the development of a sense of unity, a sense of their own solidarity, at first among the workers of a particular locality and then among the workers of the country as a whole, among the whole working class. Thirdly, this struggle develops the political consciousness of the workers. The living conditions of the mass of working people put them in a position where they can have neither the leisure nor the opportunity to reflect on any matters of state. But the workers' struggle with the factory owners for their everyday needs in itself inevitably leads the workers [to reflect on] state political questions, the questions of how the Russian state is governed, how laws and regulations are promulgated and whose interests they serve. Every confrontation in the factory inevitably leads the workers into a confrontation with the laws and the representatives of state authority. In this process the workers hear 'political speeches' for the first time. Admittedly, the first are from the factory inspectors, who explain to them that the trick employed by the factory owner to defraud them is based on a strict interpretation of the regulations, which have been approved by the relevant authority and give the owner a free hand to defraud the workers, or that the factory owner's oppressive measures are quite legal because he is merely availing himself of his right, which is based on such and such a law approved and implemented by the state authorities. The political explanations of the inspectors are occasionally supplemented by the still more beneficial 'political explanations' of the minister who reminds the workers of the feelings of 'Christian love' that they owe to the factory owners for the fact that these owners acquire their millions at the expense of the workers' labour. Later on, these explanations by the representatives of the state authorities and the workers' direct acquaintance with the preferences shown by these authorities are further supplemented by leaflets or other explanations from the Socialists, so that the workers get their political education in full from such a strike. They learn to understand not just the specific interests of the working class but also the specific place occupied by the working class in the state. Thus, this is what the *assistance* rendered by the Social Democratic Party to the workers' class struggle should consist in: the development of the workers' class self-consciousness by helping them in the struggle for their most essential needs.

The second type of *assistance* should, as stated in the programme, consist in promoting the organisation of the workers. The struggle that we have just described necessarily requires that the workers be organised. Organisation becomes necessary for a strike, so that it can be conducted with greater success, for collections on behalf of strikers, for the establishment of workers' mutual aid funds, for agitation among the workers, for the distribution among them of leaflets, declarations, manifestos, etc. Organisation is even more necessary so that the workers can defend themselves from persecution by the police and the gendarmerie, conceal from them all the workers' associations and contacts and arrange the delivery among themselves of books, brochures, newspapers, etc. Assistance in all these things is the party's second task.

The third consists in indicating the real aims of the struggle, i.e. in explaining to the workers what the exploitation of labour by capital involves, what is rests on, how the private ownership of the land and the instruments of labour leads to the pauperisation of the working masses, forces them to sell their labour to the capitalists and to give them for nothing the whole of the surplus produced by the labour of the worker over and above his upkeep. [It involves], furthermore, explaining how this exploitation inevitably leads to class struggle between the workers and the capitalists, what the conditions for this struggle and its ultimate aims are – in a word, in explaining what is stated briefly in the programme.

B. 2. What does it mean when we say that the struggle of the working class is a political struggle? It means that the working class cannot wage the struggle for its own emancipation without gaining influence over affairs of state, over the administration of the state, over the promulgation of laws. The Russian capitalists long since appreciated the need for this kind of influence and we have demonstrated how, despite all kinds of prohibitions contained in the police laws, they have been able to find thousands of ways of influencing the state authorities, and how those authorities have served the interests of the capitalist class. From this it naturally follows that the working class is also unable to wage its struggle, unable even to achieve a lasting improvement in its lot, without exerting influence on the state authorities.

We have already said that the workers' struggle with the capitalists will inevitably lead them into a confrontation with the government, and the government itself is trying very hard to prove to the workers that it is only through struggle and combined resistance that they can influence the state authorities. This was particularly clearly demonstrated in the great strikes that occurred in Russia in 1885 and 1886.[103] The government at once set about drafting regulations dealing with the workers, immediately promulgated new laws on factory practices, conceding the workers' persistent demands (e.g. regulations were introduced that limited fines and ensured the proper payment of wages).[104] In the same way the current [1896] strikes have once more provoked immediate government intervention, and the government has already realised that it cannot restrict itself to arrests and deportations, that it is absurd to regale the workers with stupid sermons about the good intentions of the factory owners (see the circular sent by the Minister of Finance, Witte, to factory inspectors in the spring of 1896). The government has realised that the 'workers united constitute a force that must be reckoned with', and so it has already undertaken a review of factory legislation and convened a congress of senior factory inspectors in St Petersburg to discuss the question of shorter working hours and other unavoidable concessions to the workers.

Thus we see that the struggle between the working class and the capitalist class must inevitably be a political struggle. This struggle is in fact already exerting an influence on the state authorities and acquiring political significance. But, as the workers' movement develops, so the workers' complete lack of political rights, which we mentioned earlier, the complete absence of any opportunity for the workers to exert any open and direct influence on the state authorities, becomes more clearly and sharply defined. For this reason the workers' most urgent demand, the primary objective of working class influence on affairs of state, must be *the achievement of political liberty*, i.e. the direct participation, guaranteed by laws (by a constitution), of every citizen in the government of the state, the guarantee for all citizens of the right freely to assemble, to discuss their own affairs and to influence affairs of state through unions and through the press. The achievement of political liberty becomes the '*vital task for the workers*' because, without it, the workers do not, and cannot, have any influence on affairs of state and thus inevitably remain without rights, a down-trodden and voiceless class. If even now, when the workers are only just beginning to fight and close their ranks, the government is already rushing to make concessions to the workers in order to slow down the further growth of the movement, then there is no doubt that, when the workers have closed their ranks and united under the leadership of a single political party, they will be able to force the government to surrender, they will be able to win political liberty for themselves and for the whole of the Russian people!

The preceding parts of the programme indicated the place occupied by the working class in contemporary society and in the contemporary state, the aim of the struggle of the working class and what constitutes the task of the party that represents the workers' interests. Under the unbridled power of the Russian government there are not, and cannot be, overtly political parties, but there are political tendencies that give expression to the interests of other classes and exert influence on public opinion and on the government. Hence, in order to clarify the position of the Social Democratic Party, we must now indicate its attitude towards the other political tendencies in Russian society, so that the workers can determine who might be their ally and to what extent, and who their enemy. This is indicated in the two following points of the programme.

B. 3. The programme declares that the allies of the workers are, first of all, all those social strata that actively oppose the unbridled power of the autocratic government.

Since this unbridled power is the principal obstacle to the workers' struggle for their own emancipation, it naturally follows that it is in the direct interest of the workers to support any social movement against absolutism ('absolute' means unbridled; 'absolutism' is the unbridled power of the government). The stronger capitalism becomes, the deeper become the contradictions between this bureaucratic rule and the interests of the propertied classes themselves, the interests of the bourgeoisie. And the Social Democratic Party declares that it will support all the strata and ranks of the bourgeoisie that are actively opposed to the absolutist government.

The exercise by the bourgeoisie of *direct influence* on affairs of state is of infinitely greater value to the workers than the present situation, where they exert their influence through a bunch of corrupt and despotic officials. The *overt* influence of the bourgeoisie on policy is of much greater value than their present *covert* influence, concealed by the allegedly all-powerful 'independent' government, which calls itself a government 'by the grace of God' and hands out 'its graces' to the suffering and hard-working landowners and the impoverished and oppressed factory owners. The workers need an *overt struggle* with the capitalist class so that the whole Russian proletariat may see whose interests the Russian workers are fighting for, so that they may learn how the struggle should be waged, and so that the intrigues and aspirations of the bourgeoisie are not concealed in the ante-rooms of grand dukes, in the salons of senators and ministers or in private departmental offices, so that they may surface and open the eyes of all and sundry to who really influences government policy and what the capitalists and landowners are aiming for. So, down with everything that conceals the present influence of the capitalist class and support for any representative of the bourgeoisie who *actively opposes* the bureaucracy, bureaucratic administration and absolutist government! But, in declarint its support for any social movement against absolutism, the Social Democratic Party recognises that it is not distinct from the workers' movement, because the working class has its own particular interests which are opposed to the interests of all other classes. In giving their support to all the representatives of the bourgeoisie in the struggle for political liberty, the workers should remember that the propertied classes can only be their allies temporarily, that the interests of the workers and the capitalists cannot be reconciled, that the workers must bring to an end the unbridled power of the government so that they can wage their struggle with the capitalist class on an open and broad basis.

The Social Democratic Party further declares that it will offer its support to all those who rebel against the class of privileged landed nobility. In Russia the landed nobility are considered to be the first estate in the land. The remnants of their feudal power over the peasants oppress the mass of the people even now. The peasants continue to make land redemption payments for their emancipation from the power of the landowners. The peasants are still tied to the land, so that the landowners do not have to suffer a shortage of cheap and servile labourers. Even now the peasants, deprived of their rights and treated as children, are at the mercy of officials who look after their own pockets and interfere in the life of the peasants to make sure that they make their redemption payments or pay their quit rent to their feudal landlords 'on the dot', and that they do not 'shirk' working for the landlords, do not dare, for instance, to move away and, in so doing, perhaps compel the landowners to employ outside workers who are not as cheap and not as oppressed by want. The landowners keep millions and tens of millions of peasants in their service, enslaving them and continuing to deprive them of their rights and, in return for their bravery, they enjoy the highest state privileges. The landed nobility are the principal holders of the highest offices of state (what is more, by law the nobility, as a social estate, enjoys priority in the civil service); the aristocratic landlords are closest to the court and they, more directly and easily than anyone else, influence government policy to their own advantage. They make use of their close links with the government to raid the state coffers and secure from public funds gifts and grants amounting to millions of roubles, sometimes in the shape of vast estates given for services rendered, at other times in the shape of 'concessions'.

28. THE WORKERS' HOLIDAY OF 1 MAY (19 APRIL BY OUR CALENDAR) (19 APRIL 1896)[105]

St Petersburg Union of Struggle

Comrades, let us take a close look at our position, let us examine the conditions in which we pass our lives. What do we see? We work a lot, we produce endless wealth, gold and cloths, brocade and velvet, we extract iron and coal from the bowels of the earth, we build machines, we construct shops and palaces, we lay the railways. The entire wealth of the world is produced by our hands, achieved through our sweat and blood. What kind of reward do we get for our backbreaking toil? In justice we should live in pleasant housing, wear decent clothes and at least not want for our daily bread. But we all know very well that our pay is scarcely enough for us to survive. Our bosses reduce our wages, compel us to work extra hours, unjustly fine us – in a word oppress us in every way – but, if we are dissatisfied, we are sacked without argument.

We have on many occasions been convinced that the people to whom we turned for protection were the servants or friends of the bosses. We workers are kept in darkness; we are not allowed an education, so that we do not learn to fight to improve our lot. We are kept in bondage – anyone who resists oppression is exiled and arrested and driven from his job – we are forbidden to fight. Darkness and bondage are the means by which we are kept in subjection by the capitalists and by the government that does everything to please them. What means do we have of improving our lot, raising our wages, shortening the working day, protecting ourselves from outrageous treatment and reading intelligent and useful books? Everyone is against us – both the bosses (because the worse our lives are, the better theirs are) and all their servants, all those who live off the favours of the capitalists and who keep us in ignorance and bondage to please them. We cannot expect help from any quarter, we can rely only on ourselves. Our strength lies in unity, our means is *combined, unanimous and persistent opposition* to the bosses. They long ago realised the source of our strength and at every opportunity they try to divide us, to prevent us from understanding that we workers have the same common interests. They reduce our wages, not all at once but bit by bit, they dispose of the older workers, introduce piece-rates and, laughing up their sleeves and seeing how our brother exerts himself over his work, they themselves gradually reduce our pay. But all good things come to an end. Nobody has endless patience. In the past year the Russian workers have shown their bosses that their slavish obedience is giving way to the steadfast courage of men who will not give in to the insolence of capitalists who are greedy for free labour. There have been many strikes in various towns: in Yaroslavl, Teikovo, Ivanovo-Voznesensk, Białystok, Vilna, Minsk, Kiev, Moscow and other towns. From the workers' point of view the majority of strikes came to a successful conclusion, but even the unsuccessful strikes only appeared to be unsuccessful. In fact they have really scared the bosses, caused them considerable losses and forced them into concessions for fear of a new strike. The factory inspectors also begin to fuss and notice the mote in the eye of the factory owners. They turned a blind eye until the workers opened their eyes with their strike. How in fact could the factory inspectors notice the disgraceful goings-on in the factories of such influential people as Mr Thornton or the shareholders of the Putilov factory? Here in Petersburg we have given our bosses a lot of trouble too. The strike of the weavers at the Thornton mill, of the cigarette-girls at the Laferme factory, at the Lebedev mill, at the mechanised shoe-factory, the disturbances among the workers at the Koenig and Voronin factories and in the port and, finally, the recent disturbances in Sestroretsk have shown that we have ceased to be meek and have taken up the struggle. As you know, workers from many factories and plants here have set up the 'Union of Struggle for the Emancipation of the Working Class', with the aim of exposing all the abuses, rooting out all the outrages, fighting the insolent restrictions and oppressive measures of our unscrupulous exploiter-bosses and achieving complete emancipation from their power. The 'Union' distributes leaflets the sight of which causes trembling in the hearts of the bosses and their faithful lackeys. It is not the leaflets that frighten them but the prospect of our united opposition, the emergence of that great strength of ours that we have never shown them. We, the workers of Petersburg, the members of the *'Union'*, call on the rest of our comrades to join our *'Union'* and help the great cause of joining the workers together to fight for their own interests. It is time for us Russian workers to tear off the chains with which the capitalists and the government have bound us to keep us in subjection; it is time for us to join in the struggle of our brothers, the workers of other states, to stand with them beneath our common banner on which is written: 'Workers of all countries, unite!'

In France, England, Germany and other countries where the workers have already joined together in strong unions and won many rights for themselves, they celebrate 19 April (which is 1 May abroad) as a general festival of labour.

Leaving their stuffy factories they parade in an orderly throng along the main streets of the city with music and banners; demonstrating their ever-increasing strength to the bosses, they gather in numerous crowded meetings, where speakers recount the victories of the previous year over the bosses and outline plans for future struggles. Fearing a strike, no factory owner would punish the workers for being away from work on that day. Similarly on that day the workers remind the bosses of their principal demand: the limiting of the working day to eight hours: eight hours' work, eight hours' sleep and eight hours' rest – that is what the workers of other states are now demanding. There was a time not so long ago when they, like us today, did not have the right to make their demands known; they too were oppressed by poverty and isolated just as we are now. But through persistent struggle and great sacrifices they won for themselves the right to discuss together their workers' cause. We wish for our brothers in other countries that the struggle should bring them to the victory they desire, to the time when there will be neither lord nor slave, neither workers nor capitalists, and when everyone will work equally and wisely enjoy life equally.

Comrades, if we unite in friendship and unanimity the time will not be far off when we too, closing our forces into orderly ranks, will be able to join openly in the general struggle of the workers in all countries, without distinction of race or creed, against the capitalists of the whole world. Our muscular arm will be raised and the shameful chains of bondage will fall away, the working people of Russia will rise up and cause trembling in the hearts of the capitalists and the government which always assiduously serves and assists them.

Union of Struggle for the Emancipation of the Working Class
19 April 1896

29. TO THE WORKERS IN ALL THE PETERSBURG COTTON MILLS (1 JUNE 1896)[106]

St Petersburg Union of Struggle

We, the workers of the Petersburg cotton mills have suffered for a long time, but at last we can no longer endure it. We can no longer tolerate working to the point of exhaustion, put up with the repressive measures of the bosses, see how they cheat and swindle us every day, how they lower our wages almost every six months. But in the last few days the greed of the bosses has shown itself to be even worse than it was before: our rich men grieved even at the pittance due to us for Coronation holidays; they did not want us to have a rest, nor did they want to pay us properly for our work — and these brutes in particular don't go short of rest. For long enough, we said to ourselves then, for long enough we have listened to our bosses in silence and without a murmur. For a long time we waited for them to improve our lot but we received nothing. Then we decided to take matters into our own hands. If *they* will not give in, then *we* shall make our demands. Above all we must demand:

1. that the working day should last from 7 a.m. to 7 p.m. with a one-and-a-half hour lunch break, i.e. ten and a half hours altogether; that on Saturdays everyone should knock off work at 2;
2. that the rate of pay should be increased so that wages do not fall;
3. that all the repressive measures that are unjust and illegal should be done away with, and that we should be paid for Coronation holidays.

We shall bide our time *peacefully* until the bosses agree to our demands. If they have not given in after a week, we shall wait another week; if they do not give in after the second, we shall wait a third; if they still have not agreed then we shall go on waiting. Our ten and a half hours of hard labour is more than they deserve; even without it they would make enough profit out of us.

Comrades, we shall recall that the eyes of the workers of the whole world are now turned on us; with pride they welcome us as warriors for the workers' cause. The workers of Petersburg are making every effort to come to our assistance, organising collections for us in the workshops. Let us then show that the working people know how to obtain their demands. *We shall act peacefully together, without disorder or violence*, and victory will certainly be ours.

Union of Struggle for the Emancipation of the Working Class
1 June 1896

30. TO ALL PETERSBURG WORKERS (3 JUNE 1896)[107]

St Petersburg Union of Struggle

The strike in Petersburg has now lasted a whole week. Our comrades, the workers in the cotton mills, could not stand the oppression of the bosses and stopped work. On the 27th the Ekaterinhof (Volynkin) factory came out because the workers had not been given full pay for Coronation holidays; a day later they were joined by workers from the Koenig, Mitrofanev and other factories, and there are at present already seventeen factories that are not working.[108]

What are the weavers after?

Perhaps they are demanding the impossible, something that will bring fatal losses to the factory owners? Not at all.

Let us just listen to what the weavers are demanding:

1. That everywhere here the working day should last from 7 a.m. to 7 p.m., instead of the present 6 a.m. to 8 p.m.
2. That lunch breaks should last an hour and a half so that the whole working day lasts ten and a half hours instead of thirteen.
3. That everyone should have a two-hour break at the same time on Saturdays.
4. That payments everywhere should be raised so that wages are not reduced.
5. That the owners should not wilfully stop, nor set the machines in motion, before time.
6. That pay for the first half of the month should be *given out correctly* and on time, and not held back.
7. That there should be full pay for Coronation holidays.

Workers of the whole of Petersburg! Tell us, are our comrades really asking for much, and don't we really have common cause with them? When the weavers demand the shortening of an excessively long working day, let us remember how many of us strain over our work for twelve to thirteen hours. And don't let us forget that payments here are being reduced everywhere year by year; and, finally, are the pressures and injustices here really so few?

See how, when the worker finds that he labours all day long, bent double and gets nothing out of it, then the authorities cry that the workers are in revolt.

Obviously they would prefer the worker to be simply a silent and docile slave, whose sole function is to work till he is exhausted and accumulate profit for the factory owner.

Far from it. A long time ago the Petersburg workers began to think about how things could be arranged in a different, and better, way. The weavers were the first to furnish an example.

Workers of Petersburg! Let us support our comrades – let us like brothers extend the hand of assistance in their difficult struggle with the robber-owners; let us start to arrange collections among ourselves for the strikers and let us not forget that similar hard times could befall us, and then the weavers would certainly remember our present support.

For all workers are brothers: stern fate has brought us all together. We all have the same general interests, the same general desires and aims. And when we understand this, when we really merge together in a single spirit and a single body, then no force in the world will overcome the workers' movement.

The Union of Struggle for the Emancipation of the Working Class
3 June 1896.

31. REPORT PRESENTED BY THE RUSSIAN SOCIAL DEMOCRATS TO THE (LONDON) INTERNATIONAL CONGRESS OF SOCIALIST WORKERS AND TRADE UNIONS (1896)[109]

G.V. Plekhanov

Note: this document is reproduced in its original 1896 translation.

Dear Comrades,

In the Report, presented to the International Socialist Congress at Brussels, by V. Zasulich and G. Plekhanov in the name of the Russian Social Democrats, it was said: 'Nous nous sommes imposé le devoir de couvrir la Russie d'un réseau de sociétés ouvrières. Jusqu'au moment où ce but sera atteint nous nous abstiendrons de prendre part à vos assises. Jusqu'à ce moment-là toute représentation de la démocratie socialiste russe sera fictive'.

At the present moment we can say, with legitimate pride, that this task has been to some extent accomplished. The first and most difficult steps towards organisation of the Russian working-class have been taken, at least in some places, with the result that delegates from the Russian Social Democrats are here at the International Workers' Congress, the largest that there has yet been.

To give some slight idea of the difficulties with which we are confronted almost at every step in working for our cause, let us first of all give a sketch of what has been taking place and what is going on now, in the capital of the Russian Empire, Petersburg. For ten years — from 1880 to 1890 — the labour movement was smouldering in the numerous but scattered and secret clubs in which the Social Democratic propaganda was being carried on; at one time gaining strength, at another dying down again, suffering immense losses, but, like the phoenix, springing ever into fresh life from its ashes. And with this varying success the propaganda went on, not getting beyond the limit of the clubs till last autumn – 1895. Thus, it was only this year that the groups found it possible to combine under one organisation. This was named 'The League of Struggle for the Emancipation of the Working Class'. Not till then had the Social Democrats of Petersburg strength enough to enter upon the wider arena of agitation among the masses.

The organisation of trade-unions, and funds to be used in cases of strikes, in the first place; the training of thoroughly competent agitators among the workmen, in the second place; and thirdly, mass agitation by means of appeals, diffusion of pamphlets, and formulation of the needs of the workers in the various workshops, factories and works – such, in few words, were the immediate practical aims which the League set before themselves. Unhappily, the conditions of secrecy under which the so-called League is forced to do its work, by the present government in Russia, enable us to speak definitely only of this side of its activity.

The periodical appearance of leaflets in great numbers had not been seen for so long in Petersburg that it had been forgotten even by the Russian police; the greater, therefore, was the impression produced by the appeals of the League, which appeared in shoals in all parts of the city. From November onwards, handbills distributed by thousands throughout the working class districts, thrown into workmen's lodgings, dropped in the streets, stuck like advertisements on the walls, and handed about in workshops and factories, produced a crushing impression on factory owners and local authorities, who made extraordinary efforts to *extirpate the sedition*. Representatives of the so-called 'intelligentsi', or advanced classes, were seized, suspected workmen were banished to their native places by tens and by hundreds, but in vain. The leaflets were issued immediately after the arrests, as though in mockery of the zealous menials of the Tsar's government.

The distinguishing feature in these appeals of the League is their concrete, practical character. Each appeal treated of some definite abuse on the part of the employers, some definite arbitrary act on the part of the administration, and each of them was supported by the details of a particular case. They aimed at formulating the demands of the workers, developing a feeling of class solidarity among them, showing the antagonism between their interests and the interests of the capitalists, and finally proving that the *Tsar's government* has shown itself and will show itself under all circumstances the zealous servant of the bourgeoisie, the zealous enemy of every intelligent movement among the Russian proletariat. Now the soil which the Petersburg Social Democratic organisation had to cultivate was full of the sap of life; the very appearance of the League served as a noteworthy symptom of the awakening of the Petersburg proletariat, and it is not surprising that the results of its systematic activity were not slow in manifesting themselves. The winter of 1895–96 in Petersburg was rich as never before in strikes and risings among the workmen; the signs of that life which characterises the *awakening conscience* of the labouring masses. In November of last year a strike broke out in Thornton's cloth factory; and the terrified owners and the bewildered police hastened to satisfy the demands of the exasperated workpeople, which had been formulated by the League in a mass of manifestos distributed by them. Almost simultaneously, the women cigarette-makers in Laferme's tobacco factory came out on strike.[110] Though at its beginning this movement was somewhat chaotic, it began to take shape; demands were made, and once more were quickly satisfied to avoid further misunderstandings.

A month later and there was the strike at the factory of a company for the manufacture of boots and shoes. Then there was a strike among the sawyers of Lebedev, and the weavers rose at the same place.[111] There was excitement among the workmen in the Putilov factory,[112] and then followed the explanation, very unpleasant for the Administration, at the cotton mills of Koenig.[113] In January a strike at Voronin's (in the island of Rezvy) was rapidly and successfully brought to an end;[114] lastly, the leaflets stirred up excitement among the workmen of the New Imperial Dockyard.[115]

The calm following all this was succeeded in the spring by a fresh outburst: the workmen of the New Imperial Dockyard were again in commotion,[116] and this time a single issue of leaflets was enough to make the administration of the imperial Alexandrov iron foundry grant concessions,[117] while threats of a strike subdued for the second time the stubbornness of Mr Voronin, the employer already mentioned.[118]

Such was the position of affairs at the beginning of May, 1896. Strikes had been made in various branches of industry on various grounds. It is not difficult, however, to recognise the general typical features in the demands put forward by the strikers. In the great majority of cases the workmen protest against direct breach of the law on the part of the employers, of the contravention of some article or other in the legislation which, generally speaking, puts the workmen in complete subjection to the employer.

They demand: first, exact fulfilment of the law; secondly, they attempt to keep up the former level of wages, to preserve the *status quo* and to oppose the downward tendency in the price of wage labour. To give an illustration of this – what did the workmen in Thornton's factory demand? They demanded, as was stated in one of the leaflets, that the law should be carried out, that the amount of the wage for which he is hired should be declared to the workman before he begins work, and that the factory inspector should see that there be no deception in the tables of payment, that there should not be two scales of payment for piece-work.[119] Again, the workmen were in commotion in the New Imperial Dockyard mentioned already. Why? Because the governor of the port, Admiral Verkhovsky, arranged for the payment of wages once a month, while the law with perfect clearness lays down: 'In cases where workmen are hired for an indefinite period, the payment of wages must take place not less often than twice a month'.

Shortly after the end of the strike at the tobacco factory of Laferme (in the beginning of December 1895), the factory inspectors had to confess the justice of the workwomen's demands, based as they were on the law, and to declare in the circular printed in the Russian newspapers of 20 December, 1895, and sent to the Russian tobacco manufacturers, that 'We allow the workwomen's grievance', and that

It is impossible to arbitrarily condemn work. If the employer regards as worthless work done, he has not the right, on account of a few spoiled cigarettes, to condemn a whole hundred. Such condemnation is absolutely arbitrary. For spoiled cigarettes (due to careless or incompetent work) the employer may impose a fine, but for waste of material he can claim only by taking the case into court.

Of this character are also the principal demands made by the workers in the Kalinsky cotton mill, in the cotton mills of Koenig, in Voronin's factory, in the Alexandrov foundry, etc.

We have already spoken of another common feature in the demands of the Petersburg workmen, i.e., their effort at least to *preserve* the present or the recently existing rate of wages. Such is their exceedingly *moderate* desire. And here we must remember with how little it is possible to content the Russian proletariat at present. This is not the place to attempt to sketch its economical position, we will merely quote two or three figures taken from the tracts circulating in Petersburg. When the weavers at Thornton's, in their crushing poverty, lost all patience and made the above-mentioned strike, many of them, owing to the stagnation in the market, were not earning more than seven roubles, 14s. 7d. a month, a figure incredible to a western European workman. Again, when at the beginning of summer there was a commotion in the so-called Russian–American india-rubber factory,[120] the leaflets circulating among the workmen referred among other things to the fact that workmen for an eleven-hour day, at an occupation which brings on spitting of blood in the course of a few years, were paid in all only 65 kopeks (1/4¼) a day. But the existence of an incredibly low standard of wages is acknowledged in a moment of candour even by the representatives of the Russian administration. At the time of the 'pacifying' of the strikers at Laferme's factory, when the cigarette makers (whose grievances the factory inspector's circular confessed to be well-founded) were in terrible poverty, when by order of the head of the police they had been drenched by fire engines, the same martial officer had the insolence, in acknowledging the insufficiency of their wage, to advise them to eke it out by means of prostitution.

Crushed by their poverty, exploited in the most infamous manner, ill-treated by the police, unorganised for the most part, the Petersburg workers listen intently to the voices of their organised, intelligent comrades. Here and there the fire has kindled and burst into flame, merely on the appearance of a leaflet of the Social Democratic organisation. The factory owners themselves, as we have seen, hastened in alarm to make concessions, while the Tsar's police with feverish hurry set to work 'to clear the atmosphere' by removing the disaffected elements, flattering themselves that they would succeed in disorganising, destroying and wiping off the face of the earth the hated League.

Indeed, from the beginning of December in last year, the government prepared a real campaign against the unknown 'malefactors'. On the night of 8 December,[121] some dozens of men 'suspected' by the police were seized, both from among the so-called 'intelligentsi', or advanced class, and the working class. The police were triumphant, supposing that they held the leaders of the movement. What followed? A manifesto of the League appeared immediately after the arrests, declaring that the police had 'made a mistake in the address', foretelling fresh strikes and concluding in the following words, the force and significance of which the Russian government appreciated only later: 'You cannot crush the labour movement by arrests and banishments; strikes and struggles will not cease till the complete emancipation of the working class from the capitalists is attained.'[122] From the date of the publication of that manifesto there has been a duel of a kind between the Petersburg police and the organisation of the 'League'. An exasperated gendarmerie has made captives right and left; single arrests went on through December; there were arrests and banishments wholesale in January;[123] and since then not a week has gone by without arrests among the mass of workers suspected of relations with the League. Meanwhile the issue of manifestos, opening the eyes of the workers to capitalist exploitation, at the arbitrary will of the servants of the Tsar, goes on in its course uninterruptedly, raising the confidence of the proletariat and their faith in its powers, while they see it striking dismay and alarm into the hearts of its adversaries.

At last the Tsar's government thought it necessary by the mouth of the Minister of Finance, Witte, to sound the alarm; he issued secret instructions, which got by chance into the columns of the Russian papers. In these he called upon factory inspectors to watch over the maintenance of the patriarchal order of relations, as though such relations still existed in Russian factories, and to guard the workmen from the machinations of agitators – 'enemies of the working class', in the words of the circular. But the circular, published and distributed by the League among the workers, destroyed the last traces of the prestige of the factory inspector, slight as it already was; it displayed the double role of this quasi-champion of the workman's interests, and manifested the real nature of the dumb slave of absolutism coquetting with the bourgeoisie. And, indeed, in general the League never lost an opportunity of discrediting the imperial government in the workmen's eyes, proving to them that in the struggle for a better future they ought to rely only on their own forces.

On the 1st of May in this year, the League issued a manifesto explaining to the workers the significance of the world-wide labour festival.[124] The Petersburg workman fastened upon the printed words, and in hot haste read the leaflets that told him of the proletariat of Western Europe, that told him of the triumphs won by workers of other lands, thanks to dogged struggle, and thanks to well-ordered organisation. And besides the leaflets written for special occasions, the League has distributed masses of pamphlets and publications of various kinds, partly imported from abroad, partly printed in secret printing-presses in Russia itself.[125] We must, however, remark that the demand for the printed word is always considerably in excess of the supply, and that, with every effort, the League is not in a position to fully satisfy the continually increasing demand of the worker for information, in the intolerably difficult conditions in which it is placed by the everlasting reprisals of the Russian government. Still the efforts of the Russian Social Democrats have not been thrown away; the seeds they have scattered have brought forth a rich harvest. In the milieu of the workers an atmosphere has been created full of discontent and protest.

Amid such conditions rose and grew the strike (colossal by Russian standards) of almost all the Petersburg cotton-spinners, a strike which plays a great part, not only in the history of Petersburg, but of the whole Russian labour movement.

As is well known, Russian manufacturers, glad to find a snug berth for themselves under the Russian system of protection, are all without exception loyal 'patriots of their country', and seize every opportunity for the expression of their loyal sentiments. 'Patriots' they showed themselves at the time of the recent coronation festivities. This 'patriotism' quickly vanished, however, when brought into contact with real, though insignificant sacrifices, where their tightly-stuffed purses were in question. Honourable representatives of Russian manufacturers, many of them at least, refused to satisfy the demands of the workers for wages during the coronation days, when they were making holiday, *not of their own free will*. Such a refusal, for instance, was received, among others, by the workers in the Ekaterinhof factory in one of the suburbs of Petersburg, and they had recourse for help to other cotton-mills, sending delegates for this purpose.[126] In a large number of cases the workers responded warmly to this appeal, and it was resolved that the representatives from the various factories should meet to formulate the general indignation.

At the end of May (old style) a meeting of delegates assembled in Ekaterinhof Park, in which one hundred persons took part, a spectacle utterly extraordinary for Petersburg, and astounding to everyone having even a slight acquaintance with the Russian police regime. At this open-air meeting the general demands of the workers in the cotton mills were put forward, and they were afterwards formulated in a manifesto published by the League, and distributed in immense numbers all over Petersburg.[127] Then began the strike. We quote the text of this manifesto, signed by the League, 30th May (old style), 1896, entitled 'What it is the Petersburg Cotton Spinners Want':

(1) We want our working-day everywhere to last from 7 o'clock a.m. to 7 o'clock p.m., instead of as at present from 6 o'clock a.m. to 8 o'clock p.m.

(2) We want our time off for dinner to last an hour and a half, so that the whole working day will consist of 10½ hours instead of 13 hours as at present.

(3) We want the rate of wages to be everywhere raised one farthing, and where possible, two farthings.

(4) We want work to stop everywhere simultaneously at 2 o'clock on Saturdays.

(5) We want the overseers not to arbitrarily stop the machines, or to set them in motion before the time.

(6) We want the wages for the first half of the month to be paid regularly and punctually, and not delayed.

(7) We want full wages to be paid for the coronation holidays.

In the course of a few days the strike had spread to seventeen cotton mills; four more were soon won over, and, with a single insignificant exception, work was at a standstill in every cotton mill in Petersburg, thirty to forty thousand men being out on strike.

The effect produced by this concerted action was an almost overwhelming dismay, and the bourgeois official world of Petersburg, dumbfounded by the utterly unexpected turn of events, began to ask itself whether it were possible that a labour question existed in Russia, and whether the restless spirit of the proletariat which allows no peace to the 'decaying West', had arisen to confront it also. Special astonishment was excited in the breasts of the respectable Petersburg citizens at the extraordinary quiet and discipline of the workers on strike. Patrols of Cossacks and special detachments of police, sent into the poorer quarters of the town, moved through empty streets in which even the din of the ordinary traffic was lessened. The very rare appeals to violence at open-air meetings were received with opposition by the workmen who had been so well-prepared for peaceful action. Even when the local police officers took the trouble to enlarge upon the services rendered to the people by the manufacturers, as though they laboured in the sweat of their brows for the public well, the crowds listened with the utmost patience and calmness. For the first time Petersburg was surprised into talk about the labour movement. The strike was criticised, attacked, defended on all sides, and the attention of many who had entirely ignored anything of the nature of a social question was now drawn to it. In the meanwhile the representatives of authority did not lose time. A special meeting of the Board of Manufacturers was summoned, and tried to determine upon a scheme of action. The Minister of Finance sent confidential communications to them assuring them of Government support. The Mayor circulated printed appeals to the workmen, the tone of which became less peremptory as the strike was prolonged, and peace and order still continued to the astonishment and anger of the police. The strike fever is infectious. There were soon rumours that the employees at the Putilov and some others of the great foundries would throw up work and thus increase the number of strikers by some tens of thousands.[128] Disturbances took place in the Vorgunin factory; a strike was imminent at the Aleksandrov iron foundry.[129] At a large gutta-percha factory incendiary leaflets were in circulation;[130] the suppressed excitement was becoming dangerous, and the authorities, with an alarmed sense of the necessity for some kind of action, made haste to pacify the workers by promises to fulfil their demands. At any cost the strike had to be stopped, the more especially as, *horribili dictu*, it was delaying the Tsar's triumphal entry into Petersburg!

And so most radical measures were taken to prevent further postponement of the Imperial visit. In many parts of the town the mayor addressed the workers in person, with promises that their demands should be examined, and all possible concessions made to them, if only they would put an end to the 'riot' before the entry of the Tsar. Where 'clemency' was felt to be of no avail, they did not hesitate to resort to force. Many of the factory yards were surrounded by soldiers, and the police burst in upon the workers who remained in their own homes, and demanded of each of them separately whether they were willing to go back to work or not. Those who were unwilling were promptly arrested, thrown into prison and exiled. Needless to add that the factories were filled with spies, such being the customary practice of the Russian police. But it was felt by the authorities that the chief blow must be aimed at the League, that organisation which had given proof of its continued life by repeated manifestos at the time of the strike. And the arrests were renewed. Persons of the enlightened classes, who, for various reasons, had incurred the suspicion of the police, were seized and thrown into prison.[131] The Minister of Finance issued a proclamation in which, after referring to the unlawfulness of the strike provoked by miscreants for their own reprehensible ends, he made the shameful assurance that 'the interests of the workers were as precious to the Government as those of the manufacturers'! This assurance was made to the Russian workman! who knows quite well that workmen's clubs and unions, as well as strikes, are forbidden by Russian law; and that the Petersburg workers, guided by the League, are even attempting, *for their own reprehensible ends*, to abolish these monstrous laws, hostile alike to culture and humanity, these laws which embody the vaunted equal treatment of workers and employers by the Tsar's Government! The workmen, having insufficient means to hold out longer, and terrorised by the reprisals of the police, began gradually to return to their work. By degrees the strike cooled down – at last it was over altogether.

'And what', it will be asked us, 'is the result of it? What has the strike gained, if it has gained anything, for the Petersburg workmen?' Some demands of the workmen were conceded, others, it was promised, should be looked into at some later time. That is little. But the true value and immense significance of the strike just over, does not lie in this. It lies in the tremendous moral effect produced by it: that is its importance and value to us. It served as a living testimony to the fact that the Russian workman knows how to stand up for his own interests, in steady union with his fellows; that he is capable of a discipline and organisation, exciting admiration even in his bitterest foes. It was – and this is the chief thing – a living object lesson to the workman himself. His continual collision with the police showed him, in a peculiarly vivid and painful manner, his helplessness under the Russian government of to-day. He learnt that behind the capitalists there stands another foe – Russian autocracy, and it became clear to him further that what he needs, before all and more than anyone, is to gain political freedom. It was the political question that came *de facto* to the surface at the time of the strike. The political question was also considered by the League which appealed to the representatives of Russian society, and declared that all true and genuine opponents of despotism should support the mass movement beginning among the Russian proletariat, with all the means at their command.

That which happened in Petersburg took place in its general features, though on a smaller scale, in other centres of manufacturing and commercial life. In the spring of 1895 the railway employés of the Kursk line at Moscow stopped work on account of their discontent with the management.[132] Early in May of the same year, there was a disturbance among the men of the Prokhorov weaving factory in Moscow. In June the workmen of Kasurik and Gerasimov's factory at Kuskovo, near Moscow, came into conflict with Cossacks and police. At the same time there broke out a strike of workmen in the depot of K. and S. Popov & Co. Our Moscow comrades, like those of Petersburg, took advantage of all such events to explain the present position of affairs to the workers, and to point out what should be their line of action for the future; and at the time of the late strike in Petersburg, the central committee of the Moscow Labour League issued manifestos in which it called upon the Moscow workmen to support their Petersburg brothers. In May 1895 there was a strike in the factory of Korsinkin at Yaroslav, with its eight thousand and ninety-nine workpeople – (4,938 men, 4,028 women, 111 boys, and 22 girls). It is sad to have to relate that this strike led to little less than a massacre. Two officers, Petrov and Kalugin, attacked with their soldiery a group of strikers, who up to that time had been perfectly peaceful. The workmen, so unexpectedly assaulted, began to defend themselves with stones. The soldiers were ordered to fire, with the result that three of the strikers were killed and eighteen wounded.[133]

Similar conflicts of workmen with the soldiers took place in the large manufacturing village of Teikovo, near the town of Ivanovo-Vosnesensk, in the Government of Vladimir, in the spring of 1895.[134] The workmen of Karesnikov's factory assembled to the number of 5,000 in the factory-yard and fell into a hot wrangle with the English overseer of the factory. In his alarm the overseer aimed a revolver at the workmen. This act proved a fatal one to himself, for he was at once thrown down and literally torn to pieces by the infuriated crowd. The local police lost no time in wiring an account of this unfortunate incident to the chief town of the Government of Vladimir. Troops of Cossacks and infantry were immediately despatched to Teikovo.

Fortunately a bloody termination of the affray was prevented by the judgement of Messrs Karesnikov. The demands of the workmen were granted, and the men went back to work. All that was left for the authorities was to set on foot an inquiry into the circumstances attending the death of the overseer.

The conduct of the authorities during the strike of the textile workers at Ivanovo-Vosnesensk, in the October of the same year,[135] was of a piece with the general despotism displayed elsewhere. The workers were absolutely compelled to return to work after a fortnight's struggle, and the strike accordingly ended in an apparent victory for the employers. Their unanimous resistance, however, was not entirely without result; and, fearing a fresh disturbance, the factory inspector persuaded the Company to slightly raise the rate of wages.

In Nizhni Novgorod, on the Volga, in the winter of 1895–6, the Social Democratic League had to enter into a campaign against a special form of the sweating system, carried on at the machine factory of Dobrov, Nacholz and Co. Their appeal to the workers made a powerful impression on the employés and caused not a little consternation to the masters and to the police; and the latter caused some of the most glaring abuses to be remedied, at least for a time.

In South Russia the awakening among the workers to an understanding of their position has gone on no less rapidly than in the North. There is not a single manufacturing centre in which, in the course of the last two or three years, strikes and other manifestations of the growing discontent have not been in evidence. Even so early as 1893 and 1894 the police of Rostov, on the Don, had much trouble with the workmen of the railway depôt of the Vladicaucasus line, who demanded, in March, 1894, an increase of wages, curtailment of the working day, and generally showed themselves very 'untrustworthy' from the point of view of the police.

In Ekaterinoslav, in the summer of 1895, the police made an attempt to break up the Social Democratic League in that place, and arrested sixteen workmen. These arrests were renewed in the winter of 1895–6, and our comrades at Ekaterinoslav suffered severe losses from arrests of about a hundred workmen at various factories and foundries.[136]

In all the South of Russia there is no more hopeful spot than Odessa for the awakening of the proletariat. Passing over many other facts we may mention that in this new capital of Russia the workmen have been in the habit of holding regular meetings in a restaurant for some time past, at which the 'Programme of the South Russian Workers' was discussed and put into shape. Discovered at last by the police, two hundred people were arrested in one day and charged with the formation of a secret society, having for its object agitation among the working classes by both legal and illegal means. The labour movement in Odessa did not by any means come to an end with these arrests, and in July of the same year the police thought it necessary to close three restaurants and one eating house, and to make other raids and captures. More arrests took place in December, and all the prisoners were accused of socialistic propaganda.

Turning now to the West of Russia we have especial pleasure in commending to the attention of our foreign comrades the progress of the Social Democratic propaganda among the Jews, who constitute a most important, and often preponderant, part of the town populations of that region of Russia. There, manufactures are but little developed, and are replaced by handicrafts and petty industries, which afford a limited field for propaganda, carried on principally by poor Jews. These pariahs, destitute even of those pitiable rights which are the heritage of the Christian subjects of the Tsar, have shown in their struggle with their exploiters an endurance and comprehension of the social and political aims of the labour movement, entitling them to be ranked as the advance guard of the great army of labour in Russia.

How clearly the advanced representatives of the Jewish Social Democracy understand the political situation is apparent from a couple of extracts from pamphlets published at the time of a certain strike:

There is no longer one Jewish people; within Judaism there are two peoples, two hostile classes, and the struggle between these two hostile classes has reached a point when it can be suppressed neither by respect for the synagogue and the Rabbis nor by the menaces of the government.

And further on:

Should we regret this? Should we try to hinder it? No; for only through this struggle with the capitalists have we become conscious of our manhood; only through this struggle have we learnt to understand our true interests; only through hatred of capital have we risen to sympathy and love for our brothers in suffering. It is only by this conflict between Capital and Labour that the sense of our class solidarity has sprung up; in that conflict it has developed and grown strong. Are we to regret those old days when, ignorant, despised and hated, ill-treated from below and oppressed from above, the Jews led the life of hunted beasts, trembling for our pitiful existence and forever expecting fresh calamity? Are we to regret the loss of ties uniting Jewish beggars and Jewish magnates, when we have gained new ties uniting us with the workers of Russia, Poland and Lithuania – with the workers, indeed, of all lands? The future will bring us a strengthening of these bonds, and a growth of our powers and our understanding. Why regret a dark past, without struggle and dissension, but also without life?[137]

These quotations need no comment. As striking examples of the political awakening of the Russian proletariat, we will, in conclusion, point to the eagerness with which the Russian worker reads every item of news of the labour movement in Western Europe, the celebration of the 1st of May in the secret societies, and the addresses in which the workers of Petersburg and Moscow saluted the French proletariat on the 25th anniversary of the Paris Commune of 1871.[138] Among the many wreaths laid on the grave at Père-Lachaise of those who fell in the Commune, were wreaths sent by the workmen of Moscow and Petersburg and the Jews of Western Russia.

So much, comrades, we can report to you of the progress of the labour movement in our country. We lay it before you without exaggeration, but without concealing the pride and hope of which our hearts are full in view of the results – humble as yet, but still significant and unmistakable – of our movement. We firmly believe that a rapid growth and powerful development await the labour movement, now just beginning among us.

At the Paris International Socialist Congress of 1889, our comrade Plekhanov said that the revolutionary movement in Russia will triumph as a labour movement or not at all. At that time his words seemed doubtful to many of our most enlightened and intelligent fellow-countrymen. Gradually, however, it has become clear that the movement among our working class is the truly revolutionary movement in the Russia of to-day. All that stands outside their desire for justice and social emancipation cannot have any durable significance. The struggle against absolutism will only be victorious when the idea of political freedom has penetrated to the masses of the working people.

We are convinced that this time is now not far off, and the day is not far distant when the Russian Tsardom, once the firmest stronghold of European reaction, will fall to the ground. We repeat, however, not desiring to deceive ourselves nor our Western comrades, that we have taken only the first, though it may be the most difficult, steps on the path that leads to the complete secret organisation of the revolutionary forces of the Russian proletariat. Between the secret Social Democratic organisations in the different towns of Russia there exists as yet no sufficient union, and often there is a lack of unity in their action.

The creation of such a union and such unity of action – the foundation of a united Social Democratic organisation in Russia – must be the great aim of our labours in the immediate future.

32.   TO ALL ST PETERSBURG WORKERS (15 SEPTEMBER 1896)[139]

St Petersburg Union of Struggle

Comrades! The whole series of disturbances during the past year at the Thornton, Laferme and other factories has ended with a huge strike of 30,000 weavers and spinners, news of which has spread far beyond the frontiers of Russia. From now on the Russian worker in his struggle is joined to the international workers' family, to the whole working class. Foreign workers at the Congress of the Socialist International in London gave an enthusiastic welcome to Plekhanov, the representative of the Petersburg 'Union', when he mentioned our strike.[140] This very strike scared our guardian government. Even if it deceives others by its foul lies, underestimating the number of strikers by more than half, asserting that the workers did not support one another – it does not deceive itself by such inventions. It has realised that the workers are no longer a submissive flock of sheep, it has understood that the united working mass, acting together in its own interests, represents a formidable force which cannot be destroyed by flattering promises or even by arms. It has understood this and has suddenly reflected. And then we read in the papers that 'the government is currently preoccupied with introducing improvements in the workers' way of life'. It is true that we know from our own bitter experience that the promises of the government are only pie in the sky and that, without insistent demands on our part, they would not even give us what they promise. But it is important to us that they recognise the workers as a force, talk with them and want to placate them. All this convinces us, comrades, that there is only one force in the whole world that can alleviate our condition – and that force is us ourselves. Only by merging our interests together, only by advancing as a whole mass in the joint common struggle, can we achieve a real alleviation of our general lot.

Working men and women of St Petersburg! Our 'Union', which has caused the factory owners and the government so much trouble and grief, the 'Union of Struggle for the Emancipation of the Working Class', is entering the second year of its existence. We have had a glorious year. The severity of the struggle has taught us a great deal. We have become more conscious, we have begun to understand better the interests and tasks that are common to us all. We now know how much we need the right to arrange, without hindrance, strikes, unions, [mutual aid] funds and collections for the discussion of our common affairs.

Henceforth this ray of consciousness in us must not be extinguished. Fathering our strength, regardless of any persecutions, we shall, by tireless struggle, step by step win for ourselves ever more concessions. We shall move cheerfully and boldly along the straight and broad path arm in arm with the workers of the whole world — towards our great final aim — *the complete emancipation of the working class from the yoke of capital.*

Union of Struggle for the Emancipation of the Working Class
15 September 1896.

33.   TO THE TSARIST GOVERNMENT (NOT LATER THAN 25 NOVEMBER 1896)[141]

V.I. Lenin

This year, 1896, the Russian government has already on two occasions made announcements to the public about the workers' struggle against the factory owners. In other countries announcements of this kind are not rare — there they do not conceal what is happening in the country and the press freely publishes news of strikes. In Russia, however, the government fears more than the plague publicity for the practices and incidents in the factories: it has forbidden the newspapers to report strikes, it has forbidden factory inspectors to publish their reports, it has even put a stop to the hearing of strike cases in the normal courts that are open to the public. In a word, it has taken every measure to preserve strict secrecy about what is happening in the factories and among the workers. But all of a sudden all these police tricks burst like soap bubbles and the government was itself forced to speak openly of the fact that the workers were engaged in a struggle against the factory owners. What caused such a *volte-face*? In 1895 there was a particularly large number of workers' strikes. Yes, but there had been strikes before, yet the government had managed to keep them secret and the mass of workers as a whole knew nothing about these strikes. The recent strikes were much larger than those that had gone before and they were concentrated in one place. Yes, but there have also been strikes as large as this before — in 1885–6, for instance, in the Moscow and Vladimir provinces.[142] Yet the government held firm and said nothing of the workers' struggle against the factory owners. What then has made it speak this time? This time the Socialists have come to the aid of the workers, helped them to explain their case, to spread news of it everywhere, both among the workers and among the public, to formulate precisely the workers' demands, to demonstrate to all the unfairness and the brutal violence of the government. The government realised that it was becoming quite ridiculous for it to remain silent, since the strikes were common knowledge, and it too has fallen into line behind everyone else. The socialist leaflets demanded a government response and the government emerged and responded.

Let us see what kind of response it was.

At first the government tried to avoid an open and public response. One of the ministers, the Minister of Finance, Witte, sent out a circular to the factory inspectors, and in this circular he called the workers and the Socialists 'the worst enemies of public order', advised the factory inspectors to try to scare the workers, to assure them that the government had forbidden the factory owners to make concessions, to point out the factory owners' good intentions and noble designs, to tell them how the factory owners are concerned about the workers and their needs, how the factory owners are full of 'good feelings'. The government said nothing about the strikes themselves, it said not a word about the causes of the strikes, about the terrible oppression by the employers and the violation of the law or about the workers' aims. In a word it simply *misrepresented* all the strikes that took place in the summer and autumn of 1895 and tried to get away with hackneyed stock phrases about the violent and 'illegal' actions of the workers, although the workers had committed no violent acts. It was the police alone who resorted to violence. The Minister wanted to keep this circular a secret, but the very officials to whom he had entrusted it failed to keep the secret and so the circular did the public rounds. Then it was printed by the Socialists. Whereupon the government, seeing that it had as usual been made to look silly with its open 'secrets', had it printed in the newspapers. This, as we have already said, was the response to the strikes of the summer and autumn of 1895. In the spring of 1896, however, the strikes were repeated on a much larger scale. The rumours about them were accompanied by socialist leaflets. At first the government maintained a cowardly silence, waiting to see how the matter would end, and then, when the workers' revolt had died down, it belatedly came out with its bureaucratic wisdom, as it might with a delayed police protocol. This time it had to speak openly and, what is more, to do so collectively as a government. Its announcement appeared in No. 158 of *Pravitel'stvennyi Vestnik* [*The Government Bulletin*, 19 July 1896]. This time, unlike previous occasions, it could not misrepresent the workers' strikes. It had to tell the whole story, to recount the oppressive measures taken by the factory owners' and the workers' demands. It had to admit that the workers had behaved 'decently'. Thus the workers taught the government to stop lying in the despicable manner of the police: they forced it to admit the truth when they rose up *en masse* and made use of leaflets to publicise their case. This was a great success. The workers will now recognise their sole means of achieving a public statement of their needs, of informing the workers throughout Russia of the struggle. The workers will now recognise that the lies of the government are only refuted by the united struggle of the workers themselves to secure their rights and by their [class] consciousness. Having told the full story, the ministers began to think up excuses and to claim in their statement that the strikes were caused purely by the 'particular circumstances of cotton spinning and cotton weaving production'. Fancy that! And not by the particular circumstances of the whole of Russian *production*, not by the circumstances of Russian state procedure that allow the police to hound and to detain peaceful workers who are defending themselves against oppression? Why then, good ministers, did the workers snap up, read and ask for the leaflets that made no mention of cotton or spinning, but instead told of the lack of rights of Russian citizens and of the arbitrary tyranny of a government that fawns on the capitalists. No, this new excuse is almost worse, almost more despicable, than the one that Finance Minister Witte got away with in his circular by blaming everything on 'troublemakers'. Minister Witte views the strike in the same way as any police official whose palm has been greased by the factory owners: the troublemakers came and there was a strike. Now that they have all seen a strike of 30,000 workers, the ministers have put their heads together and have at long last come to the conclusion that strikes do not occur because socialist troublemakers appear on the scene, but that Socialists appear on the scene because strikes occur and because the workers' struggle against the capitalists is beginning. The ministers now assert that the Socialists then 'joined' the strikes. This is a fine lesson for Finance Minister Witte. Take care, Mr Witte, learn your lesson well! Learn to sort out in advance the cause of a strike, learn to examine the workers' demands and not the reports of your police rats, whom you yourself have not the slightest faith in. The ministers assure the public that it was only 'malevolent individuals' who were trying to give the strikes a 'criminal political character' or, as they say in one passage, a 'social character'. (The ministers wanted to say 'socialist' but, either through illiteracy or bureaucratic cowardice, they said 'social' and the result is a nonsense: 'socialist' means that which supports the workers in their struggle against capital whereas 'social' simply means public. How can a strike be given a social character? It's just the same as giving ministers ministerial rank!) That is amusing! The Socialists give the strikes a political character! But, before the Socialists did anything, the government itself took all possible measures to give the strikes a political character. Did it not begin seizing peaceful workers as if they were criminals? Did it not arrest and transport them? Did it not send spies and *agents provocateurs* everywhere? Did it not arrest all those who fell into its hands? Did it not promise to help the factory owners so that they would not give in? Did it not hound workers just for collecting money for the strikers? The government itself was ahead of everyone in explaining to the workers that their war against the factory owners must inevitably be a war against the government. All the Socialists had to do was to confirm this and publish it in their leaflets. That is all. The Russian government had, however, already had extensive experience in the art of subterfuge and ministers attempted to keep quiet about the methods used by our government to 'give the strikes a political character'. It told the public the dates of the Socialists' leaflets, but why did it not tell it the dates of the orders issued by the City Governor and the other cut-throats for the arrest of peaceful workers, for putting troops under arms, for the despatch of spies and *agents provocateurs*? They gave the public details of the number of socialist leaflets, but why did they not give details of the number of workers and Socialists seized, the number of families ruined, and the number transported and imprisoned without trial? Why? Because even Russian ministers, despite their shamelessness, are wary of mentioning such criminal exploits in public. The entire strength of the power of the state – the police, the army, the gendarmerie and the public prosecutors – has been brought to bear on peaceful workers who were standing up for their rights and defending themselves from the tyranny of the factory owners. The entire strength of the state treasury has, by the promise of support for the poor factory owners, been directed against the workers who have held out on their own pennies and on the pennies of their comrades, the English, Polish, German and Austrian workers.

The workers were not united. They were unable to arrange collections, to enlist other towns and other workers. They were hounded everywhere and they had to give in to the entire strength of the power of the state. Our ministerial gentlemen are rejoicing in the victory of the government!

A fine victory! Against 30,000 peaceful workers with no money – the entire strength of the authorities, the entire wealth of the capitalists! The ministers would be wise to wait before boasting of this victory: their boasting is really redolent of that of a policeman who brags because he has got away from a strike *un*harmed.

To calm the capitalists the government triumphantly declares that the 'incitements' of the Socialists have been unsuccessful. But our reply to this is that no incitement could have produced one hundredth part of the impression that the government's behaviour in this affair has created on all the workers of St Petersburg and the whole of Russia! The workers have seen through the government's policy of keeping quiet about workers' strikes and misrepresenting them. The workers saw how their united struggle forced the abandonment of the hypocritical lies of the police. They saw whose interests were safeguarded by a government that promised assistance to the factory owners. They understood who their real enemy was, when, without their violating law and order, it sent in the army and the police against them as if they were enemies. However much ministers may awy that the struggle has been a failure, the workers see how the factory owners everywhere have quietened down and they know that the government is already summoning the factory inspectors to discuss the concessions that must be made to the workers, for it sees that concessions are unavoidable. The strikes of 1895–6 have not been in vain. They have been of immense service to the Russian workers, they have shown them how to wage the struggle for their interests. They have taught them to understand *the political situation and the political needs of the working class.*

Union of Struggle for the Emancipation of the Working Class.
November 1896.

34.   ON AGITATION (1896)[143]

A. Kremer and Yu. Martov

Our article is intended to clarify several questions relating to the practice of the Russian Social Democrats: the correct resolution of these questions is, in our opinion, a necessary precondition if social democratic activity is to attain its desired objectives. Drawing on our own experience and on the information that we have on the activity of other groups, we have come to the conclusion that the first steps taken by the Russian Social Democrats were the wrong ones and that, in the interests of the cause, their tactics must be changed. We have therefore tried in our article to show the direction in which the activity of the Social Democrats should be changed, which tasks they should set themselves in order to avoid the risk of remaining just as impotent at the end of the day as they were at the beginning.

The article was written with readers from amongst the intellectuals and advanced workers in mind; it was especially important for us to influence the convictions of this last group, because the majority of the worker Social Democrats sympathise with the practical activity that we condemn as useless. This is not the place to go into the causes of this phenomenon; this question is partly elucidated in the article itself and, in any case, we are convinced that, as long as the most advanced workers do not agree that we need to work in the direction indicated, the future of our workers' movement remains in doubt.[144] If our article does at least lead to a polemic on the question that concerns us, we shall count ourselves satisfied: in one way or another a polemic will serve its purpose, as it will have raised for examination a question that, until now, has been decided by separate closed circles.

The workers' movement is the inevitable result of the contradictions inherent in capitalist production. As far as the working mass is concerned, the contradictions in capitalist production consist in the changes in the conditions of life and the conceptions of the people brought about by the capitalist system which make this mass ever less prone to exploitation. Requiring men to be automata, unquestioningly subordinate to the will of capital, this system prepares the soil for the emergence among the workers of thinking men and instils in the workers an understanding of their interests. If capitalism requires the atomisation of the workers in order to root out the possibility of a struggle against capital, it does, in its turn, gather the workers together and join them in a single workshop, a single settlement, a single manufacturing centre. If capitalism requires that the workers should not be conscious of the opposition of the interests of capital to those of labour, the same system, with its concentration of capital, nonetheless makes the distinction between the position of the capitalists and workers ever more acute. If the differentiation of the worker suits capitalism, because it leads to atomisation, technical development at the same time destroys this differentiation and reduces the majority of workers to the level of unskilled workmen. If it suits the capitalist for the worker's family to be strong and to hold him back from too passionate a struggle with capital, then, on the other hand, the latter itself emancipates the worker from his family and melts down his wife and children in this same crucible of factory life. In a word, if capital, faced with the threat of its own ruin, is obliged to try and erect obstacles to the development of the working class, it is, on the other hand, itself destroying its own edifice and preparing a force that is hostile and dangerous to it. It is true that, at a certain level of its development, the same capitalist system prepared a strong weapon for the struggle even against the united proletariat, but then as a weapon this is double-edged. In struggling against it, the force it has itself created and developed, capitalist society suffocates and hastens its own destruction. It is sufficient to mention the reserve army of workers, which weighs on the working population like a millstone and paralyses the success of the struggle.[145] But the increase in the worker army that forms this reserve curtails the home market, since it makes it ever more difficult for the working population to bear the burden of taxes, which the transition from indirect to direct taxation gives rise to; finally, this army requires state assistance (not to mention the increases in expenditure on the police, the courts and prisons) which leads to an increase in state expenditure. The first consequence is that the capitalist is forced to seek new markets, which becomes more and more difficult, and this then leads to frequent, and then also to permanent, crises, and the crises lead to losses instead of profits, to the reduction of some capitalists to the ranks of the proletariat, to the destruction of a part of capital. The change in the system of taxation and the increase in expenditure caused by the members of the reserve army takes away an ever greater part of profit for the use of the state and, as profit is reduced, so, consequently, is accumulation. But these new contradictions result in the urge to increase exploitation and further improve technique, in increasingly bitter competition and other similar phenomena, which, as we saw above, will in their turn lead to consequences which do not contribute to the objectives of capitalism – they develop strength and a degree of hostility in the working mass towards the existing order. Thus the contradictions inherent in a certain stage of capitalist development drive the working mass against capital. The further the development of capitalist production goes, the keener this struggle must become and the further the demands and the consciousness of the working mass will extend. Hence capitalism is a school, not only training material – worker militants – but also educating them and impressing upon them its all too glaring contradictions. It has not only increased the strength of the working class by uniting the workers, but also prepared the soil for the development and dissemination of ever more extreme ideas. The idea of socialism as something concretely possible could be worked out only on the basis of the capitalist system and, in addition, only at a certain stage of its development.

But how does the school of capitalism act on the working mass? Gathering the workers together still does not mean uniting them for the struggle.

The concentration of the proletariat is fertile soil for the movement. If capitalism were able constantly to satisfy the worker in his daily needs, then this unification would not play a revolutionary role. But capitalism, which depends on competition and the absence of planning in production, constantly forces individual entrepreneurs to strive for an increase in surplus value,[146] for a reduction in the share of labour in the product, for a constant niggling struggle with the proletariat, which defends its existence and cannot but protest against the obvious encroachment on its well-being. This struggle is inevitably the main educational factor acting on the working mass and makes it, at a certain level of development, one of the principal forces undermining this system. Becoming keener, deeper and more general, this struggle takes on the character of a class struggle with the corresponding class consciousness of the proletariat, which we are now experiencing in all capitalist countries. Capital will not surrender immediately, it will not surrender until the last moment: defeated on all counts, it tries to get up again and begin the struggle with renewed strength. In this struggle the naked interests of capital emerge most boldly: at a certain level of development the struggle can no longer be conducted under the banner of high-flown ideas, capital discards its mask and, unabashed, announces that it is fighting against the claims on its pocket; at this stage capital will be waging a struggle not for predominance, but simply for existence. It snatches at the political forms of the capitalist system, just as a drowning man clutches at a straw. Only state power is still in a position to fight against the working mass, and, as long as political power remains in the hands of the bourgeoisie, it is possible to assert categorically that there can be no great improvements in the position of the workers. Therefore, however broadly based the workers' movement may be, its success will not be secured until such time as the working class stands firmly on the ground of political struggle. The achievement of political power is the principal task of the struggling proletariat.

But the working class can only be confronted with this task when the economic struggle demonstrates to it the clear impossibility of achieving an improvement in its lot in the current political circumstances. It is only when the aspirations of the proletariat collide head on with current political forms, only when the torrent of the workers' movement meets political force, that the moment of transition in the class struggle to the phase of consciously political struggle occurs. As Social Democrats, we set ourselves the task of leading the proletariat to an awareness of the need for political freedom as the preliminary condition for the possibility of its broad development.

But how is this to be achieved?

The idea of political freedom is by no means a simple and obvious one, especially in a politically backward country; the working class cannot be inspired with this idea as long as that class remains suffocated in the present political atmosphere and as long as the satisfaction of the demands that it deems vital is impossible within the limits of existing political conditions. Just as for a recognition of the opposition of interests, the emergence of this opposition is in itself not enough, but a constant struggle is necessary, so, for a recognition of the lack of political rights, the very fact of this lack of rights is in itself inadequate, until such time as it conflicts with the efforts of the working mass to improve its situation. We see the best evidence of this fact in the history of England where, thanks to the prosperity of industry, it was at a certain period necessary to struggle solely for such improvements as it was possible to achieve in existing political conditions by means of a purely economic struggle with the capitalists, who did not resort to the help of the organised strength of the state. At first sight the results turned out to be really startling. In England there is the most highly developed capitalist production, the most highly developed workers' movement, but the political character of the movement is very insignificantly developed and the majority has until now stood aside from active political struggle. The proletariat has only very recently begun to acquire a social democratic leaning, as the working class, through the very course of the struggle, arrives at a recognition of the need for reforms that cannot be realised by any means other than direct influence on the state machine. But if we take Austria, in which the workers' movement is very young, there we meet with a startlingly rapid growth of the political elements in the proletarian movement, caused by a narrower political framework within whose limits the original struggle of the proletariat had to be conducted. Or, for example, Ireland. The struggle of the small farmers, divided by capital, has for a long time had a political character, because the economic struggle for the maintenance of their level of prosperity brought the Irish people into sharp conflict with the organised force of the English state. From the above-mentioned examples it follows that it is unthinkable to expect a class movement with a political programme where the purely economic struggle is not conducted on a sufficiently large scale. It is therefore utopian to suppose that the Russian workers, in their general mass, can wage a political struggle unless they clarify with sufficient conviction the need for this in their own interests. The popular mass is drawn into the struggle not by reasoning, but by the objective logic of things, by the very course of events which drives them to struggle. The role of the party, having taken upon itself the political education and organisation of the people, is limited in this respect to determining correctly the moment at which the struggle becomes ripe for transition to the political struggle and for the preparation in the mass itself of the elements that will ensure that this transition is accomplished with the minimum loss of resources. How, for example, can the proletariat come to recognise the need for freedom of assembly? The mass does not arrive at a demand like this in a purely logical way. Freedom of assembly must be recognised as a means of struggle for the proletariat's own interests and it follows that these interests should be recognised; and practice should demonstrate before their very eyes the link between the interests of the worker and freedom of assembly. This practice reveals itself in the struggle for their own interests, a struggle in which it is necessary to face up to the kind of general questions on which their thoughts appeared, even to them, to be nonsensical. It only remains for critical thought to direct the mass to the conclusions that result from the posing by life itself of the questions that are vital to it, and to formulate the results that flow from the logic of things, from the logic of the struggle itself – in other words, to produce a programme.

But how can one explain, in this case, the proletarian movement at the end of the last century in France and in the first half of the present century in almost the whole of Europe? That was the time of the political subjection of the bourgeoisie

which encountered obstacles in its development that the political forms of absolutism or aristocracy had placed in its way. The bourgeoisie, by then already
materially strong, was lacking in purely physical strength. In fact the working
people – for example, the apprentices and the factory workers – also suffered from
the same political conditions. Discontent was prevalent among the mass: it was
encouraged by the political struggle, but this struggle occurred while the old forms
of production were being replaced by the new and the whole significance and meaning of the new was not sufficiently clear even to the educated part of society, and
even less to the backward popular mass. In these conditions the struggle could not
give the proletariat either a clear consciousness of the fatal opposition between its
interests and the interests of all the other classes or, even more, of the fact that the
fundamental causes of the misfortunes of the working class lie in the foundations of
the economic order of contemporary society. Meanwhile, the considerable
repression of the bourgeoisie provoked in it the urge to fight for emancipation,
accompanied by an idealistic enthusiasm and a flourishing of political talents in its
midst which this class has never achieved either before or since. Whole masses of
orators, politicians, writers and publicists emerged from its ranks, inspired with
ideas of freedom and equality which, in the consciousness of the propagandists
themselves, bore little relation to the material interests of the bourgeoisie. Nonetheless, it was their children, nourished on political dissatisfaction and opposition who,
admittedly, went beyond the boundaries within which the solid bourgeois had permitted himself to grumble, and not infrequently found themselves in open conflict
with the representatives of the moderation and scrupulousness of financial and
industrial liberalism, but who were nevertheless working for the benefit of the
bourgeoisie alone. These very activists, moving out among the people with all the
ardour of one who is unaware of the material roots of his idealism, found fertile
soil in the mass, which was politically immature and in a state of turmoil. It was not
difficult to convince the people that the cause of all their misfortunes resided in
political restrictions and it was all the more easy to do this when the class that was
standing over it sang in unison with the revolutionary agitators, although in truth
an octave lower. This powerful combination confirmed in the minds of the workers
the truth and significance of what the orators were saying in flysheets and at meetings. In addition the same powerful combination confirmed in their minds the idea
of a link between all their interests and the interests of the entrepreneurs. Seeing in
the owner his defender and patron, he surrendered to him completely, not suspect-
ing that they would have only a short path to follow together, that their roads
would diverge in opposite directions. Thus the bourgeoisie became the leader of a
working class that, under its direction, did not destroy a single stronghold of
'blessed' absolutism. The working class went into battle, the bourgeoisie produced
the programme and after the victory established the new foundations of order,
while taking for itself the lion's share of the plunder, culminating in political
power. Nevertheless, even those crumbs of victory that fell to the proletariat after
victory had their uses. Of still greater use to it was the political education that it
had acquired in this struggle. But these positive attributes also bring negative ones

in their train. Right up to the present the worker has seen in the honey-tongued bourgeois his ruler and natural representative in political affairs. Assisting the political education of the working class, training it for political struggle, this historical period did at the same time facilitate the weakening of its political self-consciousness as a separate class. The history of this epoch is important for us, both as a lesson and as valuable material for our own practice and the theoretical basis of the movement. We should conclude from this that only the mass can win political freedom. And, if this is the case, then the struggle for the emancipation of the proletariat must not be postponed until such time as the bourgeoisie achieves political freedom. Whether our bourgeoisie achieves it, whether there are organised conflicts between government and capital in the near future – this question is undoubtedly important. But whichever way this question is resolved should not alter the direction of our activity. In any eventuality it is most important for us that the working class be conscious, that it understands its interests that it should not become an appendage of the bourgeoisie if the latter wants to use the strength of the working mass as a protection which it will not only subsequently discard as unnecessary, but will also try to destroy, so that it cannot act against the victors themselves. If our bourgeoisie really does not know how to become revolutionary, then we should not give it the opportunity to appear as the teacher and leader of our proletariat, for an education received from the bourgeoisie will be repaid at too dear a price by the loss of class self-consciousness. If the bourgeoisie itself also advances into the arena of political struggle, then that is undoubtedly a bonus.

The worker will find a fellow-traveller along the way, but only a fellow-traveller; if not, then he will walk this part of the road before him alone, as he will also walk the whole of the rest of the road to complete emancipation. And how insignificant is this first part of the road compared to the road that stretches before him!

II

In view of the above, the task that faces us is clear: we should strive to develop political self-consciousness among the mass of workers, to interest them in political freedom. But political self-consciousness does not only mean a change in the present political system but also a change in favour of the working class. Consequently, recognition of the opposition of interests must precede political class self-consciousness. The opposition of interests will be recognised when this opposition makes itself apparent in the life of the proletariat. It must make itself felt at every step, be constantly repeated to the worker and make itself felt in every detail. But is it enough just to feel this opposition for oneself, to promote one's own interests first and foremost, and to bear them constantly in mind? Life often obscures simple and clear relationships and not infrequently it seems possible to explain the antagonism between the position of the owner and the workers purely by natural circumstances, which only confuse the worker. For instance, nothing is easier than bewildering the worker and proving to him that a reduction in the working day is impossible. Even the depressed state of trade in the particular branch of industry is cited in evidence; the impossibility of shortening the working day because of competition with other owners, small profits, the battle with large stores, and so on, are cited. These are precisely the arguments, even if they were incorrect or correct only for a particular case, that appear quite conclusive to the worker who has a limited understanding. Obviously, to feel and to understand the justice of their demands, and to promote them constantly and persistently, are far from one and the same thing. But to ensure that tricks and deceptions of various kinds do not deflect the workers from their just demands, these demands must be promoted constantly, and not only on important questions, but also – this is particularly important as preparatory work – on questions that appear very insignificant. Where petty demands are concerned, the owner will not confuse the workers in this way because the possibility of satisfying petty demands is obvious to everyone. It depends only on the particular owner and failure to satisfy a demand is easily explained to the workers as simply the unwillingness of the owner himself, and in this way the opposition of their interests to those of the owners are partially made plain. In this connection petty demands can more easily meet with success without particular persistence in the struggle for them, and this brings with it a faith in their own strength, it teaches the workers the practical concepts of struggle, it prepares and promotes individuals who were hitherto lost in the mass and gives to other workers an example of how to fight successfully with the owners. Even in the struggle for petty demands the workers must willy-nilly join together, convincing themselves in practice of the necessity for, and possibility of, unity. This practice is much more important in the education of the mass, and more convincing, than books about the same thing. In the struggle the relations between the opposing sides become acute and the owner appears in his true guise; it is only then that he throws off his mask as the paternal benefactor and reveals his genuine thoughts and aspirations. In this struggle the worker can clearly distinguish his friends from his enemies, can observe the solidarity of all the owners, the whole of the bourgeoisie in general – both big and petty bourgeoisie – against him, the worker. On the basis of the awakening that the struggle has produced, the worker is more inclined to accept the ideas that earlier seemed nonsensical to him.

This struggle for petty demands, provoked in particular by exploitation by one or several owners, is limited to the arena of one or a few workshops or factories. The struggle, which is in the majority of cases confined to a struggle only with the most immediate exploiter, who is not supported by the administration, must serve as the elementary school for the Russian proletariat, which has still not been lured into the class struggle; in the struggle it will be educated and strengthened and from it it will emerge prepared for the struggle for the more important demands even without the unity of the workers of several factories or the whole trade.

The first phase of the struggle for petty demands, towards which the worker is propelled by a calculation that is easily grasped – exploitation by the owner being easy to explain – demands from the workers a certain degree of energy and unanimity. In the second phase, when it is necessary to make common cause against the entire bourgeois class, which the government will immediately rush to help, a much greater degree of endurance, solidarity and courage will be required. More-over, a certain level of consciousness will also be demanded, the ability to link one's own interests with the interests of other workers in the same branch of production, sometimes even of another, but such consciousness can be developed only when the worker comes, through his own experience, to the conclusion that success in a par-ticular struggle for the interests of workers in separate factories is not feasible. This very struggle with separate owners will develop in the working class a degree of stability and endurance, of unity, a sense of independence and class self-confidence, which it will need when it comes face to face with the inevitability of the class struggle in the proper meaning of the word. As it enters this stage, the workers' movement will begin little by little to take on a political tinge. Indeed, as the workers advance a particular demand for significant change in the existing methods in a particular factory or in a whole branch of industry, so they join in a struggle in which the attitude towards them of not just one, not just a few owners, but of the whole of the upper classes and government will become clear to them. Conscious of the complete justice of their demand, the workers at first behave peacefully and with restraint, confident that everyone must be on their side, that everyone must sympathise with them. After all, this is all so simple, their demands are so clear, the oppression is so unjust! They send a deputation to the factory inspector. He will certainly help them, he is after all their defender, he knows all the laws, and the laws certainly speak in their favour . . . The inspector just pours a bucket of cold water over them . . . There is nothing about this in the laws; the factory owner stands on completely legal ground, I can do nothing . . . The door is closed in front of my nose . . . How is it that the laws did not intercede for us! It cannot be that our little father has not defended us! The inspector has been bribed by the factory owner, he is lying, lying insolently! . . . The workers try other ways: everywhere they meet refusal, sometimes accompanied by a threat which soon takes on a real form – the troops are sent to help the owners. The workers receive their first lesson in political science which says that right is on the side of the strong, that against the organised force of capital there must emerge a similarly organised force of labour. Broadening as they develop, enveloping whole areas of production instead of indi-vidual factories, with every step the movement conflicts ever more often with state power, the lessons of political wisdom become all the more frequent, and on each occasion their powerful moral is imprinted ever more deeply on the minds of the workers, class self-consciousness is formed, the understanding that everything the people strive for can only be achieved by the people themselves. The ground is prepared for political agitation. This agitation now finds a class, organised by life itself, with a strongly developed class egoism, with a consciousness of the com-munity of interests of all workers and their opposition to the interests of all others. Then the alteration of the political system is only a question of time. One spark – and the accumulated combustible material will produce an explosion.

Thus the task of the Social Democrats is to conduct constant agitation among the factory workers on the basis of existing petty needs and demands. The struggle aroused by such agitation will train the workers to defend their own interests, increase their courage, give them confidence in their strength, a consciousness of the need for unity, and ultimately it will place before them the more important questions which demand solutions. Having been prepared in this way for the more serious struggle, the working class proceeds to the resolution of these vital questions, and agitation on the basis of these questions must have as its aim the formation of class self-consciousness. The class struggle in this more conscious form establishes the basis for political agitation, the aim of which will be to alter existing political conditions in favour of the working class. The subsequent programme of the Social Democrats is self-evident.

III

As a result of the fact that social democracy can only become the real people's party when it bases its programme of activity on the needs that are actually felt by the working class, and of the fact that to achieve this goal – the organisation of the working class – it must begin with agitation on the basis of the most vital demands, the minor ones that are clearest to the working class and most easily attainable, we come to a new formulation of the question of what sort of individuals we should try to promote from among the workers for the leadership of the movement. In order to advance the most minor demands which could unite the workers in the struggle, we must understand what sort of demand will most easily exert a positive influence on the workers in particular conditions. We must choose the right moment to begin the struggle, we must know what methods of struggle are most appropriate to the particular conditions, place and time. Information of this kind requires constant contacts with the mass of workers on the part of the agitator, requires that he constantly interest himself in a particular branch of industry and follow its progress. There are many pressures in every factory and many trifles can interest the worker. To ascertain the most keenly felt grievance in the life of the workers, to ascertain the moment when a particular grievance should be advanced, to know in advance all the possible ramifications – this is the real task of the active agitator. Knowledge of this kind can be given only by life: theory can and must only illuminate it for him. To immerse himself constantly in the mass, to listen, to pick on the appropriate point, to take the pulse of the crowd – this is what the agitator must strive for. Knowledge of the conditions of life, knowledge of the feelings of the mass will by and large give him his influence on the mass; these will enable him to find his feet whatever the circumstances, they will promote him from the crowd and make him its natural leader. Clearly, the social democratic views of the agitator will determine which road he considers he should lead the crowd along without abandoning his convictions. He is obliged to strive with all his strength to explain to the mass the advantages and disadvantages of each of the meausres that are proposed, to preserve it from any mistakes that might harm the development of its self-consciousness. Further, he must always go one step further than the mass, he must throw light on its struggle, explaining its significance from the more general standpoint of the opposition of interests, and should in so doing broaden the horizon of the masses.

But at the same time the agitator himself should not lose sight of the final goal, he should be so theoretically prepared that, whatever misfortunes occur, the connection between his present activity and the final goal is not lost from view. For this, however, theoretical preparation alone is not enough. The latter must constantly be reinforced by practical work. It is only by this constant verification, only by constant adaptation to the task known and learnt in theory, that the agitator can say that he has understood and mastered the theory. In its turn, practical activity will reveal which questions should be more thoroughly based in theory and, by a similar extension, the man will know how to make sure of the foundation of the theory itself and of its application to particular conditions.

For this reason we identify with neither of the extremes, neither losing touch with the practical basis and only studying, nor agitating among the mass, without at the same time concerning ourselves with theory. Only parallel activity, the complementing of the one by the other, provides a real preparation and produces solid convictions. What sort of character do and did the concepts of propaganda bear in the majority of social democratic circles? Individuals raised on theory worked out for themselves correspondingly theoretical convictions that they attempted to transmit to others. But a total world view, even the world view of scientific socialism, may by no means be grasped by everyone, and it is only at a certain stage of industrial development that the propaganda of scientific socialism finds a mass of disciples and in this case the mass is prepared by a long and persistent struggle. For this reason the more able workers who had been grouped in the circles were selected and, little by little, social democratic views were passed on to them (insofar as these were grasped by the leaders themselves) and then this raw material was sent to an intellectual for its finishing touches.

What has been the result of this kind of propaganda? The best, most able men have received theoretical evidence that is only very superficially connected with real life, with the conditions in which these people live. The worker's desire for knowledge, for an escape from his darkness, has been exploited in order to accustom him to the conclusions and generalisations of scientific socialism. The latter has been taken as something mandatory, immutable and identical for all. This is why the majority of propagandised workers, for all their enthusiasm for scientific socialism, bore all the traits characteristic of the Utopian Socialists in their time – all the traits except one: the Utopians were convinced of the omnipotent power of the preaching of the new gospel and believed that the winning over of the popular mass depended on their own efforts alone, whereas our Utopian Social Democrats know perfectly well that the backward condition of Russian industry dictates narrow limits to any socialist movement, and this conviction deprives them of any energy in the task of propaganda and compels them to limit their activity to a narrow circle of the more advanced individuals. Our propagandised workers know and understand the conditions of the activity of Western social democracy much better than the conditions of their own activity.

Scientific socialism appeared in the West as the theoretical expression of the workers' movement; with us it is transformed into abstract theory, unwilling to descend from the transcendental heights of scientific generalisation.

Moreover in this formulation socialism degenerates into a sect and the system of propaganda that was being practised had other, more harmful consequences. On the one hand, with this system of propaganda the mass have remained completely on one side, being regarded as material to be tapped and tapped as much as possible. This tapping has fatally weakened the intellectual forces of the mass; the better elements have been taken away from it, and it has been deprived of those people who, though lacking in consciousness, had, through their mental and moral superiority, served it before and could still have served as leaders and as the foremost front-line fighters in its purely spontaneous struggle for existence. On the other hand, these best elements of the proletariat have formed a special group of people with all the traits that characterise our revolutionary intelligentsia, doomed to everlasting circle life and activity with the results that flow inevitably from that. Convinced that further promotion of individuals from the mass will become all the more difficult (and such a moment must certainly come), the worker intellectuals are nonplussed, they ponder on the reasons for the difficulties and naturally are inclined either to the thought that the inadequate level of their own development is the reason for the failure of their activity, or to the conviction that in our country conditions are not yet ripe for a workers' movement. In the first case they conclude that it is necessary to study and study and then to go and transmit their views to the mass; in the second case, if they do not conclude in complete disillusionment, with a reconciliation with reality, they become locked all the more irrevocably in their circles concerned with self-perfection right up until the moment when, of its own accord and without their assistance, the impending improvement in the cultural level of the mass renders it capable of understanding their teaching. In both cases these results of propaganda are an undoubted obstacle to the task of raising the class self-consciousness of the Russian proletariat. The more the worker Socialists are improved in their mental and moral attitude, the further they are removed from the mass, the more remote they become from reality and at the decisive moment, when some event or other might propel the worker mass into the movement, it and the worker Socialists will stand alienated from, and even hostile to, one another. It is difficult to foresee what this can lead to, but the history of Europe shows that in this kind of situation, when the conditions are ripe for a movement of the working mass and the genuine representatives of its interests are found to be divorced from it, it will find other leaders for itself, not theoreticians but practical men who will lead it to the detriment of its class development. For Social Democrats this prospect cannot fail to appear highly dangerous. Propaganda among the workers in order to recruit new individual adherents to socialism is no different from propaganda among the intelligentsia for the same purpose; however, as demonstrated above, this kind of propaganda has a directly harmful side – it weakens the intellectual strength of the mass. By creating a worker socialist intelli-

gentsia, alienated from the mass, we harm the cause of the development of the proletariat, we harm our own cause.

Different results must be achieved by uniting propaganda with agitation, uniting
theory with practice. Permanent unison between advanced individuals and the mass,
unity on the basis of questions vaguely comprehended by the mass and made clear
to it by an experienced agitator, will make him its natural leader. At the same time,
every success that is achieved through this kind of union of individuals with the
mass will enhance the slumbering strength of the mass, it will raise its spirit, it will
provoke in it new demands, which previously seemed alien to it; in that way it will
raise its cultural level and consequently bring it still nearer to the agitator. Constant
struggle will stimulate it to the effort of thinking: in addition the same struggle will
promote from the mass new individuals who are capable of becoming the object of
the same rational propaganda and who, without it, would remain lost in the mass.
The latter is especially true: whereas, when the mass was passive, the reserves of
people who could be turned into Socialists were rather narrowly defined, when the
movement is active, the movement itself will constantly refill the places of those
front-line fighters who have left the ranks. The task of the agitator is to try and
ensure that new thoughts are conceived in the mind of the worker, that he understands the attitudes of the owners towards him in a clearer light. The awakening,
the eternal discontent and eternal striving for an improvement of its situation,
alongside a broad understanding of the victories already achieved – it is towards
this that the agitator should lead the mass.

With propaganda in the circles it was necessary to make great sacrifices for the
achievement of insignificant results. By working among the mass the number of
sacrifices made in comparison with the results achieved decreases and, the broader
and deeper the movement becomes, the more difficult it will be to cope with it, the
more difficult it will be to uproot the socialist elements. The best example is
Poland: the strikes there are beginning to receive official recognition and the
government has decided not to apply existing laws to the participants. This proves
that an open movement can render ineffective obstacles that the law has placed in
its path. But for this the movement must have roots in the soil. He who does not
promote by his own activity the growth of class consciousness and the revolutionary demands of the proletariat is not a Social Democrat.

However it is possible to assist the one or the other solely by concerning oneself
directly with arousing the mass of the movement on economic grounds and every
step in this direction shortens the remaining road and at the same time facilitates
the further progress of the movement, removing one after another those obstacles
that now seem irremovable and that hinder even circle work, which is essentially
cultural, and that it cannot actually remove. In view of all this, we recognise the
need for social democratic circles to make the transition to the programme whose
main features we have outlined, or to cease thinking that their activity is more
useful to the cause of the development of the proletariat than the activity, for
example, of the Committee for Literacy.[147] The experience gained in these circles,

and the evidence of the workers who have been successfully propagandised by them, will make it possible to begin the struggle more or less rationally on new foundations. Intellectuals and workers should constantly discuss what demands should be advanced at a given moment in a given branch of production, and what should be the object of agitation, taking as a starting point the most vital needs of the workers. Further, there must be clarification of the means that would best facilitate the commencement of the struggle (agitation, strike, petitions to the inspector,[148] and so on). The production of agitational literature should then be the task of the intelligentsia, literature suited to the conditions in a given branch of production or a given industrial centre, literature that would speak to the worker of his needs and would serve as a corresponding supplement to oral agitation. Finally, the intellectuals should strive to impart to their study sessions with the workers a more practical character, so that for the worker the knowledge he has received in these sessions will serve to broaden his horizons and not tear him away at once from solid ground into the sphere of completely abstract scientific positions. Propagandising literature which inclines in the same direction must be created.

We have still to say a few words about the sorts of limits within which the Social Democrats should restrict their activity. There is a view that only the most advanced industrial centres can furnish the basis for agitational activity. And, indeed, in handicraft and domestic industry the workers, who are uncoordinated and dispersed find it more difficult to unite on the basis of conscious common interests and the actual common character of these interests cannot easily be recognised as the opposition of interests between employer and worker. The absence of a pronounced differentiation between the position of master and worker adds to this. Moreover, it is comparatively easy for the worker to become an owner or an independent producer; as a result the worker regards his position as temporary and is willing to make certain sacrifices. But can one conclude from this that the struggle is absolutely impossible? Again, no! Handicraft and domestic (i.e. small-scale) production has some advantages in the struggle.

Skilled workers are culturally more advanced than unskilled, they are more scarce and cannot easily be replaced by others; with a good prospect of opening their own workshops, the workers lose less if they refuse to work, and so on. Finally, a large number of small workshops in one region makes it easier to change from one boss to another. Consequently if, on the one hand, small-scale production prevents the development of active struggle then, on the other, the same production will help us to wage the struggle.

If in the large centres life itself drives the workers into battle with the capitalists, and the role of the agitator is merely to show the way, then in small-scale production the agitator has to a far greater degree still to arouse the workers. On the other hand, once the movement has begun, it has some chance of success. People will ask, is this necessary? There is a view that we shall have to wait until small-scale production has in fact been transformed into large-scale industry and then begin agitation, but until that time be satisfied with propaganda directed at the making of individual worker Socialists. But, apart from the doubt that exists as to whether we should in general strive to create a worker intelligentsia isolated from the mass, there are objections of a different sort that might be made against the suggested tactic. The fact is that small-scale production does not become a branch of industry by a sudden leap: the transition is completed very slowly and in the meantime it is not at all easy to determine whether the said small-scale or domestic production has been transformed into manufacturing industry or not. In the process of transition it is the workers above all who suffer most because of their unpreparedness. The workers are gradually caught in the iron vice of large production and it is a misfortune for them if they participate only passively in this process. Terrible sufferings, material insecurity, unemployment, the constant reduction of earnings, almost degeneration – this is what happens from day to day if the workers themselves do not take note of their descent down the slippery slope of decreasing wages and increasing insecurity, if by their own efforts they do not fight for the achievement of better living conditions. It is the workers' misfortune if, in exchange for the advantages of skilled labour, which they lose at every step, they do not acquire another weapon – the recognition of their interests, the understanding of the need to adhere solidly one to another for a successful struggle. It is true that agitation in such circumstances is much more difficult, owing to the advance of this terrible force which is crushing the workers, but it is consequently that much more important to prevent the most acute suffering and thus to create the chances of a more successful struggle with the new conditions once the latter have been established. We count ourselves fortunate that we live in an epoch when the progression of the movement is so clear that we can foresee its further stages.

To be aware of this progression, and not to use the knowledge, would be to commit an enormous historical error. Similarly, the notion of the feasibility of a strong workers' movement in a few centres is mistaken. With the greater mobility of workers, the provincial workers, reduced to the ranks of the unemployed by the first stages of capitalism, will play the part of emigrants from a less cultured country in relation to the organised workers of the large centres. Thus, to neglect workers in small-scale production is to complicate the task of organisation and of struggle in the large workers' centres. From this it follows that only widespread agitation can bear fruit. As far as the mass, which has still not been united by industrial capital, is concerned, we must exert ourselves so that capitalism, in its conquest of one branch of production after another, will not just leave ruination behind it but that following immediately on its heels the ranks of the organised workers' army should rise so that, though deprived of their skills and turned into unskilled workers, the proletarians will know how to oppose exploitation with the strength of organisation, the strength of class self-consciousness.

35. TO THE WORKERS IN THE PETERSBURG COTTON SPINNING AND WEAVING MILLS (1 JANUARY 1897)[149]

St Petersburg Union of Struggle

Comrades! Six months have passed since our great strike.[150] It is time to consider what it has done for us and what it has taught us. In the spring 30,000 men struck, as the authorities have deliberately ascertained. The authorities were afraid to reveal such a large number of strikers in the newspapers and reduced the number by half. The strike opened many people's eyes to the terrible position of the workers. In the streets, on the trams, in their homes, both in St Petersburg and elsewhere, even abroad, people talked – and still talk – about the workers.

The strike should teach us a great deal. It showed that the working people are a great force and that through concerted pressure they can improve their way of life. It also showed how the workers should act to achieve their ends. Above all we realised that we must behave in a calm and resolute manner. Our calmness and resolution served us well in two ways: our enemies were frightened and our friends learned to respect us. In other words the strike showed us that resolution and restraint are a force, and a force that is greater than guns and cannons.

The city governor tried to use the army against us. But in this he did not succeed: nobody resorted to violence and there was nothing to call the army out for. The authorities lost their nerve and started to arrest the first people who fell into their hands. Around 700 were taken. But here too the authorities were disappointed: there were no charges that could be brought against those arrested. For the workers, you see, are not serfs: even the authorities cannot drag them to work by force. In the end the authorities themselves began to act illegally. The city governor began doing all he could to scare the workers. But, scare us or not, we know that you cannot put all 30,000 men in prison. Then the authorities tried to incite the workers to disturbances and sent in its *agents provocateurs*. But we did not swallow this bait. Then the city governor took the strikers' cases out of the hands of court officials and handed them over to the gendarmes. A neat and simple trick. You see, we know that to the gendarmes anyone is a rebel if he dares to want to eat and if he yells when he is hurt or in pain, for this disturbs the peace and quiet of the authorities and the bloated factory owners. Many of our comrades who were taken by the gendarmes are still in prison and many have been sent away from St Petersburg. Why is this being done? Perhaps in this way they are going to prove to us that truth is on the side of the factory owners and not on our side. We know that people have always suffered for the common cause. In short, it has become clear to all that the transgressors were the authorities themselves. It is well known that the law is used to scare only the weak, but the strong, like the authorities, can live without the law.

Our great strike has given even the Minister a bit of a fright. Three ministers who were on leave came tearing back from far-flung corners of Russia to find out what the workers were up to. It was not for nothing that even the Minister of Finance began to tell us in his honeyed words that 'the tsarist government is concerned about improving our living conditions and making our work easier'.[151] Thank you for your concern, but this has not prevented us from showing that we too are not averse to showing concern that our work should be made easier. And by our strikes we have shown that this is necessary.

But did the ministerial gentleman keep his promise? What good has he done for us? Almost none. In several factories they tossed us a few coppers and calmed down, thinking that this would satisfy us. But they are not dreaming of granting our principal demand for a shorter working day. Why? Is it because we went on 'strike' instead of petitioning the authorities? No, that is not why: it is quite simply because the authorities have always been ill-disposed towards us, both at the time of the strike and for a long time before that. Can anyone fail to realise that all our pledges have been redeemed by our own strength, by a fear of us? But after the strike the true intentions of the authorities became even clearer. What did the authorities do after the strike? This is what they did: there were some factory owners, whose pockets we had hit, who themselves wanted at one time to introduce a ten-hour working day for us, but the Minister did not allow them to do this. The ministers want us to believe that everyone who opens our eyes to the activities of the authorities is our enemy, and everyone who teaches us to turn the other cheek, to suffer in silence, is our friend. The authorities close schools and Sunday schools[152] and arrest and remove the pupils and the men and women who teach in these schools. The authorities do not permit the publication of books and newspapers that tell the truth, which is hard for them and for the factory owners to stomach. (And at the trade and industrial congress in Nizhny Novgorod the authorities forbade the delivery and discussion of reports that mentioned the position of the workers in Russia.) What fine friends! What fool would believe it? But you do not deceive us! We understand as well as the authorities that schools and education are our salvation. We know as well as the authorities that it is easier to manage an ignorant person than one who is educated: one knows only how to submit, to cringe, while the other will have none of this and says that he too is human and wants to live just as well and just as fully as the ministerial gentleman. These are our enemies: the ministerial gentlemen, who want to please the factory owners and have arranged things so that for every rouble they make 2 or 3 roubles profit, these very factory owners, the *provocateurs* and spies sent to us by the police and the gendarmerie, gaol and the gaolers who are now guarding our comrades and teachers.

This is the true design of the authorities: as far as possible not to give us a penny more, and in future to restrain us from striking at all. The Minister advises us 'to ask and it shall be given to you. Ask individually, each one asking his inspector on his own behalf, ask the police, ask me, the Minister.' Well said. But the authorities imprison us individually and then spend whole decades wondering how they can help our brother – without embarrassing the factory owners. No, you cannot get at our authorities through the moderate requests of weak individuals. The authorities will only give in to our strength, whereas for many centuries they have ridden on the back of our moderation.

Everywhere a better life and better rights have been won by struggle. Have we asked for much? What came of it anyway? But what about this: the Minister began to make promises only after our strike. We see this and we understand it.

No, comrades, we cannot be satisfied with the Minister's honeyed words and promises. They will not be enough for you. We do not want someone else's [promises], we want our own, vital [interests]. We have demanded shorter hours for our penal labour. We wanted to do less work on the eve of holidays. We have demanded an increase in pay. We must strive for this now and all the time until we have got our way. And here is something else for us to think about.

The law permits the factory owners to organise strikes that are called by the syndicates, and the Minister even helps to arrange them by raising the price of goods or lowering pay – but, for us, strikes are forbidden. The factory owners have all sorts of discussions with ministers – but with us they do not stand on ceremony. And at present the law is not on our side, but on theirs. However, the law should protect us too, and not just the factory owners. But we can only achieve whatever we want by great strikes, arranging them in concert and at times that are particularly inconvenient for the factory owners. *We should all understand that they will only listen to us when we have done things our way and made ourselves felt through great strikes.*

Only in this way can we turn the law to our advantage. Only in this way can we force the officials to draft more just laws to defend us from the oppression of the factory owners. It is all very well for ministers to pass judgement: they make the laws themselves – today one law, tomorrow another, today something is legal that tomorrow the Minister will make illegal. But the law should be just to all. If it is unjust, it must be changed. The law must recognise that workers should also have the right to organise strikes, just like the kerosene and sugar refiners and the other manufacturers.

We too must understand this and by our common strength together ensure that the tsarist government changes the strike law. It was once the case abroad that the law forbade a worker to take any action. But there the workers themselves forced the repeal of unjust laws, organising one great strike after another. They were a long time preparing, organising funds, saving money to support themselves and their comrades during strikes. They tried to educate themselves and acquire knowledge, they got hold of good books and read them. They *decided to organise workers' unions*, they achieved a reduction in the working day to ten, or even eight hours, while in England, Germany and a few other countries representatives *elected by the workers even participate in the drafting of laws.*

In this way, comrades, we too shall obtain an improvement in our lot. *Let us too prepare for strikes.* Let us organise them until we can turn the law to our advantage.

Union of Struggle for the Emancipation of the Working Class
1 January 1897

36.   TO ALL PETERSBURG WORKERS (11 JANUARY 1897)[153]

St Petersburg Union of Struggle

You should take advantage of the appropriate occasions to explain to the workers that if they actually achieve anything by illegal or violent means this will lead, not to an improvement, but to a deterioration in their position.

Circular to factory inspectors, winter 1895.

Let the workers be assured that the interests of the government are the same as those of the factory owners and the workers.

Proclamation of the Finance Minister, summer 1896.

The government has decided to renounce the policy of non-compliance it pursued over the summer and introduce a shorter working week thanks to the goodwill of the factory owners.   *Ministerial communication, 3 January 1897.*

We order the introduction for mechanical workers of a ten-and-a-half-hour day. For weavers and spinners an eleven-and-a-half-hour day, and for the rest of Russia a twelve-hour day.   *Conference of factory owners, 5 January [1897].*

Comrades! This is the clearest expression of what is happening to us, this is the best proof of our united strength and of the fruitfulness of our combined struggle. We have celebrated the New Year with a struggle. The Petersburg factories are striking once more; there are again disturbances everywhere.

You know about the strike at Maxwell's (2 Jan.) at the Ekaterinhof, Koenig, Rossiiskaya and Stieglitz plants (all since the 7th) and at the Bolshaya Okhtenskaya (since the 8th).[154] The Aleksandrov iron works has decided on a strike as well but a conference of traction foremen decided to concede that they should finish on Saturday at 2 p.m. This was finally agreed and on the 11th work should finish at 2 p.m.

This simple fact, together with the other events of the moment tell us that we, all pulling together, are strong enough to curb the tyranny of our bosses and to limit the power of the government.

Our summer strike of 30,000 weavers and spinners forced everyone, both government and capitalists, everybody, to recognise that our demands were legal and it forced them to make promises to us. With the present strike we should force them to fulfil these legal demands of ours and to keep all their promises.[155]

Comrades!

Striking weavers and spinners! Remain steadfast and unanimous; do not allow disorders or violence. You are fighting for the common cause of all the workers of Petersburg and of Russia.

Workers of all other cotton spinning and weaving mills! You are moved by the procrastination of the government; you are angered by the intransigence of your bosses. Join together for a strike. Support your comrades: you have the same conditions and the same aims.

Workers of the other factories and plants of Petersburg! Organise help immediately. Your comrades, the weavers and spinners, are fighting for our common cause. By supporting them you will help yourselves. Their cause is also yours — one and the same workers' cause.

> Stand all together
> Stand for one another!
> In this lie your strength and might,
> In this lies the success of the strike.

Comrades, remain calm and united, let the government know that it is dealing with conscious, skilful and steadfast workers, real fighters for the workers' cause. This is not the first time that we have come into contact with them. Before us lie all the difficult conditions of a hard winter, but for the worker-warriors for a better life there are no seasons, there is only the consciousness of the justice of their cause and the decision to pursue to the end the glorious task that they have undertaken.

Union of Struggle for the Emancipation of the Working Class.
11 January 1897

37. THE WORLD-WIDE WORKERS' HOLIDAY OF 1 MAY (APRIL 1897)[156]

St Petersburg Union of Struggle

Working men and women of St Petersburg! Once more 1 May (by our calendar, 19 April) is approaching, the day that the workers of all countries, races and peoples have established so that every year they can celebrate their own international workers' holiday.

This is not, comrades, a feast-day like the ones that the priests talk to us about in church: this is not a festival of humility, obedience and prayer; it is a festival of struggle against the exploiters and oppressors of all sorts and descriptions; a festival of struggle that sooner or later will become a festival of victory. And this festival of the uncompromising struggle with the enemies of the working class is at the same time a festival of brotherhood among the workers. Every year on this day it is as if the workers of the whole world were merging into a single great army to prove to the capitalists and the governments that the workers are all brothers regardless of race or creed and that, joined together, they represent a fearsome and powerful force. Every year before 1 May a trembling seizes all our enemies, from the small factory owners to the mighty Emperor. They realise that their rule will soon be at an end and they feel that the annual celebration of 1 May is like the review and the manoeuvres of the worker battalions – these are the blows of the axe that will fell the branch they are sitting on; this is the sound of the hammer nailing the lid on their coffin.

How do workers abroad celebrate 1 May? You know, comrades, that our brothers – the English, French, German and other workers – through long years of persistent and painful struggle long ago escaped from the pitiful, unjust position we are now in. In their countries strikes are not considered a crime, they can arrange meetings and make speeches openly. On 1 May in many parts of Western Europe the roar of the machines is silent, the smoke from the plants and factories ceases, the mines and pits empty: the workers leave their work, organise well-attended meetings at which they put forward their demand for an eight-hour working day or, quietly and peacefully, they parade in an orderly fashion along the streets of the city with their red banners unfurled, singing revolutionary songs. Even here in Russia the most conscious of our brothers, the Polish, Jewish and Lithuanian workers, have for some years already been celebrating 1 May at secret gatherings.

On this day the workers usually look back on the past year and recall what it has brought them and what it has taught them. Let us too, comrades, look back on the past year. We can proudly say that there is nothing for us to be ashamed of. This year marks the beginning of a new period in the life of the Russian working class. This year of struggle is the first ray of light after the long dark years of penal labour and slavish animal existence. A whole series of almost continuous disturbances and strikes, especially the two vast strikes of the weavers and spinners, following one after the other, have spread the fame of the workers of St Petersburg far beyond the frontiers of Russia.

These strikes have rendered a great service both to us and to all the workers of Russia. They have compelled the factory owners to shorten the working day in all the weaving and spinning mills of St Petersburg from 16 April and pushed the government to the point where it will soon be forced to promulgate a law limiting the hours of work in all plants and factories in Russia.[157] These same strikes have also steeled us in the struggle and proved to us that the emancipation of the workers is a matter for the workers themselves and that we should place hope in no one but ourselves. We are convinced that the tsarist government will only ever defend the interests of the rich classes and will only agree to concessions under the pressure of our concerted struggle. *And 16 April, the day of victory for the St Petersburg weavers over the factory owners and the government,*[158] *will merge for all of us into 19 April, the festival of struggle with these factory owners and this government.* Having schooled ourselves to struggle, learning lessons from our defeats, deriving hope and strength from our recent victories, we can look the future cheerfully in the eye.

Working men and women of St Petersburg. Workers from all corners of the world are following our struggle and our successes with interest and joy; the workers of the whole of Russia look to us with hope and rapture as the foremost detachment of the revolution. And we shall not disappoint them in their expectations. We have already achieved a great deal but we must achieve more and still more so that we can at least compare with our comrades abroad.

So we shall continue firmly and unflinchingly what we have already begun. We shall join together, we shall organise ourselves so that, by saving our strength, we can demand for ourselves those *first political rights* without which any broad struggle is impossible: *the right to organise strikes, meetings and unions* and the right freely and openly to speak and write about our needs, i.e. *freedom of speech and of the press.* Let us vow, comrades, on this great and solemn day, that we shall, as in the past, wage the same stubborn struggle for a better future and not be afraid of persecution, not be discouraged by defeat and not be deceived by paltry concessions. We shall stand by this oath of unity and struggle until, together with the workers of the whole world, we have transformed the present unjust order into one in which there will no longer be either capitalists or workers, rich or poor.

Long live the international workers' holiday of 1 May.

Union of Struggle for the Emancipation of the Working Class.

38. THE FIRST OF MAY (1 MAY 1897): EXTRACTS[159]

St Petersburg Union of Struggle

Comrades!

Today is the *First of May*. Today many millions of workers in every country will abandon the stuffy atmosphere of their workshops to enjoy the first breath of spring with the other inhabitants of the earth. Proud of their past struggle and hoping for victory in the near future, they will parade in vast crowds and ordered ranks along broad streets filled with people. The eyes of their bosses will follow them in fear and curiosity from the windows of their houses but the police will clear the way for them.

Today is the *First of May* holiday, a festival for the workers of the whole world, a festival for the oppressed and exploited who have resolved to put an end to the reign of capital and to create a new life based on the principles of *justice and humanity* . . .

Comrades!

We are well aware of our recent helplessness. We well remember our lack of consciousness and our complete disunity, the full rein given to the tyranny of our bosses and our government. The chief obstacles to our unity, without which our struggle for a better life was impossible, were the oppression and injustice that resulted from our lack of consciousness.

But how quickly everything changed after the initial emergence of a mass movement among the Russian workers. Through the strikes of 1883–4 the workers won concessions from the bosses and the tsarist government for the first time.[160] By imperial decree the factory inspectorate was introduced, the foundation of Russian worker legislation was laid. 1885 was marked by the great Morozov strike and this was followed by the law of 3 June 1886, many of whose points were taken in their entirety from the list of the demands of the Morozov strikers.[161] The (in the Minister's words) 'illegal' workers' demands became law because the entire mass demanded them. Since then the workers' movement has begun to grow rapidly and in the past year it has encompassed the whole of Russia, both Orthodox and non-Orthodox.

Yes, for the Russian workers this year has been a year of glorious struggle, a year of glorious victories over the government and the factory owners. As late as the autumn of 1895 the Minister of Finance suggested to the workers that, as long as they were on strike, none of the workers' demands – not even their just demands – would be considered, and that their legal demands, if they continued on their path of illegality or force, would lead, not to an improvement, but to a deterioration in their position. This was followed by a whole series of strikes and every strike, as if to mock the Minister, was followed by a concession. Strike followed strike in St Petersburg and whole winter and early spring. The first to down tools were the weavers at the Thornton mill – and a concession was made to them. Then the cigarette-girls at the Laferme factory rebelled – and the result was a circular banning the indiscriminate rejection of sub-standard cigarettes [by the bosses]. Then there were strikes at the mechanised shoe-factory, at the Lebedev saw mill, at the Lebedev textile mill, disturbances at the Putilov factory, at Koenig's, at the Admiralty, at Voronin's, at the Admiralty again, at the Alexandrov iron foundry, at Voronin's again, at the Sestroretsk arms factory, etc., etc. And this was accompanied by explanatory leaflets from the Union of Struggle for the Emancipation of the Working Class and, not infrequently, by concessions from the factory owners.[162] Then came the vast summer mass strike of 30,000 weavers and spinners.[163] For the first time the Minister of Finance decided to talk directly to the workers and, imitating the Union of Struggle, he issued his proclamation in which he declared that the government held the interests of factory owners and workers equally dear to its heart. To underline his words the tsarist government sent the army to defend the factory owners' interests against the workers' blackmail; they tried to pacify the starving workers with prison bread and accommodation at the public expense . . .

The strike subsided but the disturbances continued all autumn for the promises were not kept. These disturbances greatly increased before the New Year.

The government sent circulars to all the factory owners, ordering them to keep watch on the workers and report any disturbances and promising to suppress any disorders with armed force. But, when a strike actually began on 2 January,[164] the

Minister of Finance had no choice but to call an extraordinary meeting which resolved to allow the factory owners to make concessions to the workers. The strike continued. The ministers soon met in conference and decided to bring in on 16 April a ten-and-a-half-hour working day for mechanised plants, an eleven-and-a-half-hour day for weaving and spinning mills and a twelve-hour day for all other establishments.[165]

This is the struggle and these are the victories of the workers of St Petersburg. In the other industrial towns of Russia the awakening of the working people, the growth of their consciousness, have progressed just as rapidly. A whole series of strikes in and around Moscow, a strike in Yaroslavl, a series of strikes in Ivanovo-Voznesensk, Smolensk, Vilna, Minsk, Kiev, Odessa, Kostroma, etc., all this has convinced us that a bright new era has dawned for our fatherland.

Yes comrades! Our latest victory is the best proof of our strength when we act together consciously. But our strength would be decimated if we did not have the chance to bring consciousness to broader masses of workers than we have done so far. Our victory would be more significant and longer lasting if our lack of [civil] rights did not stand in our way. We are the slaves of an autocratic government which limits the struggle for our interests in every way. And can we be satisfied with an eleven-and-a-half- to twelve-hour working day? Scholars long ago proved the harm in such a long working day and many factory owners admit that, even with an eight-hour day, their profit is extremely respectable. It is not for nothing that the European proletariat has inscribed on its banner the demand for an eight-hour working day.

We know, comrades, that we shall not achieve this straight away. A hard battle lies ahead for us. But many Russian factory owners have already agreed to a ten-hour working day. The Russian government, however, does not want this and has proposed to us, through its Minister, an eleven-and-a-half-hour working day.

Workers of St Petersburg!

Treat this law the way you have already treated a whole series of Russian laws; throw it back in the face of the tsarist government.

Russian workers!

Support your comrades in St Petersburg in this struggle. Let us demand:

A ten-hour working day for the whole of Russia.

But this is not enough. We must have the opportunity of fighting for the improvement of our living conditions, for higher pay and for humane treatment.

We must have the chance to unite with our comrades, to facilitate the growth in consciousness among them, for their strength is our strength and a union with the mass of Russian workers will make us invincible. Let us therefore demand:

freedom of speech and assembly,

so that we have the chance to discuss our affairs together and in public;

freedom to strike,

so that we are not subjected to all kinds of persecution, arrests, exile, etc. because of our demand for higher pay, and so on;

freedom of association,

so that we have the chance to organise mutual benefit funds in case of strikes, to resolve jointly the various issues that concern the workers' lives, to settle our arguments with the bosses, and so on.

A cruel struggle lies ahead, comrades! But it is only by struggle that we can achieve the recognition of our rights. The government has already made concessions to us because it was afraid of us. It will have to go even further, it will have to concede our new demands, to give us the freedom that we need, because it will be convinced that our strength is growing and that we shall not be frightened by any gendarmes or procurators.

So, forward, comrades, to the new struggle and to new victories!

Long live the international workers' festival!

Long live the First of May!

39. TO ALL MOSCOW WORKERS (1 JULY 1897)[166]

Moscow 'Workers' Union'

Comrades! In accordance with the new factory law, from 1 January 1898 the working day in plants and factories must not last for more than eleven and a half hours on ordinary days or more than ten hours for night work or on the eve of a holiday.[167] Previously at such times people have had to work for twelve, fourteen or even sixteen hours, but now no boss has the right to compel people to work for more than eleven and a half hours a day. This law is particularly important, comrades, because we alone, by our own strength, forced the government into promulgating it. In the course of the past two years, in every strike, in every proclamation, the workers in all the large industrial towns of Russia have, in addition to their particular demands, put forward a single, universal and constant demand – the shortening of the working day.

The strike of 30,000 Petersburg workers in June last year showed the Russian government for the first time how strong the working class is when it defends its interests and rights in a concerted and conscious manner. The terrified capitalist bosses and their lackey, the government, thought that they could get away with a few promises, assuring the workers that their demands would be met. At the beginning of the New Year, 1897, when the deadline for the promises ran out and the demands had not been fulfilled, the workers once more decided to strike. The incoming New Year was marked by a series of strikes which started with the strike of nearly 30,000 workers in the Alexandrov works in Petersburg.[168] Even the very

possibility of a vast general strike became such a terrible threat to the capitalists
and the government that the capitalist bosses made concessions and their toadies,
the government, after a few little circulars favouring the workers, have now promulgated the new factory law on an eleven-and-a-half-hour working day. The government has promulgated this new law after we have already achieved a ten-hour working day in many factories. So, comrades, we can boldly assert that we won this law
for ourselves. If we had not stood together and organised strikes, we should not
have seen this law. But this law is only the beginning of our future victories. We
demand a further shortening of the working day and an increase in pay. We demand
that the government should not prevent us from discussing our workers' affairs,
that it should not hamper our struggle with the capitalists and our advocacy of the
interests of the working class. In the light of this, we demand the freedom of the
press, the freedom of assembly and the right to strike, which is the only means and
weapon with which we can force our exploiter bosses to yield. After all, Russian
factory owners and manufacturers have the right freely to defend their interests in
newspapers and periodicals, to assemble at conferences and to organise their own
unions and strikes (e.g. the union of sugar refinery owners or the union of kerosene
refinery owners). Why should the workers be deprived of these rights? . . .

Comrades, the more firmly we stand together, the more insistently we put forward our demands, the sooner we shall achieve them.

The Workers' Union
July 1897

40.   LETTER TO ALL KIEV WORKERS
(26 NOVEMBER 1897): EXTRACTS[169]

Kiev Union of Struggle

Comrades! There is continual and implacable hostility between workers and bosses
everywhere, wherever they exist. The bosses only ever worry about how to make
the working day longer, how to reduce pay and thus increase their profits, whereas
the workers, on the other hand, would prefer to have, and must have, much greater
leisure and more pay than they have now. Both factory owners and workers try
every means to achieve their ends. In the early days of the struggle, when the
workers did not have sufficient experience or understanding of their cause, the
prize usually went to the bosses. The workers, however, have one mighty weapon –
a union. As long as each individual worker requests his own particular concessions,
they will, of course, not even begin to listen. But, when all the workers in a par-

ticular factory or workshop together demand a shortening of the working day or an increase in pay, the capitalists, i.e. the owners of the plants and factories, will become more conciliatory, more attentive: they are forced to meet the workers' demands if they do not want to drive them to the point where their patience is exhausted and they call a strike for a while, thus depriving the factory owners of their profit. Sooner or later every worker must realise that the sole, but at the same time the insuperable, strength of the workers lies in a union. The more advanced, clever and conscious the workers are, the better they will understand that they must unite and stand all for one and one for all.

Working men and women abroad – in England, Belgium, Germany, France – realised this long ago and they have achieved a great deal through their unanimity. In this respect Russian workers have fallen far behind their comrades abroad. Nevertheless, oppression and deprivation have taught even them to seek their defence against the bosses in union. So, for several years now in all the large Russian cities the workers have begun to put their demands jointly to their capitalist oppressors, to threaten them with downing their tools and organising strikes, and by doing this they have forced the factory owners into more than one concession.

The working men and women of Kiev have begun to stand up for their cause in a more conscious and concerted fashion for about two years in all. The desire of the Kiev workers to ease their lot has become particularly noticeable in the past year. During this time events have occurred in Kiev that every worker should know and think about. The struggle of the workers for a better life started here recently; nevertheless, the workers of several factories who have acted in a bolder and more concerted manner have managed to win concessions. By strike, threat, unanimous proclamation of demands or by the simple expression of dissatisfaction the workers have obtained several changes for the better in the Graff factory, the Rozhnetsky workshop, the Chimaera furniture factory, the Kogan tobacco plant, the Gretter factory, the South Russian engineering works, the Dutoit corset factory, the Shimansky factory, at Ludmer's, Kravets', Khmelnitsky's, Glosman's and in several other places. Some bosses were forced to reduce the hours worked, others to raise pay and a third group had to introduce a just method of payment, restore the money that had been illegally deducted and reduce unjustly levied fines. Some of these concessions were insignificant, but they are very important to the workers' cause: they have shown how, united, the workers make the factory owners, foremen and the factory inspectors tremble.

All these events show that in Kiev too the workers are rising in defence of their rights against the capitalists, following the example of St Petersburg, Moscow and cities abroad. The number of workers who appreciate the need for common struggle against the enemy, the number of conscious workers, is growing from day to day. The more intelligent workers are teaching less conscious comrades. Banned (illegal) booklets describing the life and struggle of the workers abroad and showing Russian workers the way to a better life are read avidly. Finally, in the last six months leaflets have started appearing at works and factories: these remind the workers that the factory owners are unjust and persuade them to demand concessions.

These leaflets (proclamations), published by the Kiev *Workers' Committee* and the Kiev *Union of Struggle for the Emancipation of the Working Class*, have so far been distributed in more than twenty-five Kiev works and factories. In many places they have appeared several times. Apart from the leaflets, books discussing the workers' cause have also been distributed in some factories. The leaflets have been found in the streets, in factory yards and at markets. They have been stuck on telegraph poles and on walls. In all 6,500 copies have been distributed. They have summoned the worker 6,500 times to the struggle for their rights, for a better life. This appeal has resounded through almost the whole of Kiev and now you find few workers who have not read the leaflets or have not at least heard of them.

The desire of the Kiev workers for a better life is growing stronger; the workers' movement in Kiev is growing in size and strength. It would have grown even faster if the workers had tackled their cause with greater courage. But they are not always sufficiently determined to put forward their demands, or to achieve them by strike action. The workers are often put out by the fact that they have to deal not with particular factory owners but with their powerful accomplices and protectors, the government. In the workers' struggle with the capitalists, the police and the gendarmerie, the factory inspectors and the ministers, the law, the courts and the army — in a word the whole government — are all on the side of the factory owners, and all against the workers. Anybody who did not appreciate this can easily be convinced by the recent events in Kiev . . .

The workers can use the same weapon against the government as they use in their struggle against the bosses, i.e. a union. When hundreds or thousands of workers organise a strike, when hundreds or thousands of workers celebrate 1 May, the government cannot put them all in prison, or try them all, or send them away from the city. When all Russian workers demand a better life (and there are millions of workers in Russia), there will not be enough prisons, police spies or gendarmes for them all and the government will be forced to meet all their demands.

The struggle of the Russian workers was originally directed exclusively against the bosses. This was a purely economic struggle: more pay, more leisure, more justice — that was all that the Russian workers demanded in the first instance. But the government itself hastened to assure the workers that it was the slave of the capitalists and the enemy of the workers. It issued a challenge to the workers to fight and the workers had only to take up this challenge.

Winning concessions from the capitalists, the workers will at the same time wage war on all the sly and illegal actions of the police and the gendarmerie, by which they help the factory owners to rob and oppress the workers. Every strike, every workers' assembly, every union will be a weapon in the struggle against not only the capitalists, but also the government that persecutes workers' unions and strikes to please the capitalists. *Apart from the struggle with the bosses — the economic struggle — the workers must engage in a struggle.* The government did well to show the worker straight away what he could expect from it. It is always better to take issue with an open enemy than with a hidden one . . .

Thus, what has happened in Kiev during the past year should teach all Kiev workers that it is time for them too to think about improving their lot. They have the strength. *This strength consists in union. This strength will bring them victory in both the economic and the political struggle for a better life and for their happiness.*

May the time soon come when the terrified hearts of the capitalists and their hangers-on – the gendarmes, policemen and officials – will shudder at the might of the workers' union.

Kiev Workers' Committee
Published by the Union of Struggle for the Emancipation of the Working Class
26 November 1897

1898-1902: political agitation and the critics of orthodoxy

41. MANIFESTO OF THE RUSSIAN SOCIAL DEMOCRATIC LABOUR PARTY (MARCH 1898)[170]

P.Struve

Fifty years ago the invigorating storm of the 1848 revolution swept across Europe.
For the first time the modern working class appeared on the scene as a major historical force. Through its efforts the bourgeoisie was able to sweep away many outmoded feudal—monarchical customs. But the bourgeoisie rapidly perceived in its new ally its most dangerous enemy, and betrayed both itself and its ally, and the cause of freedom, into the hands of reaction. It was, however, already too late: the working class, temporarily suppressed, reappeared on the stage of history ten to fifteen years later, with redoubled strength and enhanced self-consciousness as a fully mature warrior for its own ultimate liberation.

Throughout this whole period Russia apparently stood aside from the mainstream of historical development. There was no obvious class struggle in Russia but it was there and, what is important, it was continuing to mature and grow. The Russian government, with commendable zeal, itself implanted the seeds of the class struggle, treating the peasants unfairly, protecting the landowners, rearing and fattening the great capitalists at the expense of the toiling population. But the bourgeois-capitalist order is unthinkable without a proletariat or a working class. The latter comes into being at the same time as capitalism, grows with it and, as it grows, is increasingly drawn into conflict with the bourgeoisie.

The Russian factory worker, serf and freeman has always fought a covert and an overt battle with his exploiters. As capitalism has developed, the dimensions of the battle have grown, encompassing ever broader strata of the working population. The awakening of the class consciousness of the Russian proletariat and the growth of a spontaneous workers' movement coincided with the final development of international social democracy as the vehicle for the class struggle and the class ideal of the conscious workers of the whole world. In their activities, all the newly founded Russian organisations have, consciously or unconsciously, always acted in the spirit of social democratic ideas. The strength and significance of the workers' movement, and of the social democracy that it supports, have been most clearly revealed by a whole series of recent strikes in Russia and Poland, especially the famous strikes of the St Petersburg weavers and spinners in 1896 and 1897. These strikes forced the government to promulgate the law of 2 June 1897 on the length of the working day.[171] This law, however great its shortcomings, will forever remain as an unforgettable testimony to the mighty pressure that the combined efforts of the workers can bring to bear on the legislative and other functions of the government. It is futile for the government to think that it can pacify the workers by concessions. The more the working class everywhere is given, the more it demands. The Russian proletariat will do the same. In the past it has only been granted something when it has *demanded* it and in the future it will only be granted what it *demands*.

But is there anything that the Russian working class does not need? It is completely deprived of things that are enjoyed without let or hindrance by its foreign comrades: participation in government, freedom of speech and of the press, freedom of association and assembly – in a word, all the weapons and means with which the West European and American proletariat are improving their position and, at the same time, fighting for their ultimate emancipation – against private property, for socialism. Political liberty is as necessary to the Russian proletariat as fresh air is to healthy breathing. It is the fundamental condition for its free development and for a successful struggle for partial improvements and final emancipation.

But only the Russian proletariat *itself* can win the political liberty that it needs.

The further east one goes in Europe, the meaner, more cowardly and politically weak the bourgeoisie becomes, and the greater are the cultural and political tasks that fall to the proletariat. On its own sturdy shoulders the Russian working class must, and will, carry the cause of the achievement of political liberty. This is an essential, but only an initial, step towards the realisation of the great historic mission of the proletariat: the creation of a social order in which there will be no place for the exploitation of man by man.

The Russian proletariat will cast off the yoke of autocracy, so that it may continue the struggle with capitalism and the bourgeoisie with still greater energy until the complete victory of socialism.

The first steps of the Russian workers' movement and of Russian social democracy could not but be uncoordinated, somewhat random, devoid of unity and plan. Now the time has come to unite the local forces, circles and organisations of social democracy into a single Russian Social Democratic Labour Party. In recognition of this, the representatives of the Union of Struggle for the Emancipation of the Working Class,[172] the group publishing *Rabochaya Gazeta*[173] and the General Jewish Workers' Union of Russia and Poland[174] have held a congress, whose decisions are given below.

The local groups, in uniting to form a party, recognise the full significance of this step and the full meaning of the responsibility that it entails. In so doing they finally confirm the transition of the Russian revolutionary movement to a new epoch of conscious class struggle. As both a socialist movement and a tendency, the Russian Social Democratic Party is furthering the cause and the traditions of the whole preceding revolutionary movement in Russia; in defining the achievement of political liberty as the most important of the immediate tasks facing the party, social democracy is pursuing the goal clearly proclaimed by the still glorious activists of the old Narodnaya Volya.[175] But the methods and the paths chosen by social democracy are different. The choice is determined by the fact that it consciously desires to be, and to remain, the class movement of the organised working masses. It is firmly convinced that 'the emancipation of the working class can proceed only from its own efforts' and will resolutely fashion all its actions according to this fundamental principle of international social democracy.

Long live Russian, long live international social democracy!

42. DECISIONS OF THE FIRST CONGRESS OF THE RSDLP (MARCH 1898)[176]

Russian Social Democratic Labour Party

1. The organisations of the Union of Struggle for the Emancipation of the Working Class, the groups of *Rabochaya Gazeta* and the General Jewish Workers' Union in Russia and Poland are merged into a single organisation called the Russian Social Democratic Labour Party, and the General Jewish Workers' Union in Russia and Poland enters the party as an autonomous organisation, independent only in questions that specifically affect the Jewish proletariat.

2. The executive organ of the party is the Central Committee, elected by the congress of the party, to which it also reports on its activities.

3. The responsibilities of the Central Committee comprise:
   a. Concern with the regular activity of the party (the distribution of personnel and funds, the formulation and pursuit of routine demands, etc.); the Central Committee is guided in this by the general directives issued by the congresses of the party.
   b. The production and supply of literature to local committees.
   c. The organisation of such undertakings as have general significance for the whole of Russia (celebrating 1 May, publishing leaflets on important occasions, giving assistance to strikers, etc.).

4. In particularly important cases the Central Committee is guided by the following principles:
   a. In matters that may be postponed, the Central Committee is bound to turn to the party congress for instructions.
   b. In matters that may not be postponed, the Central Committee acts independently, by unanimous decision, reporting on the action taken to the next regular or extraordinary congress of the party.

5. The Central Committee has the right to co-opt new members.

6. The funds of the party, which are at the disposal of the Central Committee, consist of:

    a. voluntary once-for-all donations of local committees at the time of the formation of the party;

    b. voluntary periodic deductions from the assets of local committees and

    c. special collections for the party.

7. Local committees carry out the decisions of the Central Committee in the form that they consider most appropriate to local conditions. In exceptional circumstances local committees may be granted the right to refuse to carry out the demands of the Central Committee, having informed it of their reason for refusal. In all other matters local committees act with full independence, guided only by the party programme.

8. The party, through its Central Committee, enters into relations with other revolutionary organisations, insofar as this does not interefer with the principles of its programme or its tactical precepts. The party recognises the right of every nationality to self-determination.

Note: Local committees enter into relationships with such organisations only with the knowledge, and on the instructions, of the Central Committee.

9. The highest organ of the party is the congress of representatives of local committees. There are regular and extraordinary congresses. Every regular congress establishes the time of the next regular congress. Extraordinary congresses are convened by the Central Committee, either on its own initiative or at the request of two-thirds of the number of local committees.

10. The Union of Russian Social Democrats Abroad forms a part of the party and is its representative abroad.[177]

11. The official organ of the party is *Rabochaya Gazeta*.

43. ON THE QUESTION OF THE PRESENT TASKS AND TACTICS OF THE RUSSIAN SOCIAL DEMOCRATS (DRAFT PROGRAMME) (1898)[178]

P.B. Akselrod

First letter

November, 1897

Dear Comrades!

We shall soon be celebrating the fifteenth anniversary of the birth of Russian social democracy.[179] Not, however, in Russia itself, in the thick of the heroic struggle of a revolutionary party with the government, but among a small group of émigrés who have escaped, by the will of the fates, the lot that has befallen the majority of their friends and comrades. As yet there has been no struggle in the real sense of the word, only the noisy rejoicing of the tsar's servants who have searched out and mercilessly finished off the remnants of the recently still fearsome ranks of the Russian revolutionary party that have fallen into their hands. A revolutionary creation new to Russia emerged at the very height of the reaction, of the reaction that is not only governmental but also social. The liberal forces were frightened and cringed when they saw that there was nothing behind the Narodnaya Volya, that it represented only a vanguard of brave fighters, fighters who were admittedly fearless and filled with unflagging energy but were nonetheless without an army and power-less to conquer the enemy. While the government suffered in eternal fear and trembling under the blows of the revolutionaries, liberal society, on the quiet at least, was enthusiastic about them and offered them a certain amount of support. But, once the reaction had overcome the Narodnaya Volya Party, the liberals' sympathies for the revolutionary movement evaporated and gave way to complete indifference, if not worse. Student youth, for its part, was too stunned and dis-illusioned by the tragic outcome of the movement led by the 'Executive Com-mittee'[180] not to doubt the very advisability of the revolutionary path but, without the active support of this youth and a constant flow of militants from its ranks, the movement was unable to renew itself, because at that time the working *mass* still remained completely untouched by revolutionary agitation. The programme of the Emancipation of Labour Group was precisely an answer to the question: how to escape from this difficult situation? Where to find the resources for the renewal of the struggle with autocracy and how to wage this struggle with the best chance of victory?

'Raising their voice in the name of the people (the democratic ideologists of the upper classes) are astonished to see the people indifferent to their appeals; hence the instability of our intelligentsia's political outlook and their occasional despondency and complete disillusionment.'[181] You yourselves know the way out of this situation that the Emancipation of the Labour Group indicated. 'The formation of a revolutionary workers' party whose first task must be the overthrow of absolutism'[182] – in these words the Emancipation of Labour Group formulated the path upon which the revolutionary intelligentsia was to embark. In Plekhanov's well-known pamphlet, *Socialism and the Political Struggle*, the practical tasks of Russian social democracy were theoretically substantiated for the first time.[183] But these same circumstances that had called into life the social democratic literary current, proved to be an enormous brake on the emergence of a living social democratic movement *in Russia itself*. We may say that for a whole decade it remained in embryonic form; it is only in recent years that it has begun to show signs of life and take on forms that promise rapid and healthy growth.

In saying that until recently our movement has remained in embryonic form, I have in mind not just its immediately practical manifestations, not just the practical activity of its representatives in Russia. Both in its theory and on the questions of its *programme* it is only now beginning to take its stand on the basis of social democracy. The fact is that studies of social democracy, being international and embracing the general progress and world-historical conditions and tasks of the emancipation movement of the proletariat, give only a theoretical basis and indicate a general direction, but in no way provide an *a priori national* programme for workers' parties in each separate country.

Here, however, we must make one reservation: social democracy has emerged and grown strong in countries that have already passed through the epoch of the development of capitalism and bourgeois society that contemporary Russia is now experiencing. However much their political institutions may differ, the basic living conditions of the proletariat in them are, if not identical, then *similar*. For this reason there can be no essential difference in the practical tasks, the programme and tactics of their social democratic parties. The difference can only be in the details. Russian social democracy is in a completely different position. Russia, which is already entering the epoch of industrial capitalism, is at the same time living in its initial stages: it is still far from leaving the epoch of primitive accumulation and the Russian people has simultaneously to endure the sufferings caused by the progress of large-scale industry and the yoke of economic and political barbarism that corresponds to the periods of capitalist evolution that the advanced peoples of the West passed through long ago. The Russian industrial proletariat has to begin its historical career in the clutches of bureaucratic absolutism and under the enormous pressure of the *forced* expropriation and differentiation of the peasantry that is effected by the combined resources of the state and merchant and usury capital. The deprived and uncultured masses are fleeing to the towns and further devaluing the already cheap labour of the existing cadres of the urban working class. These characteristics of the historical position of the latter [class] alone demand a different formulation of the question of the immediate tasks of its emancipatory movement from that in the West. This idea has already been very clearly and definitely expressed in the following words in the programme promulgated by the Emancipation of Labour Group:

> The practical tasks and, consequently, the programmes of the Social Democrats are bound, of course, to be more complex in countries where modern capitalist production is still only striving for dominance and where the working masses are oppressed by a double yoke — that of rising capitalism and that of obsolescent patriarchal economy. In these countries the Social Democrats must, as a transitional stage, strive for the forms of social organisation that already exist in the advanced countries and that are necessary for the further development of the workers' party.[184]

Russia is in precisely this position.

This view of the tasks of Russian social democracy allowed the representatives of the new current in revolutionary thought to see the insurgent terrorist period of our revolutionary movement not just in a negative light. In their perception social democracy should be just a new evolution of a movement that has already begun and that has created certain traditions, an evolution that should not throw overboard but, on the contrary, should preserve and, as it were, revitalise the positive elements of revolutionary Populism with a new theory. The revolutionaries of the 70s took into account only the interests of the peasantry and they constructed their programme on a positive and negative attitude towards the remnants of the era of serfdom, almost ignoring the changes in Russian life brought about by the successes of large-scale industry. The features of this new life that struck them most of all were the growing oppression by the cavaliers of kulak and merchant capital and their enslavement of ever greater masses of the rural population. This one-sidedness, that is attributable to the rudimentary condition of industrial capitalism in the period of the emergence and elaboration of Populist teachings, had a fatal effect on the movement in the 70s. Be that as it may, the elements of Russian reality that determined the content and direction of Populism do, in their totality, shape the national-historical conditions in which our proletariat must emerge on to the historical arena. They also condition the 'more complex character' of the practical tasks of Russian social democracy. In so far as Populism was revolutionary, i.e. came out against the bureaucratic class state and the barbaric forms of exploitation and oppression of the popular masses that it supported, it had, with the appropriate alterations, to become a component element in the programme of Russian social democracy. In the interests of economy and so that I do not go into lengthy explanations I shall cite a couple more extracts from the programme of the Emancipation of Labour Group:

> The old system of natural economy is giving way to commodity production and thereby opening up an enormous home market for large-scale industry. The patriarchal communal forms of peasant land tenure are rapidly disintegrating, the village commune is being transformed into a simple medium for the enslavement of the peasant population to the state and in many localities it serves also as an instrument for the exploitation of the poor by the rich . . . The Russian revolutionary movement, whose victory would first and foremost serve the interests of the peasants, receives almost no support, sympathy or understanding from them. The main bulwark of absolutism is precisely the political indifference and intellectual backward-

ness of the peasantry. An inevitable consequence of this is the powerlessness and timidity of those educated strata of the upper classes whose material, intellectual and moral interests are incompatible with the present political system . . .

This state of affairs would be absolutely hopeless if the above-mentioned movement of Russian economic relations had not created new chances of success for those defending the interests of the working people. The disintegration of the village commune is creating in our country a new class of industrial proletariat. Being more receptive, mobile and advanced, this class responds to the appeal of the revolutionaries more rapidly than the backward peasant population . . . With this class our people achieve for the first time the economic conditions that are common to all civilised peoples and hence it is only through the agency of this class that the people can take part in the progressive efforts of civilised mankind. On these grounds the Russian Social Democrats consider their primary and principal duty to be the formation of a revolutionary workers' party.[185]

In these extracts we are struck by the positive, rather than negative, attitude of the new current in Russian revolutionary thought towards the insurgent terrorist period of our movement. The most characteristic feature of this is the declaration that the Russian revolution would 'above all serve the interests of the peasantry'. Also far from insignificant is the remark, made obliquely like something implied, that recognises the great significance of the energetic opposition of the liberal strata of society to the government, if such opposition were to exist in this country. On this point the group of Russian Social Democrats abroad expressed the tendency of the Narodnaya Volya Party which, in the person of Zhelyabov,[186] for example, considered an alliance between the revolutionaries and the liberal oppositional elements 'to achieve as democratic a constitution as possible' to be necessary. Finally, if we examine the *practical* motivation for the idea of forming a 'revolutionary workers' party' in Russia today, we see that in it too is reflected the spiritual link between the social democratic current and the preceding period of our revolutionary movement. The political organisation of the workers is motivated here not by the self-contained interests of the proletariat, nor by the distant goals of socialism, but by the urgent need for such an organisation in order [to realise] the immediate general democratic goals of the Russian revolutionary movement and to ensure success for the revolutionaries in the struggle against the contemporary state for the interests of the working class, of the class in general, i.e. of both the peasant masses and the urban workers. We might think that the workers' movement saw the notion of the first Russian social democratic group not as an end in itself or as a justification for its own existence but as a mere medium or instrument destined to serve other social forces. Clearly, such a conclusion would be mistaken. But there is no doubt that, for this group, the idea of organising a workers' party in Russia was very closely linked with the political and social tendencies and tasks that did, and do, inspire all the democratic elements among our intelligentsia.

In fact, looking at the points in the programme that we are now talking about, we see that only one of them concerns the workers wholly and exclusively and that is the one containing the demand for serious factory legislation and the organisation of a factory inspectorate 'with worker representation'. The majority of the remaining points are directed against class and social organisation and against autocracy; some of them, in their radicalism, go further than the wishes of moderately liberal elements but nonetheless embrace the interests of the whole working mass and of all strata of the democratic intelligentsia. For that very reason; of the four so-called 'economic demands', only the one mentioned above concerns the workers exclusively ('urban and rural'), all the others are, in the main, aimed at defending the peasants and handicraftsmen and only in part the industrial proletarians.

The reader knows the fervour, worthy of a better cause, with which the Populists used to spread, and still spread, the legend of the 'narrowness' of the Russian Social Democrats and their 'peasant-phobia' [*krest'yanofobiya*]. It will therefore not be without interest to the reader to juxtapose this legend and the following lines, which summarise the sense and the practical tendencies of the cited programme:

These demands are as favourable to the interests of the peasants as they are to those of the industrial workers; for this reason, by achieving their implementation, the workers' party will open up the broad path of reconciliation with the agrarian population. Thrown out of the village as an impoverished member of the commune, the proletarian will return to it as a social democratic agitator. His appearance in this role will transform the present hopeless lot of the commune. The disintegration of the latter is inevitable only until such time as this very disintegration gives rise to a new popular force that is powerful enough to put an end to the reign of capitalism. The working class and the poorest part of the peasantry, drawn along in its wake, constitute a force of this kind.[187]

In this characteristic part of the practical programme of the first Russian Social Democrats there is only one feature lacking, namely, any reference to the fact that the 'demands' listed in it are also 'favourable' to the interests of the progressive strata of the upper classes in general, and of the democratic intelligentsia in particular. The general democratic tendencies constitute an organic element in the political activity of the proletariat of all countries. But they play, or should play, in a certain sense, an even greater role in Russia, where industrial capitalism is still developing in the socio-political and cultural atmosphere of the epoch of primitive accumulation, when the bourgeoisie does not yet participate in the government of the state and the industrial proletariat, because of its composition and the conditions of its existence, is still closely linked to the countryside. Unfortunately, the difficult circumstances in which Marxism began to gain influence among our student youth prevented the latter from assimilating it at once and applying it to the concrete conditions of the life and development of the proletariat in contemporary Russia. The exhaustion of the active revolutionary forces among the intelligentsia and the complete disillusionment with the old paths focussed the thought and attention of principled youth on self-development and narrowed the circle of its interests and desires to the sphere of theoretical questions which were, of course, on the whole, 'sociological'. The ideological atmosphere of Populism, from which everything revolutionary has been effaced and which has turned into a liberal-reactionary mixture, has given a very one-sided direction to this 'self-development' and to the work of rapidly advancing revolutionary thought. Those elements among the student youth whose sympathies were drawn to social democracy have involuntarily assimilated it as a 'sociological doctrine' that unconditionally rejects everything in Populism and has nothing in common not only with its liberal-reactionary mutations but also with the insurgent terrorist period. But, by severing in this fashion every ideological connection with revolutionary Populism and its traditions, these elements by that very same action strike off the list of the real factors determining the contemporary historical position of the Russian proletariat those elements of Russian life that themselves shape the reactionary national-historical atmosphere in which the Russian people, and with it the working class, is suffocating. As a result of this logical operation there emerges an abstract doctrine that has explained the historical inevitability of capitalist progress and its revolutionary tendencies in a more or less distant perspective but has left in shadow the burning questions of the revolutionary struggle in contemporary Russia. Political indifference and a nonchalant attitude towards the sufferings and misfortunes of the popular masses that are not directly caused by the exploitation of the worker by the industrial capitalist have been the most characteristic distinguishing feature of almost a majority of Marxist youth during the past decade. But, if we look at the economic antagonism between wage labourers and capitalists in isolation from their surrounding socio-political and cultural milieu, we come directly, in theory, to an abstract conception of the relationship between labour and capital (the genesis and peculiarity of this relationship are explained to us by Marx's teaching on value and surplus value) and, in practice, to the so-called economic struggle or, put simply, to strikes, as the only, or at least the principal, means of emancipation for the proletariat. In the 80s, because of the complete exhaustion of the revolutionary forces and the need to master the basic positions of Marxism, its young adherents were not yet able to embark on this path. Instead, they racked their brains all the more diligently over the theory of value. In this process many of them got lost in a scholastic maze while seriously imagining that they were nonetheless working to help the revolution.

However, in a certain sense they were right. The best, if not all, of the representatives of our youth, drunk with Marx's teachings, brought them to the workers with the firm intention of preparing among them the elements of a 'future Russian workers' party'.

However abstractly these teachings were propagated, their revolutionary influence on the advanced workers was already beginning to make itself apparent in the first years of this decade. But so many active forces had already accumulated in their midst in the circle of Marxist youth and of propagandised workers that the demand for a change to lively revolutionary activity developed of its own accord. In the first stages it took the one-sided form of the organisation of and support for strikes almost exclusively.[188] This evolution in our social democratic movement was, to a significant extent, historically inevitable and this is especially important regardless of its one-sidedness, undoubtedly very fruitful from the point of view of the political development of the Russian proletariat and its friends among the intelligentsia. In the course of some two years the strike movement brought the awakening workers and their organisational vanguard face to face with absolutism and managed to place before them next the question of the achievement of political liberty. Thanks to this, the social democratic movement is treading on ground that should attract to it the sympathies of all true friends of progress in Russia, however negative their view of the theories and ultimate ends of social democracy. Further, agitation on the basis of economic interests will inevitably lead social democratic circles into immediate contact with facts that clearly demonstrate the closest identity of interests between our industrial proletariat and the peasant masses. On the other hand, with the success and broadening of the scope of agitation there will also come a progressive growth in social democracy's demands for an increase in its reserves and resources. Even now, mass agitation devours such a large proportion of both that we must feel a need to preserve and broaden the source of their constant replenishment and renewal. This need will become even more acute, of course, when the Russian Social Democrats broaden the limits of their activity in the direction indicated and lead the attack against absolutism, albeit under the class banner of the proletariat but in the name, and for the defence, of all those who are oppressed and deprived. But this very broadening of the sphere of the class struggle of the Russian proletariat will also serve as a reliable source for replenishing it with a constant flow of the reserves and resources that it needs.

The indifference to all the phenomena of Russian life that prevailed among Marxists in the 80s, which went beyond the sphere of the immediate antagonism between labour and capital, represented a peculiar reflection of the tactical view of Western social democracy, according to which in relation to the proletariat all classes and parties constitute 'a single, undifferentiated, reactionary mass'. This tactical slogan is logically connected to the practical efforts of the revolutionary proletariat in the West towards the 'political expropriation' of the upper classes and it expresses in somewhat exaggerated form the fact that, because of their dominant position in the state, these classes cannot fail to emerge as the principal opponents of the Social Democrats. Generally speaking, the tactic of fiercely hostile opposition between the political organisation of the workers and all the bourgeois parties is not the fruit of social democratic or other doctrinaire attitudes. It has grown organically on historical ground that is characterised, on the one hand, by a sharp and final separation of the urban workers from the general popular mass into an economically and culturally distinct class and, on the other hand, by the complete domination of large-scale capitalist production and the absence of monarchist absolutism in the government of the state. The important thing about this process is the fact that the historical movement that has given rise to this ground has at the same time raised the proletariat to an intellectual height that renders it *capable* of the organised defence of its own interests and has created the political conditions that permit it, if not to gain decisive victories over the *combined* forces of the other classes, then at least to fight against them and to grow stronger in this struggle.

In Russia we do not yet have the principal condition for the political struggle with the bourgeoisie — there are no politically dominant classes — but instead we have the tsar and his officials ruling autocratically over the whole nation. The industrial workers are in a state of irreconcilable antagonism towards the entrepreneurs, i.e. towards a single stratum of the capitalist bourgeoisie. But, as the bourgeoisie in general does not stand at the helm of the ship of state, the antagonism between it and the proletariat has, in the *immediate* sense, a purely economic character. If it carries within it an inexhaustible source of impulses towards the development of political consciousness and political passions among our working class, this is not because of the political dominance of the capitalist strata of the bourgeoisie but because they are under the special *protection* of the tsarist bureaucracy. But this relatively privileged position of the commercial and industrial bourgeoisie is one of the main sources of the antagonism of the non-aristocratic [*raznochinskii*] intelligentsia and the educated strata of the representatives of private land ownership towards the autocratic state order. Finally, our capitalist bourgeoisie, in the shape of its kulak and usurer strata, emerges as the particular oppressor and enemy of the poorest peasant masses, the enemy that once again is supported and protected by the 'social policy' of absolutism and its servants. In a word, a realistic account of matters would by no means condemn our industrial proletariat to social and political isolation. Thank God that it does not condemn them. Having only recently begun to distinguish themselves from state serfs, from the undercultured peasantry, they are even now, as a mass, still too deeply immersed in the barbarism and ignorance of the people as a whole to be in a position – in the clutches of absolutism – to raise themselves, completely independently and without any outside assistance, to the heights of conscious revolutionary strength. Our 'revolutionary workers' party' would have had even less chance of growing and energetically proclaiming its existence if it had, at the present low level of intellectual and cultural development of the popular masses in Russia and against the background of an autocratic police state, been obliged to wage a struggle against *all* the bourgeois and petty bourgeois classes as if it were fighting a 'single, undifferentiated, reactionary mass'. At the same time the Marxist youth of the 80s apparently failed completely to appreciate the significance of these points and saw the numerical growth of the factory proletariat as the sole guarantee of the successes of our social democratic movement. This point of view might have corresponded in some way with purely propagandist activity in small circles of the crack units of the working class. But it is incompatible with organisational and agitational activity among the masses. Its militant character causes enormous losses in resources and in addition requires a significant contingent of leading elements and organisers with large stocks of literature and material resources at their disposal. Lastly, for constant revolutionary struggle we also need a sympathetic atmosphere outside [our ranks], i.e. if not the overt, then at least the covert goodwill of the broad strata of society that do not identify completely with the views of the ideologists of the revolutionary proletariat.

Thus, quite apart even from broad political considerations, the everyday needs of our movement in its new phase themselves raise the question of the widest possible influence of Russian social democracy on those strata of the population that, although they do not belong to the working class, are nonetheless suffering under present arrangements. But in order to influence these strata it is by no means necessary for the Social Democrats to start operating in their midst. The Social Democrats' task of attracting supporters and overt or covert allies among the non-proletarian classes is resolved first of all and in the main by the character of agitational and propagandist activity among the *proletariat itself*. Until now this activity has revolved almost entirely around the direct economic exploitation of the workers by the employers. The task mentioned requires a broadening in the scope of agitation and propaganda to cover questions involving the main points on which are merged and interwoven the interests of both the proletariat and the other classes that are oppressed or crushed by absolutism and the capitalist bourgeoisie under its protection. But these questions prove on closer examination to be the most important and essential for our proletariat at the present time. Consequently, by emphasising and promoting them, our propaganda and agitation will be most expedient even from the point of view that considers exclusively the development of the political consciousness of the workers.

Bearing in mind the social helplessness of the peasant masses and the political impotence of our educated classes, we can tell in advance that a social democratic tactic based on the considerations just mentioned will at every step demonstrate the national significance of our workers' movement as the strongest and most decisive factor in the struggle against the backward social and political order in Russia. But this in turn emerges as the source of social democratic influence on the peasantry and among the upper classes who have to suffer under this order. As it grows in importance and popularity as the most decisive and advanced fighter for the interests of the people as a whole and for progress, the liberal strata have, in their legal activity, to take ever greater account of the demands and desires of the proletariat. This means that the legal efforts and methods by which the progressive elements of the upper classes are trying to consolidate and strengthen their influence on society and the state will also directly serve to create the conditions that favour the political development and organisation of the workers in the fetters of the despotic state.

The time and place do not permit me to dwell further on the positions stated here. They only touch upon, but by no means exhaust, the tactical questions of Russian social democracy. I have in part applied the above-mentioned tactical point of view to the field of literary propaganda among the workers in my articles in the two booklets published in the social democratic *Rabotnik* collection.[189] I hope that I shall soon have an opportunity to talk in greater detail of the current tactical tasks of Russian social democracy. For the time being allow me to restrict myself to the general remarks made above.

I must use this opportunity to express to you[190] and your whole society my sincere gratitude for the moral and material support that our Russian–American comrades have never ceased to give Russian social democracy almost from the moment of its inception right up until the present. I shake you firmly by the hand and send social democratic greetings to all our comrades.

Second letter

December 1897

Dear Comrades!

Russian social democracy is now living through a moment of the greatest significance. The strike movement of the last two years that has gripped the industrial centres of Russia and whole regions has demonstrated that the Russian Social Democrats have already put down roots among the working mass and are the organisers and leaders in its everyday confrontations with its exploiters. Thus in some two years they have been transformed from peaceful propagandists and educators and self-taught adherents of Marx into a lively and active revolutionary force. But this force is still in the first stages of its development and its further growth is still far from guaranteed.

The whole economic development of Russia vouches for the fact that our workers' movement will neither stop nor stand still under the yoke of tsarist police oppression. But whether it will advance and consolidate under the banner of social democracy is another question. Meanwhile the historical significance of the struggle between workers and employers and their political role in contemporary Russia depend upon the positive or negative resolution of this question. It is not just the class interests of the proletariat but the whole course of the internal political development of Russia that depends to a significant degree upon the character and direction that our workers' movement assumes. At the present moment we are perhaps approaching the time of decision and for this reason I consider this an extremely significant moment in the life of Russian social democracy.

Two prospects occur to me for the near future:

The workers' movement confines itself to the narrow channel of purely economic confrontations between workers and employers and is, on the whole, itself devoid of political character. But in the actual struggle for political freedom the most advanced strata of the proletariat follow the revolutionary circles or fractions of the so-called intelligentsia. In a word the emancipation movement takes a path that, if not exactly the same, is in one very important respect the same as that taken in the West in the distant past when the tyranny of monarchist bureaucracy still prevailed there too; the working masses play no independent revolutionary role in it, they follow the bourgeois intelligentsia and fight for their emancipation not under their own banner but under that of others.

The other prospect is that social democracy organises the Russian proletariat into an independent political party, fighting for emancipation, *partly side by side and in alliance with* the bourgeois revolutionary fractions, such as they might be, and partly by attracting directly into its own ranks or by carrying in its wake the most sympathetic and revolutionary elements of the intelligentsia. Obviously this latter prospect demands from the workers a far higher level of political consciousness and self-awareness than does the first, according to which the leaders of the revolutionary movement would be the representatives of the bourgeois classes and the proletariat would merely be a blind mass, led by them and following in their footsteps.

Does Russian life contain the means necessary for the development among Russian workers of the political consciousness and self-awareness that would render them capable of organising themselves into an independent and, in part, a leading revolutionary party? For this is the first, one might say, the fundamental question, upon whose resolution depends the subsequent fate of Russian social democracy. If there are not the means, in other words, if there is no possibility of giving the Russian proletariat an independent, pre-eminent role in the fight against tsarist police autocracy and arbitrary rule, then Russian social democracy has no historical right to exist. It becomes, in this event, no longer viable, and its very existence, far from assisting the growth of the revolutionary movement, retards it.

Fortunately for our proletariat, Russian life provides a fully affirmative answer to the question posed above. One of the basic conditions for the workers' development is widespread elementary education among them which, through newspapers and books, gives them the opportunity of widening their intellectual horizons, engaging in intellectual contact with the world-historical movement and receiving stimuli and the impetus to thought from the ideas and events that fill the life of educated, thinking and active mankind. In our country popular education is still at a low level; even straightforward literacy is still far from being available to the whole population. Nevertheless Russia has already made significant progress in this respect and the urgent needs of the upper classes and of the government itself vouchsafe even more rapid progress in the future. Because of these needs there has already been a significant spread and development of educational media such as public schools, public reading-rooms and libraries, popular lectures that are open to all, cheap popular literature and a periodical press. Of course, all this is far from corresponding to the needs of the population, but the movement for popular education cannot stand still: on the contrary, it will continue at an accelerated pace, enlarging and reinforcing the intellectual basis for social democratic activity among the working mass.

But literacy and even education become an instrument for arousing the popular masses to political activity only when the life of society is in full swing, when the struggle between the different classes of the population is taking place in the organs of independent public organisation, at meetings and in the press, when, finally, dissatisfaction with the government and with the whole state system exists and is manifested in varying forms and varying ways. In constitutional countries all these motors and instruments of the political development of the working masses are present in abundance and the state order itself favours a seething social and political life. In this country, clearly, there can be no such talk of seething life for the time being. Our rural assemblies [*zemskie sobraniya*] and town councils, [*gorodskie dumy*], their pleas and petitions to the government, our various congresses and social gatherings, our liberal press and the other legal organs of independent public activity are only the enzymes of constitutional life and they are enzymes that are

diluted with barrels of water full of harmful microbes. However, even these embryonic forms of independent public organisation and freedom, weak as they are, can
serve as the bases for and motors of the awakening and education of the Russian
proletariat for political life. Despite their material weakness, they constitute an
enormous revolutionary force, which is currently still concealed and underdeveloped, but which can easily be transformed into a living, active force influenced by
the energetic work done by Social Democrats among the workers. We can even say,
with certain reservations, that the *rudimentary* elements of constitutional life in
contemporary Russia directly contain more revolutionary spirit than the developed
constitutional forms of the West. All the more so because in the West the upper
classes, from the exploiters to the strata that we call the 'intelligentsia', are inclined
towards conservatism and use the legislative power in their hands, even science and
the press, for the struggle *against* the revolutionary aspirations of the proletariat. In
Russia, however, a significant section of these classes, and in particular the most
politically developed of their strata, is itself infected with 'destructive urges'[191] and
cannot help employ all the ways and means at its disposal for a covert or overt
struggle against tsarist police omnipotence and against the lack of rights for the
popular masses which is the basis of this omnipotence. Obviously this has left a
corresponding imprint both on the liberal press and on the whole social activity of
our educated circles.

In these conditions even those institutions that are in themselves harmless, such
as our organs of independent public organisation and our press, must become
instruments for revolutionising the popular masses. But clearly, in the absence of
energetic action on the part of the Social Democrats, these conditions may remain
a slow-acting, slumbering force as far as the political development of our proletariat
is concerned. In the hands of the revolutionaries from the liberal democratic intelligentsia they may, of course, help to revolutionise [the proletariat], but by no
means in the way that its present and future class interests require; these interests
require that the Russian working class should already have begun to organise itself
into an *independent* revolutionary party and should emerge as an independent
political force.

Unfortunately, our social democratic circles are still a very long way from this
tactic which is aimed at using thoroughly the progressive elements of Russian life in
the interests of the task that I have just indicated. As far as the circumstances
beyond our control are concerned, the principal obstacle to developing this kind of
tactic is the view, prevalent among them, that narrows the sphere of activity of
Russian social democratic workers' organisations to the struggle with the employers
and active participation in strikes. Of course, not all of you, dear comrades, take
such a narrow view of the matter; indeed, the majority of you in practice diverge
to some extent from this point of view. But in general it is undoubtedly far more
widespread among Russian Social Democrats than were insurgent views among the
revolutionary intelligentsia in the 70s.

We might describe it as a unique descendant of insurgency, only on new social
ground and a different theoretical foundation. The insurgency of revolutionary

Populism was utopian in practical terms, but was nonetheless revolutionary in its theoretical and logical premisses. It derived from the proposition that the peasants already carried in their heads a *ready-made* 'socialist ideal' and that struggle 'on the basis of local needs and interests' would help them to join together and direct their efforts against the *whole existing order* in the name of this ideal that had matured among the people. And what could and should this minor preparatory battle on the part of the peasantry have led to? To local, but organised, skirmishes with those who oppress the people, from the landowners and provincial authorities to the kulaks and usurers. The practical activity of revolutionary Populism rested on narrow foundations, narrow because it had not taken into consideration the new predominant forces of life, such as the industrial proletariat and the industrial bourgeoisie. But Bakuninism directly propelled the revolutionary elements into a struggle with the backward social and political conditions of Russian life; for this reason its practical activity was distinguished by its directly revolutionary character. The view that strikes should be the sole or principal form [of activity] for the emancipatory movement of the proletariat sets far narrower limits to the spontaneous activity of the latter and is in a *direct* sense far less revolutionary than insurgency.

The proletariat, on the admission of the Social Democrats themselves, does not possess a ready-made, historically developed social ideal. The 'economic struggle' with the entrepreneurs is supposed to develop such an 'ideal' slowly in its consciousness: put more plainly, to prepare the workers to understand the final goals of socialism. But even in the West, where the bourgeoisie does have legislative authority and the government of the state in its hands, even in these countries strikes are one of the principal motive forces for the revolutionary development of the proletariat. Even there, where the bourgeoisie is directly dominant in every sphere of social and political life, confrontations between the workers and their exploiters, sometimes lasting quite a long time, have not promoted the development of political class consciousness among the proletariat. If political passions and desires have emerged, they have usually been influenced by the bourgeois parties and their squabbles. It was only in Germany and Austria that the workers' movement, almost from the very beginning, assumed the character of the *political class* movement of the proletariat. But here social democracy has, almost since taking its first steps, been able to combine harmoniously and organically its energetic and tireless participation in local confrontations between workers and entrepreneurs with systematic struggle against the contemporary state and the diverse manifestations of its yoke over all the labouring masses. We may say that German and Austrian social democracy marked their emergence by immediately launching an attack on the bourgeois order from all sides.

By this I do not by any means wish to say that we should imitate our elder sisters in the advanced countries in everything. We cannot imitate them because our social order is *not yet fully* bourgeois, because it still rests on socio-political foundations bequeathed by the epoch of the nobility and the serfs. But this very circumstance renders dangerous a one-sided enthusiasm for strikes as the principal instru-

ment for revolutionary education and as the sole means of encouraging the emergence of the independent revolutionary activity of the proletariat. I consider it
dangerous precisely because, as the fruit of an inadequate attention to, as it were, a
lower order of relationships in Russian life, it facilitates the implantation and consolidation of indifference among Russian Social Democrats towards the many facts
and phenomena of Russian life that condition the historical position of our proletariat and, consequently, the current tasks of its social democratic vanguard. It is
harmful in that, by limiting the intellectual horizons of the advanced workers to
narrow class interests in the vulgar sense that the bourgeoisie of all shapes and sizes
attributes to the teachings of social democracy, it slows down these workers' own
political development and prevents them from growing beyond the stage of political
immaturity. But this in turn becomes a brake on our proletariat achieving the central and pre-eminent political significance that it might achieve in contemporary
Russia due to the political impotence of *all other classes*.

Despite its social helplessness and its completely uncultured state, our peasantry
has so far been the focus for the care and sympathies of the progressive and revolutionary strata of the intelligentsia. Why? Amongst other things because it is only
[in the peasantry] that they saw and see the social incarnation, as it were, of their
progressive aspirations and a means of deliverance from the political order that is
paralysing Russian life. But the one-sided practical activity of the Russian Social
Democrats is slowing down the development among the intelligentsia of a similar
attitude towards the working class, regardless of the fact that the latter, historically
speaking, has really been summoned to the role of principal revolutionary force in
the emancipatory movement against outmoded political customs.

To avoid misunderstandings I point out that I am far from belittling the significance of the so-called 'economic struggle'. On the contrary, for me it constitutes an
axiom, a truth that does not require proof and whose dissemination would be an
insult to the advanced reader. The preceding observations derive, therefore, from
the proposition that the paramount significance of strikes and, generally speaking,
of local confrontations between workers and capitalists for the movement for the
emancipation of the proletariat is acknowledged by all Russian Social Democrats as
something that is self-evident and has passed into their general consciousness. But in
saying that, we do not in our country notice the reverse side of the coin. Many
ignore the fact that there is nowhere else in the civilised world where strikes meet
such obstacles and require such sacrifices as they do in Russia. At the same time in
no country in the West was the working class as poor in intellectual, organisational
and material resources as it is here. Consequently there is every reason to fear that
the one-sided development of the strike movement in future might be reflected in a
temporary depletion of our resources and might entail a period of disillusionment
and reaction in our ranks and in the popular mass itself. Only a constantly increasing flow of new resources from the intelligentsia and a sympathy towards our movement on the part of the progressive strata of the upper classes in general might save
us from such a distressing prospect. But to create this kind of support for ourselves
among these classes we must show clearly and tirelessly in all our practical activity,

including the sphere of the purely economic struggle, the general democratic tasks of our movement and in this way popularise its general national revolutionary significance for contemporary Russia.

Apart from this, we must also bear in mind the prospect of a lull in strike disturbances. As 'Petersburger' has already rightly noted in his fine article 'A propos the St Petersburg strike' (nos. 3–4 of the *Rabotnik* collection): 'Events like the Petersburg strike can neither last long nor be repeated often.'[192] What will the energy of the remaining vital revolutionary resources of the proletariat be expended on, where will it go from here? At the end of the 70s these forces joined the terrorist movement and were dispersed in the general mass of the revolutionary intelligentsia, which did nothing either to encourage an increase in political consciousness among the working mass or to strengthen the inclination among the progressive strata of society towards the proletariat as the new popular revolutionary force in society. Is there any reason why this phenomenon should not repeat itself once more, since the most energetic and intelligent representatives of our proletariat find no use for their strength nor any outlet for their political aspirations – under the banner of social democracy?

It is, however, time to stop. I did not take up my pen with the intention of discussing in detail the inadequacies in our tactics and of setting forth my positive views on them. The limitations of a newspaper letter are too great for that. Besides, much of what concerns the sphere of tactical questions can be discussed in the appropriate fashion only through collective consultations among active comrades in local and general congresses.

Perhaps the discussion of tactical questions and the elaboration of a *general programme of action* marks the beginning of, or at least gives a decisive push to, the cause of unifying the revolutionary workers' circles and unions into a 'Russian workers' revolutionary party'. Until such time as a union of this kind exists on the basis of a general tactic, Russian social democracy will continue to be an embryo but far from the living organism full of strength that is entitled to bear that name.

Summarising my extremely cursory and very fragmentary remarks, I will say that the most urgent questions and tasks for our movement are now grouped around a single question or a single task that may be formulated in the following way: to expand the limits and broaden the content of our propagandist, agitational and organisational activity.

In conclusion, I ask you, dear comrades, to accept my fraternal greeting and sincere wishes for the success of the publication you have undertaken. With all my heart I wish that *Rabochaya Gazeta*[193] should be worthy of its name – should serve as the organ for all our social democratic groups – and should facilitate the more rapid transition of our movement to the period of maturity.

44. OUR REALITY (1899): EXTRACTS[194]

K.M. Takhtarev

1. The workers' movement

The movement is reality ... because the movement is life, and reality and life are
one and the same thing. The principal element in life is labour and the surest sign
of reality is practical activity.   (Chernyshevsky)

Our workers' movement derives in its entirety from the real (material and juridical)
position of the working strata of the population of Russia. It is utterly dependent
on working conditions: on the stage of development of a particular area of production and the development of mechanisation in it (large-scale, small-scale, handicraft ...), on the stability of the composition of a particular group of workers and
the scale of the flow of new workers from the villages.

For this reason our workers' movement, even at the very beginning of its development, contains the embryos of diverse forms of organisation, from the broad,
militant, though still temporary, strike associations of workers in large-scale production (the spinners, weavers, iron workers ...) right down to the always peaceful, and therefore always permitted by the Ministry of the Interior, mutual aid
societies covering illness, accident, death, unemployment and the search for a job
... etc. and the consumer societies. Further, the movement depends to a very considerable extent on purely local, and even temporary, conditions (the back of
beyond, an industrial centre, the capital ... industrial activity, industrial stagnation); apart from this, we can still accept the following subdivision of the movement into two or three basic types:

1. The broad, mass, completely independent, workers' (professional) movement, e.g. the weavers and spinners in the Vladimir province (the development of trade-unionism [*tred-yunionizm*]).
2. The workers' movement in the intellectual and administrative centres (the
   capitals), which will acquire a more definite political colouring in the
   immediate future.
3. The unique movement of Jewish handicraft workers and artisans who have
   been packed for administrative reasons into the north-western region.[195]
   This movement has been put in a unique position by Russian legislation on
   Jewish settlement and for this reason it should be called a unique 'case'
   rather than a type of workers' movement. It naturally has a special, political, character. In our further exposition we shall be speaking only of the
   first two types (of Russian workers' movement).

The tasks of the movement at the present time, the current workers' cause for
the Russian workers that stems from their actual position which they find unsatisfactory, amount to an improvement by the workers in this position by all possible
means and appropriate measures in their independent social activity: by the path of

struggle (militant strike organisations), mutual aid (mutual aid societies), self-help (consumer, educational . . . societies). As far as the mutual aid and consumer societies, that are just starting up in this country and are permitted by the Ministry of Internal Affairs, are concerned, there is no doubt that in their subsequent development these societies will be widespread and of great significance for us. The direction and the objectives pursued by these societies are clear from their very names and amount to the protection of the mainly material and moral position of every one of their members. These societies, at the present moment and in their current state (given the frequently variegated composition of the membership, the participation of the bosses and their political position), cannot make up their minds about their broad political objectives: either the legislative defence of all workers, or particular militant efforts to increase pay or shorten the working day for their members. The present unpropitious (political) conditions of Russian social life and the senseless ministerial red tape for official permission for this type of 'legal' workers' mutual aid society seriously hamper their development.

More important for us is the struggle of the workers in large-scale production, which recently attained such broad political significance (law of 2 June 1897). Beginning with local disturbances among the workers of individual factories against the oppression and robbery of their individual bosses, this struggle became apparent in the beginning in the barely conscious form of stormy protests (in the shape of factory disorders, pogroms, etc.) against the extremely unsatisfactory contemporary position of the workers and the scandalous oppression of the bosses and their administration. But, in accordance with the development and growth amongst the workers of a sense of common cause and a more realistic understanding of their own interests, this struggle, apart from being a means for the workers to express their protest, began, little by little, to acquire a more conscious form, the form of their actual attempts to improve their position by means even of the particular and temporary struggle of the workers of individual factories against their bosses with the aid of strikes on the basis of already determined demands, worked out together and presented to the bosses by specially elected workers . . . Developing further, this movement begins to assume the form of a broad, but nevertheless temporary, organised, but nonetheless local, struggle of the workers of a whole branch of production against a whole series of bosses . . . As this temporary struggle of the workers for the improvement of their present position becomes increasingly *organised* and *constant*, it is transformed into the present forward movement of the workers by way of the gradual improvement in their position. For it is only with the help of permanent organisation (constant readiness for struggle) that the workers can really retain for themselves the concessions wrung from the bosses by the temporary struggle and achieve a lasting improvement in their position. The development of workers' organisations is a necessary condition for such a lasting improvement in the present and future position of the workers. The development of workers' organisations serves at the same time as the most characteristic and reliable sign and index of the actual workers' movement. In this respect the struggle of our workers in large-scale production represents only the most elementary form of the workers' movement (the period of temporary strike organisations). The present broad but temporary strike organisations will, of course, develop in the future, as has happened abroad, into permanent workers' organisations. Transient strikers' meetings will in time be replaced by the assemblies of permanent militant workers' unions. Existing circles and groups of the most active workers, the representatives of individual factories and factory districts will become the central groups, the councils of such unions. The significance of these organisations and the importance of their development, both for the present and for the future development of the embryonic organised workers' movement in this country is obvious to all. But the stunted development of these organisations at the present time is equally obvious to all.

Now a few words about the direction of our movement. The most characteristic index of the movement consists, of course, in the demands put forward by the workers both in times of peace and in time of struggle. These demands concerning the most essential needs of the workers and their most urgent current interests, are so well known from the daily leaflets and appeals published, both by the workers themselves and by the circles of intelligentsia Social Democrats who have links with the workers, that we do not have to enlarge on them in detail. In the vast majority of cases these demands, just like the strike struggle itself during which they were in the main advanced, frequently have a local character (the demands for a local improvement in the position of the particular workers who have advanced these demands). As far as broad demands are concerned – the demands covering not just a local improvement in the position of the workers of a particular factory or factories – as far as political demands are concerned – covering legal protection for all Russian workers (covering the regulation of fines, the limitation of the oppressive measures of the administration and the police, the shortening of the working day or the freedom of the unions . . . it is all the same) – it is only in the demands of the Petersburg weavers and spinners at the time of their January mass strike in 1897,[196] followed by the law of 2 June 1897, that we see the first and still barely conscious case of our workers putting such broad political demands. This is, as it were, only a foretaste of the impending political struggle of the Russian workers for legal protection for labour.

This struggle, which requires enormous resources and sacrifices from the workers, demands from them an even greater understanding of their own interests. But so that such a political struggle might be waged by the workers with full consciousness and independence, it must be waged by the actual workers' organisations so that these workers' political demands rest on what they themselves recognise as their general political requirements and current interests, so that these demands should be the demands of the workers' (guild) organisations, so that they are really worked out by them together and advanced by all these workers' organisations together, on their own individual initiative in accordance with the collective common will of their members . . .

At present, barely conscious of their own interests and in the almost complete absence of permanent militant organisations (unions) among them, Russian workers are still very poorly prepared for this. But things are moving in this direction. The most immediate tasks of the movement, in our opinion, are the development among the workers of organisations (through the retention even in times of peace of the organisations born in times of struggle to collect money (strike fund), of assemblies (and councils of the most active workers' representatives . . .) and the transformation of these organisations from the temporary to the permanent. Similarly, the further development of existing workers' organisations, both legal and illegal, and also of the circles of advanced workers, is necessary. For, as will be clear from the above, it is only in the presence of permanent organisations that a successful struggle, both particular and general, and a really lasting improvement, both particular and general, in the present position of the workers, with a further improvement in the future, are possible. The immediate local demands of the workers are further local increases in wages, the shortening of the working day, the ending of fines . . . of the crude and oppressive behaviour of the administration, the right to have elected representatives, workers' deputies, in all cases of conflict with the bosses, with their administration and the police . . . and other local demands that depend on the local, particular conditions of the life and work of particular workers. The immediate general political demands of the workers still remain the legal shortening of the working day (to ten hours) and the restoration of the holidays abolished by the law of 2 June 1897. But we shall be accused of heresy by those who criticise the narrowness of our attitude, the revolutionaries who call us the lowest strata of the proletariat.[197] 'The economic emancipation of the proletariat,' they say, 'is a consequence of its political hegemony . . . The immediate task of the Russian workers' movement (the strike struggle? mutual aid societies? workers' circles? – we ask) is the overthrow of tsarism . . . The workers' movement must wipe out the autocracy, alleviating the economic position of the proletariat in the process' . . . etc. Very well! But let us begin at the beginning: what is Russian autocracy really and how should we understand it? For Russian autocracy is not something eternal and unchanging that stands above the laws of development (and disappearance) . . .

3. Society[198]

. . . Now a few words on the so-called revolutionary intelligentsia. It has, it is true, not once in fact demonstrated its complete willingness to 'engage in the decisive battle with tsarism'. The pity of it all is just that our revolutionary intelligentsia, mercilessly persecuted by the political police, has taken its struggle with this same political police for the political struggle with autocracy. Thus for it the question still remains unanswered: 'where do we find the resources for the struggle with autocracy?'

The multi-million mass of the de-agriculturalised PEASANTRY. Who has not heard of the enrichment of the 'clever yokels', the development of kulakism, the improvement in the circumstances of one part of the peasantry and the impoverishment [*obezloshadivanie*] and complete ruin of the other part? Russian science and literature long ago turned with particular attention and interest to the stratification of the peasant masses. Both the agricultural and urban seasonal work of the peasants, their resettlement in Siberia and the flight to the great industrial centres of new workers from the villages, which represent such obstacles to the unification and development of organisations among the more advanced urban workers – all these are current problems. The economic strength of the peasants? 'Which ones,' we ask, ' – the starving or the satiated?' The economic strength of the so-called rural bourgeoisie is, no doubt, not insignificant, but the main thing is that it is growing rapidly. The personal power of the peasants has already been idealised enough by Russian literature in the course of the last three decades, although at the crucial moment of the general excitement about the peasant question and the peasant disturbances Chernyshevsky wrote, 'The conservatism of the peasant is his entire way of life . . . ' The peasants have their own social organisation in the form of village self-government. But the ignorance and oppression of the peasant masses is such that, on the whole, this peasant self-government is used by the 'clever yokels', and even by the government itself.

The attitude of the majority of peasants towards the autocracy is purely passive. Their attitude towards the advanced strata of Russian society is, for the most part, very reactionary. Scattered throughout Russia, the one and a half million oppositionally inclined Old Believers and spiritual Christians, and especially the sectarians of the latter who have recently multiplied so rapidly (Stundists, Baptists, Dukhobors . . .) lose an important part of their social significance because of their passive, and partly even negative, attitude to everything in the world apart from the interests of their circle and the inner world.

The position of the social strata of the RURAL AND URBAN WORKERS, including factory workers, artisans and miners, is more definite. Their constantly growing number is increasing more and more rapidly. But the economic position of the majority of them is extremely grievous. Because of the very stunted development, even the non-existence, of their organisations (apart from a few mutual aid societies, the still embryonic consumer societies and the broad, certainly, but only temporary strike associations, we cannot cite any other examples of workers' organisations) the economic strength of the workers, even of the urban workers, is negligible. The workers do not have the same kind of social class organisation as the other strata of the Russian population listed above (the always inert and now completely defunct guild organisation of handicraftsmen can hardly have any significance even for the handicraft workers). The legal position of the Russian workers is intolerable: the workers, alone of all the social strata, do not yet have any social rights in this country. Even the ignorant and downtrodden peasants have their own social self-government and their representatives sit in the Zemstvo alongside the representatives of the landowners and the capitalists . . . Apart from the 'right to work' for the bosses throughout Russia, apart occasionally from thirty-five (industrial) provinces, the workers are accorded no rights. The ministries 'permit' the bosses to make laws for the workers. The degree of consciousness of their social interests and even advantages among the urban workers and even the workers in the capital leaves much to be desired. The autocratic government regards the workers as a developing social force that is directly opposed to it and extremely dangerous to it in the political sense. The workers' question, in its eyes, is an 'abyss into which mankind is rushing'. Our bureaucracy, which has already been forced to protect the societies and leagues of the factory owners and entrepreneurs in all sorts of ways, has set itself the task of persecuting even the temporary associations of the workers aimed at improving their lot and of suppressing by every means even their peaceful mutual aid and consumer societies, etc.

In arresting masses of workers, the government seems to want to give them time in prison to reflect thoroughly on their position and their attitude towards that same government that is persecuting them. In exiling the most advanced and conscious St Petersburg, Moscow and Odessa workers to the provinces and the remoter parts, the government must be concerned about a possible broad dissemination throughout the whole of Russian territory of the social and emancipatory labour teaching (socialism) whose best representatives and most active proselytisers are these workers. However, in this particular respect Muraveyv and Goremykin, and their department of police and spies, their chamber of procurators, and their directorates of gendarmes and detectives, have gone too far in withholding from 'political' workers their very 'right' to work and live not just in the capitals but also in the large industrial centres, and, further, in preventing these workers from working even in the industrial provinces, they have raised the number of forbidden provinces to thirty-five . . . 'They' try to disrupt every peaceful — orderly (organised) — workers' strike with the aid of their *agents provocateurs* by turning it into a 'workers' disturbance' or an 'insurrection', so that they have a chance to put it down by armed force, in a way that they could not put it down through their usual 'legal' measures . . . It might be thought that these gentlemen would like to drive the workers to terrorism so that they could then begin hanging the most active of them . . . The Russian bureaucracy still continues to this day to consider a workers' strike to be a crime disturbing public order and it calls the supporters of the spontaneous social activity of the workers its principal enemies. The attitude of the advanced strata of the workers to a government that assures them that 'the interests of the factory owners and the interests of the workers follow the same path'[199] is as understandable as is the attitude of the workers to the factory owners, under the pressure of whose social strength, the government determines its attitude towards the workers.

Such is Russian reality, the social conditions in which our young workers' movement, which we began this article by examining, has to develop. What kind of struggle should the workers wage? Is it not the only one they can wage in present circumstances? But is not the struggle that is possible in present circumstances the one that they are in actual fact presently waging? It is to this struggle, to the particular and the political struggle for the improvement of their lot that we now summon the workers, meaning by *particular struggle* a struggle waged by the workers of particular factories against their bosses for their particular interests, for the particular improvement of their lot (whatever the characteristics of their particular demands that they put to their bosses in this process), and meaning by *political struggle* the struggle that the workers wage in the general interest, involving an improvement in the lot of all workers, albeit by means of the legal protection of labour (whether it concerns the material side of their lives or the legal does not matter). We summon all workers to this struggle, recognising that any really *social* struggle, whichever class it is waged by, any really social activity, whichever social stratum it attaches to, is by the very social basis inherent within it (by its democratic nature) hostile to the autocratic basis of our bureaucratic government. In this respect we are in complete agreement with its representatives, who are considered by their principal enemies to be the supporters of spontaneous social activity.

In this sense we regard the development of the independent social and political activity of the workers, their particular social and political struggle for the particular and general (legislative) improvement of their position, as the best and only possible method for them, in present political conditions, of indirect, but partly also of direct, struggle with autocracy. The workers' allies in this struggle are all the progressive strata of Russian society, defending their own social interests and institutions, understanding clearly their own general political advantages, 'never forgetting' how great is the 'difference in the way any change is made – either by the independent decision of the government or by a formal *demand from society*'.

By understanding in this way the real social struggle of the Russian workers, we are ready 'not to understand' those among our comrades who consider the alleviation of the economic position of the proletariat' to be merely a 'fellow-travelling accompaniment' to the overthrow of the autocracy, and likewise those who regard their 'Emancipation of Labour' programme as a simple answer to the question, 'Where do we find the resources for the struggle with tsarism?' We shall also say that we too 'do not understand' their disregard in this connection for the remaining social strata or for their separate groups, whose economic, organisational and human resources have such significance for this struggle. We are staggered by the way in which, in these programmes, they always ascribe the greatest importance to the advantages of workers' activity in parliament (which does not exist in this country) – in their complete disregard (because of their revolutionary nihilism) for the importance of worker participation in the legislative assemblies of factory owners that do exist in this country to draft laws for the workers, in the offices for factory affairs which are composed half of officials and half of these same factory owners . . . or, be that as it may, worker participation in urban local government which, given the present plans of the government to 'grant' the franchise to all householders, acquires a certain real significance for the workers. A fact worthy of mention: they themselves were the first people in this country to talk about the significance for the workers of independent social organisation (see the letter from the worker −r −v in *Rabochaya Mysl*, no. 7).[200] We give the highest priority to the development of workers' organisations, i.e. mainly of guild (militant) workers' unions, also of mutual aid, consumer and educational societies, etc. . . .

They will say to us once more that 'the government will not permit you to start such societies for they have directly forbidden the guild workers' unions of struggle'. To this we shall reply: the first is not quite true and, as for the prohibition of these societies, as that same worker −r −v says: 'certainly, strikes (and those same, only temporary, militant societies) are forbidden, but nonetheless they occur with increasing frequency . . . '. Let us recognise this. Perhaps we shall find an even greater obstacle to the organisation of the workers in the constant flow from the villages of new, backward 'dull' workers, depressing wages, real heathens, disrupting strikes and bringing all kinds of discord and demoralisation to the already settled milieu of long-standing urban workers.[201] Despite this, we nonetheless insist on the organisation of the workers on the basis of their vital demands and current needs, on the basis of their present particular and general interests as they perceive them; for, without this kind of organisation, the workers' movement is impossible, any kind of lasting improvement in the present or future (material and legal) position of the workers is unthinkable; for it is only with the development of workers' organisations that the workers acquire the economic and human (social) resources with which alone they can make their struggle with the bosses' exploitation and the government's tyranny more successful and finally emancipate themselves from every form of enslavement.

In conclusion, a few words on our conception of workers' socialism. We see it in the workers' movement itself, in the present and future development of the independent social and political activity of the workers, in the development of workers' organisations: guild (trade-unionism [*tred-yunionizm*]), consumer (cooperative movement) associations . . . in the gradual transition from present economic production first to the social control of organised (into guild unions) workers, and then to their social management or to the management by contemporary social authority democratised by the workers, democratised by way of their active participation in offices for the analysis of all possible factory and plant affairs, in arbitration courts, in all sorts of assemblies, commissions and conferences to draw up workers' laws, by way of worker participation in independent social management and finally in the country's general representative institution.

Considering that *socialism*, deriving from the development of the social modes of contemporary production and inevitably leading to the complete socialisation (and even communalisation) of all its resources, is *only the furthest and highest development of contemporary society*, we see the essence of historical development in the fact that 'the various classes into which the population of the country is divided one after another come to manage matters until finally the identity of rights and social advantages for the whole of the population is settled . . . '.

Recognising that 'history is sad precisely because the meanness, baseness, treachery in it are the same kind of impotent mirage as bursts of generosity and self-sacrifice', we know that that same 'history even removes the possibility of despair about the future if it removes the visions of rash hopes'.

Realising that a better future depends entirely on the development of the most vital, the best, aspects of the present, recognising that a more social (socialist) life is only the further development of contemporary social life, we repeat: Do you really envisage measuring the distant future by your habits, concepts and means of production? Do you really suppose that your great-great-grandchildren will be the same as you? Have no fear, they will be cleverer than you. Concentrate on arranging your own (social) life and leave worrying about the fate of your great-great-grandchildren to your great-great-grandchildren.

R.M.[202]

45. CREDO (1899)[203]

E.D. Kuskova

The existence of the guild and manufacturing period in the West has left a clear imprint on all subsequent history, and particularly on the history of social democracy. The bourgeoisie's need to fight for free forms, its efforts to free itself from the guild regulations that fettered production, made it, the bourgeoisie, into a revolutionary element; everywhere in the West it started with *liberté, fraternité, égalité* (liberty, fraternity, equality), with the achievement of free political forms. But with these gains it, in Bismarck's expression, gave a hostage to its future opponent – the working class. There is almost nowhere in the West where the working class, as a class, has won democratic institutions [for itself] – it has made use of them. It may be argued that it took part in revolutions. Reference to history will refute this view for it was precisely in 1848, when the consolidation of constitutions took place in the West, that the working class consisted of an urban artisan element, of petty-bourgeois democracy. A factory proletariat scarcely existed, while the proletariat in large-scale industry (the German weavers depicted by Hauptmann, the weavers of Lyons) constituted a wild mass, capable only of rioting but not of putting forward any political demands. We can definitely say that the constitutions of 1848 were achieved by the bourgeoisie and the petty bourgeoisie, the artisans. On the other hand, the working class (artisans, textile workers, printers, weavers, watchmakers, etc.) have since the Middle Ages been used to participating in organisations, mutual benefit funds, religious societies, and so on. This spirit of organisation is still alive among the skilled workers in the West and it distinguishes them clearly from the factory proletariat, which succumbs to organisation badly and slowly and which is capable only of so-called *lose Organisation* – (temporary organisation), and not of permanent organisations with rules and regulations. It is these skilled manufacturing workers who have constituted the core of social democratic parties. So we get the following picture: on the one hand, the relative ease of political struggle and every opportunity for it; on the other hand, the opportunity to organise this struggle with the help of the workers who have experience from the manufacturing period. It was on this basis that theoretical and practical Marxism grew up in the West. Its starting point was the parliamentary political struggle with the prospect (only superficially resembling Blanquism[204] but with a completely different origin) on the one hand, of capturing power and, on the other, of *Zusammenbruch* (catastrophe).[205] Marxism emerged as the theoretical expression of prevailing practice: of the political struggle predominating over the economic. In Belgium, in France, and especially in Germany, the workers organised the political struggle with incredible ease, the economic struggle with terrible difficulty and tremendous friction. Even to this day the economic organisations are, in comparison with the political organisations (leaving aside England), extraordinarily weak and unstable everywhere *laissent à désirer quelque chose* (leave something to be desired). As long as energy was not completely exhausted in the political struggle, *Zusammenbruch* was an essential *Schlagwort* (slogan) destined to play an enormous historical role. The fundamental law that can be discerned from studying the workers' movement is that of the line of least resistance. In the West this line was political activity, and Marxism as formulated in *The Manifesto of the Communist Party* was the best possible form the movement could assume. But when energy in the political struggle had been completely exhausted, when the political movement had reached a point of intensity that it would be difficult and almost impossible to surpass (the recent slow increase in votes, public apathy at meetings, the note of despondency in the literature), on the other hand, the ineffectiveness of parliamentary action and the entry into the arena of the ignorant mass, of the unorganised and almost unorganisable factory proletariat, gave rise in the West to what is now called Bernsteinism, the crisis of Marxism. It is difficult to imagine a more logical course of events than the period of development of the workers' movement from *The Manifesto of the Communist Party* to Bernsteinism, and a careful study of the whole process might determine with the accuracy of astronomy the outcome of this 'crisis'. Here, of course, we are talking, not about the victory or defeat of Bernsteinism (that is of little interest), but about the radical change in practical activity that has, for a long time, gradually been taking place in the party's midst.

This change will be not only in the direction of a more energetic prosecution of the economic struggle, a consolidation of the economic organisations, but also, and this is the most essential thing, in the direction of a change in the party's attitude towards the other opposition parties. Intolerant Marxism, negative Marxism, primitive Marxism (which holds to too schematic a concept of the class division of society) will give way to democratic Marxism, and the social position of the party in the midst of contemporary society will have to change drastically. The party *will recognise* society: its narrow corporative and, in the majority of cases, sectarian tasks will broaden into social tasks and its striving to seize power will be transformed into a desire for change, for the reform of contemporary society along democratic lines that are adapted to the present state of arrairs, with the object of protecting, in the most complete and effective way, (all) the rights of the labouring classes. The concept of 'politics' will be expanded, acquiring a truly social meaning, and the practical demands of the moment will acquire greater weight and will be able to count on receiving greater attention than has hitherto been the case.

It is not difficult to draw conclusions for Russia from this short description of the course of the development of the workers' movement in the West. Here, the line of least resistance will never lead to political activity. The intolerable political oppression will prompt much talk about it and will concentrate attention precisely on this question, but it will never prompt political action. While in the West the fact that the workers were drawn into political activity strengthened and shaped their weak forces, in Russia these weak forces are, on the contrary, confronted by a wall of political oppression: not only do they lack practical ways of struggle against it, and hence also for their own development, but they are systematically stifled by it and cannot put out even weak shoots. If we add to this the fact that the working class here has not inherited the spirit of organisation that has distinguished the fighters in the West, then we get a gloomy picture, one that could drive the most optimistic Marxist to despair if he believes that another factory chimney will, by the very fact of its existence, bring great benefits. The economic struggle too is hard, infinitely hard, but it is possible to wage it, and it is in fact being waged by the masses themselves. By learning in this struggle to organise, and by coming, in the course of it, into continual contact with the political regime, the Russian worker will at last create what might be called a form of the workers' movement, the organisation best suited to Russian realities. At the moment we can say with certainty that the Russian workers' movement is still in an amoebic state and has not acquired any form. The strike movement, which exists under any form of organisation, cannot yet be described as the crystallised form of the Russian movement, while the illegal organisations are not worthy of consideration even from the purely quantitative point of view (quite apart from their usefulness under present conditions).

That is the situation. If we add to this the famine and the process of ruination in the countryside, which facilitate strike breaking and, consequently, the even greater difficulty of elevating the working masses to a more tolerable cultural level, then ... well, what is there for a Russian Marxist to do?! Talk of an independent workers' political party is nothing but the result of transplanting alien aims and alien achievements on to our soil. The Russian Marxist has, so far, been a sad spectacle. His practical tasks at the present time are paltry, his theoretical knowledge, insofar as he utilises it *not as an instrument for research* but as a pattern for activity, is of no value as far as the execution of even these paltry practical tasks is concerned. Moreover, these patterns, borrowed from abroad, are harmful from the practical point of view. Our Marxists, forgetting that in the West the working class had embarked on political activity as on a field that had already been cleared, have viewed with suspicion the radical or liberal opposition activities of all the other non-worker strata of society. The slightest attempts to concentrate attention on public manifestations of a liberal political character arouse the protest of orthodox Marxists, who forget that a whole series of historical conditions prevent us from being Western Marxists and demand of us a different kind of Marxism that is suited to, and necessary in, Russian conditions. Clearly, the absence in every Russian citizen of a feeling for, and a sense of, politics cannot be compensated by the discussion of politics or by appeals to a non-existent force. This feeling for politics can only be acquired through education, i.e. through participation in the life (however un-Marxian it may be) offered by Russian conditions. 'Abstentionism' is as harmful to us, as it was appropriate (temporarily) in the West, because abstentionism that proceeds from something harmful and possesses real power is one thing and abstentionism that proceeds from an amorphous mass of scattered individuals is another.

For the Russian Marxist there is only one way out: participation in, i.e. assistance for, the economic struggle of the proletariat and participation in liberal opposition activity. As an 'abstentionist', the Russian Marxist came early on the scene, and this abstentionism has weakened the share of his energy that should have been turned in the direction of political radicalism. For the moment this is not disastrous, but, if the class pattern prevents the Russian intellectual from participating in life and keeps him too far removed from opposition circles, this will be a serious loss for all those who are compelled to fight for legal forms separately from a working class that has not yet advanced its political aims. The political innocence that the Russian Marxist intellectual conceals behind his considered judgements on political themes may play havoc with him.

46. A PROTEST BY RUSSIAN SOCIAL DEMOCRATS (AUGUST 1899)[206]

V.I. Lenin

A meeting of Social Democrats, seventeen in number, held in a certain locality, unanimously accepted the following resolution and decided to publish it and submit it to all their comrades for their consideration.

Recently a tendency has been observed among Russian Social Democrats to depart from the fundamental principles of Russian social democracy that were proclaimed both by its founders and foremost fighters, the members of the Emancipation of Labour Group, and by the social democratic publications of the Russian workers' organisations of the nineties. The *Credo* reproduced below, which purports to express the basic views of certain (the so-called 'young') Russian Social Democrats, represents an attempt at a systematic and definite exposition of the 'new views'. There follows the full text of the *Credo*:

[See Document no. 45]

We do not know if there are many Russian Social Democrats who share these views. But there is no doubt that, generally speaking, ideas of this kind do have their adherents and, for this reason, we feel bound to protest categorically against such views and to warn all our comrades against [a position] that threatens to deflect Russian social democracy from the path that it has already charted, i.e. the formation of an independent political workers' party that is inseparable from the class struggle of the proletariat and that has as its immediate task the achievement of political liberty.

The *Credo* cited above presents, firstly, a 'brief description of the course of the development of the workers' movement in the West' and, secondly, 'conclusions for Russia'.

Above all, the authors of the *Credo* have a completely false conception of the history of the Western European workers' movement. It is not true to say that the working class in the West has not participated in the struggle for political liberty or in political revolutions. The history of Chartism[207] and the revolutions of 1848 in France, Germany and Austria prove the opposite. It is completely untrue to say that 'Marxism emerged as the theoretical expression of prevailing practice: of the political struggle predominating over the economic'. On the contrary, 'Marxism' emerged at a time when non-political socialism (Owenism, 'Fourierism', 'true socialism',[208] etc.) was the prevailing practice and *The Manifesto of the Communist Party* came out against non-political socialism straight away. Even when Marxism came out fully armed with theory (*Capital*) and organised the celebrated International Working Men's Association, the political struggle was by no means the prevailing practice (narrow trade-unionism in England, anarchism and Proudhonism[209] in the Latin countries). In Germany the great historical service rendered by Lassalle[210] consisted in his transformation of the working class from an appendage of the liberal bourgeoisie into an independent political party. Marxism joined the economic and political struggle of the working class into a single indissoluble whole, and the attempt by authors of the *Credo* to separate these forms of struggle is one of their most inept and unfortunate departures from Marxism.

Furthermore, the authors of the *Credo* also have an entirely false conception of the present state of the Western European workers' movement and of the theory of Marxism under whose banner that movement marches. To talk of a 'crisis of Marxism' is to repeat the nonsensical phrases of bourgeois hacks who do all they can to blow up every disagreement between Socialists and turn it into a schism between socialist parties. The notorious 'Bernsteinism', in the sense in which it is understood by the general public at large and the authors of the *Credo* in particular, marks an attempt to narrow the theory of Marxism, an attempt to transform the revolutionary workers' party into a reformist one, and this attempt, as was to be expected, has met with clear condemnation from the majority of German Social Democrats.[211] Opportunist tendencies have repeatedly manifested themselves in German social democracy, and on every occasion they have been repudiated by the Party, which faithfully preserves the tenets of revolutionary international social democracy. We are certain that any attempt to translate opportunist views to Russia will meet with an equally determined rejection from the vast majority of Russian Social Democrats.

Similarly there can be no question of a 'radical change in the practical activity' of the West European workers' party, despite what the authors of the *Credo* say: the tremendous importance of the economic struggle of the proletariat and the necessity for this struggle were recognised by Marxism from the very outset. Even in the forties Marx and Engels were engaged in polemics against the Utopian Socialists[212] who denied the importance of this struggle.

When the International Working Men's Association was formed about twenty years later,[213] the question of the importance of workers' trade unions and the economic struggle was raised at its very first congress, in Geneva, in 1866. The resolution adopted at that congress specifically mentioned the importance of the economic struggle, warning Socialists and workers, on the one hand, against overestimating its importance (noticeable among English workers at that time), and, on the other hand, against underestimating its importance (noticeable among the French and Germans, especially the Lassalleans). The resolution recognised that workers' trade unions were not only a natural but also a necessary phenomenon, as long as capitalism existed, and an extremely important means of organising the working class in its day-to-day struggle with capital, and of abolishing wage labour. The resolution recognised that workers' trade unions should not devote their attention exclusively to the 'immediate struggle against capital' and should not be hived off from the general political and social movement of the working class; they should not pursue 'narrow' aims, but should strive for the universal emancipation of the millions of oppressed workers. Since then this question has arisen many times, and will of course arise again and again, within the workers' parties of various countries: whether to devote more or less attention at a given moment to the economic or to the political struggle of the proletariat. But the general question, or the question of principle, remains the one posed by Marxism. The conviction that the united class struggle of the proletariat must join together the political and economic struggle has passed into the flesh and blood of international social democracy. The experience of history bears incontrovertible further witness to the fact that the absence of political liberty or the restriction of the political rights of the proletariat always make it necessary to put the political struggle first.

Still less can there be any talk of any significant change in the attitude of the workers' party towards other opposition parties. In this respect, too, Marxism has indicated the proper line, one that is as far removed from exaggerating the importance of politics as it is from conspiracy (Blanquism, etc.) and from belittling politics or reducing it to opportunist, reformist social patching-up (anarchism, utopian and petty-bourgeois socialism, state socialism, professorial socialism,[214] etc.). The proletariat should strive to found independent workers' political parties whose principal aim must be the seizure of political power by the proletariat for the purpose of organising a socialist society. The working class should not regard other classes and parties as a 'single reactionary mass': on the contrary, it should take part in all political and social life, support the progressive classes and parties against the reactionary ones, support any revolutionary movement against the existing order, defend the interests of every oppressed race or nationality, every persecuted religion, disenfranchised sex, etc. The arguments that the authors of the *Credo* advance on this subject merely reveal a desire to obscure the class character of the struggle of the proletariat, weaken this struggle by a meaningless 'recognition of society' and reduce revolutionary Marxism to a trivial reformist tendency. We are convinced that the vast majority of Russian Social Democrats will resolutely repudiate such a distortion of the fundamental principles of social democracy. Their mistaken references to the West European workers' movement lead the authors of the *Credo* to still more mistaken 'conclusions for Russia'.

The assertion that the Russian working class 'has not yet advanced its political aims' simply reveals an ignorance of the Russian revolutionary movement. Even the North Russian Workers' Union, founded in 1878, and the South Russian Workers' Union, founded in 1875,[215] put forward the demand for political liberty. After the [period of] reaction in the eighties, the working class repeatedly put forward the same demand in the nineties. The assertion that 'talk of an independent workers' political party is nothing but the result of transplanting alien aims and alien achievements to our soil' simply reveals a complete failure to understand the role of the Russian working class and the most essential tasks of Russian social democracy. Clearly the *Credo*'s own programme inclines to the view that the working class, following the 'line of least resistance', should confine itself to the economic struggle, while the 'liberal opposition elements' fight, with the Marxists' 'participation', for 'legal forms'. The realisation of such a programme would be tantamount to the political suicide of Russian social democracy: it would greatly retard and debase the Russian workers' movement and the Russian revolutionary movement (for us the two concepts are identical). The very fact that a programme like this could appear shows how well-founded were the fears expressed by one of the foremost warriors of Russian social democracy, P.B. Akselrod, when, at the end of 1897, he wrote of the possibility of this prospect:

> The workers' movement stays in the narrow rut of the purely economic conflicts between the workers and the employers and is itself, on the whole, devoid of any political character, while the advanced strata of the proletariat follow the revolutionary circles and groups of the so-called intelligentsia in the struggle for political liberty.[216]

Russian Social Democrats must declare determined war on the whole body of ideas that find their expression in the *Credo*, because these ideas lead straight to the realisation of this prospect. Russian Social Democrats must devote all their efforts to realising another prospect outlined by P.B. Akselrod in these words:

> The other prospect is that social democracy organises the Russian proletariat into an independent political party that fights for liberty *partly side by side and in alliance* with bourgeois revolutionary groups (in as far as they exist) and partly by recruiting directly into its ranks or securing the following of the most democratically inclined and revolutionary elements among the intelligentsia.[217]

At the time that P.B. Akselrod wrote these lines, the declarations made by Social Democrats in Russia clearly demonstrated that the vast majority of them showed the same view. It is true that one Petersburg paper, *Rabochaya Mysl*,[218] seemed to incline towards the ideas of the authors of the *Credo*, unfortunately expressing, in the leading article setting out its programme (no. 1, October 1897), the completely mistaken idea, and one that runs counter to social democracy, that the 'economic basis of the movement' may be 'obscured by the attempt to keep the political ideal constantly in mind'. But at the same time another St Petersburg workers' newspaper, the *S. Peterburgskii Rabochii Listok* (no. 2, September 1897),[219] emphatically expressed the view that 'the overthrow of the autocracy . . . can only be achieved by a strongly organised workers' party with a large membership, and that, in organising themselves into a strong party, the workers will 'emancipate themselves and the whole of Russia from all political and economic oppression'. A third newspaper, *Rabochaya Gazeta*[220] wrote in its leading article in issue no. 2 (November 1897): 'The fight against the autocratic government for political liberty is the most urgent task of the Russian workers' movement.' 'The Russian workers' movement will increase its strength tenfold if it acts as a single harmonious whole with a common name and a well-knit organisation.' 'The separate workers' circles should combine into a single common party.' 'The Russian workers' party will be a social democratic party.' That the vast majority of Russian Social Democrats fully shared precisely these views of *Rabochaya Gazeta* is obvious from the fact that the congress of Russian Social Democrats that met in the spring of 1898 formed the Russian Social Democratic Labour Party, published its manifesto and recognised *Rabochaya Gazeta* as the official party organ.[221] Thus, the authors of the *Credo* are taking a colossal step backwards from the stage of development that Russian social democracy has already reached and that it has enshrined in the *Manifesto of the Russian Social Democratic Labour Party*. As frenzied persecution by the Russian government has led to the present situation in which the party's activity has temporarily subsided and its official organ has ceased to appear, it is the task of all Russian Social Democrats to devote all their efforts to the final consolidation of the party, to the drafting of a party programme and to the revival of its official organ. In view of the ideological vacillations evidenced by the appearance of programmes like the above-mentioned *Credo*, we consider it particularly necessary to underline the following basic principles that were expounded in the *Manifesto* and that have immense significance for Russian social democracy. Firstly, Russian social democracy 'desires to be, and to remain, the class movement of the organised working masses'. From this it follows that the motto of social democracy should be: aid for the workers not only in the economic but also in the political struggle; agitation not only in connection with immediate economic needs but also with every manifestation of political oppression; propaganda, not only for the ideas of scientific socialism, but also propaganda for democratic ideas. Only the theory of revolutionary Marxism can be the banner of the class movement of the workers and Russian social democracy must concern itself with the further development and implementation [of this theory], at the same time safeguarding it from all the distortions and vulgarisations to which 'fashionable theories' are so often subjected. (The successes of revolutionary social democracy in Russia have already made Marxism into a 'fashionable' theory.) In concentrating all its efforts at the present time on activity among factory workers and miners, social democracy must not forget that, with the expansion of the movement, domestic servants, handicraftsmen, agricultural labourers and the millions of ruined and starving peasants must join the ranks of the movement that it is organising.

Secondly, 'On its own sturdy shoulders the Russian working class must, and will, carry the cause of the achievement of political liberty.'[222] Setting as its immediate task the overthrow of absolutism, social democracy must act as the foremost fighter for democracy and in this capacity alone must give every support to all the democratic elements in the Russian population, winning them as allies. Only an independent workers' party can be a firm bulwark in the struggle with autocracy, and by allying themselves with such a party and by supporting it that all those others fighting for political liberty can play an active part.

Thirdly and finally,

As both a socialist movement and a tendency, the Russian Social Democratic Party is furthering the cause and the traditions of the whole preceding revolutionary movement in Russia; in defining the achievement of political liberty as the most important of the immediate tasks facing the party, social democracy is pursuing the goal clearly proclaimed by the still glorious activists of the old Narodnaya Volya.[223]

The traditions of the whole preceding revolutionary movement in Russia dictate that social democracy should at the present time concentrate all its efforts on the organisation of the party, on strengthening its internal discipline and developing its technique for conspiratorial work. If the activists of the old Narodnaya Volya could play an enormous role in Russian history, despite the narrow range of social strata that supported the few heroes, despite the fact that revolutionary theory was by no means the banner of the movement, then social democracy, which relies on the class struggle of the proletariat, can become invincible. 'The Russian proletariat will cast off the yoke of autocracy, so that it may continue the struggle with capitalism and the bourgeoisie with still greater energy until the complete victory of socialism.'[224]

We invite all the social democratic groups and all the workers' circles in Russia to discuss both the *Credo* quoted above and our resolution and to express a definite opinion on the question raised, so that all differences may be resolved and the work of organising and consolidating the Russian Social Democratic Labour Party may be accelerated.

The resolutions of groups and circles may be communicated to the Union of Russian Social Democrats Abroad, which, on the basis of Point 10 of the resolution of the Congress of Russian Social Democrats in 1898 is a part of the Russian Social Democratic Party and its representative abroad.[225]

47. THE URGENT TASKS OF OUR MOVEMENT (OCTOBER/NOVEMBER 1900)[226]

V.I. Lenin

Russian social democracy has more than once declared that the immediate task of the Russian workers' party should be the overthrow of the autocracy and the achievement of political liberty. This was the view, more than fifteen years ago, of the members of the Emancipation of Labour Group, the representatives of Russian social democracy; this was the view two and a half years ago, of the representatives of the Russian social democratic organisations that, in the spring of 1898, formed the Russian Social Democratic Labour Party.[227] But, despite these repeated assertions, the question of the political tasks of social democracy in Russia is once more achieving prominence today. Many representatives of our movement are expressing their doubts about the correctness of the solution to the question that has already been mentioned. They say that the economic struggle is of paramount importance; they relegate the political tasks of the proletariat to second place, narrow these tasks down and restrict them, and they even say that to talk of forming an independent workers' party in Russia is merely to repeat the words of foreigners and that the workers should carry on only the economic struggle and leave politics to the intelligentsia in alliance with the liberals. This latest profession of a new article of faith (the notorious *Credo*)[228] amounts to a confession that the Russian proletariat has not yet come of age, and to a complete rejection of the social democratic programme. *Rabochaya Mysl* (especially in its *Separate Supplement*) has expressed essentially the same view.[229] Russian social democracy is passing through a period of vacillation, a period of doubt verging on abstentionism. On the one hand the workers' movement is losing touch with socialism: the workers are given assistance to carry on the economic struggle but nothing, or next to nothing, is done to explain to them socialist aims and the political tasks of the movement as a whole. On the other hand, socialism is losing touch with the workers' movement: Russian Socialists are again beginning to say with increasing frequency that the intelligentsia will have to carry on the struggle against the· government entirely from its own resources, because the workers are confining themselves to the economic struggle.

In our opinion, three circumstances have prepared the ground for this sad state of affairs. Firstly, in their early activity the Russian Social Democrats confined themselves solely to work in propaganda circles. When we went over to agitation among the masses we could not always stop ourselves from going to the other extreme. Secondly, in our early activity we frequently had to fight for our right to exist with the *Narodovoltsy*, who understood by 'politics' an activity that was divorced from the workers' movement and who reduced politics to mere conspiratorial struggle. In rejecting this kind of politics, the Social Democrats went to the other extreme and relegated politics to second place overall. Thirdly, because of their isolated activity in small local workers' circles, the Social Democrats did not pay enough attention to the need to organise a revolutionary party which would combine all the activities of local groups and make it possible to put revolutionary work on the right lines. The predominance of this isolated work is naturally connected with the predominance of the economic struggle.

These circumstances resulted in an enthusiasm for only one side of the movement. The 'Economist' tendency (in as far as we can call it a 'tendency') has led to attempts to elevate this narrowness into a special theory, to attempt to utilise to this end fashionable Bernsteinism and the fashionable 'critique of Marxism' that peddles the old bourgeois ideas under a new name. These attempts alone have given rise to the danger of a weakening in the link between the workers' movement and Russian social democracy, the foremost fighter for political liberty. And the most urgent task of our movement is to strengthen this link.

Social democracy is the fusion of the workers' movement with socialism. Its task is not to serve the workers' movement passively at each of its separate stages but to represent the interests of the movement as a whole, to direct this movement towards its ultimate goal, its political tasks, and to safeguard its political and ideological independence. Divorced from social democracy, the workers' movement degenerates and inevitably becomes bourgeois: in carrying on the purely economic struggle, the working class loses its political independence, becomes an appendage of the other parties and betrays the great principle that 'the emancipation of the workers should be a matter for the workers themselves'. In every country there has been a period when the workers' movement and socialism existed separately, each going its own way – and in every country this separation weakened both socialism and the workers' movement; in every country only the fusion of socialism with the workers' movement has created a lasting basis for the one and for the other. But in every country this fusion of socialism with the workers' movement has evolved historically, in a particular way, in accordance with the time and the place. In Russia the need to fuse socialism with the workers' movement was proclaimed in theory long ago – but this fusion is only now being put into practice. This evolutionary process is a very difficult one and there is nothing particularly surprising in the fact that it is accompanied by vacillations and doubts.

What lesson can we learn from the past?

The whole history of Russian socialism has led to a situation in which its most urgent task is the struggle against the autocratic government, the achievement of political liberty; our socialist movement has, as it were, concentrated itself in the struggle against autocracy. On the other hand, history has shown that the divorce between socialist thought and the most advanced representatives of the working classes is far greater in Russia than in other countries, and that such a divorce condemns the Russian revolutionary movement to impotence. From this it emerges that the task that Russian social democracy is called upon to fulfil is to instil socialist ideas and political self-consciousness into the mass of the proletariat and to organise a revolutionary party that is inseparably linked to the spontaneous workers' movement. Russian social democracy has already done a great deal in this respect; but even more remains to be done. With the growth of the movement the field of activity for Social Democrats becomes ever broader, the work becomes ever more varied, and the ever-increasing number of activists in the movement concentrate their efforts on carrying out the various particular tasks brought to light by the everyday needs of propaganda and agitation. This phenomenon is quite natural and inevitable but it compels us to pay special attention to ensuring that these particular tasks and concepts of struggle do not become an end in themselves and that preparatory work is not regarded as our main and sole work.

To facilitate the political development and the political organisation of the working class – that is our principal and fundamental task. Those who relegate this task to second place, those who refuse to subordinate to it all particular tasks and concepts of struggle, are set on a false path and cause serious harm to the movement. It is being relegated, first of all, by those who call upon revolutionaries to carry on the struggle with the government through isolated conspiratorial circles divorced from the workers' movement. It is being relegated, secondly, by those who restrict the content and scope of political propaganda, agitation and organisation, those who think it right and proper to treat the workers to 'politics' only at exceptional moments in their lives, only on ceremonial occasions, those who are too concerned to substitute demands for particular concessions from the autocracy for the political struggle against autocracy, and who do not take sufficient care to ensure that these demands for particular concessions are elevated into the systematic and irreversible struggle of a revolutionary workers' party against autocracy.

'Organise!', *Rabochaya Mysl* and all the followers of the 'Economist' tendency repeat to the workers in different ways. We, of course, wholly endorse this call but we shall certainly add: organise not only in mutual benefit societies, strike funds and workers' circles; organise also into a political party, organise for the decisive battle against the autocratic government and against the whole of capitalist society. Without such organisation the proletariat is not capable of rising to conscious class struggle, without such organisation the workers' movement is condemned to impotence and, with only funds, circles and societies, the working class will never manage to fulfil the great historic mission that has befallen it: to emancipate itself and the whole Russian people from its political and economic slavery. There is not a single class in history that has attained power without producing its own political leaders, its most advanced representatives, who are able to organise the movement and lead it. And the Russian working class has already shown that it is capable of producing such people: the widespread struggle of the Russian workers in the course of the past five or six years has demonstrated what enormous potential revolutionary forces there are concealed in the working class and shown how the most ruthless government persecution does not diminish, but increases, the number of workers who long for socialism, political consciousness and political struggle. The congress held by our comrades in 1898 correctly defined our tasks and was not merely repeating the words of others, not just expressing the enthusiasm of the 'intelligentsia' . . . We must resolutely set about fulfilling these tasks, discussing the question of the programme, organisation and tactics of the party in turn. We have already stated our views on the fundamental propositions of our programme and this is, of course, not the place to develop these propositions in detail. We intend to devote a series of articles in forthcoming issues to organisational questions.[230] For us, this is one of the most contentious issues. In this respect we lag far behind the old activists of the Russian revolutionary movement. We must frankly admit this defect and direct all our efforts to devise more secret methods in our work, to propagandise systematically rules for our conduct, methods of deceiving the gendarmes and slipping out of the police net. We must train people who will devote not just their free evenings but their whole lives to the revolution, we must build up an organisation that is large enough to allow a strict division of labour between the different aspects of our work. Finally, as far as tactics are concerned, we shall limit ourselves here to the following: social democracy does not tie its hands, it does not restrict its activity to any one preconceived plan or concept of political struggle: it recognises all methods of struggle as long as they correspond to the forces at the party's disposal and facilitate the attainment of the best possible results in the particular circumstances. If there is a strongly organised party, a single strike may be turned into a political demonstration, a political victory over the government. If there is a strongly organised party, a revolt in one particular district may grow into a victorious revolution. We should remember that our struggles with the government for particular demands and the winning of particular concessions are only minor skirmishes with the enemy, encounters between outposts, whereas the decisive battle is still ahead. In front of us, in all its strength, stands the enemy fortress, from which shot and shell rain down on us, carrying off our best fighters. We must take this fortress and we shall take it if the entire strength of the awakening proletariat is joined with the entire strength of the Russian revolutionaries into a single party that will attract everything in Russia that is vital and honest. And only then will the prophecy of the great Russian worker revolutionary, Peter Alekseev, be fulfilled: 'The muscular arm of the millions of working people shall be raised and the yoke of despotism, guarded by soldiers' bayonets, shall be reduced to dust!'[231]

48.   WHERE TO BEGIN? (MAY 1901)[232]

V.I. Lenin

In recent years the question 'What is to be done?' has confronted Russian Social Democrats with particular force. It is not a matter of which path we should choose (as it was in the late 90s) but of what practical steps we should take along a known path and how they should be taken. It is a matter of a system and plan of practical work. And we must confess that we have still not resolved this question of the character and methods of struggle which is fundamental for a party of practical activity and still provokes serious disagreements that reveal a deplorable ideological instability and vacillation. On the one hand, the 'Economist' trend, far from dying out, is still trying to curtail and restrict the work of political organisation and agitation. On the other hand, unprincipled eclecticism is rearing its head again, aping every new 'trend' and incapable of distinguishing between immediate demands and the fundamental tasks and permanent needs of the movement as a whole. As we know, this trend has built its nest in *Rabochee Delo*. Its latest declaration of 'programme', a bombastic article under the bombastic title 'A Historic Turn' (*Listok 'Rabochego Dela'*, no. 6),[233] confirms our characterisation particularly vividly. Only the other day there was a flirtation with 'Economism', anger over the resolute condemnation of *Rabochaya Mysl*, and Plekhanov's postulation of the question of the struggle against autocracy was being 'toned down'. But today we are citing Liebknecht's words: 'If the circumstances change in twenty-four hours, then the tactic too must be changed in twenty-four hours.' We are talking about 'a strong fighting organisation' for direct attack, for storming the autocracy, about 'broad revolutionary political agitation among the masses (how energetic we are now – both revolutionary and political!), about the 'constant call for street protest', about the 'organisation of street demonstrations of a pronounced (sic!) political character', etc. etc.

We could of course express our satisfaction at the fact that *Rabochee Delo* has so rapidly adopted the programme that we put forward in the first issue of *Iskra*, calling for the creation of a strong organised party that aims not just at gaining particular concessions but also at conquering the fortress of the autocracy itself, but the absence of any firm point of view among [these people] is enough to undermine our satisfaction completely.

Of course, *Rabochee Delo* mentions the name of Liebknecht in vain.[234] The tactic of agitation in relation to some special question or the tactic for the conduct of some detail of party organisation may change in twenty-four hours, but one's view of the need – generally, constantly and absolutely – for an organisation of struggle and political agitation among the mass may change in twenty-four hours, or for that matter, twenty-four months only if one has no principles at all. It is laughable to plead different circumstances and different periods: working for the creation of a fighting organisation and the conduct of political agitation are essential under any 'drab and peaceful' circumstances, in any period of 'decline in revolutionary spirit'. Moreover, it is in precisely these circumstances and precisely these periods that work of this kind is especially necessary since at moments of explosion and outburst it is already too late to create an organisation: it must be at the ready, prepared to act at a moment's notice. 'Change the tactic in twenty-four hours!' But, in order to change the tactic, you must first have a tactic and, without a strong organisation skilled in waging the political struggle under all circumstances and at all times, there can be no question of the systematic plan of action, illumined by firm principles and steadfastly carried out, that alone deserves the name of tactic. Let us look at the matter. We are now told that the 'historic moment' has presented our party with 'a completely new' question, the question of terror. Yesterday it was the question of political organisation and agitation that was 'completely new', today it is the question of terror. Is it not strange to hear people who have so obviously forgotten who their friends are holding forth on a radical change in tactic?

Fortunately, *Rabochee Delo* is wrong. The question of terror is not a new question at all: it is enough to recall briefly the established views of Russian social democracy.

We have never renounced, and cannot renounce, terror in principle. This is one form of military action that may be quite appropriate and even essential at a certain point in the battle, given a certain state of the troops and the existence of certain conditions. But the essence of the matter is precisely the fact that terror is at the present time being promoted not as a *modus operandi* for an army in the field, one that is closely connected with and integrated into the whole system of struggle, but as an independent method of occasional attack that is unrelated to any army. Given the weakness of local revolutionary organisations and the absence of a central body, terror could not be anything else. That is why we declare emphatically that in present conditions this method of struggle is inopportune and inappropriate: it distracts the most active fighters from their real task, which is most important for the interests of the movement as a whole, and it disorganises the forces of the revolution rather than those of the government. Remember recent events: before our very eyes the broad masses of workers and the 'common people' of the towns pressed forward in the struggle, while the revolutionaries had no staff of leaders and organisers. Is there not a danger in these circumstances that the most energetic revolutionaries will turn to terror and weaken the fighting detachments, on whom alone we can pin serious hopes? Is there not a danger that the link will be broken between the revolutionary organisations and the fragmented masses of the discontented, the protesting and those disposed to struggle, who are weak precisely because they are fragmented? Yet this link is the sole guarantee of our success. Far be it from us to deny the significance of individual heroic blows, but it is our duty to warn with all our energy against a passion for terror, against accepting it as the principal and basic method of struggle, as very many people are so inclined to do at present. Terror can never be a regular military *modus operandi*: at best it can serve only as one of the methods employed in the decisive storming action. But can we *issue the call* for such a storming action at the present moment? *Rabochee Delo* apparently thinks that we can. At any rate, it exclaims: 'Form assault columns!' But this again is more enthusiasm than reason. The main body of our military forces is composed of volunteers and insurgents. We have only a few small detachments of regular troops and even these are not mobilised, they are not coordinated with one another, they have not been trained to form columns at all, let alone assault columns. In these circumstances it must be clear to anyone who is capable of appreciating the general conditions of our struggle and who is mindful of them at every 'turn' in the course of historical events that at the present moment our slogan cannot be, 'To the assault', but has to be, 'Lay siege to the enemy fortress.' In other words the immediate task for our party cannot be to summon all available forces for an attack now but to call for the formation of a revolutionary organisation that is capable of uniting all forces and guiding the movement not just in name but in reality, i.e. [an organisation] that is always ready to support any protest and any outburst and to use it to build up and consolidate the fighting forces suitable for the decisive battle.

The lesson of the events of February and March[235] is so striking that it is now almost impossible to find any disagreement in principle with this conclusion. But what we need at the present time is a solution to the problem, not in principle but in practice. We must not only be clear on the kind of organisation that is needed and the kind of work it is to do, we must draw up a definite *plan* for the organisation so that we can embark on its formation from all sides. In view of the urgent importance of the question, we for our part venture to submit for the consideration of our comrades a draft plan to be developed by us in greater detail in a brochure that is now being prepared for publication.[236]

In our opinion the starting point for our activities, the first practical step towards the creation of the desired organisation or the main thread which, if followed, would enable us to develop, deepen and broaden that organisation steadily must be the establishment of an all-Russian political newspaper. We need a newspaper more than anything: without it we cannot conduct the systematic all-round propaganda and agitation, consistent in principle, that is the permanent and principal task of social democracy in general, the pressing task of the moment, when an interest in politics and in questions of socialism has been awakened among the broadest possible strata of the population. Never has the need been felt so acutely as it has today for reinforcing fragmented agitation by means of individual action, local leaflets, pamphlets, etc., by the kind of generalised and systematic agitation that can only be carried out with the aid of a periodical press. It would hardly be an exaggeration to say that the frequency and regularity with which a newspaper is published (and distributed) may serve as a precise measure of how well this cardinal and most essential branch of our militant activity is organised. Furthermore, our newspaper must be an all-Russian one. If we do not succeed, and as long as we do not succeed, in combining our pressure on the people and on the government by means of the printed word, it would be utopian to think of combining other means, more complex, more difficult, but at the same time more decisive, for exerting pressure. Our movement, in both ideological and practical organisational respects, suffers more than anything from its fragmentation, from the almost complete immersion of the vast majority of Social Democrats in purely local work which narrows their outlook, the scope of their activities and their conspiratorial skill and preparedness. It is in precisely this fragmentation that we must look for the deepest roots of the instability and vacillation that we mentioned above. The *first* step in eliminating this shortcoming, in transforming the several local movements into a single all-Russian movement must be the establishment of an all-Russian newspaper.

Finally, our newspaper must, without fail, be a *political* one. Without a political organ, a political movement worthy of the name is inconceivable in contemporary Europe. Without [such a newspaper] it would be absolutely impossible for us to fulfil our task, to concentrate all the elements of political discontent and protest and thereby to fertilise the revolutionary movement of the proletariat. We have taken the first step, we have awakened in the working class a passion for 'economic' factory revelations. We must take the next step: we must awaken in every stratum of the population that is at all politically conscious a passion for *political* revelations. We must not be discouraged by the fact that the voices of political revelations are today so weak, so timid and infrequent. The reason for this is by no means a wholesale submission to police despotism. The reason for this is that the people who are willing and able to make revelations have no tribune to speak from, no audience of eager and encouraging orators, nowhere among the people do they see the force towards which it would be worth directing their complaint against the 'omnipotent' Russian government. But now all this is changing very rapidly. There is such a force — the revolutionary proletariat which has already proved its readiness not just to listen and support the call to political struggle, but also to throw itself bravely into the battle. We are now in a position to provide a tribune for the nation-wide exposure of the tsarist government and it is our duty to do this. That tribune must be a social democratic newspaper. The Russian working class, as distinct from the other classes and strata of Russian society, displays a constant interest in political knowledge and manifests a constantly (not only in times of particular unrest) enormous demand for illegal literature. When such mass demand is evident, when the training of experienced revolutionary leaders has already begun, when the concentration of the working class makes it effectively master in the workers' districts of the big city, in the factory settlements and communities, it is quite feasible for the proletariat to establish a political newspaper. Through the proletariat the newspaper will penetrate to the urban bourgeoisie, the rural handicraftsmen and peasants and will become a real people's political newspaper.

The role of a newspaper is not, however, limited solely to the dissemination of ideas, to political education and to the enlistment of political allies. A newspaper is not only a collective propagandist and a collective agitator, it is also a collective organiser. In this last respect it may be likened to the scaffolding erected around a building under construction which marks the contours of the structure and facilitates communication between the different builders, helping them to distribute the work and to view the common results achieved by their organised labour. With the aid of the newspaper, and through it, a permanent organisation will naturally take shape that will engage not only in local but also in regular general work and will train its members to follow political events attentively, assess their significance for and influence on the various strata of the population, and develop effective means for the revolutionary party to influence those events. The purely technical task of ensuring that the newspaper is regularly supplied with copy and regularly distributed will necessitate the creation of a network of local agents of the united party, agents who will maintain constant contact with one another, know the general state of affairs, get used to performing regularly their detailed functions in all-Russian work, testing their strength in the organisation of various revolutionary actions. This network of agents[237] will form the skeleton of precisely the kind of organisation that we need: large enough to cover the whole country, sufficiently broad and varied to effect a strict and detailed division of labour, sufficiently self-possessed to be able to conduct its *own* work steadily under any circumstances, in any 'sudden turns' and unexpected contingencies, sufficiently flexible to be able, on the one hand, to avoid an open battle against an overwhelming enemy, when [the enemy] has concentrated all his forces on one spot, and yet, on the other, to take advantage of his unwieldiness to attack him when and where he least expects it. Today we are faced with the relatively easy task of supporting the students who are demonstrating on the streets of our big cities. Tomorrow, perhaps, we will have a more difficult task: for example, supporting the unemployed movement in a particular district. The day after we shall have to be at our posts to play a revolutionary part in a peasant uprising. Today we must make use of the political tension arising from the government's campaign against the Zemstvo. Tomorrow we shall have to support popular indignation against some tsarist *bashi-bazouk* on the rampage and help, through boycott, badgering, demonstrations, etc., to teach him a lesson so that he will be forced into open retreat. Such a degree of combat-readiness can be developed only through the constant activity undertaken by a regular army. If we join forces to produce a common newspaper, this work will train and promote not just the most skilful propagandists but also the most capable organisers, the most talented party leaders, capable, at the right moment, of producing the slogan for the decisive battle and of taking the lead in it.

In conclusion, a few words to avoid possible misunderstanding. We have talked the whole time only about systematic planned preparation but it is by no means our intention to imply that the autocracy can be overthrown only by a regular siege or an organised assault. Such a view would be a doctrinaire absurdity. On the contrary, it is quite possible, and historically much more likely, that the autocracy will collapse under the impact of one of the spontaneous outbursts or unforeseen political complications that constantly threaten it from all sides. But no political party wishing to avoid adventurism could base its activities on the expectation of such outbursts and complications. We must go our own way and steadfastly carry on our regular work, and the less we rely on the unexpected, the less likely we are to be caught unawares by any 'historic turns'.

49.   OUR NEW PROGRAMME (FEBRUARY 1902)[238]

Rabochee Delo

The social emancipation of the working class is impossible without its political emancipation.

Our new programme

Instructions to the editorial staff of 'Rabochee Delo'

Introduction
The First Congress of the reorganised Union of Russian Social Democrats (in the autumn of 1898) gave the editorial staff of *Rabochee Delo* the instructions that underlie its programme.[239]

The basic purpose of these instructions was to underline the need for a close link between the Social Democrats and the broad mass movement of the proletariat. The basic concent of these instructions was the discovery of the means by which the mass could be drawn into active political struggle.

The congress recognises that this purpose and this content of the instructions of 1898 are also valid for the present.

But, in view of the fact that since then the social democratic workers' movement has grown considerably in both ideological and practical terms, and that broader practical tasks have emerged to confront social democracy, the Third Congress has revised the instructions of 1898.

General principles
The Union of Russian Social Democrats Abroad acts on the basis of international scientific socialism in accordance with the *Manifesto* of the Russian Social Democratic Labour Party,[240] of which it is both a part and the foreign representative.

Social democratic activity may be expedient only in conditions when it is guided not merely by the general principles of scientific socialism, but: (1) by general political conditions and the concrete relationships between the social classes in a particular country and: (2) by the stage of development of the workers' movement.

The political growth of the workers' movement in Russia
As the struggle of the workers for what they recognise to be their interests develops and spreads, the mass workers' movement in Russia, merging with social democracy, moves on to an ever-broader path of revolutionary class struggle and becomes the increasingly dominant factor in Russian social life.

The development of the workers' movement under the banner of social democracy has made the demand for political rights increasingly tangible to the workers. But, as these rights are essentially incompatible with the autocratic regime, the overthrow of autocracy is already becoming the immediate and concrete aim of the struggle in the consciousness of the working mass. Thus, the overthrow of autocracy, which has always been an objective of the programme of Russian social democracy, arising from the whole course of Russian history and bequeathed by the earlier revolutionary movements, now passes from the field of social democratic propaganda to the field of the immediate revolutionary struggle.

The economic and political struggle

Under the autocratic regime in Russia all forms and areas of the struggle of the proletariat should fall within the sphere of activity of social democracy, which also directs them towards its immediate political aim.

If, from the point of view of social revolution, 'economical emancipation of the working class is therefore the great end to which every political movement ought to be subordinated as a means' (the Statute of the International),[241] then, from the point of view of the future political revolution in Russia, the economic struggle is a means towards the immediate political aim of the Social Democratic Party – the achievement of a democratic constitution.

In view of the fact that the economic struggle, even in present conditions, may lead to a partial, albeit minimal, improvement in the social condition of the proletariat, at the same time improving its fighting position in the struggle for its political and social emancipation; in view of the fact that the Social Democratic Party is unthinkable without a close bond with the mass struggle of the proletariat; in view of the fact that in Russian conditions the separation of the political struggle from the economic struggle, even if such a possibility were to be admitted, would significantly paralyse the party's struggle for political freedom – in view of all this, social democracy should lead the economic struggle of the proletariat, protecting it at the same time from sectional, national etc. egoism and utilising it to revolutionise the working mass.

The means of political agitation

In Russia the most broadly suitable means of attracting the mass into the political movement is the economic struggle and it is on this basis that political agitation must be conducted; but there is no need to conduct political agitation from the very beginning solely on an economic basis.

Every phenomenon and event in social and political life, everything that affects the proletariat, either directly as a distinct class or as the vanguard of all revolutionary forces in the struggle for freedom, should serve as a pretext for political propaganda and agitation.

Individual rights and the overthrow of autocracy

Social democracy should promote and support the active protests of the workers for individual political rights such as the freedom to strike, to join a union, to assemble, freedom of speech and of the press and the inviolability of the person. Such protests are a powerful agitational method of struggle with autocracy, which is itself incompatible with the political rights of the proletariat, and also a method of popularising purely proletarian rights – which will facilitate the achievement of these rights simultaneously with the fall of autocracy.

By these same considerations we must generally make concrete the content of the democratic constitution in mass propaganda, underlining those elements of the constitution which define its democratic character.

Demonstrations

The Union recognises that at the present time demonstrations and protests are the best methods of political struggle. Organised demonstrations must be arranged. If the government resorts to violence against demonstrators, the congress recognises the advisability of answering violence with violence.

The May Day holiday

In Russia May Day serves as a day of demonstration for the proletariat against the autocratic regime and the capitalist order for a democratic constitution and the international demands of the proletariat.

Terror

The congress feels that systematic offensive terror is inappropriate. If individual acts of terrorism occur, these should be used to develop the political consciousness of the proletariat.

The organisational principle

In the interests of the successful development and unification of social democracy we must underline, develop and fight for the broad democratic principle in its party organisation; this is particularly important in view of the anti-democratic tendencies that are to be found in the ranks of our party.

The instructions quoted do not in themselves require a detailed commentary. In addition many of them include their motivation. It is left to us principally to define the relationship between the new instructions and the instructions of 1898, to point to the degree and character of the changes in the old programme of *Rabochee Delo.*

The introduction to the new instructions indicates the considerations that guided the congress in revising them. The healthy growth of the social democratic workers' movement in its ideological and practical aspects, which has brought broader practical tasks before social democracy – that is an adequate and convincing reason for re-examining the resolutions which comprise *the code of tactical positions for the current struggle.*

By this very characteristic our instructions, old and new, are distinguished from the party programme, which gives a general theoretical basis for our activity and sets out the general *aims* and *demands* of the party, whereas our instructions designate the *tasks and methods of the current struggle*. Hence, among other things, it is clear that the revision of the instructions of 1898 does not affect the views of the Union on the *party programme*. As before, the Union 'acts on the basis of international scientific socialism in accordance with the *Manifesto* of the Russian Social Democratic and Labour Party', in which the fundamental principles of the programme of our party are set out.

Obviously we have spread these principles in our propaganda, in *Rabochee Delo* and in our brochures, from the very beginning of the reorganised Union. As far as our view on the means and methods of the current struggle is concerned, that must change with the progressive growth of our social democratic movement.

Three years ago the Russian social democratic movement had scarcely set out on the path of political agitation. In many places it had not yet even gone beyond the confines of circle propaganda. Everywhere in agitational activity the *local* element took precedence over the *general*: the tasks of local struggle, bearing an economic character, drove the all-party tasks of the political struggle into the background. The limited success of the First Congress of the party in the sense of a real unification of social democratic organisations is explained by this embryonic condition of our movement in 1898. In such circumstances the Union congress of 1898 had to work out a programme which adequately guaranteed the progressive political development of the movement and in addition one which *could be immediately fulfilled* by what were, at that time at least, the strongest organisations.

It is not surprising if the instructions of 1898, which answered the demands of the struggle then, have since become out of date. But it is not their basic purpose nor their basic content that is out of date, but the view of the immediate tasks of the struggle, and in addition the formulation of the means of attracting the mass into active political struggle and – partly – the formulation of the means for this very struggle.

With the increase in the political tempo of our movement, with the revolutionising of broad sections of the proletariat who have recognised the inevitability of the struggle with autocracy, the all-party tasks begin to occupy a predominant place in the agitational activity of all our advanced organisations. The spring events of this year have shown vividly enough what revolutionary strength has already been gathered in the working mass. If our party in earlier years only awakened the mass to political life, only attracted it to the political struggle, now its urgent task is the appropriate utilisation of accumulated revolutionary strength for the overthrow of autocracy, that most vital obstacle in the struggle of the proletariat for its full social emancipation, for the triumph of socialism.

Faithful to the general spirit of the whole activity of the Union – the desire to respond to the demands of the social democratic struggle which is being accomplished in Russia, the Third Union Congress altered the instructions of 1898 in accordance with the new and higher tactical aims of our movement.

As is already clear from what has been said, the basic attitude of the Union towards tactics served as the criterion for the revision of the instructions. We have in mind the formulation of the conditions appropriate for social democratic struggle, which stands at the head of both the old and the new instructions (see the 2nd of the 'general conditions' of the instructions) – the only difference being that in the latter the basic view has been purged of the ephemeral references which in the earlier formulation obscured its true, permanent sense by considerations which applied only to the condition of the Russian social democratic movement at that time or which were expressed because of their novelty at that time. In the new formulation a clear reference to the 'general political conditions'[242] has been added; further, the 'essential demands of the Russian workers' movement at a certain stage of its development' have been replaced by a general universally applicable expression: 'the stage of development of the workers' movement'. Lastly, reference to the need 'to take account of the variety of local conditions and of the level of development of different sections of the working class' has been deleted. Such a reference would at the present time have been both superfluous and harmful. Superfluous, as far as the technical concepts of agitation are concerned, because all our organisations are sufficiently experienced in this respect; harmful, in as far as this reference could be interpreted to mean that the local element should be given precedence over the all-party tasks of the political struggle.

We are aware that the new instructions may turn out to be as far in *advance* of the movement as a whole as the instructions of 1898 were in advance of the general condition of the movement at that time. This, however, is not a weakness but a strength in the programme of an organ which is aimed at the whole of Russia, which bears in mind the interests of the movement as a whole, which places in the forefront the *general tasks of the party*. In any event the new code of tactical positions corresponds to the present 'stage of development of the workers' movement', by which we should of course understand the condition of the movement in the more advanced regions and among the more advanced sections of the working mass.

The focal point of the new instructions lies in the following thought: 'In this way the overthrow of autocracy . . . now passes from the field of social democratic propaganda to the field of the immediate revolutionary struggle.' This thought runs through all the tactical resolutions of the congress. All forms and spheres of the activity of social democracy, all the methods of party struggle are in one way or another linked with the 'immediate revolutionary struggle' for a democratic constitution.

It was in this spirit above all that the relationship between the economic and political struggle was formulated; in our old programme this was formulated vaguely and therefore somewhat contradictorily. On the other hand the new instructions are based more fully and boldly than the old ones on the need for social democracy to lead the economic struggle of the proletariat. If in 1898 it was still necessary to refer to the importance of the economic struggle for the 'development of a feeling of solidarity and class consciousness among the workers, etc.', now, in view of the fears which seized a well-known sector of the Russian Social

Democrats with regard to the economic struggle, we must emphasise the need for our party organisations to conduct a more widespread form of proletarian struggle. In 1898 it was necessary to advocate a form of influence on the working mass which was still relatively new at that time, in 1901 it seems necessary to defend from irrational fears what appears as an inexhaustible source of revolutionary energy for the proletariat and what serves as the most important factor in the qualitative and quantitative growth of the social democratic movement.

Further, the instructions of the last congress, recognising the whole political significance of the leadership of the economic struggle by social democracy, clearly indicate the full possibility of instigating political agitation distinct from the economic struggle. In addition they broaden the field of political agitation in all directions right up to those phenomena and events which concern the proletariat 'as the vanguard of all revolutionary forces in the struggle for freedom' – such as, for instance, student disturbances or the protests of those who are oppressed because of their nationality. Our readers know that in Union literature the student disturbances of 1899 and 1900–1 met with a most fervent response.[243] In just the same way we urged the committees of our party to universal protest against the crime of the autocratic government in Finland.[244] Thus on this question the new instructions do not introduce a new element into our publications but merely sanction the tactical views that we have held and that were however – although in another context – expressed on the instructions of 1898, declaring that 'every enemy of autocracy is a temporary ally of the working class in its struggle for emancipation'.[245]

The most important change has occurred in the formulation of the methods of political agitation in connection with the question of 'partial' or 'immediate' rights. The old programme stated: 'The struggle of the working class for these rights forms the immediate content of its struggle with tsarist autocracy, which will lead to the conquest of complete political freedom with the participation of the whole people on a basis of equal rights on the direction of the government, i.e. to the gaining of a democratic constitution.' Here we find expressed the entirely correct idea that, as the workers' movement develops, the destruction of the immediate political interests of the proletariat by the government and the defence of them by the proletariat serve as a powerful method of attracting it into the struggle with autocracy. But alongside this the old programme speaks of 'immediate political demands' and of 'immediate political rights', as a 'necessary condition for the further development of the workers' movement on all sides'. This expression, linked with the unfortunate epithet 'immediate' could give rise, and has given rise, to the interpretation that the *achievement* of 'immediate' rights is feasible under autocracy. That is why this point was amended to a reference to the agitational significance of protests for individual political rights. To eliminate such protests from our agitation would mean making two fatal errors. Firstly, we should be renouncing 'a powerful agitational means of struggle with autocracy'; for these protests are in themselves inevitably connected with the protest against the whole autocratic order, appearing just as a concrete pretext for *general political* protest. Second, we should be transgressing against the most important duty of social democracy, the duty to strive to *ensure for the proletariat the maximum of rights upon the fall of the autocracy*.

It is well known that in Western Europe the conquest of purely proletarian rights did not correspond to the introduction of the constitutional order. The right to strike and to form workers' unions did not exist for many years and even decades after the fall of autocracy. This resulted of course from the inadequate development of the economic struggle of the proletariat and of the proletarian struggle in general. The first to gain freedom of association were the English workers in 1824–5, because capitalism, and with it the struggle of the workers with the capitalists, developed first of all in England. It was, however, only the authorisation of strikes in France in 1864 that expedited the achievement of freedom of association in other countries: in Belgium in 1866, in Germany in 1869, in Austria in 1870, in Holland in 1872. But in Russia, where the proletariat is the principal revolutionary force in the struggle for freedom and where this struggle is so closely connected with its economic struggle, we can and must achieve purely proletarian rights simultaneously with the overthrow of autocracy. But for this we must even now popularise these rights in the current workers' struggle – just as now we should already expound as the slogan of the struggle a *democratic* constitution on the basis of general, direct and equal electoral rights.

Of the methods of political struggle the congress put demonstrations in first place, which, however, the First Congress of the reorganised Union had already viewed with 'unconditional sympathy'.

In view of the ever-increasing significance of political demonstrations it was not enough to recognise them as 'the best method of political struggle'. It was necessary to take into account too the fact that the tsarist government, no less than the revolutionaries, recognises the whole danger to it from demonstrations. The forcible suppression of demonstrations becomes all the more probable, the more often they are repeated, the greater the number of people involved and the more clearly the new general political character is revealed. In these circumstances it is necessary, in organising demonstrations, to consider the possibility of violence on the part of the government and to be prepared to answer violence with violence. Were we not to do so, demonstrations would threaten to lead to a battle, which would cow the mass for a long time. On the other hand resistance to violence on the part of the demonstrators would produce a strong, and furthermore an enduring, moral effect which would besmirch the government's halo and inspire the mass to ever more daring deeds. This was shown by the still recent experience of our demonstrations, which were accompanied to a greater or lesser degree by resistance from the demonstrators, e.g. in the Kharkov May Day of 1900, in the May demonstration of 1901 in Tiflis and on 7 May this year in the Obukhov factory in Petersburg.[246]

The instructions of 1898 'recommended that 1 May be celebrated as a general demonstration in favour of the most important economic demands of the proletariat and as a most appropriate moment for the declaration of immediate political demands'. The resolution of the last congress on the May Day holiday corresponds to the general change in the statement of our tactical tasks. Furthermore, all the

May issues of *Rabochee Delo*, aimed at the whole of Russia, made propaganda for a democratic constitution alongside separate political demands.

On the question of terror our congress adhered in essence to the decision of the Fourth Congress of the Bund. We should note, however, that this decision was a compromise between two partially differing views. These views are expressed in the following two resolutions, neither of which received a majority of the votes. Here are the two rejected resolutions:

I. Without prejudging the issue of whether terror should play a role, and of what role it will play in Russia in the cause of the conquest of political freedom, we recognise that systematic political terror is incompatible, as a method of struggle, with the broad democratic principle of organisation of the Social Democratic Party. As for individual terrorist acts, these must be used to develop the political consciousness of the proletariat.
II. Without prejudging the issue of whether terror should play a role, and of what role it will play in Russia in the cause of the conquest of political freedom, we recognise that for social democracy, standing on the foundation of a mass workers' movement, terror may be expedient only in close connection with mass acts of struggle and as an expression of the mass mood. Individual terrorist acts must be used for mass political propaganda and agitation.

The resolution in favour of the democratic principle of our party organisation speaks for itself. We can only regret that such a resolution was generally necessary, that, with the advent of *Iskra*,[247] tendencies appeared in the ranks of our party or, more exactly, emerged outside, which could, with the democratic organisation of our party, have destroyed the basic condition for its successful development. The struggle of the conspirators is lacking in the dictatorial forms of organisation; the Social Democratic Workers' Party, which 'consciously wishes to be, and to remain as, the class movement of the organised working masses' (manifesto of the RSDLP), is *unthinkable* without democratic organisation. Neither one nor another so-called group should impose its will on the party, but on the contrary, every separate group should submit to the general will of the party. He who does not accept the decision of the majority advertises himself by his own slogan: 'Always in the minority', and that can only paralyse the activity of the party.

We have completed our review of the most important changes and additions made by the Union congress to the old programme. It is obvious that all the unaltered points in this programme remain in force. This applies to the decisions of the 1898 congress on the relationship of the Union (1) towards other revolutionary sections of the Russian Socialists, (2) towards the non-socialist revolutionary and opposition political groups, (3) towards the socialist organisations of different nationalities active in Russia, and also to the resolution on the agrarian question.

The continuous growth of the Russian social democratic movement over the last three years has forced the Union to re-examine the *code of tactical positions* worked out in 1898. The old instructions nevertheless remain as a signpost, marking out the first political steps of our party. This was the first attempt to gather together the tactical positions by which the separate social democratic organisations were more or less consciously guided. And, we repeat, the programme of 1898 attempted to place the tactical unity of the party on a *higher* level, which was attainable at that time, i.e. it went *ahead of the movement.*

The 1901 programme bears the same character. It formulates the *maximum* of the presently attainable tasks of our party, outlines the tactical tasks and methods of the struggle which, we hope, will be adopted universally in the near future. But this is only possible given one condition: *our organisations must renew and complete the task of the First Congress of the party.* This congress gave itself a banner – the *Manifesto* – and established a moral link between the separate committees and groups. The task of the *Second Congress* of the party should be to work out programmes and tactics which are obligatory for everyone and to establish a strong all-party link. But such a link cannot be established and maintained without a central committee, which is elected and responsible to the party, and without a central party organ under its control.

Promoting the tactical unification of the party on a higher level by the new instructions, the Third Union Congress has by that same token also assisted in the realisation of the urgent organisational tasks of the party.

The editors of *Rabochee Delo* for their part will act in the spirit of the Union instructions, bearing constantly in mind the imperative need for a Second Congress of the party. This higher authority is alone competent to decide on questions of programme and tactics, and can alone express an authoritative view on the works of the Third Union Congress.

The Editors of Rabochee Delo

1903-1906: the Bolshevik/Menshevik dispute – organisational questions and appraisals of the 1905 revolution

50. SECOND PARTY CONGRESS: THE DEBATE ON CLAUSE 1 OF THE PARTY RULES (AUGUST 1903)[248]

Russian Social Democratic Labour Party

Twenty-third session

2 (15) August, evening

(Present: 43 delegates with 51 mandates and 12 persons with consultative voice.)

MARTOV: Of all the objections raised against my formulation[249] I shall concentrate on the one about the impracticability of my Clause 1, i.e. of control by party organisations over members of the party. I think the position is quite the reverse. Control is practicable insofar as the committee, having delegated a particular function to someone, will be able to keep watch over it. On the other hand, the aim towards which Lenin's rules are directed is essentially impracticable. For Lenin there are no organisations within the party other than 'party organisations'. In my view, on the contrary, these organisations must exist. Life creates and breeds organisations more quickly than we can include them in the hierarchy of our militant organisation of professional revolutionaries. Lenin thinks that the Central Committee will confer the title of 'party organisations' only on those that are completely reliable on matters of principle. But Comrade Brouckère[250] understands very well that life will assert itself and that the Central Committee, in order to avoid leaving a large number of organisations outside the party, will have to legitimise them, despite the fact that they are not completely reliable; for this reason Comrade Brouckère goes along with Lenin. But I think that, if this kind of organisation is ready to accept the party programme and party control, then we may admit it to the party, without thereby making it a party organisation. I should regard it as a great triumph for our party if, for instance, some union of 'independents' were to declare that it accepted the viewpoint of social democracy and its programme and was joining the party, which would not, however, mean that we should consider the union as a 'party organisation'. I support Lenin's idea that, in addition to organisations of professional revolutionaries, we also need *lose Organisationen* of various sorts.[251] But only our formulation expresses the aspir-

79

ation for a series of organisations between the organisation of professional revolutionaries and the mass. It comprises that plus the sum total of the active and
advanced elements of the proletariat.

PLEKHANOV: I had no preconceived notion on the point in the rules now under
discussion. Even this morning, when I heard the supporters of the opposing views, I
found that I 'leaned, first one way and then the other'. But the more that was said
on the subject and the more attentively I reflected on the speeches, the more convinced I became that the truth is on Lenin's side. The whole question boils down to
which elements may be included in our party. In Lenin's draft, only someone who
joins a particular organisation can be considered a party member. The opponents of
this draft maintain that this will cause some kind of unnecessary difficulties. But
what are these difficulties? They talk of people who are unwilling or unable to join
one of our organisations. But why *can't* they? As someone who has himself participated in Russian revolutionary organisations, I say that I do not concede the existence of objective conditions that consistute an insuperable obstacle to anybody
joining. As far as those gentlemen who are *unwilling* are concerned, we do not need
them. It has been said here that a professor who sympathises with our views may
find it demeaning to join one of our local organisations. This reminds me of Engels
who said that when you have dealings with a professor you must be prepared in
advance for the very worst. (Laughter.) In fact, it is an extremely bad example. If
some Professor of Egyptology[252] thinks that, because he knows the names of all
the pharaohs by heart and knows all the appeals that the Egyptians made to the
bull Apis, joining our organisation is beneath his dignity, then we have no need of
that professor. But to talk of party control over people who are *outside* the organisation is playing with words. In fact, such control is impracticable. Akselrod was
wrong to cite the 1870s. At that time there was a well-organised and superbly
disciplined centre surrounded by organisations of various sorts that it had created,
and what remained outside these organisations was chaos and anarchy. The component elements of this chaos called themselves party members but this harmed
rather than benefited the cause. We should not imitate the anarchy of the 1870s,
but avoid it. The supporters of Martov's draft say that the right to call yourself a
party member has great moral significance. But I cannot agree with this. If it is at
all useful to recall the example of the 1870s, then it is in precisely this instance.
When Zhelyabov said in court that he was not a member of the Executive Committee,[253] but only one of its agents at fourth remove, this increased rather than
diminished the fascination exerted by that famous committee. The same would be
true today. If an accused person says that he sympathised with our party but did
not belong to it because, unfortunately, he could not satisfy all its requirements,
then its authority will only be enhanced.

I also do not understand why people think that Lenin's draft, if adopted, would
close the doors of our party to a large number of workers. Workers who want to
join the party are not afraid of joining an organisation. Discipline holds no terrors
for them. Many intellectuals who are thoroughly steeped in bourgeois individualism

are afraid to join an organisation. But that is a good thing. These bourgeois individualists usually also emerge as the representatives of all kinds of opportunism. We must keep them at arm's length. Lenin's draft may serve as a bulwark against their penetration of the party and, for that reason alone, all those who are opposed to opportunism should vote for it.

RUSOV:[254] I have no particular sympathy with opportunists and Bernsteinists and I should not wish to see them in the party, but I cannot agree with Comrade Plekhanov. In my view, the danger that Comrade Lenin sees in the adoption of the second formulation is quite unreal. The title of 'party member' conferred by the rules gives the person who bears it no rights in relation to the party – but a mass of obligations. Given the absence of the elective principle in all party organisations, given the strict centralisation and the accountability of everyone who works for the party to its central institutions, there is no reason to fear penetration by elements threatening the purity of our principles. After all, those members mentioned in Lenin's formulation are already in party organisations, they are registered and have duties in the sphere of competence of the organisation to which they belong. We do not need to establish a new title to count them as party members and impose upon them the obligation of helping the party. Comrade Lenin would be logical if he were to strike out the whole of Clause 1 or replace it with a clause stating that the basic unit of the party is any collective; any organisation that has been approved by the central organs of the party and that fulfils some party function. But, in accepting this, we should be leaving outside the party the mass of the proletariat and individual townspeople who, while not belonging to any party organisation, serve as instruments in the hands of these organisations for the fulfilment of their tasks. Every practical worker who is present will, if he tries to recall all the people working in the localities, agree that there are many people like that, especially among the workers. Their attachment to the party would do no harm at all to the work or the ideological purity of the party and would, at the same time, make it possible for us to know at a given time the minimum force that we could count on. In addition, their attachment would give us the opportunity to demand from all these people that they fulfil unconditionally the obligations that the party imposes upon its members. These obligations may be particular resolutions of the party, but may also be decisions of the central organs. Reminding comrades once again that a party member has no rights but, on the contrary, a mass of obligations towards the party, I invite you to support Comrade Martov's resolution.

PAVLOVICH:[255] I always treat with some caution Comrade Brouckère's declarations of solidarity with us on any question. In this instance Comrade Brouckère is with us because of a misunderstanding. Comrade Lenin's entire organisational plan is held together by the idea of centralism. But Comrade Lenin has tried to ensure that the negative aspects of centralism are reduced to a minimum. As a supporter of 'democratism', Comrade Brouckère has been misled by Clause 1 of the rules. It is by no means in our interest to dilute the party's ranks with dubious elements.

Martov is worried that our rules will embrace these dubious elements and I appreciate his good intentions . . . But his mistake lies in the fact that he views the process of the growth of social democracy statically rather than dynamically. After all, acceptance of the programme presupposes a fairly high level of political consciousness. Even if we follow Martov, we must first of all delete the clause on the acceptance of the *programme* because, before the programme can be accepted, it must be mastered and understood. Lenin's clause provides for the acceptance not merely of the programme but also of the relations laid down in the rules. Translated into simple language this means (this translation will not, perhaps, please Comrade Lieber):[256] if you want to be a member of the party, your acceptance of organisational relations must not be merely platonic. We have been told here about those individuals — professors and officials — who are not afraid of Martov's resolution but are frightened by Comrade Lenin's. But, comrades, the party rules are written not for professors but for proletarians, who are not as shy as professors, and they are not, I hope, afraid of organisation and *collective* activity. Rules are on the whole written not for individuals but for collectives. I would go further: these individuals, who do not have the *sanction* of any party organisation, cannot in any way, either in form or in essence, be called the representatives of the party. As for the affiliated organisations, of high-school pupils, writers, correspondents, and so on, that Lieber is so concerned about, I say to him that it simply needs one of our organisations to determine the degree of their social democratic commitment and give them the corresponding functions and responsibility in that particular field, and within the confines of these functions they will have to co-ordinate their actions with ours. But, if these pupils and students stick to their bourgeois outlook, then I do not see this as a loss for social democracy. If we accept Martov's formulation, we shall be irresponsibly admitting an anarchic mass to membership of the party. We must not proceed on the assumption that Russia presents a *tabula rasa*. Already there is not a single important centre in Russia where we do not have an organisation or the elements of one. How we are to reconcile the conception of our party spread throughout Russia with the existence, acting alongside it, of some *irresponsible* members who have *enrolled themselves* in the party, how we are to reconcile this anarchic conception with Martov's own statement that our party should be the conscious expression of a process, I leave to the comrades to decide.

MURAVEV:[257] I think that Comrade Rusov's objection to Lenin's draft, that it would leave a large number of people outside the party, is unfounded. Lenin's draft embraces, apart from 'party organisations' in the strict sense, a whole series of other organisations that various circles and individuals can easily join.

TROTSKY:[258] I was very surprised when Comrade Plekhanov proposed that we should vote for Lenin's formulation as a reliable defence against opportunism. I was not aware that opportunism could be exorcised by rules. I think that opportunism is the product of more complex causes. Finally, I had not realised that opportunists were organically incapable of organisation. I know the Juarèsist party,[259] and that is organised opportunism. I have not forgotten the organisations of our Economists. No, I think that this dispute is much less of a matter of principle. 'Why can't some-one join our organisations if he accepts our programme?' Comrade Plekhanov asks, and he answers, 'It's obviously a matter of intelligentsia individualism, and we must fight against that.' But the point is that Lenin's formulation, directed against intelligentsia individualism, hits a quite different target. It is much easier for intelligentsia youth, organised in one way or another, to enrol in the party. Associations of high-school pupils, Red Cross organisations and, in particular, associations of students from the same part of the country, are far longer lasting than any broad (*lose*) workers' organisations. These student associations last for years, whereas broad workers' organisations break up every day as a result of strikes, crises and migration among the working masses. Comrade Lenin's definition therefore places the intelligentsia and the workers on an unequal footing. The author of this definition main-tains that it will enable us to know at any time the forces that we can lead into battle. But I am afraid that, when Comrade Lenin consults his lists at the critical moment, he will find in them these student associations and young ladies, very good social democratic ladies, grouped in the Red Cross . . . I do not accord our rules any mystical significance and I do not think that they will shift the centre of gravity of our work to the milieu of student societies and Red Cross ladies. No, our field of work will, of course, remain, as before, the proletariat. But, if legal defi-nitions are to correspond to actual relations, then Comrade Lenin's formulation must be rejected. I repeat: it misses the mark. Its author, and in particular its defender, Comrade Plekhanov, want to make it a noose to hang those politically depraved characters from the 'intelligentsia' who call themselves Social Democrats, organise young people and hand them over to the Peter Struves.[260] Believe me, comrades, I should be the first to grasp at any formulation that would serve as a noose to hang those gentlemen and I should be the first to pull it tight with enthusi-asm. But won't these gentlemen be able to join one of our broad (*lose*) party organ-sations? Won't they be able to form some such organisation *themselves*? You will say that the Central Committee would not recognise it. Why not? Not because of the character of the organisation itself, obviously, but because of the character of the people who belong to it. That means that the Central Committee will know I.M. and N.N. as political *individuals*. But they would not then be dangerous. They would then be disposed of by a general party boycott. But what is the sense, I ask, of restricting the status rights of individual intellectuals who take their stand on the basis of the party programme and serve the party as individuals under the direction of its organisations? Must the Central Committee member reply to any such indi-vidual Social Democrat living in the town of Penza: 'Before you can enjoy your minimum rights as a party member you must join up with similar individuals in Samara and Maluga. This is because we have now thought up a formula to strangle our intelligentsia individualism.'

LENIN: First of all, I'd like to make two observations on particular points. First, with regard to Akselrod's kind proposal (I speak without irony) to 'strike a bargain'.[261] I should willingly respond to this appeal, for I do not at all regard our disagreement as a matter of life and death for the party. We shall certainly not perish because of a bad point in the rules! But, as it has come to a choice between *two* formulations, I cannot renounce my firm conviction that Martov's formulation is a *deterioration* of the original draft, a deterioration that *might*, in certain circumstances, do the party some considerable damage. My second remark concerns Comrade Brouckère. It is only natural for Comrade Brouckère, who wants to apply the elective principle everywhere, to accept my formulation, which is the only one to define the conception of a *member* of the party with any precision. I therefore cannot understand the satisfaction that Comrade Martov draws from Comrade Brouckère's agreement with me. Could it be that Comrade Martov actually takes it as his *guiding principle* to oppose whatever Brouckère says, without examining his motives and arguments?

To come to the essence of the question, I will say that Comrade Trotsky has completely misunderstood Comrade Plekhanov's basic idea and his arguments have therefore missed the heart of the matter completely. He spoke of the intelligentsia and the workers, of the class point of view and the mass movement, but he failed to notice one basic question: does my formulation narrow the conception of a party member or broaden it? If he had asked himself this question, he would have seen without any difficulty that my formulation narrows this conception, while Martov's broadens it because his conception is distinguished by its 'elasticity' (to use Martov's own, correct, expression). And in the period of party life that we are now living through it is precisely this 'elasticity' that undoubtedly opens the doors to all the elements of confusion, vacillation and opportunism. To refute this simple and obvious conclusion it would be necessary to prove that such elements do not exist and Comrade Trotsky has not thought of doing that. Nor could it be proven, for everyone knows that there are many elements of this kind and that they are to be found even in the working class. The maintenance of a firm line and of purity of principle has now become all the more urgent because, with its unity restored, the party will now recruit very many unreliable elements and their number will grow as the party grows.

Comrade Trotsky gravely misunderstood the basic idea of my book, *What Is To Be Done?*, when he said that the party is not a conspiratorial organisation (many others also raised this objection). He forgot that in my book I advocate a whole series of organisations of various types, ranging from the most conspiratorial and the most exclusive to the comparatively broad and 'loose' (*lose*). He forgot that the party should be only the vanguard, the leader of the vast mass of the working class the whole (or nearly the whole) of which works 'under the control and direction' of party organisations, but the whole of which is not, and should not be, a part of the party. Let us, in fact, look at the conclusions that Comrade Trotsky draws from his fundamental error. He has told us here that, if row upon row of workers were arrested and all these workers were to declare that they did not belong to the party then our party would be a strange one! Isn't it the other way round? Isn't it Comrade Trotsky's reasoning that is strange? He regards as sad something that any revo utionary with any experience at all could only be pleased about. If the hundreds and thousands of workers arrested for strikes and demonstrations turned out not to have belonged to party organisations that would only prove that our organisations are good, that we are accomplishing our task of keeping dark a more or less exclusive circle of leaders and attracting the broadest possible mass to the movement.

The root of the error made by those who support Martov's formulation lies in the fact that they not only overlook one of the basic evils of our party life but even give it their blessing. This evil consists in the fact that, in an atmosphere of almost universal political discontent, in conditions requiring complete secrecy for our work, when the greater part of our activity has to be confined to closely knit, secret circles and even private meetings, it is extremely difficult, almost impossible, to separate those who do the talking from those who do the work. There is scarcely any other country where the confusion of these two categories is as common and where it produces as much muddle and harm as in Russia. We suffer cruelly from this evil, not only in the intelligentsia but also among the working class, and Comrade Martov's formulation will legitimise it. This formulation inevitably aspires to make *all and sundry* into party members: Comrade Martov had to admit this himself with his reservation, 'Yes, if you want', he said. But this is precisely what we do not want! It is for precisely this reason that we are so resolute in our opposition to Martov's formulation. It would be better for ten who do work not to call themselves party members (those who really work don't run after titles!) than for one who talks to have the right and the opportunity to be a party member. That is a principle that seems irrefutable to me and that compels me to fight Martov. It has been put to me that we confer no rights on party members and that for this reason there can be no abuses. Such a view is quite untenable: while we have not indicated what precisely are the special rights granted to a party member, you should note that we have not indicated any restrictions on the rights of party members either. That is the first point. The second point, and this is the most important one, irrespective of rights, we must not forget that every party member is responsible for the party and that the *party is responsible for every one of its members*. Given the conditions in which we have to conduct our political activity, given the rudimentary state of our political organisation at the moment, it would simply be dangerous and harmful to grant the right of membership to people who are not members of an organisation and to impose upon the party the responsibility for people who have not joined an organisation (and have, perhaps, deliberately not joined one). Comrade Martov was appalled at the idea that someone who was not a member of a party organisation would not have the right, in spite of his energetic work, to declare in court that he was a party member. This does not frighten me. On the contrary, serious damage would be done if someone undesirable were to call himself a party member in court, although he does not belong to any party organisation. It would be impossible to deny that such a person was working under the control and direction of an organisation, impossible precisely because of the very vagueness of the term. In fact — and there can be no doubt about this — the words 'under the control and direction' will result in there being *neither control nor direction*. The

Central Committee will never be in a position to exercise real control over all those who work for it but do not belong to any organisation. Our task is to give the Central Committee *real* control. It is our task to safeguard the firmness, consistency and purity of our party. We must try to raise the vocation and significance of the party member high, higher and higher still, and for this reason I am against Martov's formulation.

KOSTROV:[262] The rules exist for life, not life for the rules. Let us see how far Lenin's draft of the rules corresponds with the real state of affairs. We have social democratic committees composed of a few advanced revolutionaries. These committees stand at the head of the local labour movement. Behind these committees, behind these leaders, there is a whole mass of fighters, worker revolutionaries who distribute proclamations, collect money, demonstrate on the streets, go to prison and into exile, but who are not members of the committees or of any other organisations. Are these fighters, these soldiers of ours, really not members of the party? Must we really exclude them from the party? Who will be left in the party? Only generals without an army. That means disorganising all our work in Russia and setting our own comrades against the party. Comrade Plekhanov said that in the days of Narodnaya Volya the party was identical with the organisations. I believe that, but we must not forget that the Narodnaya Volya Party was a party of the intelligentsia, whereas our party is a party of the mass, a party of the proletariat. But we cannot include the mass in the organisation; that is unthinkable in the present state of Russia. Consequently, our party must consist of the organisations, the driving forces of the party, and the mass of fighters who are outside the organisation but who are still members of the party. Therefore, to adopt Lenin's draft would mean to disorganise the entire party, and I propose that it be rejected.

AKIMOV:[263] The question of the choice between the two versions of Clause 1 of the rules has divided comrades who have hitherto always voted together. On this matter I too part company with Comrade Brouckère. This is because the two formulations on offer have essentially one and the same aim. Comrades Martov and Lenin are arguing about how best to achieve their common goal; Brouckère and I want to choose the one that is least likely to achieve that aim. For this reason I choose Martov's formulation. We've heard a lot here about which version will best protect the party from harmful elements and as an illustration we were given the example of a Professor of Archaeology who is to be admitted to, or excluded from, the party in accordance with the degree of purity of his social democratic views. This example was chosen only to conceal the fear felt by the authors of the draft at the penetration of our party by elements of an order quite different from this mythical professor. Comrade Plekhanov said only this morning that he still did not know which of the two formulations he would support, but this does not, of course, mean that he had not yet decided what kind of organisation our party needs. In his commentaries on the draft programme Plekhanov has already expressed himself quite clearly on this point. 'If we are not mistaken', he wrote, 'not a single comrade now doubts that we need a party organisation like that of Zemlya i Volya and Narodnaya Volya; the argument is only about the quickest way to achieve it' (I quote from memory). And now both authors are offering the congress two texts of Clause 1 of the rules that seek to achieve this aim. But their very aim is impracticable and harmful. Too much has changed since Narodnaya Volya died out: quite different strata of society now bear the burden of revolutionary tasks and the tasks themselves have changed significantly. Even *a priori* it seems impossible that a mass class movement of the proletariat could be satisfied with the old conspiratorial organisation. Of course, the average revolutionary worker of today must inevitably be on a lower level than the 'professional revolutionary' as far as knowledge and even consciousness are concerned, and so you want to shut yourselves up in a special 'organisation of revolutionaries' and think up rules that will prevent the non-professional revolutionary, with his uneducated conception of the tasks of our party, from spoiling all our work. I am glad that you have taken the trouble to fence yourselves in. I am quite sure that life will nonetheless force its way into our party organisation, whether you block its path with Martov's formulation or Lenin's. But, while Comrade Lenin finds that Martov's text is not such a terrible deterioration of his draft, I recognise in it an improvement, albeit a small one, because Lenin's formulation excludes from our party the whole mass of its active workers, leaving a handful of 'professional revolutionaries'.

GUSEV:[264] It is my lot to speak last. After everything that has been said, I have nothing to add. I support Lenin's formulation because it is closer to the organisational plan expressed in the rules before us.

The congress proceeded to a vote. Lenin's formulation was *rejected* (in a roll call vote) by twenty-eight votes to twenty-three. Martov's formulation was *accepted* by twenty-eight votes to twenty-two, with one abstention.

51. THE PROGRAMME OF THE RUSSIAN SOCIAL DEMOCRATIC LABOUR PARTY (1903)[265]

Russian Social Democratic Labour Party

a. The programme of the RSDLP

The development of trade has forged such a strong link between all the nations of the civilised world that the great emancipatory movement of the proletariat had to become, and long ago did become, an international movement.

Regarding itself as one detachment in the world-wide army of the proletariat, Russian social democracy is pursuing the same goal as that for which the Social Democrats of all other countries are striving.

This goal is determined by the character of contemporary bourgeois society and by the path of its development.

The principal characteristic of this society is the production of goods on the basis of capitalist productive relations, under which the most important and significant part of the means of production and exchange of goods belongs to a numerically small class of people, while the great majority of the population consists of proletarians and semi-proletarians, forced by their economic position to sell their labour either permanently or temporarily (i.e. to become the hirelings of the capitalists) and by their labour to create income for the upper classes of society.

The sphere of predominance of capitalist productive relations is expanding all the time as the constant improvement in technology, which increases the economic importance of large enterprises, leads to the exclusion of the small independent producers, transforming one section of them into proletarians and reducing the role of the remainder, making them more or less completely, more or less obviously, more or less heavily, dependent on capital.

That same technological progress gives the enterpreneurs, in addition, the opportunity of employing women and children on a large scale in the process of the production and distribution of goods. But since, on the other hand, this leads to a corresponding reduction in the entrepreneurs' need for the labour of the workers, the demand for the work force inevitably falls short of the supply and, consequently, the dependence of wage labour on capital is increased and the level of its exploitation is heightened.

Such is the state of affairs in bourgeois countries, and the increasingly fierce competition between them on the world market makes it more and more difficult to sell the goods produced in constantly increasing quantities. Overproduction, manifesting itself in more or less acute industrial crises, followed by more or less prolonged periods of industrial stagnation, appears as the inevitable consequence of the development of productive forces in bourgeois society. Crises and periods of industrial stagnation in their turn wreak further havoc on the small producers, further increase the dependence of wage labour on capital and lead more quickly to a relative, and sometimes even to an absolute, deterioration in the position of the working class.

In this way the improvement in technology, involving an improvement in labour productivity and an increase in social wealth, provokes in bourgeois society a growth in social inequality; a widening of the gap between the owners and the non-owners, and a more precarious existence, an increase in unemployment and various forms of deprivation for ever broader strata of the working masses.

But as all these contradictions peculiar to bourgeois society grow and develop, the dissatisfaction of the workers and of the exploited mass with the existing order of things also grows, the number and cohesion of the proletarians increases, and their struggle with their exploiters grows more acute. At the same time, the improvement in technology, concentrating the means of production and exchange and socialising the labour process in capitalist enterprises, is with increasing speed creating the material opportunity for the replacement of capitalist productive relations by socialist ones, i.e. by the social revolution that is the goal of the whole activity of international social democracy as a conscious expression of the class movement of the proletariat.

By replacing private ownership of the means of production and exchange by social ownership and by introducing the planned organisation of the social-productive process to ensure the welfare and all-round development of all members of society, the social revolution of the proletariat will destroy the division of society into classes and thus emancipate the whole of oppressed mankind, at the same time putting an end to all forms of exploitation of one part of society by another.

A necessary condition for this social revolution is the dictatorship of the pro-letariat, i.e. the conquest by the proletariat of the political power that will allow it to suppress any resistance by the exploiters.

Setting itself the task of making the proletariat capable of fulfilling its great historic mission, international social democracy is organising it into an independent political party in opposition to all bourgeois parties, directing all the manifestations of its class struggle, revealing to it the irreconcilable conflict between the interests of the exploiters and the interests of the exploited, and explaining to it the historic significance of, and the necessary conditions for, the impending social revolution. In addition it reveals to all the other workers and to the exploited mass the hopelessness of their position in capitalist society and the need for social revolution in the interests of its own emancipation from the yoke of capital. The party of the working class, social democracy, invites into its ranks all the working and exploited strata of the population as they come over to the proletarian point of view.

On the path to their common goal, conditioned by the hegemony of the capital-ist mode of production throughout the entire civilised world, the Social Democrats of different countries are forced to set themselves differing immediate tasks because this mode [of production] is not everywhere developed to the same degree and because its development in different countries is taking place in different socio-political conditions.

In Russia, where capitalism has already become the dominant mode of production, numerous vestiges of our old pre-capitalist order are still preserved, based on the enslavement of the working mass to the landowners, the state or the head of state. Acting as a considerable obstacle to economic progress, these vestiges prevent the all-round development of the class struggle of the proletariat and help to preserve and strengthen the most barbaric forms of exploitation of the many millions of peasants by the state and the owning classes and keep the entire people in a darkness devoid of [civil] rights.

The most important of all these vestiges and the most powerful bulwark of all this barbarism is tsarist autocracy. By its very nature it is hostile to every social movement and cannot fail to be the most insidious opponent of all the emancipatory strivings of the proletariat.

For this reason the RSDLP sets as its most urgent political task the overthrow of tsarist autocracy and its replacement by a democratic republic, whose constitution would provide for:

1. The autocracy of the people, i.e. the concentration of all supreme state power in the hands of a legislative assembly composed of representatives of the people and forming a single chamber.
2. Universal, equal and direct franchise for elections both to the legislative assembly and to all local organs of self-government for all male and female citizens who have reached the age of twenty; the secret ballot in elections; the right of every elector to be elected to all representative institutions; two-year parliaments; the [right of] petition to popular representatives.
3. Broadly based local self-government; regional self-government for those localities that are distinguished by special conditions relating to the way of life or to the composition of the population.
4. The inviolability of the person and of his dwelling-place.
5. Unlimited freedom of conscience, of speech, of the press, of assembly, of association, and to strike.
6. Freedom of movement and occupation.
7. Abolition of classes and full equal rights for all citizens without regard to sex, religion, race or nationality.
8. The right of the population to receive education in their native tongue, to be realised by the provision, at the expense of the state and the organs of self-government, of the necessary schools; the right of every citizen to use his native tongue at assemblies; the introduction of native languages on a par with the official language in all local social and state institutions.
9. The right to self-determination for all the nations that constitute the state.
10. The right of every individual to prosecute any official before a jury.
11. The election of judges by the people.
12. The replacement of the standing army by the general arming of the people.
13. Free and compulsory general and professional education for all children of

both sexes up to the age of sixteen; the provision for poor children of food, clothing and text-books at the state's expense.

The RSDLP demands, as a basic condition for the democratisation of the economy of our state: *the repeal of all indirect taxation and the introduction of progressive taxation on income and inheritance.*

To protect the working class against moral and physical degeneration and to develop its capacity for the struggle for emancipation, the party demands:

1. The limitation of the working day to eight hours a day for all wage workers.
2. The establishment by law of a weekly rest period, lasting for at least forty-two hours without interruption, for wage workers of both sexes in all sectors of the national economy.
3. A complete ban on overtime work.
4. A ban on night work (from 9 p.m. to 6 a.m.) in all sectors of the national economy, excluding those where it is absolutely necessary for technical reasons that have been approved by the workers' organisations.
5. A ban on the employment of children of school age (up to sixteen years) and the limitation of the working period for adolescents (sixteen to eighteen years) to six hours.
6. A ban on female labour in those branches where it is harmful to the female organism; the release of women from work for four weeks before and six weeks after birth with normal pay for the whole period.
7. The provision in all works, factories and other enterprises where women work of day nurseries for babies and young children; the release from work of women who are breast-feeding their babies at least once in every three hours for not less than half an hour at a time.
8. State insurance for workers, to cover their old age and cases of complete or partial loss of ability to work, in a special fund to be financed by a special tax on the capitalists.
9. A ban on the payment of wages in kind, the establishment of a weekly time for paying them out in all agreements on workers' pay, without exception, and the payment of wages during working hours.
10. A ban on the employers making cash deductions from wages, for whatever reason or purpose (fines, wastage, etc.).
11. The appointment of an adequate number of factory inspectors in all sectors of the national economy and the extension of the factory inspectorate's supervision to all enterprises employing wage labour, including those owned by the state (domestic service should also come into the sphere of this supervision); the appointment of women inspectors in those sectors where female labour is employed; the participation of elected workers and representatives paid by the state in supervising the implementation of the factory laws and also the calculation of [wage] rates, of the receipt and inspection of sub-standard material and the results of [their] work.
12. Supervision of the organs of local self-government, with the participation

of workers' elected representatives, to control the sanitary condition of the living accommodation set aside for the workers by the employers, and also to control the internal order of this accommodation and the conditions of the lease so as to protect wage workers against interference from employers and their [everyday] lives and activities as private individuals and citizens.

13. The introduction of properly organised sanitary inspection in all enterprises employing wage labour, the whole medical and sanitary organisation being completely independent from the employers; free medical aid for the workers at the employers' expense with wages maintained for the duration of the illness.

14. The establishment of the criminal responsibility of employers for breaching the labour protection laws.

15. The establishment in all sectors of the national economy of industrial courts, composed equally of representatives from the workers and the employers.

16. The organs of local self-government should be made responsible for establishing intermediary offices for the hire of local workers and new arrivals (labour exchanges) in all branches of production, with representatives of workers' organisations participating in their management.

With the aim of eliminating the vestiges of serfdom that hang directly over the peasants like a heavy burden, and in the interests of the free development of the class struggle in the countryside, the party above all demands:

1. The cancellation of redemption and quit-rent payments and of all debts now charged to the peasantry as a tax-paying estate.

2. The repeal of all laws that limit the peasant in disposing of his land.

3. The return to the peasants of the sums of money taken from them in the form of redemption and quit-rent payments; the confiscation to this end of all monastic and ecclesiastical property and also of the estates belonging to ministers, the nobility and members of the tsar's family, and at the same time the levying of a special tax on the lands of the landowning gentry who benefit from redemption loans; the diversion of the sums collected in this fashion to a special national fund for the cultural and charitable needs of the village societies.

4. The establishment of peasant committees: (a) to return to the village societies (by means of expropriation or, where the lands have passed from person to person, through purchase by the state at the expense of the nobility with large landed estates) those lands that were taken from the peasants when serfdom was abolished, and that serve in the hands of the landowners as a means to enslave them; (b) to transfer to the ownership of the peasants in the Caucasus the lands that they use as semi-serfs, labourers, and so on; (c) to eliminate the remnants of serfdom that survive in the Urals, the Altai, the Western territory and in other areas of the country.

5. The courts should be given the right to reduce excessively high rents and to declare invalid transactions that smack of one-sidedness.

In its desire to achieve its immediate aims the RSDLP supports any oppositional and revolutionary movement that is directed against the existing social and political order in Russia, and at the same time rejects all reformist projects that involve any kind of extension or reinforcement of bureaucratic police tutelage over the labouring classes.

For its part, the RSDLP is firmly convinced that the complete, consistent and lasting achievement of the political and social changes that have been mentioned is possible only *through the overthrow of autocracy* and the summoning of a *constituent assembly*, freely elected by the whole people.

52. THE ORGANISATIONAL STATUTES OF THE RSDLP (1903)[266]

Russian Social Democratic Labour Party

Resolution. The general statutes of the party are binding on all sections of the party.

The statutes

1. Membership of the Russian Social Democratic Labour Party is open to anyone who accepts its programme, offers material support to the party and renders it regular personal assistance under the guidance of one of its organisations.

2. The supreme organ of the party is the party congress. It is convened (if possible at least once every two years) by the Council of the party. The Council of the party is obliged to convene a congress if so requested by party organisations that together have a right to more than half the decisive votes.

3. The following are represented at the congress: (a) the Council of the party; (b) the Central Committee; (c) the Central Organ; (d) all local committees that have not entered special unions; (e) other organisations that, in this context, are given the same status as committees; (f) all committee unions recognised by the party. Each of the designated organisations is represented at the congress by one delegate who has two votes; the Council of the party is represented by all its members who have one vote each.

The representation of unions is governed by special statutes.

Note 1. The right of representation is enjoyed by only those organisations that have been approved at least a year before the congress.

Note 2. The Central Committee is empowered to invite to the congress, with a consultative vote, delegates from organisations that do not meet the conditions indicated in Note 1.

4. The congress nominates the fifth member of the Council, and the [whole of the] Central Committee and the editorial board of the Central Organ.

5. The Council of the party is nominated by the editorial board of the Central Organ and by the Central Committee, which send two members each to the Council: the members of the Council who leave are replaced by nominees of their institutions; the replacement for the fifth member is nominated by the Council itself.

The Council of the party is the highest institution of the party. The task of the Council is to approve and coordinate the activity of the Central Committee and the editorial board of the Central Organ, and to represent the party in its relations with other parties. The Council of the party has the right to replace the Central Committee and the editorial staff of the Central Organ in the event of the members of one of these institutions leaving all together.

The Council meets whenever one of the central organs requests this: i.e. the editorial staff of the Central Organ, or the Central Committee, or two members of the Council.

6. The Central Committee organises the committees, committee unions and all the other institutions of the party and guides their activity; it organises and guides undertakings that have significance for the whole party; it distributes the forces and resources of the party and manages the central fund of the party; it investigates conflicts, both between the different institutions of the party and within them, and generally coordinates and directs the whole practical activity of the party.

Note. Members of the Central Committee cannot simultaneously be members of any other party organisation, with the exception of the Council of the party.

7. The ideological guidance of the party is the responsibility of the editorial board of the Central Organ.

8. All organisations that are part of the structure of the party conduct independently all business that relates particularly and exclusively to the field of party activity for which they are responsible.

9. Apart from the organisations approved by the party congress, all remaining organisations are approved by the Central Committee. All Central Committee resolutions are binding for all party organisations, which are likewise bound to contribute to the central party fund the sums determined by the Central Committee.

10. Every party member, and any individual having any business with the party, has the right to demand that his statement in its original form should be passed to the Central Committee or to the editorial board of the Central Organ, or to the party congress.

11. Every party organisation is obliged to supply both the Central Committee and the editorial board of the Central Organ with the information they need to acquaint themselves with its whole activity and with its membership.

12. All party organisations and all collective institutions of the party take decisions by simple majority vote and have the right to co-opt. Two-thirds of the

votes are required to co-opt or exclude new members, in the absence of a justified protest. Appeal to the Council of the party is permitted against decisions taken by organisations on matters of the co-optation or exclusion of members.

Co-optation of new members on to the Central Committee or the editorial board of the Central Organ is effected by unanimous vote. In cases where unanimity is not reached on co-optation to the Central Committee or to the editorial board of the Central Organ, a complaint may be lodged with the Council and, if the Council quashes the decision of the relevant collective institution, the question is finally resolved by simple majority vote.

The Central Committee and the editorial board of the Central Organ notify one another of newly co-opted members.

13. The League of Russian Revolutionary Social Democracy Abroad, as the only organisation of the RSDLP abroad, has as its aim [the conduct of] propaganda and agitation abroad but, equally, [the rendering of] assistance to the Russian movement. The League has all the rights of committees, with the sole exception that it provides support for the Russian movement only through individuals and groups specially nominated by the Central Committee.

53. ORGANISATIONAL QUESTIONS OF RUSSIAN SOCIAL DEMOCRACY (1904)[267]

R. Luxemburg

I.

A unique task that is without parallel in the history of socialism has fallen to Russian social democracy: it is to work out a social democratic tactic suited to the class struggle of the proletariat in an autocratic[268] state. The customary comparison between conditions in Russia today and those in Germany at the time of the Anti-Socialist Law[269] is untenable insofar as it views Russian conditions from the police, and not from the political standpoint. The *obstacles* that the lack of democratic freedoms creates for the mass movement are, relatively speaking, of secondary importance: even in Russia the mass movement has managed to overrun the barriers of the autocratic 'constitution'[270] and create for itself an albeit crippled 'constitution' of 'street disorders'. It will continue along these lines until it has achieved its final victory over the autocracy. The principal difficulty facing the social democratic struggle in Russia consists in the fact that the class domination of the bourgeoisie is veiled by the domination of autocratic coercion; this domination by the autocracy necessarily gives the socialist doctrine of class struggle an abstract propagandistic character, and immediate political agitation a predominantly revolutionary democratic one. The Anti-Socialist Law was intended only to place the working class beyond the bounds of the constitution and to do this in a highly developed bourgeois society where class antagonisms had been laid bare and fully exposed in parliamentarism;[271] herein lay the insanity, the absurdity of Bismarck's venture. In Russia the inverse experiment must be accomplished: social democracy must be created in the absence of the direct political domination of the bourgeoisie.

This has a unique bearing not only on the question of transplanting socialist doctrine to Russian soil, not only on the question of *agitation*, but also on that of *organisation*.

For the social democratic movement even *organisation*, as distinct from the earlier utopian experiments of socialism, is viewed not as an artificial product of propaganda but as a historical product of the class struggle, to which social democracy merely brings political consciousness. Under normal circumstances, i.e. where the fully developed political class domination of the bourgeoisie precedes the social democratic movement, it is the bourgeoisie itself that to a considerable extent takes care of the initial political merger of the workers. 'At this stage', says *The Manifesto of the Communist Party*, 'the mass solidarity of the workers results not from their own unity but from the unity of the bourgeoisie'.[272] In Russia it is the task of social democracy to miss out a stage in the historical process through deliberate intervention and to lead the proletariat straight from the political atomisation that forms the basis of the autocratic regime to the highest form of organisation – a class that is conscious of its aims and fights for them. As a result the question of organisation poses particular problems for Russian social democracy, not just because it has to create an organisation in the absence of any of the formal devices of bourgeois democracy, but above all because to some extent it has to create this organisation like Almighty God 'from nothing', in a void, without the political raw material that is elsewhere prepared by bourgeois society.

The problem that has already exercised Russian social democracy for some years is that of the transition from the type of splintered and completely autonomous organisation at circle and local level, a type of organisation that suited the preparatory, predominantly propagandist phase of the movement, to the kind of organisation necessary for concerted political action by the mass throughout the state. But, as splintering, complete autonomy, and self-government for local organisations were the distinguishing feature of the burdensome and politically outmoded old organisational forms, the rallying cry for the new phase, that of the large-scale prepared organisational structure, is naturally *centralism*. The affirmation of the centralist idea was the *Leitmotiv* of the brilliant three-year campaign waged by *Iskra* in preparation for the last party congress, which was in fact the founding one; and the same idea has preoccupied the whole of the younger generation of Social Democrats in Russia. It soon became apparent at the congress, and even more apparent afterwards,[273] that centralism is a slogan that nowhere nearly covers the historical content and the peculiarities of the social democratic type of organisation; it has once more been demonstrated that the Marxist conception of socialism cannot be fitted into rigid formulas in any field, not even in the field of organisational questions.

The book before us, *One Step Forward, Two Steps Back*[274] by Comrade Lenin, one of the distinguished leaders and militants of *Iskra* in its campaign of preparation for the Russian party congress, is a systematic exposition of the views of the *ultracentralist* tendency in the Russian party. The point of view that finds forceful and exhaustive expression here is that of uncompromising centralism: its essential principle consists, on the one hand, in the rigid separation and isolation of the organised elements of outright and active revolutionaries from their, albeit unorganised, revolutionary activist milieu, and, on the other hand, in the strict discipline and the direct, decisive and definite intervention of the central authority in all the signs of life of local party organisations. Suffice it to note that in this view the Central Committee has, for instance, the right to organise all the local committees of the party and thus also to determine the membership of every individual Russian local organisation from Geneva and Liège to Tomsk and Irkutsk,[275] to provide them with a ready-made local statute, to dissolve and reconstitute them by *fiat* and hence also to exert indirect influence on the composition of the highest party organ, the congress. Thus the Central Committee emerges as the real active nucleus of the party; all the remaining organisations are merely its executive instruments.

It is in precisely this combination of the strictest organisational centralism and the social democratic mass movement that Lenin sees a specifically revolutionary Marxist principle and he can marshal a whole series of facts to support his point of view. But let us look at the matter more closely.

There is no doubt that a strong inclination towards centralism is inherent in social democracy as a whole. Growing in the economic soil of capitalism, with its centralist tendencies, and depending in its struggle on the political framework of the large centralised bourgeois state;[276] social democracy is by nature an outright opponent of all forms of particularism or national federalism. Called upon within the framework of a particular state to represent the general interests of the proletariat as a class, as opposed to all the particular and group interests of the proletariat, it everywhere has the natural desire to weld all the national, religious and professional groups within the working class into a single party; it is only in special, abnormal circumstances such as those in Austria, for instance, where it has to make an exception, a concession to the federalist principle.[277]

In this respect there was, and is, no question, for Russian social democracy either, that it should form a federative conglomerate of a multiplicity of special national and local organisations rather than a homogeneous and compact party for the Russian Empire. The question of a greater or lesser degree of centralisation and of its precise *nature*[278] within a united and homogeneous Russian social democracy is, however, a quite different one.

From the standpoint of the formal tasks of social democracy as a party of struggle, it appears from the outset that the party's battle-readiness and its energy are directly dependent on the realisation of centralism in its organisation. But in this context the specific historical conditions of the proletariat's struggle are far more important than the standpoints of the formal requirements of any organisation of struggle.

The social democratic movement is the first movement in the history of class societies to be premissed in its every aspect and in its whole development on the organisation and the independent direct action of the mass.

In this sense social democracy creates a completely different type of organisation from earlier socialist movements, e.g. those of the Jacobin–Blanquist type.

It appears that Lenin underestimates this when he writes in his book (p. 140) that the revolutionary Social Democrat is really nothing but 'the Jacobin indissolubly linked to the *organisation* of the *class conscious* proletariat'.[279] It is in the organisation and class consciousness of the proletariat, as opposed to the conspiracy of a small minority, that Lenin sees the exhaustive distinctions between social democracy and Blanquism. He forgets that this implies a complete reappraisal of our organisational concepts, a completely new concept of centralism, a completely new notion of the mutual relationship between organisation and struggle.

Blanquism was not premissed on the direct class activity of the masses and did not therefore require a mass organisation. On the contrary, as the broad popular masses were supposed to emerge on to the battlefield only at the actual moment of revolution, while the preliminary activity consisted in the preparation of a revolutionary coup by a small minority, a rigid distinction between the people appointed to this specific task and the popular mass was directly necessary for the success of their mission. But it was also possible and attainable because there was no inherent connection between the conspiratorial activity of the Blanquist organisation and the everyday life of the popular mass.[280]

At the same time both the tactics and the precise tasks of activity were worked out in advance in the minutest detail, determined and prescribed as a definite plan, because they were improvised off the cuff and at will, with no connection with the elemental class struggle. As a result the active members of the organisation were naturally transformed into the purely executive organs of a will that had been predetermined outside their own field of activity, into the *instruments* of a central committee. This also gave rise to the second characteristic of conspiratorial centralism: the absolute blind submission of the individual organs of the party to their central authority and the extension of the latter's powers right to the very periphery of the party organisation.

The conditions for social democratic activity are radically different. This derives historically from the elemental class struggle. It operates within the dialectical contradiction that here it is only in the struggle itself that the proletarian army is itself recruited and only in the struggle that it becomes conscious of the purpose of the struggle. Organisation, enlightenment and struggle are here not separate moments mechanically divided in time, as in a Blanquist movement, they are merely different facets of the same process. On the one hand, apart from the general basic principles of struggle, there is no ready-made predetermined and detailed tactic of struggle that the Central Committee could drill into the social democratic membership. On the other hand, the process of struggle that creates the organisation stipulates a constant fluctuation in the sphere of influence of social democracy.

From this it follows that social democratic centralisation cannot be based either on blind obedience or on the mechanical submission of the party's militants to their central authority and, further, that an impenetrable wall can never be erected between the nucleus of the class conscious proletariat that is already organised into tightly knit party cadres and those in the surrounding stratum who have already been caught up in the class struggle and are in the process of developing class consciousness. The establishment of centralisation in social democracy on these two principles – on the blind submission of all party organisations and their activity, down to the smallest detail, to a central authority that alone thinks, acts and decides for everyone, and also on the strict separation of the organised nucleus of the party from its surrounding revolutionary milieu, as Lenin advocates – therefore seems to us to be a mechanical transposition of the organisational principles of the Blanquist movement of conspiratorial circles to the social democratic movement of the working masses. And Lenin characterises this point of view, perhaps more astutely than any of his opponents could, when he defines his 'revolutionary Social Democrat' as a 'Jacobin *linked to* the organisation of the class conscious workers'. In fact, however, social democracy is not *linked* to the organisation of the working class, it is the working class's *own movement*. Social democratic centralism must therefore have an essentially different character from Blanquist centralism. It can be none other than the authoritative expression of the will of the conscious and militant vanguard of the workers, vis-à-vis the separate groups and individuals among them; it is, as it were, a 'self-centralism' of the leading stratum of the proletariat, the rule of its majority within the confines of its own party organisation.

From our examination of the real content of social democratic centralism it is already becoming clear that the necessary conditions for it could not yet be said to exist in full measure in Russia at the present time. These conditions are: the presence of a significant stratum of the proletariat that has already been schooled in political struggle and the opportunity to express their battle-readiness[281] through the exercise of direct influence (in public party congresses, in the party press, etc.).

The latter condition can obviously only be realised in Russia in conditions of political liberty, but the former – the creation of a judicious and class conscious proletarian vanguard – is only now in the process of emerging and should be regarded as the principal theme of immediate agitational and organisational work.

All the more surprising is Lenin's inverse conviction that all the preconditions for the realisation of a large and highly centralised workers' party are already to hand in Russia. When he optimistically exclaims that it is now 'not the proletariat but certain intellectuals in Russian social democracy who are lacking in self-education in the spirit of organisation and discipline' (p. 145), and when he praises the educational significance of the factory for the proletariat in making it completely ripe for 'discipline and organisation' (p. 147), this once again betrays an overmechanistic conception of social democratic organisation. The 'discipline' that Lenin has in mind is instilled into the proletariat not just by the factory but also by the *barracks* and by modern bureaucracy – in a word, by the entire mechanism of the centralised bourgeois state. It is quite simply a misuse of the catchword simultaneously to characterise as 'discipline' two such opposing concepts as the lack of will and thought in a body with many arms and legs that moves mechanically to the baton and the voluntary coordination of the conscious political actions of a social stratum; such concepts as the blind obedience of an oppressed class and the organised rebellion of a class that is struggling for its emancipation. It is not through the discipline instilled in the proletariat by the capitalist state, with the straightforward transfer of the baton from the bourgeoisie to a social democratic Central Committee, but only through defying and uprooting this spirit of servile discipline that the proletarian can be educated for the new discipline, the voluntary self-discipline of social democracy.

Furthermore, it is clear from the same consideration that centralism in the social democratic sense is by no means an absolute concept existing in equal measure at every stage in the workers' movement; rather it should be regarded more as a *tendency*, which is increasingly realised in accordance with the developing consciousness and political education of the working mass in the process of its struggle.

Of course the insufficient presence of the most important preconditions for the complete realisation of centralism in the Russian movement can present a tremendous obstacle. But it seems to us perverse to think that the as yet unrealisable rule of the majority of the conscious workers within their own party organisation may be 'temporarily' replaced by the 'delegated' sole power of the central party authority, and that the absence of public control by the working masses over what the party organs do and do not do might equally well be replaced by the inverse control by a Central Committee over the activity of the revolutionary workers.

The very history of the Russian movement furnishes many proofs of the doubtful value of centralism in this latter sense. An all-powerful central institution, with the almost unlimited right of intervention and control that Lenin envisages, would obviously be a nonsense if it had to confine its power exclusively to the purely *technical* aspect of social democracy, to the regulation of the day-to-day methods and expedients of agitation such as the supply of party literature and the appropriate distribution of agitational and financial resources. It would have an appreciable political purpose only if it were to use its power to organise a tactic of struggle and launch a great political action in Russia. But what do we see in the changes that the Russian movement has so far undergone? The most important and profitable changes of the last decade were not 'invented' by any of the movement's leaders, let alone the leading organisations, but were in every case the spontaneous product of the unfettered movement. This applies to the first stage of the truly proletarian movement in Russia, which began with the spontaneous outbreak of the colossal St Petersburg strike of 1896 and which first inaugurated the mass economic activity of the Russian proletariat. The same applies to the second phase, that of political street demonstrations, which began completely spontaneously with the student unrest in St Petersburg in March 1901.[282] The next significant turning-point in tactics that pointed the way to new horizons was the mass strike that broke out 'of its own accord' in Rostov-on-Don, with its improvised *ad hoc* street agitation, open-air popular assemblies and public addresses, all of which would have seemed, only a few years before, like a fantasy, like something unthinkable, even to the most enthusiastic Social Democrat. In all these cases, 'in the beginning was the deed'.[283] The *initiative* and conscious leadership of social democratic organisations played an extremely insignificant role. This arose, however, not so much from the inadequate preparedness of these special organisations for their role (although this point may have had considerable influence) and still less from the absence at that time from Russian social democracy of an all-powerful central authority in the spirit of Lenin's plan. On the contrary, such an authority would very probably only have increased the indecision of the individual party committees and provoked a split between the tempestuous mass and temporising social democracy. It is rather the case that this same phenomenon – the insignificant role of a conscious initiative by the party leadership in shaping tactics – can be observed in Germany and elsewhere. The main features of the social democratic tactic of struggle are on the whole not 'invented': on the contrary, they are the consequence of a continuing series of great creative acts of experimental, often of spontaneous, class struggle. Here too the unconscious precedes the conscious, the logic of the objective historical process precedes the subjective logic of its agents. The role of the social democratic leadership in all this has an essentially conservative character because, as experience demonstrates, once they have won new terrain for the struggle, they will work it over thoroughly and soon turn it into a bulwark against further innovation on a greater scale. The current tactics of German social democracy, for instance, are everywhere admired for their remarkable diversity, their flexibility and, at the same time, for their assuredness. But this means only that, in its everyday struggle, our party has adapted itself admirably well to contemporary parliamentary conditions down to the smallest detail, that it can make full use of the whole field of battle that parliamentarism has to offer and master it according to its own rules.[284] However this particular tactical formulation conceals the broader horizons so effectively that there plainly emerges a considerable tendency to perpetuate the parliamentary tactic and to view it as *the* tendency for the social democratic struggle. Characteristic of this mood is, for instance, the hopelessness of Parvus' long-standing efforts to provoke a discussion in the party press of the change in tactics that would be appropriate in the event of the abolition of universal suffrage, despite the fact that the party leaders view such an eventuality with deadly seriousness. This inertia is to a great extent explained by the fact that it is very difficult to present the contours and tangible forms of an as yet non-existent and, therefore, imaginary political situation in a void of abstract speculation. The important thing for social democracy as well is never to preduct and prepare a ready-made plan for future tactics but to keep alive within the party the correct historical evaluation of the forms of struggle that dominate at a particular moment and a living sense of the relativity of a particular phase in the struggle and of the necessary increase in revolutionary momentum from the standpoint of the final goal of the class struggle of the proletariat.

But to grant the party leadership the kind of absolute powers of a *negative* character that Lenin does means to strengthen, artificially and to a very dangerous degree, the conservatism that springs inevitably from its very essence. If social democratic tactics are the creation, not of a Central Committee, but of the party as a whole – or, more accurately, of the movement as a whole – then individual party organisations will need the elbow room that alone gives them the opportunity to make full use of the means to further the struggle furnished by the particular situation and to develop revolutionary initiative. The ultracentralism that Lenin advocates seems to us, in its whole essence, to be imbued, not with a positive creative spirit, but with the sterile spirit of the night-watchman state.[285] His line of thought is concerned principally with the *control* of party activity and not with its fertilisation; with *narrowing* and not with *broadening*, with *tying the movement up* and not with *drawing it together*.

It seems doubly risky for Russian social democracy to indulge in an experiment of this kind at precisely this moment. It stands on the eve of great revolutionary battles for the overthrow of the autocracy, before, or rather in, a period of the most intensive creative activity in the tactical field and – as goes without saying in a revolutionary epoch – a period of feverish and spasmodic expansion and contraction in its sphere of influence. To try and restrict the initiative for party thought and erect a barbed-wire fence around the party's capacity for sudden expansion is by that very fact to render social democracy to a considerable extent unfit from the outset for the great tasks of the movement.

We cannot yet, of course, derive a concrete draft of the paragraphs of an organisational statute for the Russian party from the general observations we have made on the characteristic features of social democratic centralism. This draft naturally depends in the final analysis on the concrete conditions in which activity proceeds at a particular period and, because in Russia it is a question of the first attempt to build up a large proletarian party organisation, [a statute of this kind] cannot lay advance claims to infallibility; rather it must in any case first undergo the trial by fire of practice. However, what we can deduce from our general conception of the social democratic type of organisation are its principal features, the *spirit* of its organisation, and this means, especially in the initial stages of the mass movement, predominantly the coordinating and rallying, and not the regulating and excluding, character of social democratic centralism. But, if this spirit of political flexibility, combined with firm loyalty to the principles of the movement and its unity, takes root in the ranks of the party, then the bumps in any organisational statute, even a badly drafted one, will very soon be ironed out by practice itself. It is not the letter of the statute, but the sense and spirit instilled into it by the active militants that determine the value of an organisational form.

II.

So far we have looked at the question of centralism from the point of view of the general principles of social democracy and, partly, of the current conditions in Russia. But the night-watchman spirit that informs the ultracentralism advocated by Lenin and his friends is not just a chance product of errors: it is related to a hostility towards *opportunism* that is carried to the minutest detail of organisational questions.

'It is a matter', says Lenin (p. 52), *'of forging a more or less pointed weapon through the paragraphs of the organisational statute.* The deeper the sources of opportunism, the sharper the point must be.'[286]

Similarly, Lenin regards the absolute power of the Central Committee and the strict statutory restriction of the party as an effective barrier against the opportunist tendency, whose specific characteristics he defines as the innate preference of the intellectual for autonomism and disorganisation and his horror at strict party discipline, at any form of 'bureaucratism' in the life of the party. In Lenin's view, it is only the socialist 'man of letters' who, because of his innate confusion and individualism, could oppose such unbridled powers for the Central Committee; a true proletarian, on the other hand, must, because of his revolutionary class instinct, feel a certain delight in the strictness, severity and resolve of his supreme party organ, and submit, with his eyes cheerfully closed, to all the rough operations of 'party discipline'. *'Bureaucratism* versus democratism', says Lenin, *'is the organisational principle of revolutionary social democracy* versus the organisational principle of the opportunist' (p. 151).[287] He emphasises that a similar conflict between the centralist and the autonomist conception manifests itself in the social democracy of every country where the revolutionary and reformist or revisionist tendencies stand in opposition to one another. He points in particular to recent events in the German party and to the discussion that has begun on the question of the autonomy of the electoral district. For this reason alone a re-examination of the parallels drawn by Lenin should not be without interest and profit.

First of all we should note that there is nothing inherently 'revolutionary Marxist' in the strong emphasis on the innate capacities of the proletarians for social democratic organisation and in the suspicion against the 'intellectual' elements in the social democratic movement; on the contrary it is just as easy to discern in them an affinity with opportunist views. The antagonism between the purely proletarian element and the non-proletarian socialist intelligentsia is the common ideological banner beneath which the French semi-anarchist pure trade-unionist, with his old call, 'Méfiez-vous de politiciens!',[288] joins hands with the mistrust of English trade-unionism for the socialist 'visionary', and lastly, if we have been correctly informed, with the pure 'economism' of the former Petersburg *Rabochaya Mysl*[289] (the newspaper *Labour Thought*), with its translation of trade-unionist narrow-mindedness to autocratic Russia.

Of course, we can detect in the hitherto existing practice of Western European social democracy an undeniable connection between opportunism and the intellectual element as well as between opportunism and decentralising tendencies in organisational questions. But anyone who separates these phenomena, which have arisen on concrete historical foundations, from this context in order to hold them up as abstract models of universal and absolute value is committing a grave sin against the 'Holy Spirit' of Marxism, namely against its historical—dialectical mode of thought.

Taken in the abstract, one can only state that the 'intellectual' as a social element that, stemming from the bourgeoisie, is by origin alien to the proletariat, cannot come to socialism in a manner consonant with his own sense of class identity but only by overcoming that sense by taking the ideological path. For this reason he is more predisposed to opportunistic aberration than is the class conscious proletarian whose immediate class instinct, insofar as he has not lost the living link with his native social milieu and with the proletarian mass, gives him firm revolutionary backbone. However, the concrete form that this inclination on the part of the intellectual towards opportunism takes and, in particular, the tangible shape that it acquires in organisational tendencies, depend in every case on the concrete social milieu of the society in question.

The phenomena in the life of German, French and Italian social democracy to which Lenin refers have arisen on a very definite social basis, namely that of *bourgeois parliamentarism*. As this is the specific breeding-ground for the present opportunist current in the social democratic movement in Western Europe, so the particular tendencies of opportunism towards disorganisation have grown out of it.

Parliamentarism not only supports all the well-known illusions of current opportunism as we have come to know it in France, Italy and Germany: the overrating of reform, of collaboration between classes and parties and of peaceful development, etc. It also prepares the ground in which these illusions can work in practice because, even within social democracy, it separates intellectuals as parliamentarians from, and to a certain extent raises them above, the proletarian mass. Lastly, as the workers' movement grows, this same parliamentarism moulds it into a springboard for political careerism, which is why it makes it into an easy refuge for ambitious castaways from the bourgeoisie.

All these factors also give rise to the definite inclination of the opportunistic intellectual of Western European social democracy towards disorganisation and lack of discipline. The second specific condition for the present opportunist current is the presence of an already highly developed socialist movement and thus also of an influential social democratic party organisation. The latter now serves as the bastion of the revolutionary class movement against bourgeois-parliamentary tendencies, one which will have to be dismantled and destroyed if the compact and active nucleus of the proletariat is to be dissolved in an amorphous mass electorate. This is how the 'autonomist' and decentralising tendencies of modern opportunism arose. They were historically well-founded and very well-suited to particular political aims and can therefore be explained, not by the innate disorderliness or effeteness of the 'intellectual', as Lenin supposes, but by the needs of the bourgeois parliamentarian, not by the *psychology* of the intellectual, but by the *politics* of the opportunist.

All these conditions look significantly different in autocratic Russia, however, where opportunism in the workers' movement is by no means a product of the strong growth in social democracy, of the disintegration of bourgeois society, as in the West, but, on the contrary, of its political backwardness.

It is understandable that the Russian intelligentsia, from which the socialist intellectual is recruited, has a much less well-defined class character, is to a far greater extent declassed, in the precise sense of the word, than the Western European intelligentsia. This, combined with the infancy of the proletarian movement in Russia, certainly results in general in a far greater scope for theoretical instability and opportunistic vacillation which sometimes turns into a complete denial of the political side of the workers' movement and sometimes into the quite opposite belief in terror as the only salvation, and which finally comes to rest in the quagmires of liberalism in the political sphere or Kantian idealism in the 'philosophical'.

In our view the Russian social democratic intellectual lacks not only the positive experience of bourgeois parliamentarism to encourage a specifically *active* tendency towards disorganisation but also the corresponding socio-psychological milieu. The modern Western European man of letters, who devotes himself to the cult of his reputed 'ego' and even drags this 'master-race morality'[290] into the world of socialist thought and struggle, is not typical of the bourgeois intelligentsia in general but of a particular phase of its existence; in other words it is the product of a decadent, putrefied bourgeoisie that has already become entwined in the vicious circles of its own class hegemony. The utopian and opportunist fantasies of the Russian socialist intellectual tend, on the contrary and for good reason, rather to an acceptance of the inverse theoretical form of self-denial and self-deprecation. Surely the one-time movement of 'going to the people',[291] i.e. the obligatory masquerading of the intellectual as a peasant, was for the old Narodniks just a despairing invention by that same intellectual, in the same way that the recent crude cult of the 'calloused hand' is for the disciples of pure 'Economism'.

If we try to solve the question of organisational forms, not by mechanistically transferring rigid patterns from Western Europe to Russia but by examining the particular concrete conditions in Russia itself, we achieve a quite different result. To attribute to opportunism, as Lenin does, general enthusiasm for any particular form of organisation, such a decentralisation, is to misapprehend its inner nature. Opportunist as it is, opportunism has, even in questions of organisation, only one principle and that is lack of principle. It always selects its methods in accordance with circumstances, as long as they suit its ends. But if, like Lenin, we define opportunism as the desire to cripple the independent revolutionary class movement of the proletariat to make it an instrument of the bourgeois intelligentsia's longing for domination, then we must also admit that in the *initial stages* of the workers' movement this end is best achieved not through decentralisation but through rigid *centralism* which puts the still indistinct proletarian movement at the mercy of a handful of intellectual leaders. It is characteristic that in Germany too in the *initial* stages of the movement, before a strong nucleus of conscious proletarians and a proven social democratic tactic existed, both organisational tendencies were represented: extreme centralism through Lassalle's General German Workers' Union,[292] and 'autonomism' through the Eisenachers.[293] It was this tactic of the Eisenachers which, despite all its admitted confusion of principle, provoked a significantly greater active participation of the proletarian element in the intellectual life of the party, a greater spirit of initiative amongst the workers themselves – among other things, the rapid development of a substantial provincial press by this group provides proof of this – and caused a much stronger and healthier *broadening* of the movement than the Lassalleans, who naturally had increasingly pathetic results with their 'dictators'.

In general it can easily be demonstrated that, in conditions where the revolutionary part of the working mass is still unorganised and the movement itself wavering, in short in conditions similar to those in Russia now, it is precisely strict despotic centralism that emerges as the organisational tendency favoured by the opportunist academic. Just as on the other hand in a later stage – against a parliamentary background and in the face of a strong united workers' party – on the other hand *decentralisation* becomes the corresponding tendency of the opportunist intellectual.

It is precisely from the standpoint of Lenin's fears of the dangerous influences exerted by the intelligentsia on the proletarian movement that his own concept of organisation presents the greatest danger to Russian social democracy.

In fact nothing will more easily and more surely deliver up a still young proletarian movement to the power-hungry intellectuals than forcing the movement into the strait-jacket of a bureaucratic centralism that reduces the militant workers to a docile instrument of a 'committee'. On the other hand, nothing will more surely protect the workers from any opportunist abuse committee by an ambitious intelligentsia than the spontaneous revolutionary activity of the workers, the heightening of their sense of political responsibility.

What Lenin sees as a spectre today may very easily become tangible reality tomorrow.

Let us not forget that the revolution imminent in Russia is not a proletarian but a bourgeois revolution that will radically alter the whole setting for the social democratic struggle. Then the Russian intelligentsia too will very soon acquire the clear stamp of its bourgeois class composition. If social democracy is currently the only leader of the Russian working mass, on the morrow of the revolution the bourgeoisie, and above all of course its intelligentsia, will want the mass to form the pedestal for its parliamentary hegemony. The less the spontaneous activity, the free initiative, the political sense of the most aware stratum of the workers is released, the more it is politically dragooned[294] and drilled by a social democratic central committee, the easier the game of the bourgeois demagogues will be in the new Russia, and the more the harvest of today's social democratic labours will find its way into the hay-lofts of the bourgeoisie.

Above all, however, the whole basic approach of the ultracentralist view, which culminates in the idea of protecting the workers' movement from opportunism through an organisational statute, is false. Under the immediate influence of recent events in French, Italian and German social democracy, a tendency has clearly emerged among the Russian Social Democrats also to view opportunism in general as an ingredient that is alien to the proletarian movement and that has only been brought into the workers' movement from outside, together with the elements of bourgeois democracy. Were this correct, statutory organisational limitations would in themselves prove to be quite ineffective against the pressure of the opportunist element. If the massive influx of non-proletarian elements into social democracy arises from such deep-seated causes as the rapid economic collapse of the petty bourgeoisie and the even more rapid political collapse of bourgeois liberalism, the extinction of bourgeois democracy, then it is a naive illusion to imagine that this tidal wave could be held back by a particular version of the paragraphs of the party statute. Paragraphs only regulate the existence of small sects or private societies – the currents of history have always known how to set themselves above the subtlest paragraph. Furthermore, it is quite wrong to think that it is only in the interests of the workers' movement to fend off the massive influx of the elements released by the progressive disintegration of bourgeois society. The idea that social democracy, a class representative of the proletariat, is at the same time the representative of all the progressive interests in society and of all the oppressed victims of the bourgeois social order, is not to be understood merely in the sense that in the programme of social democracy all these interests are brought together as an ideal. This idea becomes reality in the course of the process of historical development, in which social democracy, as a *political party*, increasingly becomes the refuge for the most varied discontented elements, so that it really becomes the party of the people against a tiny minority of the dominant bourgeoisie. It depends only on its knowing how to subjugate the present afflictions of this motley crew of fellow-travellers to the final aims of the working class on a lasting basis, to merge the spirit of non-proletarian opposition into revolutionary proletarian action, in a word, to assimilate the elements that are flooding to it and to digest them. The latter is, however, only possible when, as in Germany until now, there are already powerful trained proletarian élite troops within social democracy who set the tone and are sufficiently conscious to take the declassed and petty bourgeois fellow-travellers into revolutionary tow. In this case a stricter application of the centralist conception in the organisational statute and the sterner formulation of party discipline is very expedient as a dam against the opportunist current. In these circumstances the organisational statute can undoubtedly serve as a weapon in the struggle with opportunism, just as it did in fact serve French revolutionary social democracy against the onslaught of the Jaurèsist confusion and just as a revision of the German party statute in this direction has now become a necessity. But even in this case the party statute should not be construed as in itself a sort of weapon of defence against opportunism, but merely an external coercive instrument for the exercise of the authoritative influence of the revolutionary proletarian majority that actually exists within the party. Where such a majority is lacking, the most rigorous paper sanctions cannot be a substitute.

However, as we have mentioned, the influx of bourgeois elements is by no means the only source of the opportunist current in social democracy. The other source is located rather in the essence of the social democratic struggle itself, in its internal contradictions. The world-historical advance of the proletariat towards its victory is a process which is unique because here, for the first time in history, the popular masses are themselves carrying out their will and carrying it out in opposition to all ruling classes, but this will can only be realised above and beyond the limits of present-day society. On the other hand, however, the masses can only develop this *will* in the day-to-day struggle with the existing order and therefore only within its framework. The identification of the great popular mass with a goal that transcends the whole existing order and the identification of the day-to-day struggle with revolutionary upheaval constitute the dialectical contradiction of the social democratic movement which must, in the whole course of its development, work a way forward logically between the two pitfalls, between losing its mass character and abandoning its goal, between relapsing into sects and declining into a bourgeois reform movement.

It is therefore a quite unhistorical illusion to think that social democratic tactics in the revolutionary sense can be determined in advance once and for all, that the workers' movement can be saved once and for all from opportunist aberrations. Certainly, Marx's teaching provides devastating ammunition against all the basic types of opportunist thought. But, since the social democratic movement is a mass movement and the pitfalls that threaten it derive not from the human mind but from social conditions, no action can be taken against opportunist errors in advance: they can only be overcome, when they have taken tangible form in practice, by the movement itself, with the help, of course, of the weapons provided by Marxism. Seen from this angle, opportunism also appears as a product of the movement itself, as a necessary feature of its historical development. It is precisely in Russia, where social democracy is still young and the political conditions of the workers' movement are so abnormal, that opportunism might to a great extent arise from this source, from the unavoidable groping and experimenting in tactics, from the need to bring the present struggle in quite exceptional, unparalleled circumstances into line with basic socialist principles.

If this is so, then the idea that the emergence of opportunist currents can be prevented in the initial stages of a workers' movement by a particular version of the organisational statute seems to us all the more whimsical. The attempt to ward off opportunism by such paper means can in fact wound not opportunism but social democracy itself and, because this attempt stops the pulse of a healthy living organism, it weakens its resistance in the struggle, not just against opportunist currents, but also — and this might also be of some importance — against the existing social order. The means turn against the end.

This anxious desire of a section of the Russian Social Democrats to protect, through the tutelage of an omniscient and ever-present Central Committee, a workers' movement that is developing with such promise and vigour against making false moves, seems to us generally redolent of the same *subjectivism* that has already played more than one trick on socialist thought in Russia. The tricks that the revered human subject of history likes to perform in its own historical process are amusing. The ego, crushed and mangled by Russian autocracy, wreaks its revenge by placing itself, in its own system of thought, on the throne and declaring itself all-powerful, as a committee of conspirators in the name of a non-existent 'Narodnaya Volya'.[295] But the 'object' proves to be stronger, the knout soon triumphs since *it* proves to be the 'legitimate' expression of the particular stage of the historical process. In the end an even more 'legitimate' child of the historical process appears on the scene – the Russian workers' movement, which has made the most promising start in creating a real people's will for the first time in Russian history. But now the 'ego' of the Russian revolutionary promptly stands on its head and once more declares itself to be an all-powerful controller of history – this time in the majestic person of a Central Committee of the social democratic workers' movement. The nimble acrobat fails to see that the only subject to whom this role of controller now falls is the *mass ego* of the working class that everywhere insists on making its own mistakes and learning the dialectic of history for itself. Finally, let us speak frankly between ourselves: the mistakes that are made by a truly revolutionary workers' movement are, historically speaking, immeasurably more fruitful and more valuable than the infallibility of the best possible 'Central Committee'.

54. PETITION OF THE WORKERS AND INHABITANTS OF ST PETERSBURG TO NICHOLAS II (JANUARY 1905)[296]

G. Gapon and I. Vasimov

Sire!

We, the workers and inhabitants of various ranks of the city of St Petersburg, our wives and children and our helpless aged parents, have come to you, Sire, in search of justice and protection. We have become impoverished, we are oppressed, we are burdened with intolerable toil, we are abused, we are not regarded as human beings but are treated as slaves who should suffer their bitter fate in silence. We have suffered it, but we are being pushed ever further into the slough of poverty, injustice and ignorance, we are being stifled by despotism and tyranny, and we cannot breathe. Sire, our strength is exhausted. We have reached the limits of our endurance. We have reached that terrible moment when death is preferable to the prolongation of unbearable torture.

We have therefore stopped work and told our employers that we shall not start again until our demands have been met. We have not asked for much: we desire only that without which life is not life but slavery and endless torture. Our first request was that our employers should discuss our needs with us. But this they have refused to do: they have denied our right to speak of our needs on the grounds that this right was not recognised by law. They also considered illegal our requests to reduce the working day to eight hours, to establish wage rates in consultation with us and, with our consent, to examine our grievances against the lowest level of factory administration, to increase the daily wage for unskilled workers and women to 1 rouble, to abolish overtime, to provide medical care free from insult, to construct workshops where we could work and not meet our death from terrible draughts, rain and snow.

In the opinion of our employers and the factory administration all this was against the law; our every request was a crime, and our desire to improve our lot was an impertinence, an insult to them.

Sire, there are many thousands of us here, all of us human beings, but only in our aspect and appearance: in reality, like the whole of the Russian people, we are denied every human right, even the right to speak, think, assemble, discuss our needs or take steps to improve our lot. We have been enslaved, and we have been enslaved with the connivance of your officials, with their assistance and collaboration. Any one of us who dares to raise his voice in defence of the working class and of the people is thrown into prison or sent into exile. A kind heart, a sympathetic soul is punished as if it were a crime. To feel pity for someone who is oppressed, deprived of his rights or tortured is a serious crime. The entire working people and the peasantry are at the mercy of the tyranny of a bureaucracy composed of embezzlers and thieves who not only do not care about the interests of the people but trample them underfoot. Bureaucracy has led the country to destruction, brought upon it a shameful war, and is leading Russia further and further into ruin. We, the workers and the people, have no voice whatsoever in the expenditure of the enormous sums extracted from us. We do not even know where and on what the monies collected from the impoverished people go. The people are denied the opportunity to express their desires and demands, to participate in the raising of taxes or in deciding how they are spent. The workers are denied the opportunity to organise themselves into unions for the defence of their own interests.

Sire! Is this really in accordance with the divine laws, by whose grace You reign? And is it really possible to live under such laws? Would it not be better to die, for all of us, the toiling people of the whole of Russia, to die? This would allow the capitalists (the exploiters of the working class) and the officials (who rob the government and plunder the Russian people) to live and enjoy themselves. That is the choice before us, Sire, and that is why we have gathered before the walls of Your palace. Here we seek our last chance of salvation. Do not deny Your people succour; raise them from the grave of injustice, poverty and ignorance, give them the opportunity to control their own destiny, free them from the unbearable oppression of officialdom, tear down the wall between Yourself and Your people and permit them to rule the country in concert with You. You have been placed [on the throne] for the good of the people, but the officials have deprived us of this good, it does not reach us, and we receive only grief and humiliation. Examine our requests dispassionately and carefully: their intent is not evil, but good, both for us, and for You, Sire. We speak not from impudence but from a recognition of the need to escape from a situation that is unbearable for all. Russia is too great, her needs are too varied and numerous for her to be governed by officials alone. Popular representation is essential. The people must help themselves and govern themselves. They alone know their true needs. Do not reject their help, accept it, summon immediately, at once, the representatives of Russia from all classes, all estates, including representatives from the workers. Let both the capitalist and the worker, the official, the priest, the doctor and the teacher all be there; let them all, whoever they may be, choose their own representatives. Let everyone have a free and equal vote and, to this end, order the election of the Constituent Assembly on the basis of universal, secret and equal suffrage.

This is the most important of our requests; everything rests in and on it; this is the principal and the sole means of healing our painful wounds; without it these wounds will bleed and bring us to death's door.

But one measure alone cannot heal our wounds. Others are necessary, Sire, and we tell You, frankly and openly as to a father, in the name of all the toiling classes of Russia, what they are. [These are] necessary:

I. Measures against the ignorance and the lack of rights of the Russian people

1. The immediate release and return of all those who have suffered for their political and religious convictions, for strikes and for peasant disorders.
2. The immediate proclamation of the freedom and inviolability of the individual, freedom of speech and of the press, freedom of assembly, freedom of conscience in religious matters.
3. Universal and compulsory popular education at the expense of the state.
4. Ministerial responsibility to the people and the guarantee of legality in administration.
5. The equality of all, without exception, before the law.
6. The separation of church and state.

II. Measures against the poverty of the people

1. The repeal of indirect taxes and their replacement by a direct, progressive income tax.
2. The abolition of redemption payments, provision of cheap credit and the gradual transfer of the land to the people.
3. Orders for the Navy should be placed in Russia, and not abroad.

4. The termination of the war in accordance with the popular will.

III. Measures against the oppression of labour by capital

1. The abolition of the system of factory inspectors.
2. The establishment in works and factories of permanent commissions elected from among the workers which will, in concert with the administration, examine all claims from individual workers. It would be impossible to dismiss a worker except by decision of this commission.
3. The freedom to establish consumer-producer cooperatives and trade unions — with immediate effect.
4. An eight-hour day and the regulation of overtime.
5. Freedom for labour in its struggle against capital — with immediate effect.
6. The regulation of wages — with immediate effect.
7. The participation, without fail, of working class representatives in the drafting of a law for state insurance for workers — with immediate effect.

These, Sire, are our chief needs with which we turn to You. Only the satisfaction of these needs will make possible the liberation of our Fatherland from slavery and poverty, will make it possible for it to flourish, will make it possible for the workers to organise to defend their own interests against the obvious exploitation by the capitalists and the plundering and oppression of bureaucratic officials. Give orders, and swear that [our needs] will be met and You will make Russia both happy and glorious, and Your name will be engraved in our hearts and in the hearts of our descendants forever. But, if you do not give orders, if you do not respond to our prayer, we shall die here on this square in front of Your palace. We have nowhere else to go, and no reason to go there. Only two roads are open to us: one leads to freedom and happiness, the other to the grave . . . Let our lives be a sacrifice for a Russia worn out with suffering. We offer this sacrifice freely and without regret.

The Priest George Gapon
The Worker Ivan Vasimov.

55. ON AN ARMED UPRISING (APRIL-MAY 1905)[297]

Menshevik Conference Resolution

Setting itself the task of preparing the masses for a rising, social democracy will endeavour to bring the rising under its influence and leadership and use it to serve the interests of the working class.

Bearing in mind that:

1. it is impossible to ensure a simultaneous and widespread rising at a predetermined date and to prepare for it through conspiratorial organisation, if only because of the weak organisation of the leading ranks of the proletariat and the unavoidably spontaneous character of the revolutionary movement of those very popular masses whose rapid induction into the struggle with tsarism is the guarantee of our victory;

2. favourable conditions for a successful uprising depend above all on ceaseless ferment among the masses and the growing disorganisation of the reactionary forces;

3. social democracy, in preparing the way for a rising, must above all:
   a. extend its agitation among the masses on the basis of current political events;
   b. associate with its own political organisation, and bring under its influence any autonomous socio-economic movements that may emerge among the proletarian masses;
   c. strengthen amongst the masses the awareness of the inevitability of the revolution, the need to be ready at all times for armed resistance and the possibility of transforming it into a rising at any moment;
   d. establish the closest links between the fighting proletariat of different localities in order to make it possible for social democracy to take initiatives to transform spontaneous movements into systematic risings; establish the closest possible contact between the proletarian movement in the towns and the revolutionary movement in the countryside;
   e. by means of widespread agitation, arouse the interest of as many sections of the population as possible in the revolutionary struggle of the proletariat for a democratic republic, thus ensuring the maximum of active support from non-proletarian groups for the militant action of the proletariat, led by an independent class-based party.

It is only on the basis of such varied activity on the part of social democracy that it can bring closer the moment for an uprising and improve the chances of bringing it under our leadership; only in this way will the technical and military preparations of our party merit serious attention.[298]

56. ON THE SEIZURE OF POWER AND PARTICIPATION IN A PROVISIONAL GOVERNMENT (APRIL-MAY 1905)[299]

Menshevik Conference Resolution

The decisive victory of the revolution over tsarism may be marked either by the formation of a Provisional Government following a victorious popular uprising or by a revolutionary initiative on the part of one representative institution or another resolving, under direct revolutionary pressure from the people, to organise a National Constituent Assembly.

In either case such a victory will serve as the beginning of a new phase of the revolutionary epoch.

The task that the objective conditions of social development will set for this new phase in the immediate future is the final liquidation of the whole class-based monarchist order in the course of the internal struggle between elements of politically emancipated bourgeois society to realise their social interests and wield power directly.

For this reason even a Provisional Government that took upon itself the realisation of the tasks of what is, historically, a bourgeois revolution, would have, in regulating the internal struggle between the opposing classes of the newly liberated nation, not only to further the development of the revolution, but also to fight against those elements in it that threaten the foundations of the capitalist system.

In these circumstances social democracy must strive to maintain, throughout the course of the revolution, the position that will best preserve for it the chance to further the revolution but will not tie its hands in the struggle with the inconsistent and self-seeking policy of the bourgeois parties, and the position that will prevent it from being submerged in bourgeois democracy.

For this reason social democracy should not aim to seize power or to share it in a Provisional Government, but should remain a party of extreme revolutionary opposition.[300]

This tactic, of course, in no way rules out the expedient of a partial, episodic seizure of power and the formation of revolutionary communes in one town or another, one area or another, solely in the interests of spreading insurrection and throwing the government into disarray.

There is only one case in which social democracy should, on its own initiative, direct its efforts towards seizing power and retaining it for as long as possible: i.e. if the revolution were to spread to the advanced countries of Western Europe where conditions are to a certain extent already ripe for the realisation of socialism. In this event the restricted historical limits of the Russian revolution may be significantly extended and the possibility arises of embarking on the path of socialist transformation.[301]

By devising our tactics so as to retain for the Social Democratic Party throughout the revolutionary period a position of extreme revolutionary opposition to all the successive governments in the course of the revolution, social democracy can best prepare itself to make use of government power if it should fall into its hands.

57. TWO TACTICS OF SOCIAL DEMOCRACY IN THE DEMOCRATIC REVOLUTION (1905): EXTRACTS[302]

V.I. Lenin

Preface

In a revolutionary period it is very difficult to keep abreast of events which provide an astonishing amount of new material for an appraisal of the tactical slogans of the revolutionary parties. The present pamphlet was written before the events in Odessa.[303] We have already pointed out in *Proletarii* (no. 9, 'Revolution Teaches')[304] that these events have forced even those Social Democrats who developed the 'uprising as process' theory and who rejected propaganda for a provisional revolutionary government actually to go over, or begin to go over, to their opponents' side. Without doubt revolution teaches with a rapidity and thoroughness that appear improbable in peaceful periods of political development. And it teaches — and this is particularly important — not only the leaders, but the masses as well.

There is not the slightest doubt that the revolution will teach social democratism to the working masses in Russia. The revolution will confirm the programme and tactic of social democracy in actual practice by demonstrating the true nature of the various classes of society, by demonstrating the bourgeois character of our democracy and the real aspirations of the peasantry who are revolutionary in the bourgeois-democratic sense but carry within them not the idea of 'socialisation' but [the seeds of] a new class struggle between the peasant bourgeoisie and the rural proletariat. The old illusions of the old Populism (*Narodnichestvo*), which are so clearly visible, for instance, in the draft programme of the Socialist Revolutionary Party[305] on the question of the development of capitalism in Russia, the question of the democratic character of our 'society', and.the question of the significance of complete victory for a peasant uprising — all these illusions will be utterly and mercilessly shattered by revolution. For the first time the various classes will receive their real political baptism. These classes will emerge from the revolution with a definite political countenance, for they will have revealed themselves not only in the programmes and the tactical slogans of their ideologists but also in the open political activity of the masses.

Undoubtedly, the revolution will teach us and will teach the masses of the people. But the question that now confronts a militant political party is: shall we be able to teach the revolution anything? Shall we be able to make use of the correctness of our social democratic doctrine, of our bond with the only thoroughly revolutionary class, the proletariat, to put a proletarian imprint on the revolution, to carry the revolution to a real and decisive victory, not in word but in deed, and to paralyse the irresolution, half-heartedness, and treachery of the democratic bourgeoisie?

It is to this end that we must direct all our efforts, and the achievement of that end will depend, on the one hand, on the accuracy of our appraisal of the political situation and the correctness of our tactical slogans, and, on the other hand, on whether these slogans will be backed by the real fighting strength of the masses of the workers. All the usual, regular and current work of all organisations and groups of our party, the work of propaganda, agitation and organisation, is directed towards strengthening and expanding the ties with the masses. This work is always necessary but it cannot be considered adequate at a time of revolution. In a contingency like this the working class feels an instinctive urge for open revolutionary action, and we must learn to define the aims of this action correctly, and then make these aims as widely known and understood as possible. It must not be forgotten that the current pessimism about our ties with the masses very often serves as a screen for bourgeois ideas of the proletariat's role in the revolution. Undoubtedly, we still have a great deal to do in educating and organising the working class; but now the gist of the matter is: where should we place the main political emphasis in this work of education and organisation? On the trade unions and legally existing associations, or on an insurrection, on the work of creating a revolutionary army and a revolutionary government? Both serve to educate and organise the working class. Both are, of course, necessary. But in the present revolution the problem amounts to this: which is to be emphasised in the work of educating and organising the working class, the former or the latter?

The outcome of the revolution depends on whether the working class will play the part of a subsidiary to the bourgeoisie, a subsidiary that is powerful in the force of its onslaught against the autocracy, but impotent politically, or whether it will play the part of leader of the people's revolution. The more intelligent representatives of the bourgeoisie are perfectly aware of this. That is why *Osvobozhdenie* praises Akimovism, economism in social democracy, the trend that is *now* bringing the trade unions and legally existing associations to the forefront. That is why Mr Struve (in *Osvobozhdenie*, no. 72) welcomes the Akimovist tendency in the new-*Iskrist* ideas.[306] That is why he comes down so heavily on the detested revolutionary narrowness of the decisions of the Third Congress of the Russial Social Democratic Labour Party.[307]

It is especially important at the present time for Social Democrats to have the orrect tactical slogans to lead the masses. There is nothing more dangerous in a evolutionary period than belittling the importance of tactical slogans that are ound in principle. For example, *Iskra* in no. 104 actually goes over to the side of :s opponents in the social democratic movement and yet, at the same time, it dis-arages the importance of slogans and tactical decisions that are ahead of the times nd indicate the path along which the movement is proceeding, though with a num-er of failures, errors, etc.[308] On the contrary, the preparation of correct tactical ecisions is of immense importance for a party that wishes to lead the proletariat 1 the spirit of sound Marxist principles, and not merely to follow in the tail *khvost*] of events. In the resolutions of the Third Congress of the Russian Social)emocratic Labour Party and of the conference of the section that has split away rom the party, we have the most precise, most carefully considered and most com-lete expression of tactical views — views not casually expressed by individual vriters, but accepted by the responsible representatives of the social democratic roletariat. Our party is ahead of all others, for it has a precise and generally ccepted programme. It must also set the other parties an example of a principled ttitude to its tactical resolutions, as distinct from the opportunism of the demo-ratic *Osvobozhdenie* bourgeoisie, and the revolutionary phrase-mongering of the ocialist Revolutionaries. It was only during the revolution that they suddenly nought of coming forward with a 'draft' programme and of investigating for the rst time whether it is a bourgeois revolution that is going on before their eyes.

That is why we think it the most urgent task of the revolutionary Social Demo-rats to study carefully the tactical resolutions of the Third Congress of the Russian ocial Democratic Labour Party and of the conference, define what deviations from ne principles of Marxism they contain, and get a clear understanding of the social emocratic proletariat's concrete tasks in a democratic revolution. It is to this work nat the present pamphlet is devoted. The testing of our tactics from the standpoint f the principles of Marxism and of the lessons of the revolution is also necessary or those who really desire to pave the way for unity of tactics as a basis for the ıture complete unity of the whole Russian Social Democratic Labour Party, and ot to confine themselves solely to verbal admonitions.

N. Lenin
July 1905.

hapter 12.

ill the sweep of the democratic revolution be diminished if the bourgeoisie recoils om it?

he preceding lines were already written when a copy came to hand of the resol-tions adopted by the Caucasian Conference of the new-*Iskrists*, and published by *kra*. Even if we tried, we could not invent anything better *pour la bonne bouche* ıs a titbit).

The editors of *Iskra* rightly remark, 'On the fundamental question of tactics the

Caucasian Conference also arrived at a decision analogous' (in truth!) 'to that adopted by the All-Russian Conference' (i.e. of the new-*Iskra* group).[309] 'The question of social democracy's attitude towards a provisional revolutionary government has been settled by the Caucasian comrades in the spirit of most outspoken opposition to the new method advocated by the *Vpered*[310] group and the delegates of the so-called congress who joined it.' 'It must be admitted that the formulation of the proletarian party's tactics in a bourgeois revolution, as given by the Conference, is *most apt.*'

What is true is true. No one could have provided a more 'apt' formulation of the fundamental error of the new-*Iskra* group. We shall quote this formulation in full, first mentioning parenthetically the blossoms, and then, the fruit they finally bear.

Here is the resolution on a provisional government adopted by the Caucasian Conference of new-*Iskra* supporters:

Whereas we consider it to be our task to take advantage of the revolutionary situation so as to deepen (of course, they should have added: *à la* Martynov!')[311] social democratic consciousness in the proletariat (only to render the consciousness more profound, and not to achieve a republic? What a 'profound' conception of revolution!) and in order to secure for the party complete freedom to criticise the nascent bourgeois-state system (it is not our business to secure a republic! Our business is only to secure freedom of criticism. Anarchist ideas engender anarchist language: 'bourgeois-state' system!), the conference declares itself against forming a social democratic provisional government, and entering such a government . . . and considers it to be the most expedient course to exercise pressure from without (from below and not from above) upon the bourgeois provisional government in order to secure a feasible measure (!?) of democratisation of the state system. The conference believes that the formation of a provisional government by Social Democrats, or their entering such a government would lead, on the one hand, to the masses of the proletariat becoming disappointed with the Social Democratic Party and abandoning it, because the Social Democrats, despite the seizure of power, would not be able to satisfy the pressing needs of the working class, including the establishment of socialism (a republic is not a pressing need! The authors in their innocence do not notice that they are speaking purely anarchist language, as if they were repudiating participation in bourgeois revolutions!), and, on the other hand, *would cause the bourgeois classes to recoil from the revolution and thus diminish its sweep.*

That is the crux of the matter. That is where anarchist ideas become interwoven (as is constantly the case among the West European Bernsteinians too) with the purest opportunism. Just imagine: these people will not enter a provisional government because that would cause the bourgeoisie to recoil from the revolution, thereby diminishing the sweep of the revolution! Here, indeed, we have the new-*Iskra* philosophy as a whole, in a pure and consistent form: since the revolution is a bourgeois revolution, we must bow to bourgeois philistinism and make way for it. If we are even in part, even for a moment, guided by the consideration that our participation may cuase the bourgeoisie to recoil, we thereby simply hand over leadership of the revolution entirely to the bourgeois classes. We thereby place the proletariat entirely under the tutelage of the bourgeoisie (while retaining complete 'freedom of criticism'!!) compelling the proletariat to be moderate and meek, so that the bourgeoisie does not recoil. We emasculate the most vital needs of the proletariat, namely, its political needs – which the Economists and their imitators have never properly understood – so as not to make the bourgeoisie recoil. We go over completely from the platform of revolutionary struggle for the achievement of democracy to the extent required by the proletariat, to a platform of horse-trading with the bourgeoisie, buying the bourgeoisie's voluntary consent ('so that it should not recoil') at the price of our principles, by betraying the revolution.

In two short lines, the Caucasian new-*Iskrists* managed to express the gist of the tactic of betraying revolution and converting the proletariat into a wretched appendage of the bourgeois classes. That which we deduced above from the errors of the new-*Iskra* tendency we now see elevated to a clear and definite principle, viz. following in the wake of the monarchist bourgeoisie. Since the establishment of a republic would make the bourgeoisie recoil (and is already doing so – Mr Struve is an example), down with the fight for a republic. Since every energetic and consistent democratic demand on the part of the proletariat makes the bourgeoisie recoil, always and everywhere in the world – hide in your lairs, working men; act only from without; do not dream of using, in the interests of the revolution, the instruments and weapons of the 'bourgeois-state' system; reserve for yourselves 'freedom of criticism'!

The fundamental fallacy in their very conception of the term 'bourgeois revolution' has come to the surface. The Martynov or new-*Iskra* 'conception' of this term leads directly to the proletariat's cause being betrayed to the bourgeoisie.

Those who have forgotten the old Economism and do not study or remember it will find it difficult to understand the present resurgence of Economism. Call to mind the Bernsteinian *Credo*. From 'purely proletarian' views and programmes its authors drew the following conclusion: we Social Democrats must concern ourselves with economics, with the real working class cause, with freedom to criticise all political chicanery, with really rendering social democratic work more profound. Politics are for the liberals. God save us from falling into 'revolutionism: that will make the bourgeoisie recoil. Those who will re-read the whole *Credo* or the *Separate Supplement* to no. 9 of *Rabochaya Mysl*[312] (September 1899) will ascertain the entire course of this reasoning.

Today we have the same thing, only on a large scale, applied to an appraisal of the whole of the 'great' Russian revolution – alas, vulgarised and reduced in advance to a travesty of the theoreticians of orthodox philistinism! We Social Democrats must concern ourselves with freedom of criticism, with making class consciousness more profound, with action from without. They, the bourgeois classes, must have freedom to act, a free field for revolutionary (read: liberal) leadership, freedom to effect 'reforms' from above.

These vulgarisers of Marxism have never given thought to what Marx said about the need to replace the weapon of criticism by the criticism of weapons.[313] Taking the name of Marx in vain they in actual fact draw up resolutions on tactics wholly in the spirit of the Frankfurt bourgeois windbags, who freely criticised absolutism and deepened democratic consciousness, but failed to understand that a time of revolution is a time of action, of action from both above and below. By turning Marxism into sophistry they have turned the ideology of the advanced, the most determined and energetic revolutionary class into an ideology of its most backward strata, of those who shrink from difficult revolutionary-democratic tasks, and leave them to the Struves to take care of.

If the bourgeois classes recoil from revolution because Social Democrats enter a revolutionary government they will thereby 'diminish the sweep' of the revolution.

Listen to that, Russian workers: the sweep of the revolution will be the mightier if it is effected by the Struves, who are not scared of the Social Democrats, and want not to gain victory over tsarism but to come to terms with it. The sweep of the revolution will be mightier if the first of the two possible outcomes outlined above eventuates, i.e. if the monarchist bourgeoisie comes to terms with the autocracy on a 'constitution' *à la* Shipov![314]

Social Democrats who write such disgraceful things in resolutions for the guidance of the whole party, or who approve of such 'apt' resolutions, are so blinded by sophistry, which has driven the living spirit completely out of Marxism, that they fail to notice that these resolutions turn all their other fine words into empty phrases. Take any of their articles in *Iskra*, or even the notorious pamphlet written by our notorious Martynov[315] – there you will read about a *popular* insurrection, about carrying the revolution to *completion*, about striving to rely upon the *common people* in the struggle against the inconsistent bourgeoisie. However, all these excellent things become miserable phrases as soon as you accept or approve the idea that 'the sweep of the revolution' will be 'diminished' as a consequence of the bourgeoisie's alienation. These are the alternatives, gentlemen: either we, together with the people, must strive to carry out the revolution and win complete victory over tsarism *despite* the inconsistent, self-seeking, and cowardly bourgeoisie, or else we do not accept this 'despite', and are afraid that the bourgeoisie may 'recoil' from the revolution; in the second case we are betraying the proletariat and the people to the bourgeoisie – the inconsistent, self-seeking, and cowardly bourgeoisie.

Do not take it into your heads to misinterpret my words. Do not shout that you are being accused of deliberate treachery. No, you have always crawled towards the marsh, and have at last crawled into it, just as unconsciously as the Economists of old, who were irresistibly and irrevocably drawn down the inclined plane of 'deeper' Marxism, until it at last became an anti-revolutionary, soulless and lifeless intellectual pose.

Have you, gentlemen, ever given thought to the real social forces that determine 'the sweep of the revolution'? Let us disregard the foreign political forces, the international combinations, which have developed very favourably for us at the present time, but which we all leave out of the discussion, and rightly so, insofar as we are concerned with the question of Russia's internal forces. Examine these internal social forces. Aligned against the revolution are the autocracy, the imperial court, the police, the bureaucracy, the army and a handful of the aristocracy. The deeper the indignation of the people grows, the less reliable the troops become, and the more the bureaucracy wavers. Moreover, the bourgeoisie, on the whole, is now in favour of revolution, zealously speechifying about liberty and holding forth more and more frequently in the name of the people and even in the name of the revolution.[316] But we Marxists all know from theory and from daily and hourly observation of our liberals, *Zemstvo* people, and *Osvobozhdenie* supporters that the bourgeoisie is inconsistent, self-seeking and cowardly in its support of the revolution. The bourgeoisie, in the mass, will inevitably turn towards counter-revolution, towards the autocracy, against the revolution, and against the people, as soon as its narrow, selfish interests are met, as soon as it 'recoils' from consistent democracy (*and it is already recoiling from it!*). There remains the 'people', that is, the proletariat and the peasantry: the proletariat alone can be relied on to march on to the end, for it goes far beyond the democratic revolution. That is why the proletariat fights in the forefront for a republic and contemptuously rejects stupid and unworthy advice to take into account the possibility of the bourgeoisie recoiling. The peasantry includes a great number of semi-proletarian as well as petty-bourgeois elements. This makes it unstable too, compelling the proletariat to rally in a strictly class party. However, the instability of the peasantry differs radically from that of the bourgeoisie, for at present the peasantry is interested not so much in the absolute preservation of private property as in the confiscation of the landed estates, one of the principal forms of private property. Without thereby becoming socialist, or ceasing to be petty bourgeois, the peasantry is capable of becoming a wholehearted and most radical adherent of the democratic revolution. The peasantry will inevitably become such if only the course of revolutionary events, which brings it enlightenment, is not prematurely cut short by the treachery of the bourgeoisie and the defeat of the proletariat. Subject to this condition the peasantry will inevitably become a bulwark of the revolution and the republic, for only a completely victorious revolution can give the peasantry *everything* in the sphere of agrarian reforms — *everything* that the peasants desire, dream of and truly need (not for the abolition of capitalism as the 'Socialist Revolutionaries' imagine, but) in order to emerge from the mire of semi-serfdom, from the gloom of oppression and servitude, in order to improve their living conditions, as much as they can be improved within the system of commodity production.

Moreover, it is not only through the prospect of radical agrarian reform that the peasantry is attached to the revolution, but through all its general and permanent interests as well. Even when fighting with the proletariat, the peasantry stands in need of democracy, for only a democratic system is capable of accurately expressing its interests and ensuring its predominance as a mass, as the majority. The more enlightened the peasantry becomes (and since the war with Japan it is becoming enlightened at a pace unsuspected by many who are accustomed to measure enlightenment with the school yardstick), the more consistently and resolutely will it stand for a thorough-going democratic revolution; for, unlike the bourgeoisie, it has nothing to fear from the people's supremacy, but on the contrary stands to gain by it. A democratic republic will become the peasantry's ideal as soon as it begins to throw off its naive monarchism, because the conscious monarchism of the bourgeois stockbrokers (with an upper chamber, etc.) implies for the peasantry the same absence of rights and the same oppression and ignorance as it suffers today, only slightly polished over with the varnish of European constitutionalism.

That is why, as a class, the bourgeoisie naturally and inevitably tends to come under the wing of the liberal-monarchist party, while the peasantry, in the mass, tends to come under the leadership of the revolutionary and republican party. That is why the bourgeoisie is incapable of carrying through the democratic revolution to its consummation, while the peasantry is capable of doing so, and we must exert all our efforts to help it do so.

The objection may be raised that this goes without saying, is all ABC, something that all Social Democrats understand perfectly well. No, that is not the case; it is not understood by those who can talk about 'the diminishing sweep' of the revolution as a consequence of the bourgeoisie falling away from it. Such people repeat the words of our agrarian programme, which they have learned by rote without understanding their meaning, for otherwise they would not be frightened by the concept of the revolutionary-democratic dictatorship of the proletariat and the peasantry, which inevitably follows from the entire Marxist world outlook and from our programme; otherwise they would not restrict the sweep of the great Russian revolution to the limits to which the bourgeoisie is prepared to go. Such people defeat their abstract Marxist revolutionary phrases by their concrete anti-Marxist and anti-revolutionary resolutions.

Those who really understand the role of the peasantry in a victorious Russian revolution would not dream of saying that the sweep of the revolution will be diminished if the bourgeoisie recoils from it. For, in actual fact, the Russian revolution will begin to assume its real sweep, and will really assume the widest revolutionary sweep possible in the epoch of bourgeois-democratic revolution, only when the bourgeoisie recoils from it and when the masses of the peasantry come out as active revolutionaries side by side with the proletariat. To be consistently carried through to the end, our democratic revolution must rely on forces capable of paralysing the inevitable inconsistency of the bourgeoisie (i.e. capable precisely of 'making it recoil from the revolution', which the Caucasian adherents of *Iskra* fear so much because of their thoughtlessness).

The proletariat must carry the democratic revolution to completion, allying to itself the mass of the peasantry in order to crush the autocracy's resistance by force and paralyse the bourgeoisie's instability. The proletariat must accomplish the socialist revolution, allying to itself the mass of the semi-proletarian elements of the population, so as to crush the bourgeoisie's resistance by force and paralyse the instability of the peasantry and the petty bourgeoisie. Such are the tasks of the proletariat, so narrowly presented by the new-*Iskra* group in all their arguments and resolutions on the sweep of the revolution.

One circumstance, however, should not be forgotten, one that is frequently lost sight of in discussions about the 'sweep' of the revolution. It should not be forgotten that it is not a question of the difficulties presented by this problem but the way in which its solution is to be sought and attained. It is not a question of whether it is easy or difficult to render the sweep of the revolution mighty and invincible, but of how to act so as to make that sweep more powerful. It is on the fundamental nature of our activities, the direction they should follow, that our views differ. We emphasise this because inattentive and unscrupulous people only too frequently confuse two different problems, viz. that of the direction to be followed, i.e. the choice of one of two different roads, and that of the ease of attaining our goal, or the nearness of its attainment along a given road.

In the foregoing we have not dealt with this last problem at all because it has not evoked any disagreement or differences in the party. The problem itself is, of course, extremely important and deserving of the most serious attention from all Social Democrats. It would be unforgivable optimism to forget the difficulties involved in drawing into the movement the masses not only of the working class, but also of the peasantry. These difficulties have more than once wrecked efforts to carry through a democratic revolution to completion, the inconsistent and self-seeking bourgeoisie triumphing most of all, because it has 'made capital' in the shape of monarchist protection against the people, at the same time 'preserving the virginity' of liberalism . . . or of the *Osvobozhdenie* trend. However, difficulty does not imply impossibility. The important thing is to be confident that the path chosen is the right one, such confidence multiplying a hundredfold revolutionary energy and revolutionary enthusiasm, which can perform miracles.

The depth of the rift among present-day Social Democrats on the question of the path to be chosen can at once be seen by comparing the Caucasian resolution of the new-*Iskra* supporters with the resolution of the Third Congress of the Russian Social Democratic Labour Party. The congress resolution says: the bourgeoisie is inconsistent and will without fail try to deprive us of the gains of the revolution. Therefore, make more energetic preparations for the fight, comrades and workers! Arm yourselves, win the peasantry over to your side! We shall not surrender our revolutionary gains to the self-seeking bourgeoisie without a struggle. The resolution of the Caucasian new-*Iskra* supporters says: the bourgeoisie is inconsistent and may recoil from the revolution. Therefore, comrades and workers, please do not think of joining a provisional government, for, if you do, the bourgeoisie will certainly recoil, and the sweep of the revolution will thereby be diminished!

One side says: advance the revolution to its consummation despite resistance or passivity on the part of the inconsistent bourgeoisie.

The other side says: do not think of independently advancing the revolution to completion for, if you do, the inconsistent bourgeoisie will recoil from it.

Are these not two diametrically opposite paths? Is it not obvious that one set of tactics absolutely excludes the other, that the first tactic is the only correct tactic of revolutionary social democracy, while the second is in fact purely *Osvobozhdenie* tactics?

Conclusion

Dare we win?

People who are superficially acquainted with the state of affairs in Russian social democracy, or who judge as mere onlookers, with no knowledge of the whole history of our inner-party struggle since the days of Economism, very often dismiss the disagreements on tactics which have now taken shape, especially after the Third Congress, with the simple argument that there are two natural, inevitable and quite reconcilable trends in every social democratic movement. One side, they say, lays special emphasis on the ordinary, current and everyday work, on the necessity of developing propaganda and agitation, of preparing forces, deepening the movement, etc., while the other side lays emphasis on the militant, general political, revolutionary tasks of the movement, points to the necessity of insurrection, and advances the slogans of a revolutionary-democratic dictatorship, and a provisional revolutionary government. Neither side should exaggerate, they say; extremes are bad in both cases (and, generally speaking, everywhere in the world), etc., etc.

The cheap truisms of the pedestrian (and 'political' in quotation marks) wisdom undoubtedly contained in such arguments too often conceal an inability to understand the urgent and acute needs of the party. Take the present-day tactical differences among Russian Social Democrats. Of course, the special emphasis on the everyday routine aspect of the work, such as we see in the new-*Iskra* arguments about tactics, could not of itself present any danger or give rise to any divergence of opinion regarding tactical slogans. But it is sufficient to compare the resolutions of the Third Congress of the Russian Social Democratic Labour Party with the conference resolutions for this divergence to become striking.

What, then, is the trouble? In the first place, it is not enough to speak in the abstract of two currents in the movement, and of the harmfulness of extremes. One must know concretely what ails a given movement at a given time, and what constitutes the real political danger to the party at the present time. Secondly, one must know what real political forces profit by the tactical slogans advanced – or perhaps by the absence of certain slogans. If one were to listen to the new-*Iskrists* one would arrive at the conclusion that the Social Democratic Party is threatened with the danger of throwing overboard propaganda and agitation, the economic struggle, and criticism of bourgeois democracy, the danger of becoming inordinately absorbed in military preparations, armed attacks, the seizure of power, etc. Actually, however, real danger is threatening the party from an entirely different quarter. Anyone who is at all familiar with the state of the movement, anyone who follows it carefully and thoughtfully, cannot fail to see the ridiculous aspect of the new-*Iskrists*' fears. The entire work of the Russian Social Democratic Labour Party has already taken a definite and unchanging shape, which absolutely guarantees that our main attention will be fixed on propaganda and agitation, flysheets and mass meetings, the distribution of leaflets and pamphlets, assisting in the economic struggle and championing the slogans of that struggle. There is not a single party committee, not a single district committee, not a single central delegates' meeting or a single factory group where 99% of all the attention, energy and time is not always and invariably devoted to these functions, which have become firmly established ever since the middle of the nineties. Only those who are entirely unfamiliar with the movement do not know that. Only very naive or ill-informed people will accept new-*Iskra*'s repetition of stale truths at their face value, when that is done with an air of great importance.

The fact is that, far from displaying excessive zeal with regard to the tasks of incurrection, to general political slogans and to giving leadership to the entire popular revolution, we, on the contrary, display a most striking *backwardness* in this very respect, a backwardness which constitutes our greatest weakness and is a real danger to the movement, which may degenerate, and in some places is degenerating, from one that is revolutionary in deed into one that is revolutionary in word. Among the many, many hundreds of organisations, groups and circles that are conducting the work of the party you will not find one which has not, since its very inception, conducted the kind of day-to-day work the new-*Iskra* know-alls now talk of with the air of people who have discovered new truths. On the other hand, you will find only an insignificant percentage of groups and circles that have understood the tasks an insurrection entails, have begun to carry them out, and have realised the necessity of leading the entire popular revolution against tsarism, the necessity of advancing certain definite progressive slogans and no other, for that purpose.

We have, incredibly, fallen behind our progressive and genuinely revolutionary tasks; in very many instances we have not even become aware of them; here and there we have failed to notice that revolutionary-bourgeois democracy has gained strength owing to our backwardness in this respect. But, with their backs turned to the course of events and the requirements of the times, the new-*Iskra* writers keep insistently repeating: 'Don't forget the old! Don't let yourselves be carried away by the new!' This is the unvarying *Leitmotiv* in all the important resolutions of the conference: whereas in the congress resolutions you just as invariably read: while confirming the old (but not stopping to chew it over and over again precisely because it *is* old and has already been settled and recorded in literature, in resolutions and by experience), we bring forward a new task, draw attention to it, issue a new slogan and demand that genuinely revolutionary Social Democrats immediately set to work to put it into effect.

That is how matters really stand with regard to the question of the two trends in social democratic tactics. The revolutionary period has presented new tasks, which only the totally blind can fail to see. Some Social Democrats unhesitatingly recognise these tasks and place them on the order of the day, declaring: the armed uprising brooks no delay; prepare yourselves for it immediately and energetically; remember that it is indispensable for a decisive victory; put forward slogans for a republic, for a provisional government, for a revolutionary-democratic dictatorship of the proletariat and the peasantry. Other Social Democrats, however, draw back, mark time, write prefaces instead of giving slogans; instead of seeing what is new, while confirming what is old, they chew over the latter tediously and at great length, inventing pretexts to avoid the new, unable to determine the conditions for a decisive victory or to put forward slogans which alone are in line with a desire to achieve full victory.

The political outcome of this tailism stares us in the face. The fable about a *rapprochement* between the 'majority' of the Russian Social Democratic Labour Party and revolutionary-bourgeois democracy remains a fable unconfirmed by a single political fact, by a single important resolution of the 'Bolsheviks' or a single document of the Third Congress of the Russian Social Democratic Labour Party. On the other hand, the opportunist, monarchist bourgeoisie, as represented by *Osvobozhdenie*, has long been *welcoming* the trends in the 'principles' advocated by the new-*Iskra* group, and is now actually using their stream to drive its mill and is adopting their catchwords and 'ideas', which are directed against 'secrecy' and 'riots', against exaggerating the 'technical' aspect of the revolution, against openly proclaiming the slogan of insurrection, against the 'revolutionism' of extreme demands, etc., etc. The resolution of an entire conference of 'Menshevik' Social Democrats in the Caucasus and the endorsement of that resolution by the editors of the new-*Iskra* sums up the whole matter politically in an unmistakable way: what if the bourgeoisie should recoil in case the proletariat takes part in a revolutionary-democratic dictatorship! This puts the matter in a nutshell and gives the finishing touches to the proletariat's transformation into an appendage to the monarchist bourgeoisie. The *political significance* of the new-*Iskra*'s tailism is thereby proved in fact – not by a casual observation from some individual but by a resolution especially endorsed by an entire tendency.

Anyone who gives thought to these facts will understand the real significance of stock references to two sides and two tendencies in the social democratic movement. For a full-scale study of these tendencies one should take Bernsteinism. In exactly the same way the Bernsteinians have been drilling into us that it is they who understand the proletariat's true needs and the tasks of building up its forces, the task of deepening all the work, preparing the elements of a new society and the task of propaganda and agitation. Bernstein says: we demand a frank recognition of that which is, thus sanctifying 'movement' *without* any 'ultimate aim', sanctifying defensive tactics alone, preaching the tactics of fear 'lest the bourgeoisie recoil'. So the Bernsteinians raised an outcry against the 'Jacobinism' of the revolutionary Social Democrats, against 'publicists' who fail to understand the 'workers' initiative', etc., etc. In reality, as everyone knows, revolutionary Social Democrats have never even thought of abandoning day-to-day, petty work, the mustering of forces, etc., etc. All they demanded was a clear understanding of the ultimate aim, a clear presentation of revolutionary tasks; they wanted to raise the semi-proletarian and semi-petty-bourgeois strata to the revolutionary level of the proletariat – not to reduce the latter level to that of opportunist considerations such as 'lest the bourgeoisie recoil'. Perhaps the most vivid expression of this rift between the intellectual opportunist wing and the proletarian revolutionary wing of the party was the question: *Dürfen wir siegen?* 'Dare we win?' Is it permissible for us to win? Would it not be dangerous for us to win? Ought we to win? This question, so strange at first sight, was however raised and had to be raised, because the opportunists were afraid of victory, were frightening the proletariat away from it, predicting that trouble would come of it and ridiculing slogans that directly called for it.

The same fundamental division into an intellectual-opportunist and proletarian-revolutionary tendency exists among us too, with the very material difference, however, that here we are faced with the question of a democratic, not of a socialist revolution. The question 'dare we win?', which seems so absurd at first sight, has been raised among us as well. It has been raised by Martynov in his *Two Dictator-ships*, where he prophesies dire misfortune if we prepare well for an insurrection, and carry it out quite successfully.[317] The question has been raised in all the new-*Iskra* literature dealing with a provisional revolutionary government, and persistent if futile efforts have all the time been made to liken Millerand's participation in a bourgeois-opportunist government to Varlin's participation in a petty-bourgeois revolutionary government. It is embodied in the resolution: 'lest the bourgeoisie recoil'. And although Kautsky, for instance, now tries to wax ironical and says that our dispute about a provisional revolutionary government is like sharing out the meat before the bear is killed, this irony only proves that even clever and revolutionary Social Democrats are liable to put their foot in it when they talk about something they know of only by hearsay.[318] German social democracy is not yet so near to killing its bear (carrying out a socialist revolution), but the dispute as to whether we 'dare' kill the bear has been of enormous importance from the point of view of principles and of practical politics. Russian Social Democrats are not yet so close to being able to 'kill their bear' (carry out a democratic revolution), but the question as to whether we 'dare' kill it is of extreme importance to the whole future of Russia and that of Russian social democracy. An army cannot be energetically and successfully mustered and led unless we are sure that we 'dare' win.

Take our old Economists. They, too, clamoured that their opponents were conspirators and Jacobins (see *Rabochee Delo*, especially no. 10, and Martynov's speech at the Second Congress, in the debate on the programme), that by plunging into politics they were divorcing themselves from the masses, that they were losing sight of the fundamentals of the working class movement, ignoring the workers' initiative, etc., etc. In reality these supporters of 'workers' initiative' were opportunist intellectuals, who tried to foist on the workers their own narrow and philistine conception of the tasks of the proletariat. In reality the opponents of Economism, as everyone can see from the old *Iskra*, did not neglect or relegate into the background any of the aspects of social democratic work, nor did they in the least forget the economic struggle; at the same time they were able to present the urgent and immediate political tasks in their full scope and thus opposed the transformation of the workers' party into an 'economic' appendage of the liberal bourgeoisie.

The Economists learned by rote that politics are based on economics and 'understood' this to mean that the political struggle should be reduced to the level of the economic struggle. The new-*Iskrists* have learned by rote that in its economic essence the democratic revolution is a bourgeois revolution, and 'understand' this to mean that the democratic aims of the proletariat should be lowered to the level of bourgeois moderation, a level beyond which 'the bourgeoisie will recoil'. On the pretext of deepening their work, on the pretext of rousing the workers' initiative and pursuing a purely class policy, the Economists were actually delivering the working class into the hands of the liberal-bourgeois politicians, i.e. were leading the party along a path whose objective significance was exactly such. On the same pretexts the new-*Iskrists* are actually betraying to the bourgeoisie the interests of the proletariat in the democratic revolution, i.e. are leading the party along a path whose objective significance is exactly such. The Economists thought that leadership in the political struggle was not the concern of Social Democrats but, properly speaking, that of the liberals. The new-*Iskrists* think that the active conduct of the democratic revolution is no concern of the Social Democrats, but, properly speaking, that of the democratic bourgeoisie, for, they argue, the proletariat's guidance and pre-eminent part will 'diminish the sweep' of the revolution.

In short, the new-*Iskrists* are imitators of Economism, not only in having their origin at the Second Party Congress, but also in the manner in which they now present the tactical tasks of the proletariat in the democratic revolution. They, too, constitute an intellectual-opportunist wing of the party. In the sphere of organisation they made their *début* with the anarchist individualism of intellectuals and ended up with 'disorganisation-as-process', establishing in the 'Rules' adopted by the conference the separation of party publishing activities from the party organisation, and an indirect and practically four-stage system of elections, a system of Bonapartist plebiscites instead of democratic representation, and finally the principle of 'agreements' between the part and the whole. In party tactics they slid down the same inclined plane. In the 'plan of the *Zemstvo* campaign' they declared that addresses to the *Zemstvo*-ists were 'the highest type of demonstration', and discerned only two active forces on the political scene (on the eve of 9 January!) – the government and the bourgeois democrats. They made the urgent task of arming the people 'more profound' by replacing a direct and practical slogan with a call to arm the people with a burning desire to arm themselves. In their official resolutions they have distorted and emasculated the tasks connected with an insurrection, with the establishment of a provisional government, and with a revolutionary-democratic dictatorship. 'Lest the bourgeoisie recoil' – this final chord of their latest resolution throws clear light on the question of where their path is leading the party.

In its social and economic essence, the democratic revolution in Russia is a bourgeois revolution. It is, however, not enough merely to repeat this correct Marxist proposition. It has to be properly understood and properly applied to political slogans. In general, all political liberty founded on present-day, i.e. capitalist, relations of production is bourgeois liberty. The demand for liberty expresses primarily the interests of the bourgeoisie. Its representatives were the first to raise this demand. Its supporters have everywhere used like masters the liberty they acquired, reducing it to moderate and meticulous bourgeois doses, combining it with the most subtle suppression of the revolutionary proletariat in peaceful times, and with savage suppression in tempestuous times.

But only rebel Narodniks, anarchists and Economists could conclude from this that the struggle for liberty should be rejected or disparaged. These intellectualist-philistine doctrines could be foisted on the proletariat only for a time and against its will. The proletariat has always realised instinctively that it needs political liberty, needs it more than anyone else, although the immediate effect of that liberty will be to strengthen and organise the bourgeoisie. It is not by evading the class struggle that the proletariat expects to find its salvation, but by developing it, by extending its scope, its consciousness, organisation and resolution. Whoever disparages the tasks of the political struggle transforms the Social Democrat from a tribune of the people into a trade union secretary. Whoever disparages the proletarian tasks in a democratic bourgeois revolution transforms the Social Democrat from a leader of the people's revolution into a leader of a free labour union.

Yes, the *people's* revolution. Social democracy has fought, and is quite rightly fighting, against the bourgeois-democratic abuse of the word 'people'. It demands that this word shall not be used to cover up failure to understand class antagonisms within the people. It insists categorically on the need for complete class independence for the party of the proletariat. However, it does not divide the 'people' into 'classes' so that the advanced class will become locked up within itself, will confine itself within narrow limits, and emasculate its activity for fear that the economic rulers of the world will recoil; it does that so that the advanced class, which does not suffer from the half-heartedness, vacillation and indecision of the intermediate classes, should fight with all the greater energy and enthusiasm for the cause of the whole people, at the head of the whole people.

That is what the present-day new-*Iskrists* so often fail to understand, people who substitute for active political slogans in the democratic revolution a mere pedantic repetition of the word 'class', declined in all cases and genders!

The democratic revolution is bourgeois in nature. The slogan of a general redistribution, or 'land and freedom' – that most widespread slogan of the peasant masses, down-trodden and ignorant, yet passionately yearning for light and happiness – is a bourgeois slogan. But we Marxists should know that there is not, nor can there be, any other path to real freedom for the proletariat and the peasantry than the path of bourgeois freedom and bourgeois progress. We must not forget that there is not, nor can there be at the present time, any other means of bringing socialism nearer than complete political liberty, than a democratic republic, than the revolutionary-democratic dictatorship of the proletariat and the peasantry. As representatives of the advanced and only revolutionary class, revolutionary without any reservations, doubts or looking back, we must confront the whole of the people with the tasks of the democratic revolution as extensively and boldly as possible and with the utmost initiative. To disparage these tasks means making a travesty of theoretical Marxism, distorting it in philistine fashion, while in practical politics it means placing the cause of the revolution in the hands of the bourgeoisie, which will inevitably recoil from the task of consistently effecting the revolution. The difficulties that lie on the road to the complete victory of the revolution are very great. No one will be able to blame the proletariat's representatives if, when they have done everything in their power, their efforts are defeated by the resistance of reaction, the treachery of the bourgeoisie and the ignorance of the masses. But everybody, and, above all, the class conscious proletariat, will condemn social democracy if it curtails the revolutionary energy of the democratic revolution and dampens revolutionary ardour because it is afraid to win, because it is motivated by the consideration: lest the bourgeoisie recoil.

Revolutions are the locomotives of history, said Marx.[319] Revolutions are festivals of the oppressed and the exploited. At no other time are the mass of the people in a position to come forward as actively as creators of a new social order as at a time of revolution. At such times the people are capable of performing miracles, if judged by the limited, philistine yardstick of gradualist progress. But it is essential that leaders of the revolutionary parties too should advance their aims more comprehensively and boldly at such a time, so that their slogans will always be in advance of the revolutionary initiative of the masses, serve as a beacon, reveal to them our democratic and socialist ideal in all its magnitude and splendour and show them the shortest and most direct route to complete, absolute and decisive victory. Let us leave to the opportunists of the *Osvobozhdenie* bourgeoisie the task of inventing roundabout, circuitous paths of compromise, out of fear of the revolution and of the direct path. If we are forcibly compelled to drag ourselves along such paths we shall be able to fulfil our duty in petty, everyday work also. But first let the choice of path be decided in ruthless struggle. We shall be traitors, betrayers of the revolution, if we do not use this festive energy of the masses and their revolutionary ardour to wage a ruthless and self-sacrificing struggle for the direct and decisive path. Let the bourgeois opportunists contemplate the future reaction with craven fear. The workers will not be intimidated either by the thought that reaction intends to be terrible, or that the bourgeoisie proposes to recoil. The workers do not expect to make deals; they are not asking for petty concessions. What they are aiming at is to crush ruthlessly the reactionary forces, i.e. to set up a *revolutionary-democratic dictatorship of the proletariat and the peasantry*.

Of course in stormy times greater dangers threaten the ship of our party than in periods of the smooth 'sailing' of liberal progress, which means the painfully steady sucking of the working class's life-blood by its exploiters. Of course, the tasks of the revolutionary-democratic dictatorship are infinitely more difficult and more complex than the tasks of an 'extreme opposition', or of an exclusively parliamentary struggle. But whoever is consciously capable of preferring smooth sailing and the course of safe 'opposition' in the present revolutionary situation had better abandon social democratic work for a while, had better wait until the revolution is over, until the festive days have passed, when humdrum, everyday life starts again, and his narrow routine standards no longer strike such an abominably discordant note, or constitute such an ugly distortion of the tasks of the advanced class.

At the head of the whole people, and particularly of the peasantry – for complete freedom, for a consistent democratic revolution, for a republic! At the head of all the toilers and the exploited – for socialism! Such in practice must be the policy of the revolutionary proletariat, such is the class slogan that must permeate and determine the solution of every tactical problem, every practical step of the workers' party during the revolution.

58.   THE PEOPLE'S DUMA AND THE WORKERS' CONGRESS (OCTOBER 1905): EXTRACTS[320]

P.B. Akselrod

And so it is with a clear conscience that I can now propagandise among influential comrades my practical proposition, which is inseparably linked in my mind with agitation for an all-Russian *workers'* congress. In fact, you see, the People's Duma, although summoned on our initiative and with our most energetic participation in the election campaign, nonetheless represents various social strata and this tendency will be strengthened as the democratic principles (upon which, according to our programme, elections to the Constituent Assembly should be conducted) are increasingly carried out and put into practice. Taking this into consideration and bearing in mind the varied background of the representatives in our People's Duma, what guarantee do we have that it will manifest the resolution and steadfastness in its actions and the revolutionary democratism in its demands that are necessary to defend the interests of democracy as a whole and the proletariat in particular? For us there can be only one answer: the foremost strata of the working class must form their own political organisation which has its own centre and which rallies the working masses, in *all possible* forms, around its banner, tirelessly encouraging in them a passionate interest in the burning issues of the day and mobilising them into the arena of decisive revolutionary actions whenever questions arise that affect the vital interests of the working class and the popular masses generally. In a revolutionary period such as Russia is experiencing will there be many days when we can sense a shortage of inflammatory material for agitation among the masses and for bringing them into the movement for the joint defence of their rights and interests? But it is obvious that the political organisation of the workers that I have proposed can be put into effect only through the energetic influence and direct participation (if not on the initiative) of the Social Democrats (workers and intellectuals), as a *closely knit* nucleus, acting in accordance with a definite plan and bringing to the proletarians embraced by the social movement the meaningful inspiration of the idea of the independent emergence of his class on to the socio-political arena, which is necessary if they are to demonstrate a passionate interest in the cause of agitation for a workers' congress and for the summoning of one. Only a party that is thoroughly immersed in the slogan 'The emancipation of the working class can be a matter for the working class alone', only social democracy, for which the revolutionary emergence of the proletarian masses is not a means for alien elements and the ends that they pursue but, on the contrary, a sufficient end in itself, sufficient in the sense that it should serve as the manifestation of the class self-activity of these masses and as the lever for their political elevation; only a party that has *this* fashion can utilise the summoning of a general workers' congress in the interests of a truly political unification of its active revolutionary elements into an independent revolutionary force. That is why I am so insistent that our Organisational Commission and the local groups or committees should attract to this cause the largest possible number of social democratic workers, and I consider the summoning and the work of the congress to be closely linked to the task of the reorganisation of our party, a task that those delegates to the congress who will be elected by social democratic workers' assemblies should fulfil.

Now for the third observation. You ask: 'Are the foremost conscious workers now (at the present moment) marching with due enthusiasm with a slogan that will not attract the whole broad mass to pursue it to the very end?' In my view the very way in which the question is put is not quite correct. For the sake of brevity and clarity I shall explain my idea by an example: the Lassallean association and its First Congress[321] were summoned by a 'slogan' which attracted by no means the 'whole broad mass'. On the contrary, this mass, in as far as it made any political moves, was attracted by the slogans of liberal democracy and frequently acted violently against social democracy, including Lassalle himself. At the same time the 'foremost conscious workers' pursued Lassalle's 'slogan' with passionate enthusiasm. Why? First of all, because Lassalle's slogans (the formation of an all-German workers' union to achieve universal suffrage with the aim of transferring state power to the proletariat) were distinguished by their vitality, they had the most immediate relation to the interests and the vague desires for emancipation of the working masses who had been awakened by liberal democracy, they showed their foremost elements the path upon which they themselves should embark in order to attract increasingly broader strata of these masses to follow them; and lastly because Lassalle and his closest associates knew how to explain to the 'foremost conscious workers' the vital and directly practical significance of the slogans they advanced, how to link them with the questions that *already* interested and aroused these workers. As you see, it is not just a matter of our slogan 'workers' congress' *directly* attracting the following 'of the whole broad mass to the very end'; the centre of gravity of the question consists in whether there is among our foremost workers a conscious desire to attract the following of the 'working mass' on to the path of revolutionary struggle. If there is, then they will greedily grasp at a slogan that shows them the first step towards their unification so that they will, by following this path, form a centre that will rally and lead the whole working class. Enthusiasm for the organisation of the congress gives them a certain realisation of the necessity and enormous importance of it as the first step on the path to their fulfilment of their duties towards their own class.

The broad masses may be attracted more by a slogan contrasting the State Duma, of the officials and all sorts of oppressors and exploiters of the people, with the People's Duma, which would consist of truly popular delegates. But, in order to achieve a situation in which the working class is represented as well and fully as possible at the head of the people in this Duma and in the Constituent Assembly which it must become, it is necessary to have the *organised* participation of the foremost workers in its summoning and organisation, not to mention their broad participation as an independent, closely knit party in the agitation and in the elections. Their unification in such a party is also necessary so that the People's Duma, and then the Constituent Assembly, is surrounded by a strongly revolutionary atmosphere, which would be able to propel them forward through its own great momentum insofar as anti-revolutionary and anti-proletarian tendencies appeared in them. In a word, so that the 'foremost conscious workers' are sufficiently and with complete 'enthusiasm' attracted by the idea of an all-Russian congress, because they alone are aware of its necessity as a means for the organisation of the popular revolutionary force that might preserve for the revolution victory over all its enemies and at the same time retain for the proletariat the opportunity of achieving a maximum of the political rights and economic improvements that are attainable on the basis of capitalism. The atmosphere of general revolutionary awakening cannot but predispose the foremost elements of our proletariat towards sympathy for a cause like the summoning of a congress of its representatives with the aim of creating a unifying and leading centre for the proletariat. To utilise this atmosphere in such a way, to transform potential sympathy into a conscious and passionate desire for the creation of such a centre, to attract the above-named elements to the path indicated is also the duty of the Social Democrats as the historically already established embryo of the political party of the proletariat. In the course of the unification of the foremost strata of the proletariat it should reform itself and develop into a genuine party of the working masses, imbuing their daily struggle for particular improvements with its own principled, fundamental aspirations and emerging in that struggle as their conscious revolutionary vanguard.

My letter has expanded so much that I do not dare to dally further on the points that I have raised. Nevertheless I have not yet touched upon one very essential point that you mention as an obstacle to the realisation of the plan to organise the summoning of a workers' congress, and even more the summoning of a People's Duma. Namely, the difficulty of putting 'all this' 'into practice', especially now when once again 'even if only for a short time, perhaps, reaction is making a new attempt, worse than before, to stop it all'. But you fail to consider the extremely precarious and unstable nature of the government's policy, its contradictory character even at a particular moment in different parts of Russia.

You have only to consider such facts as the 'first open popular meeting in Tomsk', at the fact of 'emancipation' in the Caucasus, at the congress of peasant delegates in Moscow, at the attempts to form and start legal societies. But then, what does it mean from our point of view to put into practice one or another of the slogans that we have advanced? Above all, the main thing for us is the importance of agitation on behalf of these slogans, the awakening of minds that it provokes and the increase in the regular, conscious revolutionary activity of the masses to whom we address ourselves. Let us suppose that we do not succeed in summoning a congress (or People's Duma), thanks to extraordinary measures on the government's part. Will the agitational and organisational work of the party, in which the practical realisation of our slogan is expressed, turn out to be in vain? You do not have to explain and prove this to me. It is clear that it will only succeed if we use in our agitation all the concrete material that contemporary life provides us with for the political education of the working masses, to encourage their fighting spirit and to develop in them the capacity and readiness to repel violence by force in the struggle for their rights and demands. This being the nature of our agitation it may, at a certain phase, in one or another centre in Russia, even provide the impulse for a real popular uprising.

To finish the letter this time I shall mention, in a couple of words, one more factor that is utilised very little, highly sporadically and extremely superficially to further a *real* seizure by the proletariat of the right to assemble openly to discuss the affairs of the day and to take certain decisions just as the *Zemstvo* liberals, the liberal capitalists and the democratic bourgeoisie do. We shall achieve the task of 'dissociating' ourselves from bourgeois democracy by scathing castigations of its bourgeoisness and by demanding that it should declare its support for a democratic republic. But this is, firstly, only a more or less *metaphorical* 'dissociation', which is hardly capable of rendering serious assistance to the process of the political development of the working masses, their real merger into an independent political force; secondly, comrades frequently forget that at the *present* moment in history the process of the political unification of the Russian proletariat is *indissolubly* linked with the cause of social democracy attracting bourgeois democratic organisations into pacts and agreements with us *as a party* for various acts in the struggle with reaction. Individual comrades whisper with individual liberals, they sulk privately in the midst of liberal democracy. But this is not the same as discussions between two parties or organisations in their capacity as independent political collectives that differ on matters of principle with a view to mutual support on the field of battle with the common enemy. Speaking concretely, in addition to verbal assurances from liberal democracy that it is for a republic, etc., it is important to us that it offers us *actions*, *real* support on its part in our organisation and mobilisation of the working masses for revolutionary proletarian class consciousness. Active material assistance for defensive and offensive struggle, the use by liberal democracy of all its influence on official public institutions and its utilisation of all its connections with the bureaucratic and military milieux to facilitate the organisation of open political demonstrations by us and by the strata of the proletariat that are led by us — this is the primary and the principal basis for negotiations and agreement between our party and liberal organisations. On the basis of, and by means of, such a contrast between the progressive elements of the proletariat and the bourgeois oppositional and revolutionary elements we shall accomplish our task of the political dissociation of the proletariat from the bourgeoisie much more surely and much more quickly, and at the same time we shall carry out our other duty that is indissolubly linked with it: we shall push forward all the oppositional strata of the bourgeoisie and facilitate the formation of a unique coalition between these strata and the organised proletariat for a common decisive onslaught against the autocracy. We must also use the bourgeois opposition in the sense and direction indicated to realise the plan of immediate action that I have very generally and schematically outlined in the present and preceding letters.

I am afraid to re-read what I have written lest I should be tempted to alter something, to shorten, add, develop, etc. I flatter myself with the hope that you and the other *close* comrades will understand the essence and not reinterpret the content of the letters. Of course, to realise 'plans' in practice is not as straightforward as to realise them on paper.

Yours sincerely,

P. Akselrod.

P.S. I cannot remain completely silent on your latest formulation against the project for agitation for the summoning of a People's Duma, as opposed to the State Duma. You say, 'We (i.e. our party) are too weak to realise this slogan with our own resources.' But, you see, from the outset I have maintained, and I have underlined this several times, that to bring this about we must enter into an agreement (of an organisational-technical character) with the democratic associations. Even if we were five times stronger than we are we should, to ensure the success of such a *general democratic* cause, have to propose a coalition to the other groups in the radical opposition. For it is only on the basis of such a coalition, only a Duma summoned by the combined efforts of the revolutionary proletariat and the revolutionary bourgeoisie that will be a – relatively – genuine representative of the whole people. 'But', you say, 'the liberal democrats will not join us and follow such an obviously revolutionary path.' It may very well be that they will be afraid to take this path: in that case we should have to renounce our plan to summon a People's Duma. But what would we have to lose from a failed attempt to concentrate public opinion on this point, if this failure stemmed from the cowardice and indecision of bourgeois democracy? You are afraid that failure would expose our weakness and compromise us. In my view this fear would be appropriate only in the event of our deciding at our own risk, and on our own responsibility, to call upon the populace, with their arms ready, to rise on a particular day and at a particular time on the orders of the centre, or to call on their own 'committee' initiative a general political strike. But to circulate a particular practical proposal for discussion by all the active and organised elements in the democratic opposition, to try to attract them into coalition activities in order to realise that proposal – such a step, even if it failed, would in no way compromise *us*. On the contrary, since the failure would result in the rejection by bourgeois democracy of our proposal it would, or might, compromise the latter rather than us, for we should not have taken upon ourselves alone a task that can only be a matter for all the democratic parties. This will be just another argument for us to use with the workers in favour of the urgent need for an immediate start in forming our own independent centre for the conduct of our own proletarian class policy.

However, you do not realise that you are contradicting yourself when you justify the policy of a simple 'boycott' of the State Duma by reference to the fact that liberal democracy will not move after or with us to realise our project for organising the summoning of a People's Duma. You say that the boycott should be expressed in public protests against participation in the elections, in general opposition to the participation of 'politically honest' men who belong to privileged (electoral) circles in the elections; in saying this you fully admit that, only the unanimous joint actions of all shades of democracy may be crowned with success in a particular case, that we shall do nothing in this respect through our own resources. But is the path of such a decisive active revolutionary 'boycott' less hazardous than the concentration of agitation on a *positive* fully concrete slogan? There are two alternatives: either liberal democracy is really or potentially capable of the decisive actions postulated by the policy of active boycott – and in that case I do not understand why it is afraid of our positive slogan – or it is indecisive, it fears the emerging revolutionary popular masses and is afraid of sacrifice – in that case it will not embark on a boycott. But, if it were ready for decisive actions, then it would, on the whole, not embark on a 'boycott', not prevent 'politically honest' people from participating in the elections, first of all because this would mean cooperating with the government in selecting the membership of the State Duma that it wants and, secondly, it (and we) would in so doing collide with whole strata of the population, perhaps even with significant popular masses (the petty bourgeoisie and, in particular, the peasantry); the policy of simple boycott may call into being a coalition of diverse elements in which the heroes of the Black Hundreds mingle with the strata that pin their hopes on this Duma in a single united mass led and inspired by the government against the whole of democracy. I have already said to you personally: such a policy – of a purely negative character – would, in the present phase of the Russian revolution, be directly reactionary and utopian at the same time. We should concentrate the efforts of our party and of democracy in general not on the struggle for the utopian idea of preventing the emergence of Bulygin's brainchild *by means of a boycott*[322] but on the mobilisation and organisation of the forces that will be capable of turning even this concoction of the bureaucratic reactionary imagination into a weapon and base for the revolution. The policy of boycott is a policy of fragmentation, decentralisation of the elements and manifestations of revolution. To bring unity to agitation, to concentrate our fighting forces, we must have a positive slogan, a definite, concrete aim: to create a popular institution that would – until the summoning of a future Constituent Assembly – be the expression of the demands and the will of the people and would have full powers to demand in the name of the people from the State Duma that it should *officially* and decisively agree to its demands, announcing to the government the conditions on and in which a Constituent Assembly should be summoned, and that it should cease its own official existence. And, if the proposed Duma does not see the light of day, the agitation for it to be summoned would, to a significant degree, have achieved its aim, since it would have exerted the public pressure on the State Duma that is necessary if it is to become the basis for the revolution.

59.   OUR REVOLUTION (1906): EXTRACTS[323]

L. Trotsky

Results & prospects

4. Revolution & the proletariat

Revolution is an open measurement of the balance of social forces in the struggle for power.

The state is not an end in itself. It is only a working machine in the hands of the dominant social force. Like every machine the state has its mechanisms for drive, transmission and implementation. The driving force is class interest: its mechanism is agitation, the press, church and school propaganda, the party, the street meeting, the petition, the revolt. The transmission mechanism is the legislative organisation of caste, dynastic, estate or class interest under the guise of the will of God (absolutism) or the will of the nation (parliamentarism). Finally, the mechanism for implementation is the administration, with its police, the courts, with their prisons, and the army.

The state is not an end in itself. But it is the greatest medium for the organisation, disorganisation and reorganisation of social relations. It can be a lever for profound transformation of an instrument of organised stagnation, depending on who controls it.

Every political party worthy of the name strives to achieve political power and thus place the state at the service of the class whose interests it expresses. Social democracy, as the party of the proletariat, naturally strives for the political hegemony of the working class.

The proletariat grows and gains in strength as capitalism grows. In this sense the development of capitalism is also the development of the proletariat in a dictatorship. But the day and the hour when power passes into the hands of the working class *directly* depends not upon the level of productive forces but upon relations in the class struggle, upon the international situation and, lastly, upon a number of subjective factors: tradition, initiative and readiness to fight . . .

In an economically more backward country the proletariat may come to power earlier than in an advanced capitalist country. In 1871 it deliberately took control of social matters in petty-bourgeois Paris – only for two months, it is true – but it

has never held power for so much as an hour in the large-scale capitalist centres of
England or the United States. The idea that the dictatorship of the proletariat is in
some way automatically dependent on the technical capacities and resources of a
country is a prejudice of 'economic' materialism simplified to the point of absurdity. This point of view has nothing in common with Marxism.[324]

The Russian revolution will, in our view, create the conditions in which power
can – and in the event of the victory of the revolution *must* – pass into the hands
of the proletariat before the politicians of bourgeois liberalism have an opportunity
of displaying to the full their talent for governing.

Summing up the results of the revolution and counter-revolution of 1848–9 in
the American newspaper, *The Tribune*, Marx[325] wrote:

The working class in Germany is, in its social and political development, as far
behind that of England and France as the German bourgeoisie is behind the bourgeoisie of those countries. *Like master, like man.* The evolution of the conditions
of existence for a numerous, strong, concentrated and intelligent proletarian class
goes hand in hand with the development of the conditions of existence for a
numerous, wealthy, concentrated and powerful middle class. The working class
movement itself *never* is independent, never is of an exclusively proletarian character until all the different factions of the middle class, and particularly its most
progressive faction, the large manufacturers, have conquered political power, and
remodelled the state according to their wants. It is then that the inevitable conflict
between the employer and the employed becomes imminent, and cannot be
adjourned any longer.[326]

This quotation is probably familiar to the reader because it has recently been frequently abused by the textual Marxists. They have brought it forward as an
irrefutable argument against the idea of a workers' government in Russia. 'Like
master, like man.' If the Russian capitalist bourgeoisie is not strong enough to take
state power into its own hands, then still less can we talk of a workers' democracy,
i.e. the political dominance of the proletariat.

Marxism is above all a method of analysis – not the analysis of texts but the
analysis of social relations. Is it true, in the case of Russia, that the weakness of
capitalist liberalism inevitably means the weakness of the workers' movement? Is it
true, in the case of Russia, that an independent workers' movement is possible only
when the bourgeoisie gains power? It is enough to put these questions in order to
appreciate what hopeless formalism of thought lies behind the attempt to transform
a historically relative remark by Marx into a supra-historical theorem.

During periods of industrial expansion the development of factory industry in
Russia has had an 'American' character but the actual dimensions of our capitalist
industry make it look like a child when compared with the industry of the USA.
Five million people, 16.6% of the economically active population, are employed in
manufacturing industry in Russia, in the United States the corresponding figures
would be six million, 22.2%. These figures still tell us comparatively little but they
are more eloquent if we recall that the population of Russia is almost twice that of
the States. But, in order to appreciate the real dimensions of the industry of these

two countries, we should note that in 1900 American factories, plants and large-scale workshops turned out goods for sale to the value of 25 milliard roubles, while in the same period Russia produced in its factories and plants goods to the value of less than 2.5 milliard roubles.

The numbers, concentration, cultural level and political significance of the industrial proletariat undoubtedly depend on the stage of development of capitalist industry. But this dependence is not direct. At any given moment there are various social political factors of a national and international character that intervene between the productive forces of a country and the political strength of its classes, and these deflect and even completely alter the political expression of economic relations. Despite the fact that the productive forces of United States industry are ten times greater than those of this country, the political role of the Russian proletariat, its influence on the politics of its own country, the possibility of its influencing world politics in the near future are incomparably greater than are the role and significance of the American proletariat.

In his recent work on the American proletariat, Kautsky points out that there is no direct and immediate correlation between the political strength of the proletariat and the bourgeoisie, on the one hand, and the level of capitalist development on the other. 'Two states exist', he says,

diametrically opposed to one another: in the one there is a disproportionate (i.e. not corresponding to the level of the capitalist mode of production) development of one of the elements of the latter, in the other another element. In America it is the capitalist classes, in Russia the proletariat. In America more than anywhere else there is good reason to talk of the dictatorship of capital, while the militant proletariat has nowhere achieved the significance that it has in Russia and this significance should increase, and undoubtedly will increase, because this country has only recently begun to participate in the contemporary class struggle and has only recently provided a certain amount of elbow-room for this struggle.[327]

Pointing out that Germany may to some extent discern its *future* from Russia, Kautsky continues, 'It is indeed extremely strange that it is the Russian proletariat that is showing us our future, insofar as this is expressed not in the organisation of capital but in the protest of the working class. Russia is the most backward of the large states of the capitalist world and this would appear to contradict', Kautsky remarks, 'the materialist conception of history, according to which economic development is the basis of political development. But in reality', he continues, 'this only contradicts the materialist conception of history as it is depicted by our opponents and critics, who regard it not as a *method of investigation* but merely as a ready-made cliché.[328] We particularly recommend these lines to those Russian Marxists who substitute deductions from texts chosen to suit every occasion in life for independent analysis. No one compromises Marxism as much as these self-styled Marxists!

Thus, in Kautsky's evaluation, Russia is characterised in the economic sphere by a relatively low level of capitalist development and in the political sphere by the insignificance of the capitalist bourgeoisie and the might of the revolutionary proletariat. This leads to a situation in which

the struggle for the interests of the *whole* of Russia has fallen to the lot of the *only currently existing strong class in the country* – the industrial proletariat. For this reason the latter has immense political significance there and for this reason the struggle in Russia for its emancipation from the stifling incubus of absolutism has been transformed into a *single combat between the latter and the industrial working class*, a single combat in which the peasantry may provide significant support but are unable to play a leading role.

Does not all this give us the right to conclude that the Russian 'man' will come to power sooner than his 'master'?

Political optimism can take two forms. We may exaggerate our strengths and the advantages of a revolutionary situation and set ourselves tasks that the particular alignment of forces will not allow us to perform. On the other hand, we may *optimistically* set a limit to our revolutionary tasks that the logic of our position will inevitably drive us beyond.

We may limit the scope of all the questions of the revolution by maintaining that our revolution is *bourgeois* in its objective aims and consequently in its inevitable results, thereby shutting our eyes to the fact that the chief actor in this bourgeois revolution is the proletariat, which is being propelled towards power by the whole course of the revolution.

We may reassure ourselves with the thought that, within the framework of a bourgeois revolution, the political dominance of the proletariat will be only a passing episode, thereby forgetting that once the proletariat has power in its hands it will not surrender it without the most desperate resistance and not leave go until it is torn from its hands by armed force.

We may reassure ourselves with the thought that the social conditions of Russia are not yet ripe for a socialist economy, thereby overlooking the fact that, on coming to power, the proletariat must, by the whole logic of its position, inevitably be driven to state control of industry.

The general sociological term, *bourgeois revolution*, by no means solves the political and tactical problems, contradictions and difficulties that the mechanics of a *particular* bourgeois revolution create.

Within the framework of the bourgeois revolution at the end of the eighteenth century, whose objective task was the establishment of the 'dominance of capital, the dictatorship of the *sans-culottes* turned out to be feasible. This dictatorship was not simply a transient episode: it left its imprint on the whole of the century that followed, and this despite the fact that it was very quickly smashed against the boundary fences of the bourgeois revolution.

In the revolution at the beginning of the twentieth century, whose direct objective tasks are also bourgeois, we may envisage as an immediate prospect the inevitability, or at least the probability, of the political dominance of the proletariat. The proletariat itself will see to it that this dominance is no mere passing 'episode', as some realist philistines are hoping. But even now we may ask ourselves: is it inevitable that the dictatorship of the proletariat should be smashed against the boundary fences of the bourgeois revolution or can it, in particular *world-historical* conditions, open up the prospect of victory once it has broken through these fences? From this, tactical questions arise for us: should we consciously aim for a workers' government as the development of the revolution brings this stage nearer, or should we at that moment regard political power as a misfortune that the bourgeois revolution is ready to foist upon the workers and that it would be better to avoid?

Should we apply to ourselves the words that the 'realist' politician, Vollmar,[329] uttered of the Communards in 1871: 'Instead of taking power they would have done better to go to sleep'?

5. The proletariat in power & the peasantry

In the event of a decisive victory for the revolution, power will pass into the hands of the class that has played a leading role in the struggle — in other words, into the hands of the proletariat. Let us say at once that this of course in no way precludes the entry into the government of the revolutionary representatives of non-proletarian social groups. They can and should be in it; a sound policy will impel the proletariat to summon to power the influential leaders of the petty bourgeoisie, the intelligentsia and the peasantry. The vital question is: *who will determine the content of the government's policy, who will form within it a coherent majority*? It is one thing for representatives of the democratic strata of the people to participate in what is predominantly a workers' government. It is quite another thing for representatives of the proletariat to participate in what is clearly a bourgeois-democratic government in the capacity of more or less honoured hostages.

The policy of the liberal capitalist bourgeoisie, with all its hesitations, retreats and betrayals, is quite definite. The policy of the proletariat is even more definite and complete. But the policy of the intelligentsia, because of their intermediate social status and their political amorphousness, the policy of the peasantry, because of their social diversity, their intermediate status and their primitive level, and the policy of the petty bourgeoisie, again because of their characterlessness, their intermediate status and their complete lack of political tradition — the policy of these three social groups is completely undefined, unformed, completely haphazard and, therefore, full of surprises.

It is enough to try and imagine a revolutionary-democratic government without representatives of the proletariat to be struck by the utter absurdity of the idea! A refusal by the Social Democrats to participate in a revolutionary government would destroy completely the viability of such a government and would thus be a betrayal of the revolutionary cause. But the participation of the proletariat in a government is objectively more probable and permissible in principle only as a *dominant and leading* participation. We may, of course, call this government a dictatorship of the proletariat and peasantry, a dictatorship of the proletariat, peasantry and intelligentsia or, lastly, a coalition government of the working class and the petty bourgeoisie. But the question still remains: who is to wield the hegemony in the government iself and, through it, in the country? And when we speak of a workers' government we are replying that the hegemony should belong to the working class.

The Convention, as the organ of the Jacobin dictatorship, was by no means composed of Jacobins alone: more than that – the Jacobins were even in a minority in it. But the influence of the *sans-culottes* beyond the walls of the Convention, and the need for a decisive policy to save the country, gave power to the Jacobins. Thus, while the Convention was *formally* a representative national body composed of Jacobins, Girondists and the vast 'marsh', it was *essentially* the dictatorship of the Jacobins.

When we speak of a workers' government, we have in mind a government where the workers' representatives are in a dominant and leading position.

The proletariat cannot consolidate its power without broadening the base of the revolution.

Many sections of the toiling mass, particularly in the countryside, will be drawn into the revolution for the first time and become politically organised only after the urban proletariat, as the vanguard of the revolution, stands at the helm of the state. Revolutionary agitation and organisation will be conducted with the aid of state resources. Lastly, legislative power itself will become a powerful instrument for revolutionising the popular masses.

The character of our social and historical relations, which lays the whole burden of the bourgeois revolution on the shoulders of the proletariat, will not only create enormous difficulties for the workers' government in this process but, in the first period of its existence at any rate, will also give it invaluable advantages. This will affect the relations between the proletariat and the peasantry.

In the revolutions of 1789–93 and 1848 power passed first of all from absolutism to the moderate elements of the bourgeoisie. It was this latter class that emancipated the peasantry (*how* is another matter) before revolutionary democracy had received, or was even preparing to receive, power into its own hands. The emancipated peasantry lost all interest in the political ventures of the 'townspeople', i.e. in the further progress of the revolution, and, laying itself like an immovable foundation-stone at the foot of the 'order', betrayed the revolution to the Caesarist or age-old absolutist reaction.

The Russian revolution does not, and for a long time will not, permit the establishment of any kind of bourgeois constitutional order that might solve the most elementary problems of democracy. As far as the reforming bureaucrats like Witte and Stolypin are concerned, all their 'enlightened' efforts are negated by their own struggle for existence. Consequently, the fate of the most elementary revolutionary interests of the peasantry – even the peasantry *as a whole* as an *estate* – is bound up with the fate of the entire revolution, i.e. with the fate of the proletariat.

The proletariat in power will stand before the peasantry as its class emancipator.

The hegemony of the proletariat will mean not just democratic equality, free self-government, the transfer of the whole burden of taxation on to the owning classes, the dissolution of the standing army in the armed people and the abolition of compulsory church requisitions, but also the recognition of all the revolutionary changes (expropriations) in land relationships effected by the peasants. The proletariat will make these changes the starting point for further state measures in the field of agriculture. In these circumstances the Russian peasantry will in the first and most difficult period be at any rate at least as interested in maintaining the proletarian regime ('workers' democracy') as was the French peasantry in maintaining the military regime of Napoleon Bonaparte which had guaranteed to the new property owners by the force of its bayonets the inviolability of their plots of land. And this means that the popular representative body that has been summoned under the leadership of the proletariat, which has secured the support of the peasantry, will be nothing other than a democratic guise for the hegemony of the proletariat.

But could the peasantry itself push the proletariat aside and take its place?

This is impossible. All historical experience protests against this assumption. It demonstrates that the peasantry is absolutely incapable of an *independent* political role.[330]

The history of capitalism is the history of the subordination of the countryside to the town. The industrial development of European towns has in due course rendered impossible the continued existence of feudal relations in agricultural production. But the countryside itself did not produce a class that could undertake the revolutionary task of destroying feudalism. That very same town that has subordinated agriculture to capital produced the revolutionary forces that took political hegemony over the countryside into their hands and spread the revolution in state and property relations into the countryside. In its further development the countryside has finally fallen into economic enslavement to capital, and the peasantry into political enslavement to the capitalist parties. These parties are reviving feudalism in parliamentary politics, transforming the peasantry into their own political domain, a place for their electoral hunting expeditions. The contemporary bourgeois state, through taxation and militarism, is driving the peasant into the jaws of usury capital and, through state priests, state schools and the debauchery of barrack life, it makes him a victim of usury politics.

The Russian bourgeoisie will surrender all its revolutionary positions to the proletariat. It will also have to surrender its revolutionary hegemony over the peasantry. In the situation created by the transfer of power to the proletariat, the peasantry will have no alternative but to rally to the regime of workers' democracy. Let it do so, even if with no greater degree of consciousness than that with which it usually rallies to the bourgeois regime! But, while every bourgeois party that commands the votes of the peasantry hastens to use its power to swindle the peasantry and disappoint all its expectations and aspirations and then, if the worst comes to the worst, gives way to another capitalist party, the proletariat, relying on the peasantry, will use all its efforts to raise the cultural level of the countryside and to develop political consciousness among the peasantry.

From what I have said it is clear how we view the idea of the 'dictatorship of the proletariat and the peasantry'. In essence it is not a matter of whether we consider it admissible in principle, whether we 'want' or 'do not want' this form of political cooperation. We simply think that it cannot be realised in practice, at least in a direct and immediate sense.

In fact a coalition of this kind presupposes either that one of the existing bourgeois parties commands influence over the peasantry or that the peasantry is creating a powerful independent party of its own. As we have tried to demonstrate, neither the one nor the other is possible.

6. The proletarian regime

The proletariat can only achieve power by relying on a national upsurge and national ardour. The proletariat will enter the government as the revolutionary representative of the nation, as the recognised national leader in the struggle against feudalism and feudal barbarism. But, once it is in power, the proletariat will open a new epoch — the epoch of revolutionary legislation, of positive policy — and in this respect the preservation of its role as the recognised spokesman of the will of the nation is by no means guaranteed. The first measures by the proletariat, cleansing the Augean stables of the *ancien régime* and driving out the occupants, will meet with the active support of the whole nation, in spite of what the liberal eunuchs may say about the tenacity of certain prejudices among the masses of the people.

This political cleansing will be augmented by a democratic reorganisation of all social and state relations. The workers' government will be obliged, under the influence of direct pressures and demands, to intervene decisively in all relations and events . . .

Its first task must be the dismissal from the army and the administration of all those who are stained with the blood of the people and the cashiering or disbanding of the regiments that have most sullied themselves with crimes against the people. This will have to be done in the very first days, i.e. long before it is possible to introduce a system of elected and responsible officials and move to the organisation of a people's militia. Workers' democracy will immediately be faced with questions of the length of the working day, the agrarian question, and the problem of unemployment . . .

One thing is certain. Every new day will deepen the policy of the proletariat in power and define its *class character* more and more. At the same time the revolutionary bond between the proletariat and the nation will be broken, the class disintegration of the peasantry will assume political form and the antagonism between its component parts will grow as the policy of the workers' government is defined, moving from a general democratic policy to a class one.

Although the absence of accumulated bourgeois-individualist traditions and anti-proletarian prejudices among the peasantry and the intelligentsia will help the proletariat to come to power, we must bear in mind, on the other hand, that this absence of prejudices is due not to political consciousness but to political barbarism, social formlessness, primitiveness and lack of character. These are all characteristics and features that could in no way create a promising basis for a consistent, active policy for the proletariat.

The abolition of feudalism will meet with the support of the entire peasantry as the estate that bears the burden. Progressive income tax will also meet with the support of the great majority of the peasantry. But legislative measures to protect the agricultural proletariat will not only not meet with such active sympathy from the majority, but will even encounter the active opposition of a minority.

The proletariat will be forced to carry the class struggle into the countryside and thus destroy the community of interest that undoubtedly exists among all peasants, albeit within comparatively narrow limits. In the very first moments after taking power the proletariat will have to look for support in the antagonisms between the village poor and the village rich, between the agricultural proletariat and the agricultural bourgeoisie. While the heterogeneity of the peasantry will present difficulties and will narrow the basis for proletarian politics, the inadequate class differentiation of the peasantry will create obstacles to the introduction among the peasantry of a developed class struggle on which the urban proletariat might rely. The primitive level of the peasantry will display its hostile face to the proletariat.

But the cooling off of the peasantry, its political passivity and, even more, the active opposition of its upper echelons, cannot but exert some influence on part of the intelligentsia and on the urban petty bourgeoisie.

Thus, the more definite and determined the policy of the proletariat in power becomes, the more it acquires a basis, the shakier the ground beneath its feet becomes. All this is highly probable, even inevitable . . .

Two principal features of proletarian policy will meet opposition from its allies: these are *collectivism* and *internationalism*.

The petty-bourgeois character and primitive political level of the peasantry, its limited rural outlook, its isolation from world political ties and allegiances, will create terrible difficulties for the consolidation of the revolutionary policy of the proletariat in power.

To imagine that social democracy should enter a provisional government and lead it during the period of revolutionary democratic reforms, fighting for them to have the most radical character and relying in this process on the organised proletariat, and then, once the democratic programme has been carried out, that it should leave the edifice that it has constructed, making way for the bourgeois parties, and itself go into opposition, thus opening up an epoch of parliamentary politics – is to imagine things in a way that would compromise the very idea of a workers' government. This is not because it is inadmissible 'in principle' – such an abstract formulation of the question is devoid of meaning – but because it is completely unrealistic, it is utopianism of the worst sort, a kind of philistine revolutionary utopianism.

And this is why.

The division of our programme into a minimum and a maximum one[331] has an enormous significance, deeply rooted in principle, in a situation where power lies in the hands of the bourgeoisie. It is precisely this fact – the bourgeoisie being in power – that drives out of our programme all the demands that are incompatible with private ownership of the means of production. Demands of this kind constitute the content of the socialist revolution and presuppose the dictatorship of the proletariat.

But, once power is in the hands of a revolutionary government with a socialist majority, then the distinction between the minimum and maximum programmes immediately loses its significance, both in principle and in immediate practice. Under no circumstances can a proletarian government confine itself within these limits. Let us take the demand for an eight-hour working day. It is well known that this is in no way incompatible with capitalist relations and it therefore forms part of the minimum programme of social democracy. But let us imagine its actual introduction in a revolutionary period at a time when all the social passions are intensified. There is no doubt that the new law would meet the organised and persistent resistance of the capitalists in the form, shall we say, of lockouts and the closure of factories and plants. Hundreds of thousands of workers would be thrown on to the streets. What would the government do? A bourgeois government, however radical, would never let matters go this far because, confronted with closed factories and plants, it would be powerless. It would be forced to retreat, the eight-hour day would not be introduced and the disturbance among the proletariat would be put down . . .

Under the political hegemony of the proletariat the introduction of an eight-hour day should produce completely different results. The closure of factories and plants by the capitalists cannot, of course, be grounds for lengthening the working day for a government that wants to rely on the proletariat and not on capital, as liberalism does, and that does not want to play the role of an 'impartial' intermediary of bourgeois democracy. For a workers' government there would be only one way out: the expropriation of the closed factories and plants and the organisation of production in them on a socialised basis.

Of course, one can argue in the following way. Let us suppose that the workers' government, true to its programme, decrees an eight-hour working day; if capital puts up a resistance that cannot be overcome by means of a democratic programme that presupposes the preservation of private property, social democracy will resign and appeal to the proletariat. Such a solution would be a solution only from the point of view of the group that constituted the government: but it would not be a solution for the proletariat or for the development of the revolution itself. Because, after the resignation of the Social Democrats, the situation would revert to exactly what it was before – and to the situation that forced them to take power. Flight before the organised opposition of capital would be an even greater betrayal of the revolution than the refusal to take power in the first place. It would really be far better not to enter the government rather than to enter it only to expose our own weakness and then to quit.

Another example. The proletariat in power cannot help taking the most energetic measures to resolve the question of unemployment, because it is quite clear that the representatives of the workers in the government could not reply to the demands of the unemployed with remarks about the bourgeois character of the revolution.

But, if the government undertakes to maintain the unemployed – how is not important for us at the moment – this would immediately mean a substantial shift in economic power in favour of the proletariat. The capitalists, whose oppression of the proletariat has always relied upon the existence of a reserve army, would feel *economically* powerless, while the revolutionary government would at the same time condemn them to *political* impotence.

In undertaking to maintain the unemployed, the government thereby undertakes to maintain strikers. If it does not do *that*, it will immediately and irrevocably undermine the basis of its own existence.

There is nothing left for the capitalists to do then but resort to the lockout, i.e. to close the factories. It is quite clear that the factory owners can sustain the cessation of production longer than the workers, and there is only one response that a workers' government can make to a mass lockout: the expropriation of the factories and the introduction, at least in the largest of them, of state or communal production.

Similar problems will arise in agriculture from the mere fact of the expropriation of the land. In no way must we presuppose that a proletarian government that has expropriated the privately owned estates engaged in large-scale production will divide them up and sell them off to be worked by small-scale producers: the only path open to it is to organise cooperative production under communal control or directly under the state. But this is the path of socialism.

All this quite clearly shows that social democracy cannot enter a revolutionary government, having given the workers an advance undertaking that it will not *give way* on the minimum programme, and having at the same time promised the bourgeoisie that it will not *go beyond* the limits of the minimum programme. This kind of bilateral undertaking would be quite impossible to realise. The very fact that the proletariat's representatives enter the government, not as impotent hostages, but as the leading force, destroys the dividing line between the minimum and the maximum programmes: i.e. *it makes collectivism the order of the day*. The point at which the proletariat will be held up in its advance in this direction depends upon the relation of forces but in no way upon the original intentions of the proletarian party.

That is why we cannot speak of any kind of special form of proletarian dictatorship in the bourgeois revolution or, more precisely, of the democratic dictatorship of the proletariat (or of the proletariat and the peasantry). The working class cannot preserve the democratic character of its dictatorship without overstepping the limits of its democratic programme. Any illusions on this point would be fatal. They would compromise social democracy from the outset.

Once the party of the proletariat takes power, it will fight for it to the very last. While one of the instruments in this struggle for the maintenance and consolidation of power will be agitation and organisation, especially in the countryside, another will be a policy of collectivism. Collectivism will become not only the inevitable conclusion to be drawn from the party's position in power, but also a means of preserving this position with the support of the proletariat.

When the idea of *uninterrupted revolution* was formulated in the socialist press[332] — an idea that linked the liquidation of absolutism and civil feudalism to a socialist revolution, along with growing social conflicts, uprisings of new strata of the masses, constant attacks by the proletariat on the political and economic privileges of the ruling classes — our 'progressive' press raised a unanimous howl of indignation. Oh, it had suffered a lot but it could not allow this. Revolution, it cried, is not a path that can be 'legalised'. The application of exceptional measures is permissible only in exceptional cases. The goal of the emancipation movement is not to perpetuate the revolution but to lead it as quickly as possible into the channel of *law*, etc., etc.

The more radical representatives of this same democracy do not risk taking a stand against revolution from the standpoint of the constitutional 'gains' already achieved: even for them the parliamentary cretinism that precedes the rise of parliamentarism itself does not constitute a strong weapon in the struggle with the proletarian revolution. They choose a different path: they make their stand, not on the basis of law, but on what seem to them to be facts — on the basis of historical 'possibilities', on the basis of political 'realism' and finally, finally even on the basis of 'Marxism'. And why not? That pious burgher of Venice, Antonio, very aptly said: 'The devil can cite Scripture for his purpose.'

They not only regard the very idea of a workers' government in Russia as fantastic, but they even deny the possibility of socialist revolution in Europe in the historical epoch immediately ahead. The necessary 'preconditions' are not yet to hand. Is this true? The task, of course, is not to name a date for the socialist revolution but to turn it into a realistic historical prospect.

8. The workers' government in Russia & socialism

We have already shown above that the objective preconditions for socialist revolution have already been created by the economic development of the advanced capitalist countries. But what can we say of Russia in this respect? Can we anticipate that the transfer of power to the proletariat will mark the beginning of the transformation of our national economy on socialist principles?

A year ago we answered these questions in an article that was subjected to cruel crossfire from the organs of both factions of our party.[333]

'The Paris workers', Marx says, 'did not ask for miracles from the Commune.' We should not expect instant miracles from the dictatorship of the proletariat even now. State power is not omnipotent. It would be absurd to imagine that the proletariat has only to attain power and then, by passing a few decrees, replace capitalism with socialism. The economic order is not the product of the actions of the state. It is only by using all its energy that the proletariat can apply the power of the state to ease and shorten the path of economic evolution towards collectivism.

The proletariat will begin with those reforms that are included in what is known as the minimum programme and, as a direct result of these, the very logic of its position will compel it to pass on to collectivist practice.

The introduction of the eight-hour working day and a steeply progressive income tax will be a comparatively simple matter, although even here the sticking point will be not the passing of the 'act' but the organisation of its application in practice. But the principal difficulty — and herein lies the transition to collectivism! — will consist in the state organisation of production in those factories and plants that are closed by their owners in response to the passing of these acts.

The passing of a law abolishing the right of inheritance and putting this law into practice will likewise be a comparatively simple matter: the proletariat is not embarrassed by legacies in the form of money capital, nor is its economy burdened by them. But acting as the heir to land and industrial capital means that the workers' government must undertake the social organisation of the economy.

The same thing, but on a larger scale, must be said about expropriation — with or without compensation. Expropriation with compensation offers political advantages but financial difficulties: expropriation without compensation offers financial advantages but political difficulties. But, over and above these and other difficulties, there will be economic and organisational difficulties.

We repeat: a government of the proletariat is not a government of miracles.

The socialisation of production will begin with those branches [of industry] that present the fewest difficulties. In the initial period socialised production will be like a series of oases, linked to private economic enterprises by the laws of commodity circulation. The broader the area occupied by the socialised economy, the more obvious its advantages will be, the more secure the new political regime will feel, and the more daring the further economic measures of the proletariat will be. In these measures it can and will rely not merely upon national productive forces but also on international technology just as, in its revolutionary policy, it relies not only on the experience of class relations within the country but also on the entire historical experience of the international proletariat.

The political hegemony of the proletariat is incompatible with its economic enslavement. Regardless of the political banner under which the proletariat has come to power, it must take the path of socialist policy. We must recognise as the greatest utopianism the idea that the proletariat, raised to power by the internal mechanics of the bourgeois revolution, will be able, even if it so desires, to restrict its mission to the creation of democratic republican conditions for the social hegemony of the bourgeoisie. The political hegemony of the proletariat, even if only temporary, will severely weaken the resistance of capital, which always requires the support of the state, and will give the economic struggle of the proletariat grandiose dimensions. The workers will have no alternative but to demand support for strikers from the revolutionary government and a government relying on the support of the workers will be unable to refuse this demand. But this means paralysing the influence of the reserve army of labour,[334] making the workers master not only in the political but also in the economic field, and transforming private ownership of the means of production into a fiction. These inevitable social and economic consequences of the dictatorship of the proletariat will emerge rapidly, long before the democratisation of the political system has been completed. The dividing line between the 'minimum' and the 'maximum' programme will disappear as soon as the proletariat comes to power.

The proletarian regime will first of all have to deal with the settlement of the agrarian question, with which the fate of vast masses of the population of Russia is bound up. In settling this question, as in all others, the proletariat will be guided by the fundamental goal of its economic policy: to command as large a field as possible for the organisation of the socialist economy. But the forms and the tempo of this policy on the agrarian question must be determined both by the material resources at the proletariat's disposal and by the need to act in a manner that will not drive potential allies into the ranks of the counter-revolutionaries.

It is obvious that the *agrarian question*, i.e. the question of the fate of agriculture and its social relations, is by no means covered by the *land question*, i.e. the question of the forms of land ownership. There is no doubt that the settlement of the land question, even if it does not predetermine the evolution of agriculture will predetermine the agrarian policy of the proletariat: in other words, what the proletarian regime does to the land must be linked to its general attitudes towards the progress and the requirements of agricultural development. For this reason the land question comes first.

One solution, to which the Socialist Revolutionaries have given a far from unobjectionable popularity, is the socialisation of all land: relieved of its European trappings, this term means nothing other than the 'equalised use of land' or the 'Black Redistribution'.[335] The programme of the equal distribution of land thus presupposes the expropriation of all land, not only privately owned land in general, or privately owned peasant land, but even communally owned land. If we bear in mind that this expropriation would have to be carried out in the initial stages of the new regime, while commodity-capitalist relations were still completely dominant, then it would transpire that the first 'victims' of the expropriation would be, or, more accurately, would feel themselves to be, the peasantry. If we bear in mind that for several decades the peasants have been paying out redemption money that should have converted the allotted land into their own personal property, if we bear in mind that some of the more prosperous peasants, undoubtedly through great sacrifices made by the generation that is still living, have acquired large tracts of land as private property, then it is easy to imagine the resistance that the conversion of communal and small-scale privately owned holdings into state property would provoke! By acting in this way, the new regime would begin by turning the vast masses of the peasantry against it.

What is the purpose of converting communal and small-scale privately owned holdings into state property? It is to make it available, in one way or another, for 'equalised' economic exploitation by all farmers, including the peasants and labourers who have no land at present. Thus, the new regime would gain nothing *economically* from the expropriation of small-scale and communal holdings because, even after the redistribution, the state or public land would be privately cultivated. *Politically* the new regime would be making a gigantic blunder because it would at once set the mass of the peasantry against the urban proletariat as the leader in revolutionary politics.

Further, equalised distribution presupposes the legal prohibition of the employment of wage labour. The abolition of wage labour can and must be a *consequence* of the economic reforms but it cannot be predetermined by juridical prohibitions.

It is not enough to forbid the farmer capitalist to hire workers: it is necessary beforehand to create a means of livelihood for the landless labourer, a means that is rational from the social and economic standpoint. At the same time, according to the programme for equalised land use, to forbid the employment of wage labour means, on the one hand, compelling the landless labourers to settle on scraps of land and, on the other hand, obliging the government to provide these labourers with the necessary equipment for their socially irrational production.

Obviously, the intervention of the proletariat in the organisation of agriculture will begin not by binding scattered labourers to scattered scraps of land but by exploiting the large estates through the state or the communes.

Only if this socialised production is firmly on its feet can the process of further socialisation be advanced by the prohibition of the employment of wage labour. This path will render small-scale capitalist farming impossible, but there will still be room for subsistence and semi-subsistence holdings: the forcible expropriation of these in no way features among the plans of the socialist proletariat.

In any case the proletariat can under no circumstances undertake to carry out a programme of 'equalised distribution' that, on the one hand, presupposes a pointless, purely formal expropriation of smallholdings and, on the other hand, requires the complete fragmentation of the large estates into tiny pieces. Such a policy, which, from the economic point of view, is directly wasteful, would only have a reactionary utopian ulterior motive and would above all weaken the revolutionary party politically.

But how far can the socialist policy of the working class go in Russia's economic conditions? We can say one thing with certainty: it will encounter political obstacles much sooner than it will come up against the technical backwardness of the country. *Without the direct state support of the European proletariat, the working class of Russia will not be able to stay in power and convert its temporary hegemony into a lasting socialist dictatorship.* We cannot doubt this even for a minute. But, on the other hand, there can be no doubt that a socialist revolution in the West will permit us, directly and immediately, to transform the temporary hegemony of the working class into a socialist dictatorship.

In 1904, Kautsky, discussing the prospects for social development and considering the possibility of an early revolution in Russia, wrote: 'Revolution in Russia could not immediately result in a socialist regime. The economic conditions of the country are still far from ripe for this.' But the Russian revolution should give a powerful push to the proletarian movement in the rest of Europe and, as a result of the struggle that would flare up, the proletariat could achieve dominance in Germany. 'Such an outcome', Kautsky continues,

must have an influence on the whole of Europe, must lead on to the political hegemony of the proletariat in Western Europe and create for the Eastern European proletariat the opportunity of contracting the stages of its development and, following the German example, *artificially creating socialist institutions.* Society as a whole cannot artificially skip particular stages in its development but this is possible for its individual component parts, which can accelerate their retarded development by imitating the advanced countries and, thanks to this, can even stand in the forefront of development, because they are not burdened with the ballast of tradition that the old nations have to drag along . . . This *may* happen [Kautsky goes on], but, as I have already said, we have here already left the realm of *inevitability* that can be studied and entered the realm of *possibility*, so that things may happen differently.[336]

The theoretician of German social democracy penned these lines at a time when the question of whether revolution would break out first in Russia or in the West was for him still at issue.

Afterwards, the Russian proletariat revealed a colossal strength that even the most optimistic Russian Social Democrats had not expected from it. The course of the Russian revolution was defined in its fundamental characteristics. What two or three years ago had seemed a *possibility*, became an imminent *probability*, and everything suggests that this *probability* is on the brink of becoming *inevitability*.

60. THE DRIVING FORCES OF THE RUSSIAN REVOLUTION AND ITS PROSPECTS, WITH PREFACE BY V.I. LENIN (1906)[337]

K. Kautsky

V.I. Lenin, *Preface to the Russian translation*

K. Kautsky has long been known to the progressive workers of Russia as *their* writer who is able not only to substantiate and expound the theoretical teaching of revolutionary Marxism but also to apply it with a knowledge of affairs and a thorough analysis of the facts to the complex and involved issues of the Russian revolution. But now, when the attention of Social Democrats is sometimes almost entirely taken up with the idle prattle of the liberal Petrushkas and of their conscious and unconscious yes-men, when for many people petty 'parliamentary' technicalities overshadow the fundamental questions of the proletarian class struggle, and when despondency often overwhelms even decent people and impairs their intellectual and political faculties — now it is trebly important for all the Social Democrats of Russia to pay close attention to Kautsky's view of the fundamental problems of the Russian revolution. And not so much to pay attention to Kautsky's view as to reflect on the way he poses the question — for Kautsky is not so thoughtless as to hold forth on the specific issues of Russian tactics with which he is not well acquainted, and not so ignorant of Russian affairs as to dismiss them with commonplace remarks or an uncritical repetition of the latest fashionable pronouncements.

Kautsky is answering the questions that Plekhanov addressed to a number of foreign Socialists[338] and, in answering these questions, or, more accurately, in selecting from these poorly formulated questions the points that *can* be useful subjects for discussion among Socialists of all countries, Kautsky begins with a modest reservation – 'I feel like a *novice* vis-à-vis my *Russian* comrades when it comes to Russian affairs.' This is not the false modesty of a social democratic 'general' who starts off grimacing like a petit bourgeois and ends up with the demeanour of a Bourbon. Not at all, Kautsky has *in fact* confined himself to answering *only* those questions through an analysis of which he can *help* the thinking Social Democrats of Russia to work out for themselves the concrete tasks and slogans of the day. Kautsky has refused to be a general issuing orders: 'Right turn!' or 'Left turn!'. He has preferred to preserve his position as a comrade standing at a distance, but a thoughtful comrade pointing out where we ourselves should look for an answer.

Plekhanov asked Kautsky: 1. Is the 'general character' of the Russian revolution bourgeois or socialist? 2. What should the attitude of the Social Democrats towards bourgeois democracy be? 3. Should the Social Democrats support the opposition parties in the elections for the Duma?

At first sight these questions would seem to have been chosen with great 'finesse'. But, as the saying goes, 'If a thing is too fine, it breaks.' In fact, any more or less competent and observant person will see straight away the fine . . . *subterfuge* in these questions. Subterfuge, firstly, because they are fine specimens of the metaphysics against which Plekhanov is so fond of declaiming pompously, although he cannot keep it out of his own concrete historical judgements. Subterfuge, secondly, because the person questioned is artificially driven into a small and excessively narrow corner. Only those who are completely, one might even say virginally, innocent in questions of politics can fail to notice that Plekhanov deliberately starts out from a remote position and gently pushes the person he is questioning into the position of justifying . . . blocs with the Cadets![339]

To drive a simple-minded interlocutor into justifying blocs with a certain party, without naming that party; to talk of a revolutionary movement without distinguishing the revolutionary democrats from the opposition bourgeois democrats; to imply that the bourgeoisie is 'fighting' *in its own way*, i.e. differently from the proletariat, without saying plainly and clearly what the difference really is; to trap the interlocutor like a fledgling jackdaw with the bait of the Amsterdam resolution[340] which is bound to *conceal* from the foreigner the real bones of contention among the Russian Social Democrats; to declare concrete rules relating to specific tactics in a specific case and to the attitude to be adopted towards the various parties among the bourgeois democrats, from a general *phrase* about the general character of the revolution, instead of deducing this 'general character of the Russian revolution' from a precise analysis of the concrete data on the interests and

position of the different classes in the Russian revolution – is not all this a subterfuge? Is it not an open mockery of Marx's dialectical materialism?

'Yea, yea – nay, nay, and whatsoever is more than these comes from the evil
one.' Either a bourgeois revolution or a socialist one; the rest can be 'deduced' from
the main 'solution' by means of simple syllogisms!

Kautsky performs a great service in that, in answering such questions, he grasps
the point immediately and goes to the root of the mistake contained in the very
way they were formulated. Kautsky *essentially* answers Plekhanov's questions by
rejecting Plekhanov's formulation of them! Kautsky answers Plekhanov by *correct-
ing* Plekhanov's formulation of the question. The more gently and carefully he
corrects the questioner, the more deadly is his criticism of Plekhanov's formulation
of the question. 'We should do well', writes Kautsky, 'to realise that we are moving
towards completely new situations and problems for which none of the old patterns
are suitable.'

This hits the nail on the head with regard to Plekhanov's question: is our revolution bourgeois or socialist in its general character? Kautsky says that this is the old
pattern. The question must not be put in this way, it is not the Marxist way. The
revolution in Russia is not a bourgeois revolution because the bourgeoisie is not one
of the driving forces of the present revolutionary movement in Russia. And the
revolution in Russia is not a socialist revolution for there is *no way* in which it can
possibly lead the proletariat to *sole* rule or dictatorship. Social democracy is
capable of victory in the Russian revolution and *must* strive towards it. But victory
in the present revolution cannot be the victory of the proletariat alone, without the
aid of other classes. Which class then, in view of the objective conditions of the
present revolution, is the ally of the proletariat? The *peasantry*: 'a substantial common interest for the whole period of the revolutionary struggle exists however only
between the proletariat and the peasantry'.

All these propositions of Kautsky are a brilliant confirmation of the tactics of
the revolutionary wing of Russian social democracy, i.e. the tactics of the
Bolsheviks. This confirmation is all the more valuable because Kautsky, setting
aside concrete and practical questions, has concentrated all his attention on a systematic exposition of the *general principles* of socialist tactics in our revolution. He
has shown that Plekhanov's threadbare notion of an argument that 'the revolution
is a bourgeois revolusion so that we must support the bourgeoisie' has nothing in
common with Marxism. He thus recognises the principal error of our social democratic opportunism, i.e. Menshevism, which the Bolsheviks have been fighting since
the beginning of 1905.

Further, Kautsky's analysis, which proceeds not from general phrases but from
an analysis of the positions and interests of specific classes, has reaffirmed the conclusion that the yes-men of the Cadets within our ranks considered 'tactless',
namely that the bourgeoisie in Russia fears revolution more than reaction; that it
despises reaction because it gives birth to revolution; that it wants political liberty
in order to call a halt to revolution. Compare this with the naive faith in the Cadets
professed by our Plekhanov who, in his questions, has imperceptibly identified the

struggle of the opposition against the old order with the struggle against the government's attempts to crush the revolutionary movement! Unlike the Mensheviks, with their stereotyped views of 'bourgeois democracy', Kautsky has shown its revolutionary and non-revolutionary elements, has demonstrated the bankruptcy of liberalism and shown that, as the peasants become more independent and more aware, the liberals will inevitably move rapidly to the right. A bourgeois revolution, brought about by the proletariat and the peasantry despite the instability of the bourgeoisie – this fundamental principle of Bolshevik tactics – is wholly confirmed by Kautsky.

Kautsky demonstrates that in the course of the revolution it is quite possible that the Social Democratic Party will attain victory and that that party *must* inspire its supporters with confidence in victory. Kautsky's conclusion completely confounds the Menshevik fear of a social democratic victory in the present revolution. Plekhanov's laughable efforts to 'tailor' the tasks of our revolution 'to fit the Amsterdam resolution' seem particularly comical when compared to Kautsky's clear and simple proposition that 'It is impossible to fight successfully if you renounce victory in advance.'

The basic difference between Kautsky's *methods* and those of the leader of our present opportunists, Plekhanov, is even more striking when the former states: to think that 'all the classes and parties that are striving for political liberty have simply to work together to achieve it' means '*seeing only the political surface of events*'. This sounds as though Kautsky is referring directly to that small band of Social Democrats who have deserted to the liberals: Messrs Portugalov, Prokopovich, Kuskova, Logucharsky, Izgoev, Struve and others, who are committing precisely the error that Kautsky refers to (and who in the process are dragging Plekhanov with them). The fact that Kautsky is not acquainted with the writings of these gentlefolk only enhances the significance of his theoretical conclusion.

Needless to say, Kautsky is in *complete* agreement with the fundamental thesis of *all* Russian Social Democrats that the peasant movement is *non-socialist*, that socialism cannot arise from small-scale peasant production, etc. It would be very instructive for the Socialist Revolutionaries, who are fond of asserting that they 'also agree with Marx', to ponder over these words of Kautsky.

In conclusion, a few words about 'authorities'. Marxists cannot adopt the usual standpoint of the intellectual radical, with his pseudo-revolutionary abstraction: 'no authorities'.

No, the working class, which all over the world is waging a hard and persistent struggle for complete emancipation, needs authorities but, of course, only in the same sense that young workers need the experience of veteran warriors against oppression and exploitation, of men who have organised a large number of strikes, have taken part in a number of revolutions, who are versed in revolutionary traditions and who have a broad political outlook. The proletariat of every country needs the authority of the world-wide struggle of the proletariat. We need the authority of the theoreticians of international social democracy to enable us properly to understand the programme and tactics of our party. But this authority naturally has nothing in common with the official authorities in bourgeois science and police politics. It is the authority of the experience gained in the more diversified struggle waged in the ranks of the same world socialist army. Important though this authority is in broadening the horizon of those involved in the struggle, it would be impermissible in the workers' party to claim that the practical and concrete questions of its immediate policy can be solved by those standing a long way off. The collective spirit of the progressive class conscious workers immediately engaged in the struggle in each country will always remain the supreme authority in all such questions.

This is our view of the authoritativeness of the views held by Kautsky and Plekhanov. The latter's theoretical works – principally his criticism of the Narodniks and the opportunists – remain a lasting asset for social democracy throughout Russia and no 'factionalism' will blind any man who possesses the least bit of 'physical brain power' to such an extent that he might forget or deny the importance of this asset. But, as a political leader of the Russian Social Democrats in the bourgeois revolution in Russia, as a tactician, Plekhanov has proved to be beneath all criticism. In this sphere he has displayed an opportunism that is a hundred times more harmful than Bernstein's opportunism is to the German workers. It is against this Cadet-like policy of Plekhanov, who has returned to the fold of Prokopovich[341] and Co. whom he expelled from the Social Democratic Party in 1899–1900, that we must struggle most ruthlessly.

That this tactical opportunism of Plekhanov is a complete negation of the fundamentals of the Marxist method is best demonstrated by the *line of argument* pursued by Kautsky in the essay here presented to the reader.

K. Kautsky, *The driving forces of the Russian revolution and its prospects*

1. The agrarian question and the liberals

The Russian revolution can be looked at in two ways: as a movement for the overthrow of absolutism and as the awakening of the great mass of the Russian people to independent political activity. The former only scratches the surface of events: from this standpoint it looks so far as if the revolution has failed. But we can only speak of real failure if the movement runs aground when seen from the second standpoint as well. If the Russian people are once again pushed back into their old political indifference, then absolutism will certainly have won and the revolution will have lost its game. But, if that does not happen, then the victory of the revolution is assured, even if absolutism attempts to prolong for a while the illusion of its dominance by murdering its own people, squandering its own wealth and laying waste its own country.

The mass of the Russian people consists, however, of peasants. What disturbs them is the agrarian question. Hence this question comes increasingly to the fore: the fate of the revolution depends upon its resolution. This is the case at least with the mass of Russia proper, which is all we are dealing with here, but not perhaps with Poland, Finland and the Caucasus.

The peasants in Russia do not merely constitute the enormous mass of the population: the whole edifice of the economy and the state rests upon agriculture. If agriculture were to collapse, so too would this edifice. Of the Western European bourgeois observers of the revolutionary situation in Russia Martin has clearly recognised this in his work on the future of Russia and it is on this premiss that the certainty of his prophecy of the bankruptcy of the Russian state rests, the prophecy that has recently caused such a sensation in Germany, albeit only in bourgeois circles that knew nothing of the socialist critique of Russian economic policy.[342]

The peasants must be satisfied and agriculture put on a sound economic basis — these are the conditions that must be fulfilled before the population of Russia becomes quiescent again and abandons revolutionary paths.

Almost all the parties in Russia recognise this now. But they do, of course, differ considerably in the way in which they would help the peasants. A recently published essay, *On the Agrarian Movement in Russia*,[343] will give the German reader a very good explanation of the attitude of the liberals: it contains translations of two Russian articles, one by Petrunkevich, the well-known 'Cadet' politician, and one by the Moscow Professor A.A. Manuilov, and a collection of the agrarian programmes of the different Russian parties.

Like everyone else the liberals admit the backwardness and decline of Russian agriculture. Manuilov writes:

Our largest harvests seem to be half the size of average harvests in other countries. If we take the average yield of all forms of grain in Russia as 100, the yield in other countries will be: rye 230, wheat 280, oats 277, etc. The net yield of grain and potatoes for the average sowing area of the Russian peasant (0.74 desyatin) is on average 20.4 poods[344] whereas in other countries a similar area would produce 56.9 poods, more specifically in Belgium 88, in the UK 84.4, in Japan 82.8 poods, etc. . . .

Professor A.I. Chuprov has also shown that harvests on our peasant lands with their 35–40 poods of rye per desyatin are so low that even the most primitive improvements, available to all, would be enough to raise the yield by 50% above its present level. [Numerous studies by agronomists suggest that a single improved choice of seed would be almost enough to achieve this result.] But technology disposes of incomparably more powerful resources. A yield of 30 metric hundredweight of rye to the hectare or 200 poods to the desyatin is considered to be rather low in countries with a developed technology.[345]

And things are getting steadily worse, not better. Manuilov continues:

At the present time as the Department of Agriculture has noted in its report, the peasants have the absolute minimum number of cattle necessary for the existence of agriculture . . . In the fifty provinces of European Russia the number of horses in the ten years 1888 to 1898 fell from 19.6 million to 17 million, and of large horned cattle from 34.6 million to 24.5 million . . .

Local committees have furnished evidence in support of what I have said in their

Transactions. It seems, for instance, that in the Nizhny Novgorod province the supply of manure amounts of between one fifth and one third of the demand and, as a result, the average yield, regardless of the fact that the soil is suitable, is extremely low: 38 measures of rye and 49 measures of oats. In the Mikhailov district of Ryazan province only one tenth to one eighth of the surface area is manured. In the Klin district of Moscow province manuring is done at two and a half times below the normal level.[346]

Liberals and Socialists are in complete agreement in recognising the significance of these facts. But liberal half-heartedness becomes immediately apparent as soon as it comes to laying bare the *reasons* for these phenomena and proposing remedies for them. Their half-heartedness in the latter case stems from their class position, but it necessarily engenders a similar half-heartedness in the former case. A man who is not determined to root out evil by radical means must also be afraid to lay bare its deepest roots.

The liberals see the causes of the decline in Russian agriculture in the manner in which the serfs were emancipated in 1861. The peasants were then tricked out of a part of their land: they did not receive enough and what they did receive was mostly bad land. If their share then was inadequate, since then it has declined further because the population has grown considerably. On this Manuilov writes:

In 1860 the rural population consisted of 50 million souls of both sexes, but by the end of 1900 it had reached about 86 million . . . At the same time the average size of a plot was reduced. According to figures produced by the Commission of Enquiry into the impoverishment of the Centre, the average plot for an *emancipated* serf in 1860 was equivalent to 4.8 desyatins; in 1880 the average size of a plot for a man had been reduced to 3.5, and in 1900 to 2.6 desyatins.[347]

The facts cited here are true but they are only half the truth that is necessary to understand the causes of the decline in agriculture.

When the feudal yoke was lifted the peasants elsewhere were treated in just the same way as in Russia and they were tricked out of their property. In other states this frequently led to the collapse of peasant businesses but it never led to the decline of agriculture, to a deterioration in business overall. to an increase in harvest failures. On the contrary. The pauperisation of the peasantry created the rural proletariat whose existence at that particular stage of commodity production constituted one of the preconditions of capitalist agriculture based on wage labour. This pauperisation led to a situation in which one section of the peasantry descended into the proletariat, while another section rose to prosperity at its expense. From the ruins of the shattered peasant economy there arose a new and higher mode of production. Only the bare beginnings of all this are discernible in Russia. Why is this? This is the decisive question.

There is no way in which we can accuse village communism of having made the advent of capitalist agriculture impossible. Village communism rapidly fell into a decline and it did not have the strength to prevent the emergence among the villagers of landless proletarians on the one hand and profiteers on the other, or the development of the relations of capitalist exploitation of many dreadful kinds. For this reason village communism is nowadays in Russia no longer a real bulwark against the growth of capitalist methods in agriculture.

All the conditions for capitalism had already been in existence for decades, except for two and these were the two most important: the agricultural population had not hitherto had the necessary *intelligence*, the capacity, to break the bonds of tradition and to select with certainty from all the new things pressing in on it those which were most suitable and efficacious. This requires a range of knowledge and methods which it is impossible to acquire without a good school education. But the *capital* itself, the necessary money, was also not to hand. Thus the two conditions which have the greatest importance for the development of capitalist production were absent. It is precisely the latter factor, the accumulation of sufficient sums of money in individual hands, that is the most indispensable of all if higher modes of production, the application of science to production, are to develop on the basis of commodity production.

Next to the lack of *intelligence* it is the lack of *capital* that is the decisive factor in the agricultural crisis in Russia. The shortage of land explains why the peasants are pauperised, but it does not explain why the peasants nevertheless carry on in ever more miserable conditions, why a class of prosperous farmers does not emerge to replace them, a class that would buy out the impoverished smallholdings and manage them rationally with adequate resources; why also the majority of larger businesses are still managed irrationally and with inadequate resources and do not displace the ruined peasant holdings.

Why does this happen? This question must be answered.

2. The shortage of capital in Russia

The question of the reasons for Russia's economic and intellectual backwardness cannot simply be answered by reference to the fact that the modern mode of production had its origin in Western Europe and is only slowly spreading to the East. That is because this immediately raises the further question of why it is spreading so slowly to the East. At the time when Russia was coming into closer contact with Western Europe its agriculture was already at almost the same level as it is today and the Empire was full of numerous hard-working peasants. North America, on the other hand, was then a wilderness in which a few meagre tribes of savages and barbarians were submerged. Despite that it has become the greatest capitalist power in the world.

The reasons for this difference are manifold, but they all stem from the contrast between the political organisation of each country. North America was colonised by farmers and petit bourgeois who had led the struggle for democracy against the rise of absolutism in Europe and who preferred freedom in the American wilderness to subjugation to the absolute state in European civilisation. Russia was a mass of countless village communities which were concerned only with their own affairs and satisfied with democracy in their own community and which had only a very hazy conception of the power of the state and passively left it to the absolute rulers whose armies had freed them from the Mongols and were obliged to protect them against any external enemy.

In America there was unlimited political liberty which gave the individual the fullest freedom of action. The need to come to terms with, and to master, completely new conditions required of the colonists who came from Europe an enormous amount of individual spiritual and physical exertion, complete freedom of action, extreme ruthlessness and the overcoming of countless prejudices.

In Russia there has for centuries not only been no trace of political liberty but there has been police supervision of every move that the citizen makes outside the confines of his village community and only a very limited desire for freedom of movement.... There has been a 'healthy arboreal slumber', a dozing in modest inherited conditions which have not changed for generations and which have allowed all sorts of prejudices to grow deeper roots and crippled all forms of energy.

While the conditions for the European population of North America bred all the spiritual characteristics that give man the upper hand in the capitalist mode of production, conditions in Russia bred precisely those characteristics that make the captives of capitalist competition succumb and that hamper capitalist development.

In addition, since Peter the Great, Russia has adhered to a policy whose results I have already referred to in my series of articles on the American worker in the chapter that deals with Russian capitalism (*Neue Zeit*, XXIV, 1, pp. 677ff.). I can only reiterate here what I said there.

Peter I opened Russia to European civilisation, i.e. to capitalism, but he also led Russia into the ranks of Europe's Great Powers, involved it in their conflicts, forced it to compete with them in military armaments on sea and on land and to measure itself against them in military terms. That occurred at a time when capitalism was already very strong in Western Europe and the forces of production were well developed. Despite this, even in Western Europe military rivalry led a number of powers into bankruptcy, e.g. Spain and Portugal, and hindered economic development in many others, with the exception of England, which was preserved by its insular position from the need to exhaust itself in continental wars, and could devote all its resources to the navy through which it ruled the seas, made a rich profit from piracy, the slave trade, smuggling and the plunder of India, and thus made war into a highly profitable business, a means of accumulating capital, just as the Revolutionary Wars later did for France by allowing the victorious armies of the Republic and the Empire to plunder the richest countries of the European continent, Belgium, Holland and Italy, and to extract rich booty from other countries as well.

Russia has never waged such profitable wars. There were a number of serious obstacles to its development as a sea power but on land it borders only on poor neighbours. Had it succeeded in defeating Japan and tapping the riches of China, it would, for the first time in history since its emergence as a European Great Power, have been able to draw considerable economic benefit from a war. But the irony of history willed that it was precisely this war that put the seal upon its bankruptcy.

As Russia was, in economic terms, the weakest and most backward of the

European Great Powers, tsarism has since the eighteenth century had, in order to maintain its position among them, to plunder its own poor people on an increasing scale and to render it impossible for them to accumulate any wealth. The state debt soon joined with militarism so that this plundering could be increased.

There is no country in the world, not even the richest, where the yield from taxation is enough to cover the large expenditure that militarism from time to time requires and that is colossal in time of war but still considerable in periods of armament, rearmament and the like. In such instances state debts have for a long time been the tried and tested way of immediately producing the resources for these large expenditures. The interest payment on state debts is always a heavy burden on the tax-paying population but it can be a means of enriching the capitalist class of a country when it is the state's creditor. The state then expropriates the working classes, in order to enrich the capitalist class, multiplies its wealth and simultaneously increases the number of proletarians at its disposal.

But in Russia there was no capitalist class capable of covering the state's capital requirements and the constant pressure of taxation made it much more difficult for such a capitalist class to emerge on a sufficient scale. Thus money had to be borrowed mainly from *foreign* capitalists who were called upon to fill the state's coffers which had been drained by the unquenchable thirst of militarism. These capital outlays were not deployed productively: they were used only for playing soldiers and for the splendour of the court. The interest on them flowed abroad and, next to militarism, this interest soon formed an ever-widening second open wound sapping the life-blood of Russia.

The Crimean War and its consequences brought home to the Russian government after the 1860s the fact that the colossus of its power rested on feet of clay, because the display of diplomatic and military power is impossible in the long term without economic power. In modern society, however, this derives far less from agriculture than from capitalist industry, and it certainly does not derive from primitive and impoverished agriculture — that is why Russian absolutism seized on the idea of closing the gap as rapidly as possible. It sought to create large-scale capitalist industry by guaranteeing energetic state aid. But, as the state lived off agriculture, that merely meant that industry was to be supported by imposing a heavier burden on the agricultural population. Hence the peacetime policy of industrialisation became, like the wartime policy of conquest, a means of plundering and oppressing the farmers and above all the peasants.

This peacetime policy led, as the wartime policy had done, to a growing indebtedness to foreigners. The growth of domestic capital progressed too slowly for the Russian government's purposes; it wanted to achieve a rapid independence from foreign countries in those branches of industry which are most important for military armaments, which produce cannons and guns, ships and railways and which supply equipment. Since domestic capital was growing too slowly to found the necessary large-scale enterprises, the government in recent decades has tried increasingly to attract foreign capital and that capital is particularly strongly represented in the coal, iron and petroleum industries in Southern Russia. It was, however, not increased independence but dependence on abroad that resulted from this hot-house cultivation of modern large-scale industry.

The existence of credit does of course provide a powerful lever for the development of capitalist industry. When the feudal nobleman borrows money from the usurer and pays interest on his debt, his income is reduced as a consequence and he finally goes to the wall, but the industrial capitalist achieves an increased profit if he borrows money and pays interest on it because he utilises this money productively, not like the nobleman in unproductive consumption, so that, in addition to the interest on the capital, it brings him a profit. If he borrows money at 4% and invests it so that it brings him 10%, then he is gaining 6%. In this form, as finance capital, foreign capital can easily accelerate the emergence of a capitalist class in economically backward countries.

But, to acquire finance capital, you need *credit*, you must already have a going concern, and on that score Russia had nothing to offer. Foreign capital certainly flowed in thousands of millions into Russia to develop its industry but only a minute percentage of this was lent to *Russian* entrepreneurs as capital to establish and extend large-scale industrial plants. On the contrary these plants were mostly established directly by foreign capitalists and remained in their hands so that not just the interest on the capital but the whole profit accrued to them and only the wages remained in Russia. This method of attracting foreign capital resulted only in the development of a strong proletariat, but not of a strong capitalist class, inside Russia. It encouraged, rather than hindered, the impoverishment of Russia.

This tendency, however, emerged at its clearest and most decisive in agriculture which is the one great branch of earnings that is the last and least to partake of the effects of capitalist modes of production that enhance the productivity of labour and which, more than any other, requires an intelligent population if it is to take advantage of modern expedients and methods of production. Capitalism in Russia brought the peasants not improved schools, not the money to obtain artificial fertiliser or improved tools and machinery, but only increased exploitation. Whereas in Western Europe the increased exploitation of the peasant by both state and capital went hand in hand with a growth in the productivity of agricultural labour, in Russia on the contrary the increased exploitation of the peasant, which arose from the increasing competition between Russia and the developed capitalist nations, brought with it a steady decline in the productivity of agriculture. The number of harvest failures grows but in every famine the cattle are of course slaughtered before people succumb to hunger. Thus every famine leaves a reduction in the cattle stock which in turn leads to a shortage of fertiliser, a less efficient order of cultivation, and thus to a further deterioration in agriculture and new and greater harvest failures. But the whole nation descends into misery with the peasant, for with him the domestic market for Russian industry goes under and that is the only market it supplies because it is not competitive on the world market; but with the peasant's demise the state too comes face to face with its own bankruptcy despite that enormous natural wealth that the stockbrokers of Western Europe enthuse over when they are willing to lay more thousands of millions at the feet of the bloody tsar. Yes, if only these millions were used to extract this wealth and not to oppress and butcher those who through their labours are alone capable of turning that natural wealth into items of value that can be exchanged on the world market for money!

The decay of agriculture is, after the rise of the industrial proletariat, the principal cause of the present Russian revolution. It has brought the state to the verge of financial bankruptcy and created conditions that are unsatisfactory, even intolerable, to all classes, conditions that they cannot bear and from which they must try and escape, once they have started to move.

3. The solution to the agrarian question

The most obvious way to help the peasant is to increase his share of the land. Almost all parties are agreed on that. But is it enough? What use is more land to the peasant when he does not even have enough livestock or tools to work his present share properly? It might provide him with temporary relief but the old misery will soon prevail again. If the peasant is to be helped on a longer-term basis then provision must be made for him to go over to more intensive and more rational methods of cultivation. He must have livestock, tools and fertiliser at his disposal, a first-rate system of elementary education must be established: in short, the peasant must be given, as quickly and as fully as possible, what for decades has been withheld or taken away from him in the wake of the progressive mortgaging of the state, its continuing increase in taxation and its growing inability and unwillingness to carry out any kind of cultural task.

Only a regime that is capable of doing this can put Russia's peasant agriculture, and with it the whole state, back on a sound economic footing and thus put an end to the revolution.

Is absolutism capable of doing that? If it were then it could still master the revolution. If the tsar had the intelligence and the strength to become a peasant emperor like Napoleon I he would be able to secure his absolutist regime once more. In the main the peasant has no great interest in the political liberty of the nation. Normally his interest revolves around the affairs of the village. If he saw that the tsar was looking after his economic requirements he would rally round him once again.

But fortunately that is impossible. Even the first Napoleon was only in a position to betray France's political liberty with the help of the peasants and the army recruited from among them because he was *the heir to the revolution* and because the revolution had already met the peasants' demands and he simply appeared as the protector of the gains they had made in and through the revolution.

Even the most energetic and far-sighted monarch cannot defeat a political revolution by himself bringing about its economic goal. To do this he would have to be not only more far-sighted but also more powerful than the entire ruling class in whose midst he lives and at whose expense the economic goal of the revolution can alone be achieved. Even if it were possible for a single individual to think and feel in what is clearly and distinctly a completely opposite manner from that of the entourage that he has known since childhood, there is no single individual, however much feared, who is capable of defying his whole entourage single-handed. The Russian tsar has less power to do this than anyone else. As soon as he showed the slightest inclination to come to terms with the revolution the faithful servants of absolutism would do away with him.

But from Nicholas II we cannot even expect any attempt ever to break significantly with his entourage over any question.

Hence his government energetically rejects anything that could relieve the miserable lot of the peasants even to a limited degree. It offers them nothing but empty promises, swindling and miserable botching. But the time is past when the peasant would allow himself to be deceived by all this. The revolution has already achieved so much in the country that the peasant wants action and he judges each party by its actions. But what has he come to expect from the actions of the government, which he equates with the tsar? Taxes are raised but the provinces where the failure of the harvest has caused famine are offered no support. Schools and hospitals close for lack of resources, the railways deteriorate because their equipment is not replaced, while the tsar needs more money than ever for the soldiers he uses to wag wage war against his own people. Since the Napoleonic invasion the Russian peasant has not seen an enemy soldier in his country and he has felt secure against foreign enemies thanks to the power of the tsar. Now it is the soldiers of the tsar himself who lay waste the countryside as the Mongols did before them. Thus all the promises that have been made to the peasant and that have from time to time filled him with fresh hopes for final salvation prove to be a miserable deception and this discovery makes his position seem doubly infuriating and his concealed anger twice as strong. The Duma, which was presented to him as a saviour in his time of need, has been dissolved and the right to vote for the second Duma, which is currently being elected, has been taken from under his nose. In view of all this it is no wonder that the peasant's former limitless respect for the tsar has turned into an equally limitless hatred for the tsar.

But do the liberals have a chance to win the peasant over in the long term?

They are certainly offering him what he wants more than anything else: more land. At least, many of them are demanding the expropriation of the large estates and their redistribution among the peasants. But at what price? Property should be treated with consideration in as far as this is possible and that means that the landowners should be fully compensated. But who should compensate them? Who else bu the peasant, either directly if he pays interest on the purchase price of the land ceded to him, or indirectly if the *state* compensates the landowner. But then the interest on the purchase price falls once more on the proletarians and the peasants indirectly in the form of new taxes. What would the peasants have gained by increasing their share of the land? Nothing at all, because the increased net proceeds would return in the shape of interest or taxation to the former owners of the large estates. Often not even external appearances would change because many peasants already work parts of the large estates on leasehold to increase their own share. If they were to own the leasehold and, instead of interest on the lease, they had to pay a new tax, how would they be better off?

It is only through the *confiscation* of the large estates that the peasant's share of the land can be significantly increased without new burdens being imposed upon him. The expropriation of a single stratum of the ruling class without compensation is of course a harsh measure. But there is no choice. The pauperisation of the peasantry has gone so far that it is no longer possible to require it to pay compensation. If the liberal landowners had possessed the energy and selflessness to accomplish in good time both the political forms and the policy that would have facilitated an amicable discussion with the peasantry while it was still solvent, they could have preserved their property interest in one form or another. Now it is too late. Moreover they have little to complain about. Their forefathers understood perfectly how to cheat the peasants most productively when serfdom was abolished: ever since then they have taken advantage of their desperate position for the worst kind of profiteering and they have never shown the peasantry the least consideration or respect.

The confiscation of the large estates is unavoidable if the peasant is to be helped. But the liberals are striving resolutely against it. It is only the socialist parties that do not recoil in fear.

But an increase in the peasant's share of the land is still a long way from solving the Russian agrarian question. We have seen that the peasant is not just short of land, but of know-how and money as well. The decay in Russian agriculture will not be arrested in the slightest because the land and soil are divided somewhat differently. On the contrary. If the large estates, where agriculture is frequently conducted on a much more rational basis, are broken up and replaced by ignorant peasants with no resources, the decline of Russian agriculture will only be accelerated if energetic measures are not taken at the same time to increase the peasants' intelligence and their working capital.

That is, however, impossible without a thorough-going upheaval in the whole of the present political system that has been bringing about the present misery at an increasing rate for 200 years. The more deeply this misery, which absolutism is still visibly increasing even now, is rooted, the more energetic the attacks on existing institutions and property relations that will be required if we are to bring this misery under any kind of control.

Without the dissolution of the standing army and the cancellation of naval armaments, without the confiscation of all the property of the imperial family and the monasteries, without the bankruptcy of the state and without the sequestration of the large monopolies still in private hands — railways, oil wells, mines, iron works — it will not be possible to raise the enormous sums that Russian agriculture requires if it is to be snatched from its terrible decay.

But it is clear that the liberals recoil before such gigantic tasks, such decisive upheavals in current property relations. Basically all they want is to carry on with present policy without touching the foundations of Russia's exploitation by foreign capital. They adhere firmly to the standing army, which alone, in their eyes, can secure order and save their property, and they want to acquire new resources for Russia through new loans, which is impossible if the interest on the old ones is not paid on time.

The interest on the national debt and Russian militarism are now costing *two thousand million marks*. The liberals want to go on squeezing this colossal sum from the Russian people year in and year out and yet they imagine that they will be able at the same time to perform all the great cultural tasks that tsarism has neglected and has *had* to neglect in order to pay for militarism and for the national debt. They believe that the establishment of a Duma is enough to conjure up thousands of millions from the land.

They often recall the great French Revolution. Not always correctly. The relations in present-day Russia are in many ways quite different from those of France in 1789. But the difference does not lie in the fact that Russian conditions require less decisive measures than the French. On the contrary. France was not indebted to foreign countries, it was not suffering from the same kind of shortage of capital, its education, agriculture and industry were not as backward as those of Russia when compared with the rest of Europe. Nonetheless even the National Assembly could not save France from national bankruptcy and confiscations. And, if France was able to maintain its militarism, it could only do this because of its victorious revolutionary wars which put it in a position where it could plunder half Europe and thus pay for the costs of the wars. The Russian revolution has no prospect of meeting its financial requirements in this manner. It must put an end to the standing army if it is to satisfy the Russian peasant.

Liberalism is just as incapable of doing this as is tsarism. It may recover again temporarily but it must soon fade away. It will do this all the more rapidly since it is deprived of energetic democratic elements because the only class of any significance upon which it can rely is that of the large landowners, a class whose liberalism is naturally diluted as the agrarian question comes increasingly to the fore.

4. Liberalism & social democracy

Russia's liberalism is of a different order from that of Western Europe and for that reason alone is it quite erroneous to portray the great French Revolution simply as the model for the present Russian one.

The leading class in the revolutionary movements of Western Europe was the *petty bourgeoisie* and, above all, that of the large cities. Because of its hitherto frequently mentioned dual position as the representative of both property and labour it became the link between the proletariat and the capitalist class, and it joined them both for common struggle in bourgeois democracy which drew its victorious strength from it. The petty bourgeois saw himself as a budding capitalist and to that extent advocated the interests of rising capital. But he himself created the model for the proletarian, who usually originated from petty-bourgeois circles, had as yet no independent class consciousness and asked for no more than the freedom and the opportunity to be elevated to the petty bourgeoisie.

In addition the petty bourgeoisie in the towns was the most numerous, most intelligent and economically most important of the classes constituting the popular mass. But the towns themselves had become the seats of the ruling powers since the Middle Ages. The towns ruled the open country and exploited it and the petty bourgeoisie played a large part in this rule and exploitation: they succeeded in oppressing the rural craftsmen and yet at the same time asserting their position as a powerful force against the nobility and the aristocracy of the towns.

Nothing like this occurred in Russia. The towns there, weak, few in number and mostly very recent in their development, have never achieved the powerful position they achieved in Western Europe and the popular mass has never known how to distinguish itself from, and raise itself above, the rural population, as it had done there.

The mass of urban craftsmen consisted of peasants and numerous forms of handicraft were pursued more in the country than in the town. Serfdom and oppression, political helplessness and apathy were the same there as here.

It was only after the abolition of serfdom that the seeds of political interest began to germinate among the urban masses, but this occurred in the last decades of the nineteenth century at the time when in Western Europe itself the revolutionary leading role of the petty bourgeoisie had finally been played out. On the one hand the proletariat had become independent and had been powerfully strengthened while on the other hand an enormous gulf had opened up between the petty bourgeoisie and capital. The petty bourgeois no longer sees the capitalists as the class he aspires to be elevated to, but as the class that is oppressing and ruining him. But he sees wage labourers as the element whose demands are accelerating this process. He no longer constitutes the leader of democracy who joins the capitalist and worker in a common political struggle but the unprincipled malcontent who, disappointed in democracy, rages simultaneously against both proletarian and capitalist and falls into the clutches of every reactionary swindler who promises him something attractive.

In this way the petty bourgeoisie of Western Europe is becoming steadily more reactionary and unreliable in spite of its revolutionary traditions. Russia's petty bourgeoisie enters the political movement without any similar tradition and under the complete influence of the economic situation that is also making itself felt in Eastern Europe. It is, therefore, much more inclined than its Western European class comrades to anti-semitism and reaction, to weak-kneed vacillation that can be bought off by all comers, to the role that the *Lumpenproletariat*[348] played in the Western European revolution: it is that *Lumpenproletariat* to which in spirit it becomes more and more closely related and with which, even in Russia, it willingly collaborates. Through the progress of the revolution it may eventually become increasingly involved in an opposition movement but it will not constitute a secure support for the revolutionary parties.

Thus, Russia lacks the firm backbone of a bourgeois democracy and it lacks the class that, through its common economic interest, might forge bourgeoisie and proletariat together in the democratic party in the common struggle for political liberty.

Even before the revolutionary struggle began, the capitalist class and the proletariat in Russia stood in direct opposition to one another. Both had learned from the West. The proletariat came straight on to the political arena, not as part of a purely democratic party, but as social democracy, and the capitalist class has allowed itself to be intimidated by the slightest stirring on the part of the proletariat: its principal concern is for a strong government.

The nucleus of the liberal party in Russia was formed by the large-scale landowners, as distinct from the latifundia owners, i.e. precisely that class against which liberalism in Western Europe directed its principal efforts. But in Russia, in contrast to Western Europe, absolutism has recently sacrificed agriculture to capital. The same process that had been completed in Western Europe at the end of the Middle Ages and in the beginnings of absolutism, the exploitation of the country by the town, was practised increasingly by Russia's absolutist regime in the nineteenth century, and it manifestly drove the landed gentry into the opposition. This oppositional stance was made easier for the gentry because it came into direct conflict with the proletariat, the other opposition class, less frequently than did industrial capital in the towns. As long as the peasantry remained calm, the Russian landowner could afford the luxury of liberalism, just as the English Tories and some Prussian Junkers had permitted themselves the aura of friendliness towards their work force at the beginning of industrialisation.

And it remained calm for a long time. Agriculture could visibly decay, the peasant sink into misery, famine after famine decimate his ranks and ruin his business – and he remained devoted to God and the tsar. Certainly, he rose in revolt from time to time but the cause of these disturbances was taken to be particular grievances rather than the entire ruling system, which was not recognised as the source of these grievances.

But the transformation of economic relations was of course gradually preparing a change in the peasant's outlook and his sentiments in the second half of the nineteenth century. The village was linked to world trade which brought its products on to the world market. The isolation of the village came increasingly to an end. General conscription took its sons to the big city where they were exposed to new impressions and learned new demands. In the end large numbers of peasants or peasant children who had lost their land turned to the factory and the mine and thus joined the proletarian class struggle and they conveyed their impressions of it to their comrades left behind in the villages back home.

This is how the foundations on which Russian absolutism rested were gradually undermined, but it needed a powerful blow for these foundations to collapse completely. That happened as a result of the war in Manchuria and the ensuing rebellion of the urban proletariat. The events which thirty years before would have passed the Russian peasant by imperceptibly are now provoking a lively response from him. He has woken up and realised that the hour has come at last to put an end to his misery. It no longer oppresses him: it provokes him. All of a sudden he sees himself in a completely new light: he regards the government, to whose control he has hitherto trustingly submitted, as the enemy that must be overthrown. He will not allow others to think for him again, he must think for himself, must use all his wits, all his energy, all his ruthlessness and abandon all his prejudices if he is to hold his own in the whirlpool that he has been sucked into. What caused the Anglo-Saxon peasant and petty bourgeois from the seventeenth to the nineteenth centuries to migrate will bring for the Russian peasant at the beginning of the twentieth century, more rapidly and more violently, revolution and the transformation of the easy-going, sleepy and unthinking creature of habit into an energetic, restless and inexhaustible warrior for the new and the better.

This amazing transformation is developing a firm basis for the new Russian agriculture that will arise from the rubble of the old but it also furnishes the most secure guarantee for the ultimate triumph of the revolution.

In the meantime, the more revolutionary the peasant becomes, the more reactionary is the large landowner. The more that liberalism loses in him its previous supporter, the more unstable the liberal parties become and the more the liberal professor and lawyers of the towns swing to the right so that they will not completely lose touch with their previous support.

This process might lead temporarily to a strengthening of reaction but it cannot suppress the revolution in the long term. It only accelerates the bankruptcy of liberalism. It must drive the peasants increasingly into the arms of those parties that protect their interests energetically and ruthlessly and that do not permit themselves to be intimidated by liberal doubts: the socialist parties. The longer the revolution lasts, the more this process must continue to increase the influence of the socialist parties in the country as well. It can ultimately lead to a situation in which social democracy becomes the representative of the masses of the population and thus the victorious party.

5. The proletariat and its ally in the revolution

It is perhaps appropriate here, as a conclusion to this study, for me to express my view on an inquiry that my friend Plekhanov has conducted among a number of non-Russian comrades on the character of the Russian revolution and the tactics that the Russian Socialists should pursue.[349] That is, I should like to make only a few observations on these questions and not answer them precisely. While I believe that my almost three decade of intimate contact with prominent leaders of the Russian revolutionary movement puts me in a position to provide my *German* comrades with some information on this movement, I also feel like a *novice* vis-à-vis my *Russian* comrades when it comes to Russian affairs. But it is of course urgently necessary for us Western European Socialists to form a definite view of the Russian revolution for it is not a local, but an international, event, and the way we assess it will exert a profound influence on the way we view the immediate tactical tasks of our own party. But I also have no reason to hold my own view back when Russian comrades ask me for it.

The questionnaire contains the following three questions:

1. What does the general character of the Russian revolution appear to be? Are we facing a bourgeois or a socialist revolution?
2. In view of the desperate attempts by the Russian government to suppress the revolutionary movement what should be the attitude of the Social Democratic Party towards the bourgeois democratic parties, which are struggling in their own way for political liberty?
3. What tactic should the Social Democratic Party pursue in the Duma elections in order to utilise the strength of the bourgeois opposition parties in the struggle against our *ancien régime* without violating the Amsterdam Resolution?

Neither part of the first of these questions seems to me to be easy to answer. The age of *bourgeois* revolutions, i.e. of revolutions in which the bourgeoisie was the driving force, is over in Russia as well. There too the proletariat is no longer an appendage and tool of the bourgeoisie, as it was in bourgeois revolutions, but an independent class with independent revolutionary aims. But wherever the proletariat emerges in this way the bourgeoisie ceases to be a revolutionary class. The Russian bourgeoisie, insofar as it is liberal and has an independent class policy at all, certainly hates absolutism but it hates revolution even more, and it hates absolutism because it sees it as the fundamental cause of revolution; and insofar as it asks for political liberty, it does so above all because it believes that it is the only way to bring an end to the revolution.

The bourgeoisie therefore does not constitute one of the driving forces of the present revolutionary movement in Russia and to this extent we cannot call it a bourgeois one.

But we should not use this as a reason to call it a socialist one without further ado. There is no way in which it can bring the proletariat alone to political dominance, to dictatorship. Russia's proletariat is too weak and backward for that. In any case it is very possible that in the course of the revolution victory will fall to the Social Democratic Party and social democracy does very well to hold out this prospect of victory to its supporters because you cannot struggle successfully if you have renounced victory in advance. But it will not be possible for social democracy to achieve victory through the proletariat alone without the help of another class and as a victorious party it will not be able to implement any more of its programme than the interests of the class that supports the proletariat allow.

But which class should the Russian proletariat rely on in its revolutionary struggle? If you take only a superficial look at politics you may come to the view that all the classes and parties that are striving for political liberty will just have to work together to achieve it and their differences should only be settled after political liberty has been won.

But every political struggle is basically a class struggle and thus also an economic struggle. Political interests are a result of economic interests; it is to protect these, and not to realise abstract political ideas, that the masses are in revolt. Anyone who wishes to inspire the masses to the political struggle must show them how closely linked it is to their economic interests. These must never be allowed to fade into the background if the struggle for political liberty is not to be blocked. The alliance between the proletariat and other classes in the revolutionary struggle must rest above all else on a *common economic interest*, if it is to be both lasting and victorious. The tactics of Russian social democracy must also be based on that kind of common interest.

A substantial common interest for the whole period of the revolutionary struggle exists, however, only between the proletariat and the peasantry. It must furnish the basis of the whole revolutionary tactic of Russian social democracy. Collaboration with liberalism should only be considered when and where cooperation with the peasantry will not thereby be disrupted.

It is on the common interest between the industrial proletariat and the peasantry that the revolutionary strength of Russian social democracy is founded, as is the possibility of its victory and, at the same time, the limits to the possibility of its exploitation.

Without the peasants we cannot win in the near future in Russia. We must not, however, anticipate that the peasants will become Socialists. Socialism can only be constructed on the basis of big business – it is too incompatible with the conditions of small businesses for it to be able to emerge and assert itself in the midst of a predominantly peasant population. It might perhaps be possible, should it come to power in large-scale industry and agricultural big business and, through its example, convince the poorer peasants and incite them to imitation, but it cannot do without them. And in Russia, more than elsewhere, the intellectual and material conditions for it are lacking. The communism of the Russian village lies in ruins and in no way signifies community of production. It is also impossible to convert modern commodity production on the basis of the village community into a higher mode of production. For this you need at least the framework of the large state. but Russian agricultural producers are in no way capable of production on a national basis.

The present revolution can only lead to the creation in the countryside of a strong peasantry on the basis of private ownership of land and to the opening up of the same gulf between the proletariat and the landowning part of the rural population that already exists in Western Europe. It therefore seems unthinkable that the present revolution in Russia is already leading to the introduction of a socialist mode of production, even if it should bring social democracy to power temporarily.

Clearly, however, we may experience some surprises. We do not know how much longer the Russian revolution will last and the forms that it has now adopted suggest that it has no desire to come to an early end. We also do not know what influence it will exert on Western Europe and how it will enrich the proletarian movement there. Finally, we do not yet have any idea how the resulting successes of the Western European proletariat will react on the Russians. We should do well to remember that we are approaching completely new situations and problems for which no earlier model is appropriate.

We should most probably be fair to the Russian revolution and the tasks that it sets us if we viewed it as neither a bourgeois revolution in the traditional sense nor a socialist one but as a quite unique process which is taking place on the borderline between bourgeois and socialist society, which requires the dissolution of the one while preparing the creation of the other and which in any case brings all those who live in capitalist civilisation a significant step forward in their development.

Notes

The following abbreviations are used in the notes.

LCW	V.I. Lenin, *Collected Works* (45 vols., London, 1960–70)
MECW	Karl Marx, Frederick Engels, *Collected Works* (50 vols., London, 1975–)
MESW	Karl Marx, Frederick Engels, *Selected Works* (2 vols., Moscow, 1962)
RSDLP	Russian Social Democratic Labour Party
SPD	Social Democratic Party of Germany

Introduction

Words and phrases given in transliterated Russian are generally explained only when first mentioned in the notes. A glossary has therefore been provided. Full title, place and date of publication are given only when a book is first mentioned. Subsequent references are confined to the author's surname, abbreviated title and page number.

1. See Document no. 1, pp. 41–4.
2. See Document no. 7, pp. 74–80.
3. See Document no. 12, p. 108.
4. See Document no. 13, pp. 109–12.
5. Karl Marx, Frederick Engels, *Collected Works* (50 vols., London, 1975–), 3, p. 186 (hereafter MECW). At the time of writing the Marx/Engels *Collected Works* extend only to 1854. For their writings after that time I have relied upon the Marx/Engels *Selected Works* (2 vols., Moscow, 1962) and this will be abbreviated hereafter as MESW.
6. Moses Hess, 'The Philosophy of the Act', in A. Fried and R. Sanders (eds.), *Socialist Thoughs: A Documentary History* (New York, 1964), pp. 249–75.
7. MECW, 5, p. 49
8. Ibid., p. 36.
9. MECW, 6, pp. 490–1.
10. K. Marx, *Capital* (Moscow, 1961), 1, p. 763.
11. MECW, 6, p. 495.
12. MECW, 4, p. 37.
13. Ibid.
14. MECW, 6, p. 497.
15. Ibid., p. 494.
16. MECW, 10, p. 47.
17. Ibid., p. 125.

18 Ibid., p. 97.
19 Ibid., p. 127.
20 MECW, 11, p. 187.
21 MECW, 6, p. 211.
22 G.V. Plekhanov, *Selected Philosophical Works* (5 vols., Moscow, 1961–76), 1, p. 59. Plekhanov does not give the source of his quotation but it is from *The Manifesto of the Communist Party*, see MECW, 6, p. 493.
23 MECW, 6, p. 498.
24 Ibid., p. 493.
25 Cited in M. Malia, *Alexander Herzen and the Birth of Russian Socialism* (London, 1961), p. 400.
26 Apart from the rousing of the Chigrin peasants by means of a fraudulent manifesto allegedly from the tsar. On the Chigrin conspiracy see Franco Venturi's definitive study of Russian Populism: *Roots of Revolution* (London, 1964), pp. 581 *et seq.*
27 MECW, 3, p. 183.
28 Ibid., p. 182.
29 Ibid., p. 187.
30 Ibid.
31 See the report of one such polemical attack by Plekhanov in S.H. Baron, *Plekhanov: The Father of Russian Marxism* (London, 1963), pp. 23–5. For more ample treatment of Lavrov's ideas see Venturi, *Roots*, chap. 17.
32 Venturi, *Roots*, p. 458.
33 Baron, *Plekhanov*, p. 62.
34 Plekhanov, *Selected Philosophical Works*, 1, p. 96.
35 Ibid., p. 638.
36 Ibid., pp. 741–2.
37 Ibid., p. 394.
38 Ibid., p. 393.
39 Ibid., p. 405.
40 Ibid., p. 408.
41 Ibid., p. 377.
42 Ibid., p. 389.
43 Ibid., p. 111.
44 Ibid., p. 112.
45 Ibid., p. 108.
46 Ibid., p. 454.
47 See Document no. 3, pp. 56–7.
48 See Document no. 34, pp. 192–3.
49 See Document no. 41, p. 224.
50 See Document no. 43, p. 237.
51 Quoted in A. Ascher, *Pavel Axelrod and the Development of Menshevism* (Cambridge, Mass., 1972), p. 134.
52 See Document no. 45, pp. 250–3.
53 Ibid., p. 252.
54 Ibid.
55 See Document no. 24.
56 The fullest account in English of the very important work done in this connection by Krupskaya, Fotieva, Shesterina-Nevzorova and others is: R.H. McNeal, *Bride of the Revolution: Krupskaya and Lenin* (London, 1973). See also O.G. Kutsentov, *Deyateli Peterburgskogo 'Soyuza borby za osvobozhdenie rabochego klassa'* (Moscow, 1962) and N. Krupskaya, *Memories of Lenin* (London, 1942), pp. 5–6.

57   See the extracts from Plekhanov's *The Tasks of the Social Democrats in the Fight Against the Famine in Russia*, Document no. 11, pp. 100–7.
58   N. Harding, *Lenin's Political Thought* (London, 1977), 1, p. 75.
59   Peterburzhets (pseud. K.M. Takhtarev), *Ocherk Peterburgskogo rabochego dvizheniya* (London, 1902).
60   See Document no. 17, p. 142.
61   See Document no. 18, pp. 143–4.
62   *On Agitation* is translated in full as Document no. 34, pp. 192–205.
63   Ibid., p. 192.
64   Ibid., pp. 202–3.
65   Ibid., pp. 198–9.
66   See Document no. 27, pp. 153–71.
67   Ibid., p. 166.
68   Ibid., p. 167.
69   Ibid., p. 168.
70   See Document nos. 25–32.
71   R. Pipes, *Social Democracy and the St Petersburg Labor Movement, 1885–1897* (Cambridge, Mass., 1963), p. 105.
72   See Document no. 27, p. 165.
73   See Document nos. 25–32.
74   Takhtarev, *Ocherk*, p. 25.
75   See S.P. Turin, *From Peter the Great to Lenin: A History of the Russian Labour Movement with Special Reference to Trade Unionism* (London, 1968), p. 50n.
76   See Document no. 21.
77   See, e.g., Document no. 25 *To the Weavers at the Lebedev Mill*, p. 152.
78   A.K. Wildman, *The Making of a Workers' Revolution* (Chicago, 1967), p. 74. This May Day leaflet for 1896 is translated below. See Document no. 28.
79   According to Pipes, there had been nothing about the reduction of the working day in previous social democratic propaganda – a contention which even the modest selection of documents given below amply refutes.
80   See Document no. 15.
81   Turin, *From Peter the Great to Lenin*, p. 53.
82   Ibid., p. 53n.
83   Wildman, *The Making*, pp. 74–5.
84   V.I. Lenin, *The New Factory Law*, in *Collected Works* (45 vols., London, 1960–70), 2, pp. 289–90 (hereafter LCW). Lenin's forebodings were in fact confirmed in the years which followed. As Turin laments 'Unfortunately the Act of 1897, owing to its vagueness, was capable of very wide interpretation, and since it was not accompanied by provisions to ensure its proper working, it soon became practically a dead letter.' (Turin, *From Peter the Great to Lenin*, p. 51).
85   See Document no. 43, p. 237.
86   LCW, 5, p. 364.
87   See Document no. 46.
88   In G.V. Plekhanov, *Sochineniya*, 2nd edn, ed. D. Ryazanov (29 vols., Moscow, 1923–7) 12.
89   Ibid., pp. 13–14.
90   Ibid., p. 25.
91   Ibid., p. 34.
92   *Rabochaya Mysl*, no. 7 (1899), p. 6.
93   Ibid., p. 245.
94   Ibid., p. 249.

95   Ibid., p. 247.
96   See Document no. 43, p. 240.
97   Plekhanov, *Sochineniya*, 12, p. 26.
98   Ibid., p. 30.
99   Ibid., p. 36.
100   Document no. 47, 'The Urgent Tasks of Our Movement', pp. 259–62.
101   Ibid., p. 260.
102   Ibid., p. 262.
103   Ibid., p. 261.
104   N. Harding, 'Lenin's Early Writings – The Problem of Context', *Political Studies*, XXIII, no. 4 (Dec. 1975), pp. 442–58.
105   See Document no. 50, pp. 279–87.
106   Cited in Ascher, *Pavel Axelrod*, p. 176.
107   *Kommunisticheskaya Partiya Sovetskogo Soyuza v rezolyutsiyakh i resheniyakh*, pt 2, 1898–1925, 7th edn (Moscow, 1953), p. 135.
108   See Lenin's 'The Reorganisation of the Party', in LCW, 10, pp. 29–39.
109   D. Lane, *The Roots of Russian Communism* (Assen, 1968), pp. 214–15.
110   The petition they carried, though doubtless largely drawn up by George Gapon, can be taken as a fairly accurate reflection of the social and political attitudes and objectives of the mass of Petersburg workers at this time. See Document no. 54.
111   See Document no. 57.
112   LCW, 12, pp. 334–5.
113   LCW, 9, p. 28.
114   Ibid., p. 29.
115   L. Trotsky, *Our Revolution*, Document no. 59, p. 347.
116   See Kautsky's *The Driving Forces of the Russian Revolution and Its Prospects*, Document no. 60, pp. 352–72.
117   P. Akselrod, *The People's Duma and the Workers' Congress*, Document no. 58, pp. 331–7.

Documents

1   The Northern Union of Russian Workers originated as a workers' circle formed in the autumn of 1877 by Stepan Khalturin (later to achieve notoriety as the man who engineered the explosion at the Winter Palace in February 1880) and Viktor Obnorsky. Obnorsky was already a veteran socialist organiser having been involved in the South Russian Workers' Union which had been established in Odessa in 1875. These two were principally responsible for drawing up the programme. By the end of January 1879, having helped to organise and publish the demands of two strikes, the Northern Union was severely disrupted by arrests of its worker activists. Some of its surviving leaders joined the Narodnaya Volya (People's Will) Central Workers' Circle which Zhelyabov and Perovsky established in Petersburg in late 1879. The programme was published, at the Union's request, by the underground press of Zemlya i Volya (Land and Freedom) on 12 January 1879. On the Narodnaya Volya and Zemlya i Volya, see n. 36.

2   By late 1878 the Northern Union had branches in all the main industrial regions of Petersburg and comprised 200 active members and as many sympathisers. It organised delegate meetings on 23 and 30 December at which Khalturin's and Obnorsky's draft programme was discussed and amended.

3   The first four programmatic demands of the Northern Union, especially the calls for the replacement of the state by a federation of free communes and

the vesting of ownership of land in the communes, clearly reflect the strong influence of the Narodnik tradition. The ten-point programme which follows is, however, closely modelled on the Eisenach programme of the Social Democratic Party of Germany (see L.M. Ivanov, *Istoriya rabochego klassa v Rossii* (Moscow, 1972), p. 105), a text with which Obnorsky was almost certainly familiar from his travels in Western Europe.

4 *Socialism and the Political Struggle* was Plekhanov's first extended attempt as a new convert to Marxism to settle accounts with his old system of beliefs. It was written in the summer of 1883 and intended for the journal of the Narodnaya Volya Party which, understandably perhaps, declined to publish it. The Emancipation of Labour Group, which Plekhanov established in Geneva in 1883 with the aims of applying Marxism to Russian conditions and disseminating Marxist literature in Russia, published the essay as Volume 1 of its Library of Modern Socialism.

5 Note in original: 'See *Essai sur l'histoire du Tiers État* by Aug. Thierry, pp. 33–34.'

6 The Anti-Corn-Law League was the first political pressure group to elaborate effective regional and local branches.

7 Note in original: 'See *Sozialdemokratische Abhandlungen* by M. Ritting-hausen, Drittes Heft . . . p. 3.'

8 Note in original: 'See the programmes of the German and North American Workers' parties. The *Manifesto* of the British Democratic Federation also demands "direct voting on all important questions".'

9 Note in original: 'See A.E.F. Schäffle, *Bau und Leben des sozialen Körpers* (Tübingen, 4 vols., 1875–8) vol. III, pp. 91 and 102.'

10 The quotation is from Marx's famous *Preface to a Contribution to the Critique of Political Economy* written and published in 1859. See MESW, 1, p. 363.

11 Note in original: 'See *Das System der erworbenen Rechte*, Leipzig, 1880, vol. 1, Preface, p. VII.'

12 Disparaging reference to Lorenz von Stein who wrote the first comprehensive account in German of the French socialist movement: *Der Sozialismus und Communismus des heutigen Frankreichs* (Leipzig, 1843).

13 Friedrich Albert Lange (1828–75) was a German philosopher who in 1866 had published his influential critique of materialism, *Geschichte des Materialismus und Kritik seiner Bedeutung in der Gegenwart*.

14 *Zemlya i Volya* was the organ of the Narodnik or Populist Socialists. In issue no. 5 (8 April 1879) a letter from the Northern Union of Russian Workers (see nn. 1–3) was published responding to the critique made by the editors and re-affirming the Union's belief that only political liberty could guarantee the success of the workers' cause. The letter is published in A.M. Pankratova and L.M. Ivanov (eds.), *Rabochee dvizhenie v Rossii v XIX veke* (4 vols. in 8 parts, Moscow, 1955–63), 3, pt 2, pp. 243–7 (hereafter *Rab. dvizh. XIX veke*).

15 *The Manifesto of the Communist Party*, MECW, 6, p. 495. The final phrase 'in bourgeois countries' appears to have been added by Plekhanov.

16 Again a loose quotation from *The Manifesto*, MECW, 6, p. 486.

17 In a note to the 1905 edition Plekhanov refers his readers to nos. 2 and 3 of *Zarya* (*The Dawn*) – the theoretical organ of the *Iskra* (*The Spark*) Group – for elaboration of this point. On *Iskra* see nn. 197 and 226.

18 MECW, 6, p. 494.

19 Plekhanov's note to 2nd edn: 'i.e. Rodbertus'. Johann Karl Rodbertus was a Prussian Conservative who argued for the intervention of the state to improve the lot of the working class and thus ensure political stability.

20   The *Kathedersozialisten*, or 'Professorial Socialists' were a group of German academics active in the 1870s amongst whom were Adolph Wagner, Gustav Schmoller, Brentano and Schäffle. Their position was an elaboration and refinement of Rodbertus'.

21   Plekhanov's note to 2nd edn: 'I again mean Rodbertus.'

22   The quotation is from Marx's *Introduction to A Contribution to the Critique of Hegel's Philosophy of Law*, MECW, 3, p. 187.

23   Marx and Engels, *The Manifesto of the Communist Party*, MECW, 6, pp. 493–4.

24   The Emancipation of Labour Group was established as a vehicle for developing and disseminating Marxism in Russia. It was founded in Geneva in September 1883 by four ex-activists of the Populist organisation Chernyi Peredel (Black Repartition), namely Plekhanov, Akselrod, Deich and Zasulich. This programme was written by Plekhanov at the time of the formation of the group. Its membership remained unchanged until its dissolution in 1900. 'In essence, they distrusted numbers and insisted upon a kind of élite leadership of the Marxian movement!' Baron, *Plekhanov*, p. 129. This was a source of considerable annoyance to the numerous younger Marxist émigrés of the 1890s.

25   Note in original: We by no means regard the programme that we are submitting to the judgement of comrades as something finished and complete, not subject to partial changes or additions. On the contrary, we are ready to introduce into it any kinds of corrections provided that they do not contradict the basic concepts of scientific socialism and that they correspond to the practical conclusions following from these concepts concerning the work of the Socialists in Russia.'

26   The International Working Men's Association was formed in London in September 1864 at a meeting of English and continental labour and radical leaders. Marx later became Secretary of its General Council and it was the dispute between his followers and those of the anarchist Mikhail Bakunin which led to its effective demise in September 1872.

27   Note in original: 'Such actions may include, for instance, *bribery at elections*, outrageous repression of workers by employers, etc.'

28   Note in original: 'This point is logically covered by para. 4, which requires, *inter alia*, complete freedom of conscience; but we consider it necessary to set it in relief in view of the fact that there are in our country whole strata of the population, e.g. the *Jews*, who do not enjoy even the wretched "rights" made available to other "citizens".'

29   This was originally published as part of chapter 6 of *Nashi raznoglasiya* (*Our Differences*) (Geneva, 1884) pp. 303–19; the second edition appeared in 1905 and was reprinted in G.V. Plekhanov, *Sochineniya* (Moscow, 1923–7), 2, pp. 341–53 as section 2 of chapter 5 entitled 'The True Tasks of the Socialists in Russia'. This translation has been made from the 1923 edition.

30   The comparison is between two members of the Executive Committee of Narodnaya Volya – Goldenburg, who, having been careless in his conspiratorial preparations, inadvertently led the police to the other committee members, and Zhelyabov the assiduous 'professional' conspirator. (On Narodnaya Volya see n. 36.)

31   V.V. was the pseudonym of the influential neo-Populist economist V.P. Vorontsov.

32   For the programme of the Northern Union of Russian Workers see Document no. 1 of this volume. On the Union's letter to Zemlya i Volya see n. 14.

33 Plekhanov himself had taken an active part in preparing and assisting the widespread strikes of the late 1870s in the Petersburg textile plants.

34 Plekhanov quotes from the preamble to Marx's *General Rules of the International Working Men's Association*, MESW, 1, p. 386.

35 Gleb Uspensky, a Populist novelist who nonetheless believed that the passivity and fatalism of the peasant character made revolution unlikely.

36 In October 1879, after its Voronezh Conference, the general Populist organisation Zemlya i Volya (Land and Freedom), founded in 1860 and revived in 1875, was dissolved and replaced by two separate organisations. The proponents of revolutionary propaganda and agitation among the peasants and urban workers grouped themselves in the short-lived Chernyi Peredel (Black Repartition) whilst the adherents of terror, as a device to disorganise the regime and excite the mass into rebellion, formed the Narodnaya Volya (People's Will).

37 Rabochaya Biblioteka (the Workers' Library) was the publishing house of the Emancipation of Labour Group. It survived until 1901 and was, until the turn of the century at least, the principal source of illegal literature for the social democratic movement in Russia. This editorial statement of objectives appeared as a preface to the first title to be published by the Library: P. Akselrod's *Rabochee dvizhenie i sotsialnaya demokratiya* (*The Workers' Movement and Social Democracy*) (Geneva, 1884 according to title page, 1885 according to cover).

38 *Zemskii sobor* – Assembly of the Land or National Assembly, an invocation of the assembly convened in 1550 by Ivan the Terrible to hear petitions for redress of grievances from all classes. The demand for the convocation of a national representative assembly was a perennial feature of radical thought in nineteenth-century Russia.

39 In 1873 and especially in the 'mad summer' of 1874 thousands of young Russians, mainly students, participated in the 'going to the people' inspired by often conflicting hopes of discovering a simple, 'organic' way of life for themselves, educating the peasants and raising their living standards, or of unleashing a peasant socialist revolt.

40 See Document no. 1 and nn. 1–3.

41 On 7 January 1885 some 4,000 workers at the Nikolsky cotton mills in Orekhovo-Zuevo belonging to Savva Morozov struck in protest against a 25% reduction in wages promulgated by the management. P.A. Moiseenko and V. Volkov, veterans of the Northern Union of Russian Workers, had earlier established a workers' circle at the factory and they provided organisational expertise to the strikers. As the list of grievances in their petition to the Governor of the town of Vladimir makes clear, the men were incensed at the constantly escalating fines levied by the administration which, in the Morozov works, absorbed between 30% and 50% of wages. As a consequence of the strike the government hastily prepared what amounted to the first consolidated Labour Code, promulgated as the Law of 3 June 1886, which incorporated all the strikers' demands. (For the main points of this 'First Russian Labour Code' see Turin, *From Peter the Great to Lenin*, pp. 185–6). For his pains, the Minister of Finance, Bunge, who had been responsible for drafting the Code, was shortly to be driven from office for having succumbed to 'socialism'.

42 This programme was produced by the group calling itself the Party of Russian Social Democrats formed by Dimitri Blagoev in St Petersburg in the winter of 1883–4. It was the only group in Russia to establish direct contact with the Emancipation of Labour Group in the first ten years of its existence and

Akselrod and Plekhanov contributed articles to the two numbers of the journal *Rabochii* (*The Worker*) which the group managed to produce before being liquidated by police arrests in the winter of 1885–6.

43   Here, as elsewhere, the programme appears to be directly indebted to Vorontsov's neo-Populist arguments in his *The Fates of Capitalism in Russia* (*Sudby kapitalizma v Rossii* (St Petersburg, 1882)) with regard to the impossibility of an adequate home market under capitalism and the enormous difficulties, especially in Russia, of socialisation (or concentration) of labour.

44   See n. 38.

45   Note to both clauses in original: 'The allowance is granted on the assumption that the recipient will repay it when he can without interest.'

46   The *Second Draft Programme of the Russian Social Democrats* was written by Plekhanov in 1885 following discussions between the Emancipation of Labour Group and the Blagoev Group (see n. 42). It was distributed in Russia in hectographed form and published as an appendix to *What Do the Social Democrats Want?* (Geneva, 1888).

47   See n. 26.

48   In 1891 the first May Day celebrations in Russia were organised in the woods outside St Petersburg by activists of the Brusnev circle (on Brusnev see Document no. 12 and nn. 49 and 67) and attended by approximately 100 working men and students. It has been resolved at the First Congress of the Second International in 1889, at the suggestion of American trade unionists, that May the First be a day when the international solidarity of labour was celebrated and when the universal demand for the eight-hour working day should be pressed through strikes, demonstrations and meetings. From 1891 through to the revolution of 1917 May Day was to assume ever-increasing importance in Russian social democratic practical activity as well as in its literature.

49   Brusnev had an abiding admiration for the Social Democratic Party of Germany and announced the objective of his group as 'developing future Russian Bebels' from the Petersburg workers.

50   The writer N.V. Shelgunov was held in great esteem by the Petersburg worker activists, an esteem which was reciprocated when, shortly before his death, Shelgunov resolved to devote himself wholly to the workers' cause. The pamphlet, published as no. 6 of *Rabochaya Biblioteka* (Geneva, 1892), in which these speeches appeared in print, contained, as an appendix, an 'Address of the Petersburg Workers to N.V. Shelgunov'.

51   The Peter and Paul and Schlüsselburg were notorious prisons in St Petersburg where successive generations of political opponents of the autocracy had been incarcerated.

52   *Sotsial-Demokrat*, a 'Literary-Political Review', first appeared in Geneva in 1888. In 1890 Plekhanov and Akselrod revived it as a proposed three-monthly periodical. Four issues were published between 1890 and 1892.

53   In March 1881 members of the Executive Committee of Narodnaya Volya had assassinated tsar Alexander II in St Petersburg.

54   Plekhanov quotes the concluding words of Engels' *Socialism: Utopian and Scientific*, 'to impart to the now oppressed proletarian class a full knowledge of the condition and of the meaning of the momentous act it is called upon to accomplish, this is the task of the theoretical expression of the proletarian movement, scientific socialism' (MESW, 2, p. 155).

55   Plekhanov refers, no doubt, to his own considerable efforts to dispel the apolitical prejudices of much of the Populist movement set out in *Socialism and the Political Struggle* and *Our Differences*.

56   P.N. Tkachev was the foremost representative of Russian Jacobinism in the
1870s and was engaged in numerous controversies in émigré circles. For
Engels' critique of his views, which Plekhanov closely follows here, see *On
Social Relations in Russia*, MESW, 2, pp. 49–61. For a rounded analysis of
Tkachev's ideas see Venturi, *Roots*, chap. 16.

57   Plekhanov refers to the Emancipation of the Serfs in 1861 by whose terms
the peasants lost considerable areas of land which they had hitherto farmed
or on which they had enjoyed customary rights of grazing or wood-cutting
(the so-called cut-off lands).

58   Note in original: 'Engels, *La politique extérieure du czarisme russe*.'

59   Note in original: 'Dowerine-Tchernoff, *L'esprit national russe sous Alexandre
III* (Paris, 1890).'

60   The worker in question was Stepan Khalturin.

61   For the programme of the Northern Union of Russian Workers see Document
no. 1.

62   In 1891–2 severe famine afflicted the grain producing provinces of Southern
Russia.

63   Charles Fourier (1772–1837) was one of the most engaging theorists of
Utopian Socialism who offered an ingenious plan for overcoming the division
of labour and the repression of man's natural feelings and impulses in his
meticulously detailed model community or *phalanstère*.

64   It may be that Plekhanov was here paraphrasing Engels' words in *Socialism:
Utopian and Scientific* (MESW, 2, p. 121):

> The solution of the social problems, which as yet lay hidden in undeveloped economic
> conditions, the Utopians attempted to evolve out of the human brain. Society presented
> nothing but wrongs; to remove these was the task of reason. It was necessary, then, to
> discover a new and more perfect system of social order and to impose this upon society
> from without by propaganda, and, whenever it was possible, by the example of model
> experiments.

65   The so-called 'Law of Exclusion' or 'Exceptional Law' or 'Anti-Socialist
Laws', were passed in October 1878 as an emergency measure to last for three
years but were extended by successive parliaments until October 1890. Under
its provisions 'Social Democratic, Socialistic or Communistic endeavours,
aimed at the destruction of the existing order in State or society are to be forbidden.' The law went on to detail the socialistic endeavours it banned; meetings, processions and festivities, printed matter, collection of contributions or
distribution of literature. (For a fuller account of its provisions see B. Russell,
German Social Democracy (London, 1965), pp. 100–2.)

66   See n. 38.

67   M.I. Brusnev (1864–1937) had been active in the revolutionary movement
since 1881. In 1889 when a mature student at the Technological Institute in
St Petersburg he organised a Social Democratic Society which had considerable success in establishing workers' circles in the capital and in issuing leaflets on behalf of the workers at Thornton's textile plant and at the New Port.
It was Brusnev's circle that organised the first May Day celebration in May
1891 (see n. 48). In 1891 Brusnev went to Moscow where he organised new
circles and established links with like-minded groups in other towns. Arrested
in 1892 he was given six years imprisonment and ten years exile and played
no further part in the movement.

68   The distinction implied here, common enough in social democratic programmes, was between the minimum programme, or those immediate
demands the satisfaction of which would not entail the overthrow of capital-

ism, and the maximum programme which specified the ultimate objectives which assuredly would entail the supercession of capitalism and bourgeois democracy.

69   N.E. Fedoseev (1870–98) organised one of the first Marxist circles in Southern Russia in Samara in 1888. The group was short-lived, being decimated by arrests in 1890. Fedoseev himself committed suicide in prison in 1898.

70   The quotation is of course from the authors not the editors and from the conclusion not the introduction to *The Manifesto of the Communist Party*. Fedoseev has also substituted 'Social Democrats' for 'Communists' and 'revolt and victory of the workers' for 'communistic revolution' (cf. MECW, 6, p. 519).

71   Akselrod's *The Tasks of the Worker Intelligentsia in Russia* first appeared in issue no. 1 of the journal *Sotsialist* (June 1889). The second edition, from which these extracts are taken, was published in Geneva in 1893 as no. 7 of *Rabochaya Biblioteka*.

72   For the speeches at the 1891 May Day celebration see Document no. 9.

73   The reference is to the formation of the Emancipation of Labour Group in Geneva.

74   On Zemlya i Volya and Narodnaya Volya see nn. 14 and 36.

75   Note in original: 'Through the medium of that section of workers that comes to the city for a few months year after year and then goes back home to the country political propaganda can also be spread even amongst the peasants.'

76   The delegate concerned was Viktor Obnorsky one of the principal leaders of the Northern Union of Russian Workers (see n. 1) who, on his last trip abroad in 1879, managed to purchase a press from the Nabat Group in Geneva. The 'émigré writer' asked to edit the newspaper was none other than Akselrod himself.

77   See n. 1.

78   Note in original: '*The Workers' Movement and Social Democracy*, p. XV', a reference to Akselrod's book published as no. 1 of *Rabochaya Biblioteka* (Geneva, 1885).

79   The pamphlet *The Working Day* was translated into Russian from the Polish. Its author is unknown but he was undoubtedly inspired by the decisions of the First Congress of the Second International in 1889 to press the demand for the eight-hour day as the immediate objective of international labour. The booklet first appeared in Russian as no. 8 of *Rabochaya Biblioteka* (Geneva, 1894) and was subsequently produced and distributed in a large number of editions both by Social Democrats and Narodovoltsy. It was the most influential and best-known agitational booklet of the 1890s and left its clear mark on many of the other leaflets of this period as it also did on the demands voiced in the large-scale strikes of 1896–7.

80   Note in original: 'In Russia the average working day lasts thirteen to fourteen hours, in America (USA) nine to ten hours; at the same time pay for every hour worked is five times higher in America than in Russia! It is exactly the same in England: for a nine- to ten-hour day pay is four times higher than in Russia.'

81   Note in original: 'The high mortality rate among workers also results from their low earnings which are often not sufficient to satisfy their most elementary needs. But even low wages are, as we have already seen, a consequence of too long a working day.'

82   Note in original: 'Our great poet, Nekrasov, in his poem "The Cry of Children" described the factory worker's lot in these words:

The iron wheel turns
Drones and causes a draught!
The head burns and spins,
The heart beats, everything rotates.
We, in a frenzy,
Start to shout out loud,
"Stop your terrible rotation,
Let us collect our feeble thoughts."
No point in crying and imploring:
The wheel does not hear, does not hear us.
We could die and that damned wheel will turn,
We could die and it would drone and drone and drone!'

83 Note in original: 'Article 431 of the Industrial Statute, Vol. XI, Part 2.'
84 This questionnaire is not included in the Russian editions of Lenin's
Sochineniya nor in the English *Collected Works* but its attribution to Lenin is
confirmed by the memoirs of Ivan Babushkin in *Vospominaniya o Vladimire
Iliche Lenine* (3 vols., Moscow, 1956–60), 1, p. 114. Babushkin recalled how

the lecturer [Lenin] gave us lists of previously prepared questions which prompted us
to make a closer study and observation of factory and mill life. During working hours we
found excuses to go into another shop to collect material, either by personal observations, or, where possible, in conversation with the workers.

My tool box was always full of notes of all kinds; during the dinner-hour I tried to
write up the data on hours and wages in our shop.

See also *Recollections of I. V. Babushkin* (Moscow, 1957), p. 56.
85 On the day before Christmas Eve 1894 disturbances, rioting and looting
began at the Semyannikov Factory in the Nevsky Gate area of St Petersburg
over the non-payment of wages. (Babushkin was a worker at the factory and
his *Recollections*, cited above, contain the fullest available account of the
affair, see pp. 67–75.) Lenin was the social democratic organiser for the area
and he was distressed to find many worker students of his circles standing
aloof from the struggle. To help remedy the situation he wrote this leaflet.
Only part of it is extant. It was discovered in Akselrod's archive and had, presumably, been brought from Russia by Lenin when he visited Plekhanov and
Akselrod in the summer of 1895. The surviving fragment was first published
in *Letopis Marksizma*, no. 3 (1927), pp. 61–6, and later in S.N. Valk's
definitive edition of the leaflets produced by the St Petersburg Union of
Struggle, *Listovki Peterburgskogo 'Soyuza borby za osvobozhdenie rabochego
klassa' 1895–1897* (Moscow, 1934), pp. 1–6.
86 From 7 to 12 February 1895 a strike occurred at the St Petersburg New Port.
This leaflet was produced in multiple typewritten copies not later than 9
February.
87 According to Articles 7 and 8 of the Labour Code of 1886 all workers were
to be supplied with wage books or written contracts. The grievance expressed
in the text was, presumably, directed against the management practice of
levying a fee for the supply of a written contract.
88 This appeal was issued by the Moscow 'Workers' Union' in June of 1895. For
a comprehensive account of the activities of the Moscow 'Union' from 1894
to early 1897 see the Report of the Central Committee of the Moscow
'Workers Union' in *Rabotnik*, no. 3–4 (Geneva, 1897), pp. 33–52, republished in G.N. Shanshiev (ed.), *Borba za sozdanie marksistskoi partii v Rossii:
1894–1904 gody* (Moscow, 1961), pp. 78–94.

89 Another appeal issued by the Moscow 'Workers' Union' put out in November 1895 expressing in popular agitational terms the message of the pamphlet *The Working Day*.

90 On 6 November 1895 a strike of 600 workers occurred in the woollen goods department of Thornton's mill in St Petersburg. Lenin wrote this summary of the workers' grievances in consultation with N.E. Merkulov, a worker at the mill who was also responsible for its distribution on 12 November. Immediately prior to the strike the Petersburg Social Democrats had circulated a leaflet, written by G.M. Krzhizhanovsky, 'What Do the Weavers Demand', in the Thornton mill.

91 'Noils' – short-staple combings normally separated from the long wool fibres and discarded.

92 'Bieber' and 'Ural' were trade names for varieties of woollen cloth.

93 From 9 to 11 November there had occurred a strike of 1,300 women workers at the Laferme tobacco factory in Petersburg. This leaflet was produced not later than 17 November and distributed by Z.P. Nevzorova and A.A. Yakubova, disguised as women workers. Possibly because of the prominence of women in social democratic circles in Petersburg the cigarette-girls were frequently circularised with leaflets. Thus in January 1896 two flysheets 'To the Cigarette-Girls of the Laferme Factory' and 'To All St Petersburg Cigarette-Girls' were issued, and in July a further leaflet 'To the Workers at the Laferme Factory' was put out.

94 On 15 December 1895, following the arrest of Lenin, Vaneev, Zaporozhets, Krzhizhanovsky, Starkov and others on the night of 8–9 December, a meeting of the remaining leaders of the St Petersburg Union of Struggle for the Emancipation of the Working Class was convened and this leaflet – apparently issued on the 9th – was drawn up.

95 On 4 December disturbances had broken out at the huge Putilov works which was the principal heavy engineering plant in St Petersburg, following a management announcement of a cut in wages. Not later than 5 December the Union of Struggle issued two leaflets both entitled 'To the Workers of the Putilov Works' in which the general and specific demands of the workers were amplified and threats made of an all-out strike if these were not satisfied (*Rab. dvizh. XIX veke*, 4, pt 1, pp. 26–8).

96 The prediction in this case was accurate, on 17 December a ten-day strike of 450 weavers began there. The Lebedev cotton mill was another favourite target of social democratic flysheets and leaflets (see Document nos. 25 and 26).

97 Ivan Babushkin was one of Lenin's worker students and was a prominent social democratic activist in St Petersburg. The leaflet was written at the end of December 1895 and distributed early in January 1896. Later it was published in large numbers by the Emancipation of Labour Group. It is, fairly obviously, a tribute to the intellectuals arrested on 8–9 December (see n. 94).

98 From 20 to 27 December a strike of 450 weavers at the Lebedev Cotton Mills had followed a swingeing reduction of wage rates. This leaflet was put out by the Union of Struggle on 1 January.

99 Published by the Union of Struggle simultaneously with, or immediately after, Document no. 25.

100 Articles 7–8 of the 'First Russian Labour Code' of 1886 specified that workers were to receive either wages books or written contracts. See further n. 104.

101 This draft programme was written by Lenin in prison in St Petersburg. The

manuscript was written in invisible ink between the lines of a book. The 'Explanation' was written in June—July 1896.

102   Lenin was, no doubt, paraphrasing from memory Engels' *On Authority* (MESW, 1, p. 637):

> All these workers, men, women and children, are obliged to begin and finish their work at the hours fixed by the authority of the steam which cares nothing for individual autonomy . . . at least with regard to the hours of work one may write upon the portals of these factories 'Leave ye that enter in all autonomy behind!'

103   Lenin refers to the great strike at the Morozov works in Orekhovo-Zuevo in early 1885 (see Document no. 6 and n. 41). In November and December 1886 widespread strikes and disturbances had been sparked off by unrest at the Shaw and Pal works in Petersburg.

104   See n. 41. The law of 3 June 1886 conceded almost all of the Morozov strikers' demands particularly with regard to the scale and proper regulation of fines, the regular payment of wages and the right to elect *starostas* (elders or representatives) to negotiate with the management. A translated abstract of this law 'The First Fussian Labour Code' is published as appendix 4 of Turin's useful survey of the Russian labour movement, *From Peter The Great to Lenin*, pp. 185—6.

105   This pamphlet is typical of the more 'advanced' brochures put out by the Petersburg Union attempting to extend the consciousness of the workers by relating their particular grievances, especially about hours of work, to the generalised class and international demands for a shortening of the working day. It was produced in an edition of more than 2,000 at the Lahti Press of Narodnaya Volya and distributed to more than forty of the principal works in Petersburg. This brochure together with the pamphlet *The Working Day* were arguably the most successful and influential pieces of agitational material issued by the Union and their themes and demands were taken up by the great wave of strikers in the textile industry in the summer of 1896.

106   Published by the St Petersburg Union 1 June 1896 following strikes and disturbances at many of the cotton mills which were occasioned by the refusal of the owners to pay for the holidays which had been decreed to mark the coronation of tsar Nicholas II. A whole number of pamphlets protesting about this grievance and urging a reduction in the working day were produced and distributed by the Union at that time.

107   Produced in a large edition and distributed to most of the principal factories, mills and works in Petersburg in the first week of June 1896.

108   By the time this leaflet appeared, upwards of 30,000 textile and industrial workers were conducting a remarkably well-coordinated and orderly strike in Petersburg. It was far and away the largest strike ever mounted in Russia, or, for that matter, in Europe generally. The outbreak had in fact started on 23 May with a strike of 750 workers at the Rossiiskaya cotton spinning mills. By 27 May, workers at the Koenig and Ekaterinhof mills were out. On the 28 May they were joined by the Voronin, Mitrofanev and Triumfalny works and the following day by the Aleksander, Kozhevnikov, the Nevsky and the New mills. The workers at the Nevka came out on the 31st and those at the Pal Works, the Petrovsky and the Spassky mills on the 1 June to be followed by the Nobel, Putilov and Severni workers on 3 June.

109   This report was written by Plekhanov and Zasulich and submitted to the London Congress of the Second International 15—20 July 1896. It was issued in English and German and the cost of publication (as well as the expenses of

some of the Russian delegates) was borne by the Petersburg Union of Struggle. The text given here is the English original.

110   On the Thornton strike of November 1895 see Document no. 21 and n. 90. On the Laferme strike see Document no. 22 and n. 93.

111   See Document no. 25 and n. 98.

112   A reference to the disturbances at the Putilov foundry and engineering works on 4 December protesting at reductions in rates of pay.

113   The 'explanation' referred to was probably the account of the abuses prevalent in the factory published in the leaflet 'To the Workers of the Koenig Cotton Spinning Mills' published 12 or 13 Feb. 1896 (see *Rab. dvizh. XIX veke*, 4, pt 1, pp. 198–9).

114   Voronin's was a Petersburg cotton mill at which a strike had taken place in January 1896. For an account of this strike see the journal *Rabotnik*, no. 3–4 (Geneva, 1897), p. 89.

115   Disturbances had followed the distribution of socialist leaflets amongst the port workers in early January 1896.

116   On 1 March a leaflet and strike call were issued to the workers at the New Imperial Dockyard by the Petersburg Union which were followed, at the end of March, by a strike of skilled workers against excessive fines. On 12 April another leaflet was addressed to the port workers and further leaflets, followed by strikes, were issued in April.

117   The leaflet referred to was 'Comrade Workers of the Aleksandrov Iron Foundry' issued on 13 April by the Petersburg Union (published in *Rab. dvizh. XIX veke*, 4, pt 1, document 73).

118   The reference is, probably, to the one-day strike on 28 May 1896 at Voronin's to demand payment for the Coronation holidays.

119   See Document no. 21 for Lenin's exposition of the grievances of the Thornton workers.

120   See, for example, the leaflet of 6 June 1896 'To the Workers in the India-Rubber Works' (published in *Rab. dvizh. XIX veke*, 4, pt 1, pp. 230–1).

121   On the night of 8–9 December some of the most important leaders of the Petersburg Union including Lenin, Vaneev, Saporozhets, Krzhizhanovsky and Starkov were arrested. See n. 94.

122   On 9 December the Petersburg Union published an address 'To the Petersburg Workers' written by Ivan Babushkin, which concluded with these words. The address is translated in this volume: see Document no. 24 above.

123   On 5 January some of the remaining leaders of the Petersburg Union, including Babushkin and Lyakhovsky, were arrested. At the end of the month the principal leaders of the Ivanovo-Voznesensk Workers' Union were arrested.

124   Published in translation in this volume as Document no. 28.

125   Some of the pamphlets put out by the Petersburg and Moscow Union were of Polish origin, most were hectographed in rather rough copy. *Rabochaya Biblioteka* and the journal *Rabotnik* in Geneva provided considerable assistance in printing the larger editions of brochures as did the Narodnaya Volya press in Lahti, Finland.

126   For the chronology of the huge textile strike of May/June 1896 see n. 108.

127   These demands were summarised in a leaflet issued on 1 June 1896 'To the Workers in All the Petersburg Cotton Mills' which appears as Document no. 29 of the present volume. The leaflet cited here by Plekhanov and Potresov was entitled 'What Are the Workers of the Petersburg Cotton Mills Demanding?' and was drawn up from the reports of delegates to the meeting in Ekaterinhof Park on, or the day before, 30 May.

28 At the end of May, and again on 3 June, there were meetings of the Putilov workers to discuss their attitude to the strike.

29 Refers, presumably, to a leaflet 'To All Petersburg Factory Workers' distributed in large numbers at the Obukhov and Aleksandrov works on 4 June.

30 See n. 12.

31 Arrests of workers' leaders and members of the Unions of Struggle for the Emancipation of the Working Class took place all over Russia in the spring and early summer of 1896: 18 April in Nizhni Novgorod and Ivanovo-Voznesensk, and on 24 June, a bitter blow, the arrest of the Narodnaya Volya print-shop workers at Lahti.

32 See the report of the strike in *Rabotnik*, no. 3–4 (Geneva, 1897), p. 88.

33 Note in original: 'The officers responsible for this butchery received the thanks of His Imperial Majesty for their heroic deed, and the Tsar expressed his great satisfaction at the firm and orderly behaviour of the troops at the time of the factory disturbances.'

34 The strike took place 5–12 May 1895 and resulted in the killing of a Mr Crawshaw, the English overseer referred to.

35 Between 4 and 18 October 1895, some 2,000 cotton spinners struck in Ivanovo-Voznesensk.

36 On 28 June 1895, for example, twenty-two workers at the Russian–Belgian Metallurgical Works in Ekaterinoslav were arrested on the charge of preparing a strike.

37 The quotation is from an anonymous pamphlet sent to the editors of *Rabotnik* and published under the title 'Jewish Workers against Jewish Capitalists' in *Rabotnik*, no. 1–2 (Geneva, 1896), pp. 81–8. It was an account of a strike at a tobacco factory somewhere in the Jewish Pale of Settlement (Vilna?) but the editors confessed that they did not know the name of the author nor that of the factory concerned.

38 On 3 March 1896 the Petersburg Union published an 'Address of the Petersburg Workers to the French Workers on the Occasion of the 25th Anniversary of the Commune' (published in *Rab. dvizh. XIX veke*, 4, pt 1, document 70). On 6 March the Moscow Union published their 'On the Day of Celebration of the 25th Anniversary of the Commune' (ibid., document 120). Both were republished in *Rabotnik*, nos. 1–2 (Geneva, 1896), pp. 100–5.

39 Published by the Petersburg Union on the occasion of the first anniversary of its foundation, 15 September 1896.

40 See: Plekhanov's report to the International, Document no. 31.

41 Lenin's pamphlet was a considered response to the circular to factory inspectors issued in December 1895 by the Minister of Finance S.V. Witte following the strikes of summer and autumn 1895. Witte's advice to the inspectors was that they should expose the evil intentions of agitators and assure the workers of the good intentions of both the factory administration and of government to attend to their grievances sympathetically provided they were presented in a peaceful and orderly manner. At the same time, however, the inspectors were to make it plain that the full severity of the law would be brought to bear upon militant malcontents (Witte's circular is published in full in *Rab. dvizh. XIX veke*, 4, pt 1, pp. 824–5).

42 On the great Morozov strike of 1885 see Document no. 6 and n. 41.

43 The brochure *On Agitation* was written by Arkadi Kremer following a quite prolonged and self-conscious discussion in which the central circle of the Vilna Social Democrats had been engaged in the period from winter 1893 to spring 1894. The more advanced and organised workers of the Jewish Pale of

Settlement, under the immediate influence of Polish Social Democrats with whom they were in close touch, had, by this time, already begun to organise defence funds and had begun to prosecute well-organised strikes. The dilemma confronting the Vilna Socialists was whether they should re-orientate their energies to harness this movement, which hitherto they had largely ignored, or whether they should continue their attempts patiently to induct small groups of workers into the complexities of Marxist theory via propaganda in the workers' circles. Should they turn their attention to mass economic and political agitation, generalising from present grievances, in Yiddish through pamphlets and flysheets and organising strikes to get them remedied? Or should they continue to devote their energies to the 'advanced' workers and raise these latter to a broad understanding of socialism in its relation to the entire body of modern thought and culture, urilising the more 'civilised' Russian language for this purpose? They decided that the latter course had led them into an impasse and Arkadi Kremer produced a reasoned statement for the 'agitational' approach, which, after being amended by including some of the ideas of S. Gozhansk and prefaced with a two-page theoretical preamble written by Martov, was accepted as the programme of the Vilna Group. Within eighteen months its line had been accepted by the Petersburg Marxists. *On Agitation* was, without doubt, the most influential statement of the strategy and tactics of the Russian Marxists in the latter half of the 1890s. It was widely circulated in manuscript form and first published (with a cautionary afterword by Akselrod), though with some reluctance, by the Emancipation of Labour Group in Geneva, dated 1896 but in fact appearing only in late 1897.

144   Throughout the period in which the new 'agitational' tactic was being discussed the leaders of the central circle of Social Democrats in Vilna had been subjected to a mounting campaign of hostility led by a skilled worker, Moisei Gordon, who maintained that the intellectuals, by deserting the advanced workers in the propaganda circles, were seeking to protect their exclusive access to education and culture and thereby keep the working class in thrall.

145   Martov (for it was he who wrote this theoretical preamble) refers to the mass of unemployed, which, following Marx's usage, was referred to as the industrial reserve army.

146   Surplus value is, in Marxist terminology, the difference between the values created by labour power and the value which labour power itself commanded on the market.

147   The Committee for Literacy was a philanthropic body for the promotion of popular education. To this end it established evening and Sunday schools in urban centres specifically for working men. By the early 1890s these schools had been successfully infiltrated, particularly in Petersburg, by Marxist women teachers who used their classes to recruit promising workmen into social democratic circles.

148   Workers' protest in Russia, especially its early manifestations, frequently took the form of a petition for redress of grievances addressed variously to the provincial Governor, to the factory inspector or even to the Chief of Police.

149   Published by the Petersburg Union.

150   A reference to the great textile strike of June 1896.

151   On the Finance Minister's circular to factory inspectors see n. 141.

152   The Sunday schools referred to were the adult literacy classes promoted by the Committee for Literacy (see n. 140). A number of women Marxists, members of the Petersburg Union, were employed as teachers at these schools

and used their classes as a sort of front through which intelligent and active workmen could be inducted into social democratic activity.

153   Published by the Petersburg Union on 11 January 1897. On the day the leaflet was published, over sixty of the leading worker-activists of the January strikes were arrested.

154   These were all important cotton spinning and weaving mills in Petersburg. The Petrovsky and the Spassky mills had also been strike-bound since 2 January.

155   A reference to the promises made at a general meeting of the Petersburg cotton mill owners on 6 January, the most important of which was an undertaking to introduce an eleven-and-a-half-hour working day as from 16 April 1897.

156   Published on 19 April 1897 (i.e. May Day according to the Russian calendar) and still being distributed, along with a printed version of a worker's speech celebrating May Day, until the end of April.

157   For the employers' promise to shorten the working day see n. 155. The government, for its part, had repeatedly promised to review the problem of excessive working hours and, on 2 June 1897, promulgated an Act which limited the working day to eleven and a half hours, or, in the case of shift work, to ten hours. Due to inadequate supervision and the absence of statutory penalties for flouting the law 'it soon became practically a dead letter' (Turin, *From Peter the Great to Lenin*, p. 51).

158   On 16 April the eleven-and-a-half-hour working day was introduced in all Petersburg cotton mills, the spinners and weavers also won a 7% wage increase.

159   Published by the Petersburg Union, May Day 1897.

160   The strike at the huge Morozov textile works at Orekhovo-Zuevo in early 1885 had been preceded by smaller strikes at the same works in the years 1883–4.

161   For the demands of the Morozov strikers in 1885 see Document no. 6 and n. 41.

162   Some of these leaflets are translated in this volume and most of the strikes referred to have been mentioned earlier in the notes.

163   On 23 May 1896 there began a series of strikes which escalated by early June into what amounted to a general strike in the Petersburg textile industry.

164   On 2 January 1897 some 4,000 workers at the Aleksandrov Foundry began a strike which lasted for nearly a week. On the same day 2,700 workers at the Petersburg and Spassky cotton mills began a strike which lasted for nearly two weeks.

165   See n. 157.

166   Published by the Moscow Workers' Union, July 1897.

167   The New Factory Law had been promulgated on 2 June 1897; see further n. 157.

168   There seems to be something of an exaggeration here. According to the *Khronika*, in *Rab. dvizh. XIX veke* (4, pt 2, p. 736), the strike at the Aleksandrov involved some 4,000 workers. The author has, it seems, confused the numbers involved here with those involved in the summer strikes of 1896.

169   Published by the Kiev Union of Struggle for the Emancipation of the Working Class 26 November 1897. The Kiev Union was formed in March 1897 and its first leaflet appeared on 18 April in celebration of May Day. It rapidly emerged as one of the most active provincial centres of social democratic activity and a prolific producer of leaflets and pamphlets. It had a great advantage over most other centres in that, through the energy and expertise of Eidelman, it possessed its own printing press.

170   In March 1898 the foundation of the Russian Social Democratic Party took place in Minsk. It was attended by activists of the Unions of Struggle for the Emancipation of the Working Class, members of the Jewish Bund and delegates from other socialist organisations. Peter Struve, who has a publicist of the movement but who played little active part in its organisation, was given the task of writing the manifesto of the new-born party. It was first published in April 1898 as a leaflet by the 'party' press. Thereafter numerous editions appeared. Immediately after the congress widespread arrests throughout Russia decimated the veteran leadership of the movement.

171   See nn. 155 and 157.

172   The social democratic groups in Petersburg, Moscow, Kiev and other major centres styled themselves 'Union of Struggle for the Emancipation of the Working Class' up to the convocation of the First Congress of the party. Thereafter they called themselves 'Committee of the RSDLP'.

173   *Rabochaya Gazeta (Workers' Newspaper)* was the organ of the Kiev Union of Struggle. It was the only socialist newspaper produced and published in Russia. The Kiev group had been active in calling for and preparing the First Congress of the party. Its aspirations to emerge as the organisational nexus of the new party were partially realised when congress adopted *Rabochaya Gazeta* as the official organ of the party (see Document no. 42, article 11).

174   'The General Jewish Workers' Union of Russia and Poland', popularly known as the Bund, was founded in the summer of 1897 largely through the endeavours of Arkadi Kremer. It was by far the largest organisation attending the First Congress.

175   On Narodnaya Volya see n. 36.

176   The decisions of the First Congress were first published, along with the manifesto (Document no. 41) in a pamphlet issued by the party press (*Rabochaya Gazeta*) in April 1898. By that time mass arrests had effectively destroyed the capacity of the party to organise itself along the lines prescribed in these rules and they were never implemented. The movement reverted to localism and it was not to create an authoritative central body until 1903.

177   The Union of Social Democrats Abroad had been created by the members of the Emancipation of Labour Group (see n. 24) as a more inclusive organisation to accommodate the increasing number of Russian Marxist students and exiles living abroad. The Emancipation of Labour Group continued, however, to exist as an élite organisation within the Union controlling its funds and its publications.

178   Pavel Akselrod's *Present Tasks and Tactics* was one of the most influential social democratic tracts of the 1890s. It takes the form of two letters to socialist activists. The first letter was intended for the projected journal of 'The Russian Social Democratic Society of New York' which never saw the light of day. The second was written for *Rabochaya Gazeta* (see n. 173) but by the time it was received by the editors the edition for which it was intended had already been set up and printed. The letters were first published in *Rabotnik*, no. 5–6 (Geneva, 1899) with a foreword by Akselrod which explained his objective of developing those ideas 'which lie at the basis of, but were not formulated in my Afterword to the brochure *On Agitation*'.

179   The reference is to the formation of the Emancipation of Labour Group in Geneva, 1883.

180   Presumably Akselrod has in mind the assassination by the Executive Committee of Narodnaya Volya of the tsar in March 1881, following which there were widespread arrests of revolutionaries throughout Russia.

181   The quotation is from Plekhanov's *Second Draft Programme of the Russian Social Democrats*. See this volume p. 82.
182   A paraphrase rather than a precise quotation from Plekhanov's *Second Draft Programme*. See this volume p. 82.
183   See Document no. 2 of this volume. Plekhanov's *Socialism and the Political Struggle* is translated in full in Plekhanov, *Selected Philosophical Works*, 1, pp. 57–121.
184   The quotation is again from Plekhanov's *Second Draft Programme*, see this volume p. 82.
185   Ibid. See this volume p. 82.
186   On Zhelyabov see n. 30.
187   Plekhanov, *Second Draft Programme*. See this volume pp. 83–4.
188   Akselrod had made clear his opposition to what he saw as the one-sided infatuation with economic issues and the consequent over-concentration on strike activity to the detriment of the more overtly political objectives of social democracy in his 'Afterword' to the edition of *On Agitation* published by the Emancipation of Labour Group in 1897.
189   The articles referred to were 'The Objectives and Resources of Worldwide Democracy', published in *Rabotnik*, no. 1–2 (Geneva, 1896), pp. 1–52, and his 'The Struggle of the Swiss Railway Workers against their Exploiters', in *Rabotnik*, no. 3–4 (Geneva, 1897), pp. 17–46.
190   Note in original: 'The editors of the projected collection', i.e. of the projected journal of 'The Russian Social Democratic Society of New York' for whom this piece was originally written.
191   Appears to be an invocation of the concluding words of Michael Bakunin's celebrated article 'The Reaction in Germany'.
192   This quotation appears in *Rabotnik*, no. 3–4 (Geneva, 1897), p. iv.
193   On *Rabochaya Gazeta* see n. 173.
194   *Rabochaya Mysl (Workers' Thought)* became the organ of the St Petersburg Committee of the RSDLP. Sixteen issues appeared in the period October 1897 to December 1902 and this leading article appeared in the *Separate Supplement* to issue no. 7 (September 1899). It is one of the few cogent presentations of Russian 'revisionism'. Its author was K.M. Takhtarev. Wildman, in his *The Making*, gives the author as P.A. Berlin but L.I. Komissarova convincingly demonstrates that Takhtarev wrote it (see her 'Pokrytyi psevdonim', *Istoriya S.S.S.R.*, II (1970), pp. 169–70).
195   That is the area demarcated for Jewish settlement known as the Pale.
196   For the demands of the Petersburg cotton operatives in January 1897 see Document no. 35 above. Takhtarev would appear to be either ignorant of the content of many of the agitational leaflets put out in differing centres at differing times which insistently made general demands for the shortening of the working day and general claims for civil and political rights, or else he is being disingenuous to suit his case. On the next page the shortening of the working day is, curiously, listed among 'immediate local demands'.
197   It was precisely in these terms that the editors of *Iskra (The Spark)*, Plekhanov, Akselrod, Zasulich, Lenin, Martov and Potresov, were to assail their rivals on *Rabochaya Mysl*. *Iskra* was established in December 1900 and 112 issues were produced before its demise in December 1905.
198   Section 2 on the autocracy has been omitted from this edited version.
199   Note in original: 'Declaration by the Minister of Finance, 15 June 1896.'
200   Note in original: 'To the iron-foundry workers.'
201   Note in original: 'Let us note, however, that the influx of "villagers", while

seriously hindering strikes and the foundation of permanent militant (guild) workers' unions, does comparatively little harm to the mutual aid and consumer societies.'

202   The signature 'R.M.' obviously refers to the title of the journal *Rabochaya Mysl* and readers were therefore to understand that this article was a considered statement of its editorial board.

203   E.D. Kuskova and her husband S.N. Prokopovich were active in leading the 'young' social democrats in the Union of Russian Social Democrats Abroad against what were felt to be the outmoded ideas and the personal tutelage of the Emancipation of Labour Group. At the First Congress of the Union in November 1898 the 'youngsters' decisively outvoted the veteran leadership of the Emancipation of Labour Group and the latter responded by declaring that it would no longer undertake to edit the Union's publications. In the months that followed relations between the two groups became increasingly strained. Controversy over financial and organisational questions was inflamed by ideological divergencies and, in this context, the publication of Kuskova's *Credo* in early 1899 was the first shot in what was to become a bitter controversy.

204   'Blanquism', the body of ideas associated with Louis Auguste Blanqui (1805– 81) and his followers. As represented by Marxists Blanquism connoted the project of seizing power at the centre by a conspiratorial élite and the use of state power to put down opposition and to induct the mass into an awareness of their real, or socialist, objectives.

205   Eduard Bernstein, in his series of articles in *Neue Zeit* in 1898, had undertaken a withering critique of the orthodox Marxist proposition that capitalism would undergo a catastrophic breakdown and the complementary notion that it could be transformed only through violent revolution. In early 1899 he published an edited version of these articles in his famous *Die Voraussetzungen des Sozialismus und die Aufgaben der Sozialdemokratie* (translated as *Evolutionary Socialism*, London, 1909) which was to become the manifesto of 'revisionism'. Opposition to the 'Zusammenbruchstheorie' (catastrophetheory) was the distinctive mark of his followers who believed that the triumph of socialism would only arise from the gradual transformation not only of capitalism but also of the working class itself.

206   Lenin's sister Anna sent him a copy of Kuskova's *Credo* to his place of exile in Siberia. So outraged was he by its tone and content that in August– September 1899 he set about writing a riposte, which was discussed and adopted by a number of meetings of social democratic exiles in Siberia, and sent it to Plekhanov and to the journal of the Union of Social Democrats Abroad which had fallen under the control of the 'young' opposition to the Emancipation of Labour Group. They published it not in the journal but as a separate pamphlet with a dismissive postscript to the effect that the ideas of the *Credo* enjoyed little influence or currency within the Union. For their part the Emancipation of Labour Group were undisguisedly elated that sections of the movement in Russia took their position against the 'youngsters' and were inspired by Lenin's 'Protest' to begin a vicious fightback against them.

207   Chartism: the mass movement of British working men from the late 1830s to the early 1850s in pursuit of the 'People's Charter', published in May 1838, which called for universal male suffrage, equal electoral districts, annual parliaments and payment for its members. Parts of the movement became expressly socialist and revolutionary.

208   Owenism, the body of ideas associated with Robert Owen (1771–1858) and

his followers stressing the importance of environmental determinism and seeking to escape the baneful effects of capitalist industrialism through the creation of villages of cooperation. On the ideas of Charles Fourier see n. 63. 'True socialism' was the term used by Marx and Engels to describe the ideas of Karl Grün and his followers who, according to Marx, emasculated the practical and revolutionary content of European socialism in their attempt to refine and universalise its content by incorporating it in the lifeless abstractions of German philosophy (see *The German Ideology*, MESW, 5, pp. 455—539).

209 Proudhonism, the ideas associated with Pierre Joseph Proudhon (1809—65) and his followers, also called mutualism for its advocacy of a society in which contracts freely concluded between individuals and groups would replace the authoritarian nature of law. Proudhon was a vehement critic of the state and decried all socialist projects which encouraged its seizure or legitimated the use of its power. Proudhonism had a very considerable impact on Russian revolutionary Populism.

210 Ferdinand Lassalle (1825—64) populariser of Marxism in Germany, orator and organiser of the Universal German Working Men's Association founded in 1863 which was the forerunner of the Social Democratic Party of Germany (hereafter SPD).

211 Presumably a reference to the Stuttgart Congress of the SPD in October 1898 at which Karl Kautsky, the leading theoretician of the Second International, had rebutted Bernstein's proposition as set out in the latter's articles in *Neue Zeit*.

212 In *The Manifesto of the Communist Party* and elsewhere Marx and Engels criticised the socialist schemes of Saint Simon, Fourier, Owen and the German 'True Socialists' for their failure to appreciate the necessity of proletarian class struggle and political organisation, omissions which rendered their schemes utopian.

213 The International Working Men's Association, or First International, was founded in September 1864.

214 See n. 20.

215 On the North Russian Workers' Union see Document no. 1 and nn. 1 and 2. The South Russian Workers' Union was organised by E.O. Zaslavsky in 1875 and was centred in Odessa where a mutual aid fund, library and printing press were established. Zaslavsky and the other leaders were arrested in December 1875 and the Union collapsed. The statutes of the Union are to be found in *Nachalo rabochego dvizheniya 1883—1894 gg.* (Moscow, 1960), pp. 183—4.

216 Note in original: 'Akselrod, *The Present Tasks and Tactics of the Russian Social Democrats*, Geneva, 1898, p. 19.'

217 Note in original: 'ibid, p. 20'. Akselrod's pamphlet is translated as Document no. 43.

218 On *Rabochaya Mysl* see n. 194.

219 The reference is to the organ of the St Petersburg Union of Struggle of which only two issues appeared, both in 1897.

220 On *Rabochaya Gazeta* see n. 173.

221 The manifesto of the First Congress of the RSDLP (sometimes known as the 'Minsk Manifesto') is translated in full as Document no. 41.

222 See Document no. 41, p. 224.

223 See ibid., pp. 224—5.

224 See ibid., p. 224.

225 Lenin's objective in citing this point from *Decisions of the First Congress of the RSDLP* (translated as Document no. 42) was to remind the 'young'

leadership of the Union of Social Democrats Abroad of their responsibilities, as an organ of the party, to publicise all shades of social democratic opinion regardless of their personal sympathies.

226   In August 1900 Lenin arrived in Geneva for consultations with Plekhanov on his plan to establish a newspaper which would put to rout the 'young' opposition, the Economists and revisionists within the movement and rally the orthodox. The newspaper would, in his conception, create not merely an ideological centre but also an organisational structure and authoritative party centre, dominated by the orthodox. After disturbingly bitter negotiations with Plekhanov it was agreed that the 'Russian' troika of Lenin, Martov and Potresov would join the émigré Emancipation of Labour Group trio of Plekhanov, Akselrod and Zasulich, to form the editorial board of the new journal. Although Plekhanov insisted on having two votes on the board, most of the editorial work was done by Lenin and Martov. The new journal, *Iskra* (*The Spark*) was launched in December 1900 and Lenin wrote this all-important leading article for its first issue. Given the conventions of socialist newspapers we may regard the article (as its contemporary readership was bound to) as a statement of the policies and objectives of the whole editorial board.

227   On the First Congress of the RSDLP see above Document nos. 41 and 42.

228   Kuskova's *Credo* is translated as Document no. 45.

229   The leading article from this *Separate Supplement* is translated as Document no. 44.

230   The most important of articles in *Iskra* on organisational questions were, undoubtedly, those written by Lenin himself. The article 'Where to Begin?' was especially important in this connection (see Document no. 48).

231   This was a favourite quotation for Social Democrats – the concluding words of the defiant speech made by the weaver Peter Alekseevich Alekseev to the Special Session of the Senate which heard his case on 10 March 1877 (for the whole speech see *Rab. dvizh. XIX veke*, 3, pt 2, pp. 44–7).

232   Lenin's leading article for issue no. 4 of *Iskra* (May 1901). It was re-issued in considerable editions as a separate pamphlet by local social democratic organisations.

233   *Listok 'Rabochego Dela'* was a supplement of *Rabochee Delo*, the journal of the Union of Russian Social Democrats Abroad. In all, eight issues appeared between June 1900 and July 1901.

234   Wilhelm Liebknecht, one of the founding fathers of the German socialist movement, had died in August 1900. The first issue of *Iskra* had carried an obituary on its front page and subsequently disputed his legacy with *Rabochee Delo*.

235   The events referred to were the widespread student and worker protests and demonstrations which spilled over from unrest within Russian universities after 183 students at Kiev University had been drafted into the army as punishment for participation in a student protest meeting. In spite of severe repression ferment continued in the universities throughout 1901.

236   Lenin refers to his own work *What Is To Be Done?* the title of which is anticipated in the first sentence of the article translated here.

237   Note in original: 'It will of course be understood that here agents would be able to work successfully only if they were in the closest contact with the local committees (groups, circles) of our party. In general, the whole plan that we are proposing can of course only be realised with the most active support of the committees who have more than once taken steps to unify the

party and who, we are sure, will achieve this unification, if not today, then the day after, if not in one way then in another.'

238   The new programme of the Union of Russian Social Democrats Abroad was first published in issues 11 and 12 of its journal *Rabochee Delo* (Geneva, February 1902) and subsequently published as a separate pamphlet under the title *The Old and New Programmes of Rabochee Delo* (Paris, n.d.).

239   The First Congress of the Union of Russian Social Democrats Abroad was held in November 1898 against the background of mounting acrimony between the 'young' emigration and the veteran Emancipation of Labour Group. At the congress the veterans were outvoted on all the contentious issues and withdrew from editing the Union's publications. The congress therefore elected a new editorial board of Krichevsky, Teplov and Ivanshin.

240   For this *Manifesto* see Document no. 41.

241   The quotation is from the Preamble to the *General Rules of the International Working Men's Association* (MESW, 1, p. 386).

242   Note in original: 'Although our general political conditions, i.e. the Russian autocratic regime, are implicitly included in "the concrete relationships of social classes", the congress wanted, by a clear reference to them, to express the thought that the existence of the autocracy should define the struggle of social democracy, not only by its class character, but also as a system of tyranny having self-contained interests.'

243   See for example, the article 'The Students and the Autocracy', in *Rabochee Delo*, no. 11 (Geneva, 1901), p. 28.

244   Note in original: 'No. 2–3 *Rabochee Delo*, August 1899, leading article: "The New Crime of Autocracy".'

245   Note in original: 'Resolution on the relationship between the Union and non-socialist revolutionary and political opposition groups.'

246   In January 1901 *Iskra* published a leaflet 'May Days in Kharkov' celebrating the large-scale demonstrations that had occurred on May Day 1900 and particularly emphasising the overt political demands which the worker and student demonstrators had voiced. The political tone of the Petersburg demonstrations of 1901 and the pitched battle fought between workers and police at the huge Obukhov works were taken by most sections of the party as indicators that a new period of political revolutionary struggle was at hand.

247   On the emergence of *Iskra* see n. 226.

248   The convocation of a Second Party Congress had long been canvassed by a number of groups within the RSDLP. An Organising Committee, set up in March 1902, came to be dominated by the group around *Iskra* which set itself the task of proposing a new programme for the party (see Document no. 51), drawing up an agenda and ending the organisational disarray into which, they felt, the party had lapsed. The congress eventually convened in Brussels on 30 July 1903 but, after police harassment, transferred to London and concluded its business on 23 August.

249   Lenin and Martov, though both members of the *Iskra* caucus at the congress, had proposed differing drafts of Article 1 of the party's rules, the object of which was to define the qualifications for party membership. According to the formulation Lenin used in the draft rules he submitted to the congress (see further n. 266), a party member was one 'who recognises the party's programme and supports it by material means and by personal participation in one of the party's organisations'. According to Martov's draft, a member 'recognises the party programme and supports it by material means and by regular assistance under the direction of one of the party organisations'.

250 'Comrade Brouckère' was the revolutionary pseudonym of Lydia Makhnovets a delegate from the Petersburg Union of Struggle who had, in the previous session of the congress, criticised Martov's formulation. She was the sister of V.P. Makhnovets (Akimov), who was the most dogged and persuasive critic of the Iskrists at the congress. See n. 263.

251 In *What Is To Be Done?* Lenin had stressed the importance of establishing, wherever and whenever possible, broad inclusive working class organisations operating within the bounds of legality as a necessary complement to the activities of the underground professional revolutionaries. In the previous session of the congress he had declared that 'We need the most diverse organisations of all types, ranks and shades, beginning with extremely narrow and secret ones and ending with broad, free *lose Organisationen*.'

252 In the previous session Akselrod mentioned that Lenin's formulation would exclude 'a professor who regards himself as a Social Democrat' and 'those who, even if they cannot be directly admitted to an organisation, are nevertheless party members'.

253 On Zhelyabov see n. 30. Plekhanov's general point was to dispute Akselrod's assertion, made in the previous session, that the hallowed revolutionary organisations of Zemlya i Volya and Narodnaya Volya were successful only because the secret and centralised leadership was surrounded by sympathisers 'who were regarded as party members'.

254 'Rusov' was the pseudonym of B.M. Knunyants (1878–1911), a veteran of the Petersburg Union of Struggle and delegate from the Baku Committee.

255 'Pavlovich' was the pseudonym of P.A. Krasikov (1870–1939), one of Lenin's lieutenants both before and after the October Revolution.

256 M.I. Lieber was the principal spokesman for the Bund at the Second Congress.

257 'Muravev' was the pseudonym of G.M. Mishenov, a delegate of the Ufa Committee of the party.

258 Trotsky was present as a delegate of the Siberian Association of the party for whom he wrote a report of the congress bitterly hostile to Lenin and Plekhanov.

259 Jean Jaurès, a prominent leader at the time of the 'Confédération des Socialistes indépendants' one of the six important socialist organisations in France. Subsequently Jaurès, along with the Marxist, Guesde, became a leader of the united French Socialist Party.

260 Peter Struve had been one of the early publicists of Marxism in Russia and had assisted in the foundation of *Iskra*. He was, however, always on the periphery of the social democratic movement and was considered by the revolutionaries to be a purely 'academic' Marxist with liberal inclinations. He was subsequently to be a founder and publicist of the liberal Constitutional Democratic Party (*Kadety*).

261 Lenin, in conciliatory mood, refers to Akselrod's statement in the previous session where he had said that 'Comrade Lenin, with his peripheral circles which are to be regarded as part of the party organisation, goes out to meet my demand . . . here we could make a bargain.' (*Vtoroi sezd RSDRP: Protokoly*, (Moscow, 1959), p. 267).

262 Kostov was the pseudonym of Noi Nikolaevich Zhordania (1870–1953) who was to become the leader of the Menshevik government of Georgia, 1918–21.

263 Akimov was the pseudonym of V.P. Makhnovets (1872–1921) a delegate of the Union of Russian Social Democrats Abroad who had for some time been a leader of the 'young' opposition to the Emancipation of Labour Group in the émigré movement.

264   Gusev was the pseudonym of Ya.D. Drabkin (1874–1933) a delegate of the Don Committee of the party.

265   The *Iskra* group had, almost from its inception, recognised the need for a more comprehensive statement of the party's beliefs and objectives than had been expressed in the manifesto of the First Congress (see Document no. 41) which had served this function hitherto. In the summer of 1901 Lenin urged Akselrod and Plekhanov to draft a new programme and in January 1902 Plekhanov submitted his draft to the editorial board of *Iskra*. Both Lenin and Martov expressed strong objections to its content and after bitter dispute both Lenin and Plekhanov submitted new drafts which were eventually submitted to a committee of the editors which included neither of the protagonists. It was this committee of *Iskra* which drew up the programme which was adopted at the Twenty-First Session of the Second Party Congress on 1 August 1903 after it had been debated for three days.

266   It was Lenin who, on behalf of the *Iskra* group, prepared and submitted to congress a draft of the organisational rules of the RSDLP. Martov too prepared a very lengthy draft of the rules which he did not, however, submit to the congress (for Martov's draft rules see LCW, 7, pp. 246–9). After initial discussion of Lenin's draft at the Fourteenth Session of the congress it was decided to elect a Rules Commission which was composed of Lenin, Martov, Yegorov (E.Y. Levin), Popov (V.N. Rozanov) and Glebov (V.A. Noskov). Discussion of the rules resumed at the Twenty-Second Session and the difference with regard to paragraph 1, defining a party member clarified at the Twenty-Third Session (see Document no. 50).

267   Rosa Luxemburg (1870–1919) was a Marxist theorist and activist of Polish origin who had, by the time of the Second Congress of the RSDLP, emerged as an expert within the SPD on Russian affairs. It was in this capacity that the editors of the Menshevik-dominated *Iskra* invited her to reflect on the split within the RSDLP. Luxemburg responded by offering them a lengthy article written for the principal SPD journal *Neue Zeit* and published by it in issues 42, pp. 484–92, and 43, pp. 529–35 (1904). Potresov translated the article into Russian and it was published in *Iskra*, no. 69 (10 July 1904), pp. 2–7. The present translation has been done from the German and checked against the Russian version. It was felt necessary to include a new translation of this fairly accessible document in view of the frequently misleading inaccuracies of existing translations. In view of this, and in view of the importance this document has assumed, translator's notes are given in full.

268   Translator: the German refers throughout to *Absolutismus* (absolutism), the Russian to *samoderzhavie* (autocracy). I have used 'autocracy' as this is the term normally employed in English to describe tsarist 'absolutism'.

269   The Anti-Socialist Laws were a series of repressive measures directed against the propagation of socialist ideas enacted by Bismarck in 1878 and not suspended until 1890.

270   Translator: Ger. *Verfassung*: constitution. Russ. *poryadok*: order.

271   Translator: Ger. *Parlamentarismus*: parliamentarism. Russ. *parlamentskaya borba*: parliamentary combat.

272   Luxemburg is not quoting but paraphrasing *The Manifesto of the Communist Party* (MECW, 6, p. 492) which has it that:

At this stage the labourers still form an incoherent mass scattered over the whole country, and broken up by their mutual competition. If anywhere they unite to form more compact bodies this is not yet the consequence of their own active union, but of the union of the bourgeoisie, which class, in order to attain its political ends is compelled to set the whole proletariat in motion, and is moreover yet, for a time, able to do so.

273   Translator: 'Afterwards' is emphasised in the Russian.

274   Lenin's *One Step Forward, Two Steps Back* was published in May 1904. It was a detailed and lengthy review of the crisis which had arisen within the RSDLP at its Second Congress and which had been exacerbated in the following months (see LCW, 7, pp. 203–524).

275   Translator: The Russian has 'from Geneva to Liège, from Tomsk to Irkutsk'.

276   Translator: Ger. *Grossstaat*: large state. Russ. *krupnyi gorod*: big city (i.e. a mistranslation for Ger. *Grossstadt*).

277   The Austrian Socialists, on the premiss that the Austro-Hungarian Empire was an artificial construct repressive of its numerous ethnic minorities, had elaborated a federal party structure which allowed considerable autonomy to its national sections.

278   Translator: no emphasis in the Russian.

279   Lenin, in *One Step Forward* (LCW, 7, p. 383), was in fact berating Akselrod for employing Bernstein's hackneyed phrases about 'Jacobinism, Blanquism and so on':

> These 'dreadful words' – Jacobinism and the rest – are expressive of *opportunism* and nothing else. A Jacobin who wholly identifies himself with the *organisation* of the proletariat – a proletariat *conscious* of its class interests – is a *revolutionary Social Democrat*. A Girondist who sighs after professors and high-school students, who is afraid of the dictatorship of the proletariat, and who yearns for the absolute value of democratic demands is an *opportunist*.

280   On Blanqui see n. 204. Luxemburg here employs a well-worn Marxist analysis of Blanquism which would, however, be difficult to sustain by reference to Blanqui's own writings and activities.

281   Translator: Ger. *Dispositionsfähigkeit*: qualification to act (legal term). Russ. *samodeyatel'nost'*: self-activity.

282   On student unrest in Petersburg in 1901 see n. 245.

283   The quotation is from Goethe's *Faust*. It was a favourite quotation among Socialists: Moses Hess had used it in his 'The Philosophy of the Act' and Marx, Bakunin, Herzen and Plekhanov had also employed it. See p. 14 above.

284   Translator: i.e. the rules of parliamentarism. The Russian translation interprets the German *'den Grundsätzen entsprechend'* to mean 'true to its own principles' (*vernoi svoim printsipam*), i.e. the principles of the party.

285   Translator: Ger. *Nachtwächtergeist*: literally 'night-watchman spirit'. The term 'night-watchman state' was employed by Lassalle and other German Social Democrats to suggest authoritarian government.

286   Luxemburg quotes from a footnote in which Lenin takes issue with Martov's defence against the charge that his formulation of Paragraph 1 of the rules would encourage opportunism. Opportunism, Martov declared, had deeper causes. 'The point is', Lenin replied, 'not that clauses in the rules may produce opportunism, but that with their help a more or less trenchant weapon against opportunism can be forged. The deeper its causes, the more trenchant should its weapon be. Therefore to *justify* a formulation which opens the door to opportunism on the grounds that opportunism has "deep causes" is tailism of the first order.' (LCW, 7, pp. 273–4n.)

287   LCW, 7, p. 396.

288   'Beware of politicians!', a French syndicalist slogan.

289   On *Rabochaya Mysl* see n. 194.

290   Translator: Ger. *Herrenmenschmoral*. Luxemburg appears here to confuse *Herrenmensch*, a member of the *Herrenvolk* (master race), with the

Nietzschean *Übermensch*, the 'superman' or 'overman', the extension of the human ego in a world without God.

291   On the 'going to the people' see n. 39.

292   On Ferdinand Lassalle see n. 210. His General German Workers' Union was founded in May 1863 in Leipzig. 'The statutes which Lassalle drew up himself, gave him, as president, dictatorial power' (B. Russell, *German Social Democracy* (London, 1965), p. 59).

293   By 1869 increasing numbers of the General German Workers' Union had become disenchanted with Lassalle's authoritarian successor von Schweitzer. In that year the dissidents joined forces with August Bebel's League of German Working Men's Societies to form the Social Democratic Party of Germany at a congress in Eisenach.

294   Translator: Ger. *geleithammelt*, a verb Luxemburg has derived from the noun *Leithammel* meaning a bell-wether sheep, metaphorically also a ring-leader.

295   On Narodnaya Volya see n. 36.

296   On 3 Jan. 1905 a strike broke out at the massive Putilov works in Petersburg. 'The Assembly of Russian Factory and Mill Workers', a legalised society organising mutual aid clubs and cultural and religious activities, came to the support of the strikers. Father George Gapon, the leader of the assembly, sought to contain the spread of protest meetings and demonstrations in which the workers' initial grievances were becoming radicalised and politicised. He proposed that the workers, in solemn procession, should supplicate their defender, the tsar, for redress of their grievances, which would be presented to him as a petition. The petition was drafted by Gapon and the worker Ivan Masimov and discussed at district meetings of the assembly where, according to Theodore Dan (*The Origins of Bolshevism* (London, 1964), pp. 301–2), Social Democrats were instrumental in injecting a more radical political tone into the petition.
On 9 January 1905, a vast procession of some 150,000–200,000 workers and their families, singing hymns, carrying icons and led by priests, advanced to the Winter Palace where they were met with a rain of bullets which left 1,000 dead and 2,000 wounded. Bloody Sunday, as it was hereafter known, started the revolution of 1905.

297   The First All-Russian Conference of Party Workers was convened under Menshevik auspices in Geneva, April–May 1905, and its resolutions were published as a separate supplement to *Iskra*, no. 100 (Geneva, 1905).

298   The Menshevik insistence that military-technical preparation should be a product of, or at least directly related to, extensive popular agitation and organisation was meant to distinguish their position from what they represented as the 'adventurist' or excessively militant programme of the Bolsheviks.

299   Separate supplement to *Iskra*, no. 100 (Geneva, 1905), pp. 23–4.

300   This brief paragraph formed the basis of Menshevik strategy throughout 1905–6. It was fiercely criticised, from their differing vantage points, by Lenin, by Trotsky and Parvus, and by Kautsky.

301   This was not so much an echo of Trotsky's and Parvus' theory of permanent or uninterrupted revolution as a reiteration of the orthodox injunction of Marx and Engels that Russia would only bypass a prolonged period of bourgeois dominance on the basis of a prior socialist revolution in Western Europe.

302   Lenin wrote his *Two Tactics of Social Democracy in the Democratic Revolution* in Geneva in June–July 1905. It was published in late July 1905 and was swiftly re-issued in large editions by local committees of the RSDLP. See LCW, 9, for complete text.

303   Lenin refers to the mutiny in June 1905 of the crew of the battleship 'Prince Potemkin' and the general strike in Odessa which the mutinous sailors attempted to assist.

304   See LCW, 9, pp. 146–55.

305   The Party of Socialist Revolutionaries, or SRs, was formed in the winter of 1901–2 from the merger of a number of Populist groups. Its draft programme was, however, only elaborated in the summer of 1904 by the editors (Viktor Chernov especially) of the party's main journal *Revolyutsionnaya Rossiya (Revolutionary Russia)*. This draft formed the basis of the programme adopted by the SRs at their first congress in December 1905. The SRs perpetuated many of the ideas and organisational structures associated with revolutionary Populism especially its peasant orientation and commitment to individual terror.

306   *Osvobozhdenie (Liberation)* was the journal of the first radical middle class political grouping to emerge in Russia – the Union of Liberation which came into existence in the autumn of 1904. Many of its leaders; Kuskova, Prokopovich and Struve, who was the editor of *Osvobozhdenie*, had previously been active Marxists. On Akimov see n. 263.

307   The Third Congress of the RSDLP, convened by the Bolsheviks and attended solely by them, was held in London in April and May 1905.

308   Lenin refers to the Mensheviks who refused to recognise or attend the so-called Third Congress and had organised their own 'Conference' in Geneva. Some of the resolutions of this Menshevik Conference are published as Document nos. 55 and 56.

309   See previous note.

310   *Vpered (Forward)* was a Bolshevik organ. As the Bolsheviks referred to the Mensheviks as the new-*Iskrists* so the Mensheviks used '*Vpered* group' as a synonym for the Bolsheviks.

311   A.S. Martynov had been one of the 'young' opposition to the Emancipation of Labour Group in the Union of Social Democrats Abroad. He had, at the Second Congress of the RSDLP, sharply criticised Lenin's *What Is To Be Done?* and had, subsequently, been co-opted onto the editorial board of the 'New' *Iskra*. He became one of the most prolific publicists of Menshevism.

312   Kuskova's *Credo* and the lead article for the *Separate Supplement* of *Rabochaya Mysl* no. 7 are translated as Documents number 45 and 44 of this volume. It was issue no. 7, and not, as Lenin maintains, no. 9, which appeared with its notorious *Separate Supplement* in September 1899 (see n. 194).

313   'The weapon of criticism cannot, of course, replace criticism by weapons, material force must be overthrown by material force; but theory also becomes a material force as soon as it had gripped the masses.' K. Marx, *Contribution to the Critique of Hegel's Philosophy of Law. Introduction*, MECW, 3, p. 182.

314   D. Shipov was a moderate liberal leader who drew up constitutional proposals for a consultative assembly based on a broader franchise than the 'Bulygin Duma' (see further n. 322).

315   A.S. Martynov (see n. 311) had, in his *Dve dikatury* (Geneva, 1905), urged Social Democrats to moderate their demands 'lest the bourgeoisie recoils'.

316   Note in original: 'Of interest in this connection is Mr Struve's open letter to Jaurès recently published by the latter in *L'Humanité* and by Mr Struve in *Osvobozhdenie* no. 72.'

317   See n. 315.

318   Kautsky was later to endorse the Bolshevik strategy in the period 1905–6 –

see his *The Driving Forces of the Russian Revolution and Its Prospects* translated as Document no. 60 of this volume.

319 MECW, 10, p. 122.

320 Akselrod had first mooted the idea of Social Democrats concentrating their energies on the convocation of a Workers' Congress in April and May of 1905. He had sent a proposal to this effect to the Organisation Committee elected by the Mensheviks Conference (see n. 297) and it was their favourable response which prompted him to write the pamphlet.

321 See nn. 210 and 292.

322 A.I. Bulygin was the Minister of the Interior who had been charged by the tsar with the task of drawing up the details for the electoral procedures for and powers to be enjoyed by the representative assembly or 'Duma' which the tsar proposed to convene. Bulygin's proposals were published on 6 August. The Duma was to have a purely advisory role, it was to be elected through a complex system of indirect elections, the constituency for which was to be extremely narrow and wholly excluded the urban workers. Consequently nearly all the principal socialist leaders, both of the Mensheviks and of the Bolsheviks, favoured a boycott of the elections for the 'Bulygin Duma'.

323 Trotsky, under the strong influence of Alexander Helphand (Parvus) had, by the middle of 1905, already begun to develop his theory of uninterrupted revolution in articles for the journal *Nachalo* (*The Beginning*). In 1906 Trotsky reflected at length on the revolutionary process in his book *Nasha revolyutsiya* (*Our Revolution*) from which this extract is taken.

324 The brunt of Trotsky's case is directed against Plekhanov. Anticipating his stance of 1917, Plekhanov argued that there still existed considerable potential for the development of productive forces in Russia, that therefore the revolution should not transcend its bourgeois-democratic phase.

325 In fact the author of these articles was, as we now know, Engels not Marx.

326 F. Engels, *Revolution and Counter Revolution in Germany*, MECW, 11, p. 10.

327 K. Kautsky, 'Der Amerikanische Arbeiter', in *Neue Zeit*, XXIV (1905–6), 1, pp. 676–7.

328 Ibid. Kautsky had, in a number of articles for *Neue Zeit* reflected on the extraordinary political development of the Russian proletariat and had by early 1905 arrived at the conclusion that 'permanent revolution is thus exactly what the proletariat in Russia needs'. *Neue Zeit*, XXIII (1904–5), 2, p. 492.

329 Georg von Vollmar was regarded by the revolutionary Marxists as the prototype revisionist. He was the leader of the Bavarian organisation of the SPD and had been one of the first to call for a policy of moderation and accommodation *vis à vis* the existing state.

330 Note in original: 'Does the fact of the rise and development first of the Peasant Union and then of the *Trudovik* in the Duma contradict these and subsequent ideas? Not at all. What is the Peasant Union? A Union of some elements of radical democracy who are searching for a mass and the more conscious elements of the peasantry – obviously *not* the lowest strata – on a platform of democratic revolution and agrarian reform.

As to the agrarian programme of the Peasant Union ("equality in the use of land"), which is the meaning of its existence, the following must be said. The broader and deeper the development of the agrarian movement and the sooner it comes to the point of confiscation and distribution, the sooner the Peasant Union will disintegrate because of a thousand contradictions of a class, local, everyday and technical character. Its members will exert their share of influence in the *Peasants' Committees*, the organs of the agrarian revolution in the villages, but it goes without saying that the Peasants' Committees, *economic and administrative* institutions, will not be able to abolish the *political* dependence of the countryside on the town, which is one of the basic characteristics of contemporary society.

The radicalism and shapelessness of the *Trudoviki* was the expression of the contradictory nature of the revolutionary aspirations of the peasantry. During the period of constitutional illusions it helplessly followed the Cadets [Constitutional Democrats]. When the Duma was dissolved the *Trudoviki* naturally came under the guidance of the social democratic grouping. The lack of independence on the part of the peasant representatives will be demonstrated with particular clarity when the most decisive initiative is needed – when power is passing into the hands of the revolution.'

331   Social democratic programmes often adopted the distinction, first employed by the SPD, between those objectives which were realisable without exploding private property relations, and those which would require social ownership of the means of production. Those objectives compatible with the continued existence of bourgeois democracy were included in the minimum programme, those expressing the final goals of socialism comprised the maximum programme.

332   Trotsky probably refers to Parvus' leading article in the first issue of *Nachalo* (St Petersburg 1905; republished in his collection *Rossiya i revolyutsiya* (St Petersburg 1906)).

333   In late 1904 Trotsky came to the conclusion that it would be impossible to contain the forthcoming revolution in Russia within the framework of bourgeois democracy. In December 1904 he completed a brochure outlining his views which the Mensheviks refused to publish. It was published with a preface by Parvus as *Do 9-go yanvarya* (*Up to the 9th of January*) (Geneva, 1905) and was immediately criticised by Bolsheviks and Mensheviks alike.

334   'The industrial reserve army' was Marx's term for the pool of unemployed created by capitalism.

335   'The Black Repartition' or Chernyi Peredel refers to the redistribution of land in the Black Earth regions. It was the name taken by the orthodox Lavrist wing of Zemlya i Volya after the latter split into two groups in 1879.

336   Trotsky quotes from Kautsky's article 'Allerhand Revolutionäres', in *Neue Zeit*, XXII (1904), 1, pp. 625–7.

337   Lenin's Preface is translated from the Russian edition of Kautsky's essay *Dvizhushchie sily i perspektivy russkoi revolyutsii* (Moscow, 1907), pp. 1–7. Kautsky's essay is translated from the original articles in *Neue Zeit*, XXV (1906–7), 1, pp. 284–90, 324–33.

338   In the hope that leading European Marxists would bolster his position by agreeing with him that the Russian revolution was a democratic revolution which ought therefore to be led by the bourgeoisie, Plekhanov sent them a list of (rather leading) questions. Kautsky cites the three most important of these on p. 369.

339   The Constitutional Democratic Party (whose members were known as Cadets) was a radical liberal grouping formed in October 1905 with a view to fighting the elections for the forthcoming First Duma in which they emerged as the largest party.

340   At the Amsterdam Congress of the Second International in August 1904 the SPD and the French Marxists had combined to move a forthright condemnation of revisionism and of socialist participation in bourgeois governments. Plekhanov had invoked the authority of this resolution, which insisted 'that

Social Democracy ... cannot *aim at* participating in governmental power within capitalist society' against the projects of Bolsheviks and permanent revolutionists alike.

341 Prokopovich, at one time a leader of the young opposition to the Emancipation of Labour Group, had, by this time, emerged as a publicist of the Cadets.

342 Note in original: 'Rudolf Martin, *Die Zukunft Russlands.*'

343 Note in original: '*Zur Agrarbewegung in Russland* (Teutonia-Verlag, Leipzig, 1905).' These essays are included in the Russian collection *Agrarnyi Vopros*, eds. P.D. Dolgorukov and I.I. Petrunkevich (2 vols., Moscow, 1905).

344 Note in original: 'One desyatin is slightly more than a hectare and one pood slightly more than 16 kilograms.' (In imperial measurements, 2.7 acres and 36 pounds respectively.)

345 Note in original: A.A. Manuilov, in P.D. Dolgorukov and P.P. Petrunkevich, *Agrarnyi i Vopros*, 1, p. 43.

346 Note in original: Ibid., p. 46.

347 Note in original: Ibid., pp. 24–5.

348 The *Lumpenproletariat* was, in Marx's account, that section of the class of non-owners of the means of production which, through deficiencies of organisation, articulation and consciousness fell easy prey to the bribery and demagogy of dictators like Louis Bonaparte. In unusually graphic vein Marx described this dangerous, if colourful, group thus:

Alongside decayed roués with dubious means of subsistence and of dubious origin, alongside ruined and adventurous offshoots of the bourgeoisie, were vagabonds, discharged soldiers, discharged jailbirds, escaped galley slaves, rogues, mountebanks, *lazzaroni*, pickpockets, tricksters, gamblers *maquereaus* [pimps], brothel keepers, porters, *literati*, organ-grinders, rag-pickers, knife grinders, tinkers, beggars – in short, the whole indefinite, disintegrated mass, thrown hither and thither, which the French term *la bohème*.

(MECW, 11, p. 149).

349 See n. 338.

Sources

The following list gives the source for all the documents translated in this collection.

1. N.V. Ershkov and N.E. Petukhov (eds.), *Nachalo rabochego dvizheniya i rasprostranenie marksizma v Rossii 1883–1894 gody* (Moscow, 1960), pp. 193–6 (hereafter *Nachalo rabochego dvizheniya*).
2. G.V. Plekhanov, *Sochineniya*, 2nd edn (29 vols., Moscow, 1923–7), 2, pp. 51–9.
3. Plekhanov, *Sochineniya*, 2, pp. 357–62.
4. Plekhanov, *Sochineniya*, 2, pp. 341–53.
5. P. Akselrod, *Rabochee dvizhenie i sotsialnaya demokratiya* (Geneva, 1884).
6. *Nachalo rabochego dvizheniya*, pp. 91–2.
7. *Nachalo rabochego dvizheniya*, pp. 235–42.
8. Supplement to the pamphlet *Chego khotyat sotsial-demokraty?* (Geneva, 1898).
9. *Rabochaya biblioteka*, no. 6 (Geneva, 1892).
10. Plekhanov, *Sochineniya*, 9, pp. 341–51.
11. Plekhanov, *Sochineniya*, 3, pp. 388–97, 413–17.
12. *Nachalo rabochego dvizheniya*, pp. 261–2.
13. N.E. Fedoseev, *Stati i pisma* (Moscow, 1958), pp. 267–73.
14. P.B. Akselrod, *Zadachi rabochei intelligentsii v Rossii* (Geneva, 1889; 2nd edn 1893).
15. *Rabochii den* (Geneva, 1894).
16. A.M. Pankratova and L.M. Ivanov (eds.), *Rabochee dvizhenie v Rossii v XIX veke* (4 vols. in 8 parts, Moscow, 1955–63), 4, pt 1, pp. 1–2 (hereafter *Rab. dvizh. XIX veke*).
17. S.N. Valk (ed.), *Listovki Peterburgskogo 'Soyuza borby za osvobozhdenie rabochego klassa' 1895–1897* (Moscow, 1934), pp. 1–6.
18. *Rab. dvizh. XIX veke*, 4, pt 1, pp. 2–4.
19. *Rab. dvizh. XIX veke*, 4, pt 1, pp. 2–3.
20. *Rab. dvizh. XIX veke*, 4, pt 1, pp. 71–2.
21. Valk, *Listovki*, pp. 6–12.
22. Valk, *Listovki*, pp. 12–13.
23. Valk, *Listovki*, pp. 14–16.
24. Valk, *Listovki*, pp. 20–1.
25. Valk, *Listovki*, pp. 22–3.
26. Valk, *Listovki*, p. 23.
27. V.I. Lenin, *Sochineniya*, 3rd edn (30 vols., Moscow, 1926–35), 1, pp. 449–71.
28. Valk, *Listovki*, pp. 42–5.

29. Valk, *Listovki*, pp. 52–5.
30. Valk, *Listovki*, pp. 56–7.
31. G.V. Plekhanov, *Report Presented by the Russian Social Democrats to the International Congress of Socialist Workers and Trade Unions* (London, 1896). The original English translation is here reproduced without alteration.
32. Valk, *Listovki*, pp. 93–4.
33. Valk, *Listovki*, pp. 99–106.
34. A. Kremer and Iu. Martov, *Ob agitatsii* (Geneva, 1896).
35. Valk, *Listovki*, pp. 121–5.
36. Valk, *Listovki*, pp. 128–9.
37. *Rab. dvizh. XIX veke*, 4, pt 1, pp. 597–9.
38. *Rab. dvizh. XIX veke*, 4, pt 1, pp. 526–30.
39. *Rab. dvizh. XIX veke*, 4, pt 1, pp. 646–8.
40. *Rab. dvizh. XIX veke*, 4, pt 1, pp. 762–7.
41. *Pervyi sezd R.S.D.R.P. Dokumenty i materialy* (Moscow, 1958), pp. 78–92.
42. *Pervyi sezd*, pp. 82–3.
43. P.B. Akselrod, *K voprosu o sovremennykh zadachakh i taktike russkikh sotsial-demokratov* (Geneva, 1898).
44. K.M. Takhtarev (pseudonym 'R.M.'), *Nasha deistvitelnost*, in the *Separate Supplement* to *Rabochaya Mysl*, no. 7 (1899).
45. Supplement to *Rabochee Delo*, no. 4–5 (1899).
46. Ibid.
47. *Iskra*, no. 1 (December 1900), p. 1.
48. *Iskra*, no. 4 (May 1901), p. 1.
49. *Rabochee Delo*, no. 11–12 (1902), pp. 1–14.
50. *Vtoroi sezd R.S.D.R.P.* (Moscow, 1959), pp. 267–8.
51. *Programma i ustav Rossiiskoi sotsial-demokraticheskoi partii* (Paris, 1909), pp. 3–11.
52. *Programma i ustav*, pp. 11–12.
53. R. Luxemburg, 'Organisationsfragen der russischen Sozialdemokratie', *Neue Zeit*, no. 42 (1904), pp. 484–92, and no. 43, pp. 529–35. Potresov's Russian translation appeared as 'Organizatsionnye voprosy russkoi sotsial-demokratii' in *Iskra*, no. 69 (10 July 1904), pp. 2–7.
54. *Revolyutsiya 1905–1907 gg. v Rossii. Dokumenty i materialy* (Moscow, 1955), pp. 28–31.
55. *Iskra*, no. 100 (1905), pp. 18–19.
56. *Iskra*, no. 100 (1905), pp. 23–4.
57. *Dve taktiki sotsial-demokratii v demokraticheskoi revolyutsii* (Geneva, 1905).
58. P.B. Akselrod, *Narodnaya Duma i rabochii sezd* (Geneva, 1905).
59. L.D. Trotsky, *Nasha revolyutsiya* (St Petersburg, 1906).
60. K. Kautsky, 'Triebkräfte und Aussichten der russischen Revolution', *Neue Zeit*, no. 9 (1906–7), pp. 284–9, and no. 10, pp. 324–33. Lenin's *Preface* is translated from the Russian version, *Dvizhushchie sily i perspektivy russkoi revolyutsii* (Moscow, 1907), pp. 1–7.

Guide to further reading

The purpose of this note is simply to point the interested reader towards some of the more important commentaries, biographies and source books on the development of Marxism in Russia. Their more detailed and specialised bibliographies and sources will, in turn, disclose how ample the literature is.

Perhaps the best book to begin with is still Leopold Haimson's *The Russian Marxists and the Origins of Bolshevism* (Cambridge, Mass., 1955), a work which set new standards for English language studies. It was followed by rather more specialised and more thoroughly documented studies of the practical and, to a lesser extent, the theoretical problems faced by the movement in Russia amongst which Richard Pipes' *Social Democracy and the St Petersburg Labor Movement, 1885–1897* (Cambridge, Mass., 1963) and John Keep's *The Rise of Social Democracy in Russia* (Oxford, 1963) were the most important. More recently Allan Wildman's *The Making of a Workers' Revolution: Russian Social Democracy 1891–1903* (Chicago, 1967) presents new evidence and a more sympathetic interpretation which challenges some of the conclusions of Pipes and Keep.

There can be few modern political movements which can compete with Russian Marxism in the excellence of the biographies of its principal contributors. Samuel Baron's *Plekhanov: The Father of Russian Marxism* (London, 1963) combines erudition with readability and is an invaluable reference book. Plekhanov's life-long comrade-in-arms, Akselrod, found his biographer in Abraham Ascher. His painstaking study, *Pavel Axelrod and the Development of Menshevism* (Cambridge, Mass., 1972) is, like Baron's book, essential reading for reconstructing the intellectual milieu of the Emancipation of Labour Group. Another of the main contributors to Menshevism is the subject of Israel Getzler's fine study, *Martov: A Political Biography of a Russian Social Democrat* (Cambridge, 1967). Between them these three biographies with their ample notes and sources provide a comprehensive introduction to what we might term the mainstream centre of the movement in this period.

The more overtly revolutionary left has its own galaxy of distinguished biographers and commentators. Trotsky in particular has been covered by Isaac Deutscher's modern classic *The Prophet Armed: Trotsky 1879–1921* (London, 1954) and, more latterly by Baruch Knei-Paz's sophisticated and exhaustive *The Social and Political Thought of Leon Trotsky* (Oxford, 1978). Trotsky's fellow-formulator of the theory of uninterrupted revolution is the subject of W.B. Scharlau's and Z.A.B. Zeman's evocative *Merchant of Revolution: A Life of Alexander Israel Helphand (Parvus)* (London, 1965). Rosa Luxemburg has become not merely a legend but almost an industry but little has been added in the more recent literature that was not well said by J.P. Nettl in his authoritative two-volume study *Rosa Luxemburg* (London, 1966). On Lenin, Tony Cliff's four-volume study *Lenin* (London, 1975–9) is exhaustive enough for all but the most dedicated and for this reason the novice might prefer to start with A.B. Ulam's flowing account *Lenin and the Bolsheviks* (London, 1969) or David Shub's admirable short biography *Lenin* (Harmondsworth, 1966). The more theoretical problems of the structure of Lenin's thought are dealt with in Alfred Meyer's *Leninism* (Cambridge, Mass., 1954), Marcel Liebman's *Leninism Under Lenin* (London, 1975) and the present writer's *Lenin's Political Thought*, vol. 1 *Theory and Practice in the Democratic Revolution* (London, 1977), vol. 2 *Theory and Practice in the Socialist Revolution* (London, 1981).

The more 'revisionist wing' of the movement has also had its share of scholarly attention most notably in Richard Kindersley's *The First Russian Revisionists: A Study of 'Legal Marxism' in Russia* (Oxford, 1962), in Jonathan Frankel's excellent introduction to *Vladimir Akimov on the Dilemmas of Russian Marxism 1895–1903* (Cambridge, 1969) and Richard Pipes' *Struve: Liberal on the Left, 1870–1905* (Cambridge, Mass., 1970).

Soviet literature abounds in thorough monographs on particular incidents in the development of Russian Marxism but is evidently wary of the possible political implications of offering historical reassessments of this period as a whole. It is perhaps significant that the one towering work of Soviet scholarship which attempts a broader sweep, Yuri Z. Polevoi's *Zarozhdenie marksizma v Rossii, 1883–1894 gg.* (*The Origins of Marxism in Russia, 1883–1894*) (Moscow, 1959) ends precisely at the point when the movement was beginning to attract a mass following and at the moment when theoretical controversies about the direction it should assume first became acute. Exactly the same period is covered in the useful collection *Nachalo rabochego dvizheniya i rasprostranenie marksizma v Rossii* (*The Beginning of the Workers' Movement and the Dissemination of Marxism in Russia*), eds. N.V. Ershkov and N.E. Petukhov (Moscow, 1960). The workers' movement in Russia in the nineteenth century has been meticulously documented in the eight parts of the four-volume *Rabochee dvizhenie v Rossii v XIX veke*, eds. A.M. Pankratova and L.M. Ivanov, (Moscow, 1955–63). The appendices to part 2 of volume 4 of this enormous work are particularly valuable, especially the 150 page *Khronika* of the years 1895 to 1900.

There is, surprisingly, no full-scale study in English of the Russian labour movement. S.P. Turin's *From Peter the Great to Lenin: A History of the Russian Labour Movement with Special Reference to Trade Unionism* (London 1935, reprinted 1968) remains the best available source. Nor is there a comprehensive study of the all-important relationship between the labour movement and the intelligentsia-dominated Russian Social Democratic Labour Party. Hopefully it will not be too long before these gaps are filled.

Glossary

Chernyi Peredel (Black Repartition): the name taken by the orthodox revolutionary Populists of Zemlya i Volya after the latter organisation split into two groupings in 1879.

Duma (Representative Assembly): summoned by the tsar to convene in April 1906. Survived in emasculated form until 1917.

Iskra (*The Spark*): journal of the 'orthodox' Marxists. From issue 52 (1903) it became the organ of the Menshevik wing of the RSDLP. Leipzig, Munich, London, Geneva. Dec. 1900–Dec. 1905, 112 issues.

Kadety (Cadets): members of the liberal Constitutional Democratic Party, founded in October 1905. The name was derived from KD, the Russian initials of the party.

Nachalo (*The Beginning*): short-lived Menshevik daily newspaper edited by Trotsky and Parvus. St Petersburg, 13 Nov.–2 Dec. 1905, 16 issues.

Narodnaya Volya (People's Will): a group founded at the split in Zemlya i Volya advocating 'excitative terror' to be organised by a tightly organised conspiratorial party.

Narodnik (from *narod* – people): Populist.

Narodovolets, Narodovoltsy: adherent, adherents, of Narodnaya Volya.

Osvobozhdenie (*Liberation*): journal of the radical middle class group known as The Union of Liberation which came into existence in 1902 and was edited by Peter Struve.

Rabochaya Biblioteka (The Workers' Library): the publishing house of the Emancipation of Labour Group prolific in its publications issued from Geneva 1884–1901.

Rabochaya Gazeta (*Workers' Newspaper*): the organ of the Kiev Union of Struggle for the Emancipation of the Working Class which became, briefly, the official organ of the newly formed RSDLP. Kiev, 1897, 2 issues.

Rabochaya Mysl (*Workers' Thought*): became the organ of the Economist-dominated Petersburg Committee of the RSDLP. St Petersburg, Berlin. Oct. 1897–Dec. 1902, 16 issues.

Rabochee Delo (*The Workers' Cause*): the organ of the Union of Russian Social Democrats Abroad which fell under the control of opponents of the Emancipation of Labour Group. Geneva. Apr. 1899–Feb. 1902, 12 issues.

Rabotnik (*The Worker*): an occasional miscellany published by the Union of Russian Social Democrats Abroad. Geneva, 1896–9, 6 issues.

Trudoviki (Labourites): name adopted by large group of radical peasant delegates to the Dumas.

Zarya (*The Dawn*): theoretical organ of the Iskra Group. Stuttgart, 1901–2, 4 issues.

Zemlya i Volya (Land and Freedom): the organisation of revolutionary Populists founded in 1860, revived in 1875 and splitting into two wings, Chernyi Peredel and Narodnaya Volya, in 1879.

Zemskii sobor: Assembly of the Land, or National Assembly. See p. 379, n. 38.

Index

agitation, *see* economic agitation; propaganda
Akimov, *see* Makhnovets, V.P.
Akselrod, P.B., 2, 25, 27, 32, 35, 37, 280,
  283; on economic agitation, 232–3,
  239–40, 391; on political struggle,
  236–41; on Populism, 229–32, 238–9
  texts: *The Present Tasks and Tactics of
  the Russian Social Democrats*, xiii, xiv,
  29, translated, 227–41, quoted, 256,
  390; *The Tasks of the Worker Intelligentsia in Russia*, extracts, 113–19;
  *The People's Duma and the Workers'
  Congress*, 331–7, 401
Aleksandrov iron foundry, 178, 182, 209,
  213, 215
Alexander II, 62, 94, 97
artel, 89, 108, 138
Ascher, A., 406

Babushkin, I.V., 151, 382, 384, 386
Bakunin, M.A., 1; influence in Russia, 10–11,
  12, 92–4, 96, 99
Baron, S., 406
Bellamy, E., 89
Bernstein, E., 1, 26, 251, 254, 260, 281, 318,
  319, 326, 356, 392
Bismarck, O. von, 101, 250
Blagoev, D., xiii, 2; draft programme of his
  group, 74–80, 379–80
Blanqui, L.A., Blanquism, 7, 93, 251, 255,
  392; Luxemburg on Blanquism, 298–9
bourgeoisie, 15–16, 33–4, 45–6, 61, 95–6,
  170, 196–7, 216, 218, 288–9, 295–9,
  316, 318–23, 343; Plekhanov on, 35,
  44–54; Akselrod on, 234, 334–5;
  Lenin on, 320–1, 323, 327–8;
  Trotsky on, 339–41, 343; Kautsky on,
  364–72
Brouckère, *see* Makhnovets, L.
Brusnev, M.I., xiii, 2; *Manuscript Programme
  for Studies with the Workers*, 108,
  380, 381

Bulygin, A.I., 336, 401
Bund, the, 31, 390; *see also* Jewish Social
  Democracy

Cadets (Constitutional Democrats), 35, 353,
  354, 356, 357, 402
capitalism, 56, 75, 82, 153–4, 156–65,
  192–4, 228–30, 288–90, 337–40,
  359–63, 365–6
Chartism, 254, 392
Chernyshevsky, N.G., 242, 246
Christianity, 43
Cliff, T., 407
Cobden, R., 45
commune (Russian peasant), 10, 11, 42,
  63–4, 82, 84, 108, 350
consciousness: Marx on, 3–9; Plekhanov on,
  14, 39–40, 47–8, 55–6, 81, 101–3,
  107; Kremer and Martov on, 20–2;
  strikes and, 24–5, 214, 217, 223–5;
  Rabochaya Mysl and, 28–9; Akselrod
  on, 29, 117, 236–40; Lenin on, 30–1,
  38, 165–9, 260–1, 315–17; *On
  Agitation* and, 197–200
Constituent Assembly, 311, 333, 336

democratic revolution, 15–17, 32–8, 42; programme of according to: Emancipation
  of Labour Group, 57–8, 60–1, 83,
  Blagoev Group, 75–6, Lenin, 155–6,
  163–5, 269–70, 273–5, 315–31,
  1903 RSDLP programme, 290–3,
  1905 strikers, 311–12, Trotsky,
  340–53, Kautsky, 365–72; *see also*
  political struggle
dictatorship of the proletariat, 36–7, 289; in
  Lenin's modification, 322, 328, 330,
  354; and Trotsky, 337–8, 341–2,
  345–9; and Kautsky, 370
Deutscher, I., 406
Drabkin, Ya.D. (pseud. Gusev), 287, 397

410

Duma, 69; Akselrod and People's Duma, 37, 331–7, 353, 364, 401

economic agitation: and *On Agitation*, 19–21, 197–205; Plekhanov on, 103–6; Lenin on, 166–8, 324–5; in Kiev, 216–19; Akselrod on, 232–3, 239–40; Takhtarev on, 242–5
Economism, 15, 26–31, 255–67, 283, 305, 319, 324, 327–8, 329
Ekaterinhof (Volynkin) factory, 175, 209
Emancipation of Labour Group, 26–7, 68, 248, 259, 378
    texts: programmes of, 55–8, 227–30
Engels, F., 93
Ershkov, N.V., 407

Fedoseev, N.E., xiii, 2; *Programme of Action for the Workers*, 109–12, 382
fines (on workers), 72, 139, 143, 148–9, 155, 168, 171, 179
First International, *see* International Working Men's Association
Fourier, C.M., 10, 100, 254, 381
Frankel, J., 407

Gapon, G., 32
    text: 1905 petition, 309–12, 399
Getzler, I., 406
Goethe, J.W. von, 14, 398
'Going to the People', 10, 12, 70, 379
Gordon, M., 387
Gozhansky, S., 388
Gusev, *see* Drabkin, Ya.D.

Haimson, L., 406
Harding, N., 407
Haxthausen, A. von, 10
Herzen, A., 10, 11
Hess, M., 4, 373

intelligentsia, 2, 6, 9–10, 12, 18–20, 28, 36, 77, 85, 245, 283, 303–6, 388; Lavrov on, 13–14; Plekhanov on, 13–15, 29–30, 57–8, 59, 62, 63, 66–7, 70, 84, 94, 95, 99; worker, 68, 70, 71, 85, 201–4; Akselrod on, 115–19
International Working Men's Association, 55, 56, 81, 254, 255, 378, 380, 382, 393
Iskra, 27, 36, 408; as vehicle of orthodoxy, 30–1; Lenin's plan for, 259–67, 275, 296, 394, 397; new-*Iskra*, 316–31
Ivanov, L.M., 407

Jaurès, J., 282, 307, 396
Jewish social democracy, 19–20, 26–7, 185–6, 224, 225, 242, 387–8, 390

Kadety, *see* Cadets
Kalinsky mill, 179
Kant, I., 305
kassy (workers' funds), 86, 177; model statutes for, 78–80
Kathedersozialisten, 51, 255, 378
Kautsky, K., 32, 37, 327, 352–6, 339–40, 351–2
    text: *The Driving Forces of the Russian Revolution*, 356–72
Keep, J., 406
Khalturin, S., 117, 376
Kiev Union of Struggle for the Emancipation of the Working Class, 216–19, 389, 390
Kindersley, R., 407
Knei-Paz, B., 406
Knunyants, B.M. (pseud. Rusov), 281, 282
Koenig factory, 23, 172, 175, 178, 179, 209, 213
Kostrov, *see* Zhordania, N.N.
Krasikov, P.A. (pseud. Pavlovich), 281–2, 396
Kremer, A., xiii; *On Agitation*, xiv, 19–21; text, 192–205, 387–8, 390
kulaks, 76, 87, 90, 107, 118
Kuskova, E.D., xiv, 17, 26, 392, 400; Lenin on, 253–8, 259, 319
    text: 'Credo', 250–3

Laferme factory, 19, 172, 178, 179, 213, 384; demands of strikers, 149, 150
Lange, O., 48
Lassalle, F., 1, 47, 62, 254, 255, 306, 332, 393, 399
Lavrov, P., 12–13, 374
League of Russian Revolutionary Social Democracy Abroad, 295
Lebedev mill, 150, 152–3, 172, 178, 213
Lenin, V.I., 19, 26; and consciousness, 30–1, 38, 159–69, 260–1, 315–17, 320–5; and democratic revolution, 32–4, 36, 153–6; on revisionism, 253–8; on newspaper, 259–67, 275, 296, 394; on party rules, 279–87; Luxemburg on, 297–309; on Menshevism, 316–31
    texts: *Questionnaire on the Situation of the Workers in Enterprises*, 138–9, cited 383; *To the Workers of the Semyannikov Factory*, 140–2, cited 383; *To the Working Men and Women of the Thornton Mill*, 146–9, cited 23; *Draft and Explanation of a Programme for the Social Democratic Party*, 153–71, cited 21–2, 384–5; *To the Tsarist Government*, 188–91; *A Protest by Russian Social Democrats*, 253–8, cited 27; *The Urgent Tasks of*

412   *Index*

Lenin, V.I. (*cont.*)
  Our Movement, 259–62; *Where to Begin?*, 263–8; *Two Tactics of Social Democracy in the Democratic Revolution*, 315–31; Preface to K. Kautsky, *The Driving Forces of the Russian Revolution and its Prospects*, 352–6
Lieber, M.I., 282
Liebknecht, K., 263
Liebman, M., 407
Luxemburg, R., xiii, 397
  text: *Organisational Questions of Russian Social Democracy*, 295–309

Makhnovets, L. (pseud. Brouckère), 279, 281, 284, 396
Makhnovets, V.P. (pseud. Akimov), 286–7, 316, 396
Manuilov, A.A., 357–8
Martov, Yu., xiii, xiv, 2, 19–21, 30, 31; at 2nd RSDLP Congress, 279–80, 282, 284
  text: *On Agitation*, 192–205
Martynov, A.S. (pseud. Piker), 35, 318–20, 327, 400
Marx, K.: on proletariat, 3–9, 49, 56, 111; on alienation, 4–5; on democratic revolution, 32–4, 38; on state, 46–7; Lenin on, 254–5, 330, 338, 348–9
  works cited: *Critique of Hegel's Philosophy of Law*, 3–4, 12, 53, 319; *The German Ideology*, 4; *Economic and Philosophical Manuscripts of 1844*, 5; *The Class Struggles in France*, 6, 7, 8; *The Holy Family*, 6, 36; *The Eighteenth Brumaire of Louis Bonaparte*, 8; *The Poverty of Philosophy*, 8; *The Manifesto of the Communist Party*, 8, 9, 49, quoted, 54, 111, 251, 254, 296
Masimov, I., 309–12, 399
May Day, xiii, xiv, 23, 113, 163, 218, 270, 274, 380; four May Day Speeches 1891, 84–91; St Petersburg 1896 brochure, 171–3, 180; 1897 brochures, 210–15
Maxwell factory, 209
Menshevism, 31–2, 35–8; 1905 Resolutions, 313–15; Lenin's attack on, 318–31, 354–5
Meyer, A., 407
Mikhailovsky, N.K., 15
Mishenov, G.M. (pseud. Muravev), 282, 396
Mitrofanev factory, 175
Morozov works, demands of strikers, 72–3, 213, 385
Moscow Rising, 1905, 36
Moscow 'Workers' Union', 145–6, 215–16, 383, 384
Muravev, *see* G.M. Mishenov

Napoleon III, 61, 343
Narodnaya Volya, Narodvoltsy, 11, 58, 65, 94, 114, 225, 227, 230, 258, 259, 286, 287, 309, 379, 380, 390
Narodniks, *see* Populism
Nekrasov, N., 91, 382–3
Nettl, J.P., 407
New Imperial Dockyard, 178
Nicholas II, 96–7
Northern Union of Russian Workers, 48, 60, 70, 256, 376–7, 379
  text: programme of, 41–4

Obnorsky, V., 376, 377, 382
Obukhov factory, 274, 395
Oriental despotism, 92
Orlov, V.I., 11
Osvobozhdenie, 316, 317, 323, 400
Owen, R., 10, 254, 392–3

Pankratova, A.M., 407
Paris Commune, 186, 337, 348
parliamentarianism, 304–5, 330, 345
Parvus, A.I., 34, 301, 401, 402
Pavlovich, *see* Krasikov, P.A.
peasantry, 10, 11, 33, 58, 66, 69–70, 77, 82, 84, 97, 229–35, 240, 245–6; Plekhanov on, 35, 63–4; Lenin on, 155–6, 157, 170–1, 321–2; in 1903 party programme, 292–3; Trotsky on, 341–5; Kautsky on, 357–9, 362–6, 368, 371
Peterburzhets, *see* Takhtarev, K.M.
Petukhov, N.E., 407
Piker, *see* Martynov, A.S.
Pipes, R., 22, 375, 406, 407
Plekhanov, G.V., 2; on political struggle, 8–9, 15–16, 25, 29–30, 44–54, 60–4, 67, 81–2; and application of Marxism to Russia, 9–16; and Lavrov, 12–13; on intelligentsia, 13–14, 57–8, 59, 62–4, 66–7, 68, 70–1, 84, 94, 95, 98–9, 101–3, 107; and opposition to reformism, 26–8, 30, 280–1; in 1905, 35–6, 36–7, 352–6, 369–70; on propaganda and agitation, 59–63, 103–6; on Populism, 63–7, 94–5; on liberals, 95–6, 107; on strikes in Russia, 117–86
  texts: *Socialism and the Political Struggle*, extracts, 44–54, cited, 9, 228, 377; *Programme of the Social Democratic Emancipation of Labour Group*, 57–8, cited, 16; *Our Differences*, extracts, 59–67; *From the Publishers of the 'Workers' Library'*, 68–72; *Second Draft Programme of the Russian Social Democrats*, 81–4; *Report [to the*

International] *by the Editorial Board of the Journal Sotsial-Demokrat*, 92–9; *The Tasks of the Social Democrats in the Struggle Against the Famine*, extracts, 100–7; *Report Presented by the Russian Social Democrats to the* (*London*) *International Congress of Socialist Workers and Trade Unions*, 176–87

Polevoi, Yu.Z., 407

political struggle, 8–9, 10; Plekhanov on, 15–16, 25, 29–30, 44–54, 60–4, 67, 81–2; centrality to Russian Marxism of, 16–17, 25, 224–5; *On Agitation* and, 20–1, 194–5, 199–200; Akselrod on, 25, 29–30, 236–41; *Rabochaya Mysl* on, 28–9; Lenin on, 32–4, 153–4, 161–2, 168–71, 255–8, 259–67; Fedoseev on, 110–11; Takhtarev, on difficulties of, 244–5, 247–8; Kuskova on, 250–3; *Rabochee Delo* on, 270–5; Luxemburg on, 300–1; Kautsky on, 370–2

Populism, 10, 58, 61, 63–4, 65–7, 229–32, 238–9, 305, 315; *see also* Narodnaya Volya, Zemlya i Volya

praktiki ('Young' Social Democrats), 26–7, 392, 393–4, 400

Prokopovich, S.N., 26, 355, 356, 392, 400, 403

proletariat: consciousness, Marx on, 3–9; Plekhanov on relationship to intelligentsia, 13–14, 57–8, 69–71, 82, 84, 93, 96, 98–9, 101–3, 107; and economic agitation and political struggle, 20–5, 28, 33–6, 37; dictatorship of, 33, 36–7, 76–7, 322, 328, 330, 354; Plekhanov on situation of, 47–54, 66; Blagoev Group on, 77; Fedoseev on, 109–12; Akselrod on, 117–18, 228–9, 236–41; workers' situation, 123–38; Lenin on, 154, 157–69, 260–75; *On Agitation* and, 192–200; and peasantry, 229–35, 242–5, 248–50; Takhtarev and tasks of, 243–5; Trotsky on, 339–52, 369–72

Proletarii, 315

propaganda: in workers' circles, 18–19; *On Agitation* and, 20–1, 200–3; Plekhanov on, 59–67, 99; distinction between and agitation, 103–4; Akselrod on, 114–16; Lenin on, 259–60, 266–7

Proudhon, P.J., 1, 8, 46, 254, 393

Putilov works, 150, 172, 178, 182, 213, 384, 399

Rabochaya biblioteka, *see* Workers' Library

Rabochaya Gazeta, 224, 225, 226, 241, 257, 390

Rabochaya Mysl, as vehicle of Economism and revisionism, 26–31, 248, 256–7, 259, 261, 263, 303, 319, 391
    text: K.M. Takhtarev, *Our Reality*, extracts, 242–50

Rabochee Delo: and Plekhanov's opposition, 27; Lenin on, 263–5; *see also praktiki*
    text: new programme of, 268–76, 327, 394

Rabotnik, 235, 241, 386, 408

railway workers, 184, 185

Ricardo, D., 51, 52

R.M., *see* Takhtarev, K.M.

Rodbertus, J.K., 53

Rusov, *see* Knunyants, B.M.

Russian Social Democratic Labour Party (RSDLP), xiii; First Congress, 25, 26, 31, 390; Second Congress, 31, 36, 276, 395; and debate on paragraph 1 of rules, 279–87, 395, 398; Third Congress, 316–17, 323, 324, 400; Fourth (Unity) Congress, 32; Luxemburg on organisational questions of, 295–309; maximum and minimum programmes, 345–7, 349, 381–2, 402
    texts: *Manifesto* (1898), 223–5, cited, 257, 259, 261–2, 268, 271, 275–6; *Decisions of the First Congress*, 225–6; *Programme* (1903), 288–93, cited, 397

Russian–American india-rubber factory, 179, 182

St Petersburg Union of Struggle for the Emancipation of the Working Class, 22–3, 149–51, 152–3, 171–3, 174, 175–6, 177, 187–8, 206–15

S. Petersburgskii Rabochii Listok, 257

Schäffle, A., 46, 89

Scharlau, W.B., 406

Second International: and May Day pamphlets, 23–4; Plekhanov's reports to (1891), 92–9 (1896), 176–87

Semyannikov works, 19, 383

Shelgunov, N.V., 87, 380

Shipov, D., 320, 400

Shub, D., 407

Sismondi, S., 51

Slavophiles, 92, 97, 98

Smith, A., 52

Social Democratic Party of Germany, 85, 90, 101, 254

Socialist Revolutionaries (SRs), 321, 350, 400

South Russian Workers' Union, 185, 256, 393

standing army, 76, 88

Stein, L. von, 48, 377

strikes: and development of consciousness,
21–2; extensiveness of, 24, 42, 61;
Morozov strikers' demands, 72–3; as
pressure on government, 110, 168–9,
172, 179–80, 189–91, 207–8, 209,
211, 215–16, 223–4; and working
day, 136–8, 139, 150–1; Lenin on
Semyannikov strike, 140–2, on
Thornton strike, 146–9; Laferme
strike, 149; Lebedev strike, 150,
152–3; consciousness according to
Lenin, 166–8; Plekhanov on, 177–86;
résumé of 1896 strikes, 206–8, 213,
chronology, 385; Akselrod on, 232–3,
239–40, 300; petition of 1905
strikers, 309–12; and workers' government, 349
Struve, P., 316, 319, 320, 335, 390, 396
    text: manifesto of First RSDLP Congress,
    223–5

tailism, 71, 317, 326
Takhtarev, K.M. (pseuds. R.M.; Peterburzhets), xiii, xiv, 29, 259, 319; as
historian, 19, 375, 391
    text: *Our Reality*, 242–50
terror, 62, 65, 78, 83, 94, 264; *see also*
Narodnaya Volya
Thornton mill, 23, 172, 178, 179, 213, 384;
demands of strikers, 146–9, 150
Tkachev, P., 93–4, 381
trade unionism, 242, 249, 254, 316; *see also*
strikes; economic agitation
Trotsky, L.: position of in 1905, 34–5, 36;
at Second RSDLP Congress, 282–3,
284
    text: *Our Revolution*, 337–52, cited, 401
Turin, S.P., 407

Ulam, A.B., 407
Union of Russian Social Democrats Abroad,
26, 27, 226, 258, 268, 392, 394, 395
Uspensky, G., 63

Vasimov, I., 1905 petition to tsar, 309–12
Voronin factory, 172, 178, 179, 213
Vorontsov, V.P. (pseud. V.V.), 59, 380
Vpered, 318
V.V., *see* Vorontsov, V.P.

Wildman, A.K., 24, 375, 406
Witte, S., 180, 189, 190, 387
workers' circles, 18–19
Workers' Congress, *see* Duma
Workers' Library (*Rabochaya biblioteka*),
379, 386, 408
    text: *From the Publishers . . .* , 68–72
working day, 42, 103, 104, 146, 155, 174,
175, 181, 197–8, 214, 245, 291, 312,
346, 349, 389, 391; brochure of this
name, xii, xiv, 23–5; as agitational
focus, 23–4; and strikes, 136–8; 139
    text: 123–39, cited, 382

'Young' Social Democrats, *see praktiki*

Zasulich, V., *Report [to the International]
by the Editorial Board of the Journal
Sotsial-Demokrat* (1891), 92–9
Zeman, Z.A.B., 406
Zemlya i Volya, 10, 17, 48, 60, 66, 99, 114,
379, 409; journal of, 377
Zemskii sobor, 69, 76, 106, 114, 119, 155,
409
Zemstvo, 246, 267, 321, 328, 334
Zhelyabov, A., 59, 230, 280, 376, 378
Zhordania, N.N. (pseud. Kostrov), 286, 396